UNCLE $CROOGE
and
Donald Duck

The

Don Rosa

Library

Volume One

Walt Disney

UNCLE $CROOGE
and
Donald Duck

The Son of the Sun

FANTAGRAPHICS BOOKS

Fantagraphics Books
7563 Lake City Way NE
Seattle, Washington 98115

Editor: David Gerstein
Supervising Editor: Gary Groth
Color Restoration: Rich Tommaso, David Gerstein, Kneon Transitt
Production: Paul Baresh and Tony Ong
Associate Publisher: Eric Reynolds
Publisher: Gary Groth

For a free full-color catalogue of comics and cartooning, call 1-800-657-1100. Our books may be viewed–and purchased–on our website at www.fantagraphics.com.

Special thanks to: Randall Bethune, Big Planet Comics, Black Hook Press of Japan, Nick Capetillo, Kevin Czapiewski, John DiBello, Juan Manuel Domínguez, Mathieu Doublet, Dan Evans III, Thomas Eykemans, Scott Fritsch-Hammes, Coco and Eddie Gorodetsky, Karen Green, Ted Haycraft, Eduardo Takeo "Lizarkeo" Igarashi, Nevdon Jamgochian, Andy Koopmans, Philip Nel, Vanessa Palacios, Kurt Sayenga, Anne Lise Rostgaard Schmidt, Christian Schremser, Secret Headquarters, Paul van Dijken, Mungo van Krimpen-Hall, Jason Aaron Wong, and Thomas Zimmermann

The editor would like to thank: Thomas Jensen, Dan Shane, Jesper Sichlau, Anders Christian Sivebæk, David Terzopoulos, Solveig Thime, and Bernard Voorzichtig.

First Fantagraphics Books edition: July 2014

ISBN 978-1-60699-742-0

Printed in Malaysia

Table of Contents

All stories and text features written and drawn by Don Rosa except where noted.
All stories lettered by John Clark except where noted.

6   *Preface*

13   **"The Son of the Sun"**
     Uncle Scrooge 219, cover date July
     1987. Colors by Nea Aktina A. E. and
     Rich Tomasso with David Gerstein

39   **"Nobody's Business"**
     Uncle Scrooge 220, August 1987.
     Letters by Bill Spicer; Colors by
     Nea Aktina A. E., Rich Tomasso, and
     David Gerstein

49   **"Mythological Menagerie"**
     Walt Disney's Comics and Stories
     523, October 1987. Colors by Scott
     Rockwell and Rich Tomasso

59   **"Recalled Wreck"**
     Walt Disney's Comics and Stories
     524, December 1987. Colors by Mike
     McCormick with Rich Tomasso

69   **"Cash Flow"**
     Uncle Scrooge 224, December 1987.
     Colors by Nea Aktina A. E. and Rich
     Tomasso with David Gerstein

95   **"Fit To Be Pied"**
     Walt Disney's Comics and Stories
     526, February 1988. Colors by Scott
     Rockwell with Rich Tomasso

105 **"Fir-Tree Fracas"**
     Mickey and Donald 1, March 1988.
     Colors by Nea Aktina A. E. with Rich
     Tomasso

109 **"Oolated Luck"**
     Walt Disney's Comics and Stories 528,
     April 1988. Colors by Susan Daigle-
     Leach with Rich Tomasso

119 **"The Paper Chase"**
     Uncle Scrooge 226, May 1988. Story by
     Gary Leach; Colors by Nea Aktina A. E.
     with Rich Tomasso and David Gerstein

121 **"Last Sled to Dawson"**
     Uncle Scrooge Adventures 5, June
     1988. Colors by Susan Daigle-Leach
     and Rich Tomasso

149 **"Rocket Reverie"**
     Donald Duck Adventures [series 1] 5,
     July 1988. Story by Gary Leach; Colors
     by Nea Aktina A. E. with Rich Tomasso

151 **"Fiscal Fitness"**
     Uncle Scrooge 227, July 1988. Story by
     Gary Leach; Colors by Gary Leach with
     Rich Tomasso

153 **"Metaphorically Spanking"**
     Walt Disney's Comics and Stories 531,
     August 1988. Colors by Susan Daigle-
     Leach with Rich Tomasso

163 *Behind the Scenes*

186 *This Should Cover It All!*
     Additional Covers, 1987-1989

198 *The Life and Times of Don Rosa: Last
     of the Clan Rosa*

Preface

By Don Rosa

As I gathered material for this Library—looking through everything I'd drawn or written prior to 1986, and rereading old interviews I'd given over those years to newspapers and fanzines—I became even more aware than ever that creating comics based on Carl Barks' Scrooge McDuck was, simply put, my destiny. I had been reading them (or just looking at them!) literally since birth; I had spent my childhood creating Barks-type comedy-adventure comics; I had even copied my favorite Barks adventures panel-by-panel, simply for the thrill of telling the same story with my own hand. And in every fanzine column I wrote, and in every interview I'd ever given, I would profess my love of Barks' Ducks as the greatest comic stories of all time.

There are many other cartoonists who work and have worked on these characters, practically all of them better artists than I am, but I think that I'm the only one who knew from birth that this is what I would someday do.

Two of the first Disney comic books published by Gladstone: *Walt Disney's Comics and Stories* 511 and *Uncle Scrooge* 210 (both 1986). Rosa's discovery of the *Walt Disney's Comics* issue in a comic shop helped to inspire his first professional Disney comics works.

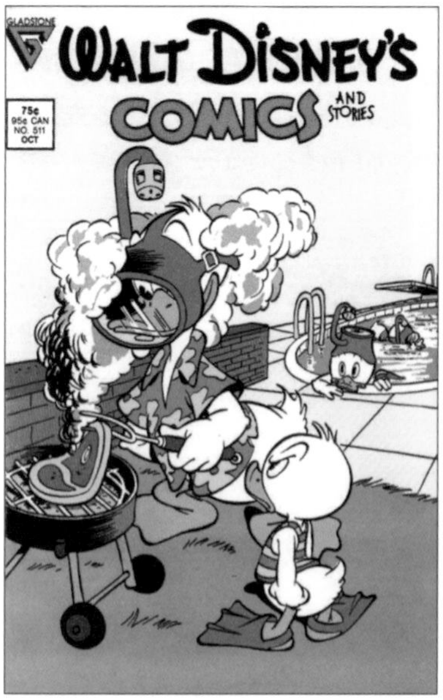
WALT DISNEY'S
COMICS AND STORIES
75¢ 95¢ CAN NO. 511 OCT

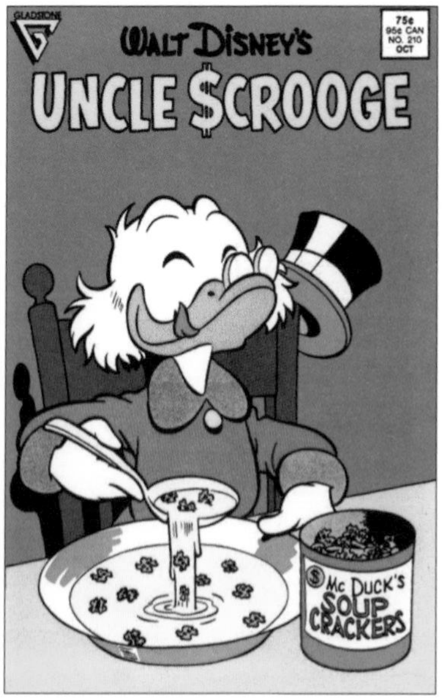
WALT DISNEY'S
UNCLE $CROOGE
75¢ 95¢ CAN NO. 210 OCT
Mc DUCK'S SOUP CRACKERS

So... why didn't I do it before 1987? Several reasons! I had no idea that Disney comics were still being published anywhere on Earth. In America, as the comic market collapsed in the 1970s, they had degenerated into hackwork and finally ceased publication altogether. But even if Dell Comics had still been in business, producing the same fabulous comics they had produced prior to the late 1960s, I *still* would not have sought work with them, because I *knew* my future—I was to take over the nearly century-old family business. Like millions or even *billions* of other people, I knew that my lifetime dream was impossible to fulfill.

Then... in August of 1986 came the turning point in my life. I was in a comic shop, and there in the rack was a *new* issue of *Walt Disney's Comics and Stories*, the first new issue in years! Not only that, but it had a Barks cover which I had *never* seen, which was *impossible* since I had amassed a full set of American Disney comics. Obviously, I bought it instantly. The first thing I noticed was that this Disney comic revealed the names of the writers and artists, and I saw that the "Barks" cover had been drawn by Daan Jippes, a superb present-day cartoonist who could mimic Barks' style.

Furthermore, I saw that the comic's publisher was Bruce Hamilton, an old friend whom I had seen for years at comic conventions and whom I knew was as big a Barks lover as I was. He had formed a tiny comic publishing company which he named Gladstone for luck (after Donald's lucky cousin), and had gotten the license to publish Disney comic books in America because... no other publisher was interested! Bruce's comics—as I knew they would—showed love and respect for the material, and gave much information about the writers, artists and the history of Disney comics in general. Bruce also brought back all the main Disney titles including *Uncle Scrooge*, which naturally became a showcase for Barks' greatest work! *Fantastic!!!*

I NEVER THOUGHT I'D SEE YOU DONATE ANYTHING TO ANYBODY, UNCLE SCROOGE!
WELL, I'M PROUD OF MY MANY TRIUMPHS! BESIDES, THE EXHIBITS ARE ON LOAN--I ONLY DONATED THE SIGN! YOU THINK I'VE LOST MY MIND?
HANDS OFF!
CANDY STRIPED RUBY
I BUILT MY VAST FORTUNE IN MANY WAYS! THIS EXHIBIT PROVES I WASN'T AFRAID TO GO AFTER TREASURES THAT THE SOFTIES THOUGHT WERE IRRETRIEVABLY LOST!
GOLD BULLION
HANDS OFF!
JUST LOOK AT THE LEGENDARY PRIZES I'VE UNCOVERED IN MY TRAVELS... KING SOLOMON'S MINES!... THE CROWN OF GENGHIS KHAN!... THE PHILOSOPHER'S STONE!... THE GOLDEN FLEECE!
GOLDEN FLEECE
1916 QUARTER ONLY ONE AROUND
FOR SALE BUT HANDS OFF!
HANDS OFF!

Walt Disney's
Donald Duck in "BIG FEET!"
IT'S ABOUT TIME YOU GOT HERE! I CALLED FIVE MINUTES AGO!
AR 101
BUT UNCLE SCROOGE, I'M EARLY! I LIVE TEN MINUTES FROM HERE!
I PAY YOU TOP WAGES OF THIRTY CENTS AN HOUR, SO YOU CAN DARNWELL GET HERE IN THREE!

Top, bottom, and overleaf: a gallery of line art from early Rosa Duck comics; compare with color versions later in this book.

Above: "Big Feet!" by Marty Greim (*Donald Duck* 249), the story that drove Rosa to pitch his first professional *Uncle Scrooge* material.

A few months later, in an issue of *Donald Duck*, there appeared a new story by someone I knew as a comic fan like myself. The story, "Big Feet" by Marty Greim, was entirely made up of copies of Barks poses, and looked quite amateurish—it was obviously fan art. Even though I had given up cartooning four years earlier, seeing that Bruce would publish art by another mere fan like me did the trick! I called up his editor, another comics fan I knew named Byron Erickson, and told him that I was *born* to write and draw an Uncle Scrooge adventure—that it was my *manifest destiny!*

I know that this story has been told enough times that it begins to sound like an urban legend, even to me; but that's *exactly* what I told him, as he will attest. Byron asked me to submit some examples of Duck drawings, which I immediately sent him. But this was a mere formality, since he had already been seeing my fanzine art for years, and in no time he gave me the go-ahead to produce a long Scrooge adventure story to appear in an issue of *Uncle Scrooge*.

That's all there was to it. One day I was quite certain that the rest of my life would be devoted to only the Keno Rosa Co, my family construction firm—and that I'd never even do any drawing again. And the next day I was writing and drawing an actual issue of *Uncle Scrooge*, realizing my fondest childhood dream. How could this be real? But it *was*.

Due to the unanimous acclaim that met my very first professional comic work, "The Son of the Sun," I soon decided to do a second Uncle Scrooge story. Then a Donald Duck story. Bruce Hamilton's small company could not afford to pay me much, but I didn't care. I was still dividing my time between doing comics and working at the Keno Rosa Co.

Soon, my partner—my uncle's stepson—suggested that if I was more interested in being a cartoonist than in the Keno Rosa Co., which was even in *my* name, maybe we should just liquidate the company and go our separate ways. I would never have had the courage (or disrespect

Ahhh...THE APPETIZERS! CURRIED RHUBARB PULP IN CURDLED MILKWEED SAUCE! WILTED CABBAGE STALKS WITH STRAW-BERRY AND ONION SYRUP!
NEXT WE'LL HAVE A TOSSED TUMBLEWEED SALAD IN COD LIVER OIL DRESSING!
REALLY, MR. DUCK, THERE'S NO NEED TO...
DON'T TALK! EAT! HERE COME THE MAIN COURSES!
SULPHURED SAUERBRATEN IN VINEGAR GRAVY!
BLOWFISH BLOATED WITH BLACK BEANS AND BOK-CHOY!
STEAK TARTAR SMOTHERED IN POACHED HUMMINGBIRD EGGS!
START ON THE NEXT PAGE, WAITER—AND DON'T FORGET OUR PITCHER OF WARM MANATEE MILK!

to my grandfather) to have suggested that myself, but at *his* suggestion I readily agreed. But how could I live on such low wages? I recall sitting down and figuring it out on paper—at what Gladstone Publishing paid me, and if I then sold my original artwork to collectors, I could maybe make about a half to two-thirds of my previous income, and that might just barely be enough. Now, truth be told— a vitally important aspect of this, I admit, was that my wife was a teacher which meant a steady income and job security for her, and health insurance through her job for me. There would be no money left for vacations or any other niceties of life... but we probably (?) wouldn't starve. What sort of life would that be?

With the Keno Rosa Co. I had a boring job that held no meaning to me, and at the end of the year the only result would be *money*—which would soon be spent on things I loved but didn't need, like big TVs or antique cars. If I became a cartoonist, at the end of each year I would have no spare money; but there'd be a year's worth of my Uncle Scrooge stories that would exist forever! To me, that was *cosmic*.

So began my life as a professional cartoonist, and a cartoonist who only created stories based on Carl Barks' wonderful Ducks. Almost literally overnight I had stumbled into living the dream of my lifetime. And people even liked my stories despite my amateurish artwork!

Another matter I might discuss in this first volume is why I insist on setting my stories about talking ducks in the real world, with real history, rather than in the traditional funny-animal Disney universe with talking chipmunks and giant mice wearing clothes. You can blame Carl Barks and my sister for that. It's Barks' "fault" that I saw his characters as human beings due to how realisti- cally he depicted their personalities and backgrounds.

Furthermore, his greatest adventures (such as my beloved "Golden Helmet") were set in the real world, with actual places and historical figures.

It was in the *other* comic books that my sister would lend me that I saw *true* "funny animals"—Bugs Bunny was naked, lived in a hole in the ground and stole carrots from farmer Fudd; equally nude Daffy Duck was shot at by duck hunters and flew south for the winter (and I don't mean in an airplane). They were obviously animals. But Barks' Donald lived in a house and had trouble holding down a job, and his Scrooge had an office staff and had to pay taxes. To my young mind, these were obviously human beings—I decided that cartoonists simply drew humans in different such manners. While I thought that one way to draw a human was in the form of Donald or Scrooge, I could also see the more ordinary appearing humans who populated Duckburg. So, when I started drawing my own comics with my own human characters at around age five, I gave them all round black noses, because I thought that's how humans were supposed to be drawn.

Therefore I have always known that Donald and Scrooge were human beings. As an example, if I had written some plot where, to save his life in some predicament, Donald needed a feather... I guess he'd need to hunt down a pillow somewhere, because to have him simply pluck a feather off his tail would seem utterly bizarre to me! In some early stories I would make gags referring to the characters' "bills" or their large feet, but I soon realized that, even for the sake of an extra laugh, I felt uncomfortable making any references to these characters as anything but ordinary humans.

My too-serious attitude towards these characters seems to annoy a few Disney comics readers, and I'm sorry for

HERE COMES FIVE-FINGER RAPIDS! SHOVE THAT BERG DOWN THE WEST CHANNEL! THAT'LL KNOCK THOSE DUCKS INTO THE DRINK!
RIGHT, BOSS!
WHUMP!
HEY! LOOK OUT!
OH, MY SAINTED AUNT PINTAIL!
WAAAHOOO! REMINDS ME OF THE TIME I SURVEYED DAM SITES IN NEW ZEALAND!
GOOD FOR YOU!

that. But... I guess they'd just better just read all the other Donald Duck comics and give mine a pass.

Another quirk I have, though it's not too obvious, is that my Duck stories are all set in the *past*, not the present. This is not readily apparent unless you spot tiny details in the backgrounds, such as dates on calendars or business ledgers in Scrooge's office. The reasons for this are twofold.

First, I've always seen my job as not simply writing and drawing stories of Scrooge McDuck, but of creating stories of only *Carl Barks'* Scrooge McDuck. The Barks stories I grew up with stated word-for-word that Scrooge was a Yukon Sourdough in 1897, a cowboy in 1882, and a riverboat crewman in 1880. Therefore he would be at *least* 140-150 years old in my stories if they took place in the present. Other fans or writers like to explain this paradox by saying that the Ducks are "fairy-tale creatures" who are immortal and live in a fairy tale world. To me that seems like a needlessly complicated (and plain silly) way to deal with the problem. I personally would have no interest in creating (or reading) adventure stories about immortal fairy-tale creatures. I also think the "fairy tale" notion spoils the charm of the realistic personalities and environment of these Carl Barks characters. I have a bit of trouble thinking of Donald as the "average guy" if he's immortal. For me, the simple solution is that I treat the characters as normal flesh and blood beings, but set the stories in the past. That clears up every possible paradox. Other comics writers or readers can regard their Duck stories as they choose—that's absolutely their privilege! But all of my stories take place in an indefinite swirl of the mid-1950s.

The second reason is even simpler—the 1950s were the decade when I was first reading Barks' original stories myself. It's just another personal thrill to imagine that I am

THEY'RE FIGMENTS OF THE IMAGINATION—LIKE FAUNS AND SATYRS! YOU KNOW, GUYS LIKE THIS! BAA! BAA!

Above: From Carl Barks' "Trail of the Unicorn" (*Four Color* 263). Like Rosa, Barks always drew a very clear distinction between the Ducks and traditional creatures of fairy tales and folklore.

YESSIR! I'M GONNA TRY FOR THAT PRIZE!
YOU'VE CONVINCED ME, CUZ! I'LL ENTER THE CONTEST, TOO!
PLEASE! SOMEONE TELL ME THAT ISN'T MY DISGUSTINGLY LUCKY COUSIN, GLADSTONE!
IF IT ISN'T, SOMEONE'S DOING A GREAT IMPRESSION OF HIM!
YOU GOOD FOR NOTHING LOAFER! YOU SPOIL EVERY CONTEST YOU ENTER... BY WINNING!
IT'S A DIRTY JOB, BUT SOMEONE'S GOT TO DO IT!

UM...ER...YOU OWN THIS...AH...HOTEL?
YES, SCROOGE! YOU RECALL THE MONEY I CAME INTO A WHILE BACK?
WELL, I RETURNED TO DAWSON AND BOUGHT THE OLD BLACKJACK BALLROOM TO SAVE IT FROM DEMOLITION! IT'S NOW A TOURIST HOTEL!
YOU NEED A PLACE TO STAY TONIGHT, SCROOGE?

sending my stories back through a time warp to myself to read when I was young. Or another way I think of it is with an example of a kid who was so inspired by his favorite baseball team of his youth, the 1953 New York Yankees, that he grows up wanting to become a professional baseball player. And decades later, he succeeds in joining the Yankees team. Well, I've topped what that baseball fanboy did—what I did was the equivalent of going back in time joining *the* 1953 Yankees team itself!

There may always be some new readers to join the ranks, so I need to mention the acronymic dedication I put in all my work with Barks' Ducks. "D.U.C.K."... that stands for "Dedicated to Unca Carl from Keno," Keno being my actual first name (as you'll have seen above in the name of my old family business). I put that dedication into the last panel of my first story in plain sight. But it looked like it might be a penname, so it was removed by the editor—since back in 1986, the only signature allowed in a Disney comic was Walt's. After the "D.U.C.K." was removed a few times, I started hiding it so the editor would not spot it. Soon I settled on always hiding it in the first ("splash") panel of the story, and then later adding it to cover art as well. Each story and cover in this book will be accompanied by a mention of where the "D.U.C.K." dedication can be found. If you enjoy hunting down the dedication without help, don't look at the solution. But be forewarned—for one reason or another, the "D.U.C.K." is sometimes *not there* to be found. Please don't make yourself crazy. •

GLADSTONE
WALT DISNEY'S
95¢
NO. 219
JULY
02661
UNCLE
$CROOGE

Cover to "The Son of the Sun" as originally published on *Uncle Scrooge* 219 (1987). Only a small percentage of copies—like this one—correctly colored Scrooge's and Flintheart Glomgold's canes brown. Most copies in circulation mysteriously make the canes green.

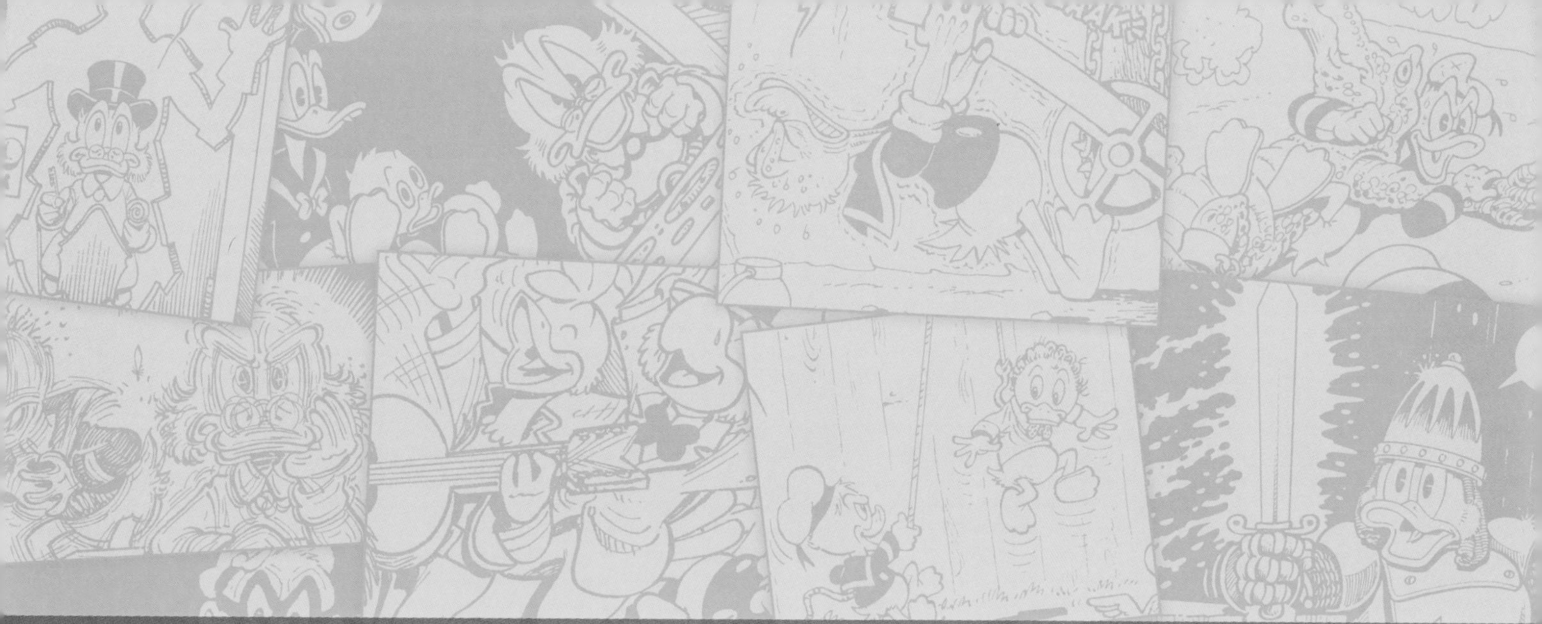

The Stories

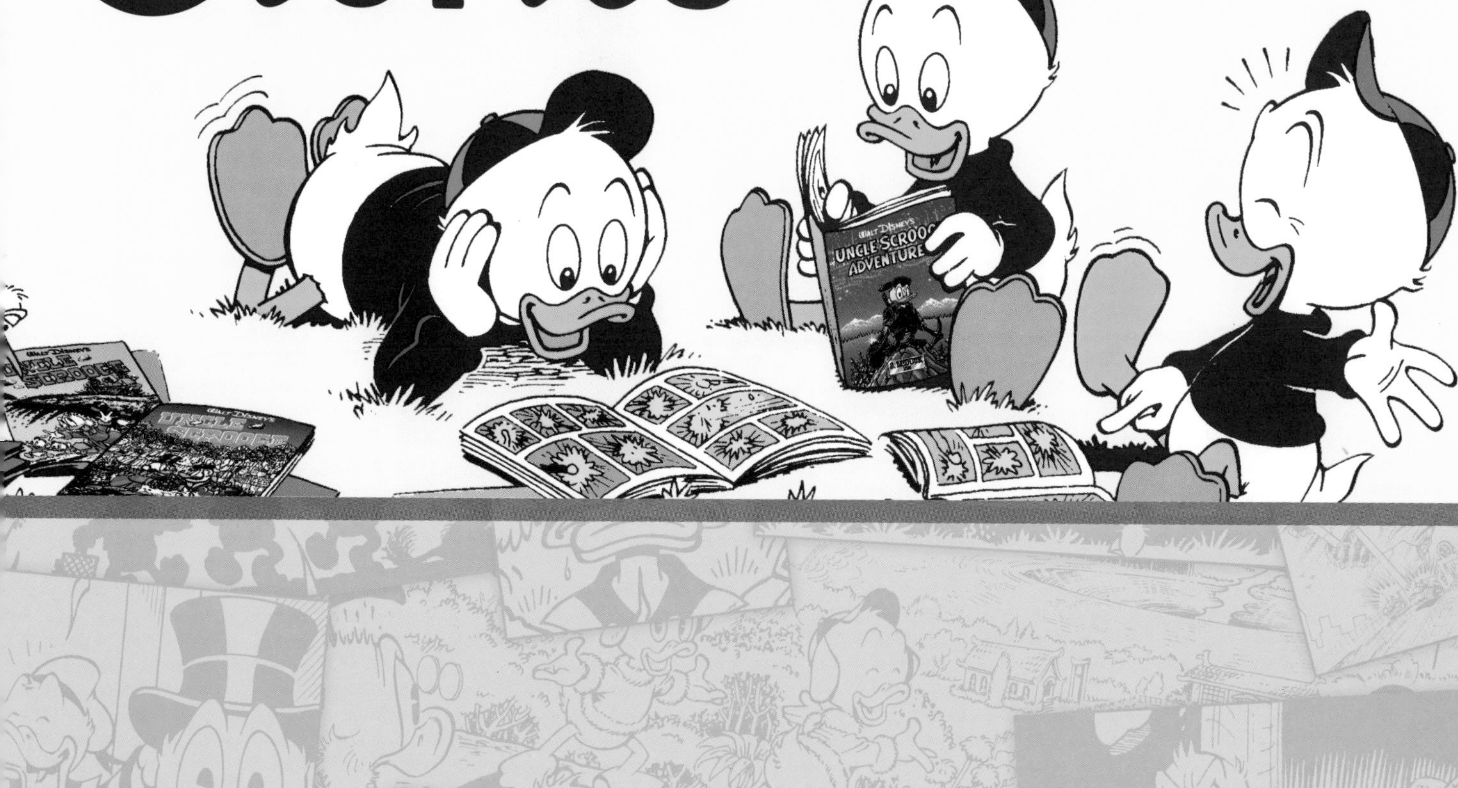
WALT DISNEY'S
UNCLE SCROOGE ADVENTURES

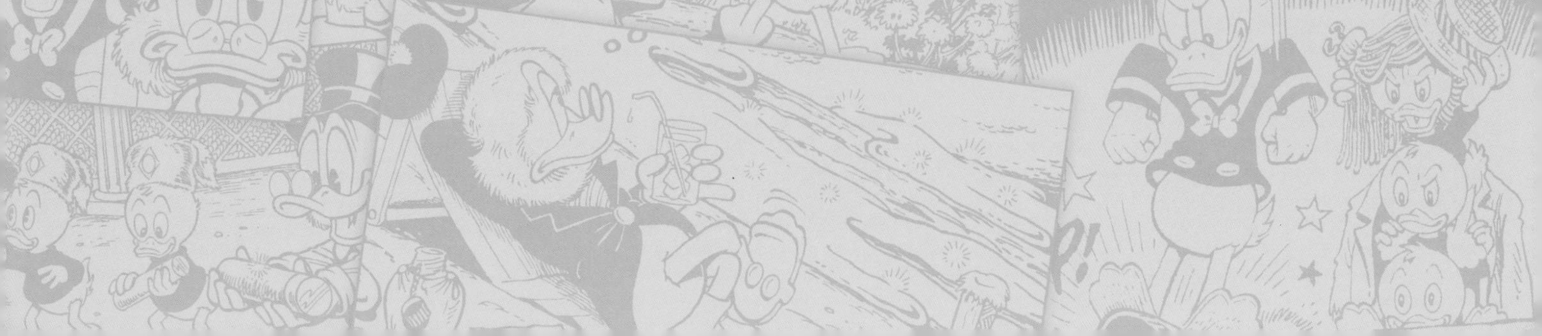

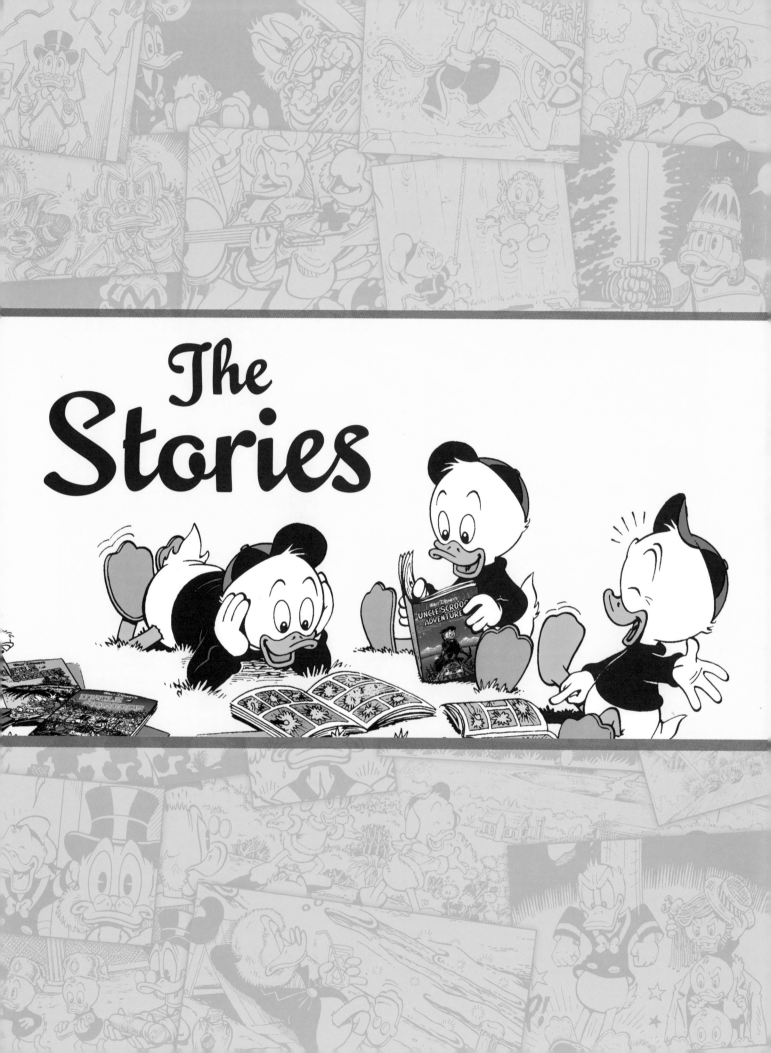

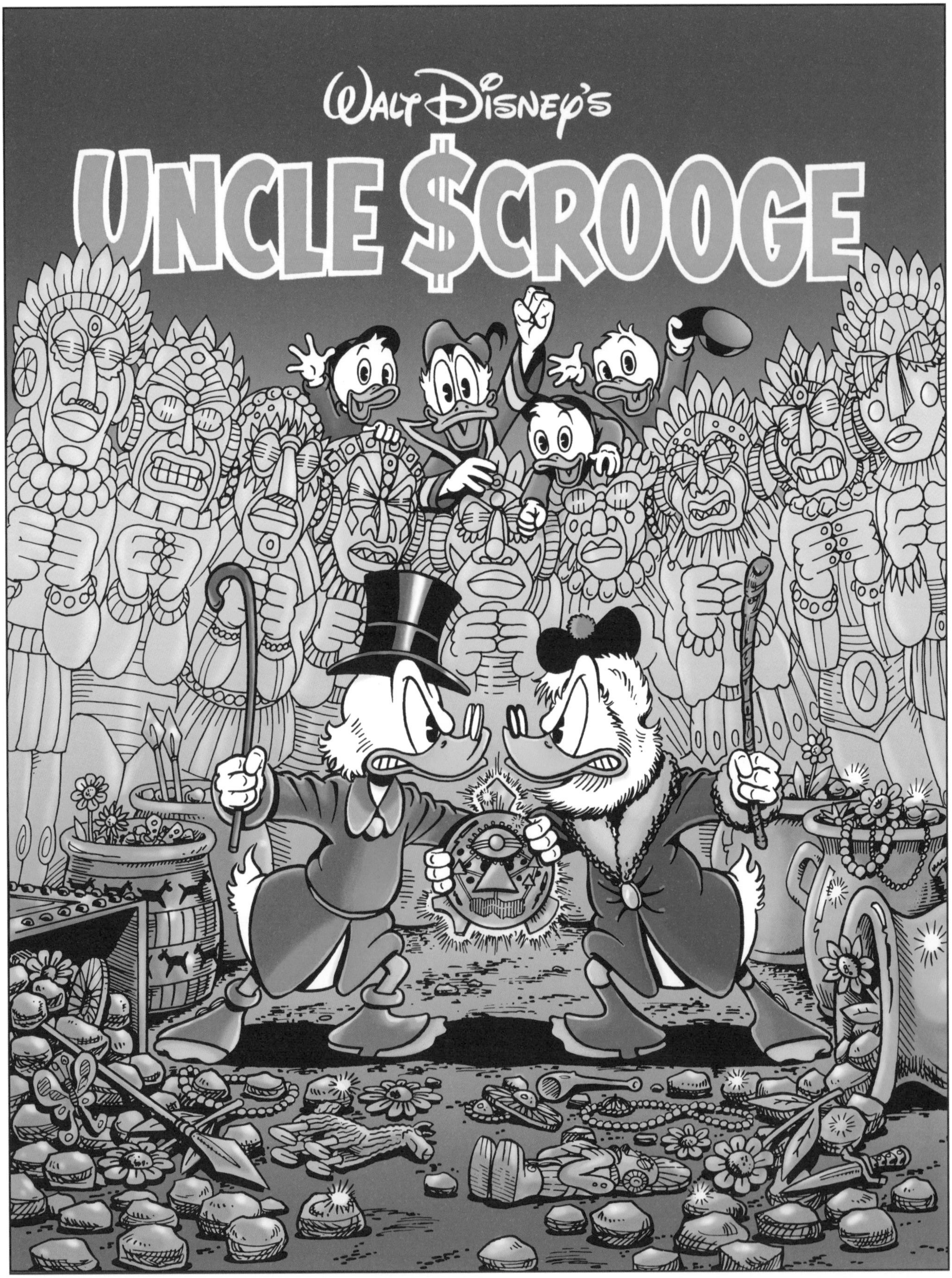
WALT DISNEY'S
UNCLE $CROOGE

THE SON OF THE SUN
Gladstone Giant Comic Album Special 4, April 1990; new color by Kneon Transitt.
The first Duck comic book cover drawn by Don Rosa. See page 164 for a variant drawn later but published earlier.

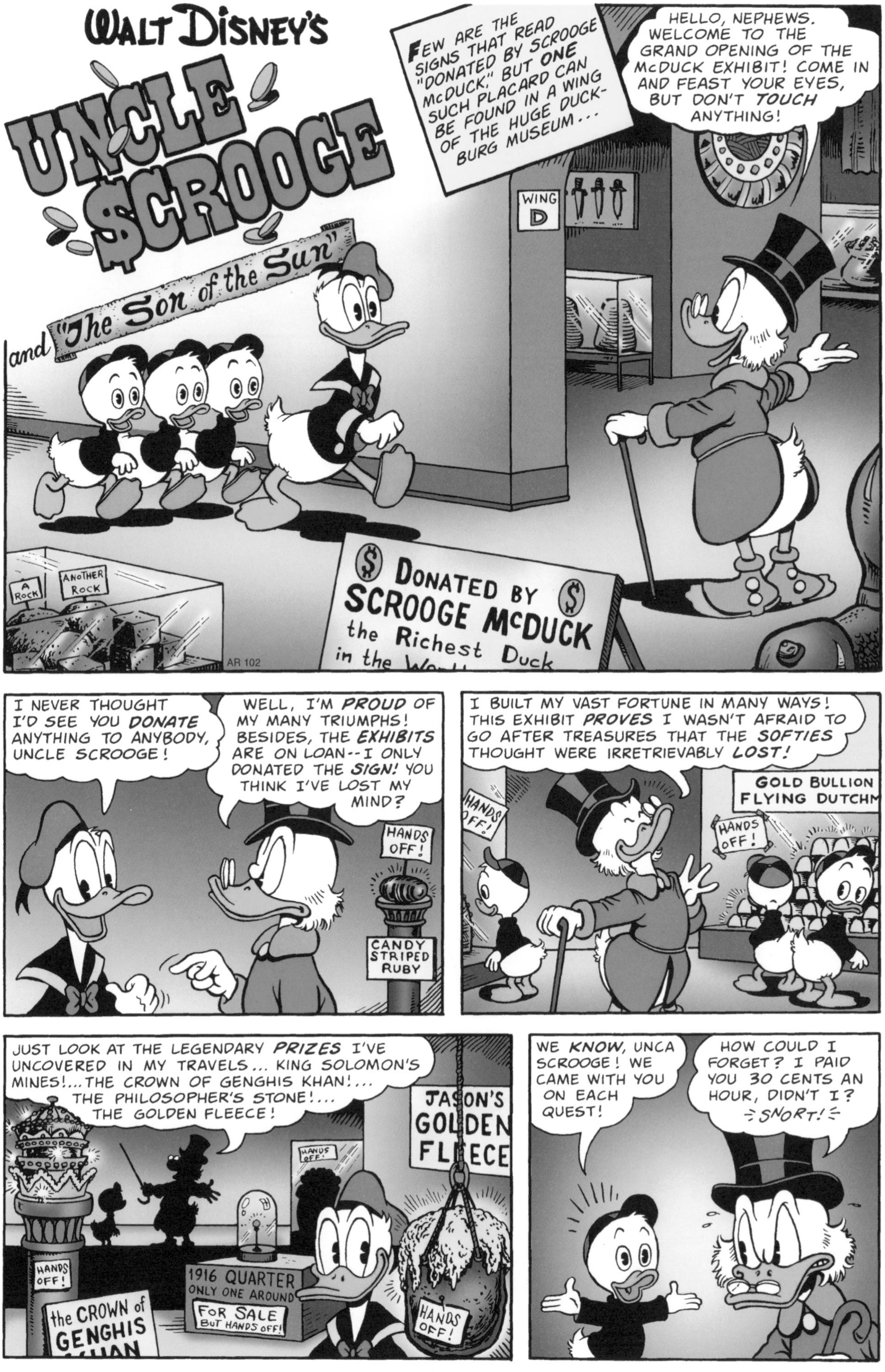
WALT DISNEY'S
UNCLE $CROOGE
and "The Son of the Sun"
FEW ARE THE SIGNS THAT READ "DONATED BY SCROOGE McDUCK," BUT ONE SUCH PLACARD CAN BE FOUND IN A WING OF THE HUGE DUCKBURG MUSEUM...
HELLO, NEPHEWS. WELCOME TO THE GRAND OPENING OF THE McDUCK EXHIBIT! COME IN AND FEAST YOUR EYES, BUT DON'T TOUCH ANYTHING!
WING D
A ROCK
ANOTHER ROCK
DONATED BY SCROOGE McDUCK the Richest Duck in the
AR 102
I NEVER THOUGHT I'D SEE YOU DONATE ANYTHING TO ANYBODY, UNCLE SCROOGE!
WELL, I'M PROUD OF MY MANY TRIUMPHS! BESIDES, THE EXHIBITS ARE ON LOAN--I ONLY DONATED THE SIGN! YOU THINK I'VE LOST MY MIND?
HANDS OFF!
CANDY STRIPED RUBY
I BUILT MY VAST FORTUNE IN MANY WAYS! THIS EXHIBIT PROVES I WASN'T AFRAID TO GO AFTER TREASURES THAT THE SOFTIES THOUGHT WERE IRRETRIEVABLY LOST!
HANDS OFF!
GOLD BULLION FLYING DUTCHM
HANDS OFF!
JUST LOOK AT THE LEGENDARY PRIZES I'VE UNCOVERED IN MY TRAVELS... KING SOLOMON'S MINES!... THE CROWN OF GENGHIS KHAN!... THE PHILOSOPHER'S STONE!... THE GOLDEN FLEECE!
JASON'S GOLDEN FLEECE
HANDS OFF!
HANDS OFF!
the CROWN of GENGHIS
1916 QUARTER ONLY ONE AROUND
FOR SALE BUT HANDS OFF!
HANDS OFF!
WE KNOW, UNCA SCROOGE! WE CAME WITH YOU ON EACH QUEST!
HOW COULD I FORGET? I PAID YOU 30 CENTS AN HOUR, DIDN'T I?
SNORT!

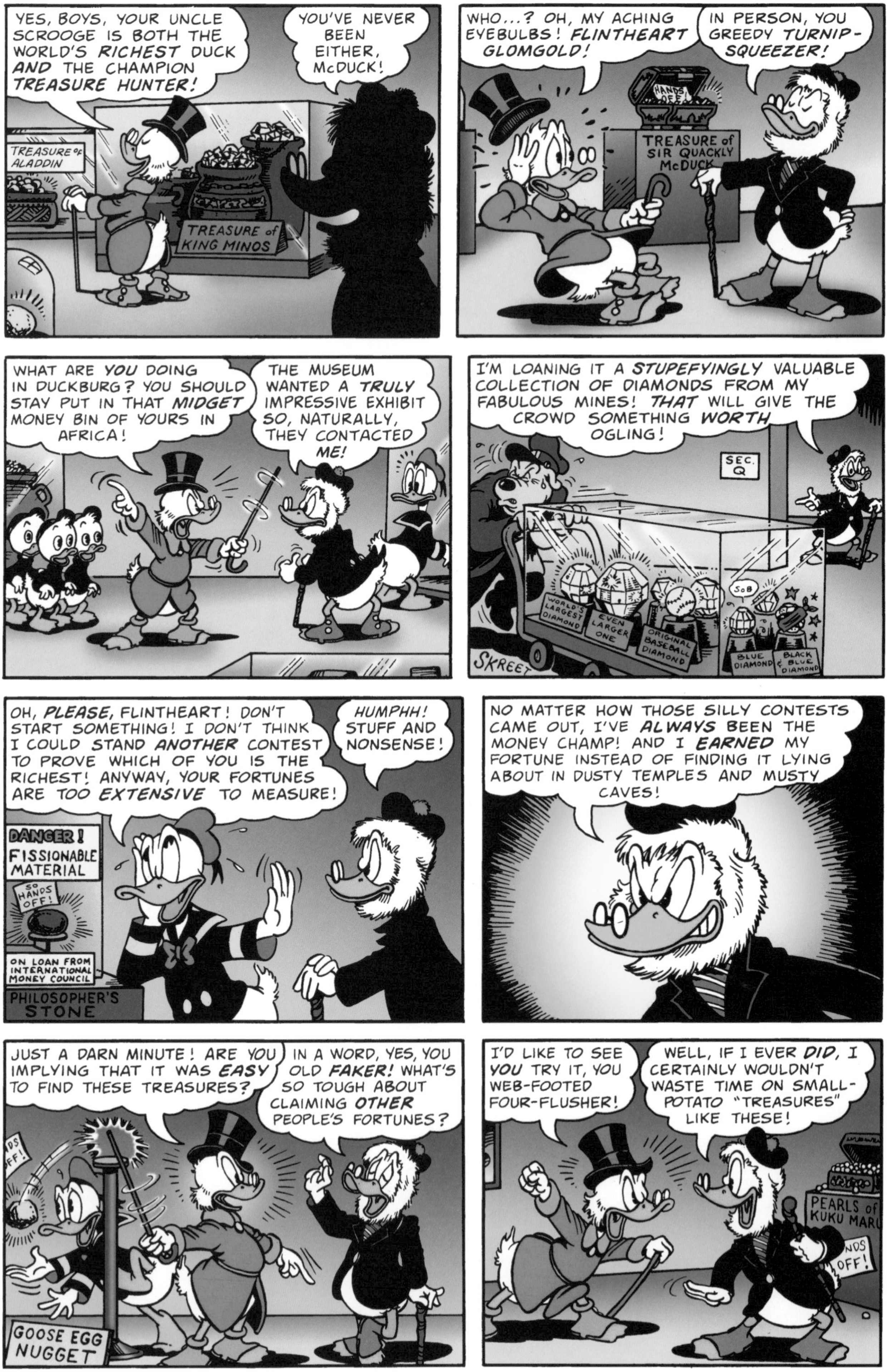
YES, BOYS, YOUR UNCLE SCROOGE IS BOTH THE WORLD'S RICHEST DUCK AND THE CHAMPION TREASURE HUNTER!
YOU'VE NEVER BEEN EITHER, McDUCK!
TREASURE of ALADDIN
TREASURE of KING MINOS
WHO...? OH, MY ACHING EYEBULBS! FLINTHEART GLOMGOLD!
IN PERSON, YOU GREEDY TURNIP-SQUEEZER!
HANDS OFF!
TREASURE of SIR QUACKLY McDUCK
WHAT ARE YOU DOING IN DUCKBURG? YOU SHOULD STAY PUT IN THAT MIDGET MONEY BIN OF YOURS IN AFRICA!
THE MUSEUM WANTED A TRULY IMPRESSIVE EXHIBIT SO, NATURALLY, THEY CONTACTED ME!
I'M LOANING IT A STUPEFYINGLY VALUABLE COLLECTION OF DIAMONDS FROM MY FABULOUS MINES! THAT WILL GIVE THE CROWD SOMETHING WORTH OGLING!
SEC. Q
WORLD'S LARGEST DIAMOND
EVEN LARGER ONE
ORIGINAL BASEBALL DIAMOND
SoB
BLUE DIAMOND
BLACK & BLUE DIAMOND
SKREET
OH, PLEASE, FLINTHEART! DON'T START SOMETHING! I DON'T THINK I COULD STAND ANOTHER CONTEST TO PROVE WHICH OF YOU IS THE RICHEST! ANYWAY, YOUR FORTUNES ARE TOO EXTENSIVE TO MEASURE!
HUMPHH! STUFF AND NONSENSE!
DANGER! FISSIONABLE MATERIAL
SO HANDS OFF!
ON LOAN FROM INTERNATIONAL MONEY COUNCIL
PHILOSOPHER'S STONE
NO MATTER HOW THOSE SILLY CONTESTS CAME OUT, I'VE ALWAYS BEEN THE MONEY CHAMP! AND I EARNED MY FORTUNE INSTEAD OF FINDING IT LYING ABOUT IN DUSTY TEMPLES AND MUSTY CAVES!
JUST A DARN MINUTE! ARE YOU IMPLYING THAT IT WAS EASY TO FIND THESE TREASURES?
IN A WORD, YES, YOU OLD FAKER! WHAT'S SO TOUGH ABOUT CLAIMING OTHER PEOPLE'S FORTUNES?
GOOSE EGG NUGGET
I'D LIKE TO SEE YOU TRY IT, YOU WEB-FOOTED FOUR-FLUSHER!
WELL, IF I EVER DID, I CERTAINLY WOULDN'T WASTE TIME ON SMALL-POTATO "TREASURES" LIKE THESE!
PEARLS of KUKU MARU

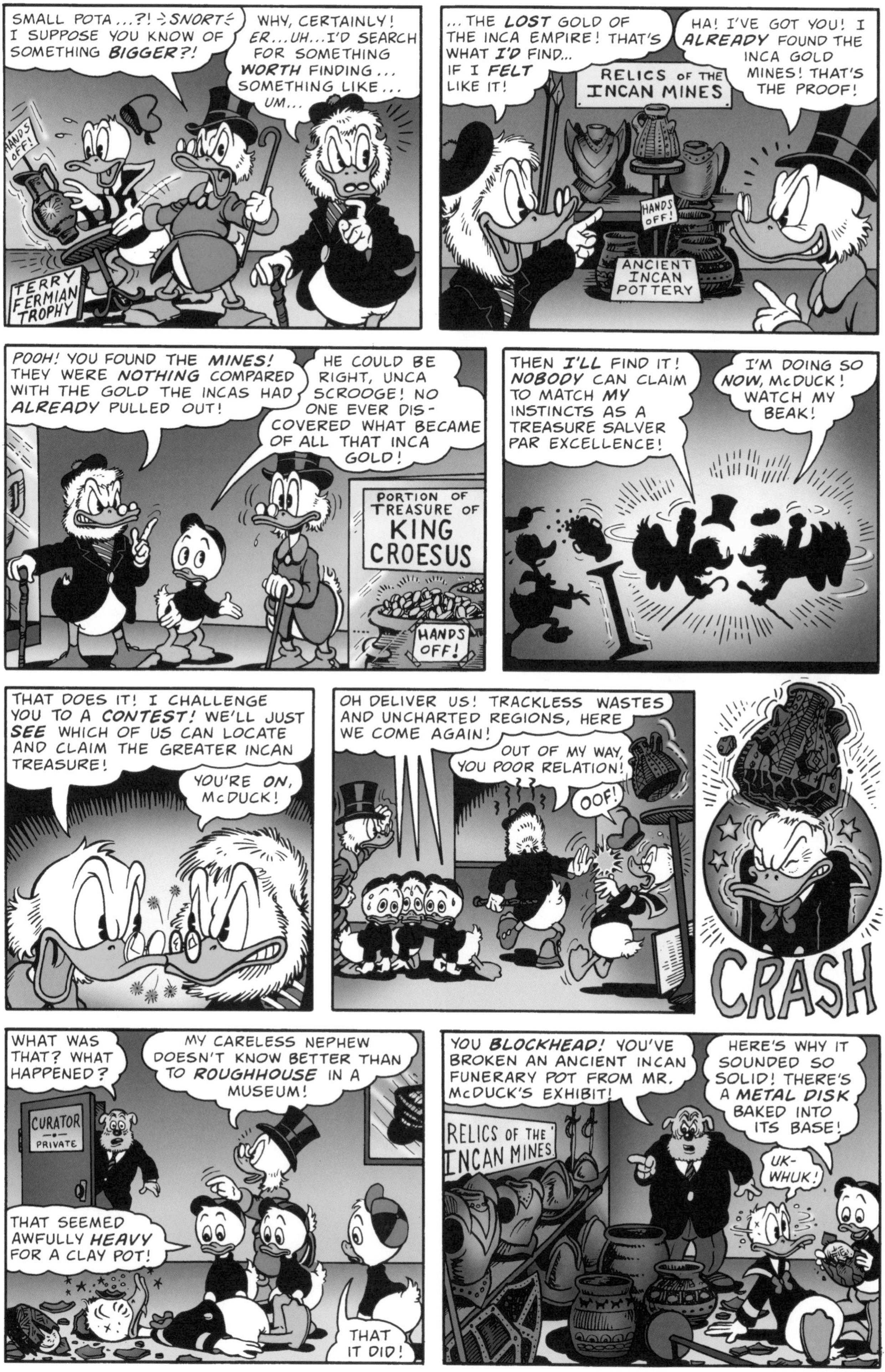
SMALL POTA...?! SNORT I SUPPOSE YOU KNOW OF SOMETHING BIGGER?!
WHY, CERTAINLY! ER...UH...I'D SEARCH FOR SOMETHING WORTH FINDING... SOMETHING LIKE... UM...
HANDS OFF!
TERRY FERMIAN TROPHY
...THE LOST GOLD OF THE INCA EMPIRE! THAT'S WHAT I'D FIND... IF I FELT LIKE IT!
HA! I'VE GOT YOU! I ALREADY FOUND THE INCA GOLD MINES! THAT'S THE PROOF!
RELICS OF THE INCAN MINES
HANDS OFF!
ANCIENT INCAN POTTERY
POOH! YOU FOUND THE MINES! THEY WERE NOTHING COMPARED WITH THE GOLD THE INCAS HAD ALREADY PULLED OUT!
HE COULD BE RIGHT, UNCA SCROOGE! NO ONE EVER DISCOVERED WHAT BECAME OF ALL THAT INCA GOLD!
PORTION OF TREASURE OF KING CROESUS
HANDS OFF!
THEN I'LL FIND IT! NOBODY CAN CLAIM TO MATCH MY INSTINCTS AS A TREASURE SALVER PAR EXCELLENCE!
I'M DOING SO NOW, McDUCK! WATCH MY BEAK!
THAT DOES IT! I CHALLENGE YOU TO A CONTEST! WE'LL JUST SEE WHICH OF US CAN LOCATE AND CLAIM THE GREATER INCAN TREASURE!
YOU'RE ON, McDUCK!
OH DELIVER US! TRACKLESS WASTES AND UNCHARTED REGIONS, HERE WE COME AGAIN!
OUT OF MY WAY, YOU POOR RELATION!
OOF!
CRASH
WHAT WAS THAT? WHAT HAPPENED?
MY CARELESS NEPHEW DOESN'T KNOW BETTER THAN TO ROUGHHOUSE IN A MUSEUM!
CURATOR PRIVATE
THAT SEEMED AWFULLY HEAVY FOR A CLAY POT!
THAT IT DID!
YOU BLOCKHEAD! YOU'VE BROKEN AN ANCIENT INCAN FUNERARY POT FROM MR. McDUCK'S EXHIBIT!
HERE'S WHY IT SOUNDED SO SOLID! THERE'S A METAL DISK BAKED INTO ITS BASE!
RELICS OF THE INCAN MINES
UK-WHUK!

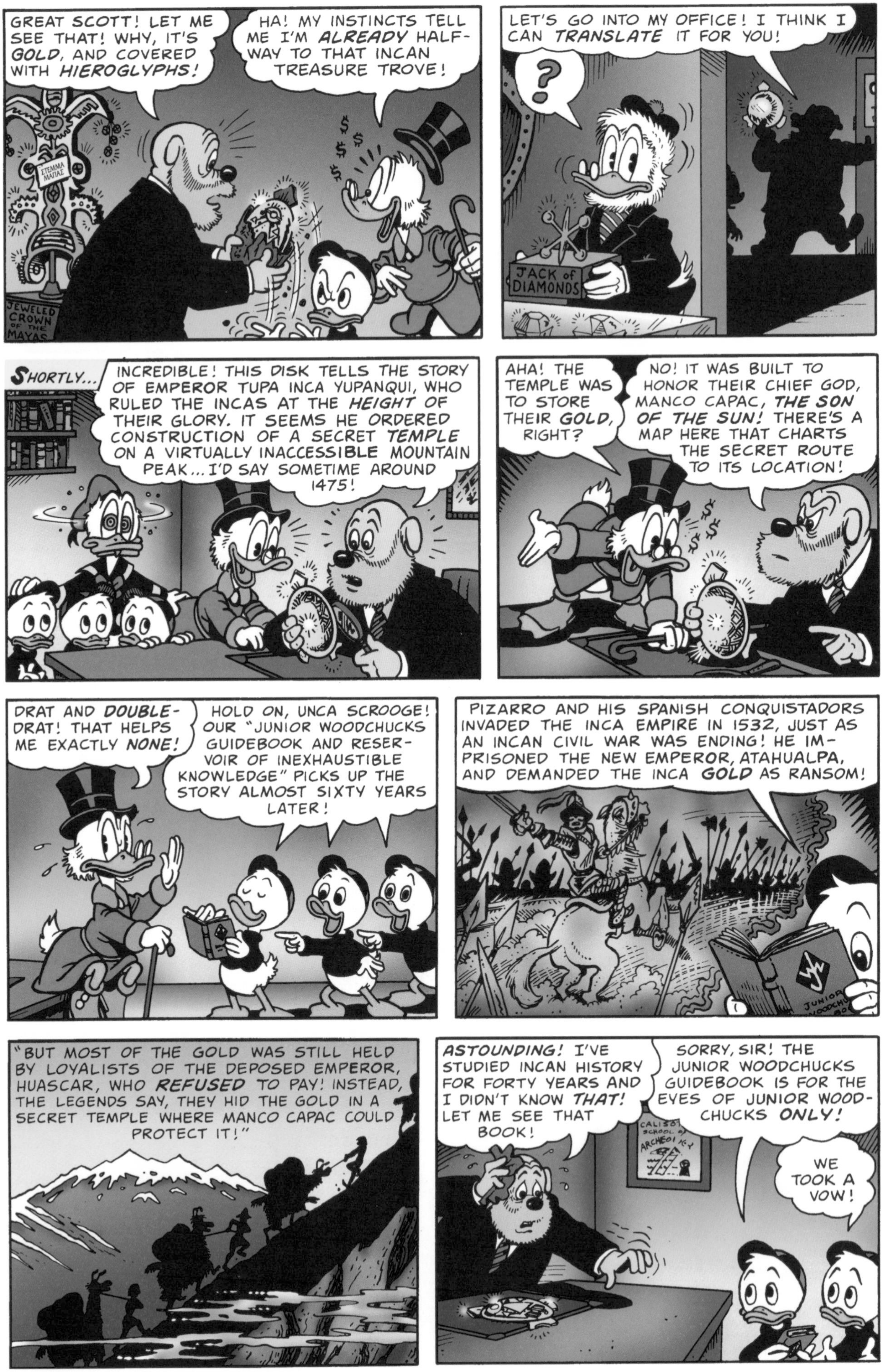
GREAT SCOTT! LET ME SEE THAT! WHY, IT'S GOLD, AND COVERED WITH HIEROGLYPHS!
HA! MY INSTINCTS TELL ME I'M ALREADY HALF-WAY TO THAT INCAN TREASURE TROVE!
JEWELED CROWN OF THE MAYAS
LET'S GO INTO MY OFFICE! I THINK I CAN TRANSLATE IT FOR YOU!
?
JACK of DIAMONDS
SHORTLY...
INCREDIBLE! THIS DISK TELLS THE STORY OF EMPEROR TUPA INCA YUPANQUI, WHO RULED THE INCAS AT THE HEIGHT OF THEIR GLORY. IT SEEMS HE ORDERED CONSTRUCTION OF A SECRET TEMPLE ON A VIRTUALLY INACCESSIBLE MOUNTAIN PEAK... I'D SAY SOMETIME AROUND 1475!
AHA! THE TEMPLE WAS TO STORE THEIR GOLD, RIGHT?
NO! IT WAS BUILT TO HONOR THEIR CHIEF GOD, MANCO CAPAC, THE SON OF THE SUN! THERE'S A MAP HERE THAT CHARTS THE SECRET ROUTE TO ITS LOCATION!
DRAT AND DOUBLE-DRAT! THAT HELPS ME EXACTLY NONE!
HOLD ON, UNCA SCROOGE! OUR "JUNIOR WOODCHUCKS GUIDEBOOK AND RESER-VOIR OF INEXHAUSTIBLE KNOWLEDGE" PICKS UP THE STORY ALMOST SIXTY YEARS LATER!
PIZARRO AND HIS SPANISH CONQUISTADORS INVADED THE INCA EMPIRE IN 1532, JUST AS AN INCAN CIVIL WAR WAS ENDING! HE IM-PRISONED THE NEW EMPEROR, ATAHUALPA, AND DEMANDED THE INCA GOLD AS RANSOM!
"BUT MOST OF THE GOLD WAS STILL HELD BY LOYALISTS OF THE DEPOSED EMPEROR, HUASCAR, WHO REFUSED TO PAY! INSTEAD, THE LEGENDS SAY, THEY HID THE GOLD IN A SECRET TEMPLE WHERE MANCO CAPAC COULD PROTECT IT!"
ASTOUNDING! I'VE STUDIED INCAN HISTORY FOR FORTY YEARS AND I DIDN'T KNOW THAT! LET ME SEE THAT BOOK!
SORRY, SIR! THE JUNIOR WOODCHUCKS GUIDEBOOK IS FOR THE EYES OF JUNIOR WOOD-CHUCKS ONLY!
WE TOOK A VOW!

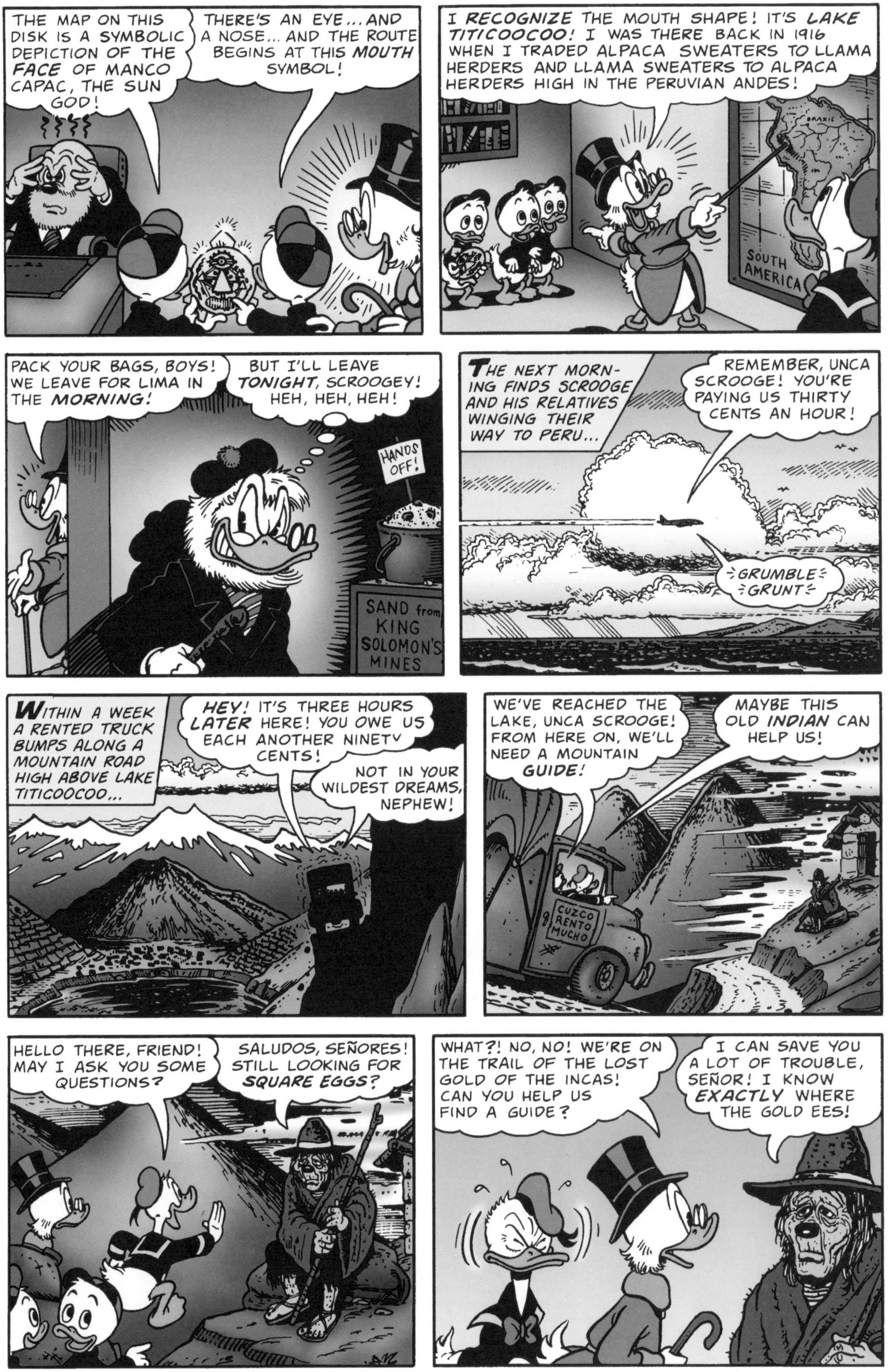
THE MAP ON THIS DISK IS A SYMBOLIC DEPICTION OF THE FACE OF MANCO CAPAC, THE SUN GOD!
THERE'S AN EYE... AND A NOSE... AND THE ROUTE BEGINS AT THIS MOUTH SYMBOL!
I RECOGNIZE THE MOUTH SHAPE! IT'S LAKE TITICOOCOO! I WAS THERE BACK IN 1916 WHEN I TRADED ALPACA SWEATERS TO LLAMA HERDERS AND LLAMA SWEATERS TO ALPACA HERDERS HIGH IN THE PERUVIAN ANDES!
SOUTH AMERICA
PACK YOUR BAGS, BOYS! WE LEAVE FOR LIMA IN THE MORNING!
BUT I'LL LEAVE TONIGHT, SCROOGEY! HEH, HEH, HEH!
HANDS OFF!
SAND from KING SOLOMON'S MINES
THE NEXT MORNING FINDS SCROOGE AND HIS RELATIVES WINGING THEIR WAY TO PERU...
REMEMBER, UNCA SCROOGE! YOU'RE PAYING US THIRTY CENTS AN HOUR!
GRUMBLE GRUNT
WITHIN A WEEK A RENTED TRUCK BUMPS ALONG A MOUNTAIN ROAD HIGH ABOVE LAKE TITICOOCOO...
HEY! IT'S THREE HOURS LATER HERE! YOU OWE US EACH ANOTHER NINETY CENTS!
NOT IN YOUR WILDEST DREAMS, NEPHEW!
WE'VE REACHED THE LAKE, UNCA SCROOGE! FROM HERE ON, WE'LL NEED A MOUNTAIN GUIDE!
MAYBE THIS OLD INDIAN CAN HELP US!
CUZCO RENTO MUCHO
HELLO THERE, FRIEND! MAY I ASK YOU SOME QUESTIONS?
SALUDOS, SEÑORES! STILL LOOKING FOR SQUARE EGGS?
WHAT?! NO, NO! WE'RE ON THE TRAIL OF THE LOST GOLD OF THE INCAS! CAN YOU HELP US FIND A GUIDE?
I CAN SAVE YOU A LOT OF TROUBLE, SEÑOR! I KNOW EXACTLY WHERE THE GOLD EES!

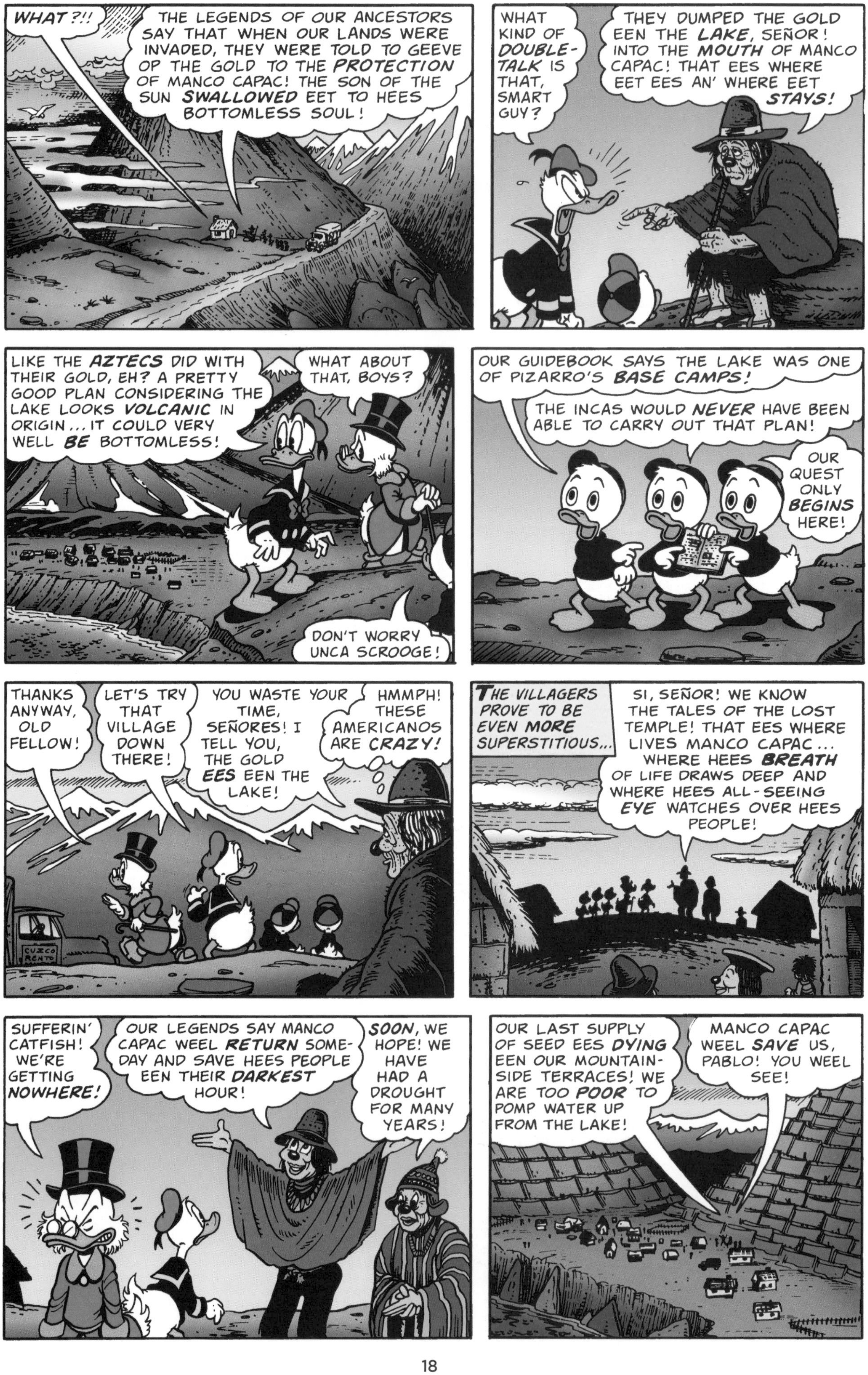
WHAT?!!
THE LEGENDS OF OUR ANCESTORS SAY THAT WHEN OUR LANDS WERE INVADED, THEY WERE TOLD TO GEEVE OP THE GOLD TO THE PROTECTION OF MANCO CAPAC! THE SON OF THE SUN SWALLOWED EET TO HEES BOTTOMLESS SOUL!
WHAT KIND OF DOUBLE-TALK IS THAT, SMART GUY?
THEY DUMPED THE GOLD EEN THE LAKE, SEÑOR! INTO THE MOUTH OF MANCO CAPAC! THAT EES WHERE EET EES AN' WHERE EET STAYS!
LIKE THE AZTECS DID WITH THEIR GOLD, EH? A PRETTY GOOD PLAN CONSIDERING THE LAKE LOOKS VOLCANIC IN ORIGIN... IT COULD VERY WELL BE BOTTOMLESS!
WHAT ABOUT THAT, BOYS?
DON'T WORRY UNCA SCROOGE!
OUR GUIDEBOOK SAYS THE LAKE WAS ONE OF PIZARRO'S BASE CAMPS!
THE INCAS WOULD NEVER HAVE BEEN ABLE TO CARRY OUT THAT PLAN!
OUR QUEST ONLY BEGINS HERE!
THANKS ANYWAY, OLD FELLOW!
LET'S TRY THAT VILLAGE DOWN THERE!
YOU WASTE YOUR TIME, SEÑORES! I TELL YOU, THE GOLD EES EEN THE LAKE!
HMMPH! THESE AMERICANOS ARE CRAZY!
CUZCO RENTO
THE VILLAGERS PROVE TO BE EVEN MORE SUPERSTITIOUS...
SI, SEÑOR! WE KNOW THE TALES OF THE LOST TEMPLE! THAT EES WHERE LIVES MANCO CAPAC... WHERE HEES BREATH OF LIFE DRAWS DEEP AND WHERE HEES ALL-SEEING EYE WATCHES OVER HEES PEOPLE!
SUFFERIN' CATFISH! WE'RE GETTING NOWHERE!
OUR LEGENDS SAY MANCO CAPAC WEEL RETURN SOME-DAY AND SAVE HEES PEOPLE EEN THEIR DARKEST HOUR!
SOON, WE HOPE! WE HAVE HAD A DROUGHT FOR MANY YEARS!
OUR LAST SUPPLY OF SEED EES DYING EEN OUR MOUNTAIN-SIDE TERRACES! WE ARE TOO POOR TO POMP WATER UP FROM THE LAKE!
MANCO CAPAC WEEL SAVE US, PABLO! YOU WEEL SEE!

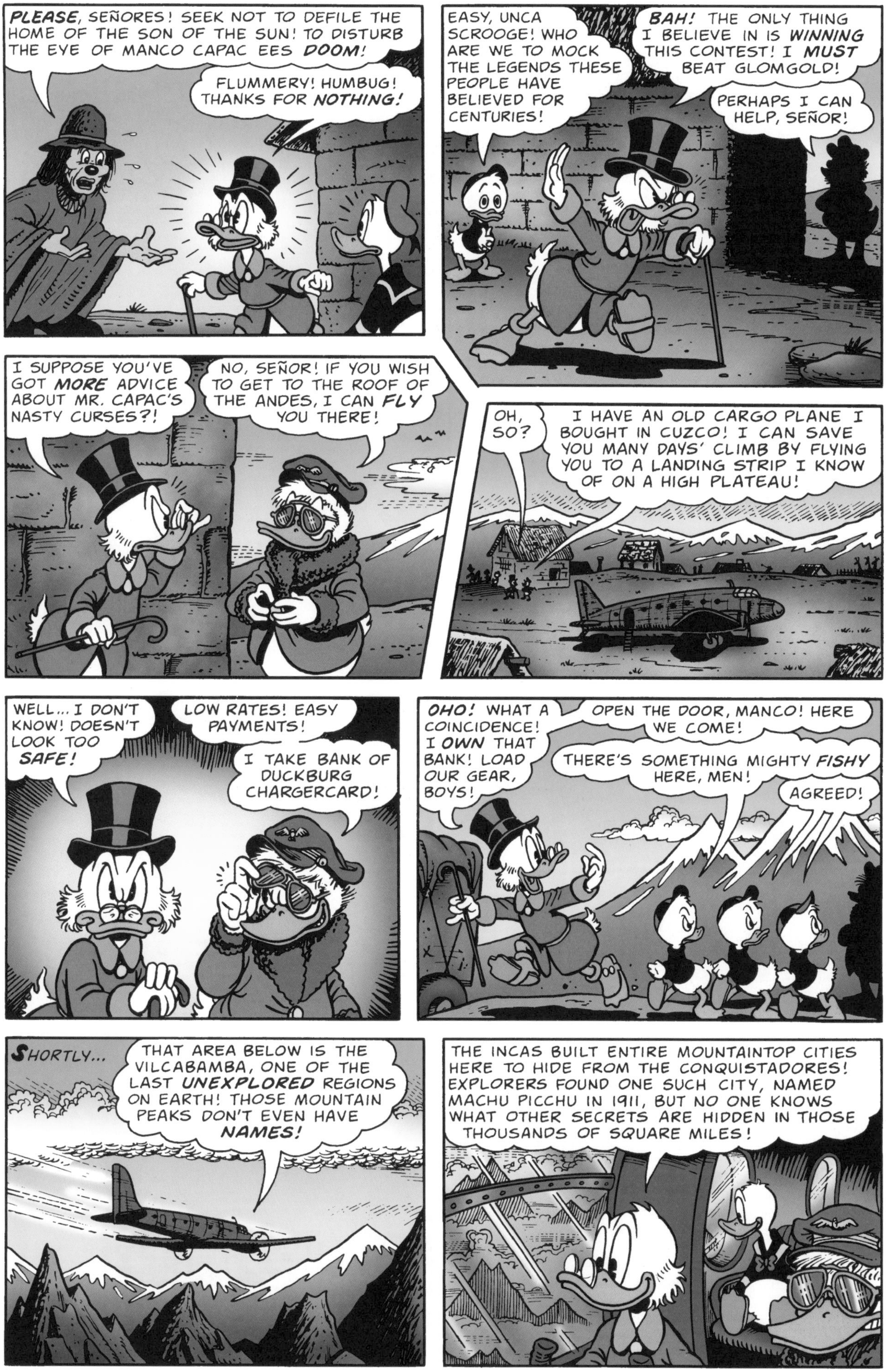

PLEASE, SEÑORES! SEEK NOT TO DEFILE THE HOME OF THE SON OF THE SUN! TO DISTURB THE EYE OF MANCO CAPAC EES DOOM!
FLUMMERY! HUMBUG! THANKS FOR NOTHING!
EASY, UNCA SCROOGE! WHO ARE WE TO MOCK THE LEGENDS THESE PEOPLE HAVE BELIEVED FOR CENTURIES!
BAH! THE ONLY THING I BELIEVE IN IS WINNING THIS CONTEST! I MUST BEAT GLOMGOLD!
PERHAPS I CAN HELP, SEÑOR!
I SUPPOSE YOU'VE GOT MORE ADVICE ABOUT MR. CAPAC'S NASTY CURSES?!
NO, SEÑOR! IF YOU WISH TO GET TO THE ROOF OF THE ANDES, I CAN FLY YOU THERE!
OH, SO?
I HAVE AN OLD CARGO PLANE I BOUGHT IN CUZCO! I CAN SAVE YOU MANY DAYS' CLIMB BY FLYING YOU TO A LANDING STRIP I KNOW OF ON A HIGH PLATEAU!
WELL... I DON'T KNOW! DOESN'T LOOK TOO SAFE!
LOW RATES! EASY PAYMENTS!
I TAKE BANK OF DUCKBURG CHARGERCARD!
OHO! WHAT A COINCIDENCE! I OWN THAT BANK! LOAD OUR GEAR, BOYS!
OPEN THE DOOR, MANCO! HERE WE COME!
THERE'S SOMETHING MIGHTY FISHY HERE, MEN!
AGREED!
SHORTLY...
THAT AREA BELOW IS THE VILCABAMBA, ONE OF THE LAST UNEXPLORED REGIONS ON EARTH! THOSE MOUNTAIN PEAKS DON'T EVEN HAVE NAMES!
THE INCAS BUILT ENTIRE MOUNTAINTOP CITIES HERE TO HIDE FROM THE CONQUISTADORES! EXPLORERS FOUND ONE SUCH CITY, NAMED MACHU PICCHU IN 1911, BUT NO ONE KNOWS WHAT OTHER SECRETS ARE HIDDEN IN THOSE THOUSANDS OF SQUARE MILES!

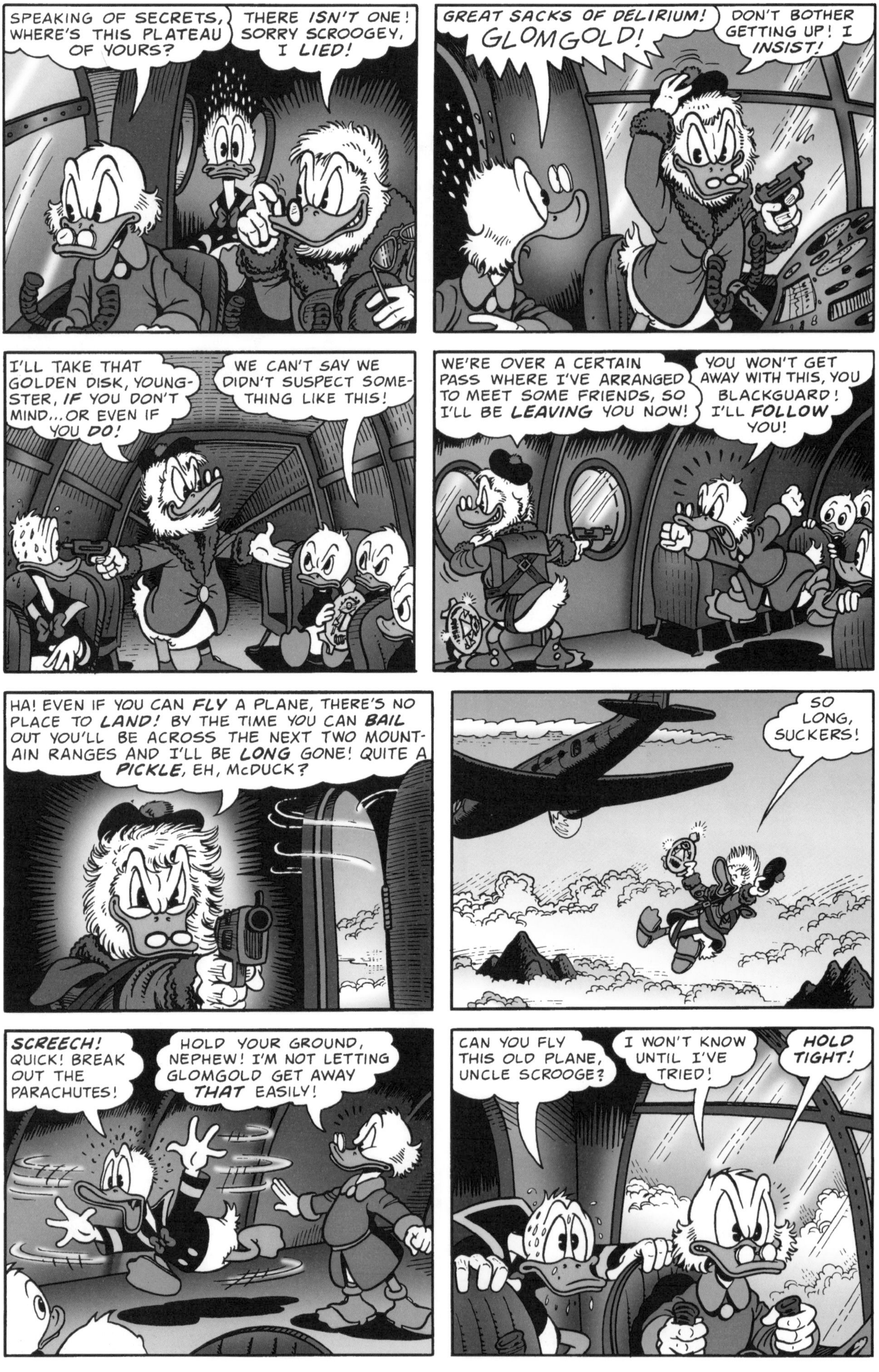
SPEAKING OF SECRETS, WHERE'S THIS PLATEAU OF YOURS?
THERE ISN'T ONE! SORRY SCROOGEY, I LIED!
GREAT SACKS OF DELIRIUM! GLOMGOLD!
DON'T BOTHER GETTING UP! I INSIST!
I'LL TAKE THAT GOLDEN DISK, YOUNGSTER, IF YOU DON'T MIND...OR EVEN IF YOU DO!
WE CAN'T SAY WE DIDN'T SUSPECT SOMETHING LIKE THIS!
WE'RE OVER A CERTAIN PASS WHERE I'VE ARRANGED TO MEET SOME FRIENDS, SO I'LL BE LEAVING YOU NOW!
YOU WON'T GET AWAY WITH THIS, YOU BLACKGUARD! I'LL FOLLOW YOU!
HA! EVEN IF YOU CAN FLY A PLANE, THERE'S NO PLACE TO LAND! BY THE TIME YOU CAN BAIL OUT YOU'LL BE ACROSS THE NEXT TWO MOUNTAIN RANGES AND I'LL BE LONG GONE! QUITE A PICKLE, EH, McDUCK?
SO LONG, SUCKERS!
SCREECH! QUICK! BREAK OUT THE PARACHUTES!
HOLD YOUR GROUND, NEPHEW! I'M NOT LETTING GLOMGOLD GET AWAY THAT EASILY!
CAN YOU FLY THIS OLD PLANE, UNCLE SCROOGE?
I WON'T KNOW UNTIL I'VE TRIED!
HOLD TIGHT!

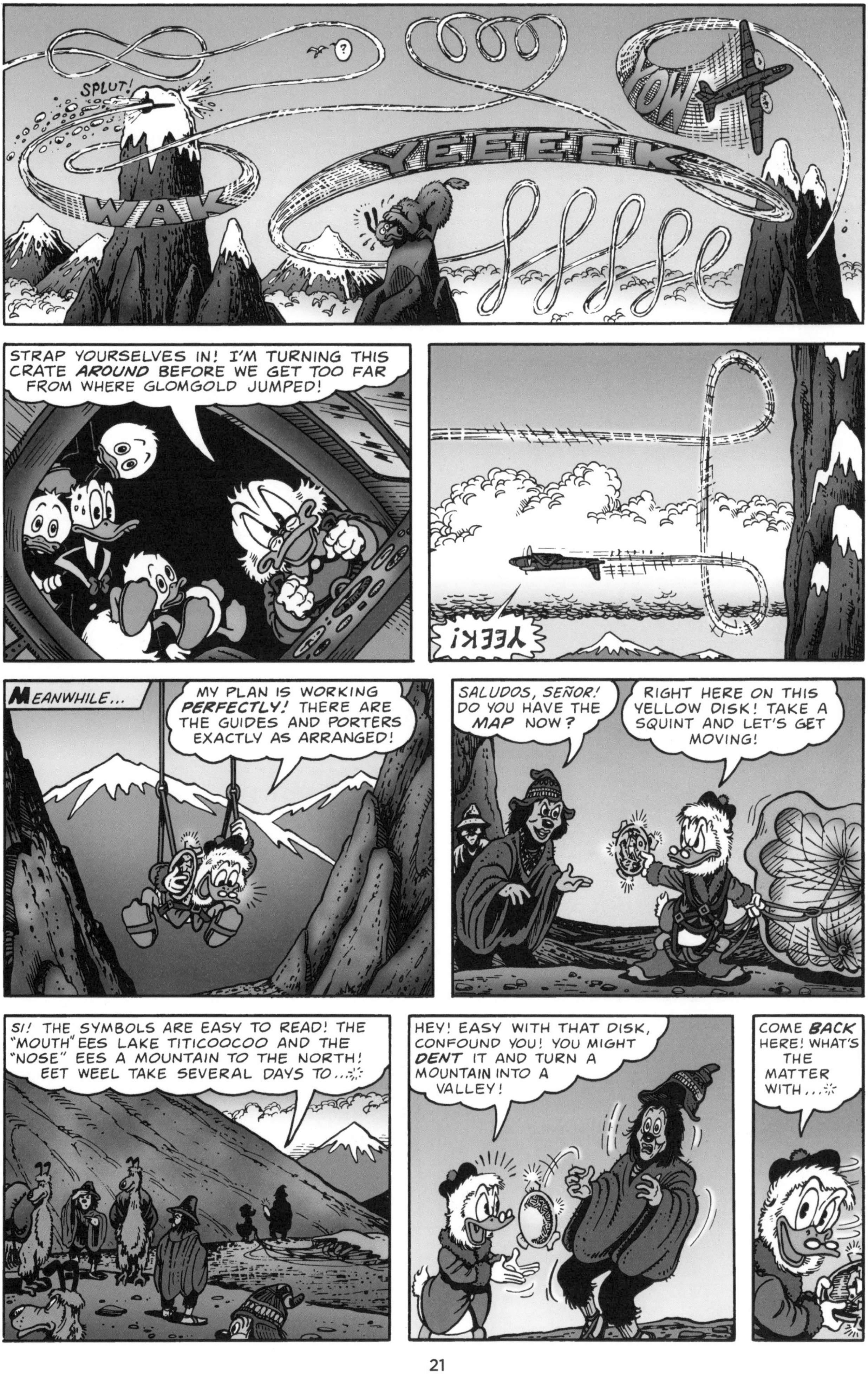
SPLUT!
?
YOW
YEEEEK
WAK
STRAP YOURSELVES IN! I'M TURNING THIS CRATE AROUND BEFORE WE GET TOO FAR FROM WHERE GLOMGOLD JUMPED!
YEEK!
MEANWHILE...
MY PLAN IS WORKING PERFECTLY! THERE ARE THE GUIDES AND PORTERS EXACTLY AS ARRANGED!
SALUDOS, SEÑOR! DO YOU HAVE THE MAP NOW?
RIGHT HERE ON THIS YELLOW DISK! TAKE A SQUINT AND LET'S GET MOVING!
SI! THE SYMBOLS ARE EASY TO READ! THE "MOUTH" EES LAKE TITICOOCOO AND THE "NOSE" EES A MOUNTAIN TO THE NORTH! EET WEEL TAKE SEVERAL DAYS TO...
HEY! EASY WITH THAT DISK, CONFOUND YOU! YOU MIGHT DENT IT AND TURN A MOUNTAIN INTO A VALLEY!
COME BACK HERE! WHAT'S THE MATTER WITH...

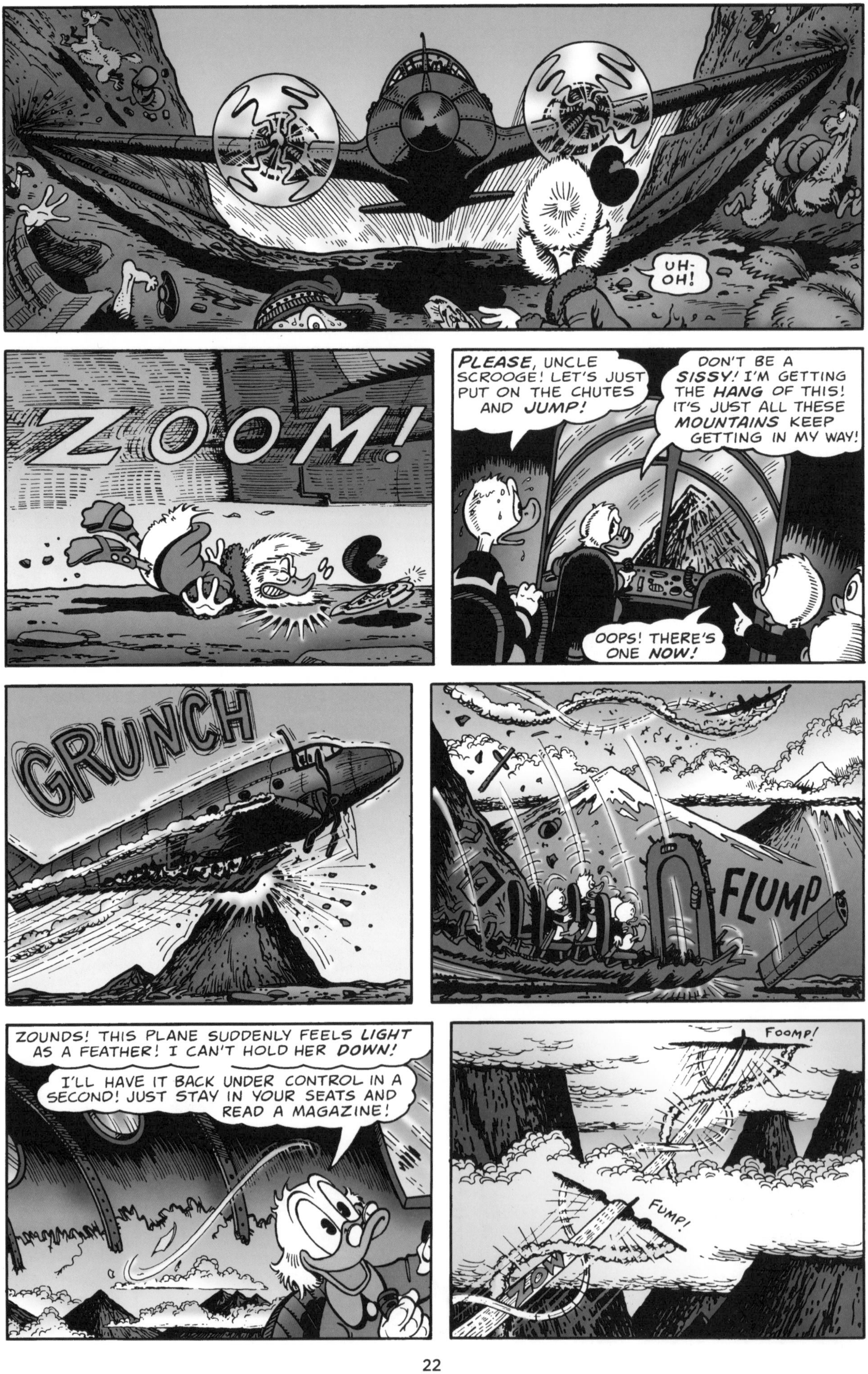
UH-OH!
ZOOM!
PLEASE, UNCLE SCROOGE! LET'S JUST PUT ON THE CHUTES AND JUMP!
DON'T BE A SISSY! I'M GETTING THE HANG OF THIS! IT'S JUST ALL THESE MOUNTAINS KEEP GETTING IN MY WAY!
OOPS! THERE'S ONE NOW!
GRUNCH
FLUMP
ZOUNDS! THIS PLANE SUDDENLY FEELS LIGHT AS A FEATHER! I CAN'T HOLD HER DOWN!
I'LL HAVE IT BACK UNDER CONTROL IN A SECOND! JUST STAY IN YOUR SEATS AND READ A MAGAZINE!
FOOMP!
FUMP!

THAT WAS OUR UNCLE SCROOGE DISAPPEARING INTO THE MIST!

AND HERE *WE* ARE!

LOST IN THE ANDES, EH? THAT'S *ALWAYS* GRAND!

YOU BLASTED *MEDDLERS!* MY PORTERS AND LLAMAS WON'T STOP RUNNING UNTIL THEY HIT THE *AMAZON RIVER!*

GLOMGOLD! CAN'T WE EVER GET *RID* OF YOU?

NOT *NOW*, YOU CAN'T! YOU'RE HELPING *ME* INSTEAD OF THAT SMALL-TOWN TYCOON UNCLE OF YOURS!

PICK UP THAT GEAR AND HEAD NORTH!

I'M A *CINCH* TO REACH THE TEMPLE FIRST! I'VE GOT McDUCK'S MAP *AND* HIS HELPERS! AND BY THE TIME THAT PLANE COMES DOWN HE'LL BE SO *DIZZY* HE WON'T KNOW PERU FROM CALISOTA!

IF HE'S *ABLE* TO FEEL DIZZY WHEN HE COMES DOWN!

POOR, POOR UNCA SCROOGE!

*L*ONG DAYS PASS SLOWLY AS THE DUCKS CLIMB EVER HIGHER INTO THE ANDES, ALWAYS FOLLOWING THE SYMBOLS ON THE GOLDEN DISK!

*U*NTIL FINALLY...

WHAT'S THAT UP AHEAD?

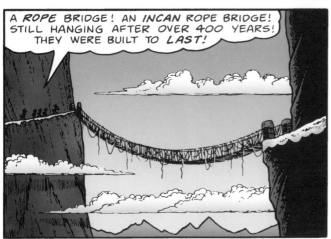

A *ROPE* BRIDGE! AN *INCAN* ROPE BRIDGE! STILL HANGING AFTER OVER 400 YEARS! THEY WERE BUILT TO *LAST!*

WE...WE'RE NOT GOING TO TRY TO CROSS IT...*ARE* WE?

YOU DON'T HAVE A *CHOICE!* KEEP MARCHING! IT'S *PROBABLY* SAFE IF WE SPACE OURSELVES OUT!

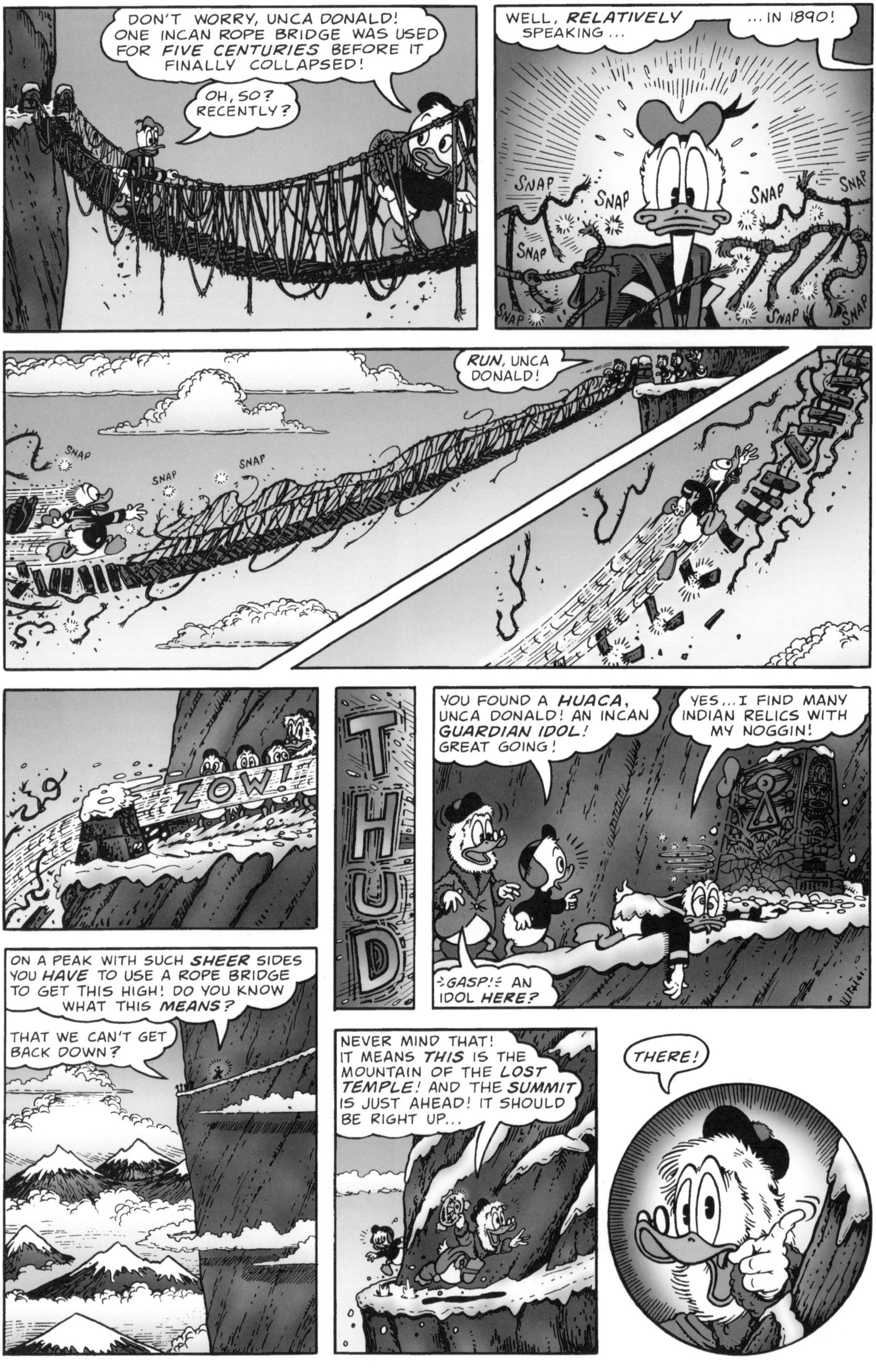
DON'T WORRY, UNCA DONALD! ONE INCAN ROPE BRIDGE WAS USED FOR FIVE CENTURIES BEFORE IT FINALLY COLLAPSED!
OH, SO? RECENTLY?
WELL, RELATIVELY SPEAKING...
...IN 1890!
SNAP
SNAP
SNAP
SNAP
SNAP
SNAP
SNAP
SNAP
RUN, UNCA DONALD!
SNAP
SNAP
SNAP
ZOW!
THUD
YOU FOUND A HUACA, UNCA DONALD! AN INCAN GUARDIAN IDOL! GREAT GOING!
YES... I FIND MANY INDIAN RELICS WITH MY NOGGIN!
GASP! AN IDOL HERE?
ON A PEAK WITH SUCH SHEER SIDES YOU HAVE TO USE A ROPE BRIDGE TO GET THIS HIGH! DO YOU KNOW WHAT THIS MEANS?
THAT WE CAN'T GET BACK DOWN?
NEVER MIND THAT! IT MEANS THIS IS THE MOUNTAIN OF THE LOST TEMPLE! AND THE SUMMIT IS JUST AHEAD! IT SHOULD BE RIGHT UP...
THERE!

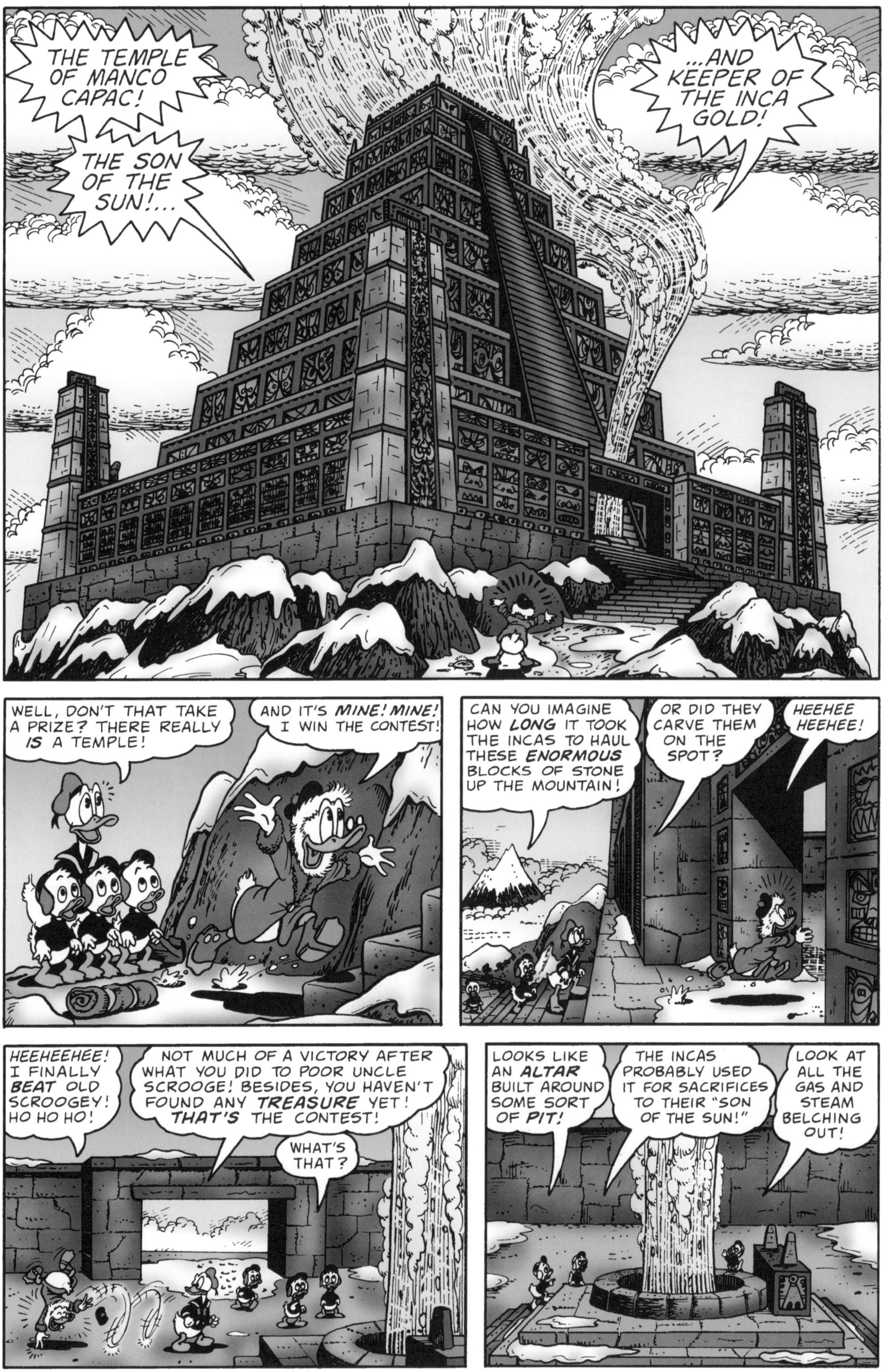
THE TEMPLE OF MANCO CAPAC!
THE SON OF THE SUN!...
...AND KEEPER OF THE INCA GOLD!
WELL, DON'T THAT TAKE A PRIZE? THERE REALLY IS A TEMPLE!
AND IT'S MINE! MINE! I WIN THE CONTEST!
CAN YOU IMAGINE HOW LONG IT TOOK THE INCAS TO HAUL THESE ENORMOUS BLOCKS OF STONE UP THE MOUNTAIN!
OR DID THEY CARVE THEM ON THE SPOT?
HEEHEE HEEHEE!
HEEHEEHEE! I FINALLY BEAT OLD SCROOGEY! HO HO HO!
NOT MUCH OF A VICTORY AFTER WHAT YOU DID TO POOR UNCLE SCROOGE! BESIDES, YOU HAVEN'T FOUND ANY TREASURE YET! THAT'S THE CONTEST!
WHAT'S THAT?
LOOKS LIKE AN ALTAR BUILT AROUND SOME SORT OF PIT!
THE INCAS PROBABLY USED IT FOR SACRIFICES TO THEIR "SON OF THE SUN!"
LOOK AT ALL THE GAS AND STEAM BELCHING OUT!

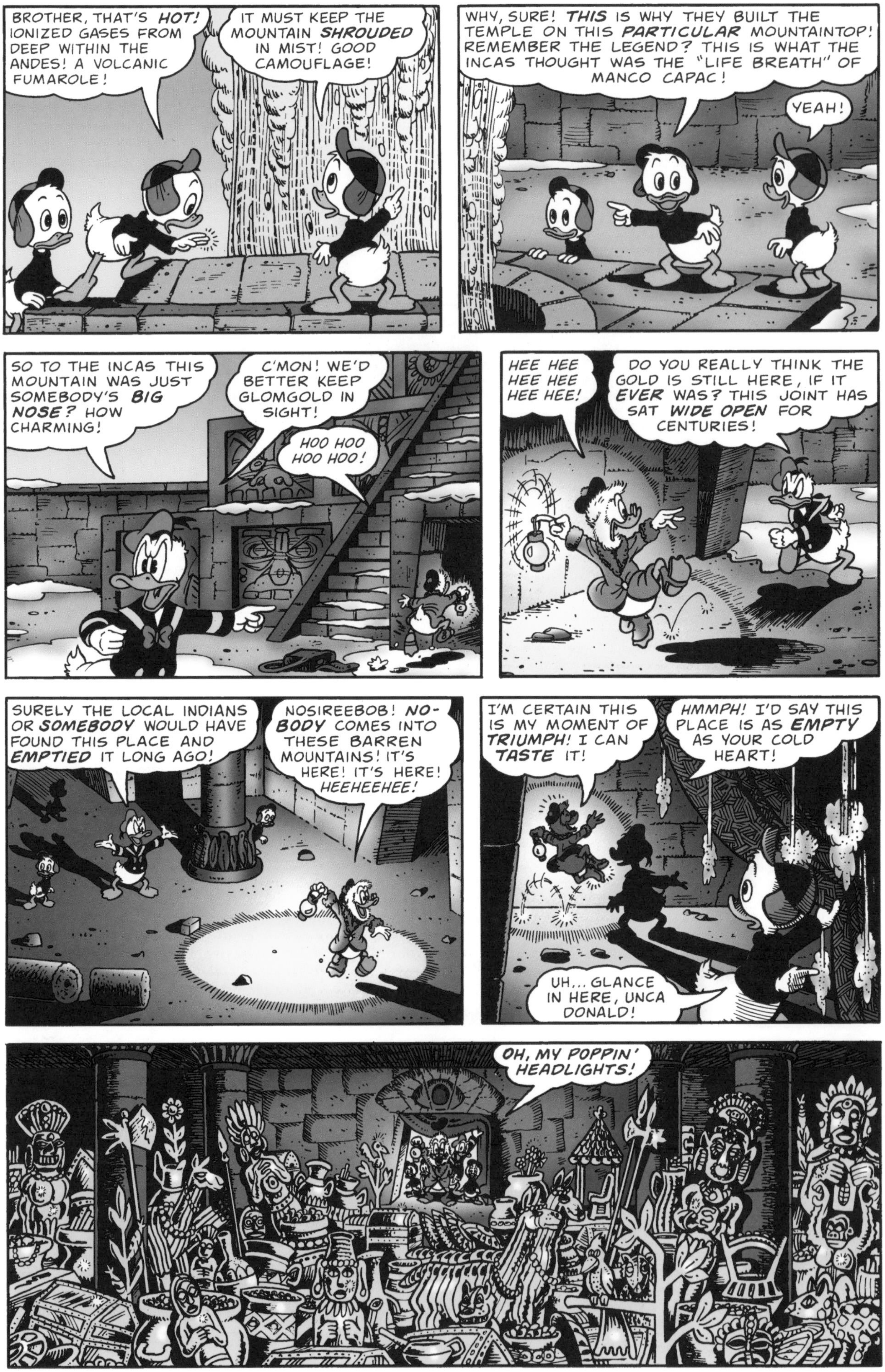
BROTHER, THAT'S HOT! IONIZED GASES FROM DEEP WITHIN THE ANDES! A VOLCANIC FUMAROLE!
IT MUST KEEP THE MOUNTAIN SHROUDED IN MIST! GOOD CAMOUFLAGE!
WHY, SURE! THIS IS WHY THEY BUILT THE TEMPLE ON THIS PARTICULAR MOUNTAINTOP! REMEMBER THE LEGEND? THIS IS WHAT THE INCAS THOUGHT WAS THE "LIFE BREATH" OF MANCO CAPAC!
YEAH!
SO TO THE INCAS THIS MOUNTAIN WAS JUST SOMEBODY'S BIG NOSE? HOW CHARMING!
C'MON! WE'D BETTER KEEP GLOMGOLD IN SIGHT!
HOO HOO HOO HOO!
HEE HEE HEE HEE HEE HEE!
DO YOU REALLY THINK THE GOLD IS STILL HERE, IF IT EVER WAS? THIS JOINT HAS SAT WIDE OPEN FOR CENTURIES!
SURELY THE LOCAL INDIANS OR SOMEBODY WOULD HAVE FOUND THIS PLACE AND EMPTIED IT LONG AGO!
NOSIREEBOB! NO-BODY COMES INTO THESE BARREN MOUNTAINS! IT'S HERE! IT'S HERE! HEEHEEHEE!
I'M CERTAIN THIS IS MY MOMENT OF TRIUMPH! I CAN TASTE IT!
HMMPH! I'D SAY THIS PLACE IS AS EMPTY AS YOUR COLD HEART!
UH,.. GLANCE IN HERE, UNCA DONALD!
OH, MY POPPIN' HEADLIGHTS!

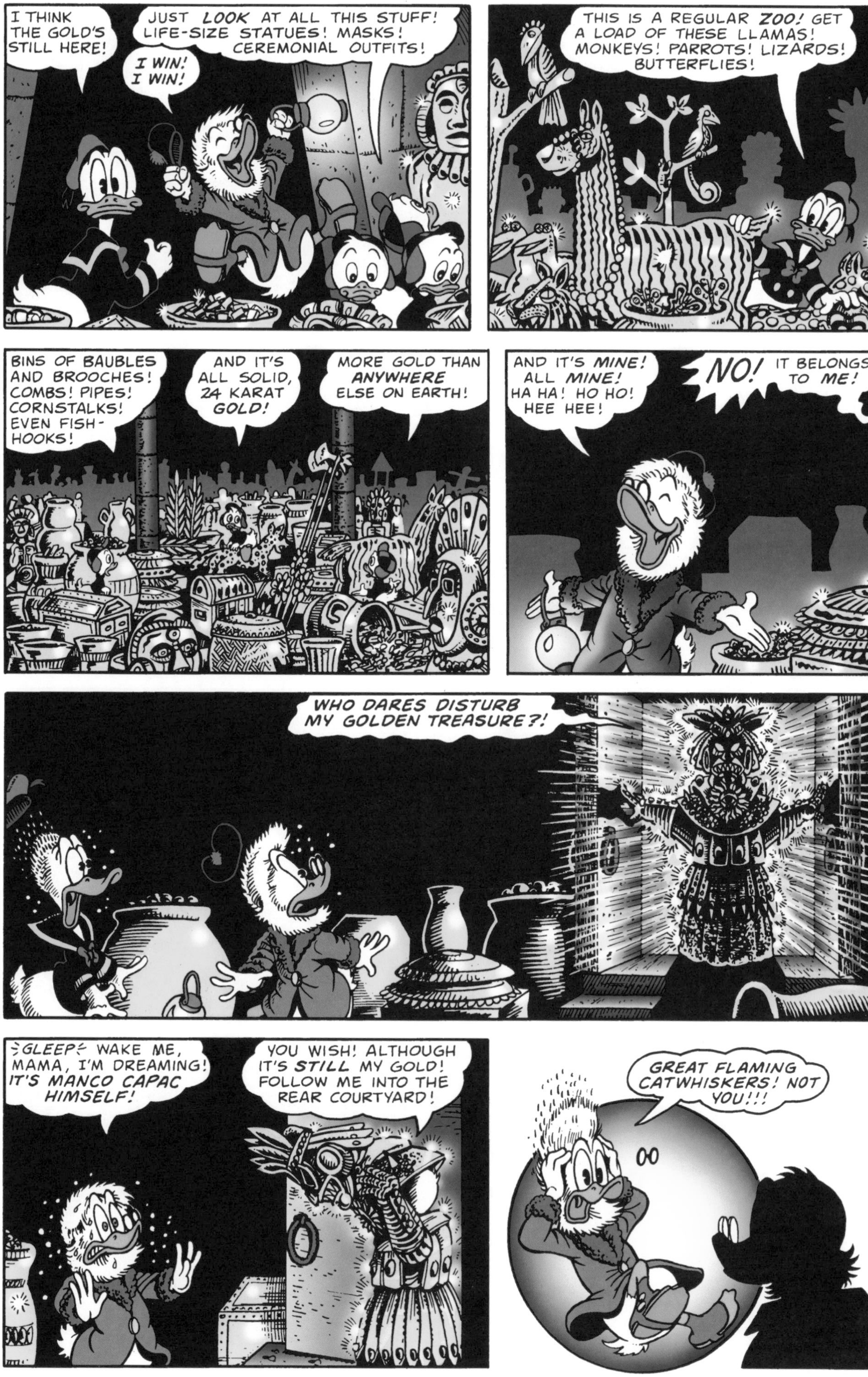
I THINK THE GOLD'S STILL HERE!
JUST LOOK AT ALL THIS STUFF! LIFE-SIZE STATUES! MASKS! CEREMONIAL OUTFITS!
I WIN! I WIN!
THIS IS A REGULAR ZOO! GET A LOAD OF THESE LLAMAS! MONKEYS! PARROTS! LIZARDS! BUTTERFLIES!
BINS OF BAUBLES AND BROOCHES! COMBS! PIPES! CORNSTALKS! EVEN FISH-HOOKS!
AND IT'S ALL SOLID, 24 KARAT GOLD!
MORE GOLD THAN ANYWHERE ELSE ON EARTH!
AND IT'S MINE! ALL MINE! HA HA! HO HO! HEE HEE!
NO! IT BELONGS TO ME!
WHO DARES DISTURB MY GOLDEN TREASURE?!
GLEEP WAKE ME, MAMA, I'M DREAMING! IT'S MANCO CAPAC HIMSELF!
YOU WISH! ALTHOUGH IT'S STILL MY GOLD! FOLLOW ME INTO THE REAR COURTYARD!
GREAT FLAMING CATWHISKERS! NOT YOU!!!

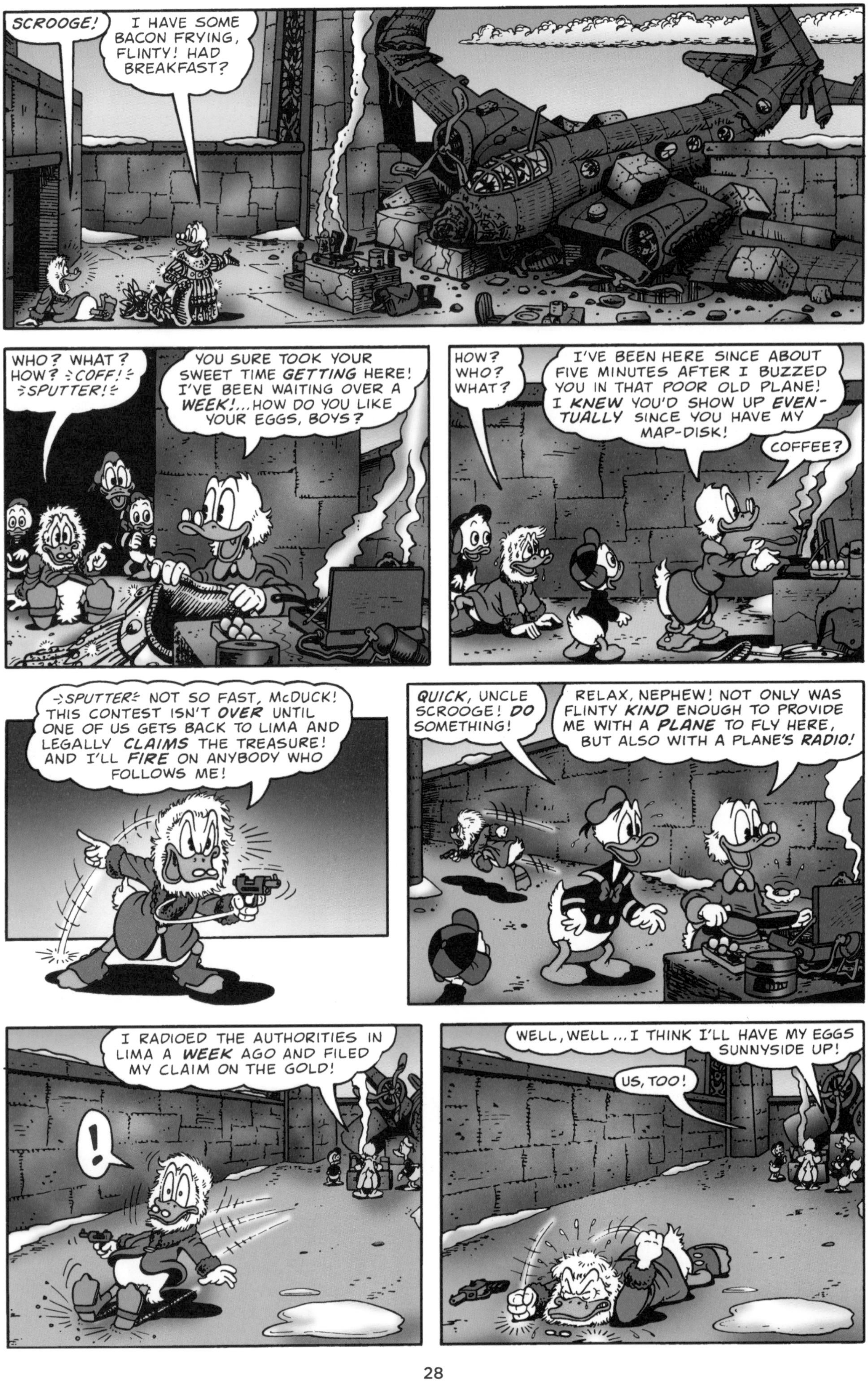
SCROOGE!
I HAVE SOME BACON FRYING, FLINTY! HAD BREAKFAST?
WHO? WHAT? HOW? -COFF!- -SPUTTER!-
YOU SURE TOOK YOUR SWEET TIME GETTING HERE! I'VE BEEN WAITING OVER A WEEK!... HOW DO YOU LIKE YOUR EGGS, BOYS?
HOW? WHO? WHAT?
I'VE BEEN HERE SINCE ABOUT FIVE MINUTES AFTER I BUZZED YOU IN THAT POOR OLD PLANE! I KNEW YOU'D SHOW UP EVEN-TUALLY SINCE YOU HAVE MY MAP-DISK!
COFFEE?
-SPUTTER- NOT SO FAST, McDUCK! THIS CONTEST ISN'T OVER UNTIL ONE OF US GETS BACK TO LIMA AND LEGALLY CLAIMS THE TREASURE! AND I'LL FIRE ON ANYBODY WHO FOLLOWS ME!
QUICK, UNCLE SCROOGE! DO SOMETHING!
RELAX, NEPHEW! NOT ONLY WAS FLINTY KIND ENOUGH TO PROVIDE ME WITH A PLANE TO FLY HERE, BUT ALSO WITH A PLANE'S RADIO!
I RADIOED THE AUTHORITIES IN LIMA A WEEK AGO AND FILED MY CLAIM ON THE GOLD!
!
WELL, WELL... I THINK I'LL HAVE MY EGGS SUNNYSIDE UP!
US, TOO!

ANOTHER EASY VICTORY FOR SCROOGE McDUCK, WORLD'S RICHEST DUCK AND CHAMPION TREASURE HUNTER! OR SO IT SEEMS!

YES, BOYS! I MIGHT HAVE FLOWN THAT PLANE INTO ANY ONE OF *HUNDREDS* OF MISTY CLOUDS! BUT WHY DO YOU THINK I HAPPENED TO PICK THE ONE SHROUDING *THIS* MOUNTAINTOP?

IT WAS *INSTINCT!* THE INSTINCT THAT HAS MADE *ME* THE WORLD'S RICHEST DUCK!

WHAT ARE YOU KIDS SO INTERESTED IN?

THIS *DISK*, UNCA DONALD! THERE'S STILL SOMETHING WE CAN'T FIGURE!

NAMELY, WHY DOES IT REFER TO MANCO CAPAC'S "TREASURE" WHEN IT WAS ENGRAVED OVER A HALF-CENTURY *BEFORE* THE GOLD WAS HIDDEN HERE?

WELL, PUT THAT STUFF DOWN! WE NEED TO TRY TO FIND A WAY OFF THIS MOUNTAIN!

YES, UNCA DONALD!

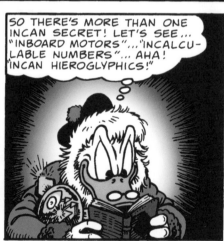

SO THERE'S MORE THAN ONE INCAN SECRET! LET'S SEE... "INBOARD MOTORS"..."INCALCULABLE NUMBERS"... AHA! "INCAN HIEROGLYPHICS!"

*S*OON, A DUCK MAKES HIS WAY UP THE TEMPLE'S EXTERIOR STAIRCASE! HE CARRIES THE GOLDEN DISK AND A JUNIOR WOODCHUCKS' GUIDEBOOK, YET HE IS *NOT* A MEMBER OF TROOP ONE OF THE DUCKBURG PATROL!

PANT! PANT!

THIS LITTLE BOOK MAKES THINGS SO *SIMPLE!* ACCORDING TO THE DISK, THIS IS THE *THRONE ROOM* OF MANCO CAPAC!

I'D BETTER WORK *FAST!* THE SUN IS ALMOST IN POSITION!

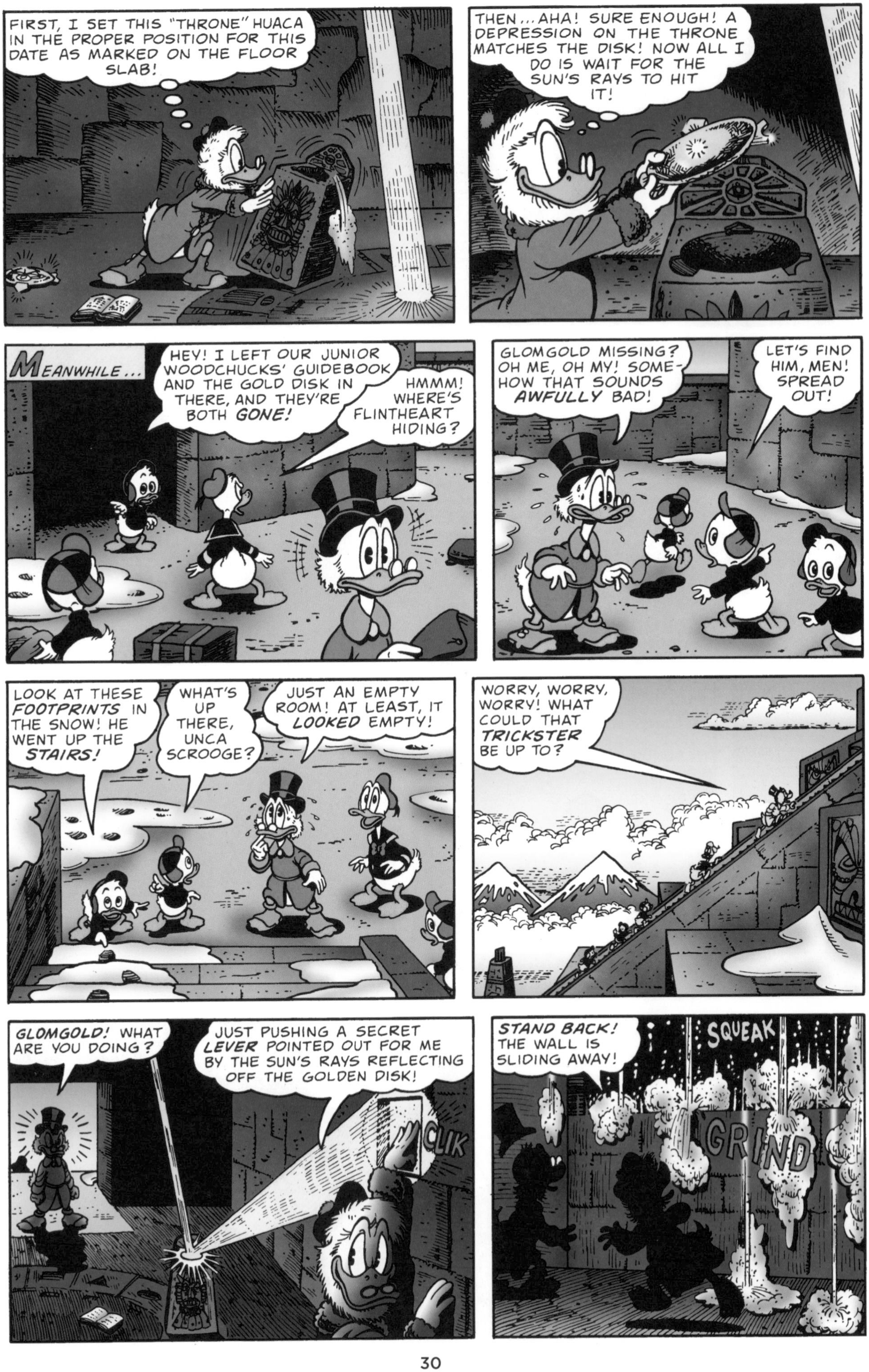

FIRST, I SET THIS "THRONE" HUACA IN THE PROPER POSITION FOR THIS DATE AS MARKED ON THE FLOOR SLAB!
THEN... AHA! SURE ENOUGH! A DEPRESSION ON THE THRONE MATCHES THE DISK! NOW ALL I DO IS WAIT FOR THE SUN'S RAYS TO HIT IT!
MEANWHILE...
HEY! I LEFT OUR JUNIOR WOODCHUCKS' GUIDEBOOK AND THE GOLD DISK IN THERE, AND THEY'RE BOTH GONE!
HMMM! WHERE'S FLINTHEART HIDING?
GLOMGOLD MISSING? OH ME, OH MY! SOMEHOW THAT SOUNDS AWFULLY BAD!
LET'S FIND HIM, MEN! SPREAD OUT!
LOOK AT THESE FOOTPRINTS IN THE SNOW! HE WENT UP THE STAIRS!
WHAT'S UP THERE, UNCA SCROOGE?
JUST AN EMPTY ROOM! AT LEAST, IT LOOKED EMPTY!
WORRY, WORRY, WORRY! WHAT COULD THAT TRICKSTER BE UP TO?
GLOMGOLD! WHAT ARE YOU DOING?
JUST PUSHING A SECRET LEVER POINTED OUT FOR ME BY THE SUN'S RAYS REFLECTING OFF THE GOLDEN DISK!
CLIK
STAND BACK! THE WALL IS SLIDING AWAY!
SQUEAK
GRIND

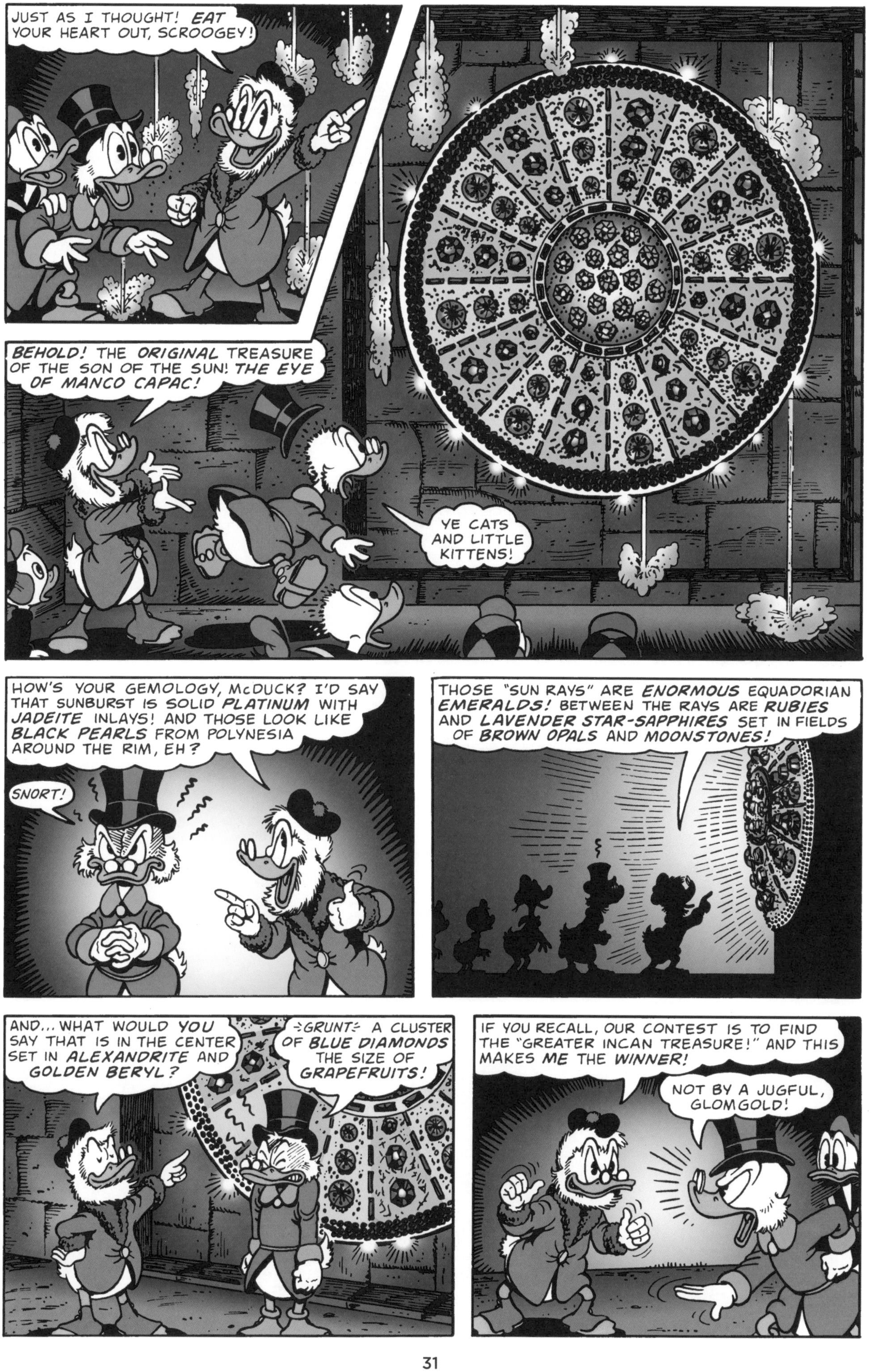

JUST AS I THOUGHT! EAT YOUR HEART OUT, SCROOGEY!
BEHOLD! THE ORIGINAL TREASURE OF THE SON OF THE SUN! THE EYE OF MANCO CAPAC!
YE CATS AND LITTLE KITTENS!
HOW'S YOUR GEMOLOGY, McDUCK? I'D SAY THAT SUNBURST IS SOLID PLATINUM WITH JADEITE INLAYS! AND THOSE LOOK LIKE BLACK PEARLS FROM POLYNESIA AROUND THE RIM, EH?
SNORT!
THOSE "SUN RAYS" ARE ENORMOUS EQUADORIAN EMERALDS! BETWEEN THE RAYS ARE RUBIES AND LAVENDER STAR-SAPPHIRES SET IN FIELDS OF BROWN OPALS AND MOONSTONES!
AND... WHAT WOULD YOU SAY THAT IS IN THE CENTER SET IN ALEXANDRITE AND GOLDEN BERYL?
GRUNT A CLUSTER OF BLUE DIAMONDS THE SIZE OF GRAPEFRUITS!
IF YOU RECALL, OUR CONTEST IS TO FIND THE "GREATER INCAN TREASURE!" AND THIS MAKES ME THE WINNER!
NOT BY A JUGFUL, GLOMGOLD!

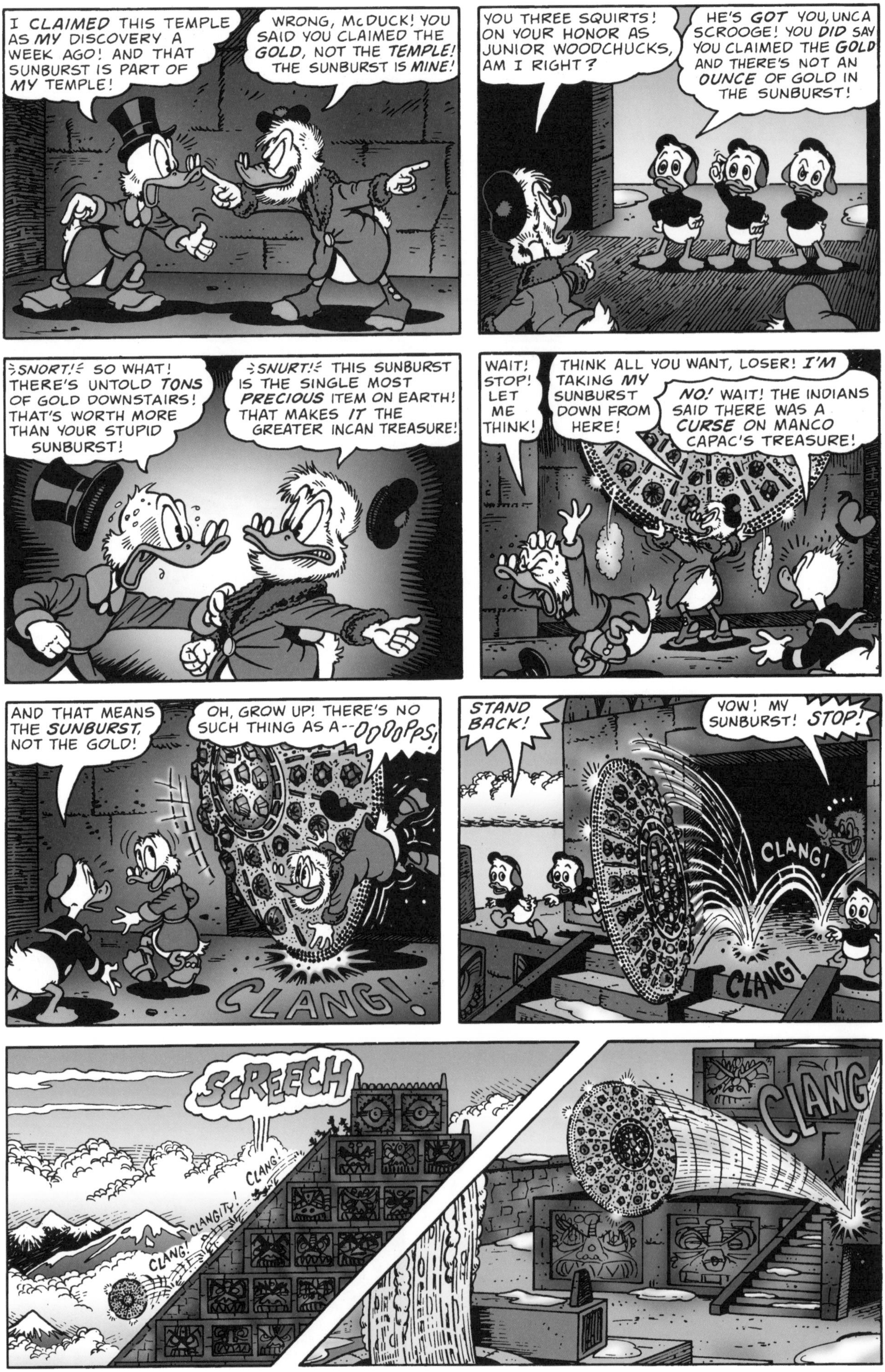
I CLAIMED THIS TEMPLE AS MY DISCOVERY A WEEK AGO! AND THAT SUNBURST IS PART OF MY TEMPLE!
WRONG, McDUCK! YOU SAID YOU CLAIMED THE GOLD, NOT THE TEMPLE! THE SUNBURST IS MINE!
YOU THREE SQUIRTS! ON YOUR HONOR AS JUNIOR WOODCHUCKS, AM I RIGHT?
HE'S GOT YOU, UNCA SCROOGE! YOU DID SAY YOU CLAIMED THE GOLD AND THERE'S NOT AN OUNCE OF GOLD IN THE SUNBURST!
SNORT! SO WHAT! THERE'S UNTOLD TONS OF GOLD DOWNSTAIRS! THAT'S WORTH MORE THAN YOUR STUPID SUNBURST!
SNURT! THIS SUNBURST IS THE SINGLE MOST PRECIOUS ITEM ON EARTH! THAT MAKES IT THE GREATER INCAN TREASURE!
WAIT! STOP! LET ME THINK!
THINK ALL YOU WANT, LOSER! I'M TAKING MY SUNBURST DOWN FROM HERE!
NO! WAIT! THE INDIANS SAID THERE WAS A CURSE ON MANCO CAPAC'S TREASURE!
AND THAT MEANS THE SUNBURST, NOT THE GOLD!
OH, GROW UP! THERE'S NO SUCH THING AS A--OOOOPPS!
CLANG!
STAND BACK!
YOW! MY SUNBURST! STOP!
CLANG!
CLANG!
SCREECH
CLANG!
CLANG!
CLANGITY!
CLANG!
CLANG

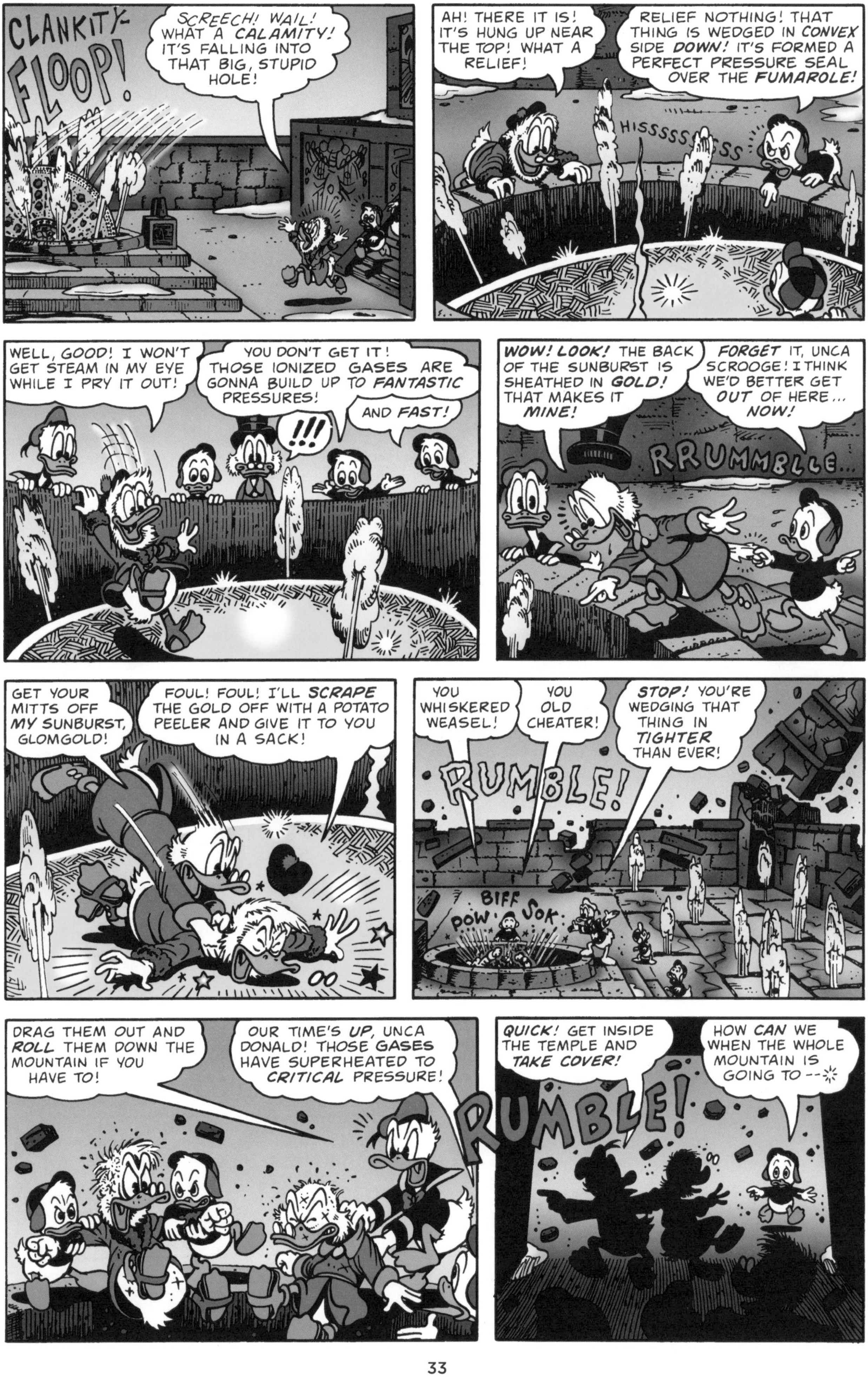
CLANKITY-FLOOP!
SCREECH! WAIL! WHAT A CALAMITY! IT'S FALLING INTO THAT BIG, STUPID HOLE!
AH! THERE IT IS! IT'S HUNG UP NEAR THE TOP! WHAT A RELIEF!
RELIEF NOTHING! THAT THING IS WEDGED IN CONVEX SIDE DOWN! IT'S FORMED A PERFECT PRESSURE SEAL OVER THE FUMAROLE!
HISSSSSSSSSS
WELL, GOOD! I WON'T GET STEAM IN MY EYE WHILE I PRY IT OUT!
YOU DON'T GET IT! THOSE IONIZED GASES ARE GONNA BUILD UP TO FANTASTIC PRESSURES!
!!!
AND FAST!
WOW! LOOK! THE BACK OF THE SUNBURST IS SHEATHED IN GOLD! THAT MAKES IT MINE!
FORGET IT, UNCA SCROOGE! I THINK WE'D BETTER GET OUT OF HERE... NOW!
RRUMMBLLE...
GET YOUR MITTS OFF MY SUNBURST, GLOMGOLD!
FOUL! FOUL! I'LL SCRAPE THE GOLD OFF WITH A POTATO PEELER AND GIVE IT TO YOU IN A SACK!
YOU WHISKERED WEASEL!
YOU OLD CHEATER!
STOP! YOU'RE WEDGING THAT THING IN TIGHTER THAN EVER!
RUMBLE!
BIFF
POW
SOK
DRAG THEM OUT AND ROLL THEM DOWN THE MOUNTAIN IF YOU HAVE TO!
OUR TIME'S UP, UNCA DONALD! THOSE GASES HAVE SUPERHEATED TO CRITICAL PRESSURE!
RUMBLE!
QUICK! GET INSIDE THE TEMPLE AND TAKE COVER!
HOW CAN WE WHEN THE WHOLE MOUNTAIN IS GOING TO --

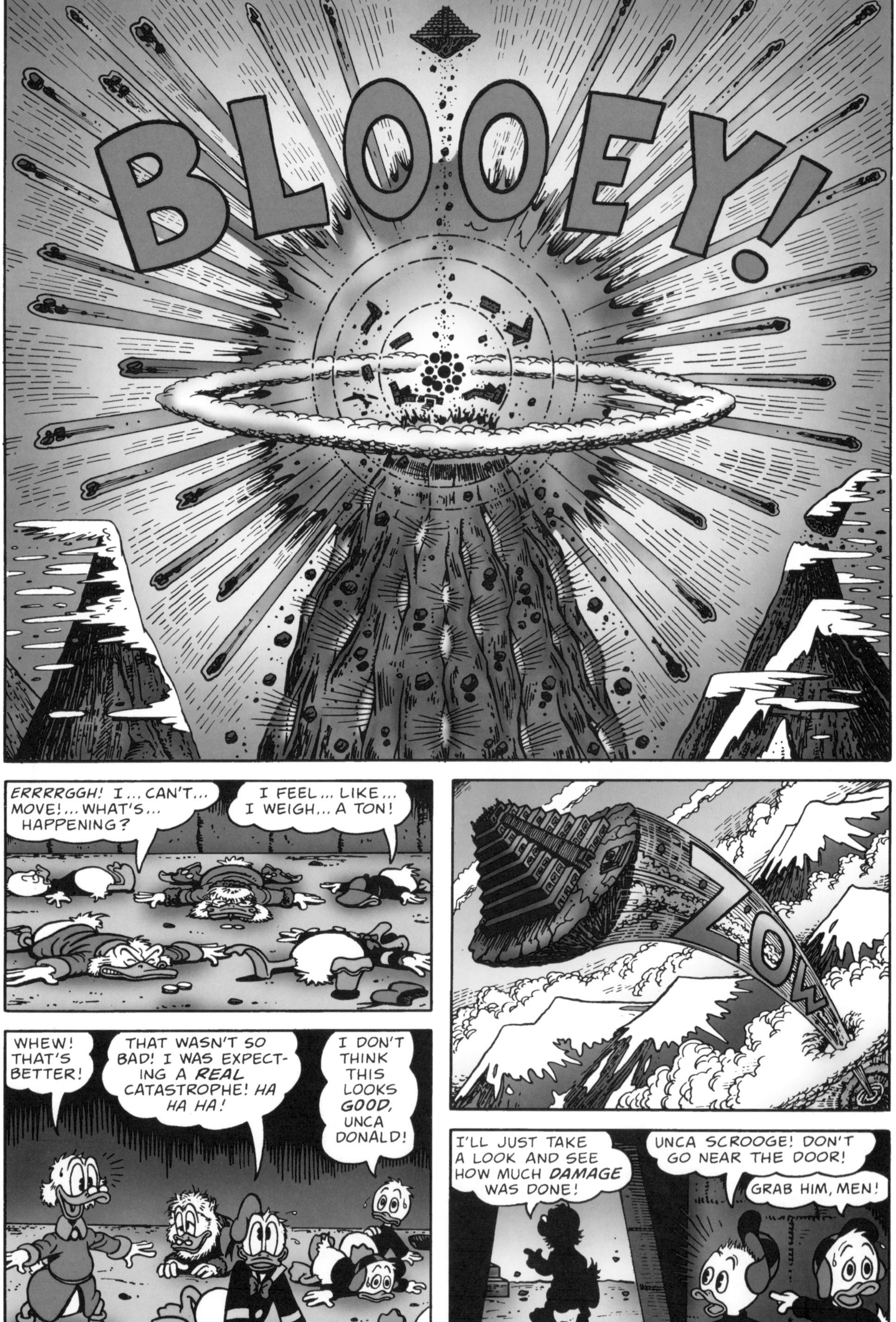
BLOOEY!
ERRRRGGH! I... CAN'T... MOVE!... WHAT'S... HAPPENING?
I FEEL... LIKE... I WEIGH... A TON!
ZOW
WHEW! THAT'S BETTER!
THAT WASN'T SO BAD! I WAS EXPECTING A REAL CATASTROPHE! HA HA HA!
I DON'T THINK THIS LOOKS GOOD, UNCA DONALD!
I'LL JUST TAKE A LOOK AND SEE HOW MUCH DAMAGE WAS DONE!
UNCA SCROOGE! DON'T GO NEAR THE DOOR!
GRAB HIM, MEN!

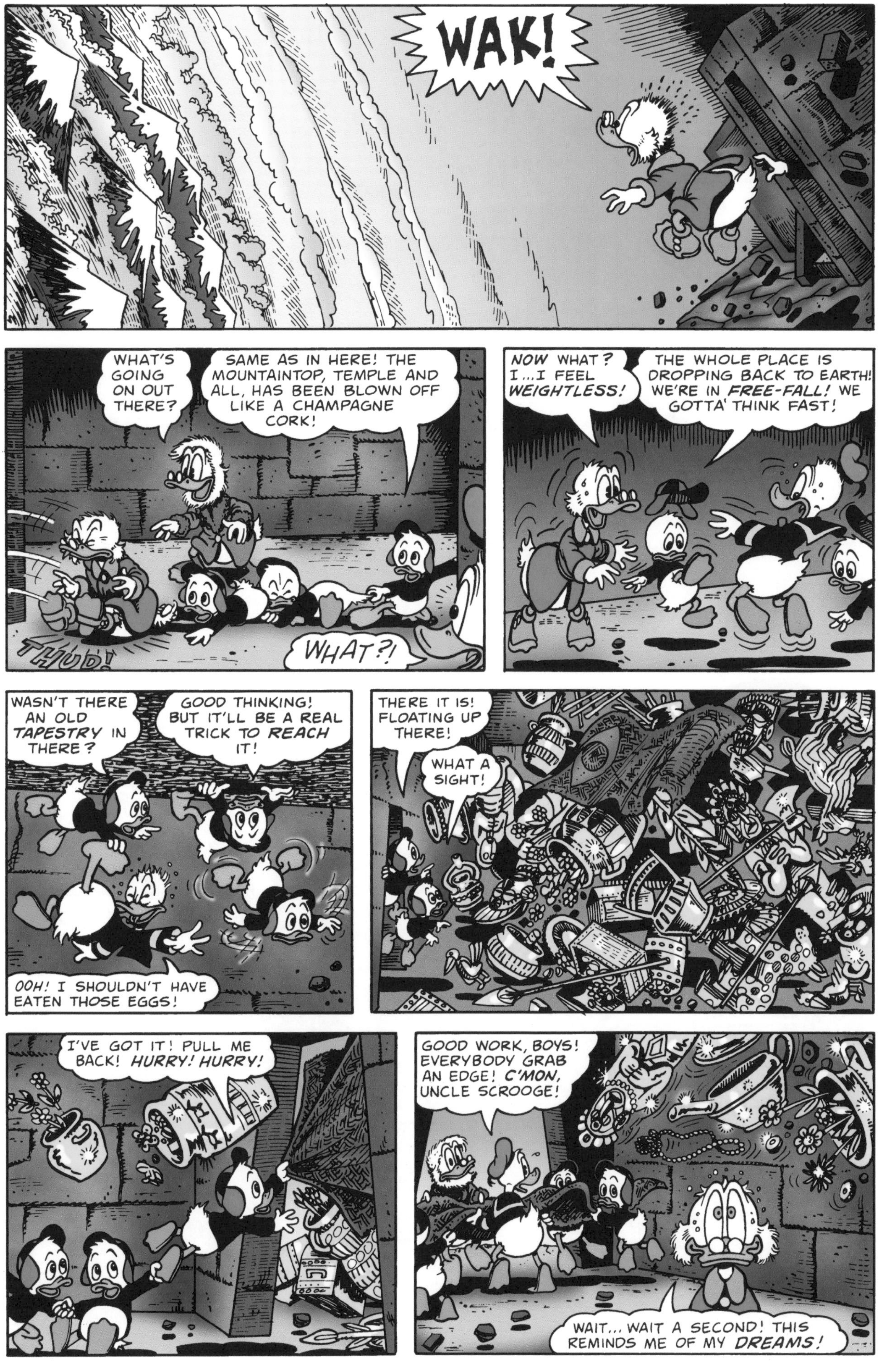
WAK!
WHAT'S GOING ON OUT THERE?
SAME AS IN HERE! THE MOUNTAINTOP, TEMPLE AND ALL, HAS BEEN BLOWN OFF LIKE A CHAMPAGNE CORK!
THUD!
WHAT?!
NOW WHAT? I...I FEEL WEIGHTLESS!
THE WHOLE PLACE IS DROPPING BACK TO EARTH! WE'RE IN FREE-FALL! WE GOTTA' THINK FAST!
WASN'T THERE AN OLD TAPESTRY IN THERE?
GOOD THINKING! BUT IT'LL BE A REAL TRICK TO REACH IT!
OOH! I SHOULDN'T HAVE EATEN THOSE EGGS!
THERE IT IS! FLOATING UP THERE!
WHAT A SIGHT!
I'VE GOT IT! PULL ME BACK! HURRY! HURRY!
GOOD WORK, BOYS! EVERYBODY GRAB AN EDGE! C'MON, UNCLE SCROOGE!
WAIT... WAIT A SECOND! THIS REMINDS ME OF MY DREAMS!

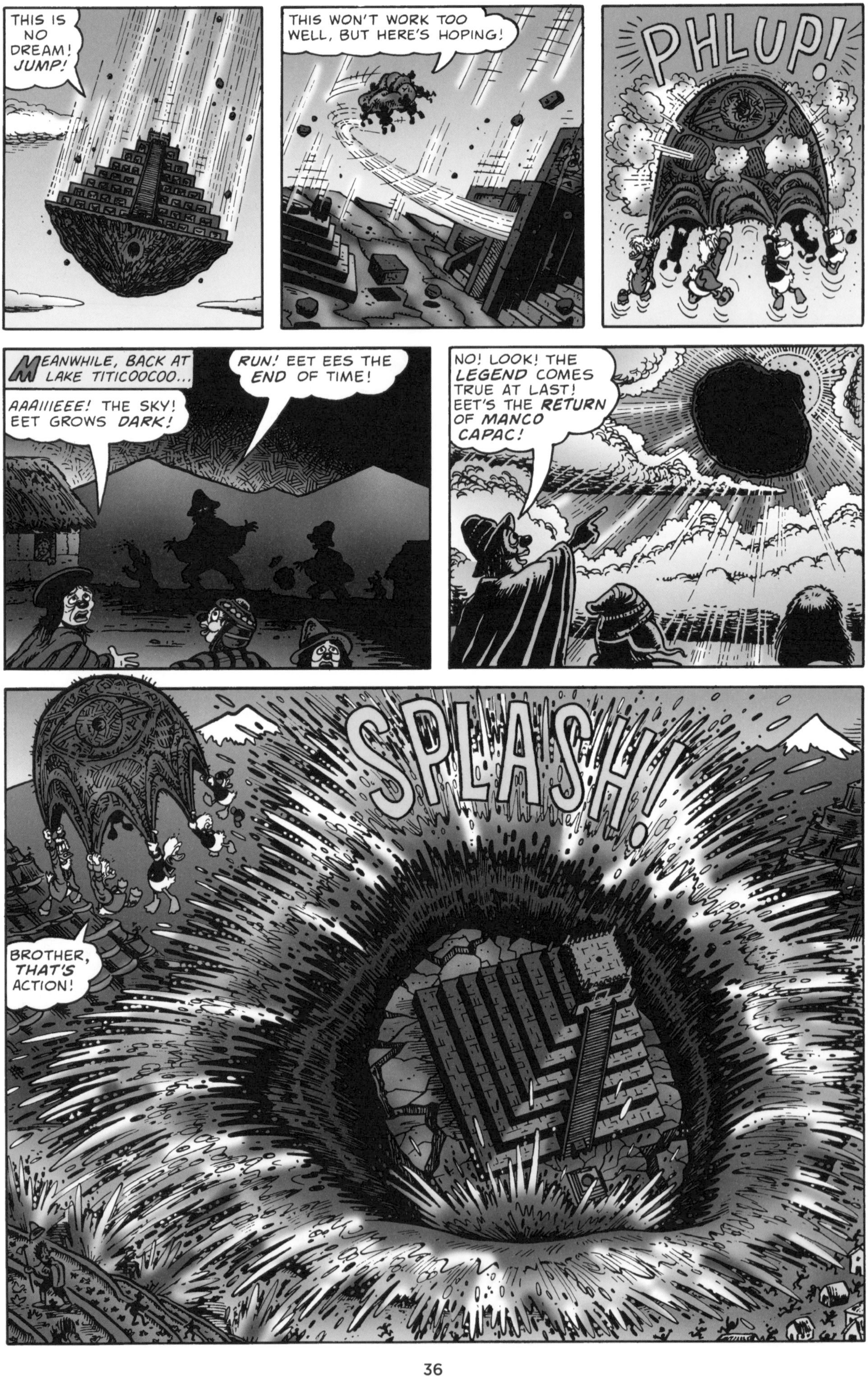
THIS IS NO DREAM! JUMP!
THIS WON'T WORK TOO WELL, BUT HERE'S HOPING!
PHLUP!
MEANWHILE, BACK AT LAKE TITICOOCOO...
AAAIIIEEE! THE SKY! EET GROWS DARK!
RUN! EET EES THE END OF TIME!
NO! LOOK! THE LEGEND COMES TRUE AT LAST! EET'S THE RETURN OF MANCO CAPAC!
SPLASH!
BROTHER, THAT'S ACTION!

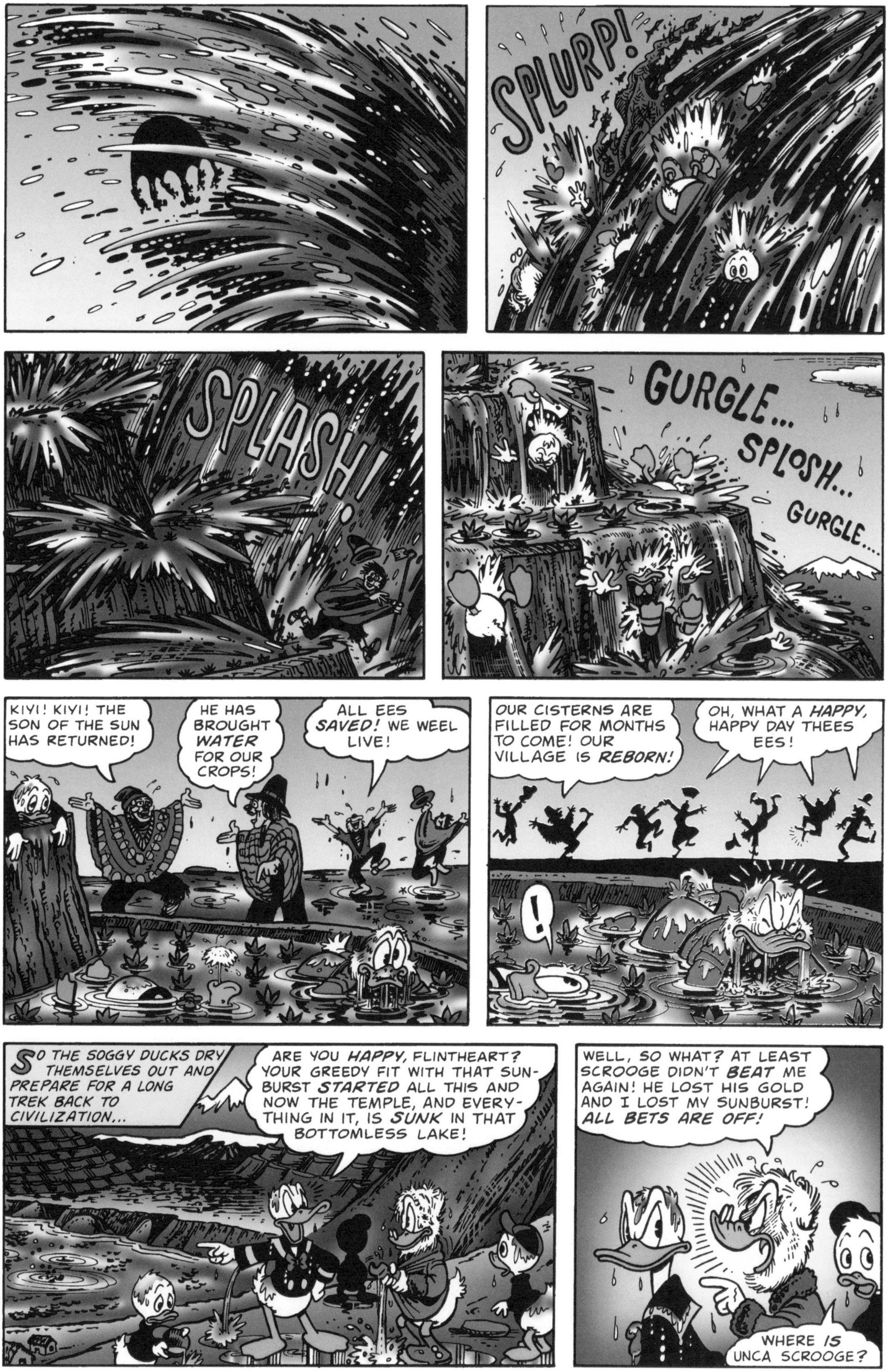
SPLURP!
SPLASH!
GURGLE...
SPLOSH...
GURGLE...
KIYI! KIYI! THE SON OF THE SUN HAS RETURNED!
HE HAS BROUGHT WATER FOR OUR CROPS!
ALL EES SAVED! WE WEEL LIVE!
OUR CISTERNS ARE FILLED FOR MONTHS TO COME! OUR VILLAGE IS REBORN!
OH, WHAT A HAPPY, HAPPY DAY THEES EES!
!
SO THE SOGGY DUCKS DRY THEMSELVES OUT AND PREPARE FOR A LONG TREK BACK TO CIVILIZATION...
ARE YOU HAPPY, FLINTHEART? YOUR GREEDY FIT WITH THAT SUNBURST STARTED ALL THIS AND NOW THE TEMPLE, AND EVERYTHING IN IT, IS SUNK IN THAT BOTTOMLESS LAKE!
WELL, SO WHAT? AT LEAST SCROOGE DIDN'T BEAT ME AGAIN! HE LOST HIS GOLD AND I LOST MY SUNBURST! ALL BETS ARE OFF!
WHERE IS UNCA SCROOGE?

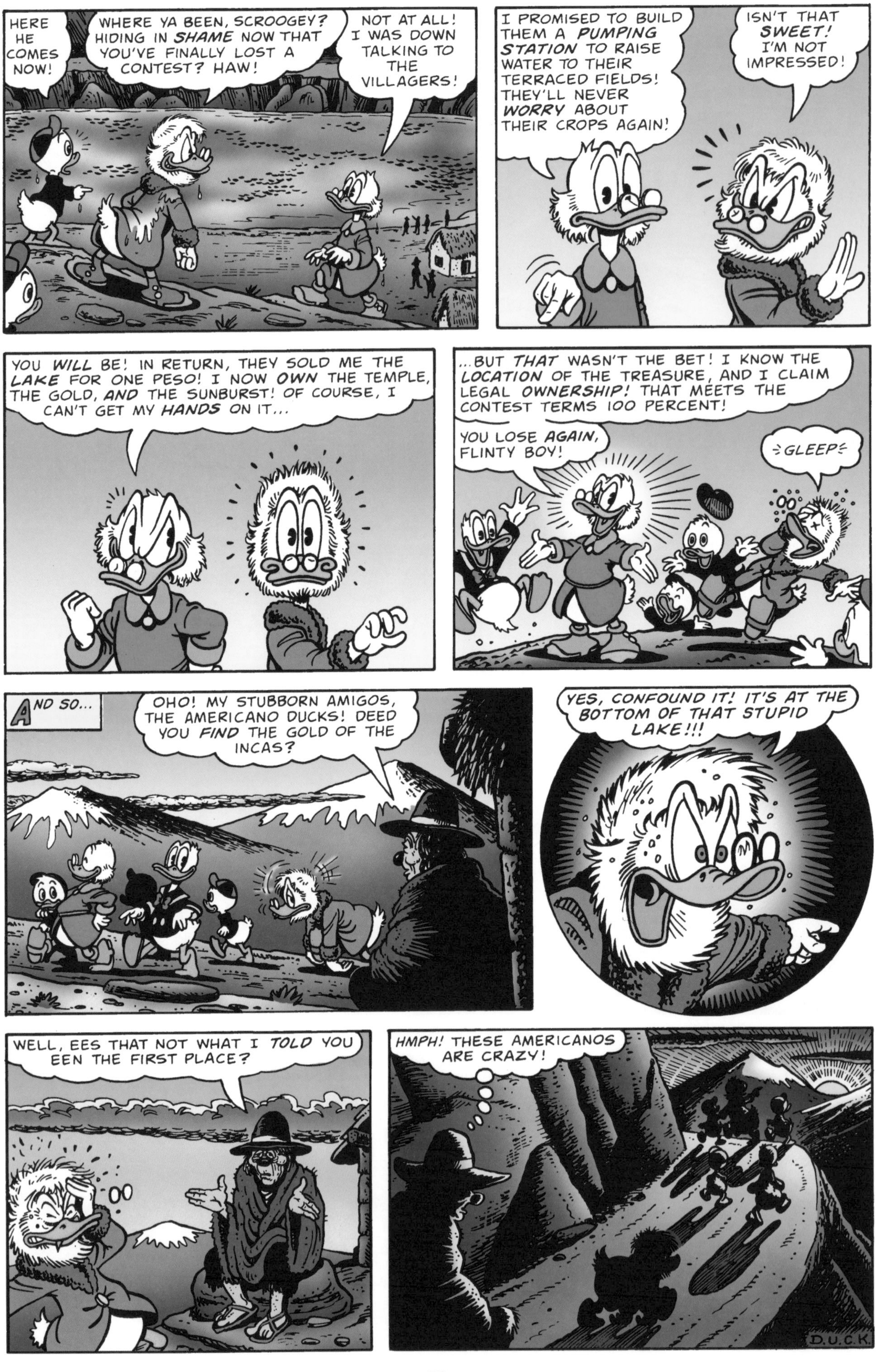
HERE HE COMES NOW!
WHERE YA BEEN, SCROOGEY? HIDING IN SHAME NOW THAT YOU'VE FINALLY LOST A CONTEST? HAW!
NOT AT ALL! I WAS DOWN TALKING TO THE VILLAGERS!
I PROMISED TO BUILD THEM A PUMPING STATION TO RAISE WATER TO THEIR TERRACED FIELDS! THEY'LL NEVER WORRY ABOUT THEIR CROPS AGAIN!
ISN'T THAT SWEET! I'M NOT IMPRESSED!
YOU WILL BE! IN RETURN, THEY SOLD ME THE LAKE FOR ONE PESO! I NOW OWN THE TEMPLE, THE GOLD, AND THE SUNBURST! OF COURSE, I CAN'T GET MY HANDS ON IT...
...BUT THAT WASN'T THE BET! I KNOW THE LOCATION OF THE TREASURE, AND I CLAIM LEGAL OWNERSHIP! THAT MEETS THE CONTEST TERMS 100 PERCENT!
YOU LOSE AGAIN, FLINTY BOY!
GLEEP
AND SO...
OHO! MY STUBBORN AMIGOS, THE AMERICANO DUCKS! DEED YOU FIND THE GOLD OF THE INCAS?
YES, CONFOUND IT! IT'S AT THE BOTTOM OF THAT STUPID LAKE!!!
WELL, EES THAT NOT WHAT I TOLD YOU EEN THE FIRST PLACE?
HMPH! THESE AMERICANOS ARE CRAZY!
D.U.C.K.

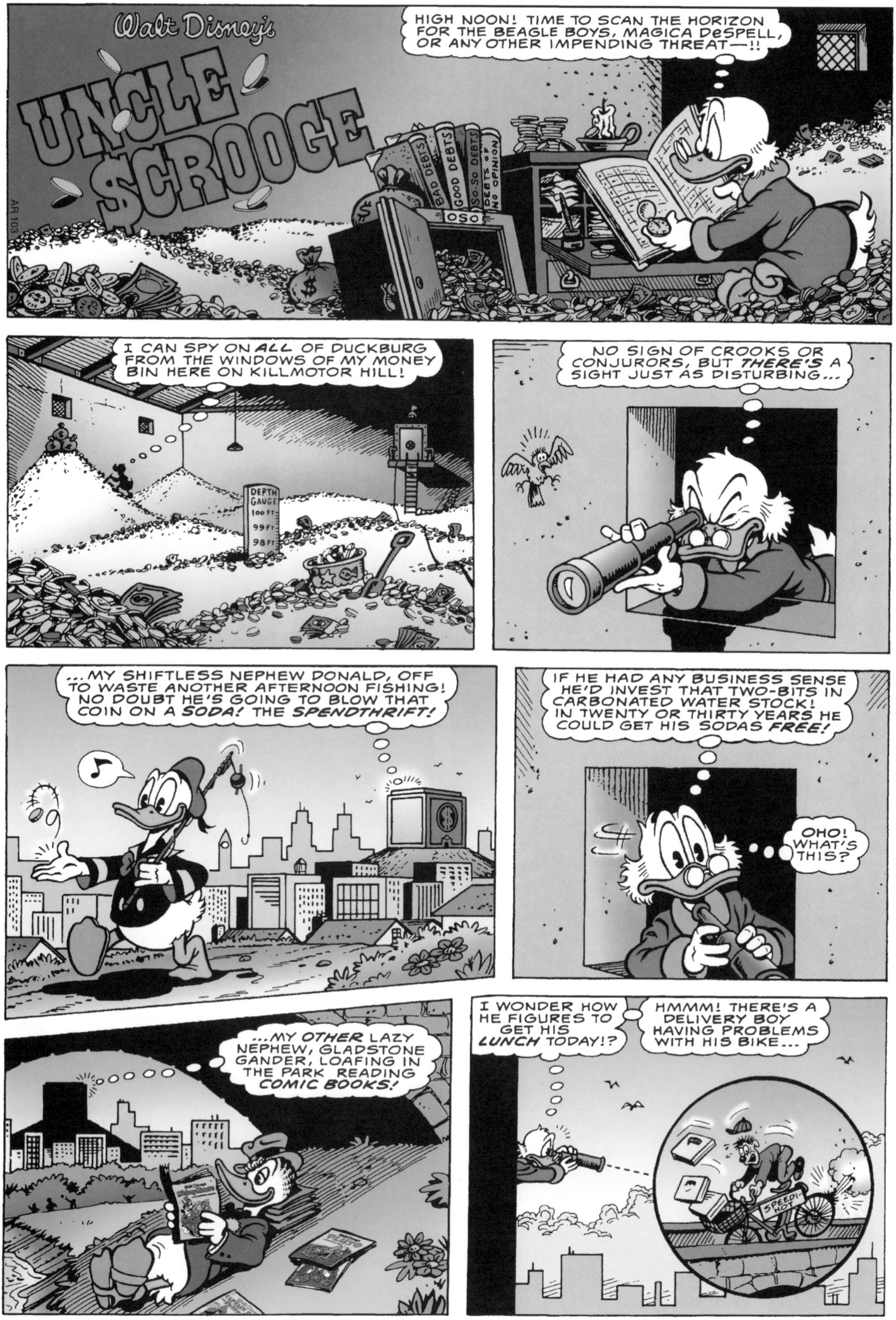
Walt Disney's
UNCLE $CROOGE
HIGH NOON! TIME TO SCAN THE HORIZON FOR THE BEAGLE BOYS, MAGICA DeSPELL, OR ANY OTHER IMPENDING THREAT—!!
BAD DEBTS
GOOD DEBTS
So-So DEBTS
DEBTS of NO OPINION
OSO
AR 103
I CAN SPY ON ALL OF DUCKBURG FROM THE WINDOWS OF MY MONEY BIN HERE ON KILLMOTOR HILL!
DEPTH GAUGE
100 FT
99 FT
98 FT
NO SIGN OF CROOKS OR CONJURORS, BUT THERE'S A SIGHT JUST AS DISTURBING...
...MY SHIFTLESS NEPHEW DONALD, OFF TO WASTE ANOTHER AFTERNOON FISHING! NO DOUBT HE'S GOING TO BLOW THAT COIN ON A SODA! THE SPENDTHRIFT!
IF HE HAD ANY BUSINESS SENSE HE'D INVEST THAT TWO-BITS IN CARBONATED WATER STOCK! IN TWENTY OR THIRTY YEARS HE COULD GET HIS SODAS FREE!
OHO! WHAT'S THIS?
...MY OTHER LAZY NEPHEW, GLADSTONE GANDER, LOAFING IN THE PARK READING COMIC BOOKS!
I WONDER HOW HE FIGURES TO GET HIS LUNCH TODAY!?
HMMM! THERE'S A DELIVERY BOY HAVING PROBLEMS WITH HIS BIKE...
SPEEDI-HOT

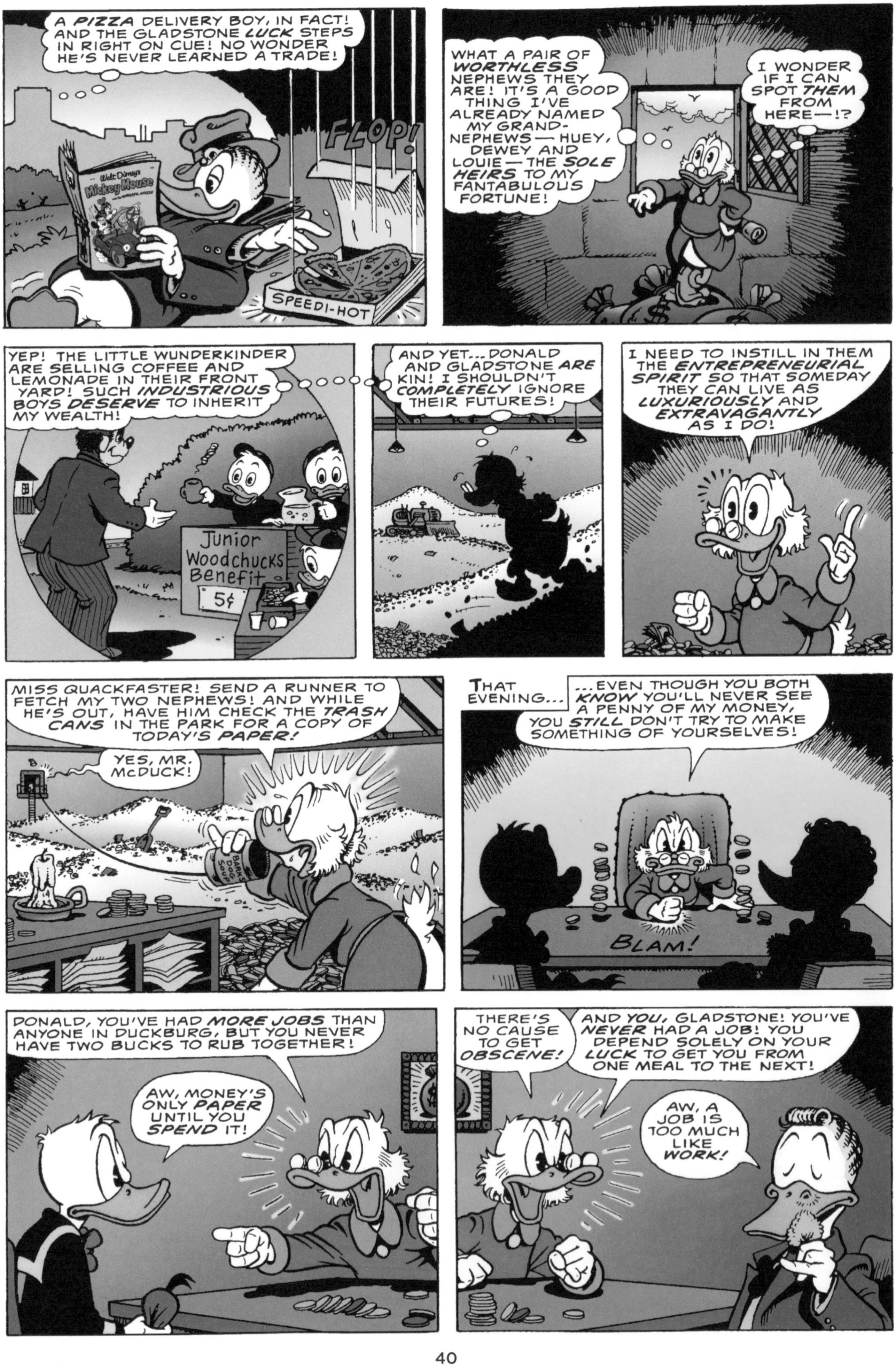

A PIZZA DELIVERY BOY, IN FACT! AND THE GLADSTONE LUCK STEPS IN RIGHT ON CUE! NO WONDER HE'S NEVER LEARNED A TRADE!
FLOP!
SPEEDI-HOT
WHAT A PAIR OF WORTHLESS NEPHEWS THEY ARE! IT'S A GOOD THING I'VE ALREADY NAMED MY GRAND-NEPHEWS — HUEY, DEWEY AND LOUIE — THE SOLE HEIRS TO MY FANTABULOUS FORTUNE!
I WONDER IF I CAN SPOT THEM FROM HERE—!?
YEP! THE LITTLE WUNDERKINDER ARE SELLING COFFEE AND LEMONADE IN THEIR FRONT YARD! SUCH INDUSTRIOUS BOYS DESERVE TO INHERIT MY WEALTH!
Junior Woodchucks Benefit
5¢
AND YET... DONALD AND GLADSTONE ARE KIN! I SHOULDN'T COMPLETELY IGNORE THEIR FUTURES!
I NEED TO INSTILL IN THEM THE ENTREPRENEURIAL SPIRIT SO THAT SOMEDAY THEY CAN LIVE AS LUXURIOUSLY AND EXTRAVAGANTLY AS I DO!
MISS QUACKFASTER! SEND A RUNNER TO FETCH MY TWO NEPHEWS! AND WHILE HE'S OUT, HAVE HIM CHECK THE TRASH CANS IN THE PARK FOR A COPY OF TODAY'S PAPER!
YES, MR. McDUCK!
BARKS DOG SOUP
THAT EVENING...
...EVEN THOUGH YOU BOTH KNOW YOU'LL NEVER SEE A PENNY OF MY MONEY, YOU STILL DON'T TRY TO MAKE SOMETHING OF YOURSELVES!
BLAM!
DONALD, YOU'VE HAD MORE JOBS THAN ANYONE IN DUCKBURG, BUT YOU NEVER HAVE TWO BUCKS TO RUB TOGETHER!
AW, MONEY'S ONLY PAPER UNTIL YOU SPEND IT!
THERE'S NO CAUSE TO GET OBSCENE!
AND YOU, GLADSTONE! YOU'VE NEVER HAD A JOB! YOU DEPEND SOLELY ON YOUR LUCK TO GET YOU FROM ONE MEAL TO THE NEXT!
AW, A JOB IS TOO MUCH LIKE WORK!

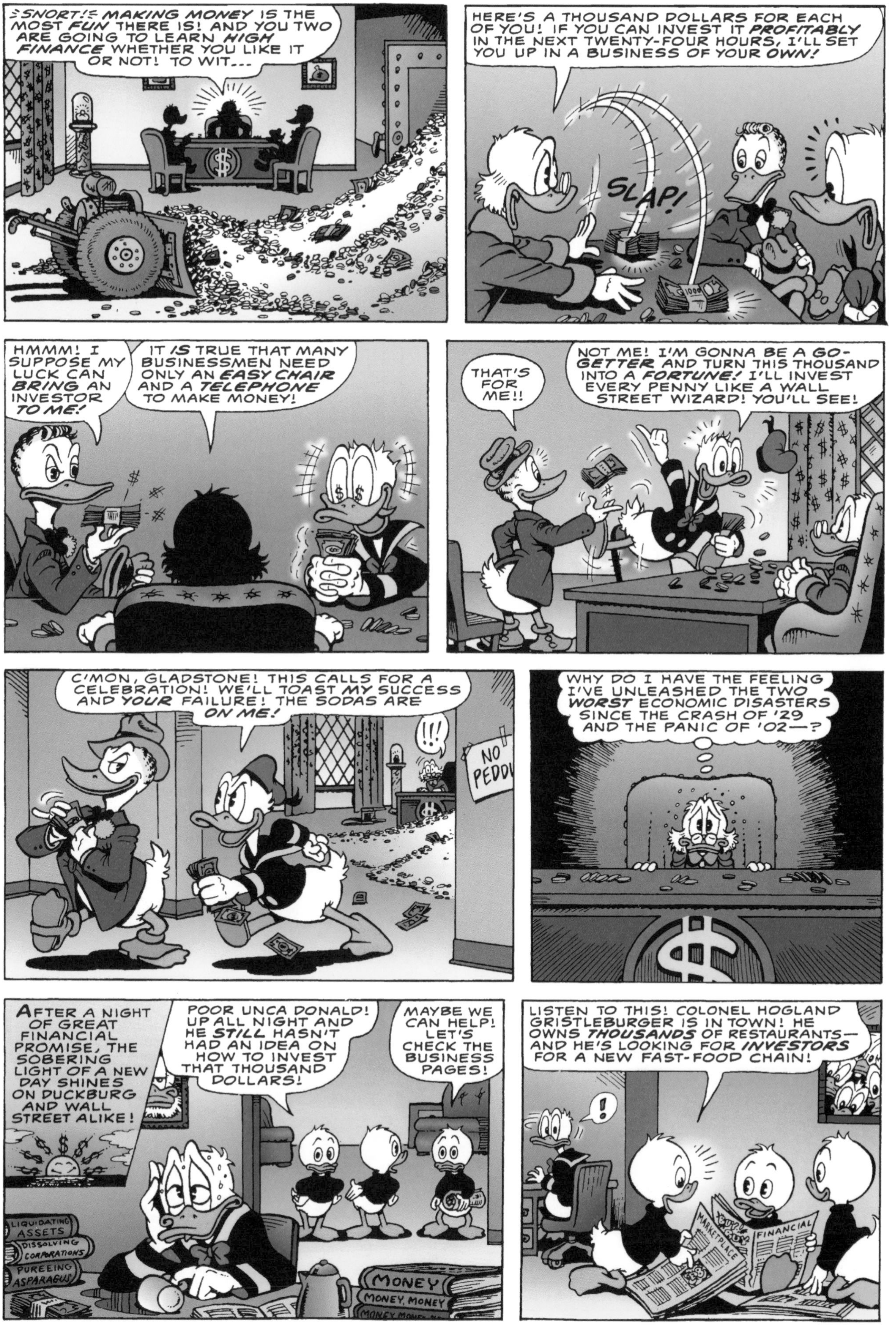
SNORT! MAKING MONEY IS THE MOST FUN THERE IS! AND YOU TWO ARE GOING TO LEARN HIGH FINANCE WHETHER YOU LIKE IT OR NOT! TO WIT...
HERE'S A THOUSAND DOLLARS FOR EACH OF YOU! IF YOU CAN INVEST IT PROFITABLY IN THE NEXT TWENTY-FOUR HOURS, I'LL SET YOU UP IN A BUSINESS OF YOUR OWN!
SLAP!
HMMM! I SUPPOSE MY LUCK CAN BRING AN INVESTOR TO ME!
IT IS TRUE THAT MANY BUSINESSMEN NEED ONLY AN EASY CHAIR AND A TELEPHONE TO MAKE MONEY!
THAT'S FOR ME!!
NOT ME! I'M GONNA BE A GO-GETTER AND TURN THIS THOUSAND INTO A FORTUNE! I'LL INVEST EVERY PENNY LIKE A WALL STREET WIZARD! YOU'LL SEE!
C'MON, GLADSTONE! THIS CALLS FOR A CELEBRATION! WE'LL TOAST MY SUCCESS AND YOUR FAILURE! THE SODAS ARE ON ME!
!!!
NO PEDDL
WHY DO I HAVE THE FEELING I'VE UNLEASHED THE TWO WORST ECONOMIC DISASTERS SINCE THE CRASH OF '29 AND THE PANIC OF '02—?
AFTER A NIGHT OF GREAT FINANCIAL PROMISE, THE SOBERING LIGHT OF A NEW DAY SHINES ON DUCKBURG AND WALL STREET ALIKE!
POOR UNCA DONALD! UP ALL NIGHT AND HE STILL HASN'T HAD AN IDEA ON HOW TO INVEST THAT THOUSAND DOLLARS!
MAYBE WE CAN HELP! LET'S CHECK THE BUSINESS PAGES!
LIQUIDATING ASSETS
DISSOLVING CORPORATIONS
PUREEING ASPARAGUS
MONEY
MONEY, MONEY
LISTEN TO THIS! COLONEL HOGLAND GRISTLEBURGER IS IN TOWN! HE OWNS THOUSANDS OF RESTAURANTS— AND HE'S LOOKING FOR INVESTORS FOR A NEW FAST-FOOD CHAIN!
!
MARKETPLACE
FINANCIAL

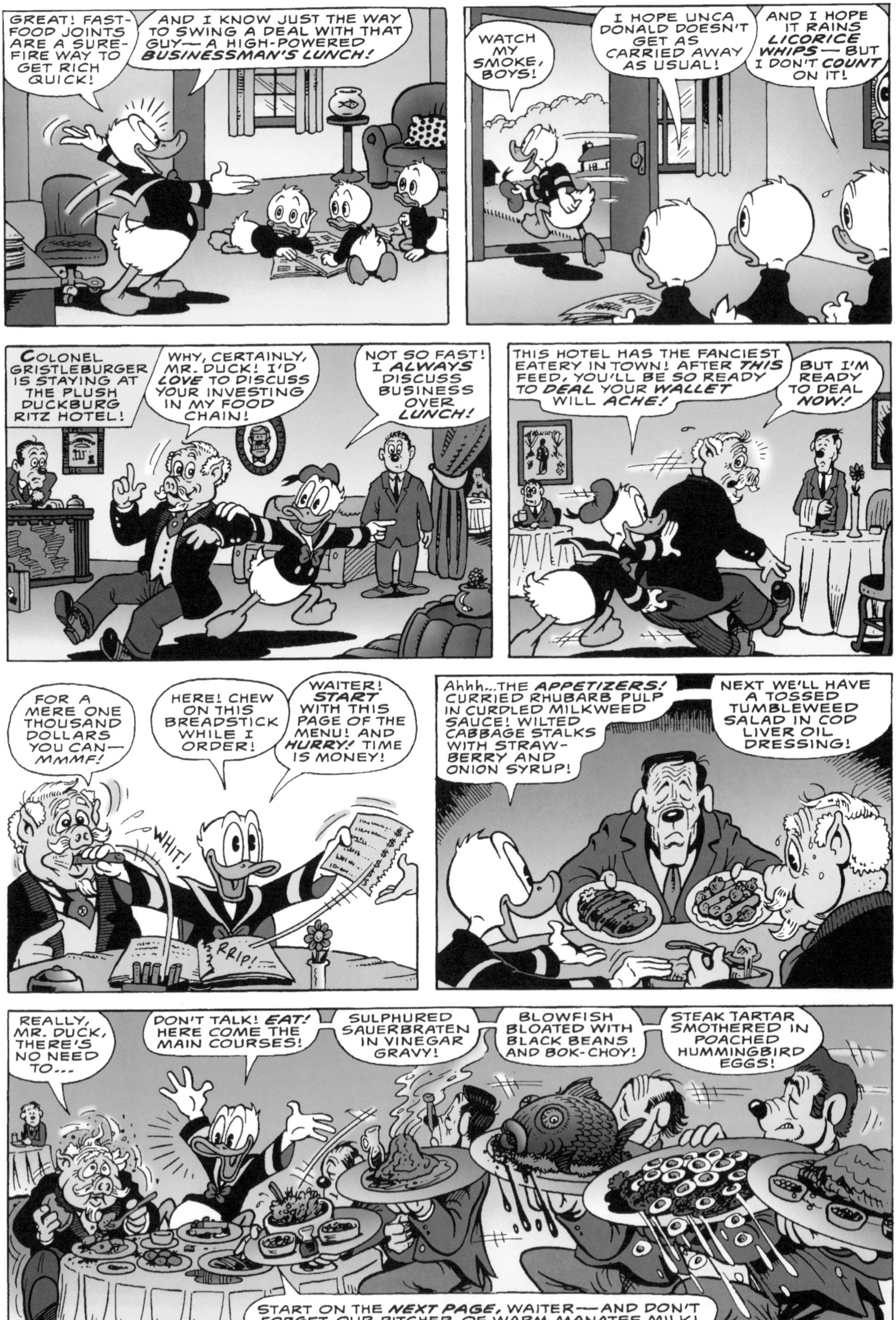

GREAT! FAST-FOOD JOINTS ARE A SURE-FIRE WAY TO GET RICH QUICK!
AND I KNOW JUST THE WAY TO SWING A DEAL WITH THAT GUY— A HIGH-POWERED BUSINESSMAN'S LUNCH!
WATCH MY SMOKE, BOYS!
I HOPE UNCA DONALD DOESN'T GET AS CARRIED AWAY AS USUAL!
AND I HOPE IT RAINS LICORICE WHIPS — BUT I DON'T COUNT ON IT!
COLONEL GRISTLEBURGER IS STAYING AT THE PLUSH DUCKBURG RITZ HOTEL!
WHY, CERTAINLY, MR. DUCK! I'D LOVE TO DISCUSS YOUR INVESTING IN MY FOOD CHAIN!
NOT SO FAST! I ALWAYS DISCUSS BUSINESS OVER LUNCH!
THIS HOTEL HAS THE FANCIEST EATERY IN TOWN! AFTER THIS FEED, YOU'LL BE SO READY TO DEAL YOUR WALLET WILL ACHE!
BUT I'M READY TO DEAL NOW!
FOR A MERE ONE THOUSAND DOLLARS YOU CAN— MMMF!
HERE! CHEW ON THIS BREADSTICK WHILE I ORDER!
WAITER! START WITH THIS PAGE OF THE MENU! AND HURRY! TIME IS MONEY!
WHIT!
RRIP!
Ahhh... THE APPETIZERS! CURRIED RHUBARB PULP IN CURDLED MILKWEED SAUCE! WILTED CABBAGE STALKS WITH STRAW-BERRY AND ONION SYRUP!
NEXT WE'LL HAVE A TOSSED TUMBLEWEED SALAD IN COD LIVER OIL DRESSING!
REALLY, MR. DUCK, THERE'S NO NEED TO...
DON'T TALK! EAT! HERE COME THE MAIN COURSES!
SULPHURED SAUERBRATEN IN VINEGAR GRAVY!
BLOWFISH BLOATED WITH BLACK BEANS AND BOK-CHOY!
STEAK TARTAR SMOTHERED IN POACHED HUMMINGBIRD EGGS!
START ON THE NEXT PAGE, WAITER— AND DON'T FORGET OUR PITCHER OF WARM MANATEE MILK!

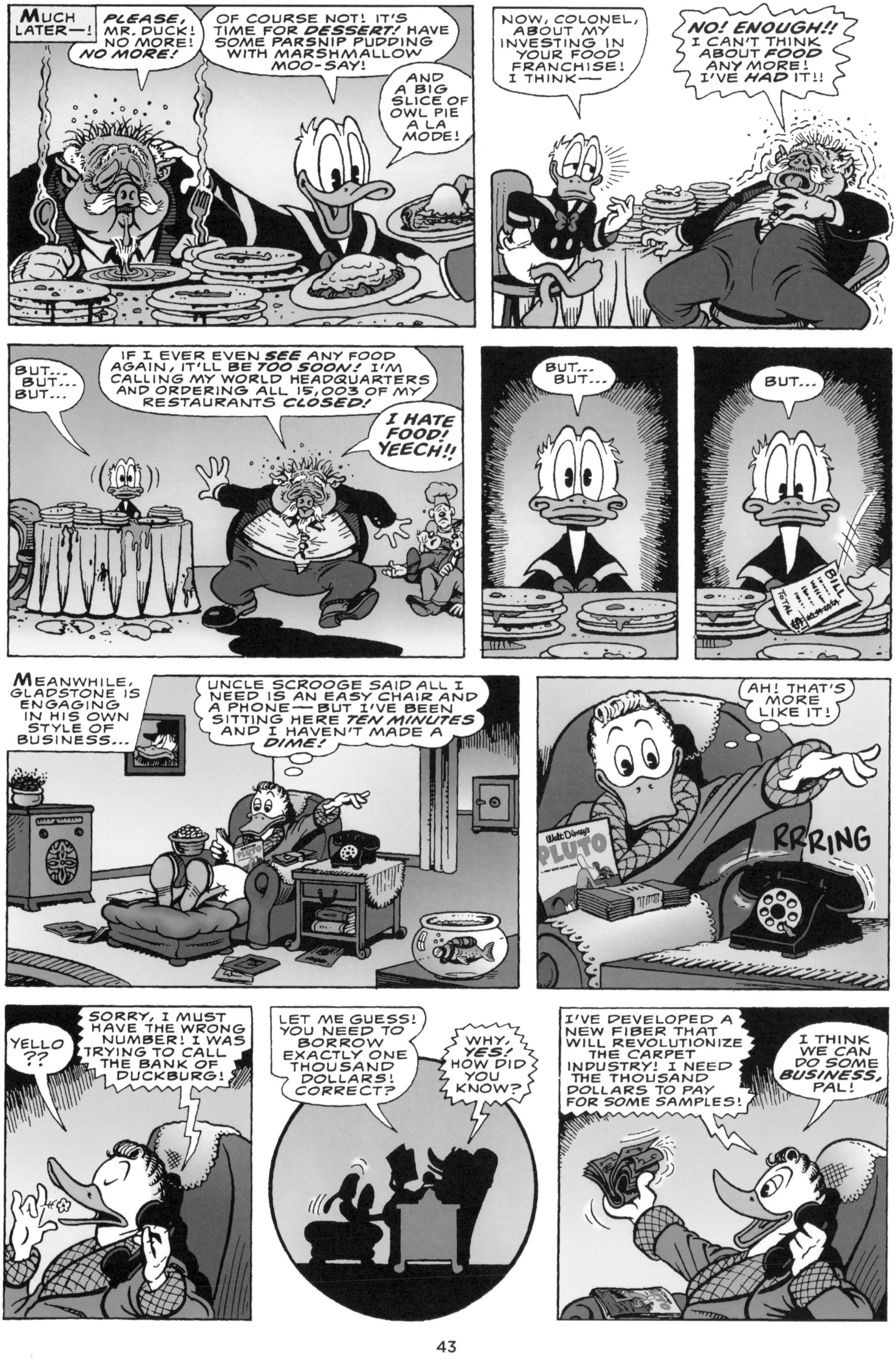
MUCH LATER—!
PLEASE, MR. DUCK! NO MORE! NO MORE!
OF COURSE NOT! IT'S TIME FOR DESSERT! HAVE SOME PARSNIP PUDDING WITH MARSHMALLOW MOO-SAY!
AND A BIG SLICE OF OWL PIE A LA MODE!
NOW, COLONEL, ABOUT MY INVESTING IN YOUR FOOD FRANCHISE! I THINK——
NO! ENOUGH!! I CAN'T THINK ABOUT FOOD ANY MORE! I'VE HAD IT!!
BUT... BUT... BUT...
IF I EVER EVEN SEE ANY FOOD AGAIN, IT'LL BE TOO SOON! I'M CALLING MY WORLD HEADQUARTERS AND ORDERING ALL 15,003 OF MY RESTAURANTS CLOSED!
I HATE FOOD! YEECH!!
BUT... BUT...
BUT...
BILL
TOTAL
MEANWHILE, GLADSTONE IS ENGAGING IN HIS OWN STYLE OF BUSINESS...
UNCLE SCROOGE SAID ALL I NEED IS AN EASY CHAIR AND A PHONE—BUT I'VE BEEN SITTING HERE TEN MINUTES AND I HAVEN'T MADE A DIME!
PLUTO
AH! THAT'S MORE LIKE IT!
Walt Disney's PLUTO
RRRING
YELLO ??
SORRY, I MUST HAVE THE WRONG NUMBER! I WAS TRYING TO CALL THE BANK OF DUCKBURG!
LET ME GUESS! YOU NEED TO BORROW EXACTLY ONE THOUSAND DOLLARS! CORRECT?
WHY, YES! HOW DID YOU KNOW?
I'VE DEVELOPED A NEW FIBER THAT WILL REVOLUTIONIZE THE CARPET INDUSTRY! I NEED THE THOUSAND DOLLARS TO PAY FOR SOME SAMPLES!
I THINK WE CAN DO SOME BUSINESS, PAL!

LATER... UNCA DONALD! DID YOU HEAR THE MID-DAY FINANCIAL NEWS? GLADSTONE SOLD AN INTEREST IN A RUG FACTORY FOR A *BIG* PROFIT!

≥SNORT!≤ SO WHAT? I'VE DECIDED THE *REALLY BIG* MONEY IS IN *REAL ESTATE!*

LISTEN TO THIS DESCRIPTION OF A LOT I BOUGHT FROM SIDEWALK SAM, THE REAL ESTATE MAN... "TWO ACRES IN *INDUSTRIAL PARK*, FLAT, DRY, SOLID *BEDROCK!*"

YOU DIDN'T BUY IT WITHOUT *SEEING* IT, DID YOU—?

WHY NOT? A GOOD BUSINESSMAN LIKE ME KNOWS A GOOD THING WHEN HE HEARS IT!

HERE! HOLD THIS TAPE MEASURE SO I CAN LOCATE MY PLOT!

THE SURVEY SAYS THE NORTH BOUNDARY IS TEN FEET FROM THAT CORNER!

SEVEN... EIGHT... NINE...

IT *ALSO* SAYS THE *SOUTH* BOUNDARY IS TEN FEET, *ONE INCH* FROM THERE!

WAK!

YOU SHOULD HAVE READ THE *FINE PRINT!* YOU OWN TWO ACRES, TRUE, BUT IT ALL DEPENDS ON YOUR *POINT OF VIEW!*

WHAT? HOW? WHO??

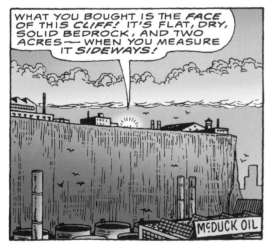

WHAT YOU BOUGHT IS THE *FACE* OF THIS *CLIFF!* IT'S FLAT, DRY, SOLID BEDROCK, AND TWO ACRES— WHEN YOU MEASURE IT *SIDEWAYS!*

McDUCK OIL

≥SPUTTER!≤ THAT SIDEWALK SAM!! WHEN I GET MY HANDS ON HIM I'LL—

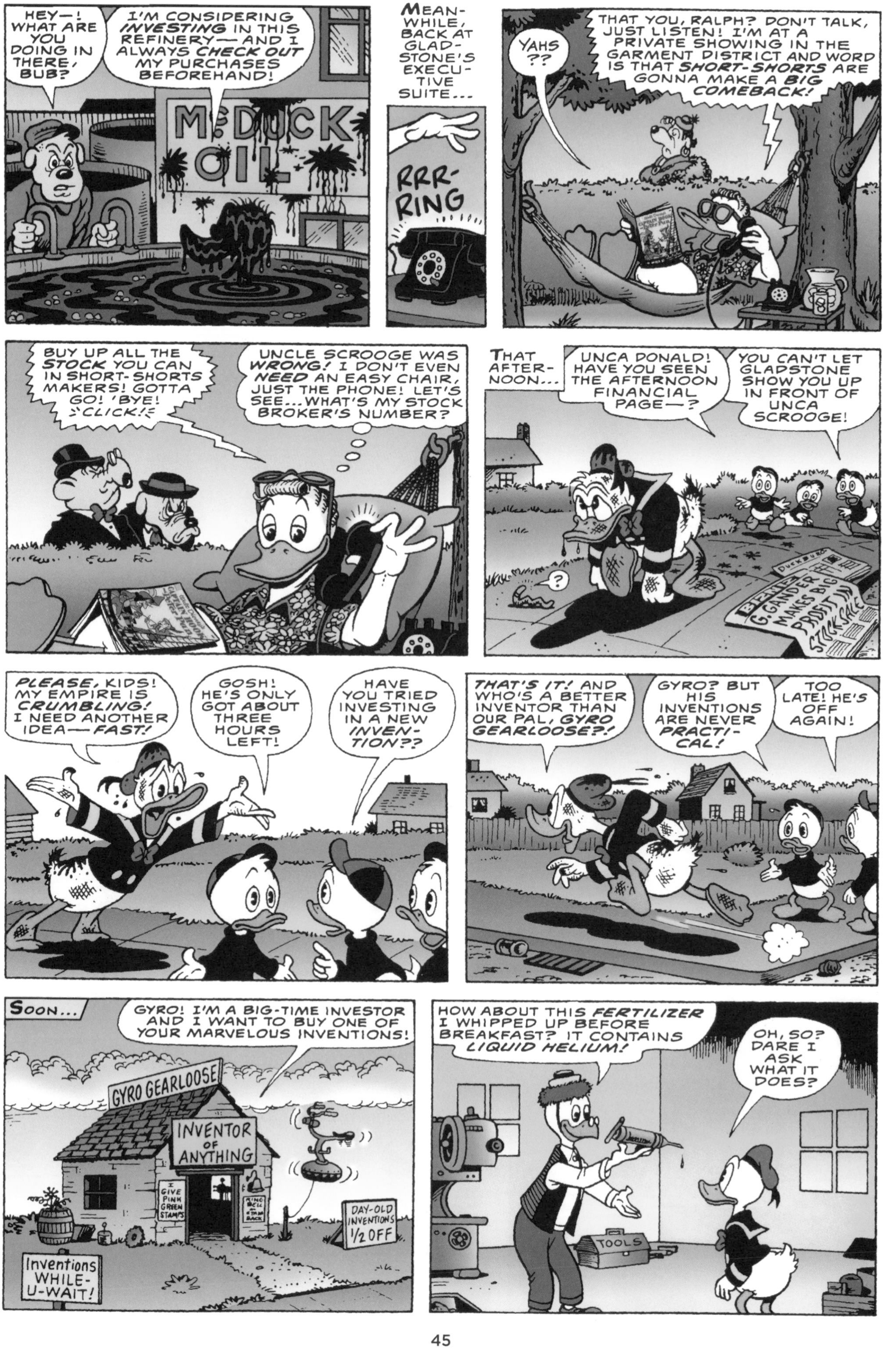
HEY—! WHAT ARE YOU DOING IN THERE, BUB?
I'M CONSIDERING INVESTING IN THIS REFINERY—AND I ALWAYS CHECK OUT MY PURCHASES BEFOREHAND!
McDUCK OIL
MEANWHILE, BACK AT GLADSTONE'S EXECUTIVE SUITE...
RRR-RING
YAHS ??
THAT YOU, RALPH? DON'T TALK, JUST LISTEN! I'M AT A PRIVATE SHOWING IN THE GARMENT DISTRICT AND WORD IS THAT SHORT-SHORTS ARE GONNA MAKE A BIG COMEBACK!
BUY UP ALL THE STOCK YOU CAN IN SHORT-SHORTS MAKERS! GOTTA GO! 'BYE! CLICK!
UNCLE SCROOGE WAS WRONG! I DON'T EVEN NEED AN EASY CHAIR, JUST THE PHONE! LET'S SEE... WHAT'S MY STOCK BROKER'S NUMBER?
THAT AFTERNOON...
UNCA DONALD! HAVE YOU SEEN THE AFTERNOON FINANCIAL PAGE—?
YOU CAN'T LET GLADSTONE SHOW YOU UP IN FRONT OF UNCA SCROOGE!
?
G. GANDER MAKES BIG PROFIT IN STOCK SALE
PLEASE, KIDS! MY EMPIRE IS CRUMBLING! I NEED ANOTHER IDEA—FAST!
GOSH! HE'S ONLY GOT ABOUT THREE HOURS LEFT!
HAVE YOU TRIED INVESTING IN A NEW INVENTION??
THAT'S IT! AND WHO'S A BETTER INVENTOR THAN OUR PAL, GYRO GEARLOOSE?!
GYRO? BUT HIS INVENTIONS ARE NEVER PRACTICAL!
TOO LATE! HE'S OFF AGAIN!
SOON...
GYRO! I'M A BIG-TIME INVESTOR AND I WANT TO BUY ONE OF YOUR MARVELOUS INVENTIONS!
GYRO GEARLOOSE
INVENTOR OF ANYTHING
I GIVE PINK GREEN STAMPS
RING BELL & STAND BACK
DAY-OLD INVENTIONS 1/2 OFF
Inventions WHILE-U-WAIT!
HOW ABOUT THIS FERTILIZER I WHIPPED UP BEFORE BREAKFAST? IT CONTAINS LIQUID HELIUM!
OH, SO? DARE I ASK WHAT IT DOES?
TOOLS

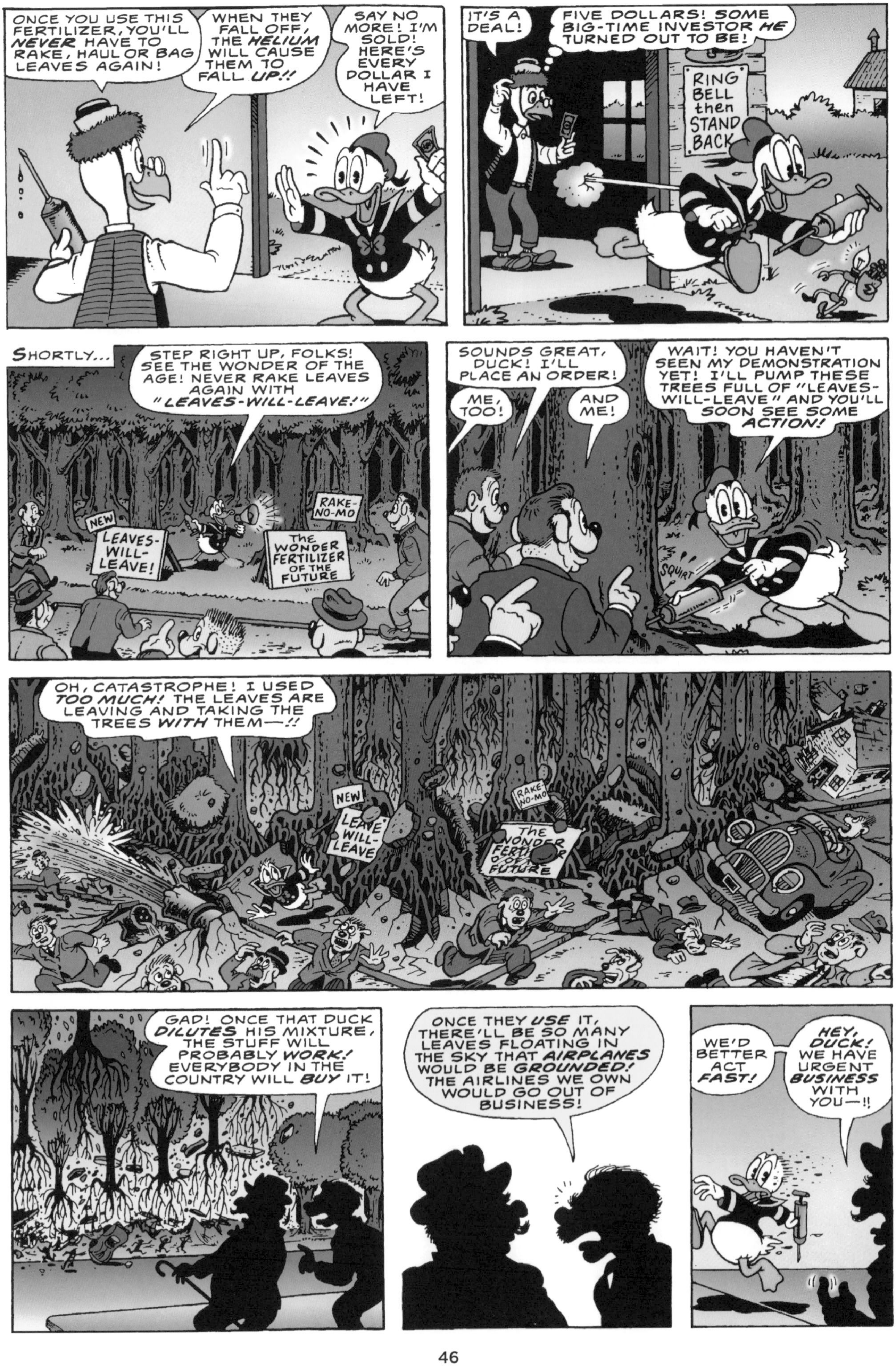
ONCE YOU USE THIS FERTILIZER, YOU'LL NEVER HAVE TO RAKE, HAUL OR BAG LEAVES AGAIN!
WHEN THEY FALL OFF, THE HELIUM WILL CAUSE THEM TO FALL UP!!
SAY NO MORE! I'M SOLD! HERE'S EVERY DOLLAR I HAVE LEFT!
IT'S A DEAL!
FIVE DOLLARS! SOME BIG-TIME INVESTOR HE TURNED OUT TO BE!
RING BELL then STAND BACK
SHORTLY...
STEP RIGHT UP, FOLKS! SEE THE WONDER OF THE AGE! NEVER RAKE LEAVES AGAIN WITH "LEAVES-WILL-LEAVE!"
NEW
LEAVES-WILL-LEAVE!
RAKE-NO-MO
The WONDER FERTILIZER OF THE FUTURE
SOUNDS GREAT, DUCK! I'LL PLACE AN ORDER!
ME, TOO!
AND ME!
WAIT! YOU HAVEN'T SEEN MY DEMONSTRATION YET! I'LL PUMP THESE TREES FULL OF "LEAVES-WILL-LEAVE" AND YOU'LL SOON SEE SOME ACTION!
SQUIRT
OH, CATASTROPHE! I USED TOO MUCH! THE LEAVES ARE LEAVING AND TAKING THE TREES WITH THEM—!!
NEW
RAKE-NO-MO
LEAVE WILL LEAVE
GAD! ONCE THAT DUCK DILUTES HIS MIXTURE, THE STUFF WILL PROBABLY WORK! EVERYBODY IN THE COUNTRY WILL BUY IT!
ONCE THEY USE IT, THERE'LL BE SO MANY LEAVES FLOATING IN THE SKY THAT AIRPLANES WOULD BE GROUNDED! THE AIRLINES WE OWN WOULD GO OUT OF BUSINESS!
WE'D BETTER ACT FAST!
HEY, DUCK! WE HAVE URGENT BUSINESS WITH YOU—!!

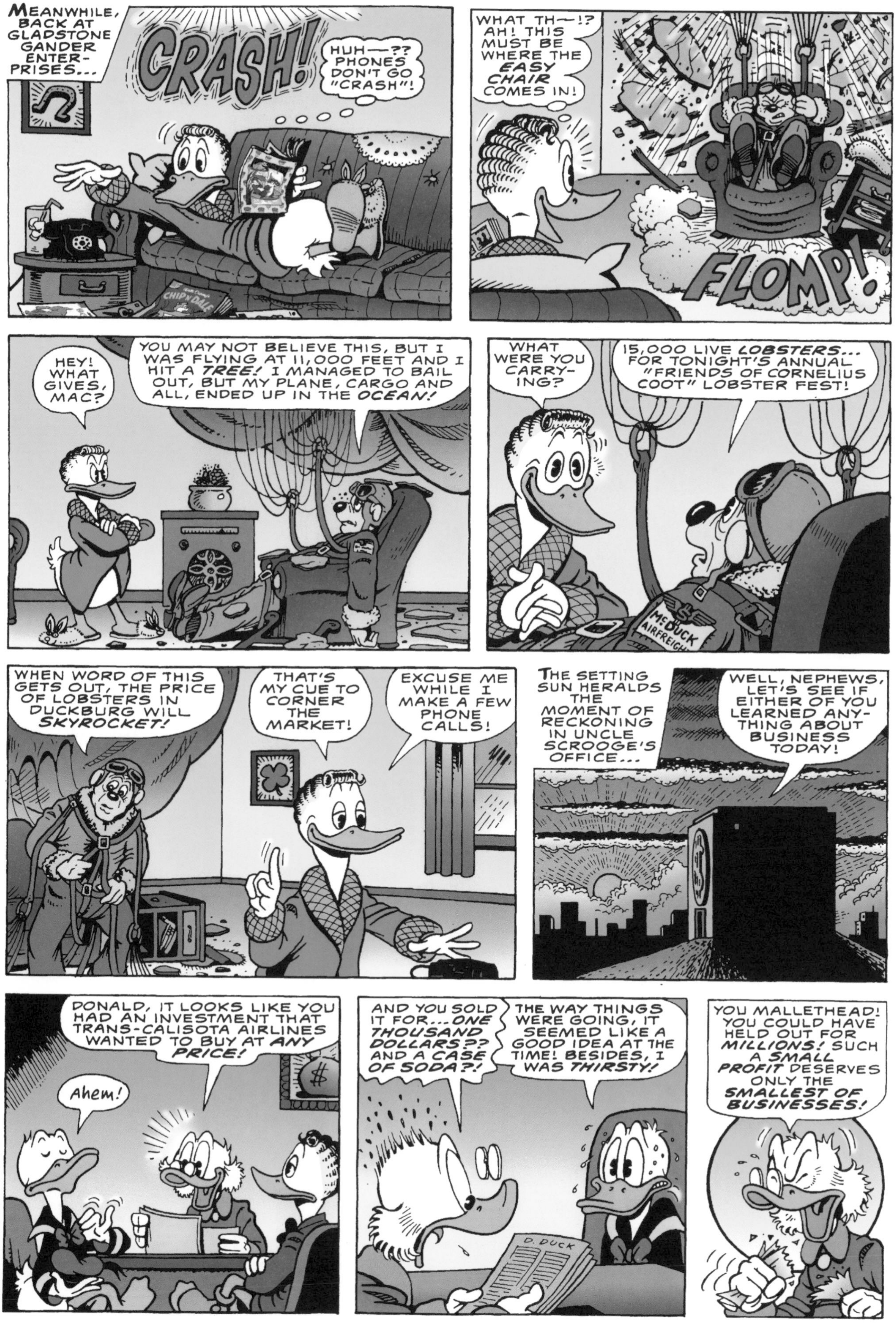
MEANWHILE, BACK AT GLADSTONE GANDER ENTER-PRISES...
CRASH!
HUH—?? PHONES DON'T GO "CRASH"!
WHAT TH—!? AH! THIS MUST BE WHERE THE EASY CHAIR COMES IN!
FLOMP!
HEY! WHAT GIVES, MAC?
YOU MAY NOT BELIEVE THIS, BUT I WAS FLYING AT 11,000 FEET AND I HIT A TREE! I MANAGED TO BAIL OUT, BUT MY PLANE, CARGO AND ALL, ENDED UP IN THE OCEAN!
WHAT WERE YOU CARRY-ING?
15,000 LIVE LOBSTERS... FOR TONIGHT'S ANNUAL "FRIENDS OF CORNELIUS COOT" LOBSTER FEST!
McDUCK AIRFREIGH
WHEN WORD OF THIS GETS OUT, THE PRICE OF LOBSTERS IN DUCKBURG WILL SKYROCKET!
THAT'S MY CUE TO CORNER THE MARKET!
EXCUSE ME WHILE I MAKE A FEW PHONE CALLS!
THE SETTING SUN HERALDS THE MOMENT OF RECKONING IN UNCLE SCROOGE'S OFFICE...
WELL, NEPHEWS, LET'S SEE IF EITHER OF YOU LEARNED ANY-THING ABOUT BUSINESS TODAY!
DONALD, IT LOOKS LIKE YOU HAD AN INVESTMENT THAT TRANS-CALISOTA AIRLINES WANTED TO BUY AT ANY PRICE!
Ahem!
AND YOU SOLD IT FOR... ONE THOUSAND DOLLARS?? AND A CASE OF SODA?!
THE WAY THINGS WERE GOING, IT SEEMED LIKE A GOOD IDEA AT THE TIME! BESIDES, I WAS THIRSTY!
D. DUCK
YOU MALLETHEAD! YOU COULD HAVE HELD OUT FOR MILLIONS! SUCH A SMALL PROFIT DESERVES ONLY THE SMALLEST OF BUSINESSES!

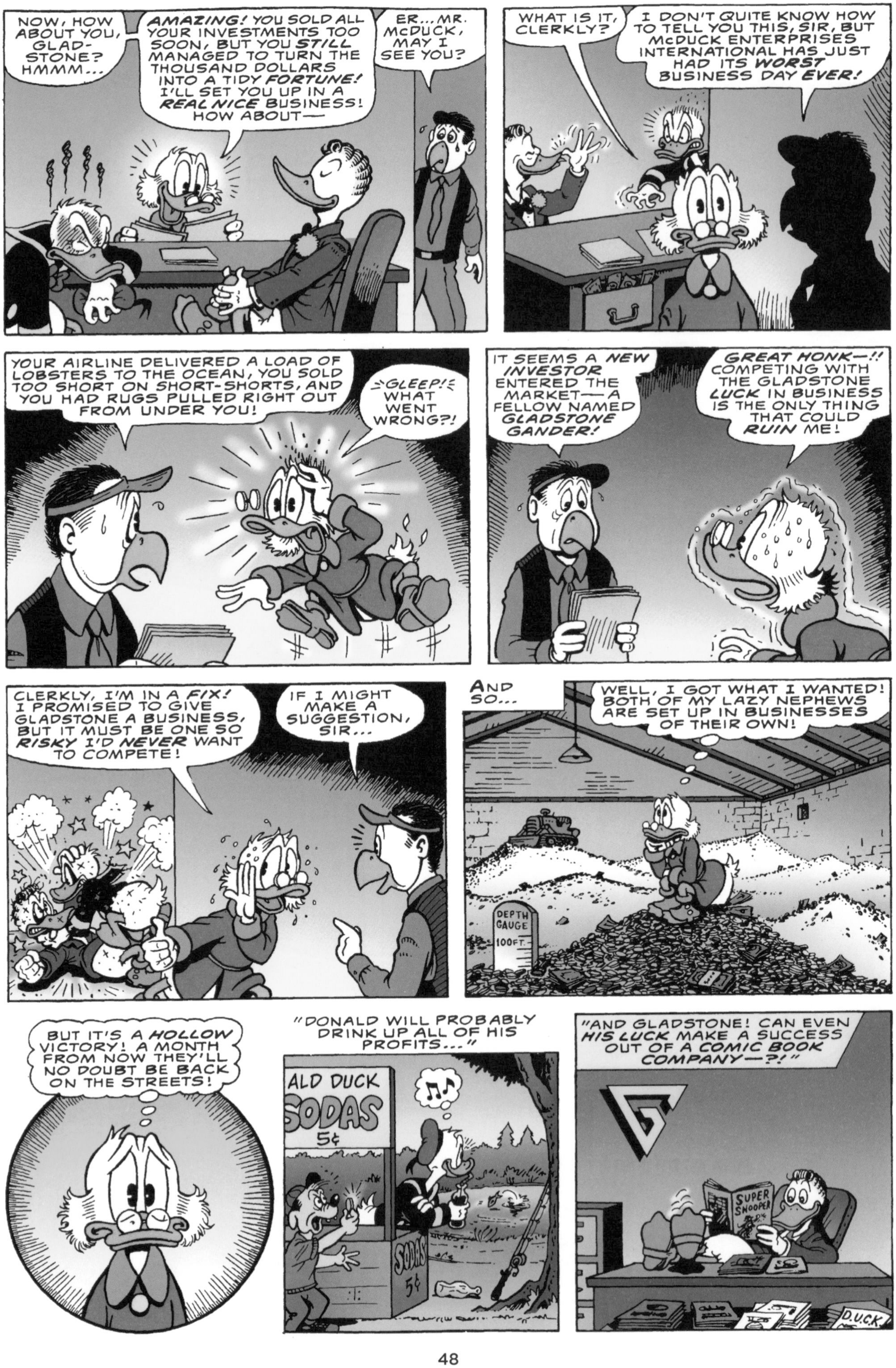
NOW, HOW ABOUT YOU, GLAD-STONE? HMMM...
AMAZING! YOU SOLD ALL YOUR INVESTMENTS TOO SOON, BUT YOU STILL MANAGED TO TURN THE THOUSAND DOLLARS INTO A TIDY FORTUNE! I'LL SET YOU UP IN A REAL NICE BUSINESS! HOW ABOUT—
ER... MR. McDUCK, MAY I SEE YOU?
WHAT IS IT, CLERKLY?
I DON'T QUITE KNOW HOW TO TELL YOU THIS, SIR, BUT McDUCK ENTERPRISES INTERNATIONAL HAS JUST HAD ITS WORST BUSINESS DAY EVER!
YOUR AIRLINE DELIVERED A LOAD OF LOBSTERS TO THE OCEAN, YOU SOLD TOO SHORT ON SHORT-SHORTS, AND YOU HAD RUGS PULLED RIGHT OUT FROM UNDER YOU!
GLEEP! WHAT WENT WRONG?!
IT SEEMS A NEW INVESTOR ENTERED THE MARKET—A FELLOW NAMED GLADSTONE GANDER!
GREAT HONK—!! COMPETING WITH THE GLADSTONE LUCK IN BUSINESS IS THE ONLY THING THAT COULD RUIN ME!
CLERKLY, I'M IN A FIX! I PROMISED TO GIVE GLADSTONE A BUSINESS, BUT IT MUST BE ONE SO RISKY I'D NEVER WANT TO COMPETE!
IF I MIGHT MAKE A SUGGESTION, SIR...
AND SO...
WELL, I GOT WHAT I WANTED! BOTH OF MY LAZY NEPHEWS ARE SET UP IN BUSINESSES OF THEIR OWN!
DEPTH GAUGE
100FT.
BUT IT'S A HOLLOW VICTORY! A MONTH FROM NOW THEY'LL NO DOUBT BE BACK ON THE STREETS!
"DONALD WILL PROBABLY DRINK UP ALL OF HIS PROFITS..."
ALD DUCK
SODAS
5¢
SODAS
5¢
"AND GLADSTONE! CAN EVEN HIS LUCK MAKE A SUCCESS OUT OF A COMIC BOOK COMPANY—?!"
SUPER SNOOPER
D.U.C.K

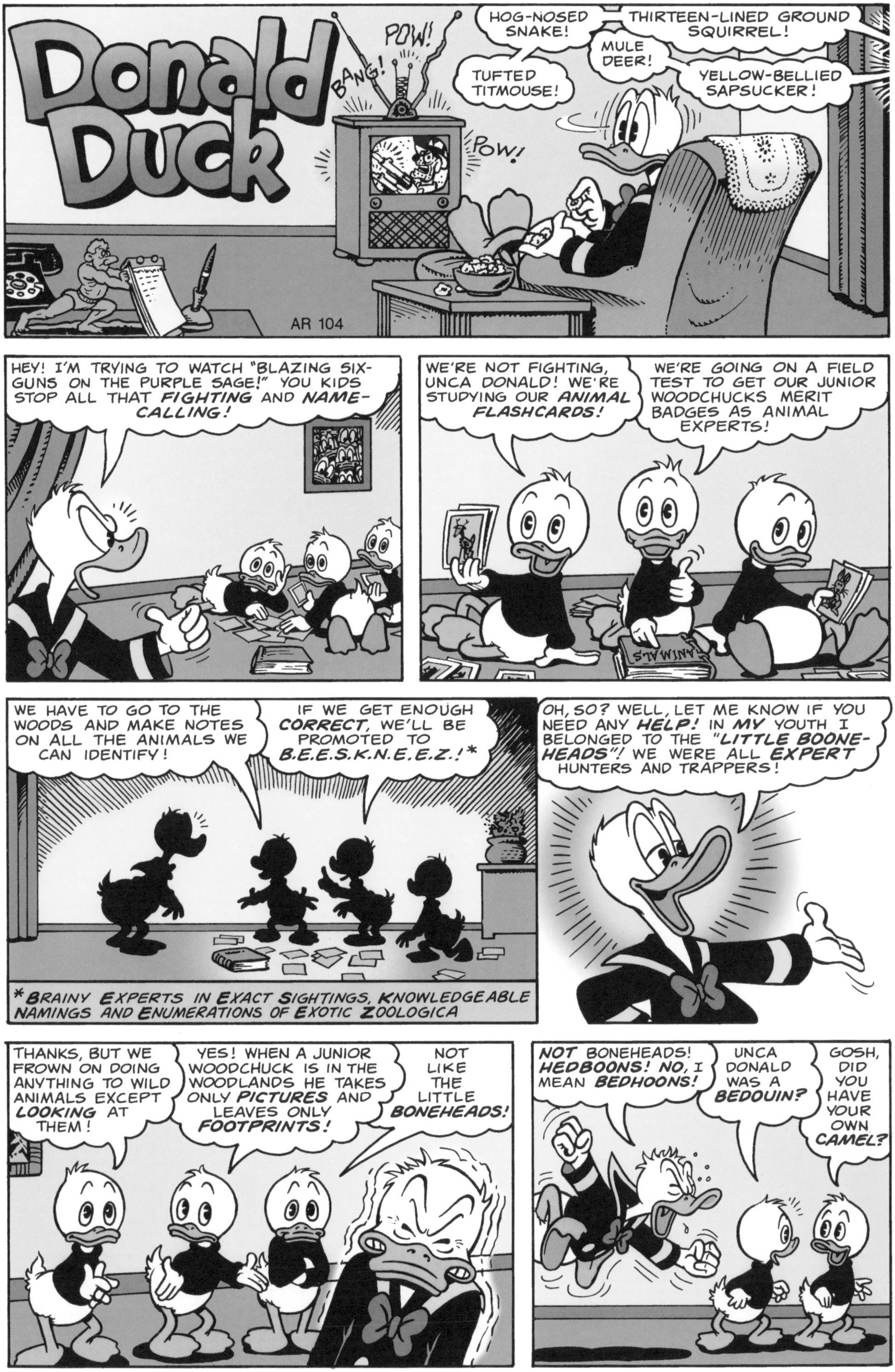
Donald Duck
POW!
BANG!
POW!
HOG-NOSED SNAKE!
THIRTEEN-LINED GROUND SQUIRREL!
MULE DEER!
TUFTED TITMOUSE!
YELLOW-BELLIED SAPSUCKER!
AR 104
HEY! I'M TRYING TO WATCH "BLAZING SIX-GUNS ON THE PURPLE SAGE!" YOU KIDS STOP ALL THAT FIGHTING AND NAME-CALLING!
WE'RE NOT FIGHTING, UNCA DONALD! WE'RE STUDYING OUR ANIMAL FLASHCARDS!
WE'RE GOING ON A FIELD TEST TO GET OUR JUNIOR WOODCHUCKS MERIT BADGES AS ANIMAL EXPERTS!
ANIMALS
WE HAVE TO GO TO THE WOODS AND MAKE NOTES ON ALL THE ANIMALS WE CAN IDENTIFY!
IF WE GET ENOUGH CORRECT, WE'LL BE PROMOTED TO B.E.E.S.K.N.E.E.Z.!*
*BRAINY EXPERTS IN EXACT SIGHTINGS, KNOWLEDGEABLE NAMINGS AND ENUMERATIONS OF EXOTIC ZOOLOGICA
OH, SO? WELL, LET ME KNOW IF YOU NEED ANY HELP! IN MY YOUTH I BELONGED TO THE "LITTLE BOONE-HEADS"! WE WERE ALL EXPERT HUNTERS AND TRAPPERS!
THANKS, BUT WE FROWN ON DOING ANYTHING TO WILD ANIMALS EXCEPT LOOKING AT THEM!
YES! WHEN A JUNIOR WOODCHUCK IS IN THE WOODLANDS HE TAKES ONLY PICTURES AND LEAVES ONLY FOOTPRINTS!
NOT LIKE THE LITTLE BONEHEADS!
NOT BONEHEADS! HEDBOONS! NO, I MEAN BEDHOONS!
UNCA DONALD WAS A BEDOUIN?
GOSH, DID YOU HAVE YOUR OWN CAMEL?

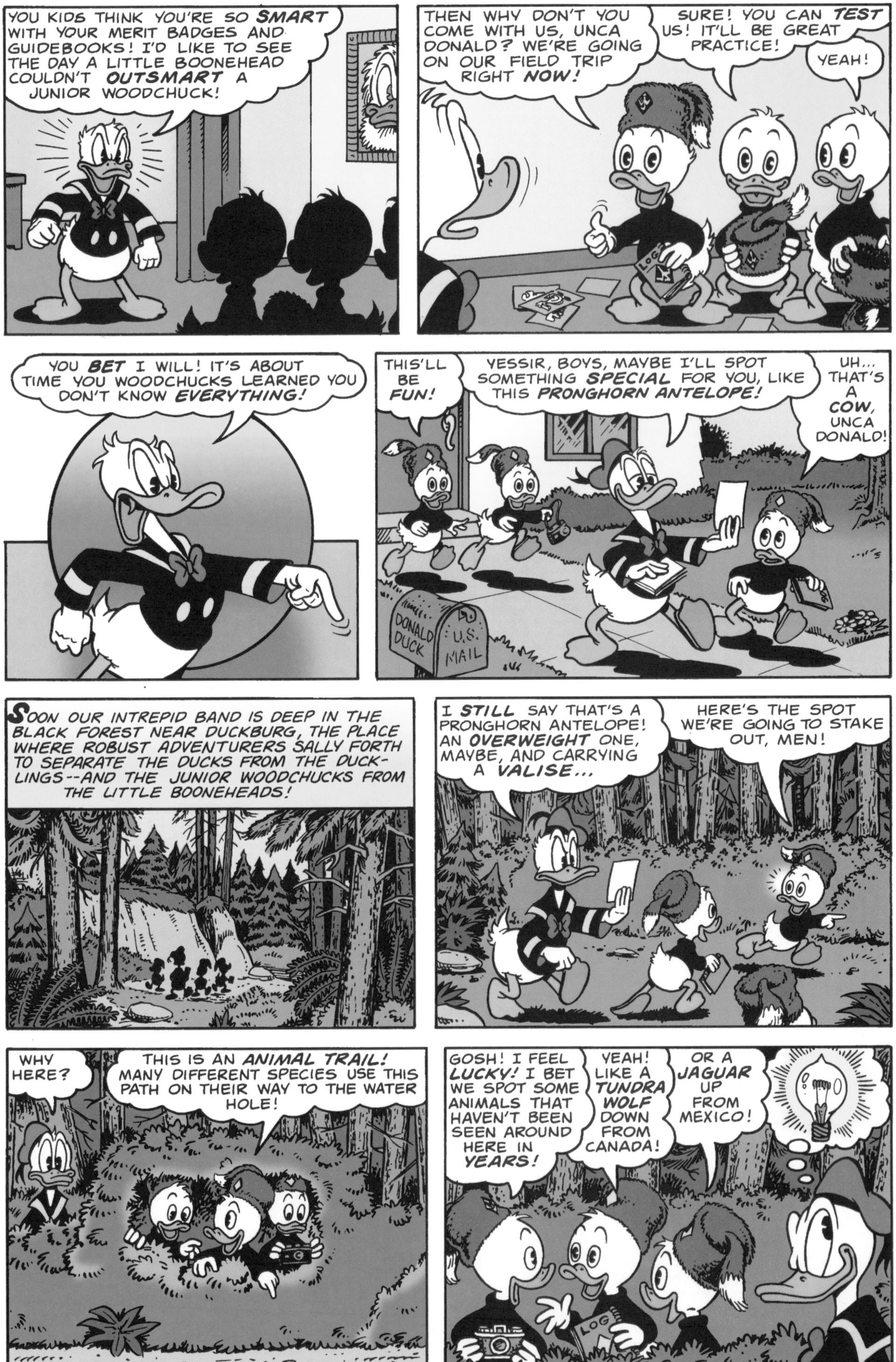
YOU KIDS THINK YOU'RE SO SMART WITH YOUR MERIT BADGES AND GUIDEBOOKS! I'D LIKE TO SEE THE DAY A LITTLE BOONEHEAD COULDN'T OUTSMART A JUNIOR WOODCHUCK!
THEN WHY DON'T YOU COME WITH US, UNCA DONALD? WE'RE GOING ON OUR FIELD TRIP RIGHT NOW!
SURE! YOU CAN TEST US! IT'LL BE GREAT PRACTICE!
YEAH!
LOG
YOU BET I WILL! IT'S ABOUT TIME YOU WOODCHUCKS LEARNED YOU DON'T KNOW EVERYTHING!
THIS'LL BE FUN!
YESSIR, BOYS, MAYBE I'LL SPOT SOMETHING SPECIAL FOR YOU, LIKE THIS PRONGHORN ANTELOPE!
UH... THAT'S A COW, UNCA DONALD!
DONALD DUCK
U.S. MAIL
SOON OUR INTREPID BAND IS DEEP IN THE BLACK FOREST NEAR DUCKBURG, THE PLACE WHERE ROBUST ADVENTURERS SALLY FORTH TO SEPARATE THE DUCKS FROM THE DUCK-LINGS--AND THE JUNIOR WOODCHUCKS FROM THE LITTLE BOONEHEADS!
I STILL SAY THAT'S A PRONGHORN ANTELOPE! AN OVERWEIGHT ONE, MAYBE, AND CARRYING A VALISE...
HERE'S THE SPOT WE'RE GOING TO STAKE OUT, MEN!
WHY HERE?
THIS IS AN ANIMAL TRAIL! MANY DIFFERENT SPECIES USE THIS PATH ON THEIR WAY TO THE WATER HOLE!
GOSH! I FEEL LUCKY! I BET WE SPOT SOME ANIMALS THAT HAVEN'T BEEN SEEN AROUND HERE IN YEARS!
YEAH! LIKE A TUNDRA WOLF DOWN FROM CANADA!
OR A JAGUAR UP FROM MEXICO!
LOG

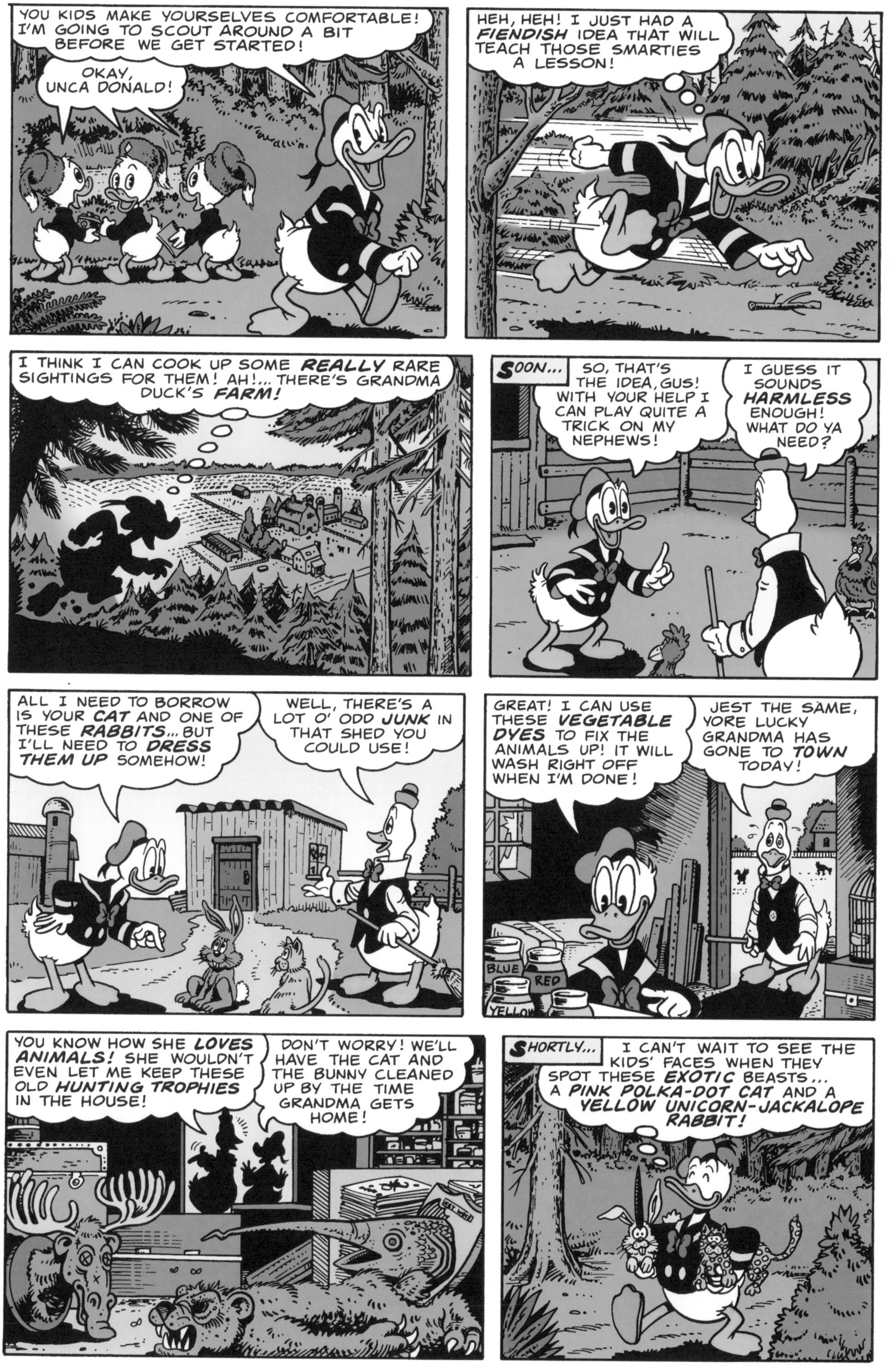
YOU KIDS MAKE YOURSELVES COMFORTABLE! I'M GOING TO SCOUT AROUND A BIT BEFORE WE GET STARTED!
OKAY, UNCA DONALD!
HEH, HEH! I JUST HAD A FIENDISH IDEA THAT WILL TEACH THOSE SMARTIES A LESSON!
I THINK I CAN COOK UP SOME REALLY RARE SIGHTINGS FOR THEM! AH!... THERE'S GRANDMA DUCK'S FARM!
SOON...
SO, THAT'S THE IDEA, GUS! WITH YOUR HELP I CAN PLAY QUITE A TRICK ON MY NEPHEWS!
I GUESS IT SOUNDS HARMLESS ENOUGH! WHAT DO YA NEED?
ALL I NEED TO BORROW IS YOUR CAT AND ONE OF THESE RABBITS... BUT I'LL NEED TO DRESS THEM UP SOMEHOW!
WELL, THERE'S A LOT O' ODD JUNK IN THAT SHED YOU COULD USE!
GREAT! I CAN USE THESE VEGETABLE DYES TO FIX THE ANIMALS UP! IT WILL WASH RIGHT OFF WHEN I'M DONE!
JEST THE SAME, YORE LUCKY GRANDMA HAS GONE TO TOWN TODAY!
BLUE
RED
YELLOW
YOU KNOW HOW SHE LOVES ANIMALS! SHE WOULDN'T EVEN LET ME KEEP THESE OLD HUNTING TROPHIES IN THE HOUSE!
DON'T WORRY! WE'LL HAVE THE CAT AND THE BUNNY CLEANED UP BY THE TIME GRANDMA GETS HOME!
SHORTLY...
I CAN'T WAIT TO SEE THE KIDS' FACES WHEN THEY SPOT THESE EXOTIC BEASTS... A PINK POLKA-DOT CAT AND A YELLOW UNICORN-JACKALOPE RABBIT!

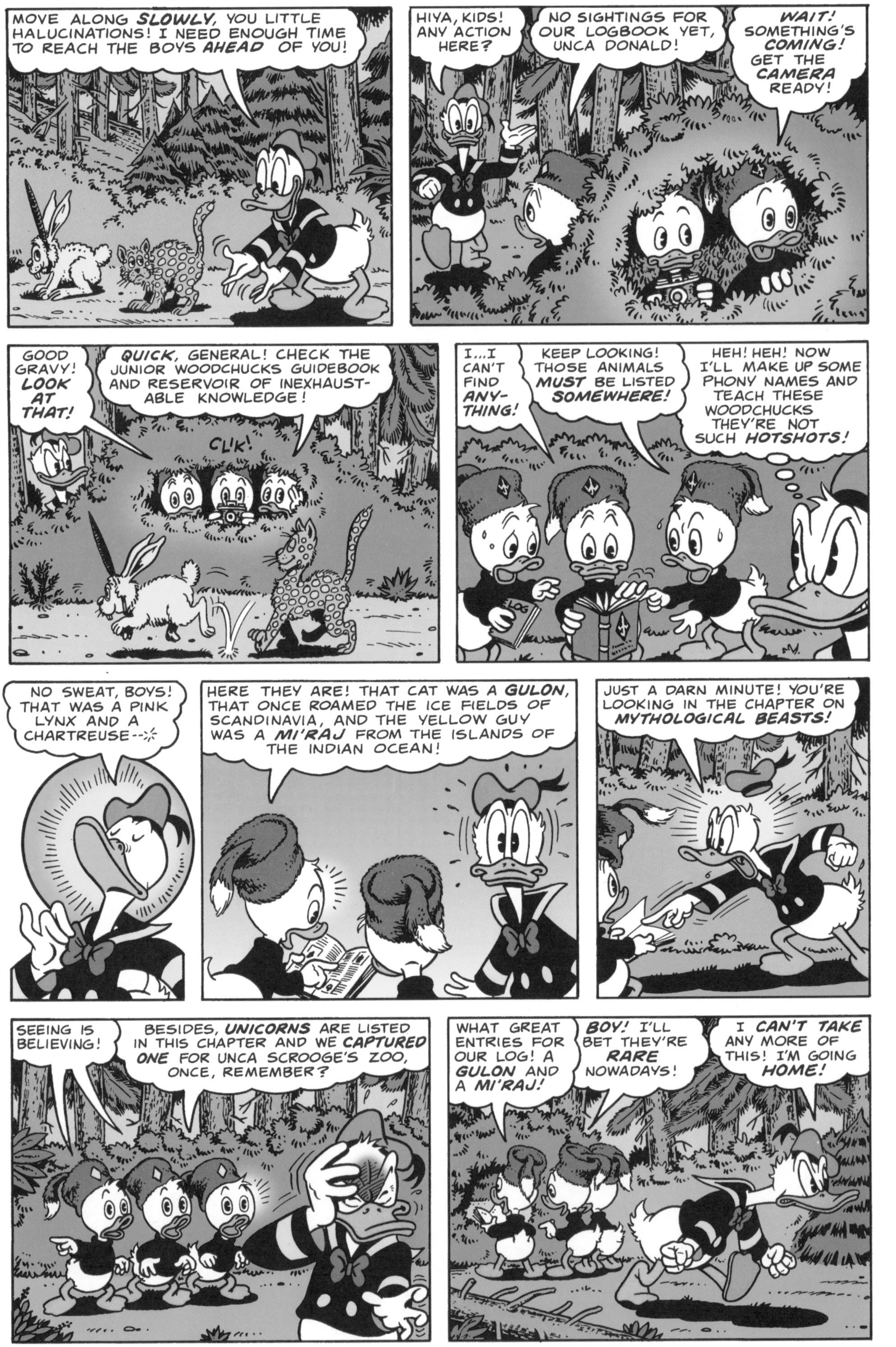
MOVE ALONG SLOWLY, YOU LITTLE HALUCINATIONS! I NEED ENOUGH TIME TO REACH THE BOYS AHEAD OF YOU!
HIYA, KIDS! ANY ACTION HERE?
NO SIGHTINGS FOR OUR LOGBOOK YET, UNCA DONALD!
WAIT! SOMETHING'S COMING! GET THE CAMERA READY!
GOOD GRAVY! LOOK AT THAT!
QUICK, GENERAL! CHECK THE JUNIOR WOODCHUCKS GUIDEBOOK AND RESERVOIR OF INEXHAUSTABLE KNOWLEDGE!
CLIK!
I...I CAN'T FIND ANYTHING!
KEEP LOOKING! THOSE ANIMALS MUST BE LISTED SOMEWHERE!
HEH! HEH! NOW I'LL MAKE UP SOME PHONY NAMES AND TEACH THESE WOODCHUCKS THEY'RE NOT SUCH HOTSHOTS!
LOG
NO SWEAT, BOYS! THAT WAS A PINK LYNX AND A CHARTREUSE--
HERE THEY ARE! THAT CAT WAS A GULON, THAT ONCE ROAMED THE ICE FIELDS OF SCANDINAVIA, AND THE YELLOW GUY WAS A MI'RAJ FROM THE ISLANDS OF THE INDIAN OCEAN!
JUST A DARN MINUTE! YOU'RE LOOKING IN THE CHAPTER ON MYTHOLOGICAL BEASTS!
SEEING IS BELIEVING!
BESIDES, UNICORNS ARE LISTED IN THIS CHAPTER AND WE CAPTURED ONE FOR UNCA SCROOGE'S ZOO, ONCE, REMEMBER?
WHAT GREAT ENTRIES FOR OUR LOG! A GULON AND A MI'RAJ!
BOY! I'LL BET THEY'RE RARE NOWADAYS!
I CAN'T TAKE ANY MORE OF THIS! I'M GOING HOME!

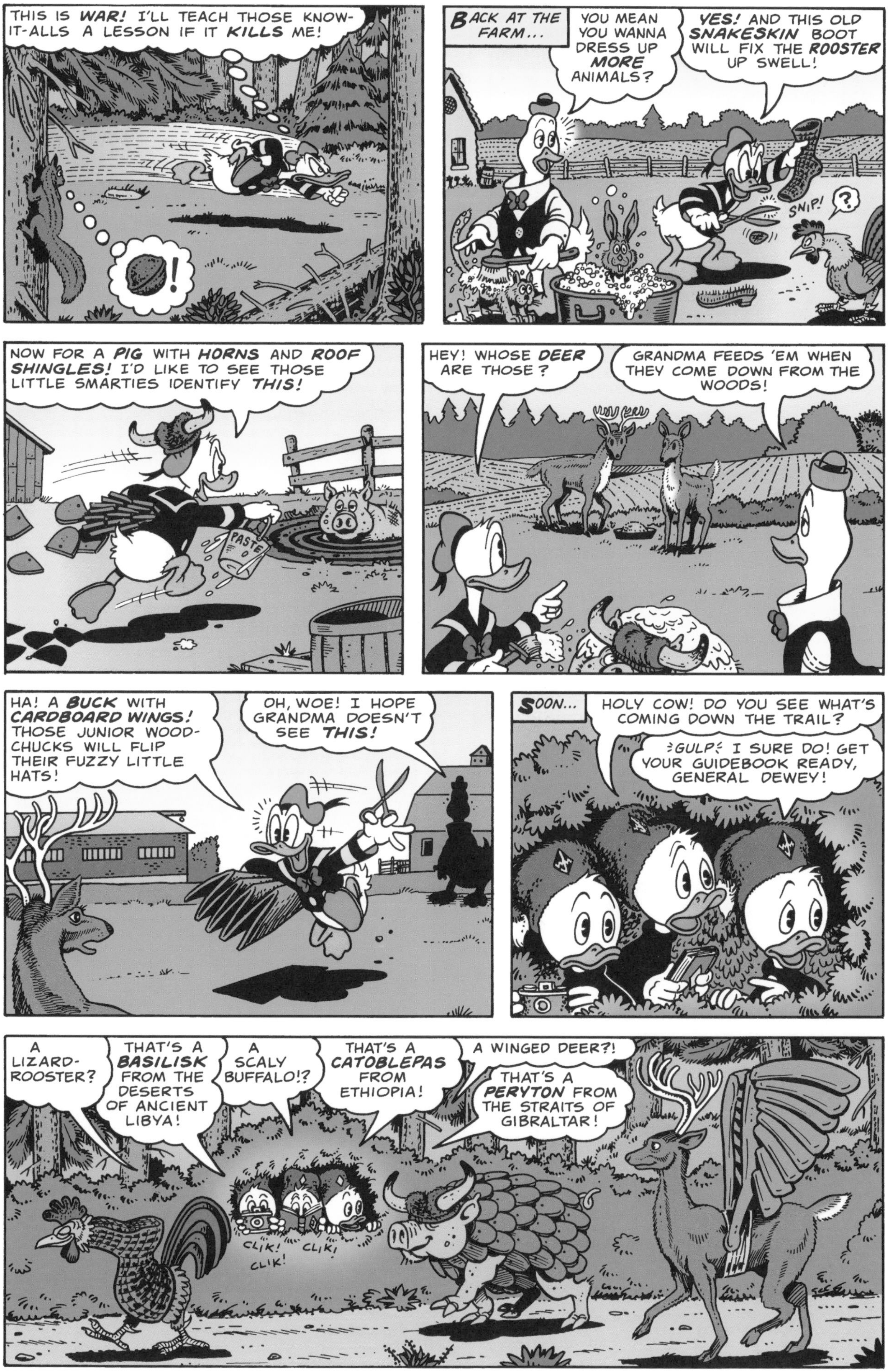
THIS IS WAR! I'LL TEACH THOSE KNOW-IT-ALLS A LESSON IF IT KILLS ME!
!
BACK AT THE FARM...
YOU MEAN YOU WANNA DRESS UP MORE ANIMALS?
YES! AND THIS OLD SNAKESKIN BOOT WILL FIX THE ROOSTER UP SWELL!
SNIP!
?
NOW FOR A PIG WITH HORNS AND ROOF SHINGLES! I'D LIKE TO SEE THOSE LITTLE SMARTIES IDENTIFY THIS!
PASTE
HEY! WHOSE DEER ARE THOSE?
GRANDMA FEEDS 'EM WHEN THEY COME DOWN FROM THE WOODS!
HA! A BUCK WITH CARDBOARD WINGS! THOSE JUNIOR WOODCHUCKS WILL FLIP THEIR FUZZY LITTLE HATS!
OH, WOE! I HOPE GRANDMA DOESN'T SEE THIS!
SOON...
HOLY COW! DO YOU SEE WHAT'S COMING DOWN THE TRAIL?
GULP I SURE DO! GET YOUR GUIDEBOOK READY, GENERAL DEWEY!
A LIZARD-ROOSTER?
THAT'S A BASILISK FROM THE DESERTS OF ANCIENT LIBYA!
A SCALY BUFFALO!?
THAT'S A CATOBLEPAS FROM ETHIOPIA!
A WINGED DEER?!
THAT'S A PERYTON FROM THE STRAITS OF GIBRALTAR!
CLIK! CLIK! CLIK!

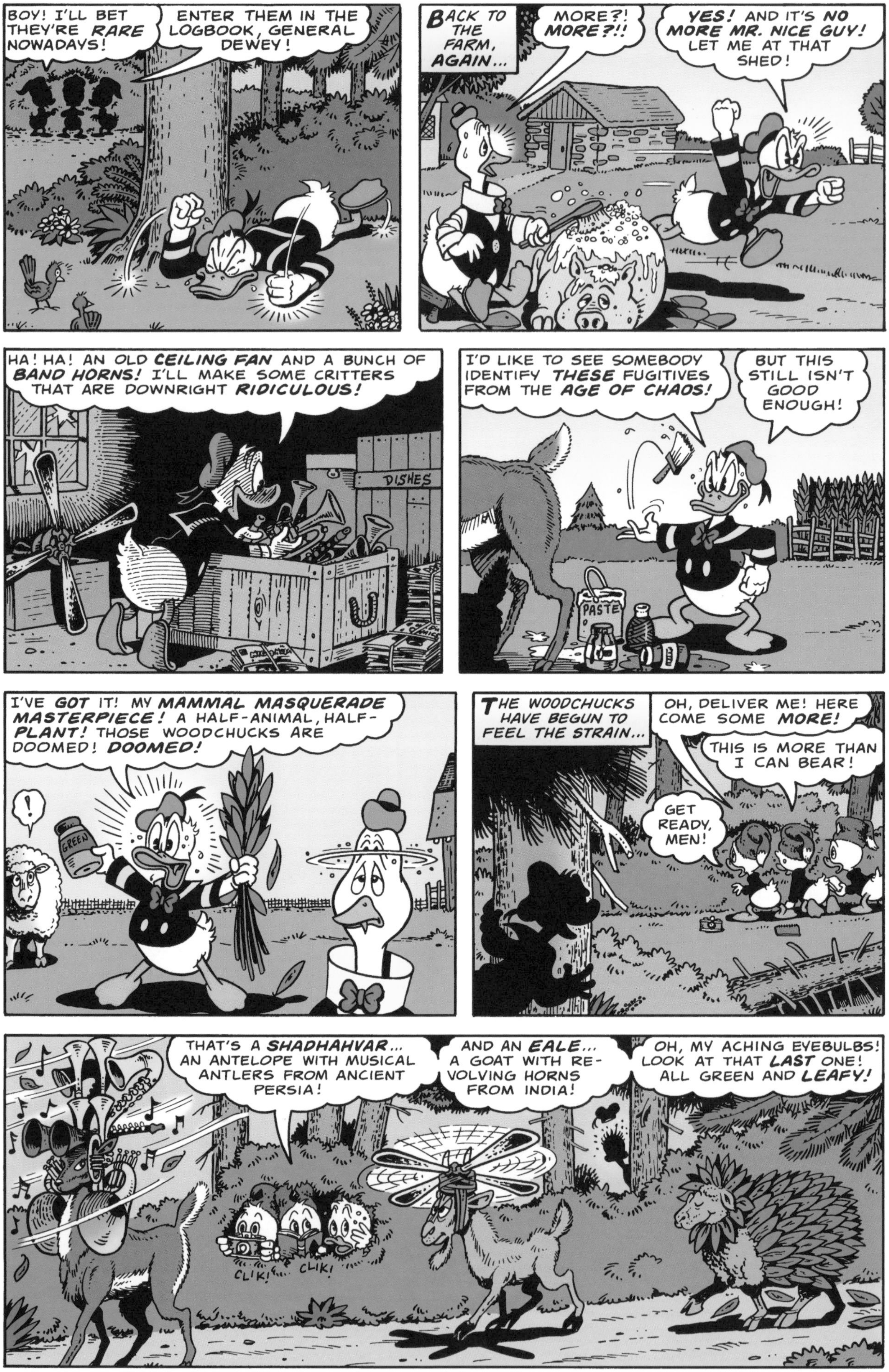
BOY! I'LL BET THEY'RE RARE NOWADAYS!
ENTER THEM IN THE LOGBOOK, GENERAL DEWEY!
BACK TO THE FARM, AGAIN...
MORE?! MORE?!!
YES! AND IT'S NO MORE MR. NICE GUY! LET ME AT THAT SHED!
HA! HA! AN OLD CEILING FAN AND A BUNCH OF BAND HORNS! I'LL MAKE SOME CRITTERS THAT ARE DOWNRIGHT RIDICULOUS!
DISHES
I'D LIKE TO SEE SOMEBODY IDENTIFY THESE FUGITIVES FROM THE AGE OF CHAOS!
BUT THIS STILL ISN'T GOOD ENOUGH!
PASTE
I'VE GOT IT! MY MAMMAL MASQUERADE MASTERPIECE! A HALF-ANIMAL, HALF-PLANT! THOSE WOODCHUCKS ARE DOOMED! DOOMED!
!
GREEN
THE WOODCHUCKS HAVE BEGUN TO FEEL THE STRAIN...
OH, DELIVER ME! HERE COME SOME MORE!
THIS IS MORE THAN I CAN BEAR!
GET READY, MEN!
THAT'S A SHADHAHVAR... AN ANTELOPE WITH MUSICAL ANTLERS FROM ANCIENT PERSIA!
AND AN EALE... A GOAT WITH RE-VOLVING HORNS FROM INDIA!
OH, MY ACHING EYEBULBS! LOOK AT THAT LAST ONE! ALL GREEN AND LEAFY!
CLIK! CLIK!

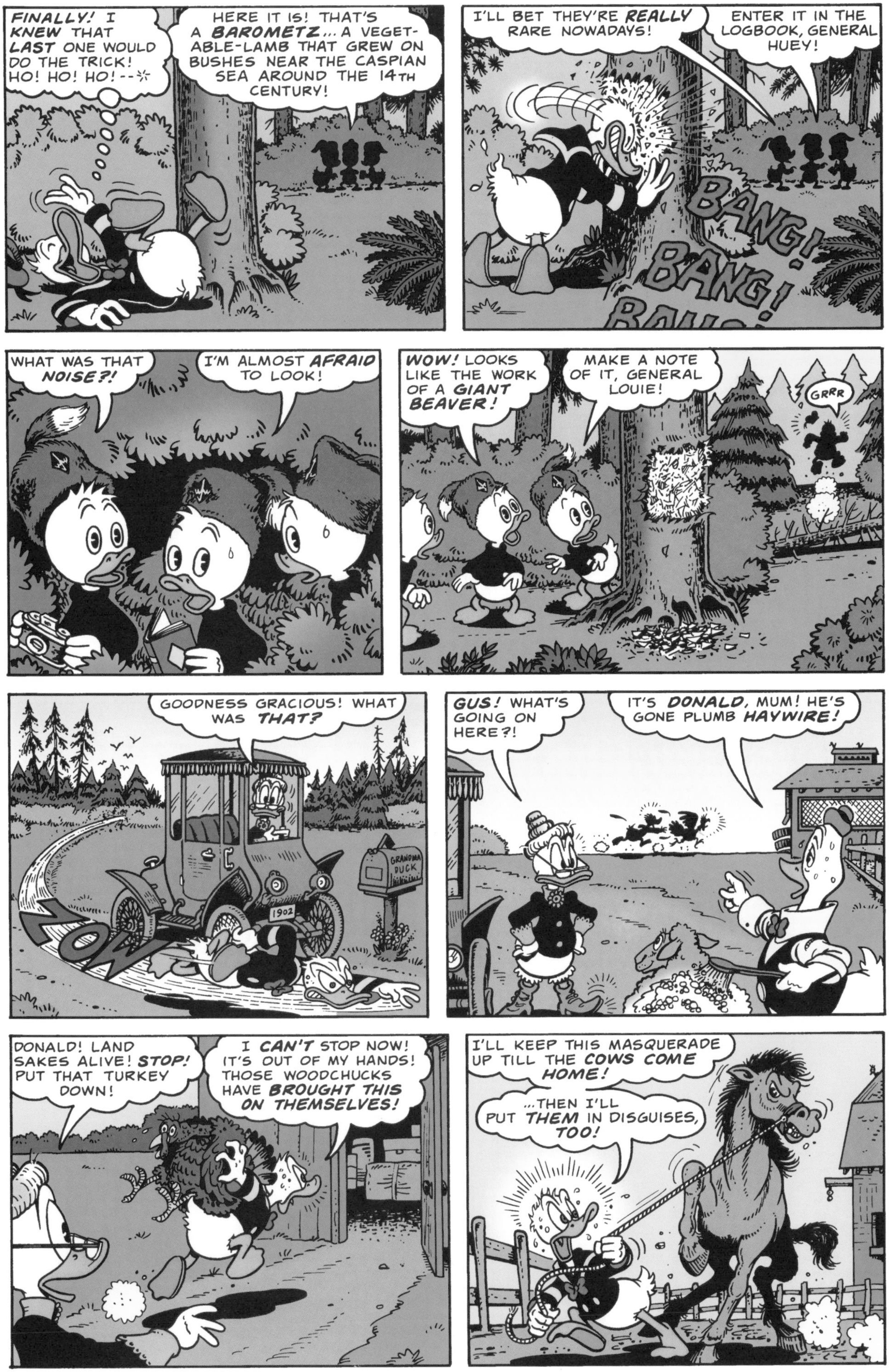
FINALLY! I KNEW THAT LAST ONE WOULD DO THE TRICK! HO! HO! HO! --
HERE IT IS! THAT'S A BAROMETZ... A VEGETABLE-LAMB THAT GREW ON BUSHES NEAR THE CASPIAN SEA AROUND THE 14TH CENTURY!
I'LL BET THEY'RE REALLY RARE NOWADAYS!
ENTER IT IN THE LOGBOOK, GENERAL HUEY!
BANG!
BANG!
WHAT WAS THAT NOISE?!
I'M ALMOST AFRAID TO LOOK!
WOW! LOOKS LIKE THE WORK OF A GIANT BEAVER!
MAKE A NOTE OF IT, GENERAL LOUIE!
GRRR
GOODNESS GRACIOUS! WHAT WAS THAT?
GRANDMA DUCK
1902
ZOW
GUS! WHAT'S GOING ON HERE?!
IT'S DONALD, MUM! HE'S GONE PLUMB HAYWIRE!
DONALD! LAND SAKES ALIVE! STOP! PUT THAT TURKEY DOWN!
I CAN'T STOP NOW! IT'S OUT OF MY HANDS! THOSE WOODCHUCKS HAVE BROUGHT THIS ON THEMSELVES!
I'LL KEEP THIS MASQUERADE UP TILL THE COWS COME HOME!
...THEN I'LL PUT THEM IN DISGUISES, TOO!

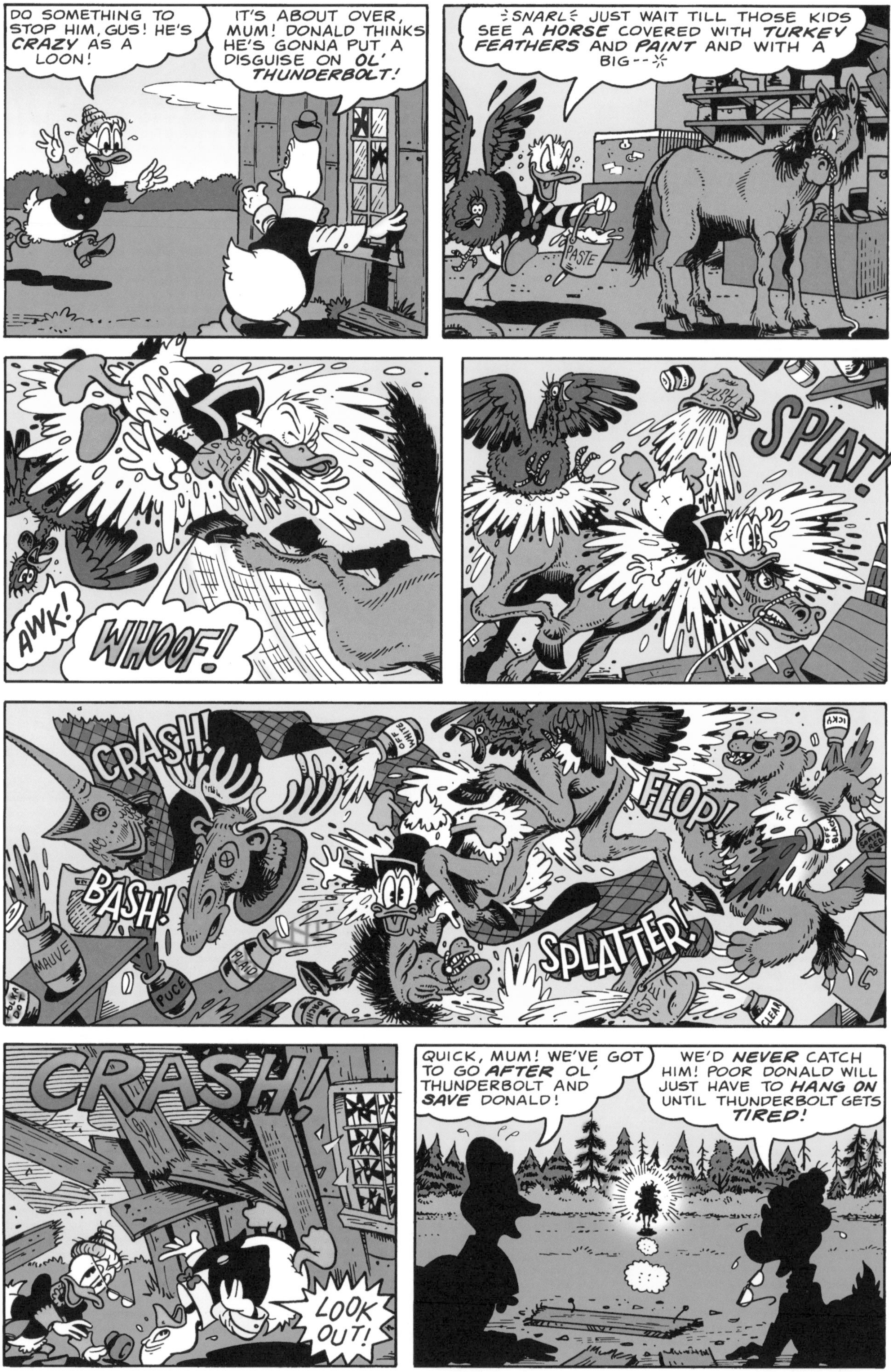
DO SOMETHING TO STOP HIM, GUS! HE'S CRAZY AS A LOON!
IT'S ABOUT OVER, MUM! DONALD THINKS HE'S GONNA PUT A DISGUISE ON OL' THUNDERBOLT!
SNARL JUST WAIT TILL THOSE KIDS SEE A HORSE COVERED WITH TURKEY FEATHERS AND PAINT AND WITH A BIG--
PASTE
AWK!
WHOOF!
SPLAT!
PASTE
CRASH!
OFF WHITE
FLOP!
ICKY
BASH!
MAUVE
PUCE
PLAID
SPLATTER!
OFF BLACK
CLEAR
CRASH!
LOOK OUT!
QUICK, MUM! WE'VE GOT TO GO AFTER OL' THUNDERBOLT AND SAVE DONALD!
WE'D NEVER CATCH HIM! POOR DONALD WILL JUST HAVE TO HANG ON UNTIL THUNDERBOLT GETS TIRED!

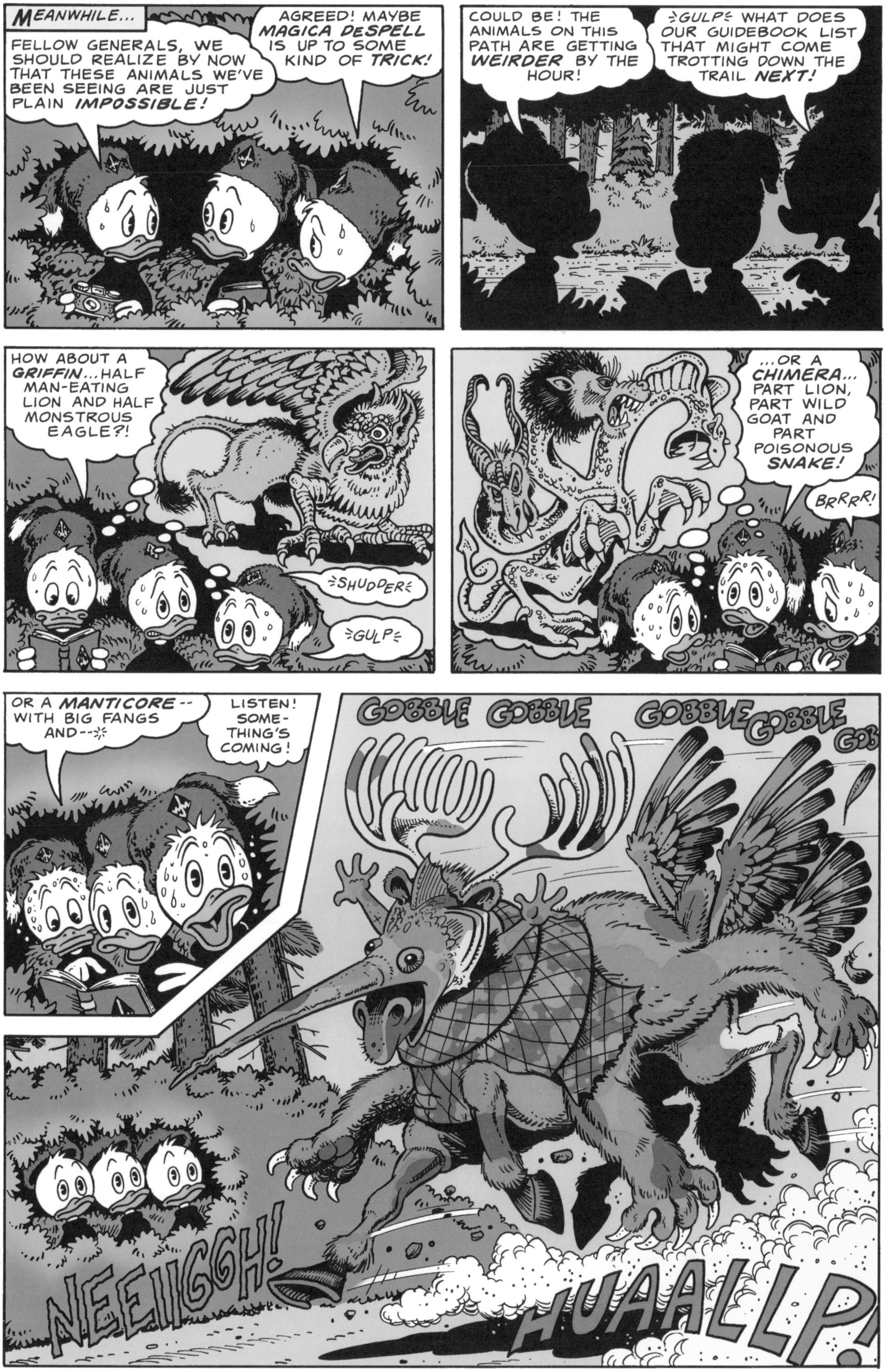
MEANWHILE...
FELLOW GENERALS, WE SHOULD REALIZE BY NOW THAT THESE ANIMALS WE'VE BEEN SEEING ARE JUST PLAIN IMPOSSIBLE!
AGREED! MAYBE MAGICA DESPELL IS UP TO SOME KIND OF TRICK!
COULD BE! THE ANIMALS ON THIS PATH ARE GETTING WEIRDER BY THE HOUR!
GULP WHAT DOES OUR GUIDEBOOK LIST THAT MIGHT COME TROTTING DOWN THE TRAIL NEXT!
HOW ABOUT A GRIFFIN... HALF MAN-EATING LION AND HALF MONSTROUS EAGLE?!
SHUDDER
GULP
...OR A CHIMERA... PART LION, PART WILD GOAT AND PART POISONOUS SNAKE!
BRRRR!
OR A MANTICORE -- WITH BIG FANGS AND --
LISTEN! SOME-THING'S COMING!
GOBBLE GOBBLE GOBBLE GOBBLE
NEEIIGGH!
HUAALLP!

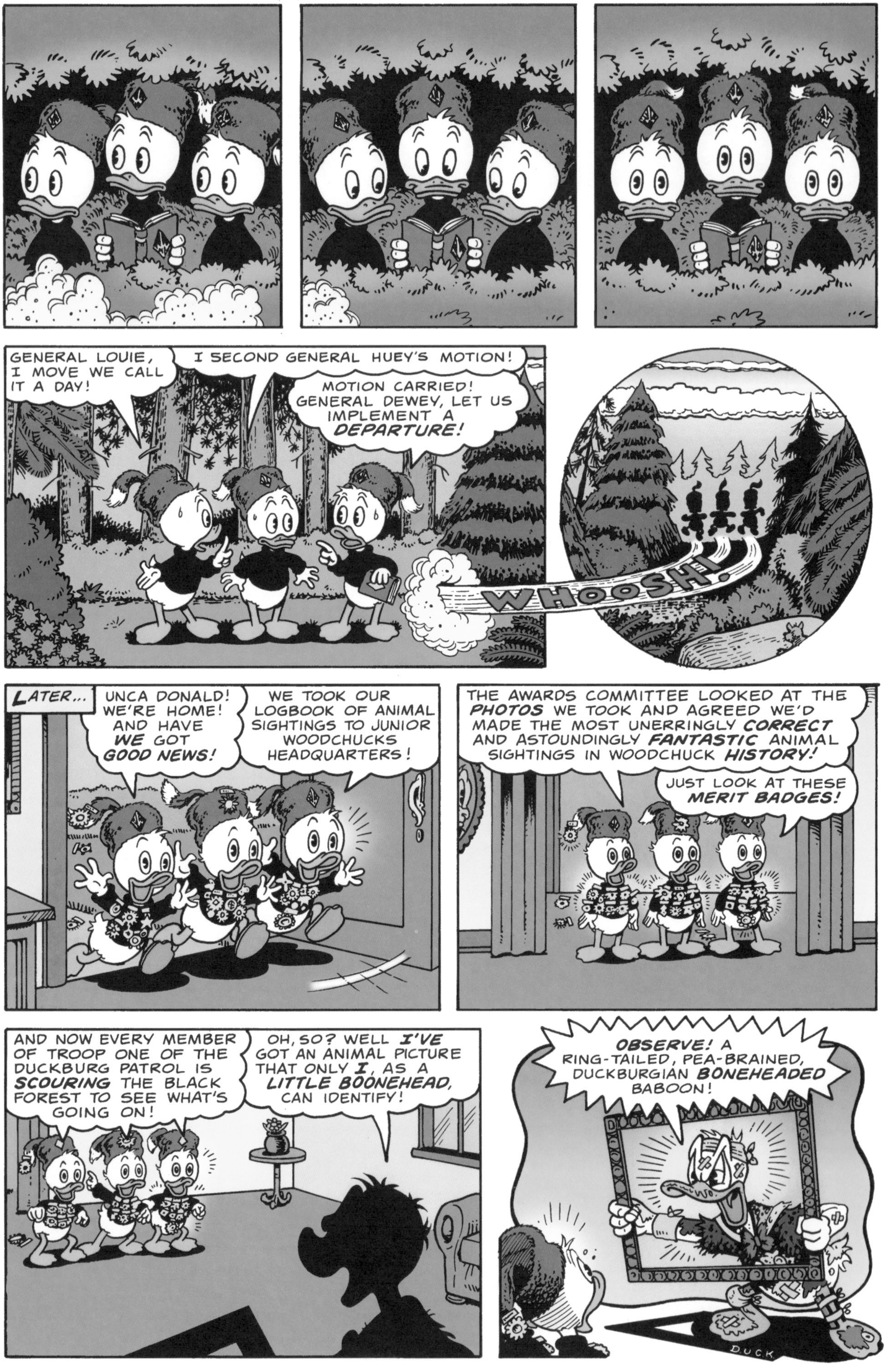
GENERAL LOUIE, I MOVE WE CALL IT A DAY!
I SECOND GENERAL HUEY'S MOTION!
MOTION CARRIED! GENERAL DEWEY, LET US IMPLEMENT A DEPARTURE!
WHOOSH!
LATER...
UNCA DONALD! WE'RE HOME! AND HAVE WE GOT GOOD NEWS!
WE TOOK OUR LOGBOOK OF ANIMAL SIGHTINGS TO JUNIOR WOODCHUCKS HEADQUARTERS!
THE AWARDS COMMITTEE LOOKED AT THE PHOTOS WE TOOK AND AGREED WE'D MADE THE MOST UNERRINGLY CORRECT AND ASTOUNDINGLY FANTASTIC ANIMAL SIGHTINGS IN WOODCHUCK HISTORY!
JUST LOOK AT THESE MERIT BADGES!
AND NOW EVERY MEMBER OF TROOP ONE OF THE DUCKBURG PATROL IS SCOURING THE BLACK FOREST TO SEE WHAT'S GOING ON!
OH, SO? WELL I'VE GOT AN ANIMAL PICTURE THAT ONLY I, AS A LITTLE BOONEHEAD, CAN IDENTIFY!
OBSERVE! A RING-TAILED, PEA-BRAINED, DUCKBURGIAN BONEHEADED BABOON!
DUCK

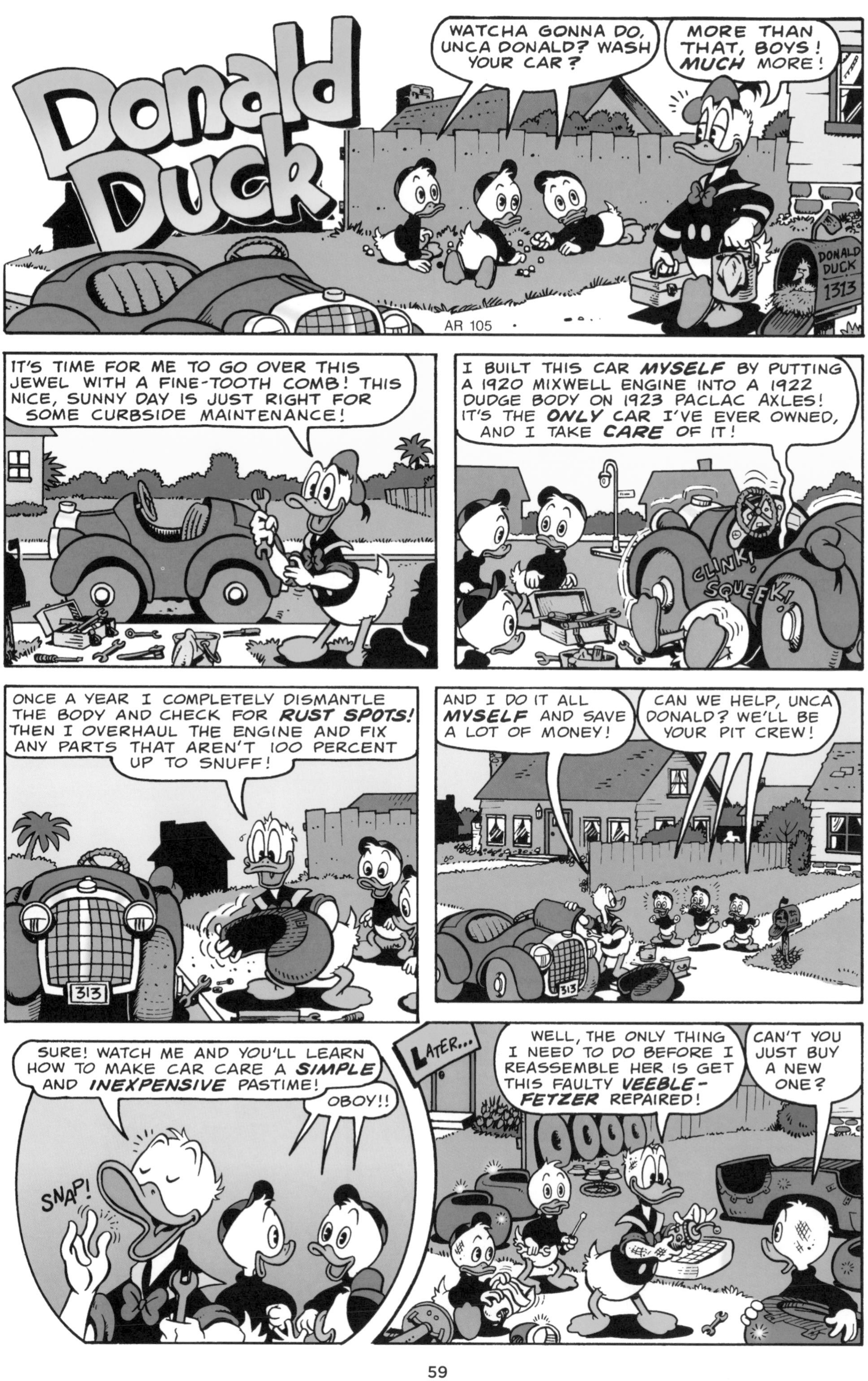
Donald Duck
WATCHA GONNA DO, UNCA DONALD? WASH YOUR CAR?
MORE THAN THAT, BOYS! MUCH MORE!
DONALD DUCK 1313
AR 105
IT'S TIME FOR ME TO GO OVER THIS JEWEL WITH A FINE-TOOTH COMB! THIS NICE, SUNNY DAY IS JUST RIGHT FOR SOME CURBSIDE MAINTENANCE!
I BUILT THIS CAR MYSELF BY PUTTING A 1920 MIXWELL ENGINE INTO A 1922 DUDGE BODY ON 1923 PACLAC AXLES! IT'S THE ONLY CAR I'VE EVER OWNED, AND I TAKE CARE OF IT!
CLINK! SQUEEK!
ONCE A YEAR I COMPLETELY DISMANTLE THE BODY AND CHECK FOR RUST SPOTS! THEN I OVERHAUL THE ENGINE AND FIX ANY PARTS THAT AREN'T 100 PERCENT UP TO SNUFF!
313
AND I DO IT ALL MYSELF AND SAVE A LOT OF MONEY!
CAN WE HELP, UNCA DONALD? WE'LL BE YOUR PIT CREW!
313
SURE! WATCH ME AND YOU'LL LEARN HOW TO MAKE CAR CARE A SIMPLE AND INEXPENSIVE PASTIME!
OBOY!!
SNAP!
LATER...
WELL, THE ONLY THING I NEED TO DO BEFORE I REASSEMBLE HER IS GET THIS FAULTY VEEBLE-FETZER REPAIRED!
CAN'T YOU JUST BUY A NEW ONE?

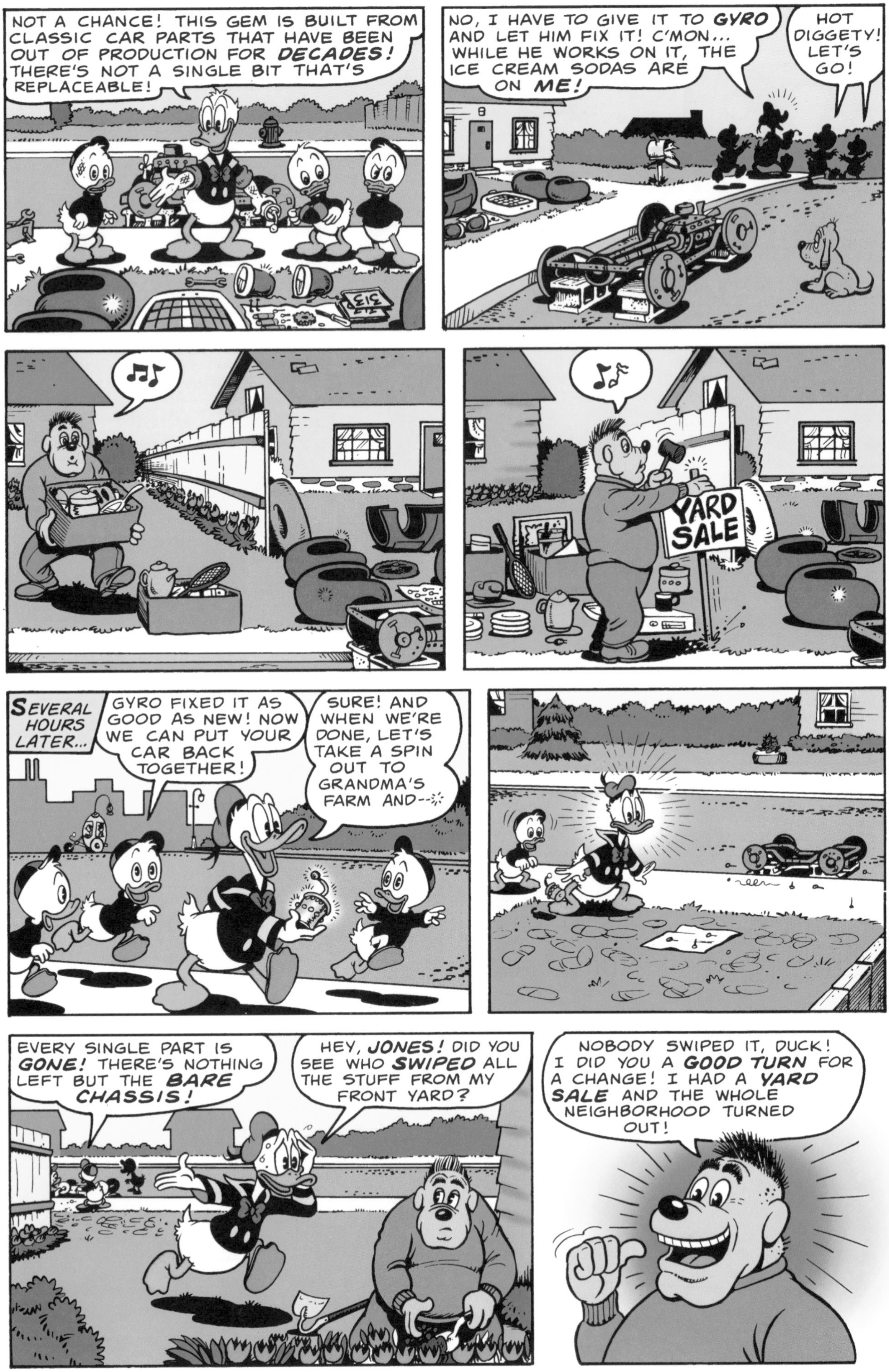
NOT A CHANCE! THIS GEM IS BUILT FROM CLASSIC CAR PARTS THAT HAVE BEEN OUT OF PRODUCTION FOR DECADES! THERE'S NOT A SINGLE BIT THAT'S REPLACEABLE!
NO, I HAVE TO GIVE IT TO GYRO AND LET HIM FIX IT! C'MON... WHILE HE WORKS ON IT, THE ICE CREAM SODAS ARE ON ME!
HOT DIGGETY! LET'S GO!
YARD SALE
SEVERAL HOURS LATER...
GYRO FIXED IT AS GOOD AS NEW! NOW WE CAN PUT YOUR CAR BACK TOGETHER!
SURE! AND WHEN WE'RE DONE, LET'S TAKE A SPIN OUT TO GRANDMA'S FARM AND--
EVERY SINGLE PART IS GONE! THERE'S NOTHING LEFT BUT THE BARE CHASSIS!
HEY, JONES! DID YOU SEE WHO SWIPED ALL THE STUFF FROM MY FRONT YARD?
NOBODY SWIPED IT, DUCK! I DID YOU A GOOD TURN FOR A CHANGE! I HAD A YARD SALE AND THE WHOLE NEIGHBORHOOD TURNED OUT!

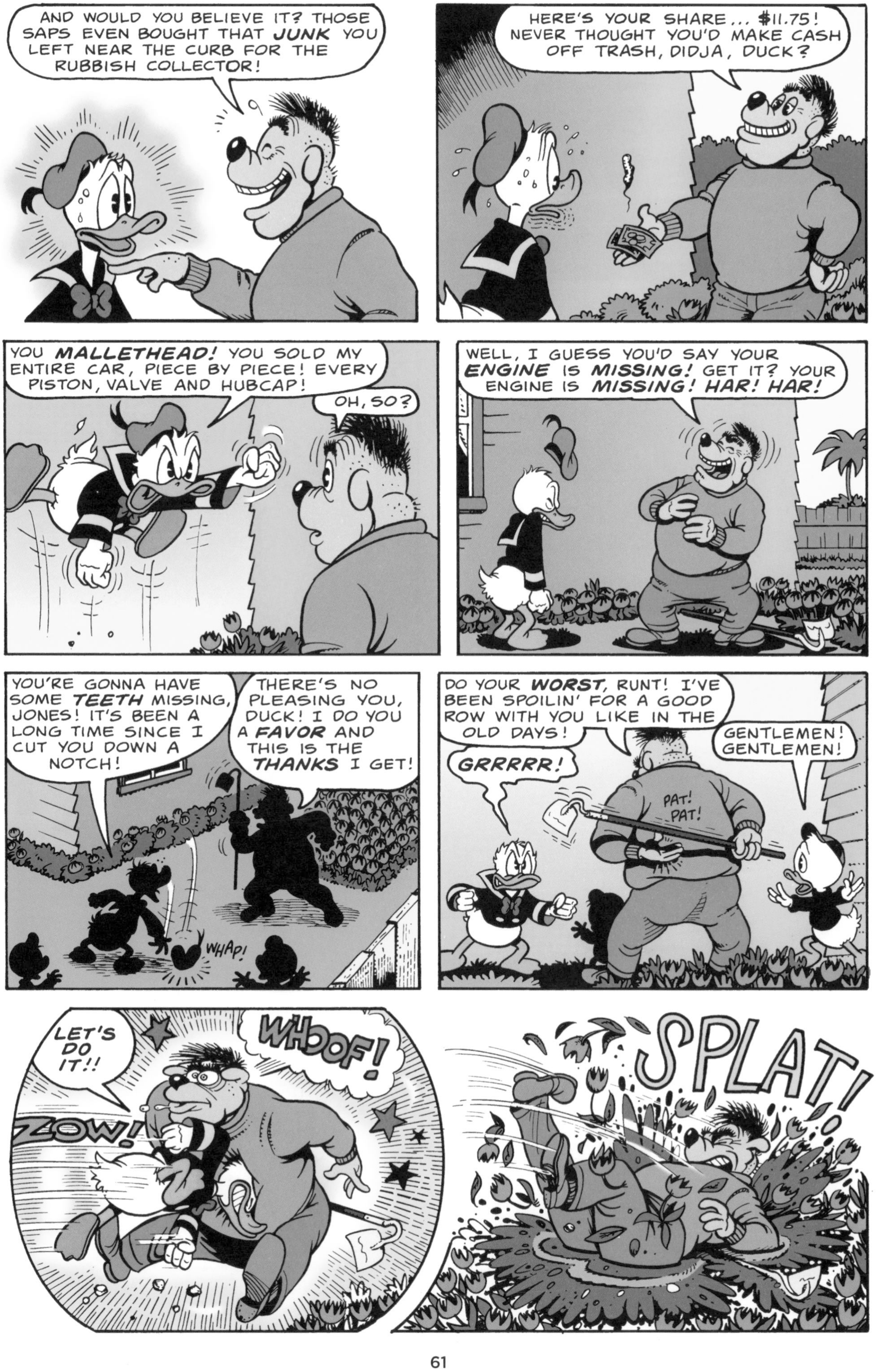
AND WOULD YOU BELIEVE IT? THOSE SAPS EVEN BOUGHT THAT JUNK YOU LEFT NEAR THE CURB FOR THE RUBBISH COLLECTOR!
HERE'S YOUR SHARE... $11.75! NEVER THOUGHT YOU'D MAKE CASH OFF TRASH, DIDJA, DUCK?
YOU MALLETHEAD! YOU SOLD MY ENTIRE CAR, PIECE BY PIECE! EVERY PISTON, VALVE AND HUBCAP!
OH, SO?
WELL, I GUESS YOU'D SAY YOUR ENGINE IS MISSING! GET IT? YOUR ENGINE IS MISSING! HAR! HAR!
YOU'RE GONNA HAVE SOME TEETH MISSING, JONES! IT'S BEEN A LONG TIME SINCE I CUT YOU DOWN A NOTCH!
THERE'S NO PLEASING YOU, DUCK! I DO YOU A FAVOR AND THIS IS THE THANKS I GET!
WHAP!
DO YOUR WORST, RUNT! I'VE BEEN SPOILIN' FOR A GOOD ROW WITH YOU LIKE IN THE OLD DAYS!
GRRRRR!
GENTLEMEN! GENTLEMEN!
PAT! PAT!
LET'S DO IT!!
WHOOF!
ZOW!
SPLAT!

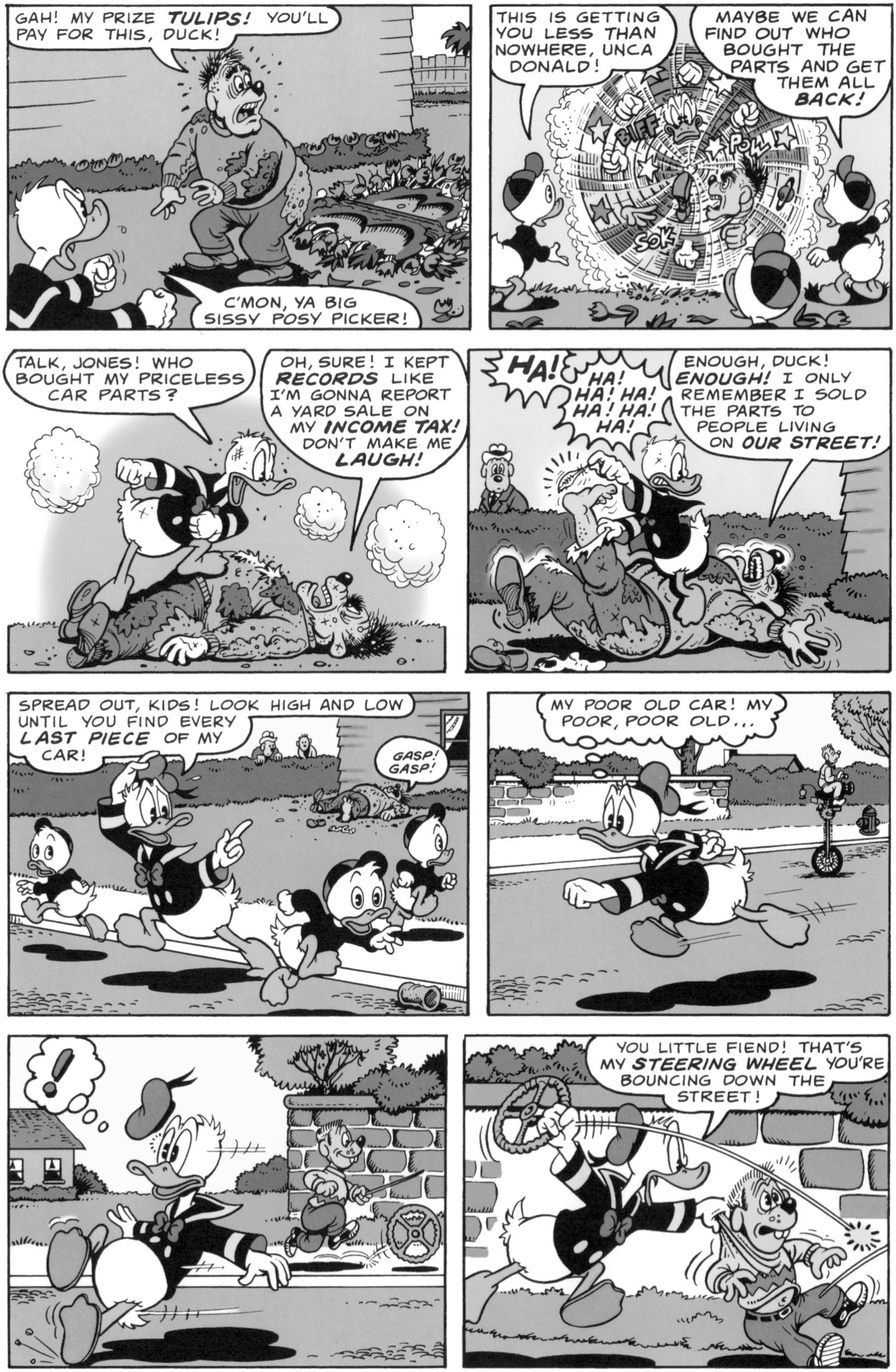
GAH! MY PRIZE TULIPS! YOU'LL PAY FOR THIS, DUCK!
C'MON, YA BIG SISSY POSY PICKER!
THIS IS GETTING YOU LESS THAN NOWHERE, UNCA DONALD!
MAYBE WE CAN FIND OUT WHO BOUGHT THE PARTS AND GET THEM ALL BACK!
BIFF
POW
SOK
TALK, JONES! WHO BOUGHT MY PRICELESS CAR PARTS?
OH, SURE! I KEPT RECORDS LIKE I'M GONNA REPORT A YARD SALE ON MY INCOME TAX! DON'T MAKE ME LAUGH!
HA!
HA! HA! HA! HA! HA! HA!
ENOUGH, DUCK! ENOUGH! I ONLY REMEMBER I SOLD THE PARTS TO PEOPLE LIVING ON OUR STREET!
SPREAD OUT, KIDS! LOOK HIGH AND LOW UNTIL YOU FIND EVERY LAST PIECE OF MY CAR!
GASP! GASP!
MY POOR OLD CAR! MY POOR, POOR OLD...
!
YOU LITTLE FIEND! THAT'S MY STEERING WHEEL YOU'RE BOUNCING DOWN THE STREET!

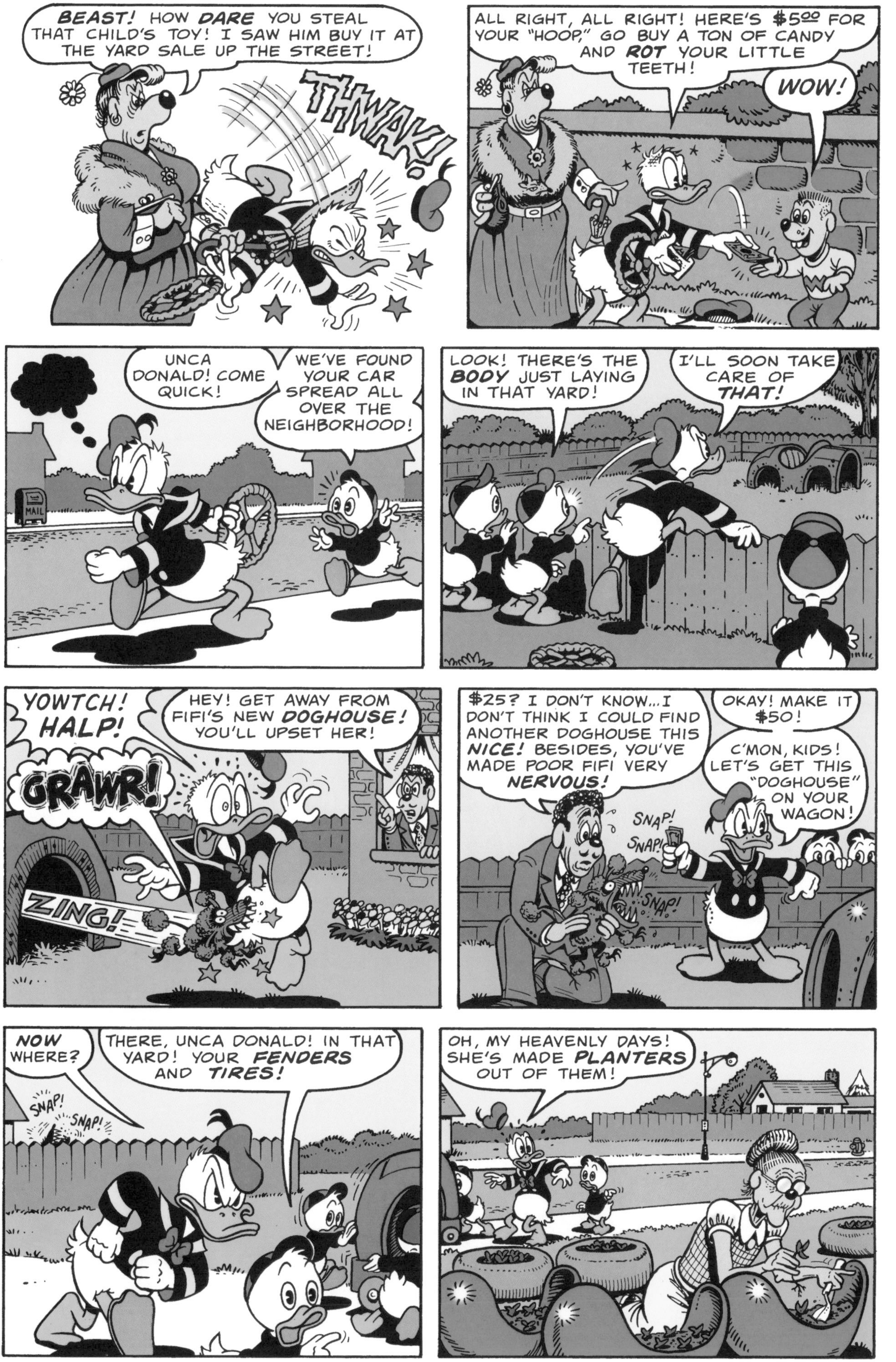
BEAST! HOW DARE YOU STEAL THAT CHILD'S TOY! I SAW HIM BUY IT AT THE YARD SALE UP THE STREET!
THWAK!
ALL RIGHT, ALL RIGHT! HERE'S $5⁰⁰ FOR YOUR "HOOP," GO BUY A TON OF CANDY AND ROT YOUR LITTLE TEETH!
WOW!
UNCA DONALD! COME QUICK!
WE'VE FOUND YOUR CAR SPREAD ALL OVER THE NEIGHBORHOOD!
MAIL
LOOK! THERE'S THE BODY JUST LAYING IN THAT YARD!
I'LL SOON TAKE CARE OF THAT!
YOWTCH! HALP!
HEY! GET AWAY FROM FIFI'S NEW DOGHOUSE! YOU'LL UPSET HER!
GRAWR!
ZING!
$25? I DON'T KNOW...I DON'T THINK I COULD FIND ANOTHER DOGHOUSE THIS NICE! BESIDES, YOU'VE MADE POOR FIFI VERY NERVOUS!
OKAY! MAKE IT $50!
C'MON, KIDS! LET'S GET THIS "DOGHOUSE" ON YOUR WAGON!
SNAP! SNAP! SNAP!
NOW WHERE?
THERE, UNCA DONALD! IN THAT YARD! YOUR FENDERS AND TIRES!
SNAP! SNAP!
OH, MY HEAVENLY DAYS! SHE'S MADE PLANTERS OUT OF THEM!

GET THAT **DIRT** OUT OF MY FENDERS! IT'LL START **RUST SPOTS** ALL OVER THEM!

WAK!

THAT'S OUR UNCLE, MA'AM! HE'S A LITTLE EXCITED, BUT I'M SURE HE'D LIKE TO MAKE YOU AN **OFFER** FOR YOUR NEW PLANTERS!

OH, DEAR ME! I'M SORRY MR. DUCK, BUT I'VE ALREADY PLANTED **DELICATE** ORCHID SEEDLINGS IN THEM--SEEDLINGS THAT I NURTURED ALL SPRING! I CAN'T JUST--

NOT EVEN FOR **$100**?

AND **HOW**, JACK!

WHERE NEXT?

FOLLOW YOUR **NOSE**, UNCA DONALD! SMELL THAT STEAK COOKING?

GLOM

YOW! THAT'S MY **RADIATOR GRILL!**

POP! SIZZLE!

SUPER CHEF

STOP! STOP! I HAVE A **STAKE** IN THE **GRILL** YOU'RE USING TO **GRILL** THAT **STEAK!**

RUN THAT BY ME AGAIN?

SIZZLE!

SUPER

IT'S THAT CRAZY DONALD DUCK FROM ACROSS THE STREET, HARRY!

WHY, HELLO, MR. DUCK! HOW WOULD YOU LIKE YOUR STEAK? RARE, MEDIUM, OR--

YOU'LL BURN MY LOVELY **CHROME! STOP!**

CRASH!

SUPER CHEF

DON'T FIX HIM A STEAK, HARRY! I DON'T LIKE HIS **MANNERS!**

HERE! GO BUY A **GAS** GRILL AND A **SIDE OF BEEF!** JUST STOP USING **THIS** TO COOK ON!

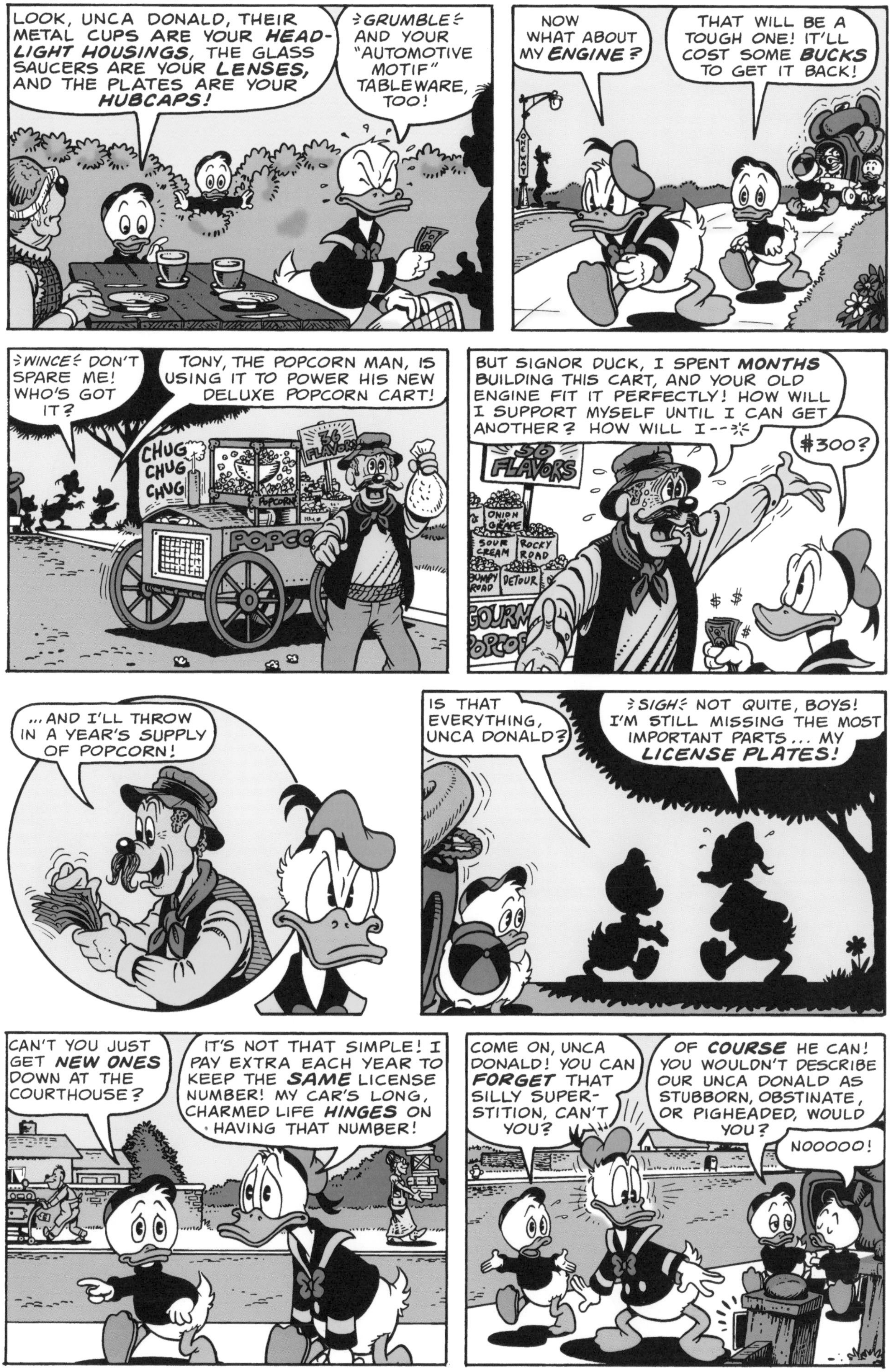
LOOK, UNCA DONALD, THEIR METAL CUPS ARE YOUR HEAD-LIGHT HOUSINGS, THE GLASS SAUCERS ARE YOUR LENSES, AND THE PLATES ARE YOUR HUBCAPS!
GRUMBLE AND YOUR "AUTOMOTIVE MOTIF" TABLEWARE, TOO!
NOW WHAT ABOUT MY ENGINE?
THAT WILL BE A TOUGH ONE! IT'LL COST SOME BUCKS TO GET IT BACK!
ONE WAY
WINCE DON'T SPARE ME! WHO'S GOT IT?
TONY, THE POPCORN MAN, IS USING IT TO POWER HIS NEW DELUXE POPCORN CART!
CHUG CHUG CHUG
36 FLAVORS
POPCORN
BUT SIGNOR DUCK, I SPENT MONTHS BUILDING THIS CART, AND YOUR OLD ENGINE FIT IT PERFECTLY! HOW WILL I SUPPORT MYSELF UNTIL I CAN GET ANOTHER? HOW WILL I--
$300?
36 FLAVORS
ONION GRAPE
SOUR CREAM
ROCKY ROAD
BUMPY ROAD
DETOUR
...AND I'LL THROW IN A YEAR'S SUPPLY OF POPCORN!
IS THAT EVERYTHING, UNCA DONALD?
SIGH NOT QUITE, BOYS! I'M STILL MISSING THE MOST IMPORTANT PARTS... MY LICENSE PLATES!
CAN'T YOU JUST GET NEW ONES DOWN AT THE COURTHOUSE?
IT'S NOT THAT SIMPLE! I PAY EXTRA EACH YEAR TO KEEP THE SAME LICENSE NUMBER! MY CAR'S LONG, CHARMED LIFE HINGES ON HAVING THAT NUMBER!
COME ON, UNCA DONALD! YOU CAN FORGET THAT SILLY SUPER-STITION, CAN'T YOU?
OF COURSE HE CAN! YOU WOULDN'T DESCRIBE OUR UNCA DONALD AS STUBBORN, OBSTINATE, OR PIGHEADED, WOULD YOU?
NOOOOO!

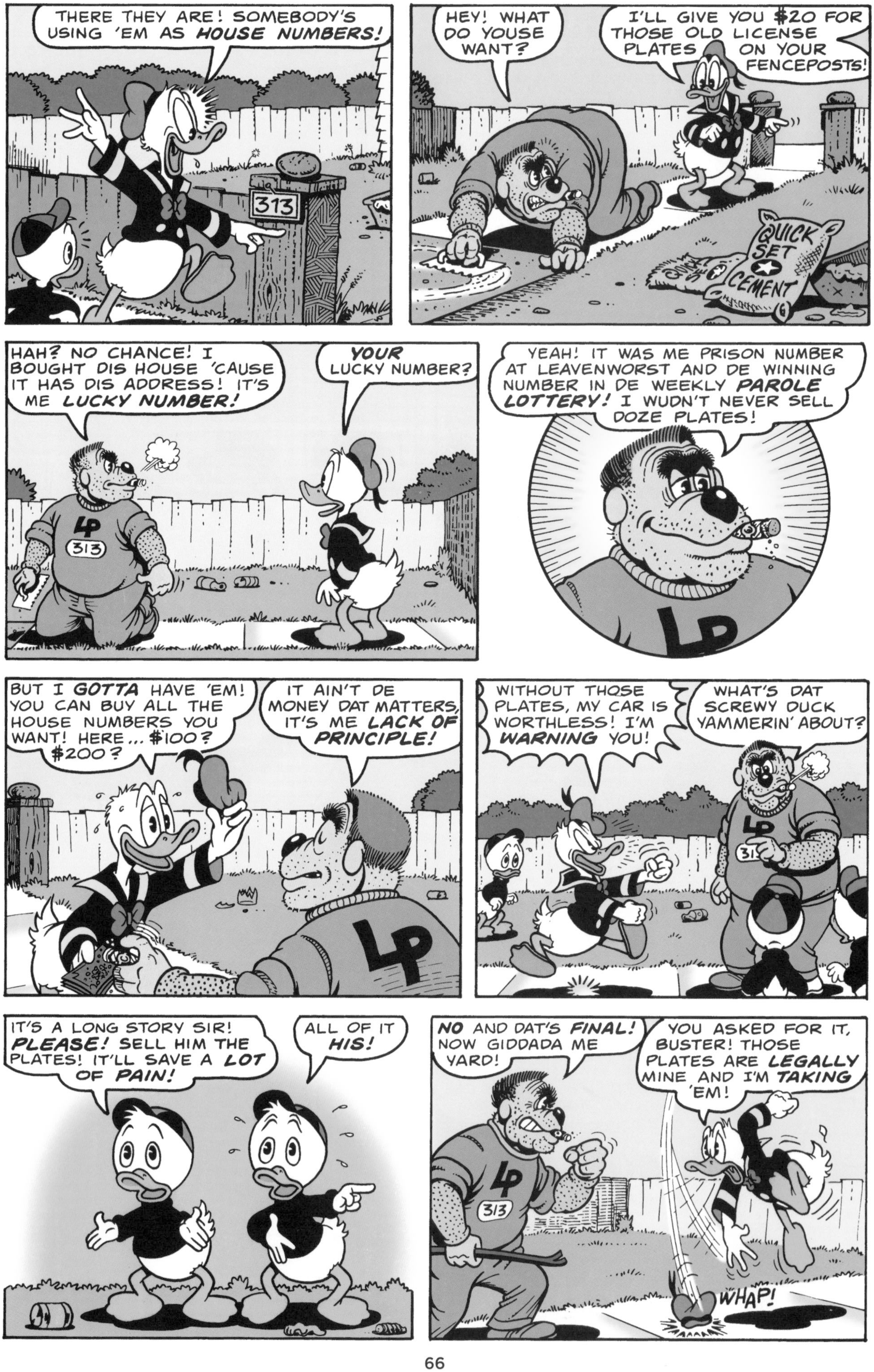
THERE THEY ARE! SOMEBODY'S USING 'EM AS HOUSE NUMBERS!
313
HEY! WHAT DO YOUSE WANT?
I'LL GIVE YOU $20 FOR THOSE OLD LICENSE PLATES ON YOUR FENCEPOSTS!
QUICK SET CEMENT
HAH? NO CHANCE! I BOUGHT DIS HOUSE 'CAUSE IT HAS DIS ADDRESS! IT'S ME LUCKY NUMBER!
YOUR LUCKY NUMBER?
YEAH! IT WAS ME PRISON NUMBER AT LEAVENWORST AND DE WINNING NUMBER IN DE WEEKLY PAROLE LOTTERY! I WUDN'T NEVER SELL DOZE PLATES!
BUT I GOTTA HAVE 'EM! YOU CAN BUY ALL THE HOUSE NUMBERS YOU WANT! HERE... $100? $200?
IT AIN'T DE MONEY DAT MATTERS, IT'S ME LACK OF PRINCIPLE!
WITHOUT THOSE PLATES, MY CAR IS WORTHLESS! I'M WARNING YOU!
WHAT'S DAT SCREWY DUCK YAMMERIN' ABOUT?
IT'S A LONG STORY SIR! PLEASE! SELL HIM THE PLATES! IT'LL SAVE A LOT OF PAIN!
ALL OF IT HIS!
NO AND DAT'S FINAL! NOW GIDDADA ME YARD!
YOU ASKED FOR IT, BUSTER! THOSE PLATES ARE LEGALLY MINE AND I'M TAKING 'EM!
WHAP!

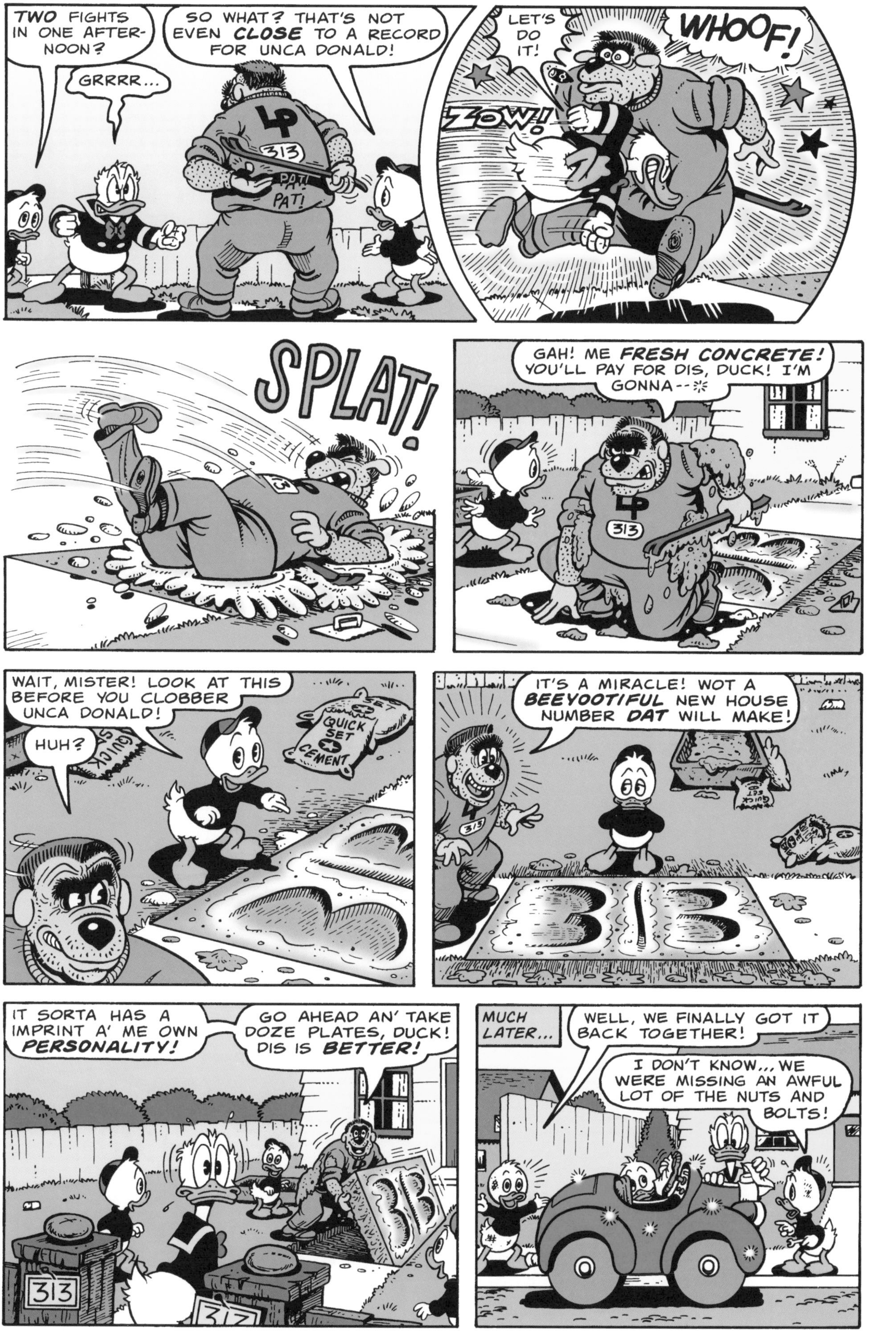
TWO FIGHTS IN ONE AFTER-NOON?
SO WHAT? THAT'S NOT EVEN CLOSE TO A RECORD FOR UNCA DONALD!
GRRRR...
PAT! PAT!
LET'S DO IT!
WHOOF!
ZOW!!
SPLAT!
GAH! ME FRESH CONCRETE! YOU'LL PAY FOR DIS, DUCK! I'M GONNA--
WAIT, MISTER! LOOK AT THIS BEFORE YOU CLOBBER UNCA DONALD!
HUH?
QUICK SET CEMENT
IT'S A MIRACLE! WOT A BEEYOOTIFUL NEW HOUSE NUMBER DAT WILL MAKE!
IT SORTA HAS A IMPRINT A' ME OWN PERSONALITY!
GO AHEAD AN' TAKE DOZE PLATES, DUCK! DIS IS BETTER!
MUCH LATER...
WELL, WE FINALLY GOT IT BACK TOGETHER!
I DON'T KNOW.., WE WERE MISSING AN AWFUL LOT OF THE NUTS AND BOLTS!

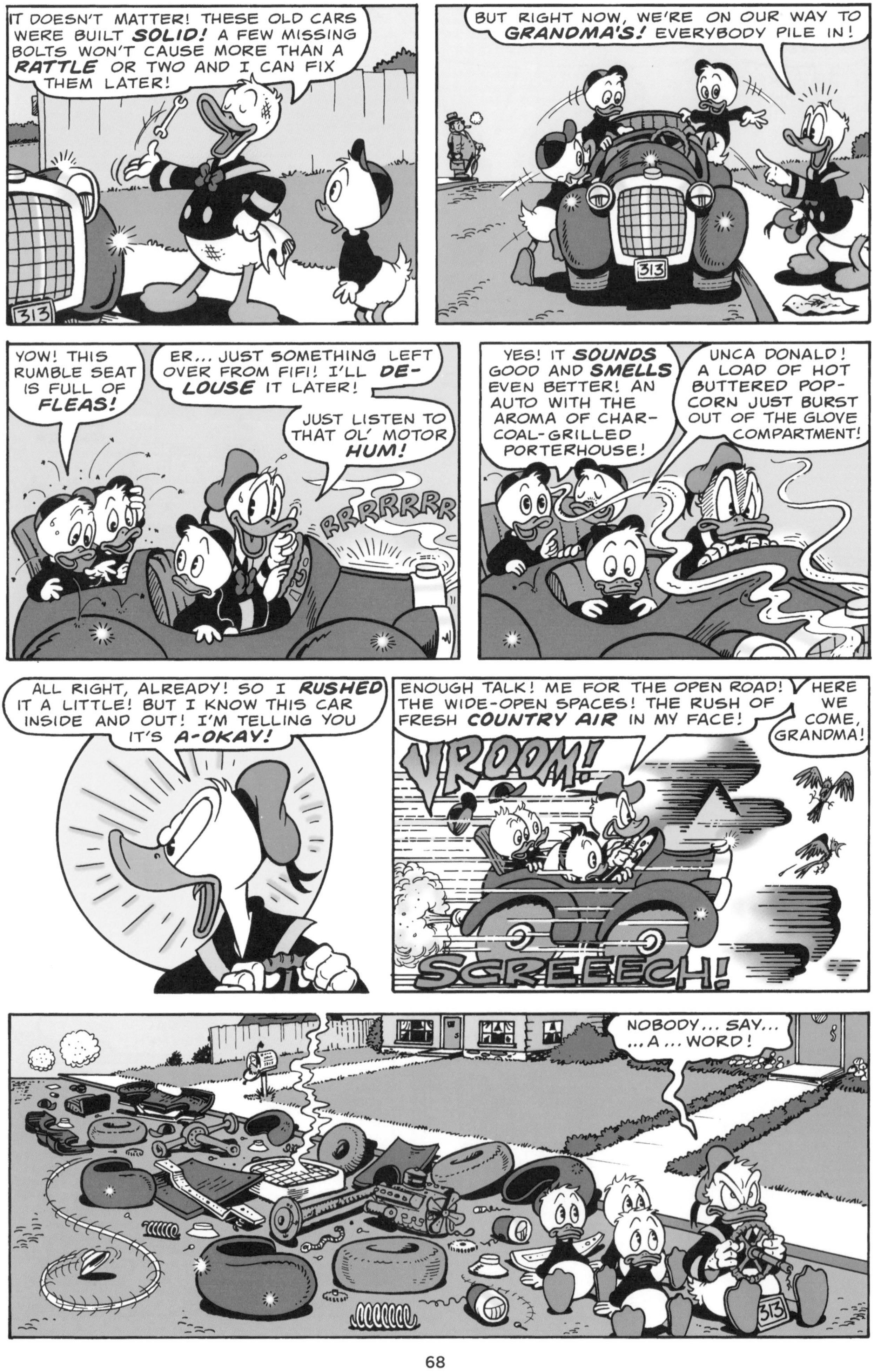
IT DOESN'T MATTER! THESE OLD CARS WERE BUILT SOLID! A FEW MISSING BOLTS WON'T CAUSE MORE THAN A RATTLE OR TWO AND I CAN FIX THEM LATER!
BUT RIGHT NOW, WE'RE ON OUR WAY TO GRANDMA'S! EVERYBODY PILE IN!
YOW! THIS RUMBLE SEAT IS FULL OF FLEAS!
ER... JUST SOMETHING LEFT OVER FROM FIFI! I'LL DE-LOUSE IT LATER!
JUST LISTEN TO THAT OL' MOTOR HUM!
RRRRRRRR
YES! IT SOUNDS GOOD AND SMELLS EVEN BETTER! AN AUTO WITH THE AROMA OF CHAR-COAL-GRILLED PORTERHOUSE!
UNCA DONALD! A LOAD OF HOT BUTTERED POP-CORN JUST BURST OUT OF THE GLOVE COMPARTMENT!
ALL RIGHT, ALREADY! SO I RUSHED IT A LITTLE! BUT I KNOW THIS CAR INSIDE AND OUT! I'M TELLING YOU IT'S A-OKAY!
ENOUGH TALK! ME FOR THE OPEN ROAD! THE WIDE-OPEN SPACES! THE RUSH OF FRESH COUNTRY AIR IN MY FACE!
HERE WE COME, GRANDMA!
VROOM!
SCREEECH!
NOBODY... SAY... ...A... WORD!

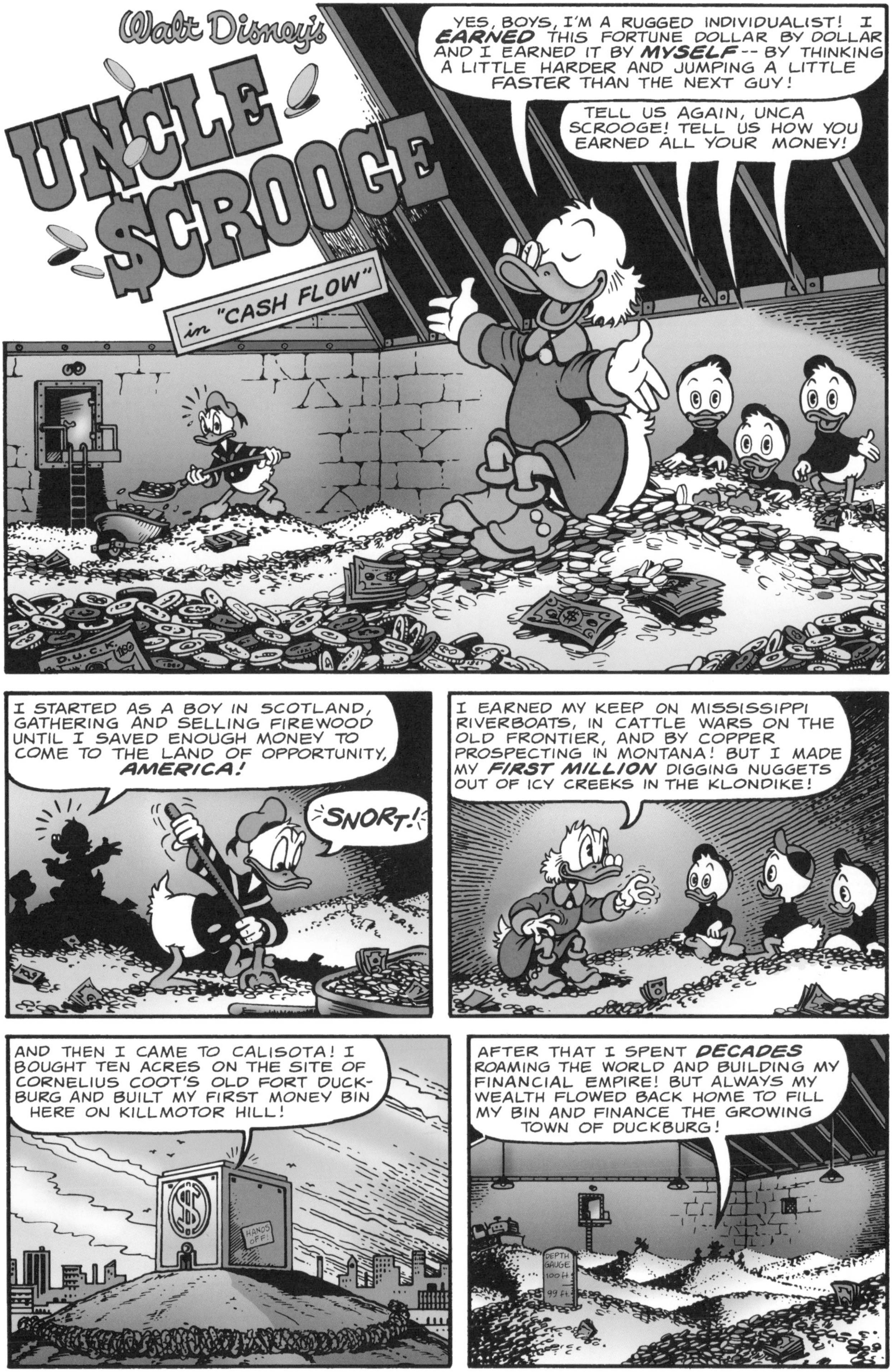

Walt Disney's
UNCLE $CROOGE
in "CASH FLOW"
YES, BOYS, I'M A RUGGED INDIVIDUALIST! I EARNED THIS FORTUNE DOLLAR BY DOLLAR AND I EARNED IT BY MYSELF -- BY THINKING A LITTLE HARDER AND JUMPING A LITTLE FASTER THAN THE NEXT GUY!
TELL US AGAIN, UNCA SCROOGE! TELL US HOW YOU EARNED ALL YOUR MONEY!
I STARTED AS A BOY IN SCOTLAND, GATHERING AND SELLING FIREWOOD UNTIL I SAVED ENOUGH MONEY TO COME TO THE LAND OF OPPORTUNITY, AMERICA!
SNORT!
I EARNED MY KEEP ON MISSISSIPPI RIVERBOATS, IN CATTLE WARS ON THE OLD FRONTIER, AND BY COPPER PROSPECTING IN MONTANA! BUT I MADE MY FIRST MILLION DIGGING NUGGETS OUT OF ICY CREEKS IN THE KLONDIKE!
AND THEN I CAME TO CALISOTA! I BOUGHT TEN ACRES ON THE SITE OF CORNELIUS COOT'S OLD FORT DUCKBURG AND BUILT MY FIRST MONEY BIN HERE ON KILLMOTOR HILL!
HANDS OFF!
AFTER THAT I SPENT DECADES ROAMING THE WORLD AND BUILDING MY FINANCIAL EMPIRE! BUT ALWAYS MY WEALTH FLOWED BACK HOME TO FILL MY BIN AND FINANCE THE GROWING TOWN OF DUCKBURG!
DEPTH GAUGE
100 ft.
99 ft.

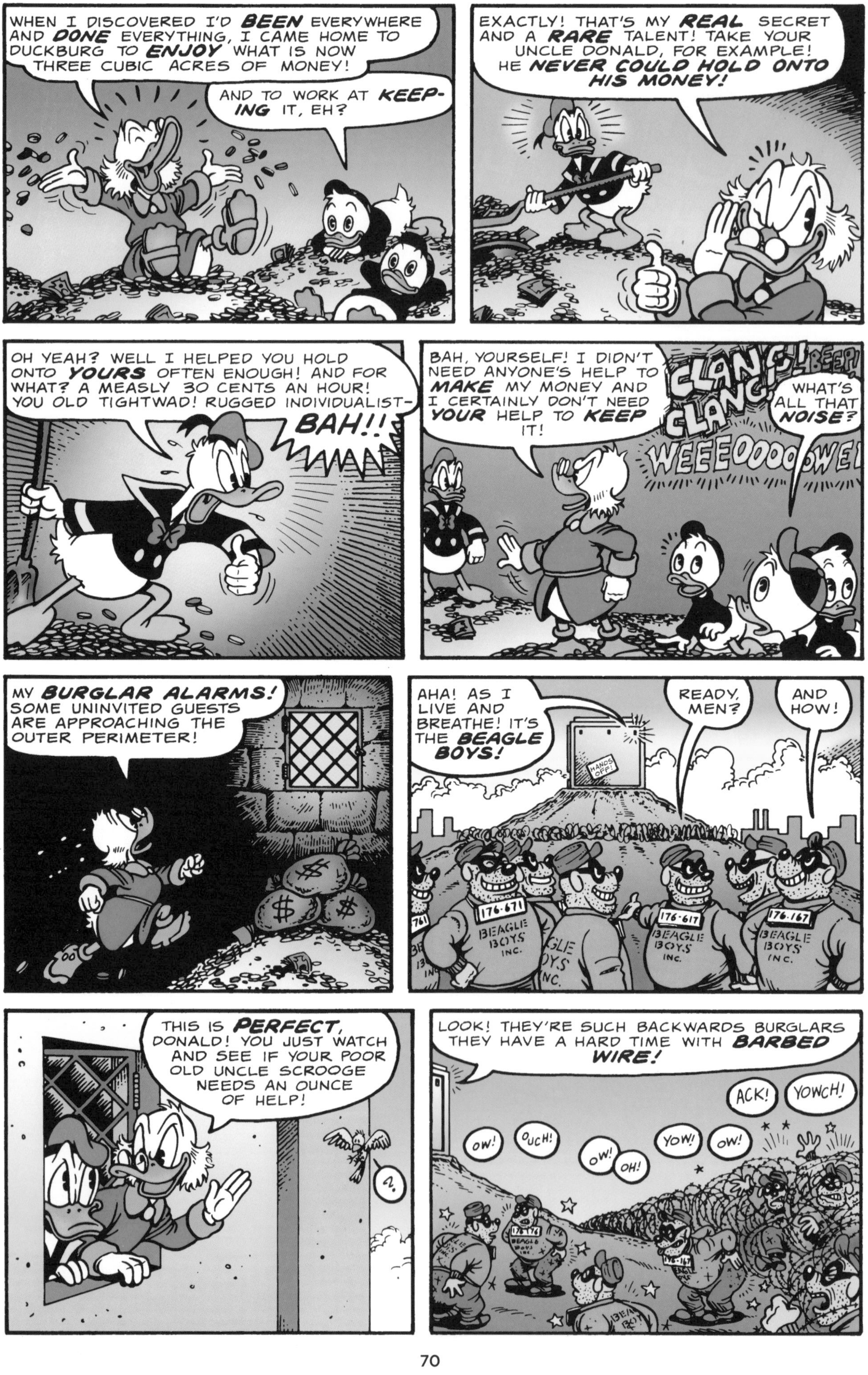
WHEN I DISCOVERED I'D BEEN EVERYWHERE AND DONE EVERYTHING, I CAME HOME TO DUCKBURG TO ENJOY WHAT IS NOW THREE CUBIC ACRES OF MONEY!
AND TO WORK AT KEEP-ING IT, EH?
EXACTLY! THAT'S MY REAL SECRET AND A RARE TALENT! TAKE YOUR UNCLE DONALD, FOR EXAMPLE! HE NEVER COULD HOLD ONTO HIS MONEY!
OH YEAH? WELL I HELPED YOU HOLD ONTO YOURS OFTEN ENOUGH! AND FOR WHAT? A MEASLY 30 CENTS AN HOUR! YOU OLD TIGHTWAD! RUGGED INDIVIDUALIST-
BAH!!
BAH, YOURSELF! I DIDN'T NEED ANYONE'S HELP TO MAKE MY MONEY AND I CERTAINLY DON'T NEED YOUR HELP TO KEEP IT!
CLANG! CLANG!
BEEP!
WHAT'S ALL THAT NOISE?
WEEEOOOOWEE
MY BURGLAR ALARMS! SOME UNINVITED GUESTS ARE APPROACHING THE OUTER PERIMETER!
AHA! AS I LIVE AND BREATHE! IT'S THE BEAGLE BOYS!
HANDS OFF!
READY, MEN?
AND HOW!
176-671
176-617
176-167
BEAGLE BOYS INC.
THIS IS PERFECT, DONALD! YOU JUST WATCH AND SEE IF YOUR POOR OLD UNCLE SCROOGE NEEDS AN OUNCE OF HELP!
?
LOOK! THEY'RE SUCH BACKWARDS BURGLARS THEY HAVE A HARD TIME WITH BARBED WIRE!
ACK!
YOWCH!
OW!
OUCH!
OW!
OH!
YOW!
OW!

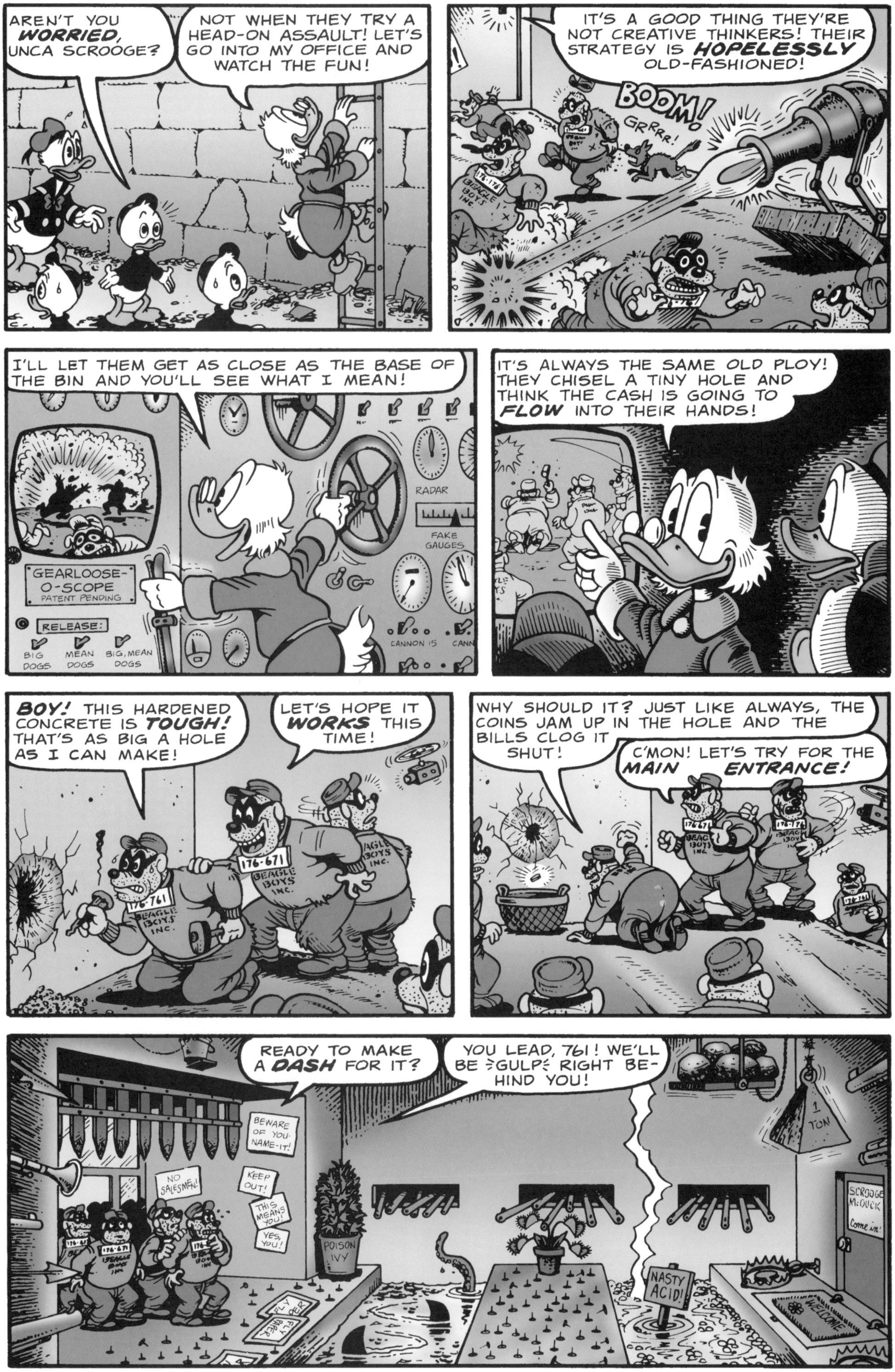

AREN'T YOU WORRIED, UNCA SCROOGE?
NOT WHEN THEY TRY A HEAD-ON ASSAULT! LET'S GO INTO MY OFFICE AND WATCH THE FUN!
IT'S A GOOD THING THEY'RE NOT CREATIVE THINKERS! THEIR STRATEGY IS HOPELESSLY OLD-FASHIONED!
BOOM!
GRRRR!
BEAGLE BOYS INC.
I'LL LET THEM GET AS CLOSE AS THE BASE OF THE BIN AND YOU'LL SEE WHAT I MEAN!
GEARLOOSE-O-SCOPE
PATENT PENDING
RELEASE:
BIG DOGS
MEAN DOGS
BIG, MEAN DOGS
RADAR
FAKE GAUGES
CANNON 15
IT'S ALWAYS THE SAME OLD PLOY! THEY CHISEL A TINY HOLE AND THINK THE CASH IS GOING TO FLOW INTO THEIR HANDS!
BOY! THIS HARDENED CONCRETE IS TOUGH! THAT'S AS BIG A HOLE AS I CAN MAKE!
LET'S HOPE IT WORKS THIS TIME!
176-761
176-671
BEAGLE BOYS INC.
WHY SHOULD IT? JUST LIKE ALWAYS, THE COINS JAM UP IN THE HOLE AND THE BILLS CLOG IT SHUT!
C'MON! LET'S TRY FOR THE MAIN ENTRANCE!
READY TO MAKE A DASH FOR IT?
YOU LEAD, 761! WE'LL BE GULP RIGHT BEHIND YOU!
BEWARE OF YOU-NAME-IT!
NO SALESMEN!
KEEP OUT!
THIS MEANS YOU!
YES, YOU!
POISON IVY
1 TON
SCROOGE McDUCK
Come in!
NASTY ACID!
FLY PAPER
WELCOME

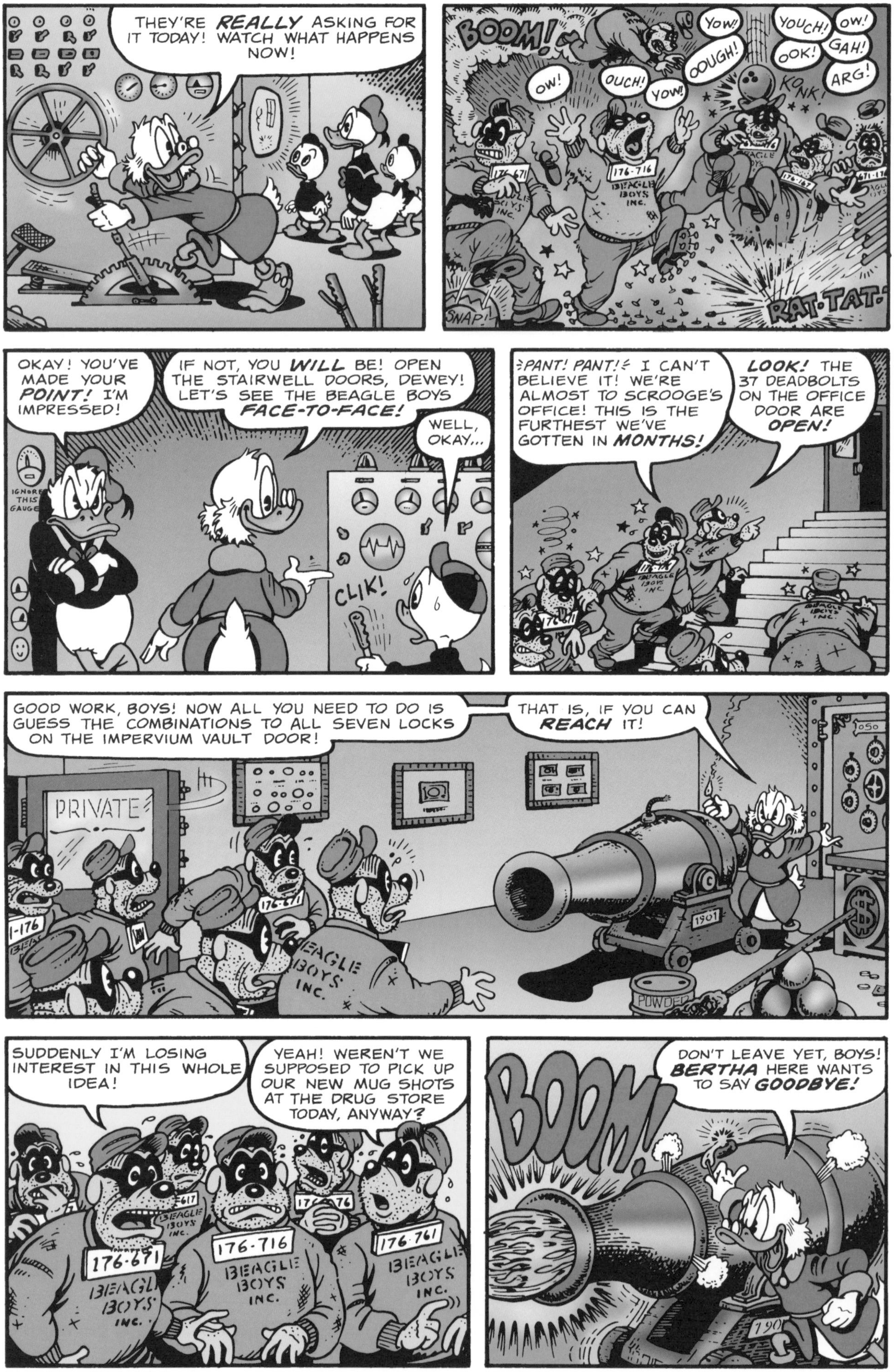
THEY'RE REALLY ASKING FOR IT TODAY! WATCH WHAT HAPPENS NOW!
BOOM!
YOW!
OW!
OUCH!
YOW!
OOUGH!
YOUCH!
OW!
OOK!
GAH!
ARG!
KONK!
SNAP!
RAT-TAT-
OKAY! YOU'VE MADE YOUR POINT! I'M IMPRESSED!
IF NOT, YOU WILL BE! OPEN THE STAIRWELL DOORS, DEWEY! LET'S SEE THE BEAGLE BOYS FACE-TO-FACE!
WELL, OKAY...
CLIK!
IGNORE THIS GAUGE
PANT! PANT! I CAN'T BELIEVE IT! WE'RE ALMOST TO SCROOGE'S OFFICE! THIS IS THE FURTHEST WE'VE GOTTEN IN MONTHS!
LOOK! THE 37 DEADBOLTS ON THE OFFICE DOOR ARE OPEN!
GOOD WORK, BOYS! NOW ALL YOU NEED TO DO IS GUESS THE COMBINATIONS TO ALL SEVEN LOCKS ON THE IMPERVIUM VAULT DOOR!
THAT IS, IF YOU CAN REACH IT!
PRIVATE
1901
POWDER
SUDDENLY I'M LOSING INTEREST IN THIS WHOLE IDEA!
YEAH! WEREN'T WE SUPPOSED TO PICK UP OUR NEW MUG SHOTS AT THE DRUG STORE TODAY, ANYWAY?
176-671
176-716
176-761
BEAGLE BOYS INC.
BOOM!
DON'T LEAVE YET, BOYS! BERTHA HERE WANTS TO SAY GOODBYE!

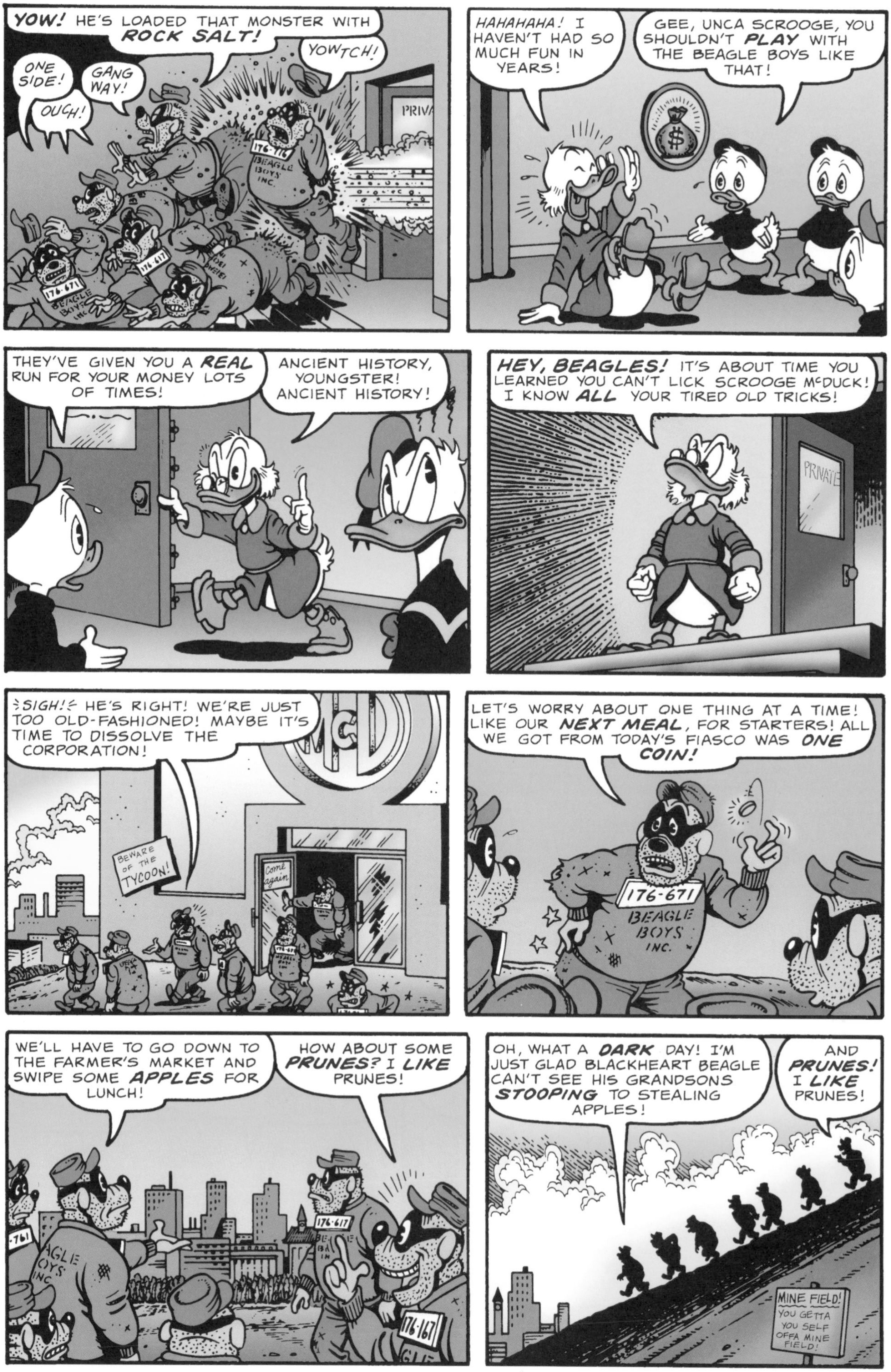
YOW! HE'S LOADED THAT MONSTER WITH ROCK SALT!
YOWTCH!
ONE SIDE!
GANG WAY!
OUCH!
HAHAHAHA! I HAVEN'T HAD SO MUCH FUN IN YEARS!
GEE, UNCA SCROOGE, YOU SHOULDN'T PLAY WITH THE BEAGLE BOYS LIKE THAT!
THEY'VE GIVEN YOU A REAL RUN FOR YOUR MONEY LOTS OF TIMES!
ANCIENT HISTORY, YOUNGSTER! ANCIENT HISTORY!
HEY, BEAGLES! IT'S ABOUT TIME YOU LEARNED YOU CAN'T LICK SCROOGE McDUCK! I KNOW ALL YOUR TIRED OLD TRICKS!
PRIVATE
SIGH! HE'S RIGHT! WE'RE JUST TOO OLD-FASHIONED! MAYBE IT'S TIME TO DISSOLVE THE CORPORATION!
BEWARE OF THE TYCOON!
Come again
LET'S WORRY ABOUT ONE THING AT A TIME! LIKE OUR NEXT MEAL, FOR STARTERS! ALL WE GOT FROM TODAY'S FIASCO WAS ONE COIN!
176-671
BEAGLE BOYS INC.
WE'LL HAVE TO GO DOWN TO THE FARMER'S MARKET AND SWIPE SOME APPLES FOR LUNCH!
HOW ABOUT SOME PRUNES? I LIKE PRUNES!
OH, WHAT A DARK DAY! I'M JUST GLAD BLACKHEART BEAGLE CAN'T SEE HIS GRANDSONS STOOPING TO STEALING APPLES!
AND PRUNES! I LIKE PRUNES!
MINE FIELD! YOU GETTA YOU SELF OFFA MINE FIELD!

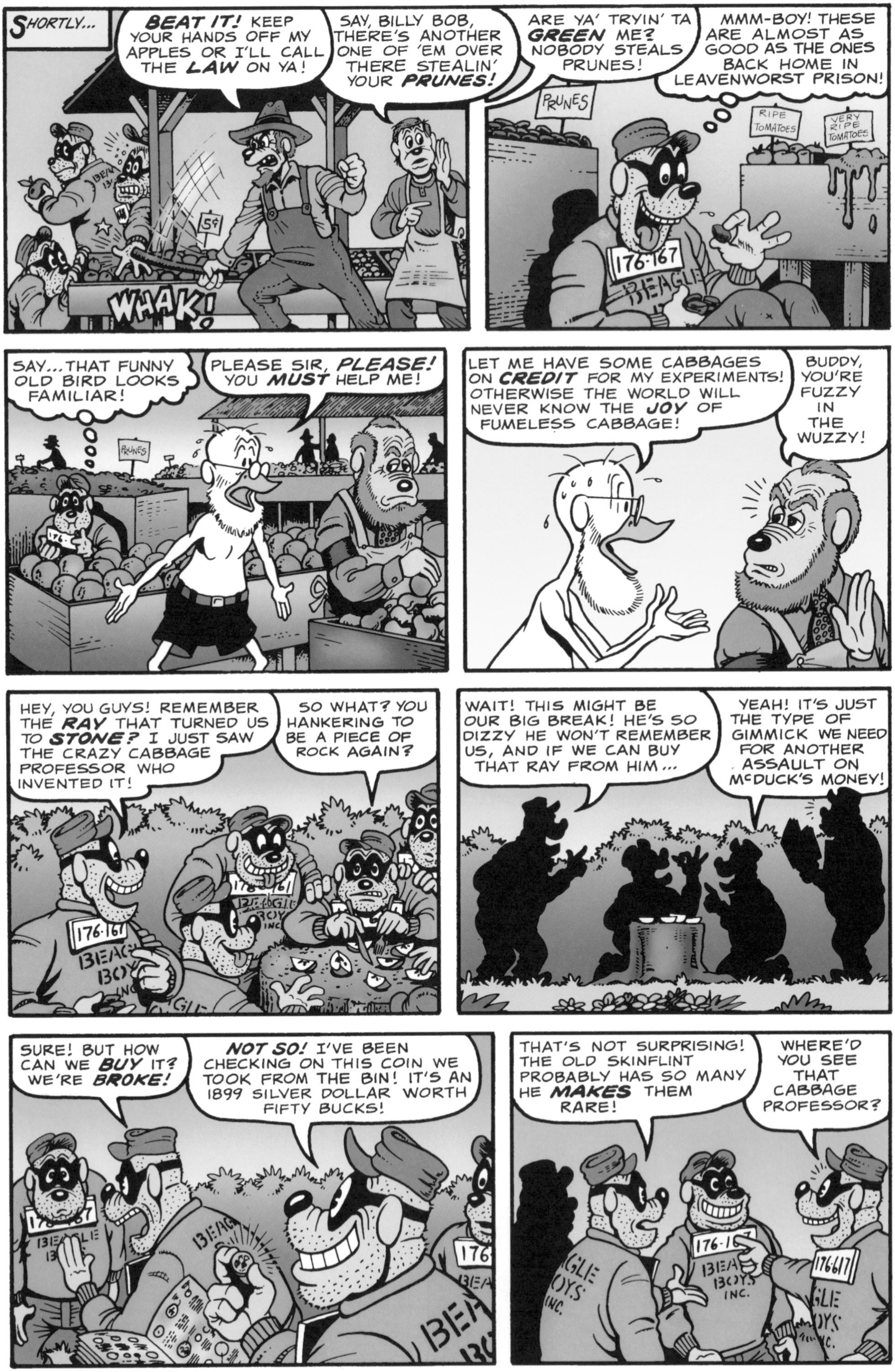
SHORTLY...
BEAT IT! KEEP YOUR HANDS OFF MY APPLES OR I'LL CALL THE LAW ON YA!
SAY, BILLY BOB, THERE'S ANOTHER ONE OF 'EM OVER THERE STEALIN' YOUR PRUNES!
5¢
WHAK!
ARE YA' TRYIN' TA GREEN ME? NOBODY STEALS PRUNES!
MMM-BOY! THESE ARE ALMOST AS GOOD AS THE ONES BACK HOME IN LEAVENWORST PRISON!
PRUNES
RIPE TOMATOES
VERY RIPE TOMATOES
176-167
SAY...THAT FUNNY OLD BIRD LOOKS FAMILIAR!
PLEASE SIR, PLEASE! YOU MUST HELP ME!
PRUNES
LET ME HAVE SOME CABBAGES ON CREDIT FOR MY EXPERIMENTS! OTHERWISE THE WORLD WILL NEVER KNOW THE JOY OF FUMELESS CABBAGE!
BUDDY, YOU'RE FUZZY IN THE WUZZY!
HEY, YOU GUYS! REMEMBER THE RAY THAT TURNED US TO STONE? I JUST SAW THE CRAZY CABBAGE PROFESSOR WHO INVENTED IT!
SO WHAT? YOU HANKERING TO BE A PIECE OF ROCK AGAIN?
176-161
WAIT! THIS MIGHT BE OUR BIG BREAK! HE'S SO DIZZY HE WON'T REMEMBER US, AND IF WE CAN BUY THAT RAY FROM HIM...
YEAH! IT'S JUST THE TYPE OF GIMMICK WE NEED FOR ANOTHER ASSAULT ON McDUCK'S MONEY!
SURE! BUT HOW CAN WE BUY IT? WE'RE BROKE!
NOT SO! I'VE BEEN CHECKING ON THIS COIN WE TOOK FROM THE BIN! IT'S AN 1899 SILVER DOLLAR WORTH FIFTY BUCKS!
THAT'S NOT SURPRISING! THE OLD SKINFLINT PROBABLY HAS SO MANY HE MAKES THEM RARE!
WHERE'D YOU SEE THAT CABBAGE PROFESSOR?
176617

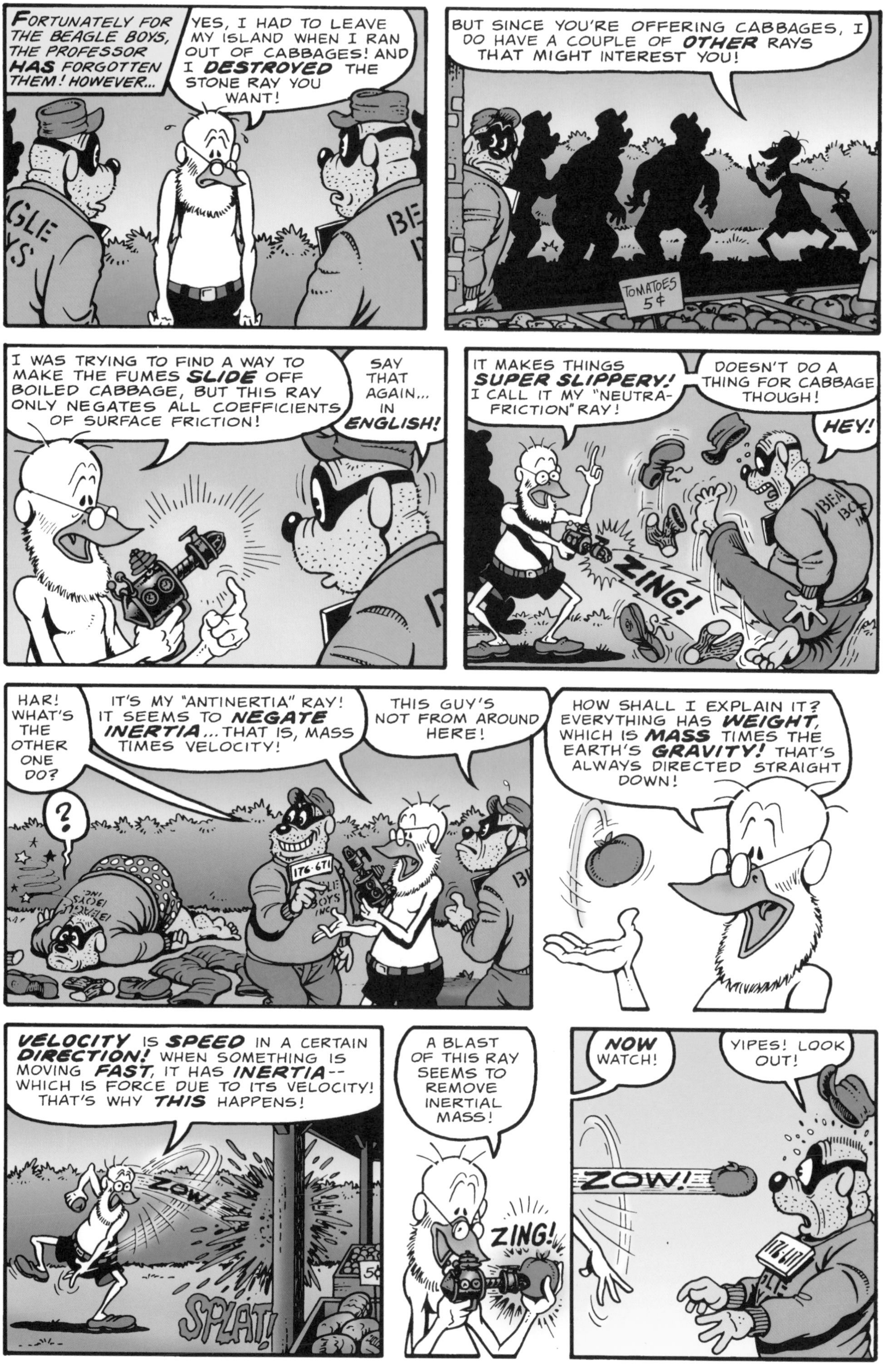
FORTUNATELY FOR THE BEAGLE BOYS, THE PROFESSOR HAS FORGOTTEN THEM! HOWEVER...
YES, I HAD TO LEAVE MY ISLAND WHEN I RAN OUT OF CABBAGES! AND I DESTROYED THE STONE RAY YOU WANT!
BUT SINCE YOU'RE OFFERING CABBAGES, I DO HAVE A COUPLE OF OTHER RAYS THAT MIGHT INTEREST YOU!
TOMATOES 5¢
I WAS TRYING TO FIND A WAY TO MAKE THE FUMES SLIDE OFF BOILED CABBAGE, BUT THIS RAY ONLY NEGATES ALL COEFFICIENTS OF SURFACE FRICTION!
SAY THAT AGAIN... IN ENGLISH!
IT MAKES THINGS SUPER SLIPPERY! I CALL IT MY "NEUTRA-FRICTION" RAY!
DOESN'T DO A THING FOR CABBAGE THOUGH!
HEY!
ZING!
HAR! WHAT'S THE OTHER ONE DO?
IT'S MY "ANTINERTIA" RAY! IT SEEMS TO NEGATE INERTIA... THAT IS, MASS TIMES VELOCITY!
THIS GUY'S NOT FROM AROUND HERE!
?
176-671
HOW SHALL I EXPLAIN IT? EVERYTHING HAS WEIGHT, WHICH IS MASS TIMES THE EARTH'S GRAVITY! THAT'S ALWAYS DIRECTED STRAIGHT DOWN!
VELOCITY IS SPEED IN A CERTAIN DIRECTION! WHEN SOMETHING IS MOVING FAST, IT HAS INERTIA-- WHICH IS FORCE DUE TO ITS VELOCITY! THAT'S WHY THIS HAPPENS!
ZOW!
SPLAT!
A BLAST OF THIS RAY SEEMS TO REMOVE INERTIAL MASS!
ZING!
NOW WATCH!
YIPES! LOOK OUT!
ZOW!

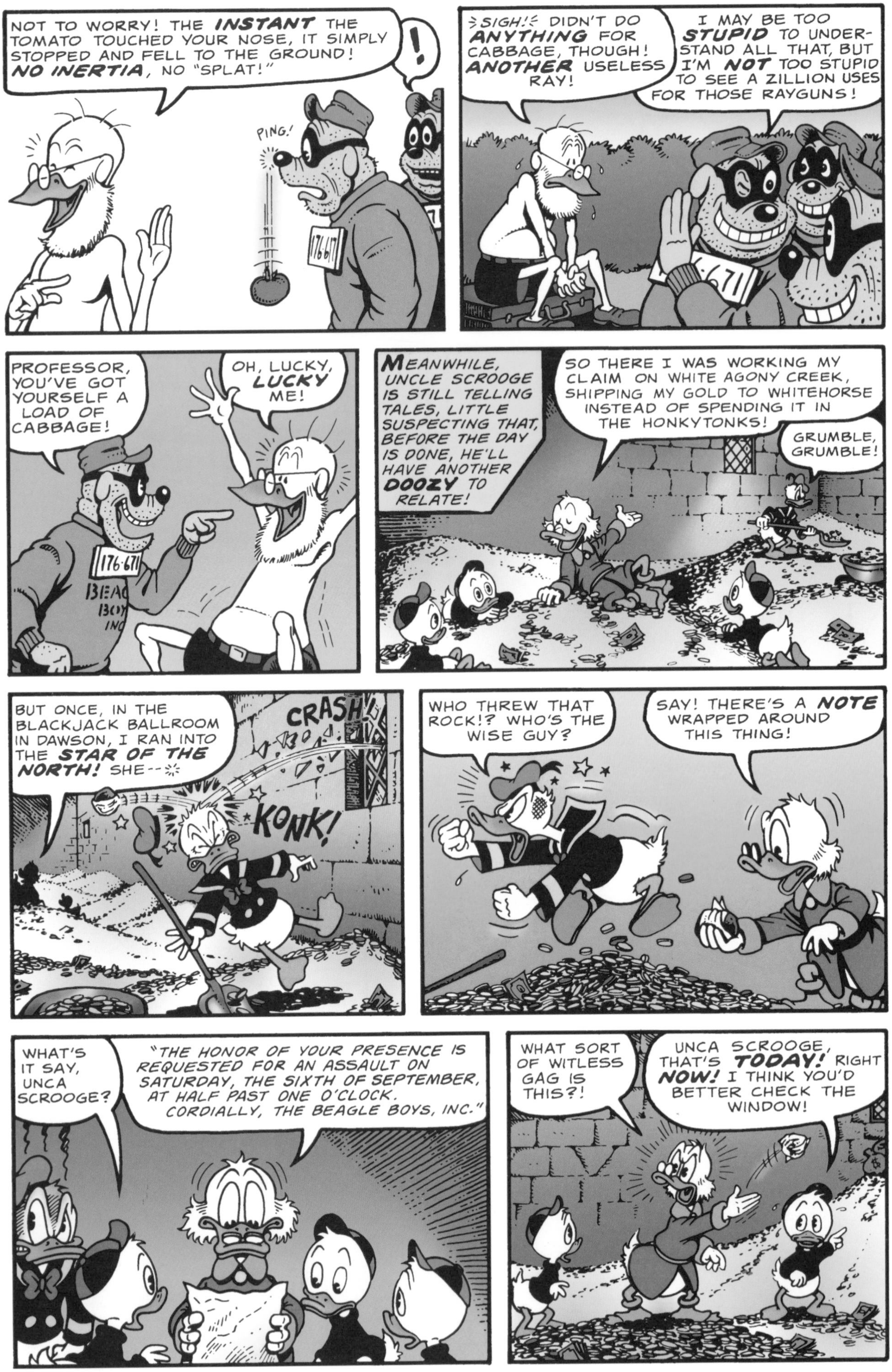
NOT TO WORRY! THE INSTANT THE TOMATO TOUCHED YOUR NOSE, IT SIMPLY STOPPED AND FELL TO THE GROUND! NO INERTIA, NO "SPLAT!"
!
PING!
176-671
SIGH! DIDN'T DO ANYTHING FOR CABBAGE, THOUGH! ANOTHER USELESS RAY!
I MAY BE TOO STUPID TO UNDERSTAND ALL THAT, BUT I'M NOT TOO STUPID TO SEE A ZILLION USES FOR THOSE RAYGUNS!
PROFESSOR, YOU'VE GOT YOURSELF A LOAD OF CABBAGE!
OH, LUCKY, LUCKY ME!
176-671
MEANWHILE, UNCLE SCROOGE IS STILL TELLING TALES, LITTLE SUSPECTING THAT, BEFORE THE DAY IS DONE, HE'LL HAVE ANOTHER DOOZY TO RELATE!
SO THERE I WAS WORKING MY CLAIM ON WHITE AGONY CREEK, SHIPPING MY GOLD TO WHITEHORSE INSTEAD OF SPENDING IT IN THE HONKYTONKS!
GRUMBLE, GRUMBLE!
BUT ONCE, IN THE BLACKJACK BALLROOM IN DAWSON, I RAN INTO THE STAR OF THE NORTH! SHE--
CRASH!
KONK!
WHO THREW THAT ROCK!? WHO'S THE WISE GUY?
SAY! THERE'S A NOTE WRAPPED AROUND THIS THING!
WHAT'S IT SAY, UNCA SCROOGE?
"THE HONOR OF YOUR PRESENCE IS REQUESTED FOR AN ASSAULT ON SATURDAY, THE SIXTH OF SEPTEMBER, AT HALF PAST ONE O'CLOCK. CORDIALLY, THE BEAGLE BOYS, INC."
WHAT SORT OF WITLESS GAG IS THIS?!
UNCA SCROOGE, THAT'S TODAY! RIGHT NOW! I THINK YOU'D BETTER CHECK THE WINDOW!

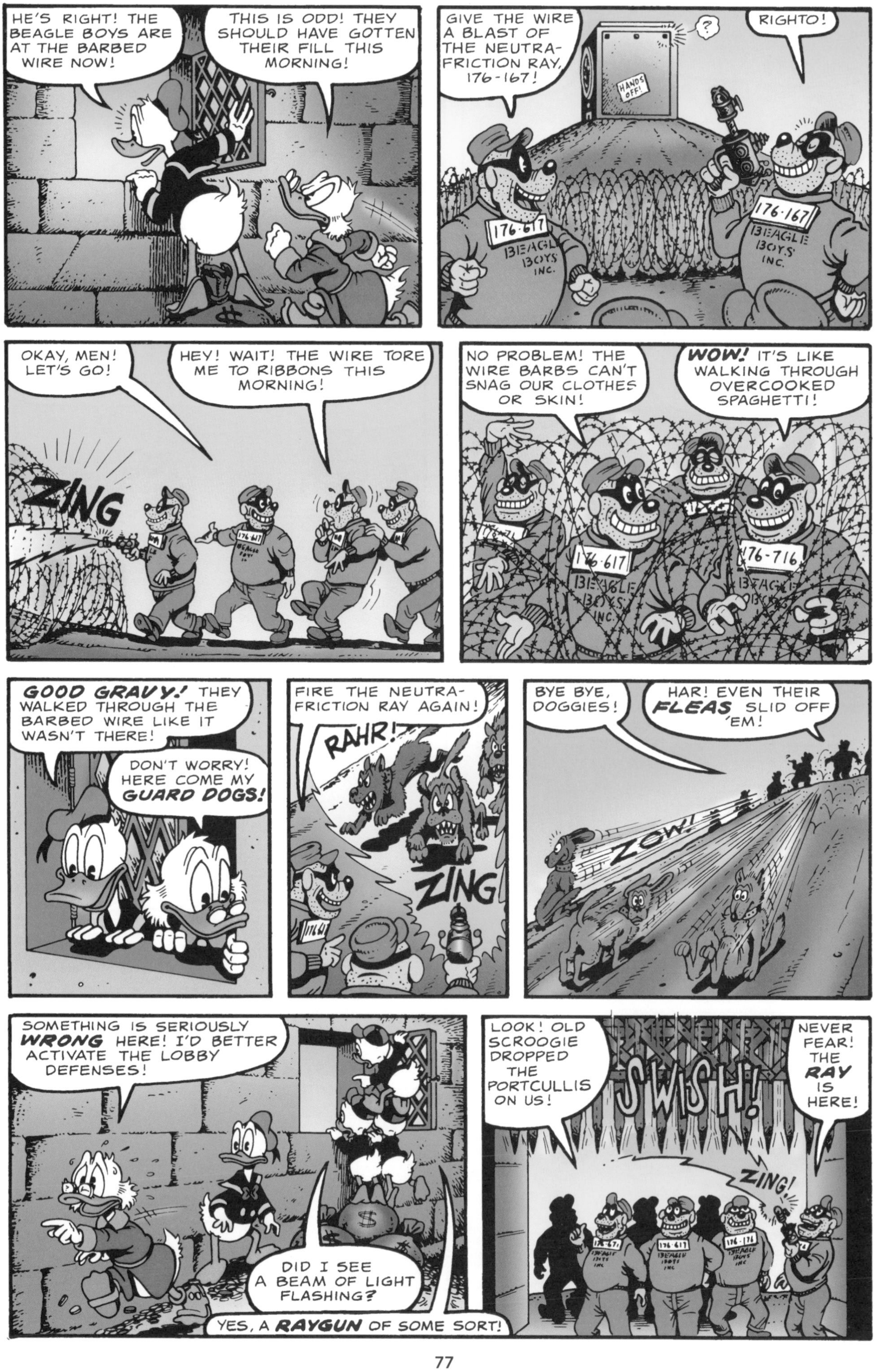
HE'S RIGHT! THE BEAGLE BOYS ARE AT THE BARBED WIRE NOW!
THIS IS ODD! THEY SHOULD HAVE GOTTEN THEIR FILL THIS MORNING!
GIVE THE WIRE A BLAST OF THE NEUTRA-FRICTION RAY, 176-167!
?
RIGHTO!
HANDS OFF!
176-617
BEAGLE BOYS INC.
176-167
BEAGLE BOYS INC.
OKAY, MEN! LET'S GO!
HEY! WAIT! THE WIRE TORE ME TO RIBBONS THIS MORNING!
ZING
176-617
NO PROBLEM! THE WIRE BARBS CAN'T SNAG OUR CLOTHES OR SKIN!
WOW! IT'S LIKE WALKING THROUGH OVERCOOKED SPAGHETTI!
176-617
BEAGLE BOYS INC.
176-716
BEAGLE
GOOD GRAVY! THEY WALKED THROUGH THE BARBED WIRE LIKE IT WASN'T THERE!
DON'T WORRY! HERE COME MY GUARD DOGS!
FIRE THE NEUTRA-FRICTION RAY AGAIN!
RAHR!
ZING
BYE BYE, DOGGIES!
HAR! EVEN THEIR FLEAS SLID OFF 'EM!
ZOW!
SOMETHING IS SERIOUSLY WRONG HERE! I'D BETTER ACTIVATE THE LOBBY DEFENSES!
DID I SEE A BEAM OF LIGHT FLASHING?
YES, A RAYGUN OF SOME SORT!
LOOK! OLD SCROOGIE DROPPED THE PORTCULLIS ON US!
SWISH!
NEVER FEAR! THE RAY IS HERE!
ZING!

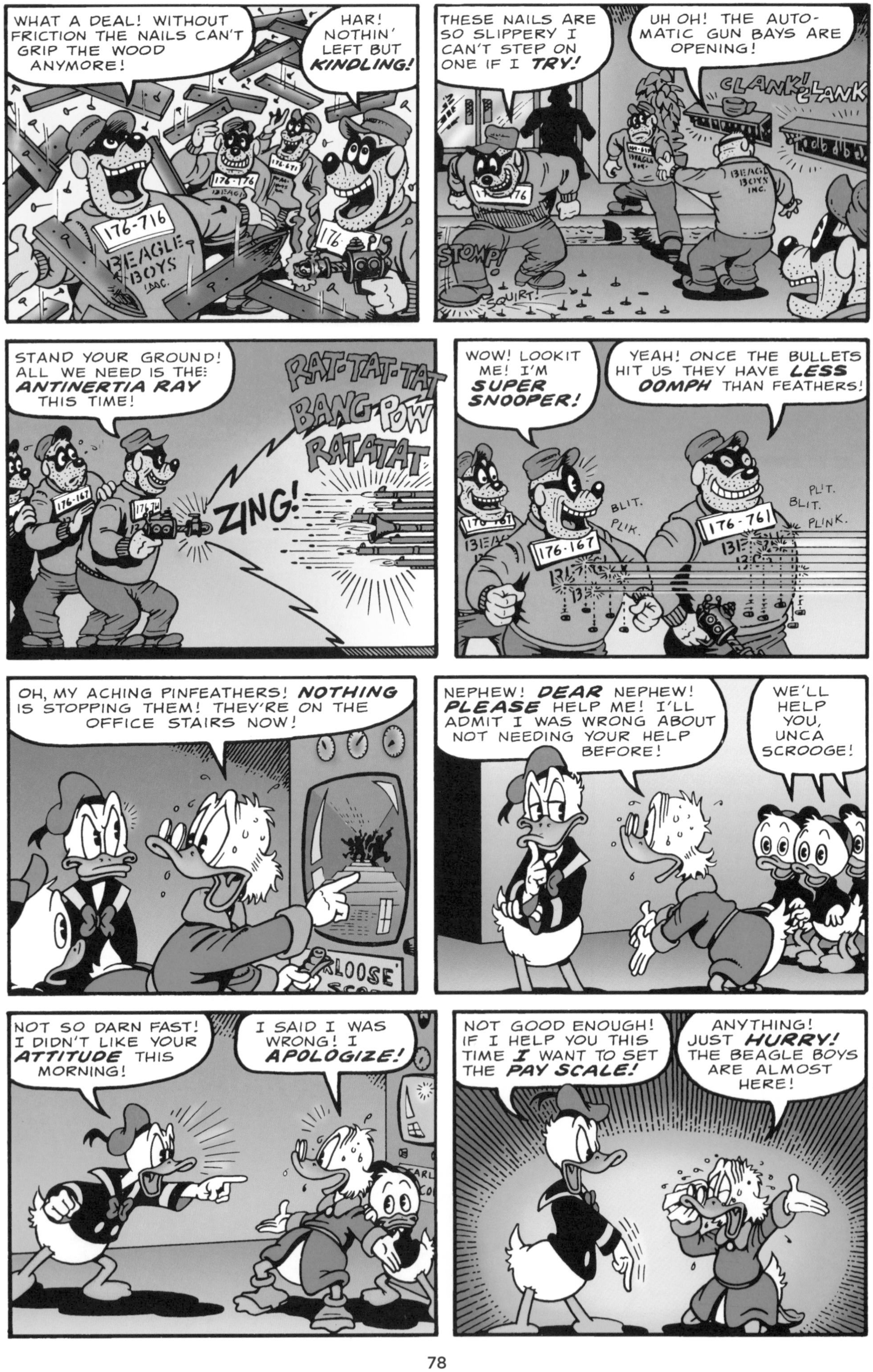
WHAT A DEAL! WITHOUT FRICTION THE NAILS CAN'T GRIP THE WOOD ANYMORE!
HAR! NOTHIN' LEFT BUT KINDLING!
176-716
BEAGLE BOYS INC.
THESE NAILS ARE SO SLIPPERY I CAN'T STEP ON ONE IF I TRY!
UH OH! THE AUTOMATIC GUN BAYS ARE OPENING!
CLANK! CLANK
STOMP!
SQUIRT!
STAND YOUR GROUND! ALL WE NEED IS THE ANTINERTIA RAY THIS TIME!
RAT-TAT-TAT
BANG POW
RATATAT
ZING!
WOW! LOOKIT ME! I'M SUPER SNOOPER!
YEAH! ONCE THE BULLETS HIT US THEY HAVE LESS OOMPH THAN FEATHERS!
BLIT.
PLIK.
PLIT.
BLIT.
PLINK.
176-167
176-761
OH, MY ACHING PINFEATHERS! NOTHING IS STOPPING THEM! THEY'RE ON THE OFFICE STAIRS NOW!
NEPHEW! DEAR NEPHEW! PLEASE HELP ME! I'LL ADMIT I WAS WRONG ABOUT NOT NEEDING YOUR HELP BEFORE!
WE'LL HELP YOU, UNCA SCROOGE!
NOT SO DARN FAST! I DIDN'T LIKE YOUR ATTITUDE THIS MORNING!
I SAID I WAS WRONG! I APOLOGIZE!
NOT GOOD ENOUGH! IF I HELP YOU THIS TIME I WANT TO SET THE PAY SCALE!
ANYTHING! JUST HURRY! THE BEAGLE BOYS ARE ALMOST HERE!

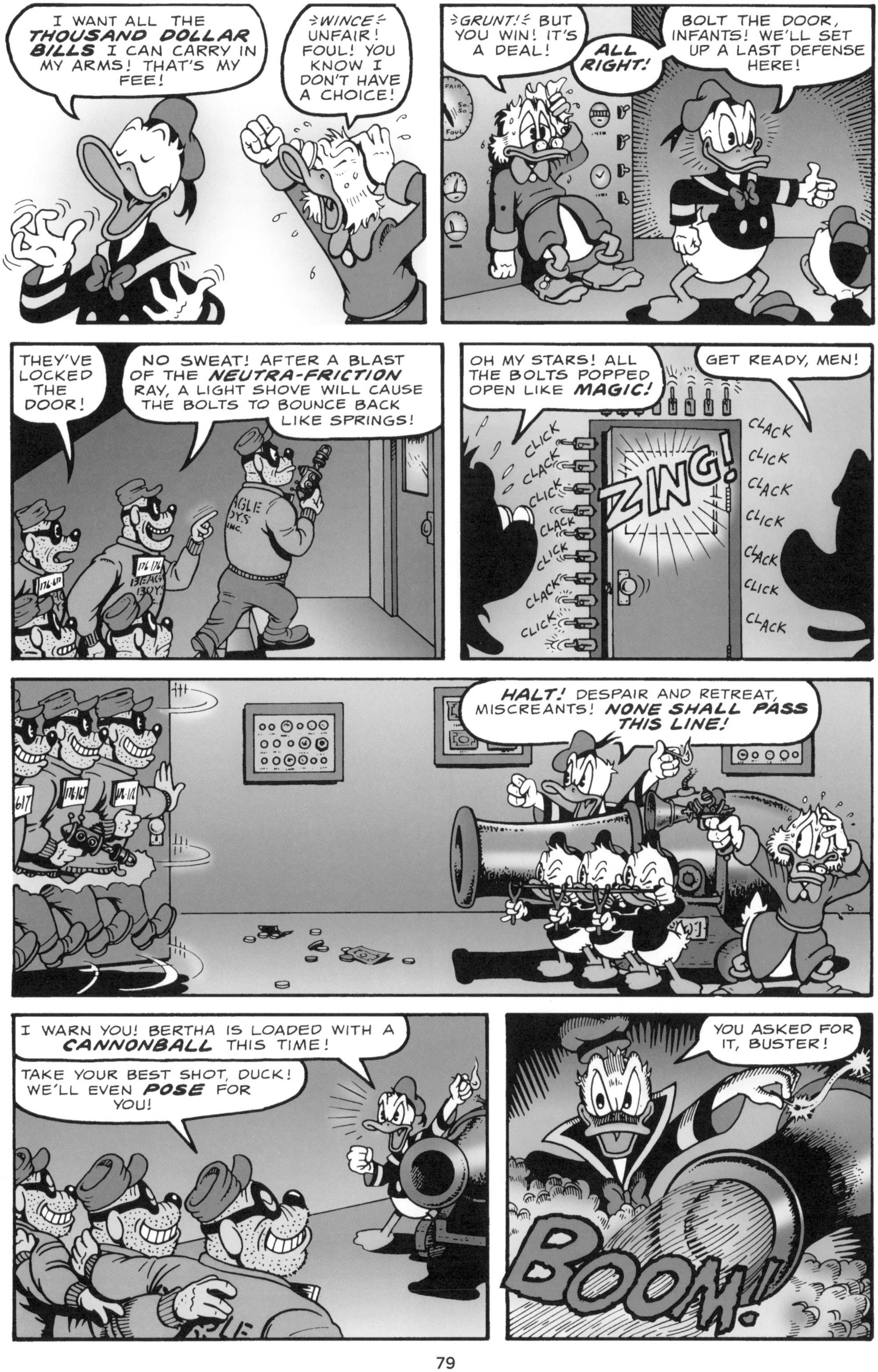

I WANT ALL THE THOUSAND DOLLAR BILLS I CAN CARRY IN MY ARMS! THAT'S MY FEE!
WINCE UNFAIR! FOUL! YOU KNOW I DON'T HAVE A CHOICE!
GRUNT! BUT YOU WIN! IT'S A DEAL!
ALL RIGHT!
BOLT THE DOOR, INFANTS! WE'LL SET UP A LAST DEFENSE HERE!
THEY'VE LOCKED THE DOOR!
NO SWEAT! AFTER A BLAST OF THE NEUTRA-FRICTION RAY, A LIGHT SHOVE WILL CAUSE THE BOLTS TO BOUNCE BACK LIKE SPRINGS!
OH MY STARS! ALL THE BOLTS POPPED OPEN LIKE MAGIC!
GET READY, MEN!
CLICK CLACK CLICK CLACK CLICK CLACK CLICK
ZING!
CLACK CLICK CLACK CLICK CLACK CLICK CLACK
HALT! DESPAIR AND RETREAT, MISCREANTS! NONE SHALL PASS THIS LINE!
I WARN YOU! BERTHA IS LOADED WITH A CANNONBALL THIS TIME!
TAKE YOUR BEST SHOT, DUCK! WE'LL EVEN POSE FOR YOU!
YOU ASKED FOR IT, BUSTER!
BOOM!!

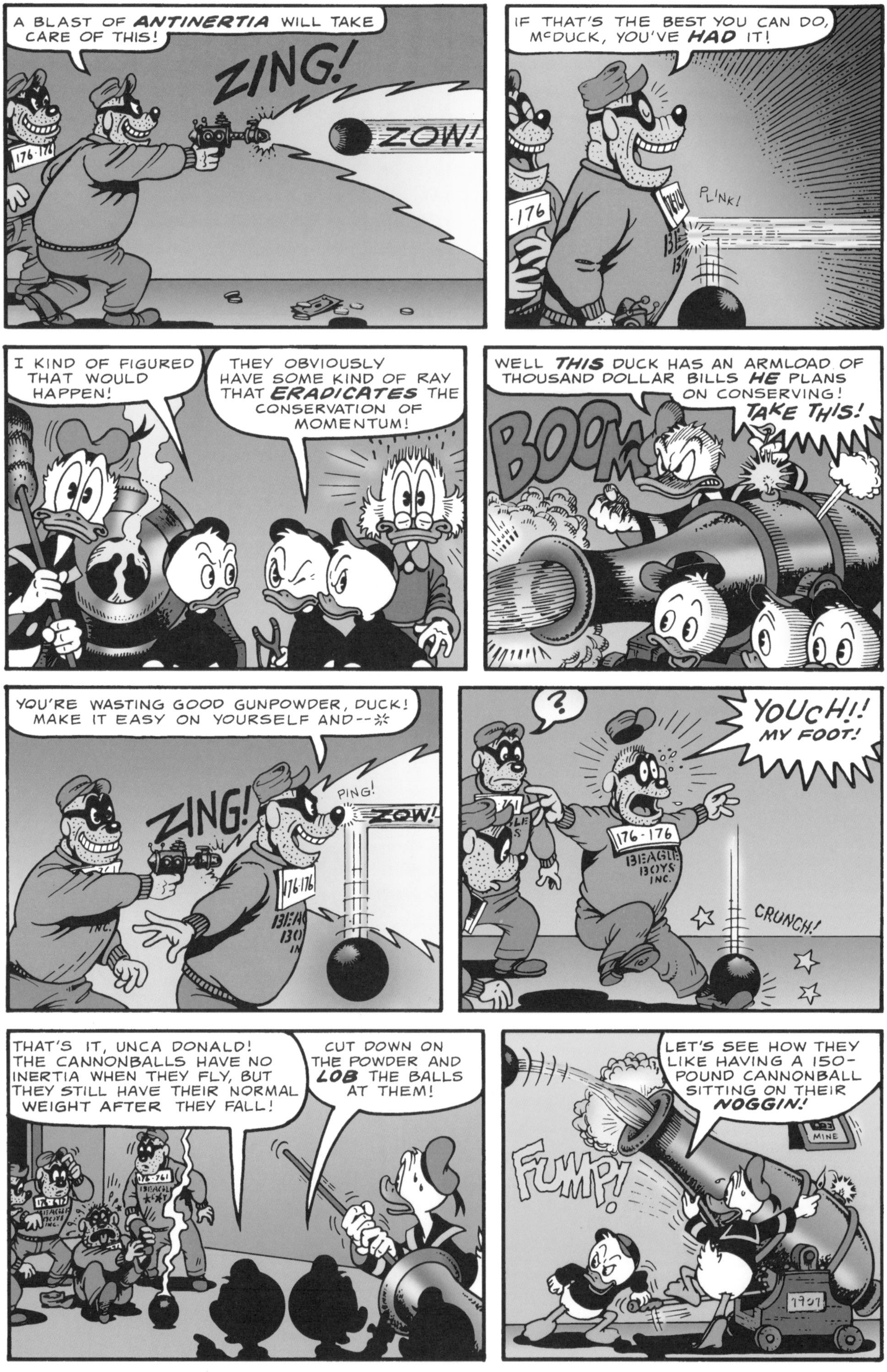
A BLAST OF ANTINERTIA WILL TAKE CARE OF THIS!
ZING!
ZOW!
IF THAT'S THE BEST YOU CAN DO, McDUCK, YOU'VE HAD IT!
PLINK!
I KIND OF FIGURED THAT WOULD HAPPEN!
THEY OBVIOUSLY HAVE SOME KIND OF RAY THAT ERADICATES THE CONSERVATION OF MOMENTUM!
WELL THIS DUCK HAS AN ARMLOAD OF THOUSAND DOLLAR BILLS HE PLANS ON CONSERVING!
TAKE THIS!
BOOM
YOU'RE WASTING GOOD GUNPOWDER, DUCK! MAKE IT EASY ON YOURSELF AND--
ZING!
PING!
ZOW!
?
YOUCH!! MY FOOT!
176-176
BEAGLE BOYS INC.
CRUNCH!
THAT'S IT, UNCA DONALD! THE CANNONBALLS HAVE NO INERTIA WHEN THEY FLY, BUT THEY STILL HAVE THEIR NORMAL WEIGHT AFTER THEY FALL!
CUT DOWN ON THE POWDER AND LOB THE BALLS AT THEM!
LET'S SEE HOW THEY LIKE HAVING A 150-POUND CANNONBALL SITTING ON THEIR NOGGIN!
FUMP!
MINE

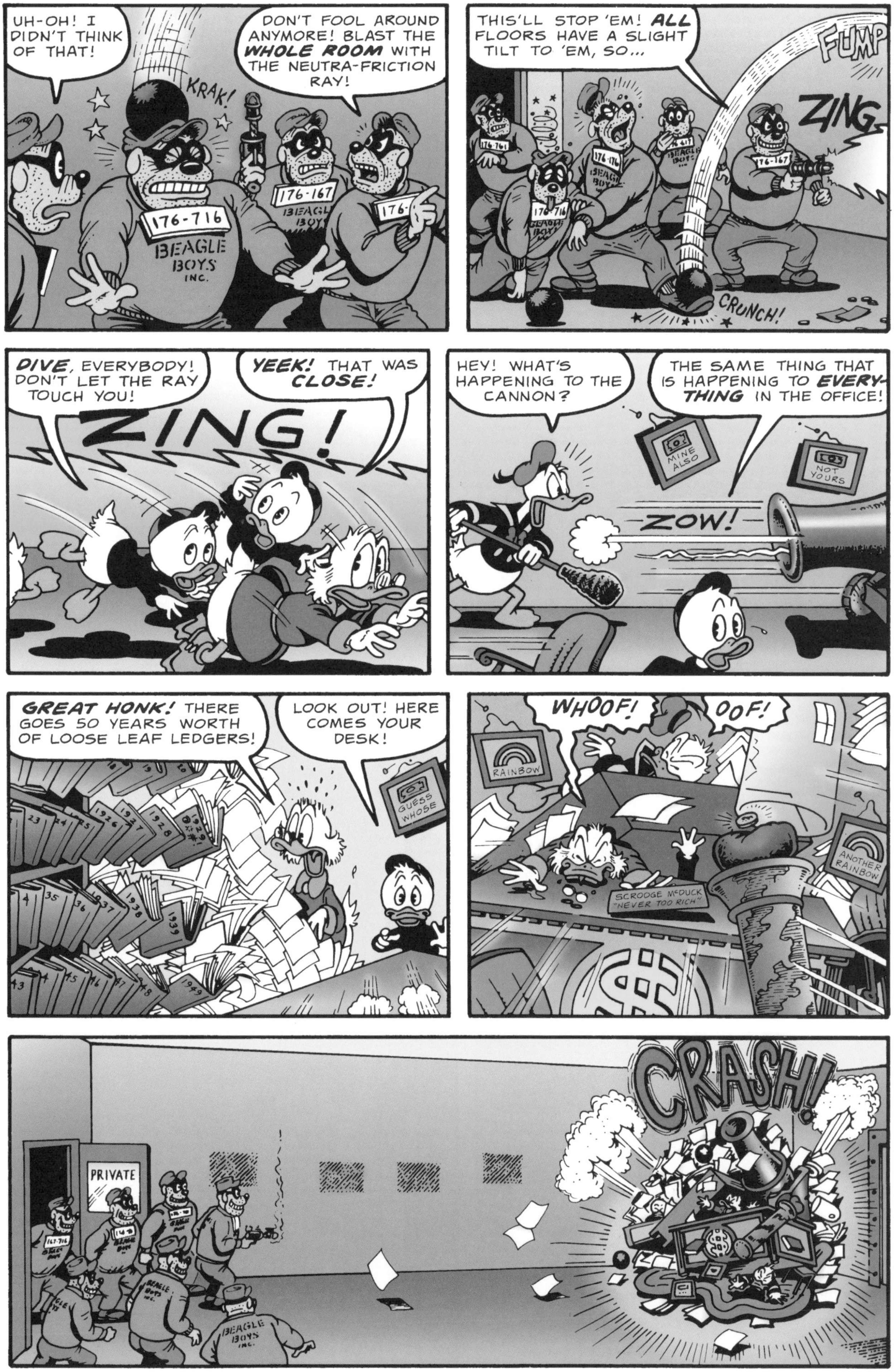
UH-OH! I DIDN'T THINK OF THAT!
KRAK!
DON'T FOOL AROUND ANYMORE! BLAST THE WHOLE ROOM WITH THE NEUTRA-FRICTION RAY!
176-716
BEAGLE BOYS INC.
176-167
THIS'LL STOP 'EM! ALL FLOORS HAVE A SLIGHT TILT TO 'EM, SO...
FUMP
ZING
CRUNCH!
DIVE, EVERYBODY! DON'T LET THE RAY TOUCH YOU!
YEEK! THAT WAS CLOSE!
ZING!
HEY! WHAT'S HAPPENING TO THE CANNON?
THE SAME THING THAT IS HAPPENING TO EVERY-THING IN THE OFFICE!
MINE ALSO
NOT YOURS
ZOW!
GREAT HONK! THERE GOES 50 YEARS WORTH OF LOOSE LEAF LEDGERS!
LOOK OUT! HERE COMES YOUR DESK!
GUESS WHOSE
WHOOF!
OOF!
RAINBOW
ANOTHER RAINBOW
SCROOGE McDUCK "NEVER TOO RICH"
CRASH!
PRIVATE
BEAGLE BOYS INC.

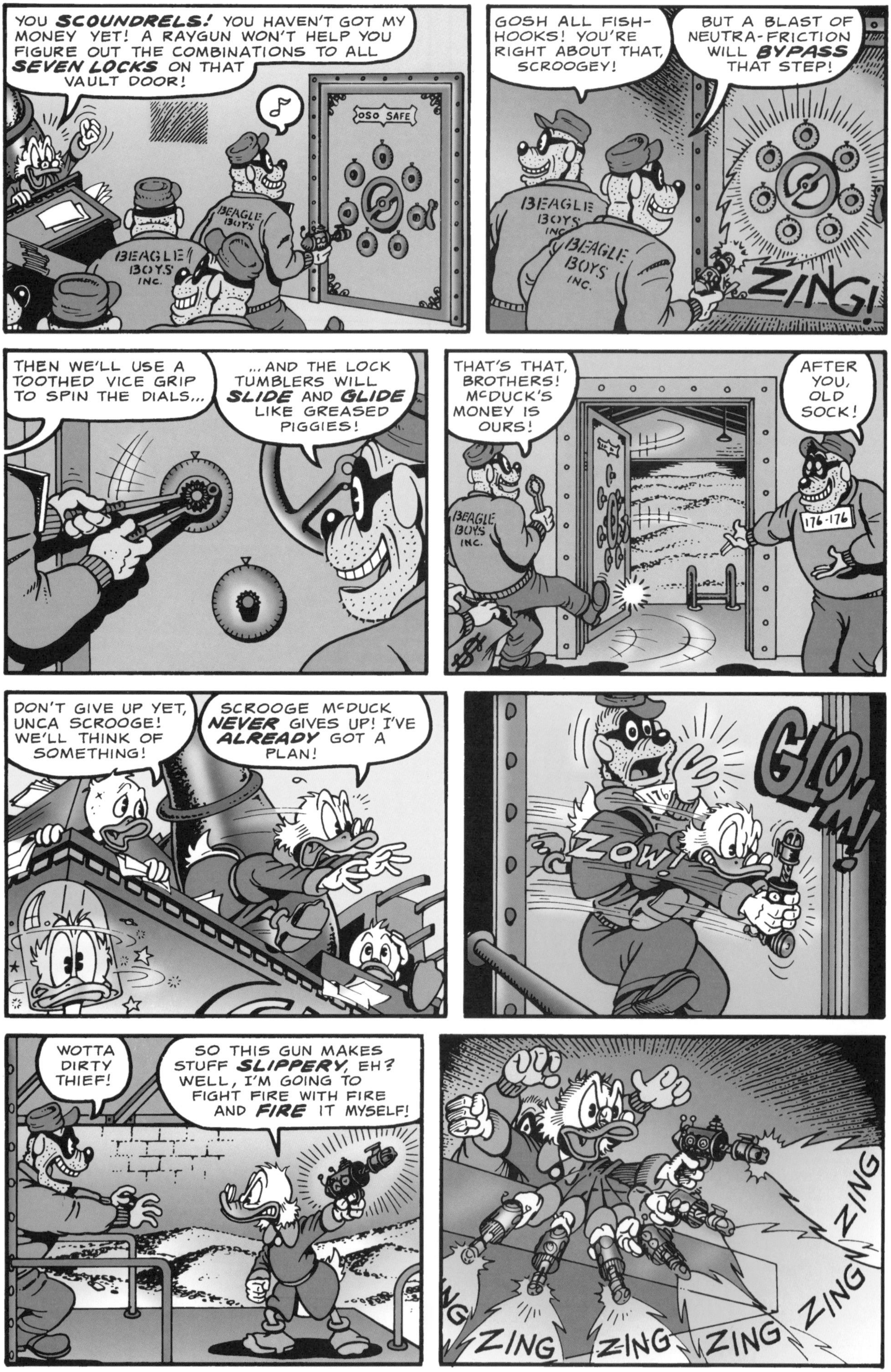
YOU SCOUNDRELS! YOU HAVEN'T GOT MY MONEY YET! A RAYGUN WON'T HELP YOU FIGURE OUT THE COMBINATIONS TO ALL SEVEN LOCKS ON THAT VAULT DOOR!
OSO SAFE
BEAGLE BOYS INC.
BEAGLE BOYS INC.
GOSH ALL FISH-HOOKS! YOU'RE RIGHT ABOUT THAT, SCROOGEY!
BUT A BLAST OF NEUTRA-FRICTION WILL BYPASS THAT STEP!
BEAGLE BOYS INC.
BEAGLE BOYS INC.
ZING!
THEN WE'LL USE A TOOTHED VICE GRIP TO SPIN THE DIALS...
...AND THE LOCK TUMBLERS WILL SLIDE AND GLIDE LIKE GREASED PIGGIES!
THAT'S THAT, BROTHERS! McDUCK'S MONEY IS OURS!
AFTER YOU, OLD SOCK!
BEAGLE BOYS INC.
176-176
DON'T GIVE UP YET, UNCA SCROOGE! WE'LL THINK OF SOMETHING!
SCROOGE McDUCK NEVER GIVES UP! I'VE ALREADY GOT A PLAN!
GLOM!
ZOW!
WOTTA DIRTY THIEF!
SO THIS GUN MAKES STUFF SLIPPERY, EH? WELL, I'M GOING TO FIGHT FIRE WITH FIRE AND FIRE IT MYSELF!
ZING
ZING
ZING
ZING
ZING
ZING

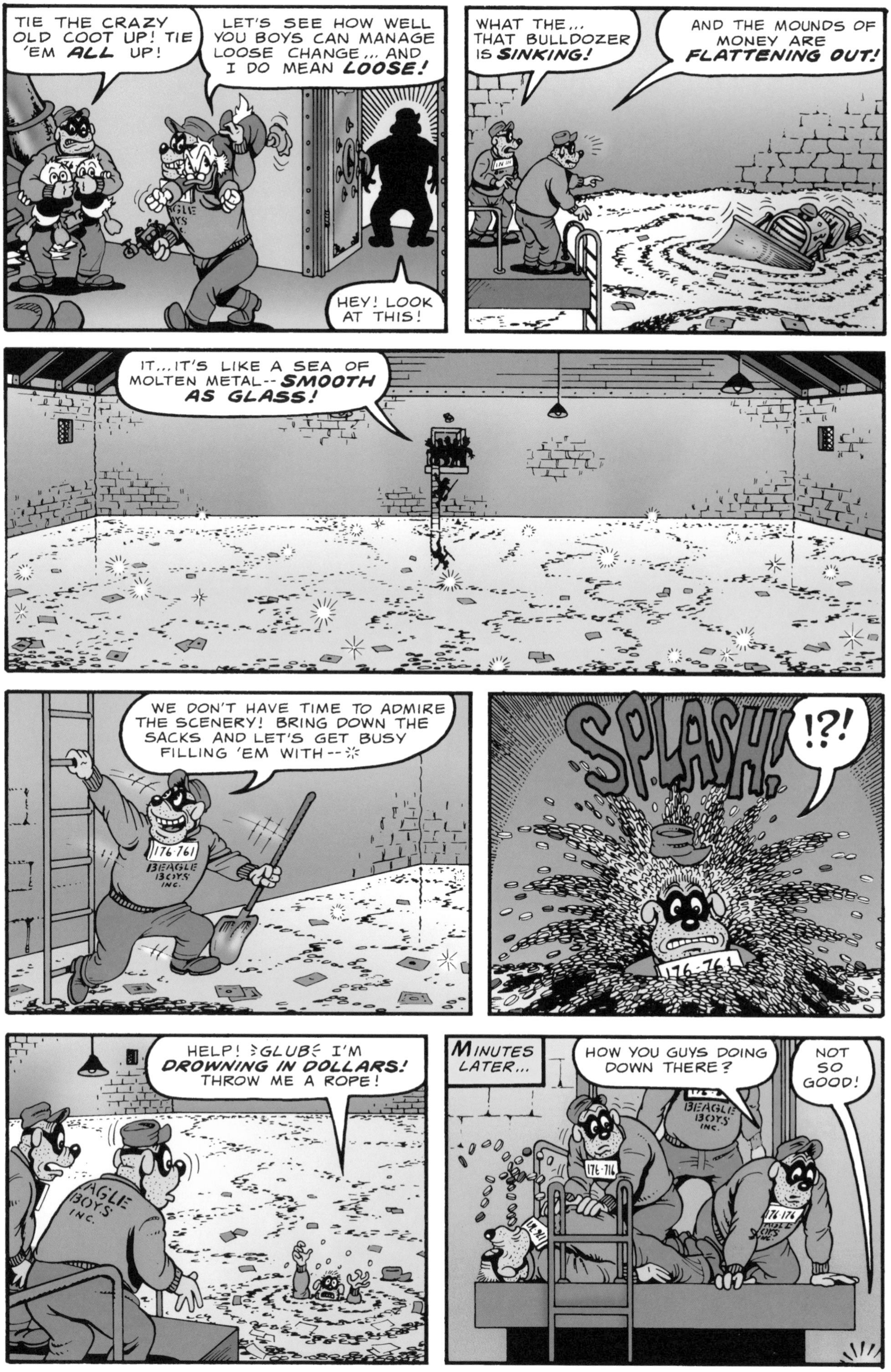
TIE THE CRAZY OLD COOT UP! TIE 'EM ALL UP!
LET'S SEE HOW WELL YOU BOYS CAN MANAGE LOOSE CHANGE... AND I DO MEAN LOOSE!
HEY! LOOK AT THIS!
WHAT THE... THAT BULLDOZER IS SINKING!
AND THE MOUNDS OF MONEY ARE FLATTENING OUT!
IT... IT'S LIKE A SEA OF MOLTEN METAL-- SMOOTH AS GLASS!
WE DON'T HAVE TIME TO ADMIRE THE SCENERY! BRING DOWN THE SACKS AND LET'S GET BUSY FILLING 'EM WITH--
176-761
BEAGLE BOYS INC.
SPLASH!
!?!
HELP! GLUB I'M DROWNING IN DOLLARS! THROW ME A ROPE!
MINUTES LATER...
HOW YOU GUYS DOING DOWN THERE?
NOT SO GOOD!

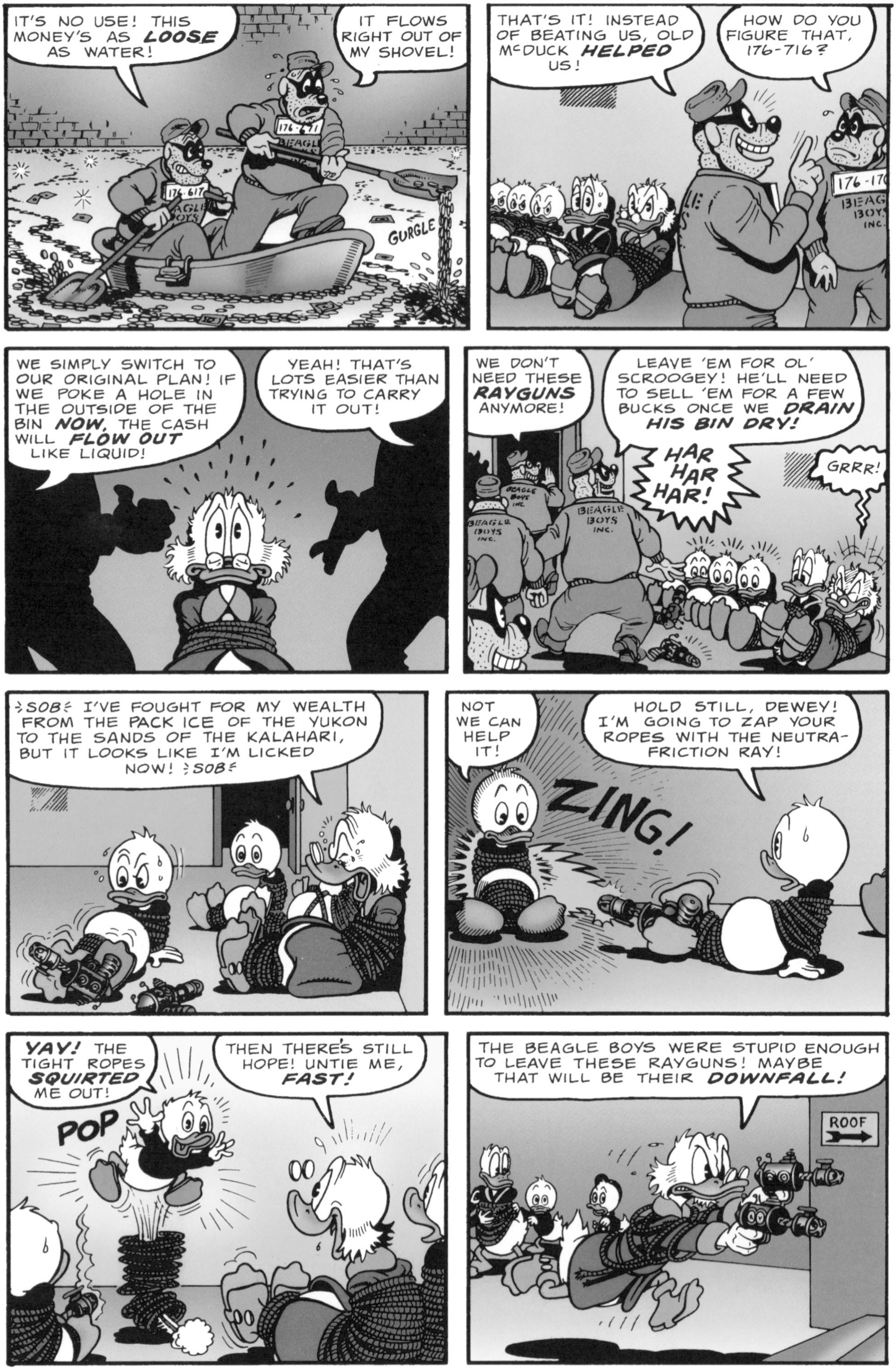
IT'S NO USE! THIS MONEY'S AS LOOSE AS WATER!
IT FLOWS RIGHT OUT OF MY SHOVEL!
GURGLE
THAT'S IT! INSTEAD OF BEATING US, OLD McDUCK HELPED US!
HOW DO YOU FIGURE THAT, 176-716?
WE SIMPLY SWITCH TO OUR ORIGINAL PLAN! IF WE POKE A HOLE IN THE OUTSIDE OF THE BIN NOW, THE CASH WILL FLOW OUT LIKE LIQUID!
YEAH! THAT'S LOTS EASIER THAN TRYING TO CARRY IT OUT!
WE DON'T NEED THESE RAYGUNS ANYMORE!
LEAVE 'EM FOR OL' SCROOGEY! HE'LL NEED TO SELL 'EM FOR A FEW BUCKS ONCE WE DRAIN HIS BIN DRY!
HAR HAR HAR!
GRRR!
SOB I'VE FOUGHT FOR MY WEALTH FROM THE PACK ICE OF THE YUKON TO THE SANDS OF THE KALAHARI, BUT IT LOOKS LIKE I'M LICKED NOW! SOB
NOT WE CAN HELP IT!
HOLD STILL, DEWEY! I'M GOING TO ZAP YOUR ROPES WITH THE NEUTRA-FRICTION RAY!
ZING!
YAY! THE TIGHT ROPES SQUIRTED ME OUT!
THEN THERE'S STILL HOPE! UNTIE ME, FAST!
POP
THE BEAGLE BOYS WERE STUPID ENOUGH TO LEAVE THESE RAYGUNS! MAYBE THAT WILL BE THEIR DOWNFALL!
ROOF

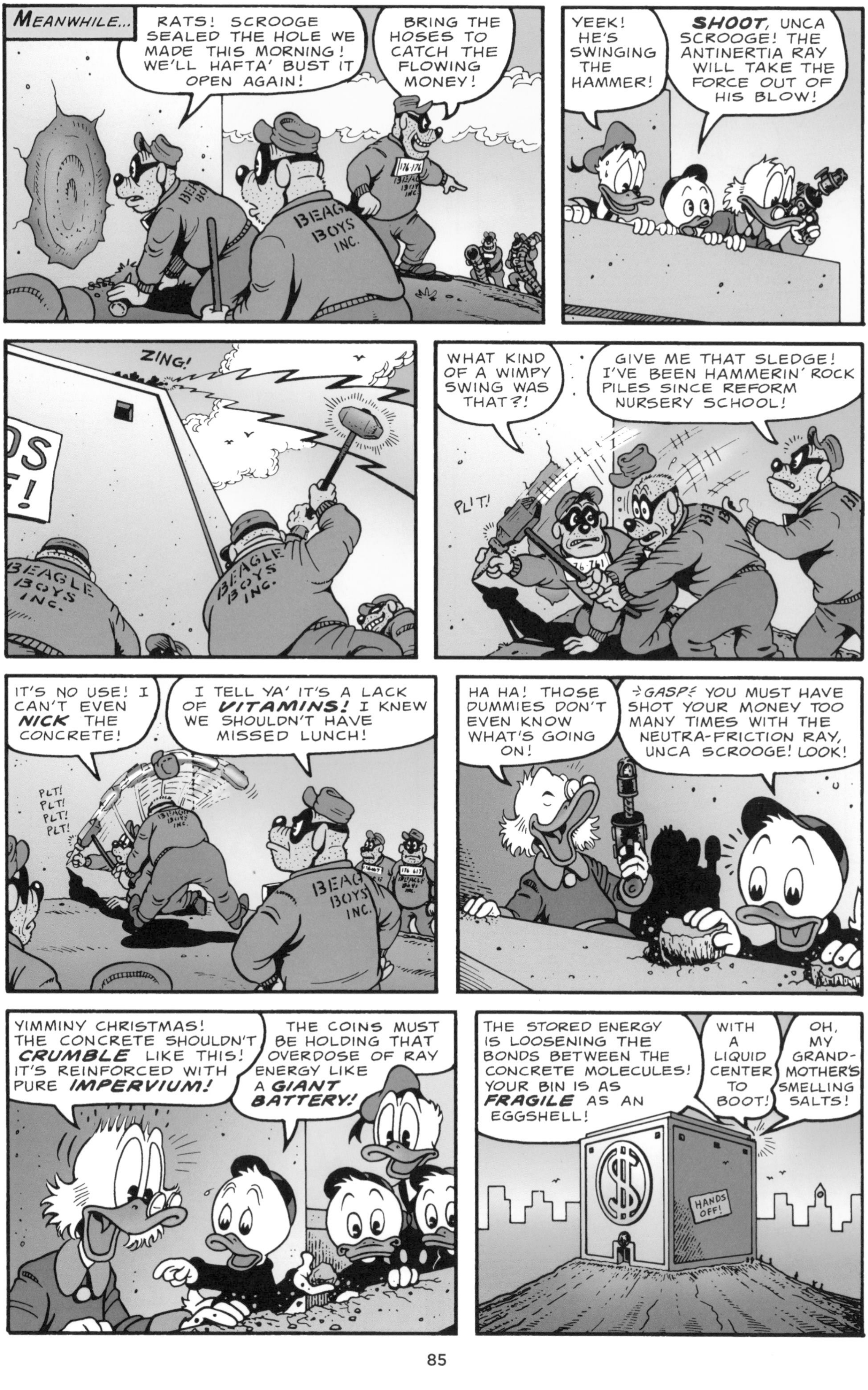
MEANWHILE...
RATS! SCROOGE SEALED THE HOLE WE MADE THIS MORNING! WE'LL HAFTA' BUST IT OPEN AGAIN!
BRING THE HOSES TO CATCH THE FLOWING MONEY!
YEEK! HE'S SWINGING THE HAMMER!
SHOOT, UNCA SCROOGE! THE ANTINERTIA RAY WILL TAKE THE FORCE OUT OF HIS BLOW!
ZING!
WHAT KIND OF A WIMPY SWING WAS THAT?!
GIVE ME THAT SLEDGE! I'VE BEEN HAMMERIN' ROCK PILES SINCE REFORM NURSERY SCHOOL!
PLIT!
IT'S NO USE! I CAN'T EVEN NICK THE CONCRETE!
I TELL YA' IT'S A LACK OF VITAMINS! I KNEW WE SHOULDN'T HAVE MISSED LUNCH!
PLT! PLT! PLT! PLT!
HA HA! THOSE DUMMIES DON'T EVEN KNOW WHAT'S GOING ON!
GASP YOU MUST HAVE SHOT YOUR MONEY TOO MANY TIMES WITH THE NEUTRA-FRICTION RAY, UNCA SCROOGE! LOOK!
YIMMINY CHRISTMAS! THE CONCRETE SHOULDN'T CRUMBLE LIKE THIS! IT'S REINFORCED WITH PURE IMPERVIUM!
THE COINS MUST BE HOLDING THAT OVERDOSE OF RAY ENERGY LIKE A GIANT BATTERY!
THE STORED ENERGY IS LOOSENING THE BONDS BETWEEN THE CONCRETE MOLECULES! YOUR BIN IS AS FRAGILE AS AN EGGSHELL!
WITH A LIQUID CENTER TO BOOT!
OH, MY GRAND-MOTHER'S SMELLING SALTS!
HANDS OFF!

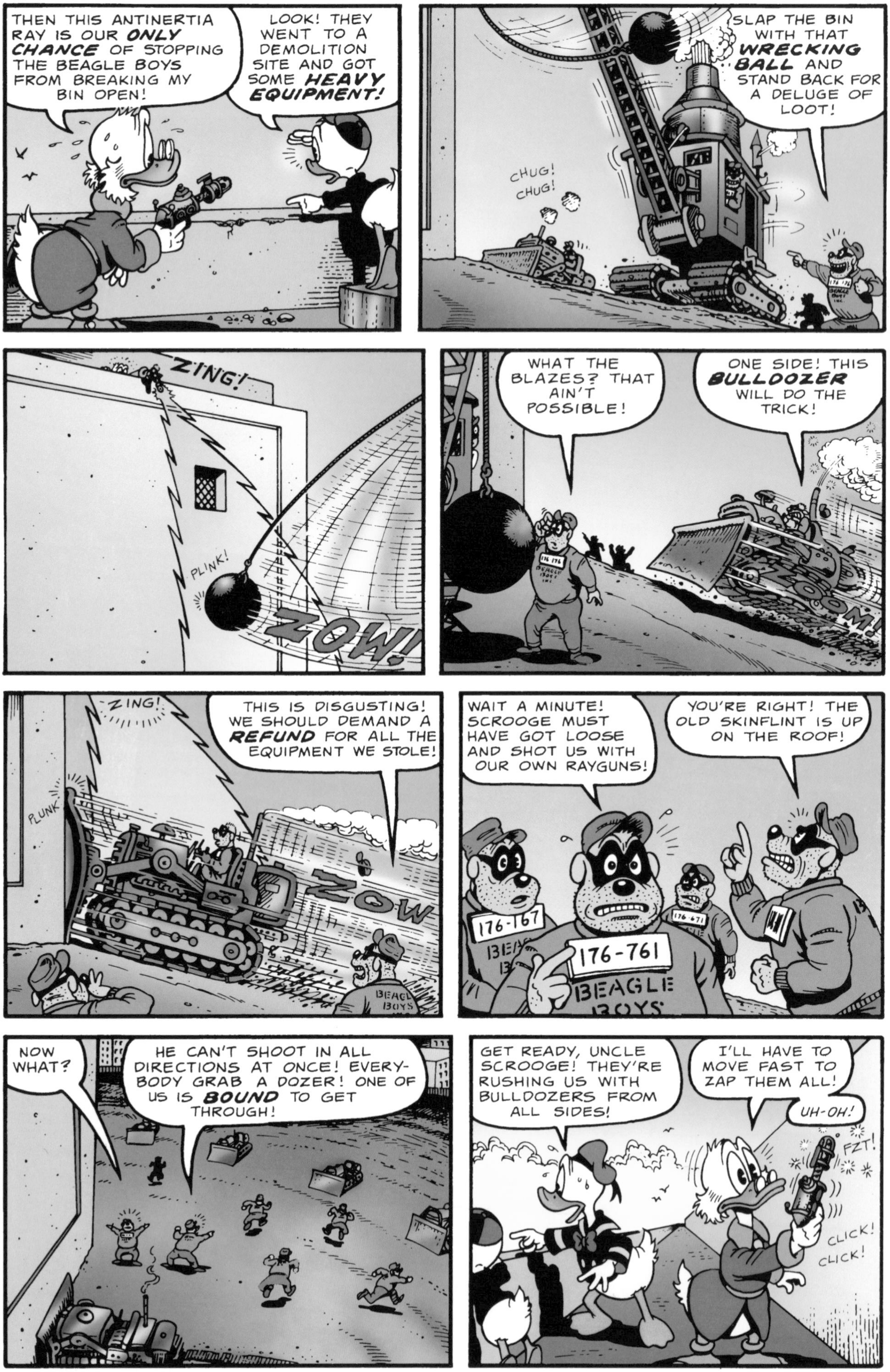
THEN THIS ANTINERTIA RAY IS OUR ONLY CHANCE OF STOPPING THE BEAGLE BOYS FROM BREAKING MY BIN OPEN!
LOOK! THEY WENT TO A DEMOLITION SITE AND GOT SOME HEAVY EQUIPMENT!
SLAP THE BIN WITH THAT WRECKING BALL AND STAND BACK FOR A DELUGE OF LOOT!
CHUG! CHUG!
ZING!
PLINK!
ZOW!
WHAT THE BLAZES? THAT AIN'T POSSIBLE!
ONE SIDE! THIS BULLDOZER WILL DO THE TRICK!
ZOOM!
ZING!
PLUNK
THIS IS DISGUSTING! WE SHOULD DEMAND A REFUND FOR ALL THE EQUIPMENT WE STOLE!
ZOW
WAIT A MINUTE! SCROOGE MUST HAVE GOT LOOSE AND SHOT US WITH OUR OWN RAYGUNS!
YOU'RE RIGHT! THE OLD SKINFLINT IS UP ON THE ROOF!
176-167
176-761
BEAGLE BOYS
NOW WHAT?
HE CAN'T SHOOT IN ALL DIRECTIONS AT ONCE! EVERYBODY GRAB A DOZER! ONE OF US IS BOUND TO GET THROUGH!
GET READY, UNCLE SCROOGE! THEY'RE RUSHING US WITH BULLDOZERS FROM ALL SIDES!
I'LL HAVE TO MOVE FAST TO ZAP THEM ALL!
UH-OH!
FZT!
CLICK! CLICK!

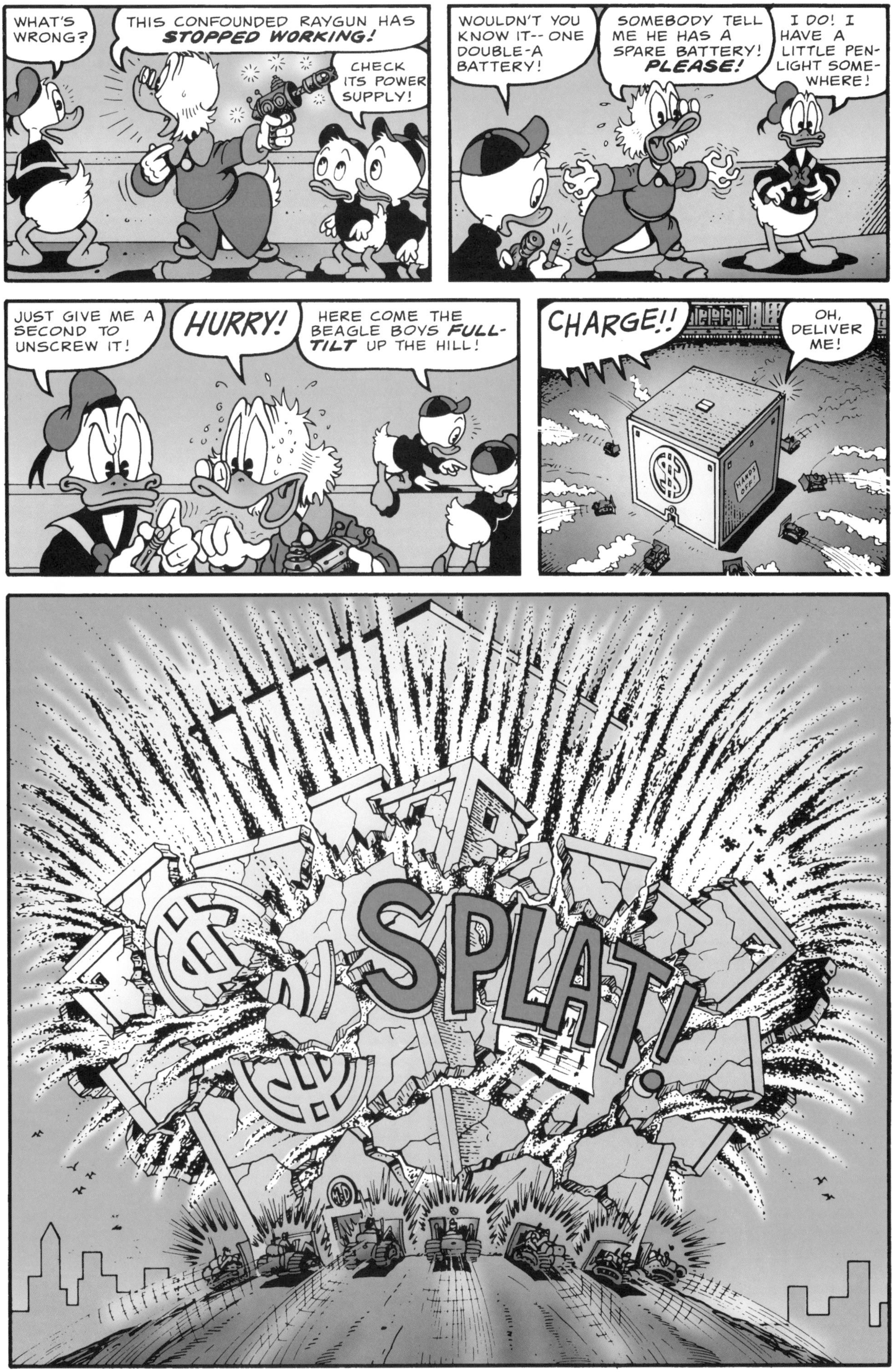

WHAT'S WRONG?
THIS CONFOUNDED RAYGUN HAS STOPPED WORKING!
CHECK ITS POWER SUPPLY!
WOULDN'T YOU KNOW IT-- ONE DOUBLE-A BATTERY!
SOMEBODY TELL ME HE HAS A SPARE BATTERY! PLEASE!
I DO! I HAVE A LITTLE PEN-LIGHT SOME-WHERE!
JUST GIVE ME A SECOND TO UNSCREW IT!
HURRY!
HERE COME THE BEAGLE BOYS FULL-TILT UP THE HILL!
CHARGE!!
OH, DELIVER ME!
SPLAT!

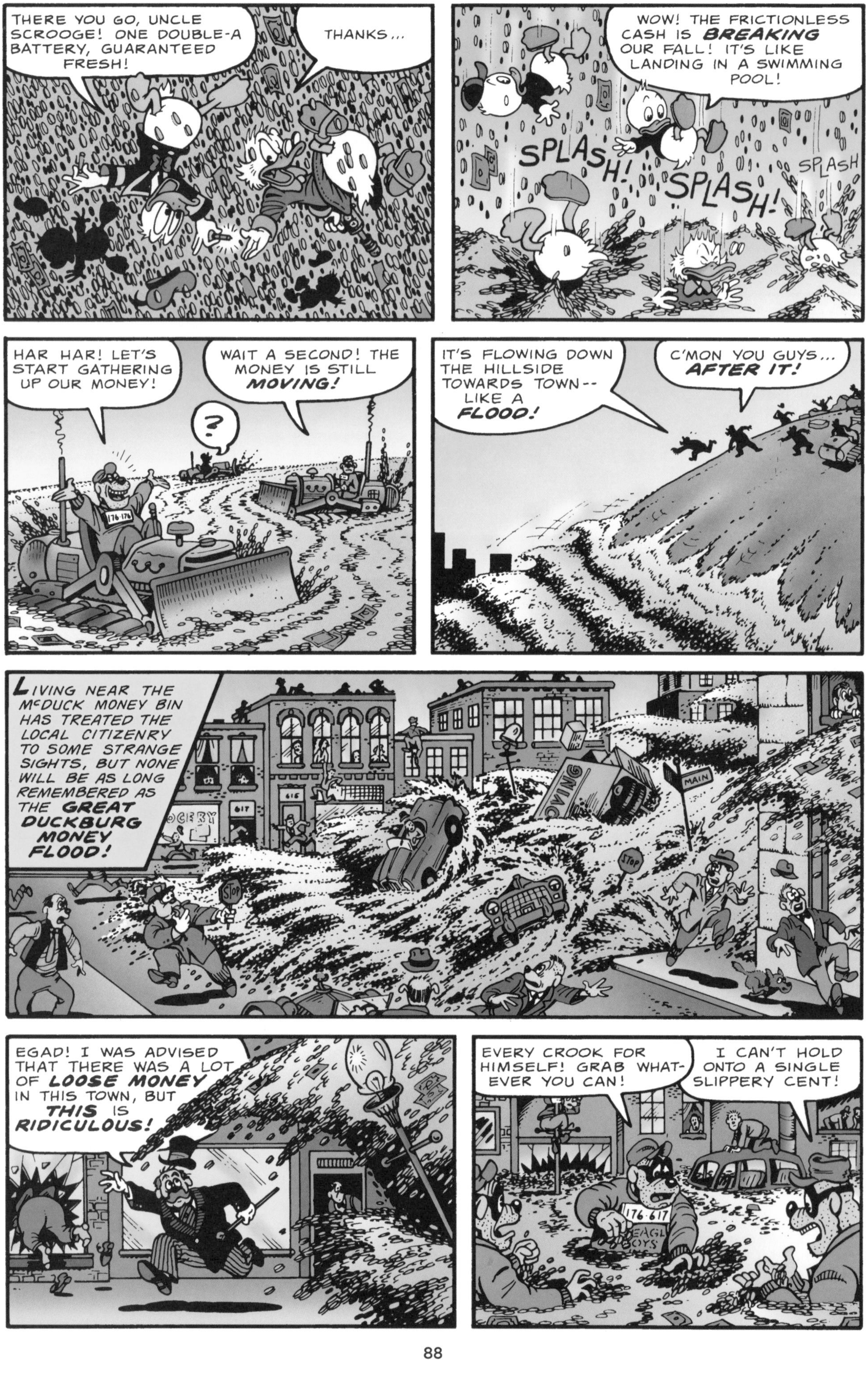
THERE YOU GO, UNCLE SCROOGE! ONE DOUBLE-A BATTERY, GUARANTEED FRESH!
THANKS...
WOW! THE FRICTIONLESS CASH IS BREAKING OUR FALL! IT'S LIKE LANDING IN A SWIMMING POOL!
SPLASH! SPLASH! SPLASH
HAR HAR! LET'S START GATHERING UP OUR MONEY!
WAIT A SECOND! THE MONEY IS STILL MOVING!
?
176-176
IT'S FLOWING DOWN THE HILLSIDE TOWARDS TOWN-- LIKE A FLOOD!
C'MON YOU GUYS... AFTER IT!
LIVING NEAR THE McDUCK MONEY BIN HAS TREATED THE LOCAL CITIZENRY TO SOME STRANGE SIGHTS, BUT NONE WILL BE AS LONG REMEMBERED AS THE GREAT DUCKBURG MONEY FLOOD!
617
615
MAIN
OVING
STOP
STOP
EGAD! I WAS ADVISED THAT THERE WAS A LOT OF LOOSE MONEY IN THIS TOWN, BUT THIS IS RIDICULOUS!
EVERY CROOK FOR HIMSELF! GRAB WHAT-EVER YOU CAN!
I CAN'T HOLD ONTO A SINGLE SLIPPERY CENT!
176-617

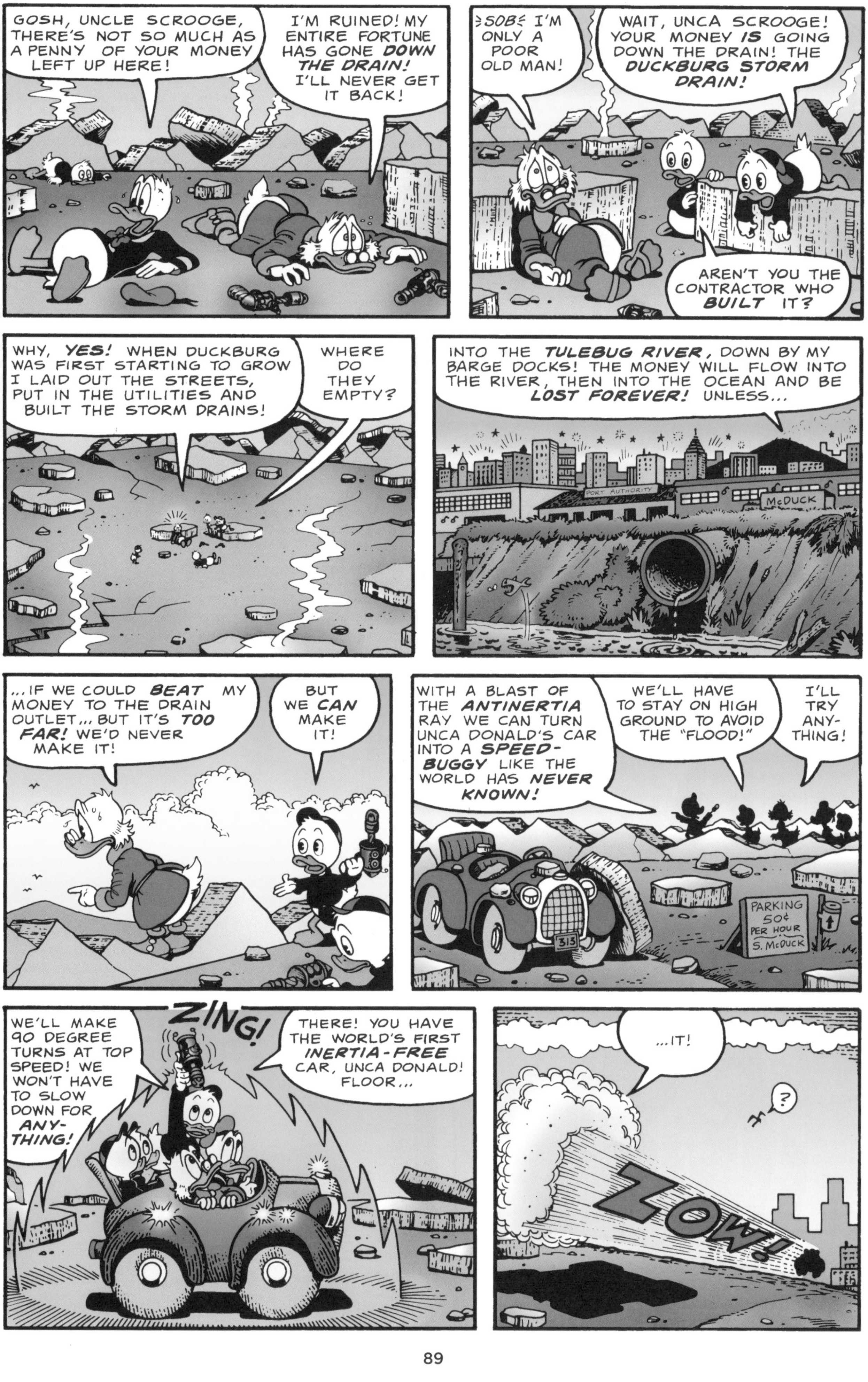
GOSH, UNCLE SCROOGE, THERE'S NOT SO MUCH AS A PENNY OF YOUR MONEY LEFT UP HERE!
I'M RUINED! MY ENTIRE FORTUNE HAS GONE DOWN THE DRAIN! I'LL NEVER GET IT BACK!
SOB I'M ONLY A POOR OLD MAN!
WAIT, UNCA SCROOGE! YOUR MONEY IS GOING DOWN THE DRAIN! THE DUCKBURG STORM DRAIN!
AREN'T YOU THE CONTRACTOR WHO BUILT IT?
WHY, YES! WHEN DUCKBURG WAS FIRST STARTING TO GROW I LAID OUT THE STREETS, PUT IN THE UTILITIES AND BUILT THE STORM DRAINS!
WHERE DO THEY EMPTY?
INTO THE TULEBUG RIVER, DOWN BY MY BARGE DOCKS! THE MONEY WILL FLOW INTO THE RIVER, THEN INTO THE OCEAN AND BE LOST FOREVER! UNLESS...
PORT AUTHORITY
McDUCK
...IF WE COULD BEAT MY MONEY TO THE DRAIN OUTLET... BUT IT'S TOO FAR! WE'D NEVER MAKE IT!
BUT WE CAN MAKE IT!
WITH A BLAST OF THE ANTINERTIA RAY WE CAN TURN UNCA DONALD'S CAR INTO A SPEED-BUGGY LIKE THE WORLD HAS NEVER KNOWN!
WE'LL HAVE TO STAY ON HIGH GROUND TO AVOID THE "FLOOD!"
I'LL TRY ANY-THING!
PARKING 50¢ PER HOUR S. McDUCK
313
WE'LL MAKE 90 DEGREE TURNS AT TOP SPEED! WE WON'T HAVE TO SLOW DOWN FOR ANY-THING!
ZING!
THERE! YOU HAVE THE WORLD'S FIRST INERTIA-FREE CAR, UNCA DONALD! FLOOR...
...IT!
?
ZOW!

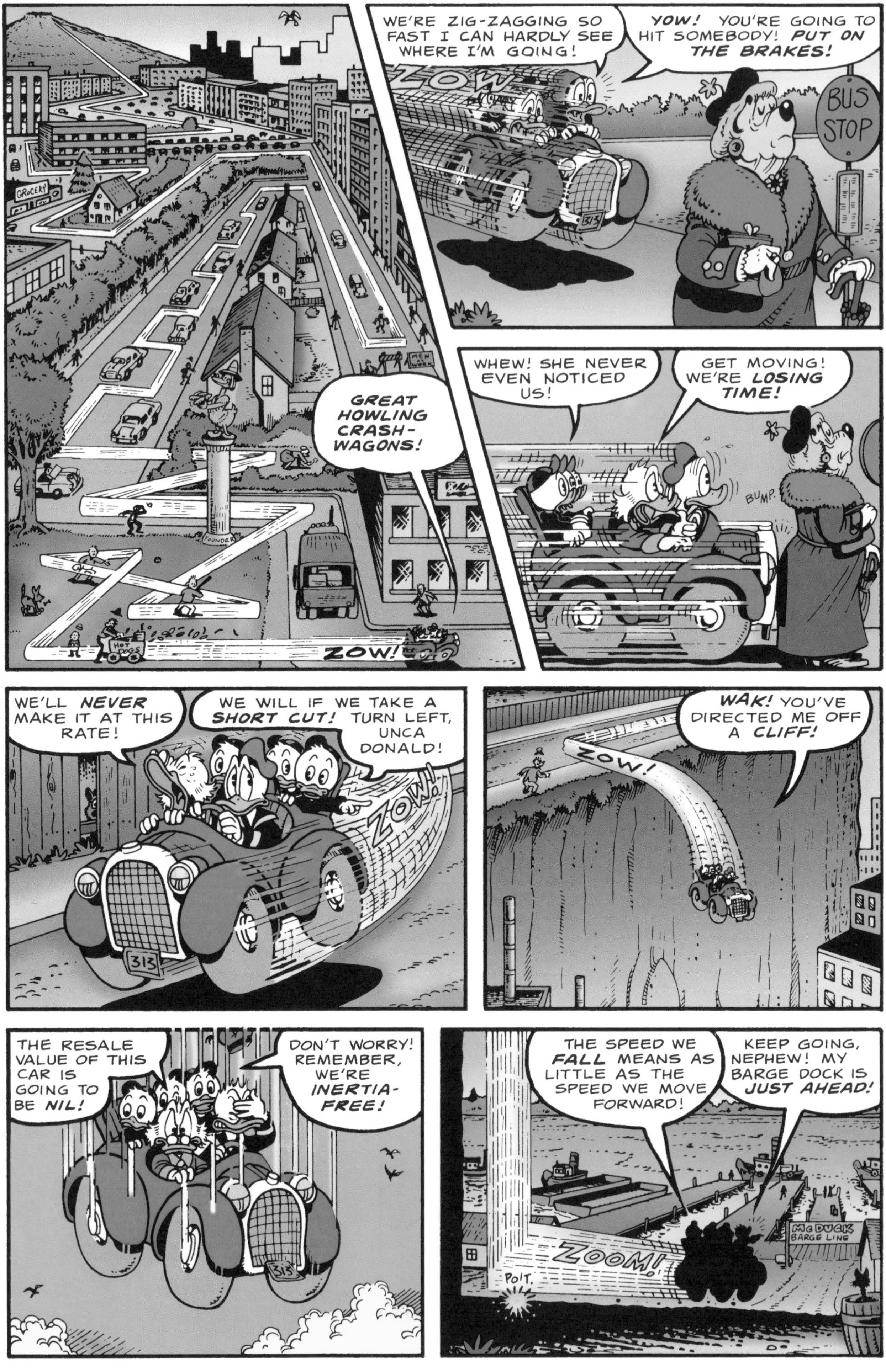
GROCERY
MEN AT WORK
FOUNDER
HOT DOGS
GREAT HOWLING CRASH-WAGONS!
ZOW!
WE'RE ZIG-ZAGGING SO FAST I CAN HARDLY SEE WHERE I'M GOING!
YOW! YOU'RE GOING TO HIT SOMEBODY! PUT ON THE BRAKES!
ZOW
BUS STOP
313
WHEW! SHE NEVER EVEN NOTICED US!
GET MOVING! WE'RE LOSING TIME!
BUMP.
WE'LL NEVER MAKE IT AT THIS RATE!
WE WILL IF WE TAKE A SHORT CUT! TURN LEFT, UNCA DONALD!
ZOW!
313
WAK! YOU'VE DIRECTED ME OFF A CLIFF!
ZOW!
THE RESALE VALUE OF THIS CAR IS GOING TO BE NIL!
DON'T WORRY! REMEMBER, WE'RE INERTIA-FREE!
313
THE SPEED WE FALL MEANS AS LITTLE AS THE SPEED WE MOVE FORWARD!
KEEP GOING, NEPHEW! MY BARGE DOCK IS JUST AHEAD!
McDUCK BARGE LINE
ZOOM!
POIT.

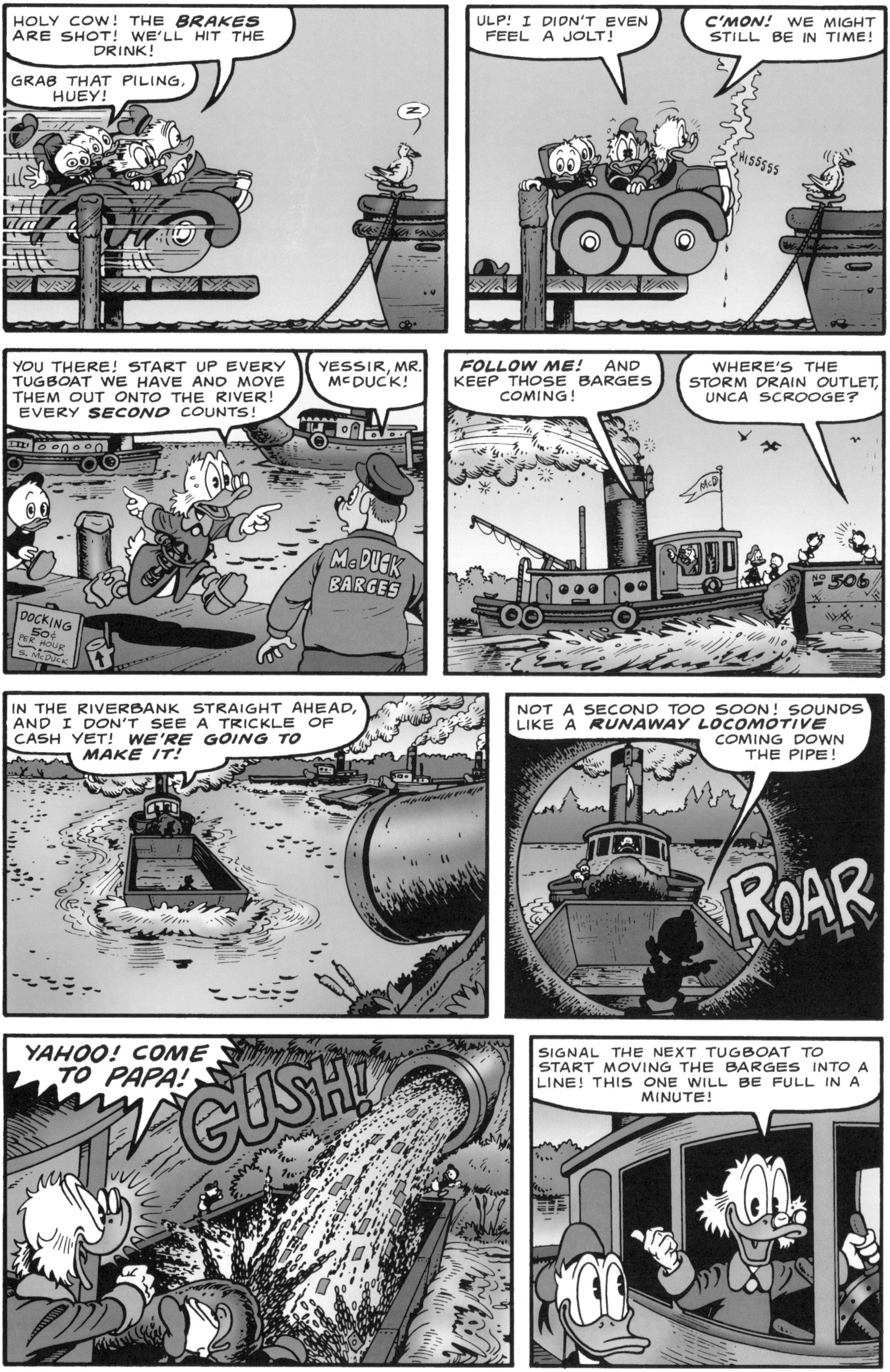
HOLY COW! THE BRAKES ARE SHOT! WE'LL HIT THE DRINK!
GRAB THAT PILING, HUEY!
Z
ULP! I DIDN'T EVEN FEEL A JOLT!
C'MON! WE MIGHT STILL BE IN TIME!
HISSSSS
YOU THERE! START UP EVERY TUGBOAT WE HAVE AND MOVE THEM OUT ONTO THE RIVER! EVERY SECOND COUNTS!
YESSIR, MR. McDUCK!
McDUCK BARGES
DOCKING 50¢ PER HOUR S. McDUCK
FOLLOW ME! AND KEEP THOSE BARGES COMING!
WHERE'S THE STORM DRAIN OUTLET, UNCA SCROOGE?
McD
No 506
IN THE RIVERBANK STRAIGHT AHEAD, AND I DON'T SEE A TRICKLE OF CASH YET! WE'RE GOING TO MAKE IT!
NOT A SECOND TOO SOON! SOUNDS LIKE A RUNAWAY LOCOMOTIVE COMING DOWN THE PIPE!
ROAR
YAHOO! COME TO PAPA!
GUSH!
SIGNAL THE NEXT TUGBOAT TO START MOVING THE BARGES INTO A LINE! THIS ONE WILL BE FULL IN A MINUTE!

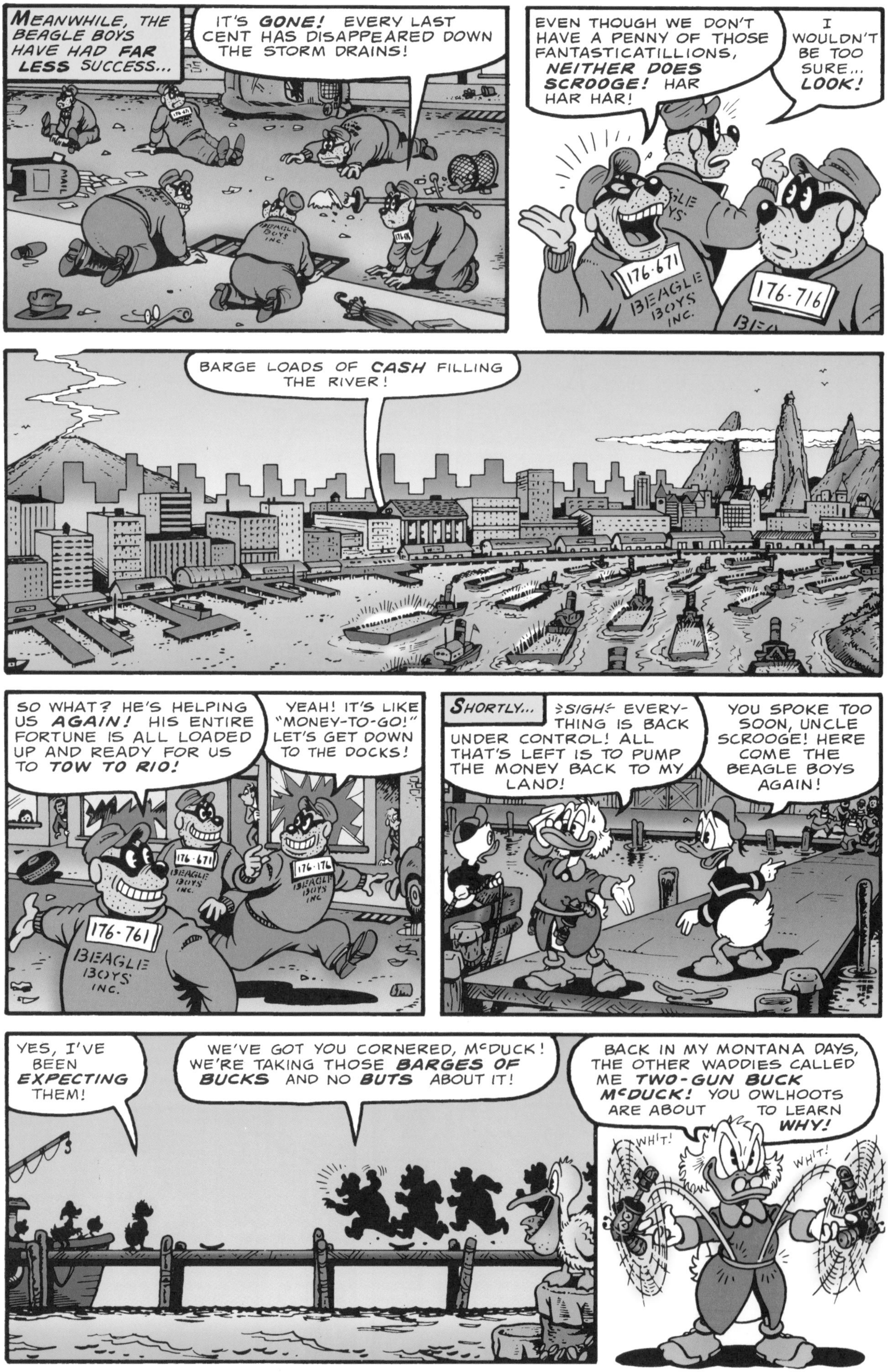
MEANWHILE, THE BEAGLE BOYS HAVE HAD FAR LESS SUCCESS...
IT'S GONE! EVERY LAST CENT HAS DISAPPEARED DOWN THE STORM DRAINS!
MAIL
EVEN THOUGH WE DON'T HAVE A PENNY OF THOSE FANTASTICATILLIONS, NEITHER DOES SCROOGE! HAR HAR HAR!
I WOULDN'T BE TOO SURE... LOOK!
176-671
BEAGLE BOYS INC.
176-716
BARGE LOADS OF CASH FILLING THE RIVER!
SO WHAT? HE'S HELPING US AGAIN! HIS ENTIRE FORTUNE IS ALL LOADED UP AND READY FOR US TO TOW TO RIO!
YEAH! IT'S LIKE "MONEY-TO-GO!" LET'S GET DOWN TO THE DOCKS!
176-671
176-176
176-761
BEAGLE BOYS INC.
SHORTLY...
⪢SIGH⪡ EVERY-THING IS BACK UNDER CONTROL! ALL THAT'S LEFT IS TO PUMP THE MONEY BACK TO MY LAND!
YOU SPOKE TOO SOON, UNCLE SCROOGE! HERE COME THE BEAGLE BOYS AGAIN!
YES, I'VE BEEN EXPECTING THEM!
WE'VE GOT YOU CORNERED, McDUCK! WE'RE TAKING THOSE BARGES OF BUCKS AND NO BUTS ABOUT IT!
BACK IN MY MONTANA DAYS, THE OTHER WADDIES CALLED ME TWO-GUN BUCK McDUCK! YOU OWLHOOTS ARE ABOUT TO LEARN WHY!
WH'T!
WH'T!

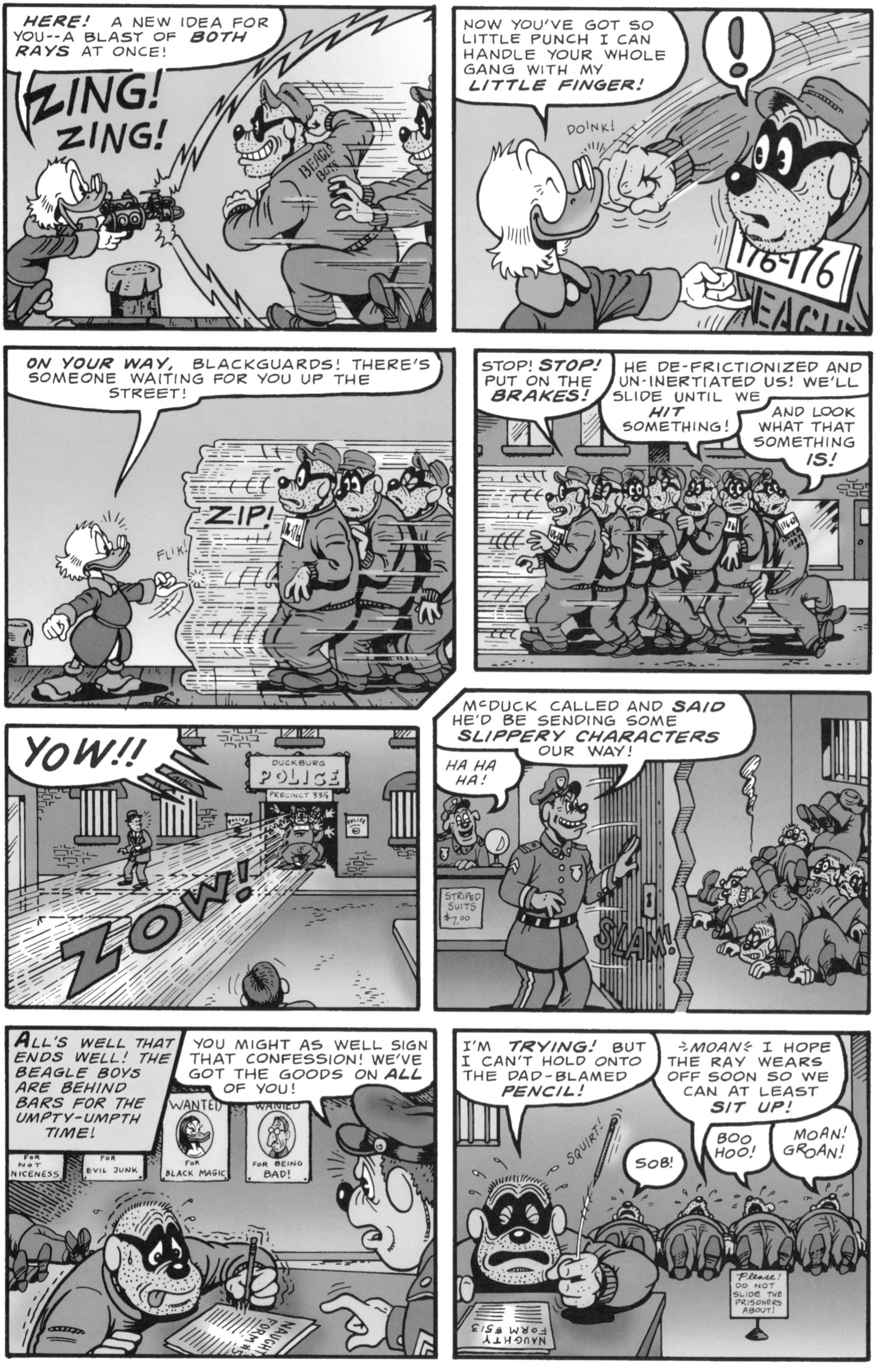
HERE! A NEW IDEA FOR YOU--A BLAST OF BOTH RAYS AT ONCE!
ZING! ZING!
BEAGLE BOYS
NOW YOU'VE GOT SO LITTLE PUNCH I CAN HANDLE YOUR WHOLE GANG WITH MY LITTLE FINGER!
!
DOINK!
176-176
ON YOUR WAY, BLACKGUARDS! THERE'S SOMEONE WAITING FOR YOU UP THE STREET!
ZIP!
FLIK!
STOP! STOP! PUT ON THE BRAKES!
HE DE-FRICTIONIZED AND UN-INERTIATED US! WE'LL SLIDE UNTIL WE HIT SOMETHING!
AND LOOK WHAT THAT SOMETHING IS!
YOW!!
DUCKBURG POLICE
PRECINCT 33½
ZOW!
McDUCK CALLED AND SAID HE'D BE SENDING SOME SLIPPERY CHARACTERS OUR WAY!
HA HA HA!
STRIPED SUITS $7.00
SLAM!
ALL'S WELL THAT ENDS WELL! THE BEAGLE BOYS ARE BEHIND BARS FOR THE UMPTY-UMPTH TIME!
YOU MIGHT AS WELL SIGN THAT CONFESSION! WE'VE GOT THE GOODS ON ALL OF YOU!
WANTED FOR BLACK MAGIC
WANTED FOR BEING BAD!
FOR NOT NICENESS
FOR EVIL JUNK
NAUGHTY FORM #
I'M TRYING! BUT I CAN'T HOLD ONTO THE DAD-BLAMED PENCIL!
SQUIRT!
≈MOAN≈ I HOPE THE RAY WEARS OFF SOON SO WE CAN AT LEAST SIT UP!
SOB!
BOO HOO!
MOAN! GROAN!
Please! DO NOT SLIDE THE PRISONERS ABOUT!
NAUGHTY FORM #513

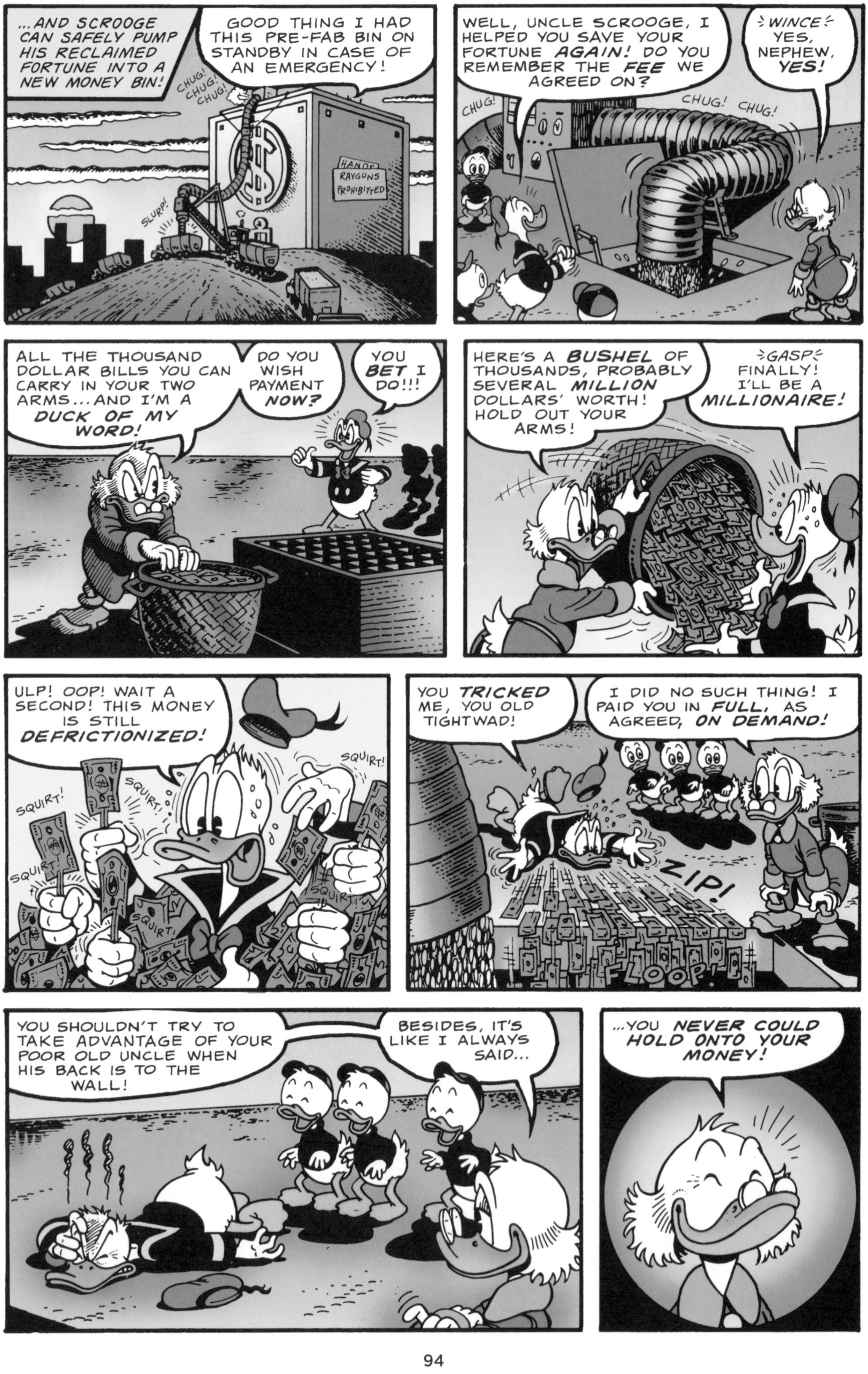
...AND SCROOGE CAN SAFELY PUMP HIS RECLAIMED FORTUNE INTO A NEW MONEY BIN!
GOOD THING I HAD THIS PRE-FAB BIN ON STANDBY IN CASE OF AN EMERGENCY!
CHUG! CHUG! CHUG!
SLURP!
RAYGUNS PROHIBITTED
WELL, UNCLE SCROOGE, I HELPED YOU SAVE YOUR FORTUNE AGAIN! DO YOU REMEMBER THE FEE WE AGREED ON?
WINCE YES, NEPHEW, YES!
CHUG! CHUG! CHUG!
ALL THE THOUSAND DOLLAR BILLS YOU CAN CARRY IN YOUR TWO ARMS... AND I'M A DUCK OF MY WORD!
DO YOU WISH PAYMENT NOW?
YOU BET I DO!!!
HERE'S A BUSHEL OF THOUSANDS, PROBABLY SEVERAL MILLION DOLLARS' WORTH! HOLD OUT YOUR ARMS!
GASP FINALLY! I'LL BE A MILLIONAIRE!
ULP! OOP! WAIT A SECOND! THIS MONEY IS STILL DEFRICTIONIZED!
SQUIRT! SQUIRT! SQUIRT! SQUIRT! SQUIRT! SQUIRT! SQUIRT!
YOU TRICKED ME, YOU OLD TIGHTWAD!
I DID NO SUCH THING! I PAID YOU IN FULL, AS AGREED, ON DEMAND!
ZIP!
FLOOP!
YOU SHOULDN'T TRY TO TAKE ADVANTAGE OF YOUR POOR OLD UNCLE WHEN HIS BACK IS TO THE WALL!
BESIDES, IT'S LIKE I ALWAYS SAID...
...YOU NEVER COULD HOLD ONTO YOUR MONEY!

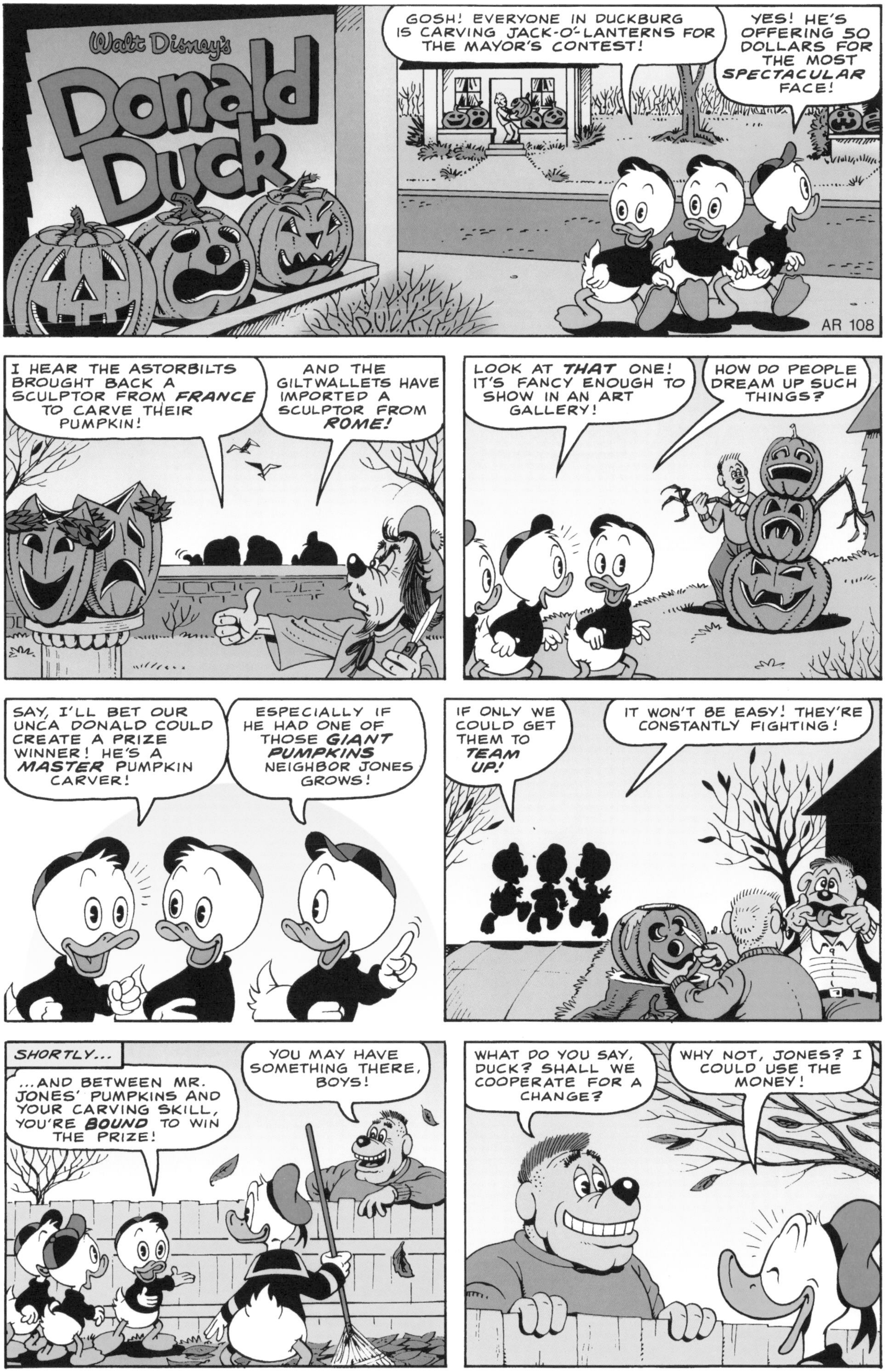

Walt Disney's
Donald Duck
GOSH! EVERYONE IN DUCKBURG IS CARVING JACK-O'-LANTERNS FOR THE MAYOR'S CONTEST!
YES! HE'S OFFERING 50 DOLLARS FOR THE MOST SPECTACULAR FACE!
AR 108
I HEAR THE ASTORBILTS BROUGHT BACK A SCULPTOR FROM FRANCE TO CARVE THEIR PUMPKIN!
AND THE GILTWALLETS HAVE IMPORTED A SCULPTOR FROM ROME!
LOOK AT THAT ONE! IT'S FANCY ENOUGH TO SHOW IN AN ART GALLERY!
HOW DO PEOPLE DREAM UP SUCH THINGS?
SAY, I'LL BET OUR UNCA DONALD COULD CREATE A PRIZE WINNER! HE'S A MASTER PUMPKIN CARVER!
ESPECIALLY IF HE HAD ONE OF THOSE GIANT PUMPKINS NEIGHBOR JONES GROWS!
IF ONLY WE COULD GET THEM TO TEAM UP!
IT WON'T BE EASY! THEY'RE CONSTANTLY FIGHTING!
SHORTLY...
...AND BETWEEN MR. JONES' PUMPKINS AND YOUR CARVING SKILL, YOU'RE BOUND TO WIN THE PRIZE!
YOU MAY HAVE SOMETHING THERE, BOYS!
WHAT DO YOU SAY, DUCK? SHALL WE COOPERATE FOR A CHANGE?
WHY NOT, JONES? I COULD USE THE MONEY!

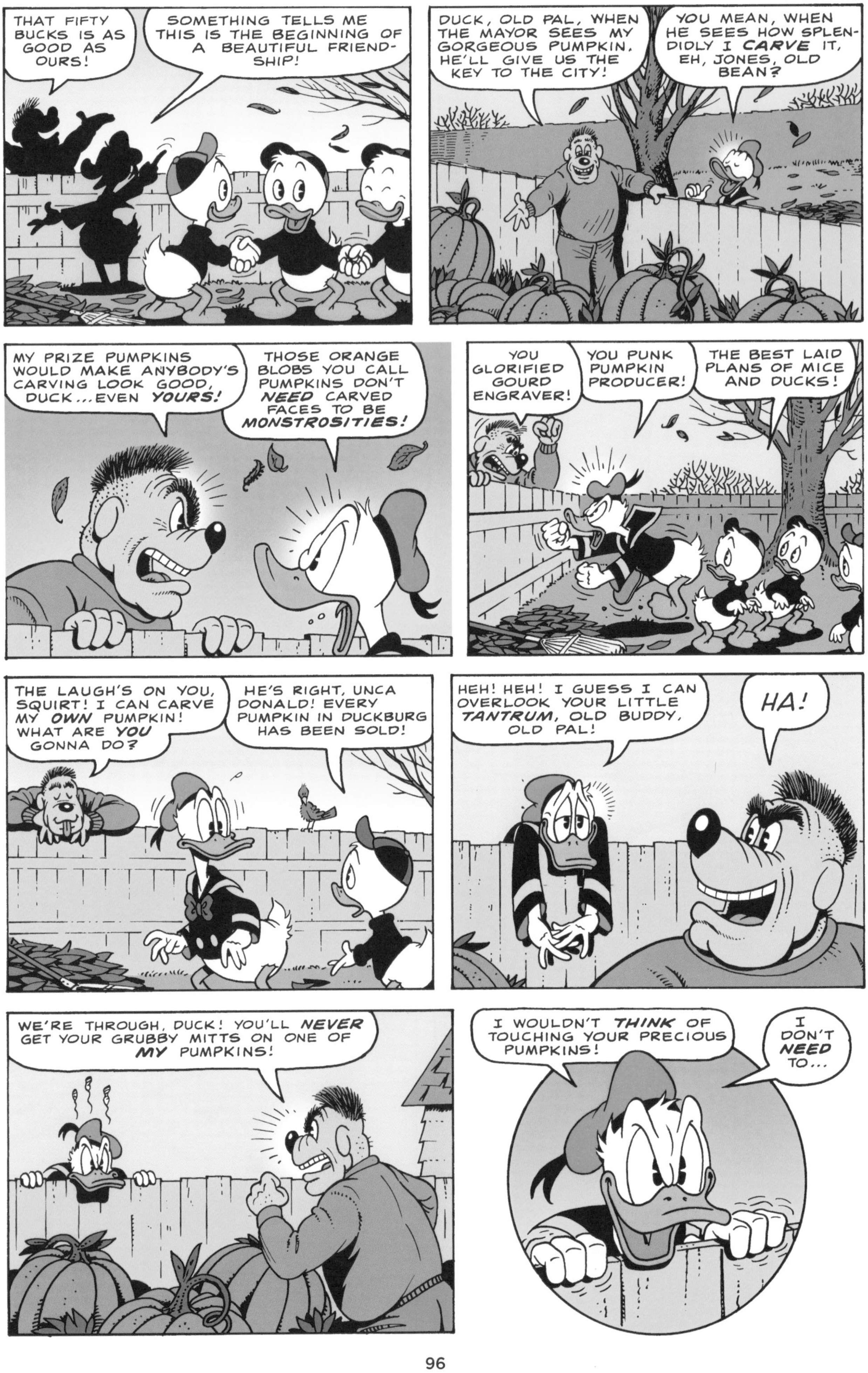
THAT FIFTY BUCKS IS AS GOOD AS OURS!
SOMETHING TELLS ME THIS IS THE BEGINNING OF A BEAUTIFUL FRIEND-SHIP!
DUCK, OLD PAL, WHEN THE MAYOR SEES MY GORGEOUS PUMPKIN, HE'LL GIVE US THE KEY TO THE CITY!
YOU MEAN, WHEN HE SEES HOW SPLEN-DIDLY I CARVE IT, EH, JONES, OLD BEAN?
MY PRIZE PUMPKINS WOULD MAKE ANYBODY'S CARVING LOOK GOOD, DUCK... EVEN YOURS!
THOSE ORANGE BLOBS YOU CALL PUMPKINS DON'T NEED CARVED FACES TO BE MONSTROSITIES!
YOU GLORIFIED GOURD ENGRAVER!
YOU PUNK PUMPKIN PRODUCER!
THE BEST LAID PLANS OF MICE AND DUCKS!
THE LAUGH'S ON YOU, SQUIRT! I CAN CARVE MY OWN PUMPKIN! WHAT ARE YOU GONNA DO?
HE'S RIGHT, UNCA DONALD! EVERY PUMPKIN IN DUCKBURG HAS BEEN SOLD!
HEH! HEH! I GUESS I CAN OVERLOOK YOUR LITTLE TANTRUM, OLD BUDDY, OLD PAL!
HA!
WE'RE THROUGH, DUCK! YOU'LL NEVER GET YOUR GRUBBY MITTS ON ONE OF MY PUMPKINS!
I WOULDN'T THINK OF TOUCHING YOUR PRECIOUS PUMPKINS!
I DON'T NEED TO...

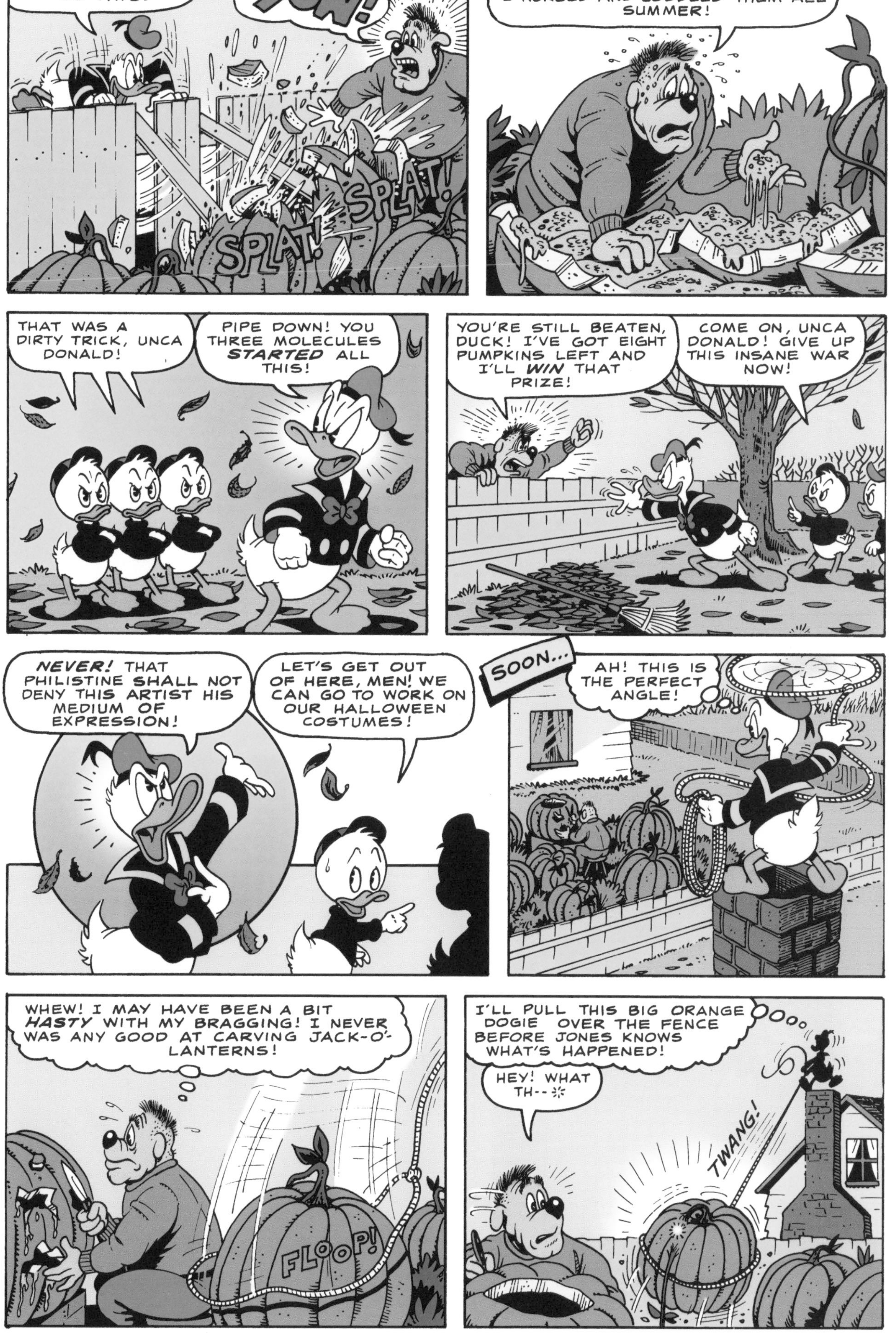
...NOT WHEN I CAN DO THIS!
YOW!
SPLAT! SPLAT!
MY POOR, POOR PUMPKINS! SOB I NURSED AND CODDLED THEM ALL SUMMER!
THAT WAS A DIRTY TRICK, UNCA DONALD!
PIPE DOWN! YOU THREE MOLECULES STARTED ALL THIS!
YOU'RE STILL BEATEN, DUCK! I'VE GOT EIGHT PUMPKINS LEFT AND I'LL WIN THAT PRIZE!
COME ON, UNCA DONALD! GIVE UP THIS INSANE WAR NOW!
NEVER! THAT PHILISTINE SHALL NOT DENY THIS ARTIST HIS MEDIUM OF EXPRESSION!
LET'S GET OUT OF HERE, MEN! WE CAN GO TO WORK ON OUR HALLOWEEN COSTUMES!
SOON...
AH! THIS IS THE PERFECT ANGLE!
WHEW! I MAY HAVE BEEN A BIT HASTY WITH MY BRAGGING! I NEVER WAS ANY GOOD AT CARVING JACK-O'-LANTERNS!
FLOOP!
I'LL PULL THIS BIG ORANGE DOGIE OVER THE FENCE BEFORE JONES KNOWS WHAT'S HAPPENED!
HEY! WHAT TH--
TWANG!

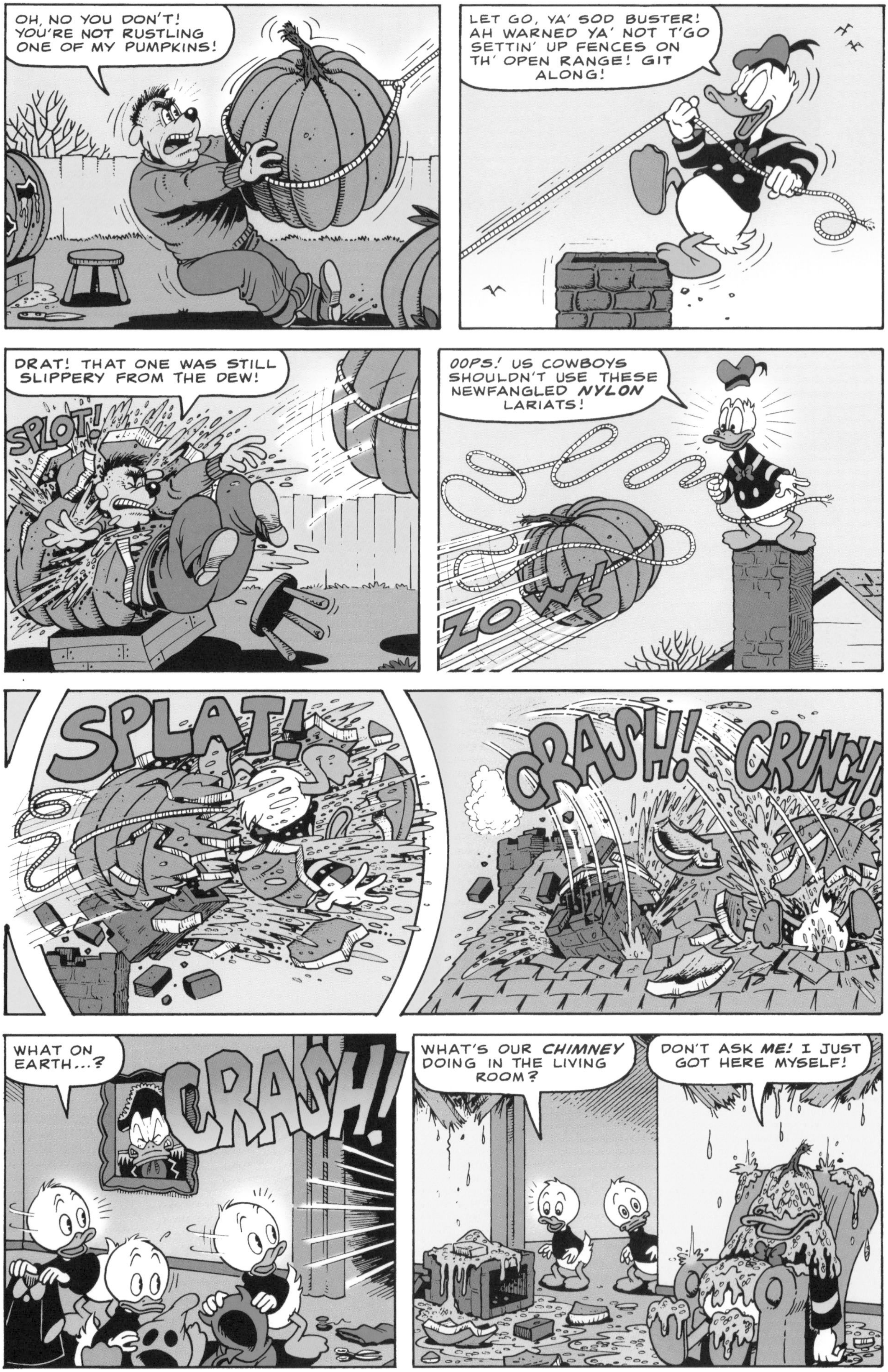
OH, NO YOU DON'T! YOU'RE NOT RUSTLING ONE OF MY PUMPKINS!
LET GO, YA' SOD BUSTER! AH WARNED YA' NOT T'GO SETTIN' UP FENCES ON TH' OPEN RANGE! GIT ALONG!
DRAT! THAT ONE WAS STILL SLIPPERY FROM THE DEW!
SPLOT!
OOPS! US COWBOYS SHOULDN'T USE THESE NEWFANGLED NYLON LARIATS!
ZOW!
SPLAT!
CRASH!
CRUNCH!
WHAT ON EARTH...?
CRASH!
WHAT'S OUR CHIMNEY DOING IN THE LIVING ROOM?
DON'T ASK ME! I JUST GOT HERE MYSELF!

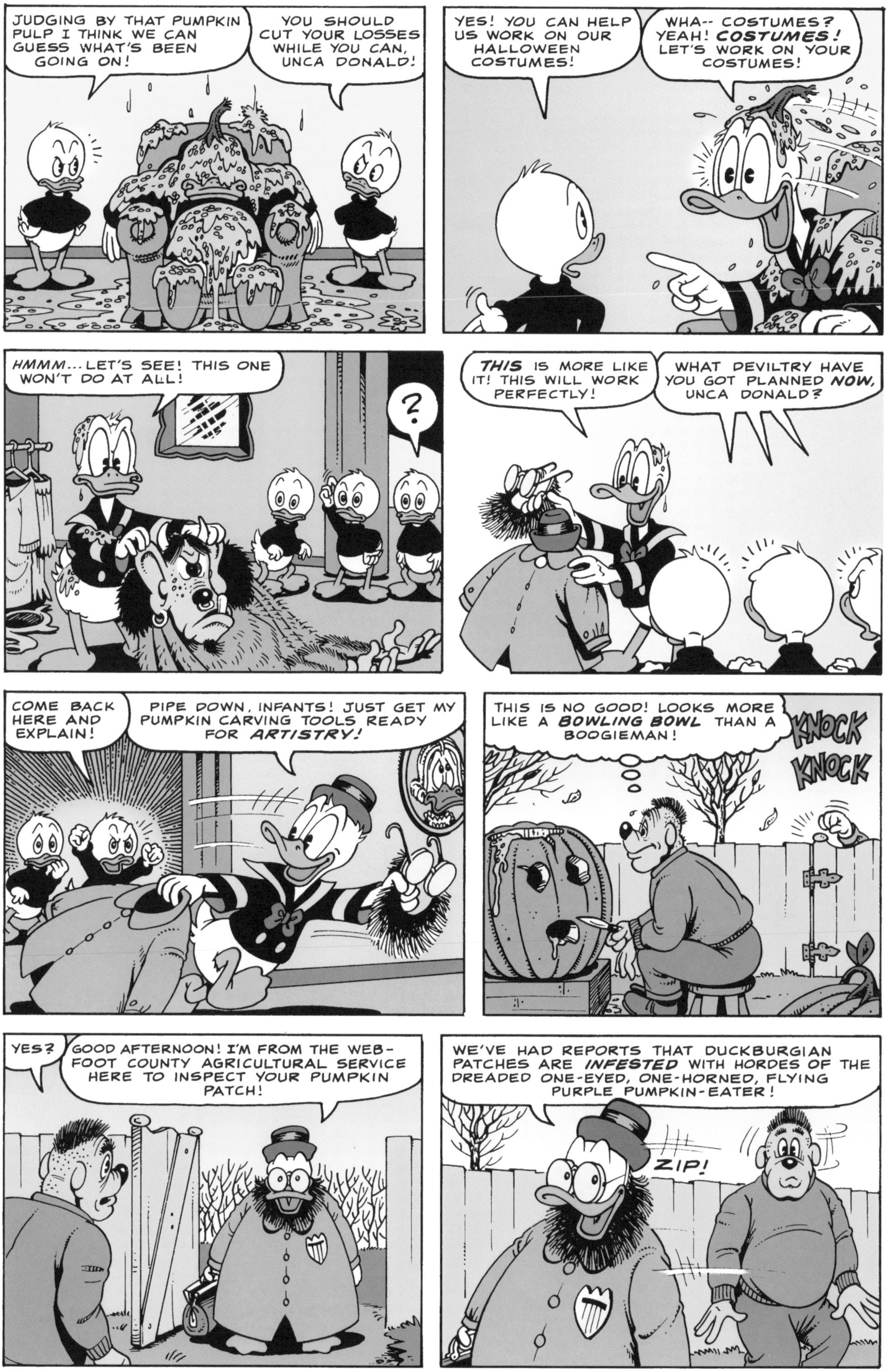
JUDGING BY THAT PUMPKIN PULP I THINK WE CAN GUESS WHAT'S BEEN GOING ON!
YOU SHOULD CUT YOUR LOSSES WHILE YOU CAN, UNCA DONALD!
YES! YOU CAN HELP US WORK ON OUR HALLOWEEN COSTUMES!
WHA-- COSTUMES? YEAH! COSTUMES! LET'S WORK ON YOUR COSTUMES!
HMMM... LET'S SEE! THIS ONE WON'T DO AT ALL!
?
THIS IS MORE LIKE IT! THIS WILL WORK PERFECTLY!
WHAT DEVILTRY HAVE YOU GOT PLANNED NOW, UNCA DONALD?
COME BACK HERE AND EXPLAIN!
PIPE DOWN, INFANTS! JUST GET MY PUMPKIN CARVING TOOLS READY FOR ARTISTRY!
THIS IS NO GOOD! LOOKS MORE LIKE A BOWLING BOWL THAN A BOOGIEMAN!
KNOCK
KNOCK
YES?
GOOD AFTERNOON! I'M FROM THE WEB-FOOT COUNTY AGRICULTURAL SERVICE HERE TO INSPECT YOUR PUMPKIN PATCH!
WE'VE HAD REPORTS THAT DUCKBURGIAN PATCHES ARE INFESTED WITH HORDES OF THE DREADED ONE-EYED, ONE-HORNED, FLYING PURPLE PUMPKIN-EATER!
ZIP!

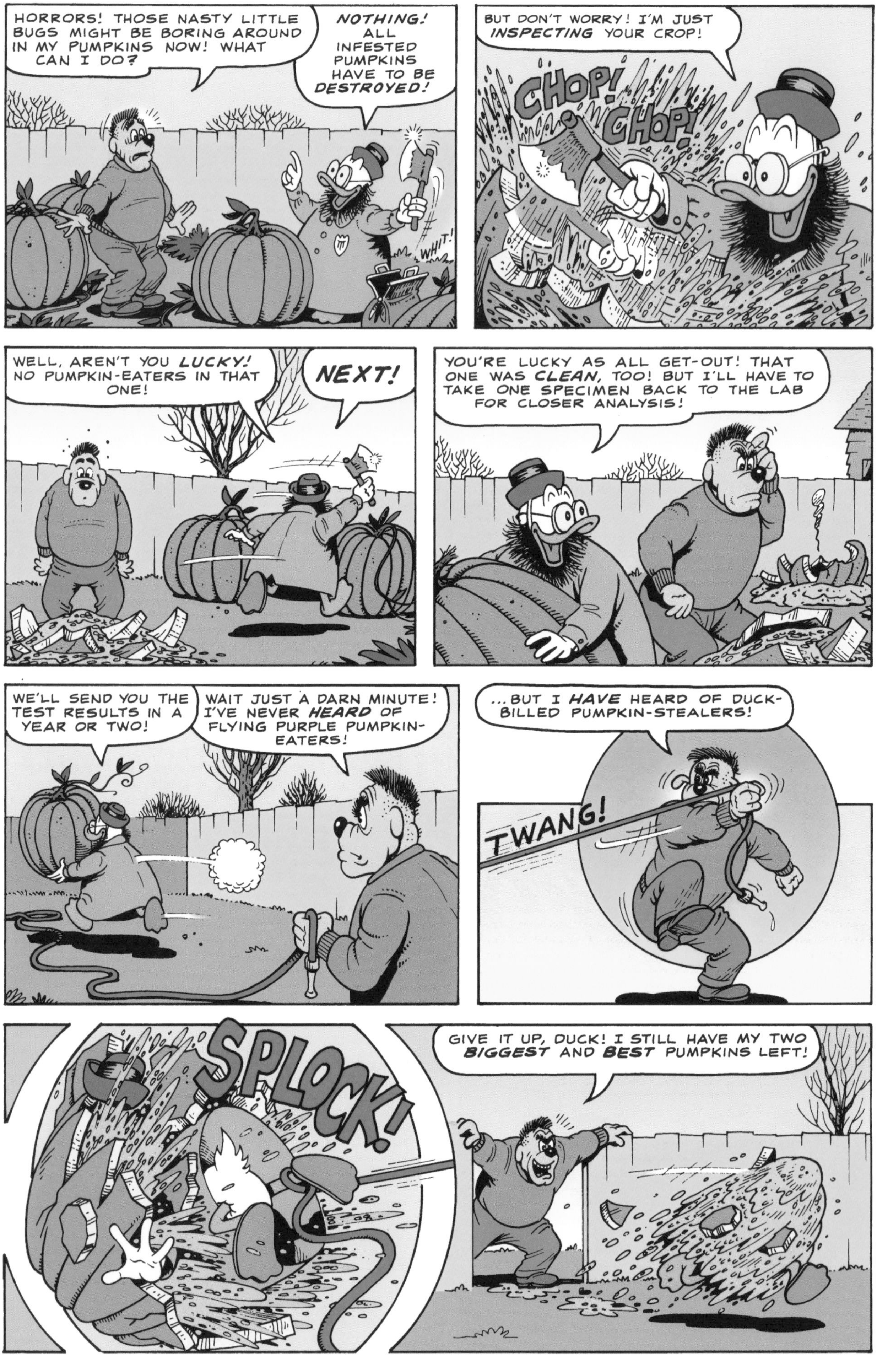
HORRORS! THOSE NASTY LITTLE BUGS MIGHT BE BORING AROUND IN MY PUMPKINS NOW! WHAT CAN I DO?
NOTHING! ALL INFESTED PUMPKINS HAVE TO BE DESTROYED!
WHIT!
BUT DON'T WORRY! I'M JUST INSPECTING YOUR CROP!
CHOP! CHOP!
WELL, AREN'T YOU LUCKY! NO PUMPKIN-EATERS IN THAT ONE!
NEXT!
YOU'RE LUCKY AS ALL GET-OUT! THAT ONE WAS CLEAN, TOO! BUT I'LL HAVE TO TAKE ONE SPECIMEN BACK TO THE LAB FOR CLOSER ANALYSIS!
WE'LL SEND YOU THE TEST RESULTS IN A YEAR OR TWO!
WAIT JUST A DARN MINUTE! I'VE NEVER HEARD OF FLYING PURPLE PUMPKIN-EATERS!
...BUT I HAVE HEARD OF DUCK-BILLED PUMPKIN-STEALERS!
TWANG!
SPLOCK!
GIVE IT UP, DUCK! I STILL HAVE MY TWO BIGGEST AND BEST PUMPKINS LEFT!

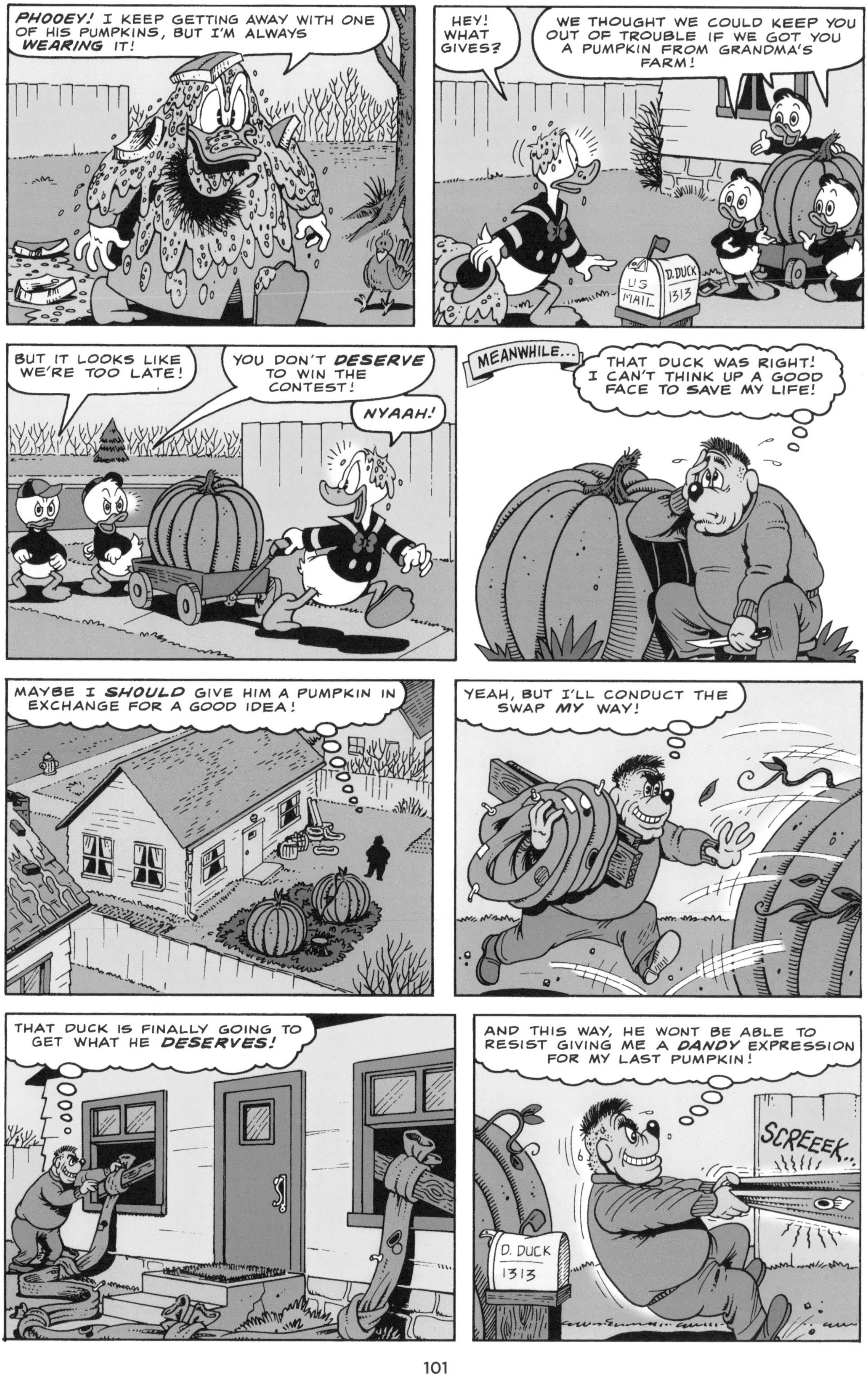
PHOOEY! I KEEP GETTING AWAY WITH ONE OF HIS PUMPKINS, BUT I'M ALWAYS WEARING IT!
HEY! WHAT GIVES?
WE THOUGHT WE COULD KEEP YOU OUT OF TROUBLE IF WE GOT YOU A PUMPKIN FROM GRANDMA'S FARM!
D. DUCK 1313
US MAIL
BUT IT LOOKS LIKE WE'RE TOO LATE!
YOU DON'T DESERVE TO WIN THE CONTEST!
NYAAH!
MEANWHILE...
THAT DUCK WAS RIGHT! I CAN'T THINK UP A GOOD FACE TO SAVE MY LIFE!
MAYBE I SHOULD GIVE HIM A PUMPKIN IN EXCHANGE FOR A GOOD IDEA!
YEAH, BUT I'LL CONDUCT THE SWAP MY WAY!
THAT DUCK IS FINALLY GOING TO GET WHAT HE DESERVES!
AND THIS WAY, HE WONT BE ABLE TO RESIST GIVING ME A DANDY EXPRESSION FOR MY LAST PUMPKIN!
SCREEEK...
D. DUCK 1313

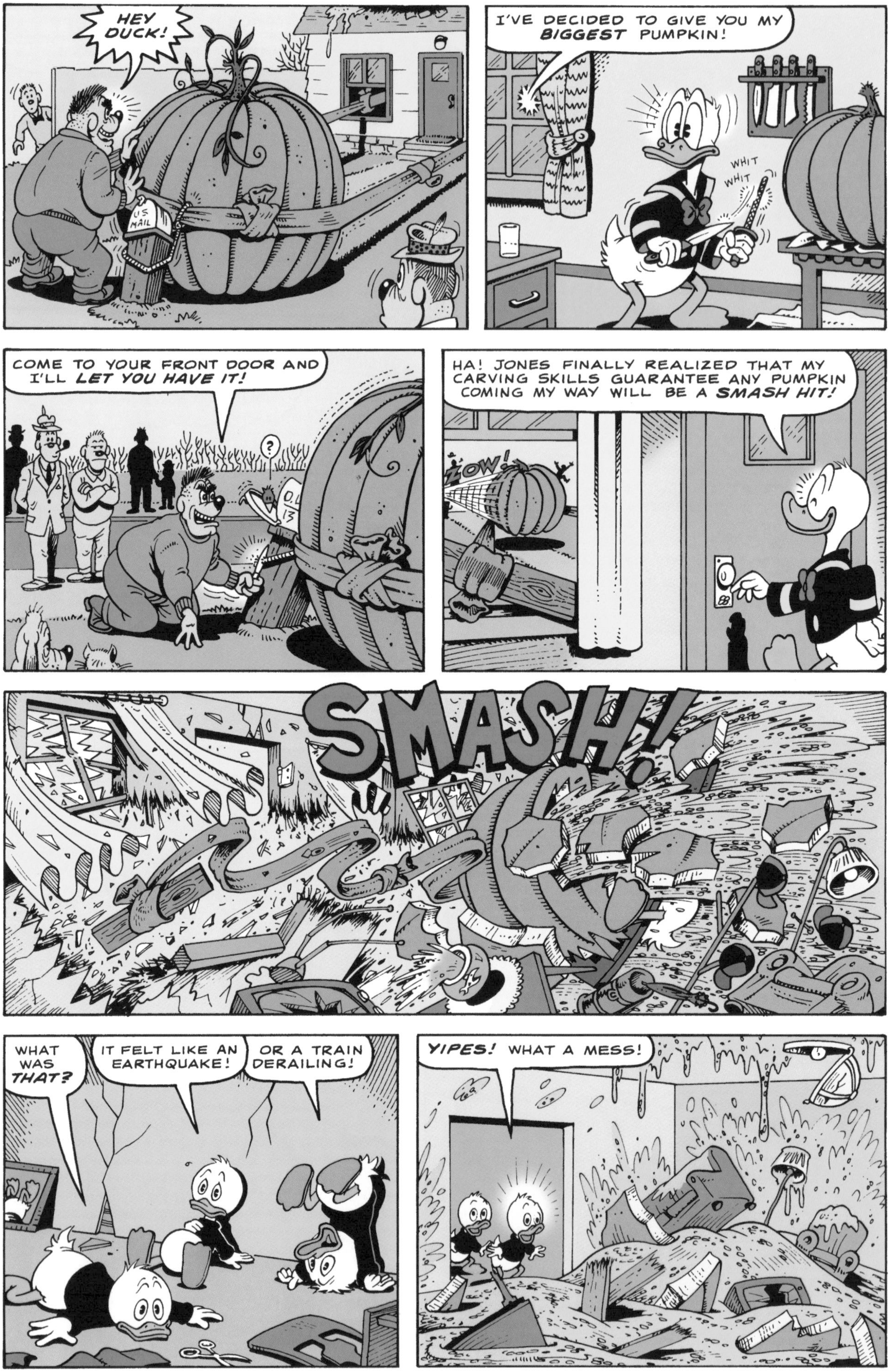
HEY DUCK!
I'VE DECIDED TO GIVE YOU MY BIGGEST PUMPKIN!
WHIT WHIT
U.S. MAIL
COME TO YOUR FRONT DOOR AND I'LL LET YOU HAVE IT!
?
HA! JONES FINALLY REALIZED THAT MY CARVING SKILLS GUARANTEE ANY PUMPKIN COMING MY WAY WILL BE A SMASH HIT!
ZOW!
SMASH!
WHAT WAS THAT?
IT FELT LIKE AN EARTHQUAKE!
OR A TRAIN DERAILING!
YIPES! WHAT A MESS!

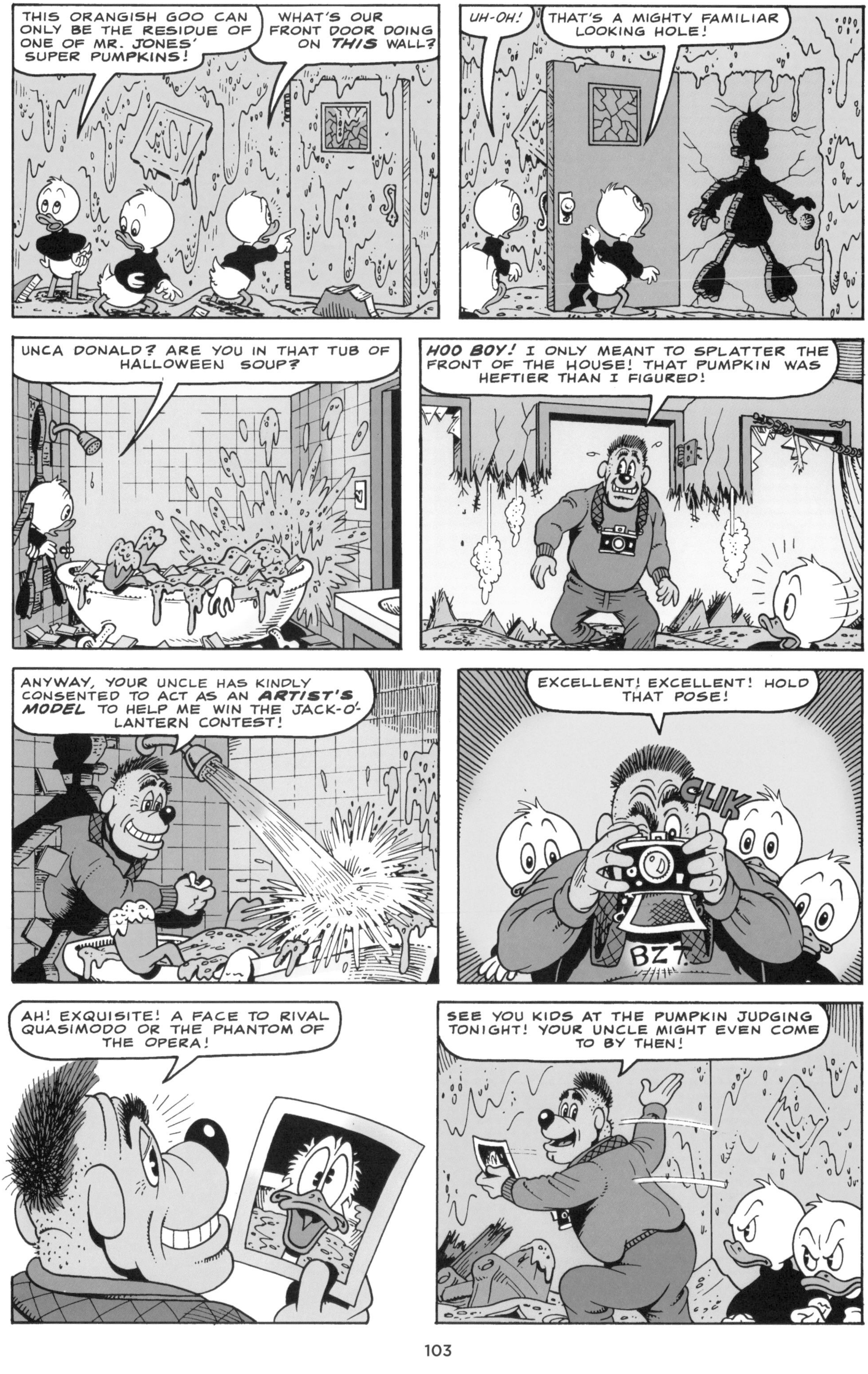
THIS ORANGISH GOO CAN ONLY BE THE RESIDUE OF ONE OF MR. JONES' SUPER PUMPKINS!
WHAT'S OUR FRONT DOOR DOING ON THIS WALL?
UH-OH!
THAT'S A MIGHTY FAMILIAR LOOKING HOLE!
UNCA DONALD? ARE YOU IN THAT TUB OF HALLOWEEN SOUP?
HOO BOY! I ONLY MEANT TO SPLATTER THE FRONT OF THE HOUSE! THAT PUMPKIN WAS HEFTIER THAN I FIGURED!
ANYWAY, YOUR UNCLE HAS KINDLY CONSENTED TO ACT AS AN ARTIST'S MODEL TO HELP ME WIN THE JACK-O'-LANTERN CONTEST!
EXCELLENT! EXCELLENT! HOLD THAT POSE!
CLIK
BZZT
AH! EXQUISITE! A FACE TO RIVAL QUASIMODO OR THE PHANTOM OF THE OPERA!
SEE YOU KIDS AT THE PUMPKIN JUDGING TONIGHT! YOUR UNCLE MIGHT EVEN COME TO BY THEN!

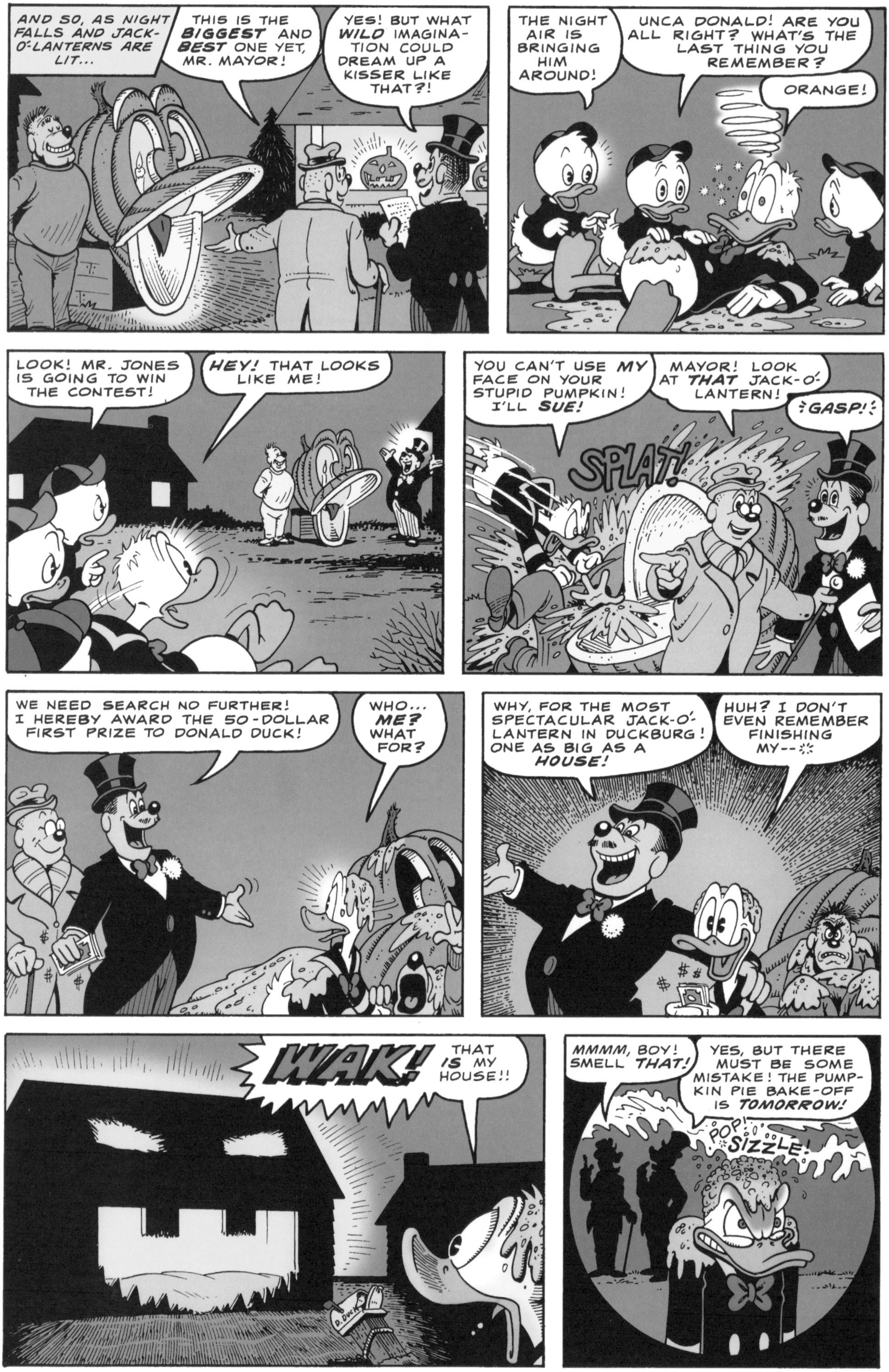
AND SO, AS NIGHT FALLS AND JACK-O'-LANTERNS ARE LIT...
THIS IS THE BIGGEST AND BEST ONE YET, MR. MAYOR!
YES! BUT WHAT WILD IMAGINATION COULD DREAM UP A KISSER LIKE THAT?!
THE NIGHT AIR IS BRINGING HIM AROUND!
UNCA DONALD! ARE YOU ALL RIGHT? WHAT'S THE LAST THING YOU REMEMBER?
ORANGE!
LOOK! MR. JONES IS GOING TO WIN THE CONTEST!
HEY! THAT LOOKS LIKE ME!
YOU CAN'T USE MY FACE ON YOUR STUPID PUMPKIN! I'LL SUE!
SPLAT!
MAYOR! LOOK AT THAT JACK-O'-LANTERN!
GASP!
WE NEED SEARCH NO FURTHER! I HEREBY AWARD THE 50-DOLLAR FIRST PRIZE TO DONALD DUCK!
WHO... ME? WHAT FOR?
WHY, FOR THE MOST SPECTACULAR JACK-O'-LANTERN IN DUCKBURG! ONE AS BIG AS A HOUSE!
HUH? I DON'T EVEN REMEMBER FINISHING MY--
WAK!
THAT IS MY HOUSE!!
D. DUCK
MMMM, BOY! SMELL THAT!
YES, BUT THERE MUST BE SOME MISTAKE! THE PUMPKIN PIE BAKE-OFF IS TOMORROW!
POP
SIZZLE!

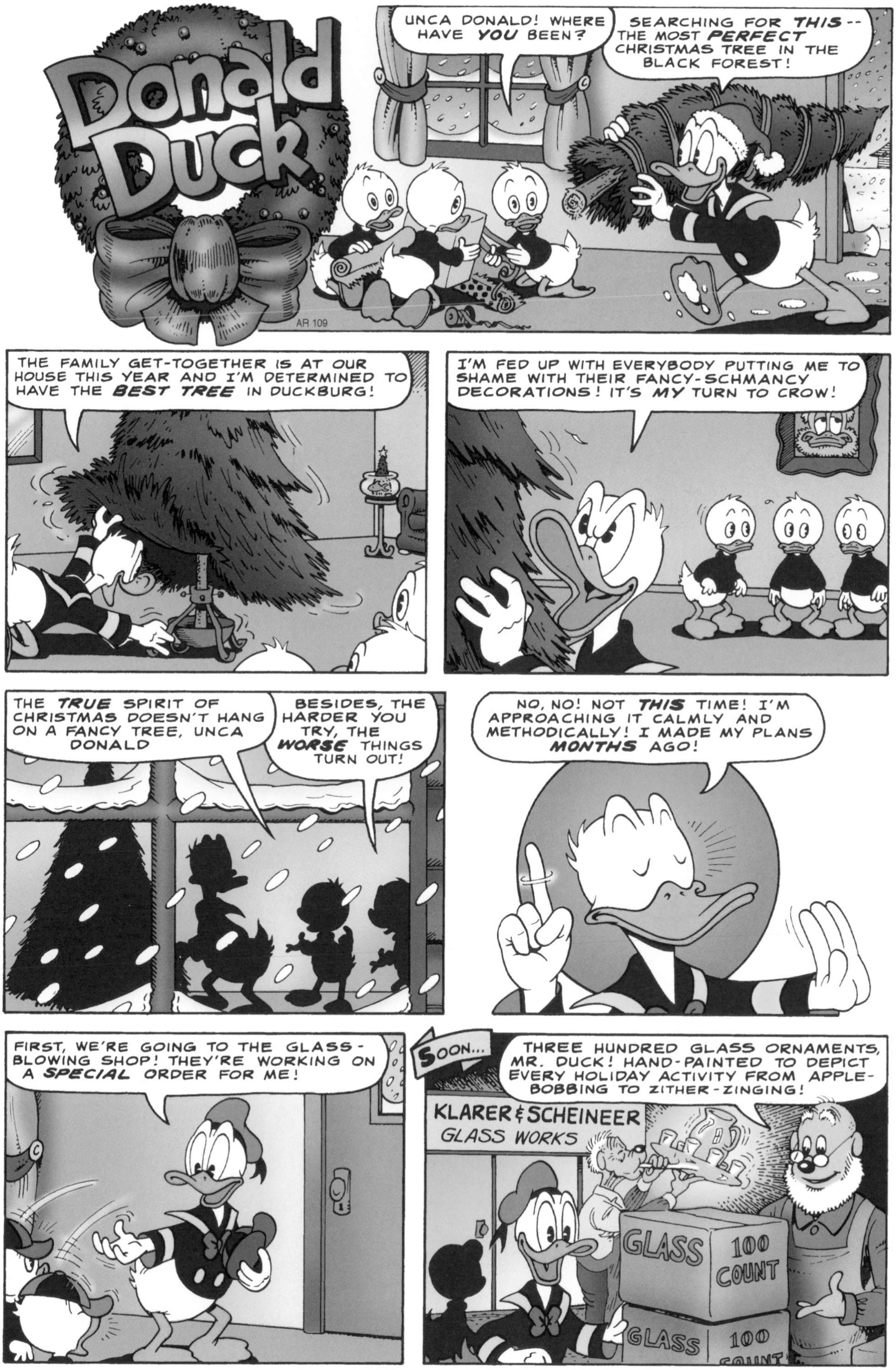
Donald Duck
AR 109
UNCA DONALD! WHERE HAVE YOU BEEN?
SEARCHING FOR THIS -- THE MOST PERFECT CHRISTMAS TREE IN THE BLACK FOREST!
THE FAMILY GET-TOGETHER IS AT OUR HOUSE THIS YEAR AND I'M DETERMINED TO HAVE THE BEST TREE IN DUCKBURG!
I'M FED UP WITH EVERYBODY PUTTING ME TO SHAME WITH THEIR FANCY-SCHMANCY DECORATIONS! IT'S MY TURN TO CROW!
THE TRUE SPIRIT OF CHRISTMAS DOESN'T HANG ON A FANCY TREE, UNCA DONALD
BESIDES, THE HARDER YOU TRY, THE WORSE THINGS TURN OUT!
NO, NO! NOT THIS TIME! I'M APPROACHING IT CALMLY AND METHODICALLY! I MADE MY PLANS MONTHS AGO!
FIRST, WE'RE GOING TO THE GLASS-BLOWING SHOP! THEY'RE WORKING ON A SPECIAL ORDER FOR ME!
SOON...
THREE HUNDRED GLASS ORNAMENTS, MR. DUCK! HAND-PAINTED TO DEPICT EVERY HOLIDAY ACTIVITY FROM APPLE-BOBBING TO ZITHER-ZINGING!
KLARER & SCHEINEER GLASS WORKS
GLASS
100 COUNT
GLASS
100

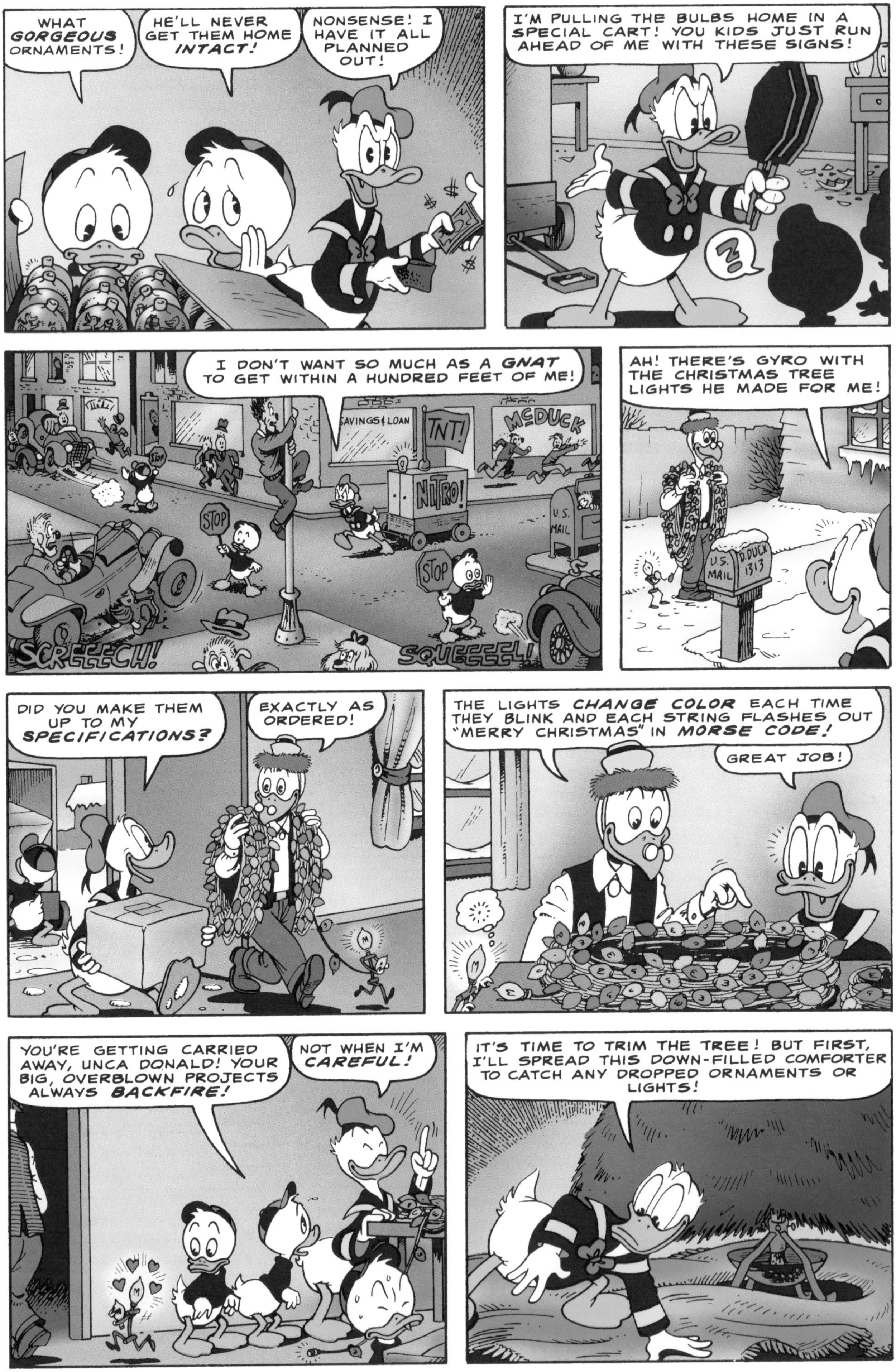
WHAT GORGEOUS ORNAMENTS!
HE'LL NEVER GET THEM HOME INTACT!
NONSENSE! I HAVE IT ALL PLANNED OUT!
I'M PULLING THE BULBS HOME IN A SPECIAL CART! YOU KIDS JUST RUN AHEAD OF ME WITH THESE SIGNS!
I DON'T WANT SO MUCH AS A GNAT TO GET WITHIN A HUNDRED FEET OF ME!
SAVINGS & LOAN
TNT!
McDUCK
NITRO!
STOP
STOP
STOP
U.S. MAIL
SCREEECH!
SQUEEEEL!
AH! THERE'S GYRO WITH THE CHRISTMAS TREE LIGHTS HE MADE FOR ME!
U.S. MAIL
D. DUCK 1313
DID YOU MAKE THEM UP TO MY SPECIFICATIONS?
EXACTLY AS ORDERED!
THE LIGHTS CHANGE COLOR EACH TIME THEY BLINK AND EACH STRING FLASHES OUT "MERRY CHRISTMAS" IN MORSE CODE!
GREAT JOB!
YOU'RE GETTING CARRIED AWAY, UNCA DONALD! YOUR BIG, OVERBLOWN PROJECTS ALWAYS BACKFIRE!
NOT WHEN I'M CAREFUL!
IT'S TIME TO TRIM THE TREE! BUT FIRST, I'LL SPREAD THIS DOWN-FILLED COMFORTER TO CATCH ANY DROPPED ORNAMENTS OR LIGHTS!

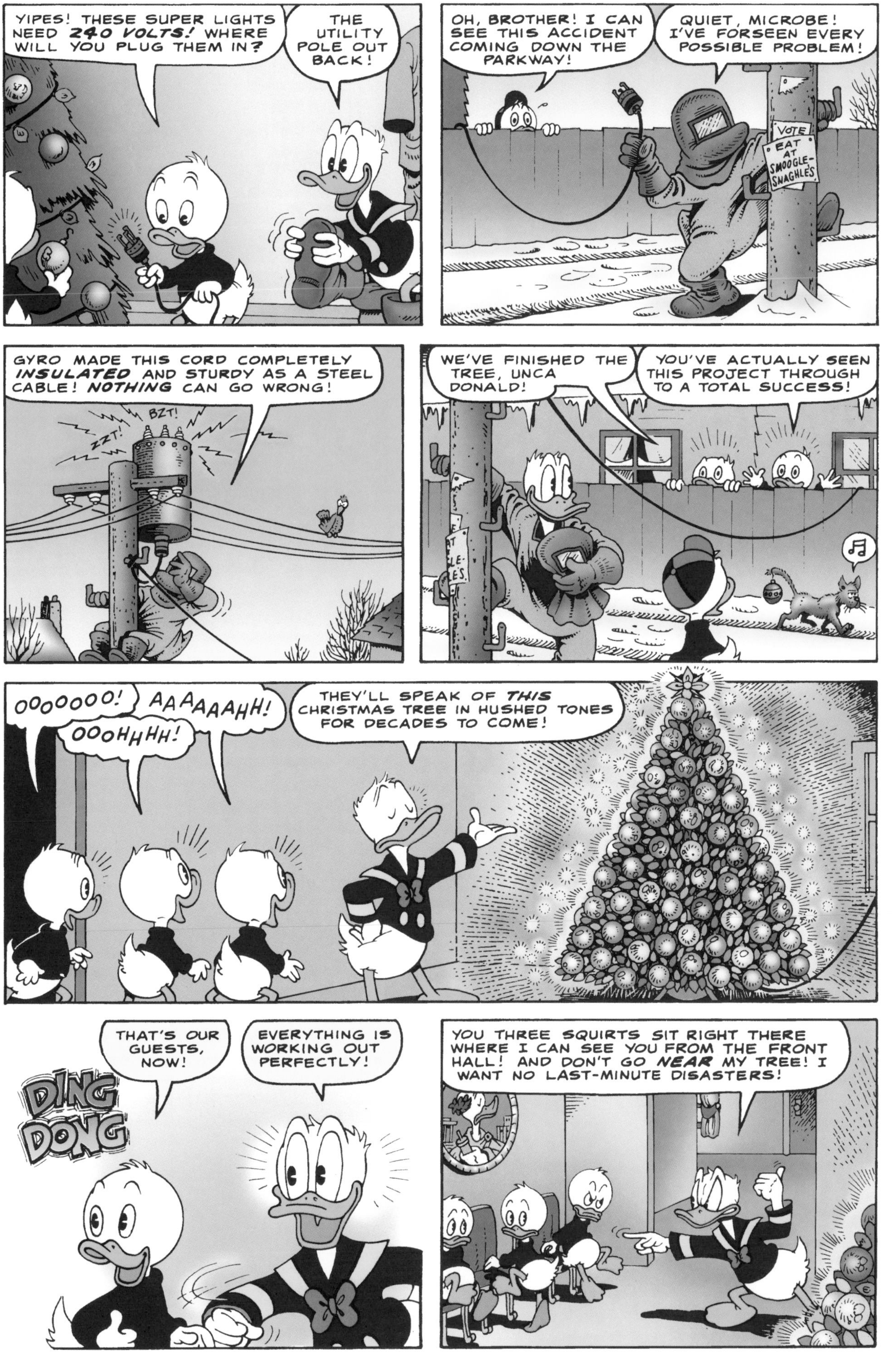
YIPES! THESE SUPER LIGHTS NEED 240 VOLTS! WHERE WILL YOU PLUG THEM IN?
THE UTILITY POLE OUT BACK!
OH, BROTHER! I CAN SEE THIS ACCIDENT COMING DOWN THE PARKWAY!
QUIET, MICROBE! I'VE FORSEEN EVERY POSSIBLE PROBLEM!
VOTE
EAT AT SMOOGLE-SNAGHLE'S
GYRO MADE THIS CORD COMPLETELY INSULATED AND STURDY AS A STEEL CABLE! NOTHING CAN GO WRONG!
BZT!
ZZT!
WE'VE FINISHED THE TREE, UNCA DONALD!
YOU'VE ACTUALLY SEEN THIS PROJECT THROUGH TO A TOTAL SUCCESS!
OOOOOOO!
AAAAAAHH!
OOOHHHH!
THEY'LL SPEAK OF THIS CHRISTMAS TREE IN HUSHED TONES FOR DECADES TO COME!
DING DONG
THAT'S OUR GUESTS, NOW!
EVERYTHING IS WORKING OUT PERFECTLY!
YOU THREE SQUIRTS SIT RIGHT THERE WHERE I CAN SEE YOU FROM THE FRONT HALL! AND DON'T GO NEAR MY TREE! I WANT NO LAST-MINUTE DISASTERS!

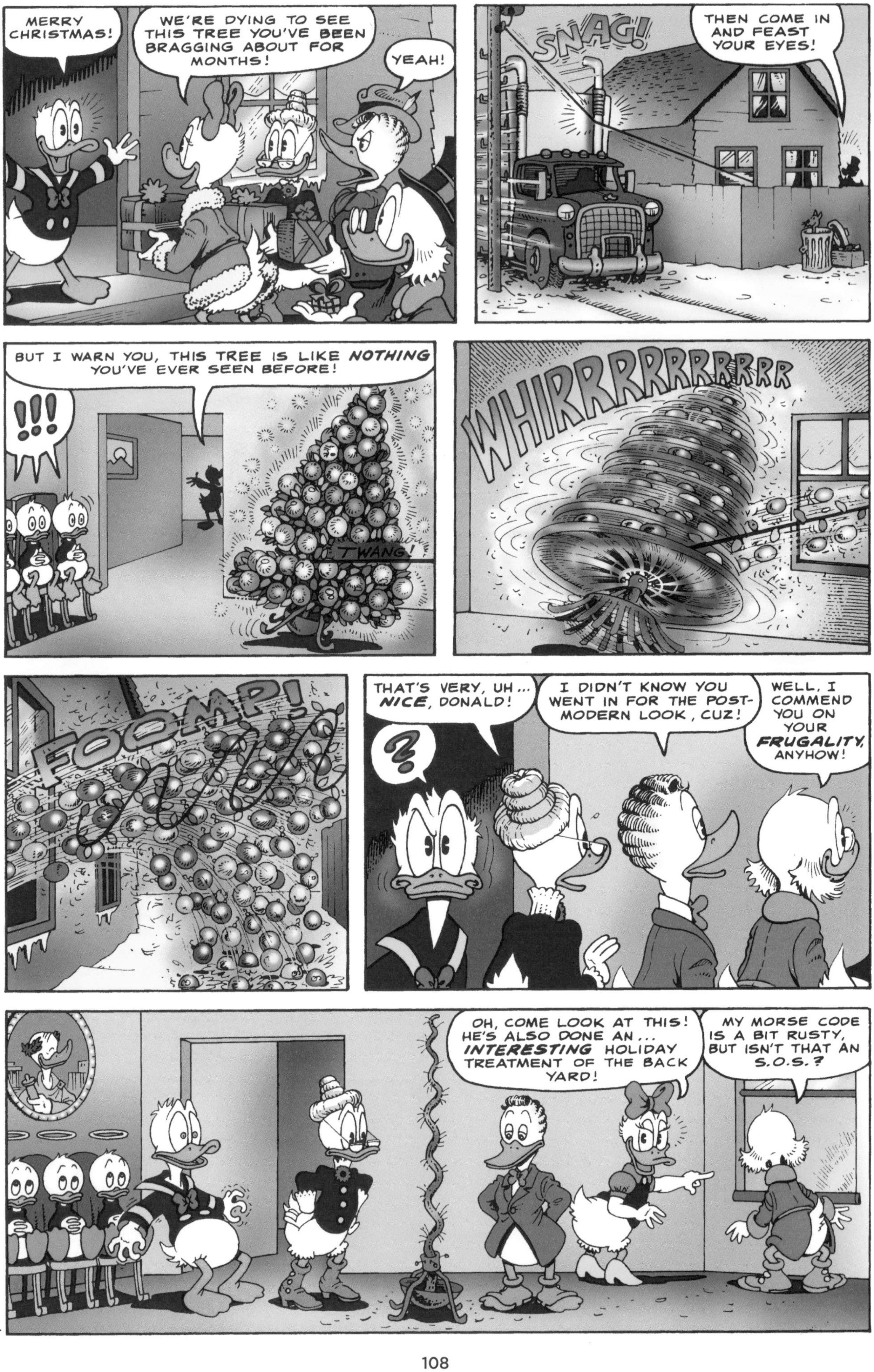
MERRY CHRISTMAS!
WE'RE DYING TO SEE THIS TREE YOU'VE BEEN BRAGGING ABOUT FOR MONTHS!
YEAH!
SNAG!
THEN COME IN AND FEAST YOUR EYES!
BUT I WARN YOU, THIS TREE IS LIKE NOTHING YOU'VE EVER SEEN BEFORE!
!!!
TWANG!
WHIRRRRRRRRRR
FOOMP!
THAT'S VERY, UH ... NICE, DONALD!
I DIDN'T KNOW YOU WENT IN FOR THE POST-MODERN LOOK, CUZ!
WELL, I COMMEND YOU ON YOUR FRUGALITY, ANYHOW!
OH, COME LOOK AT THIS! HE'S ALSO DONE AN ... INTERESTING HOLIDAY TREATMENT OF THE BACK YARD!
MY MORSE CODE IS A BIT RUSTY, BUT ISN'T THAT AN S.O.S.?

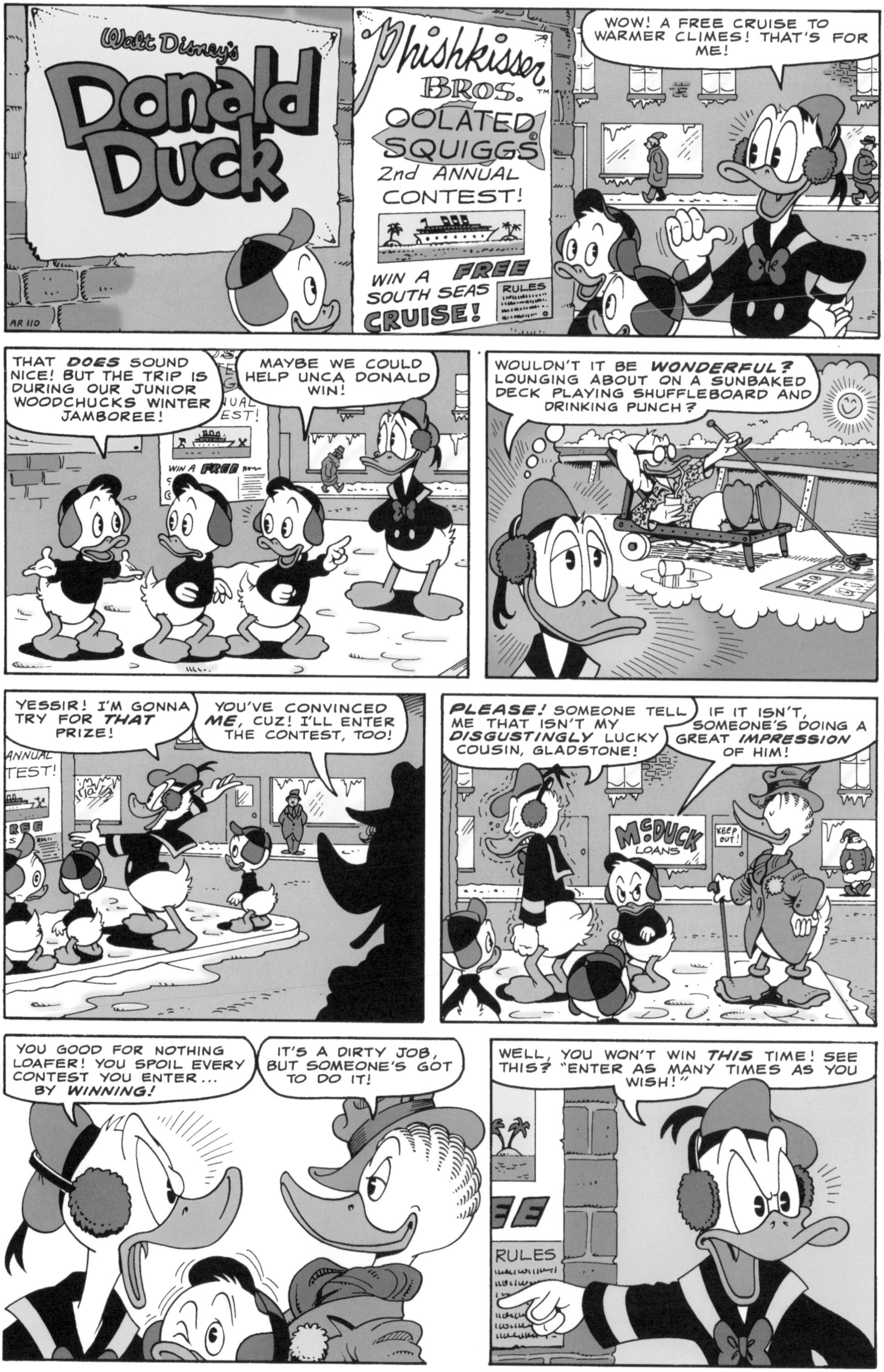
Walt Disney's
Donald Duck
Phishkisser
BROS.
OOLATED SQUIGGS
2nd ANNUAL
CONTEST!
WIN A FREE
SOUTH SEAS
CRUISE!
RULES
WOW! A FREE CRUISE TO WARMER CLIMES! THAT'S FOR ME!
THAT DOES SOUND NICE! BUT THE TRIP IS DURING OUR JUNIOR WOODCHUCKS WINTER JAMBOREE!
MAYBE WE COULD HELP UNCA DONALD WIN!
WOULDN'T IT BE WONDERFUL? LOUNGING ABOUT ON A SUNBAKED DECK PLAYING SHUFFLEBOARD AND DRINKING PUNCH?
YESSIR! I'M GONNA TRY FOR THAT PRIZE!
YOU'VE CONVINCED ME, CUZ! I'LL ENTER THE CONTEST, TOO!
PLEASE! SOMEONE TELL ME THAT ISN'T MY DISGUSTINGLY LUCKY COUSIN, GLADSTONE!
IF IT ISN'T, SOMEONE'S DOING A GREAT IMPRESSION OF HIM!
McDUCK LOANS
KEEP OUT!
YOU GOOD FOR NOTHING LOAFER! YOU SPOIL EVERY CONTEST YOU ENTER... BY WINNING!
IT'S A DIRTY JOB, BUT SOMEONE'S GOT TO DO IT!
WELL, YOU WON'T WIN THIS TIME! SEE THIS? "ENTER AS MANY TIMES AS YOU WISH!"
RULES

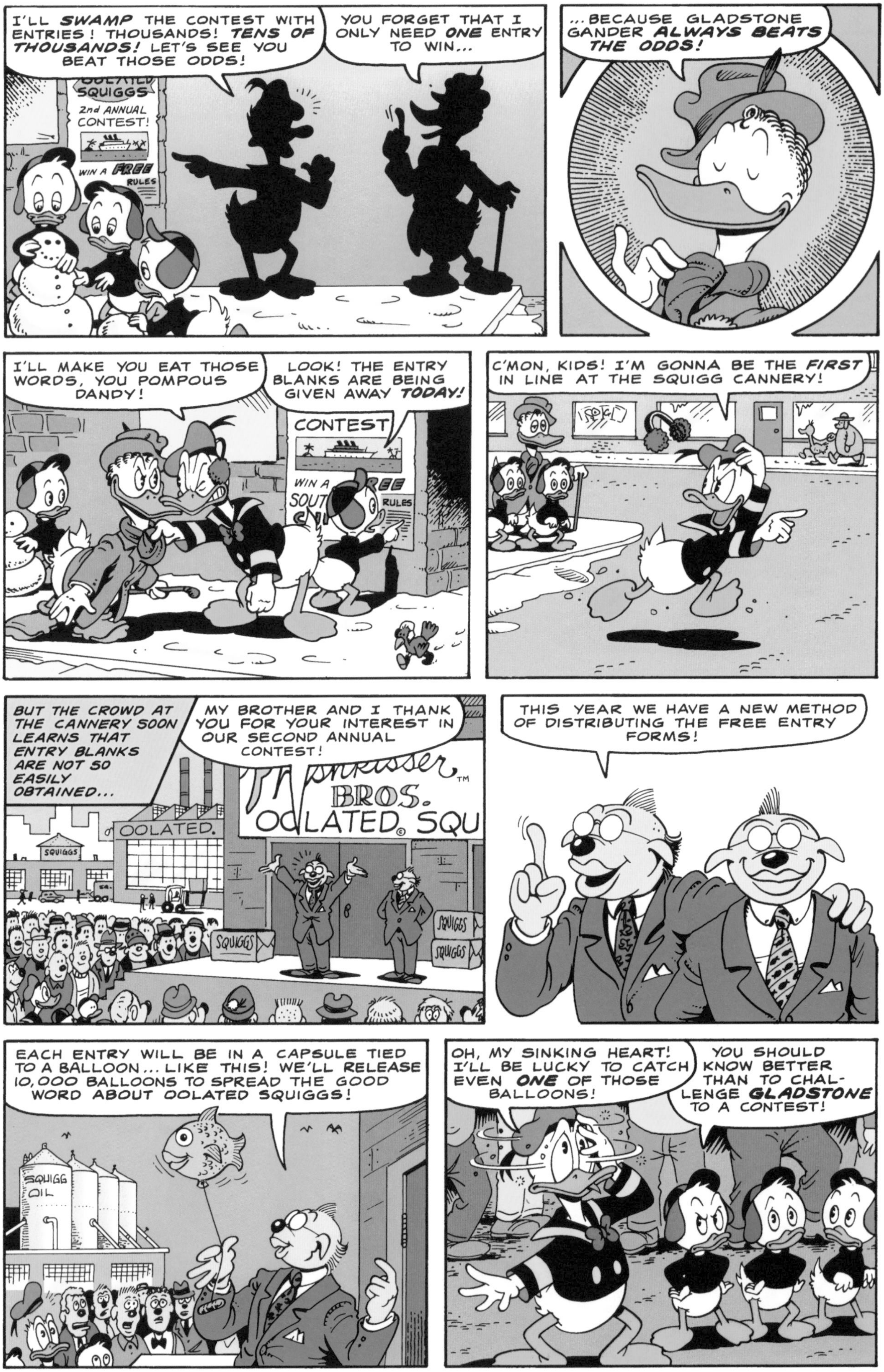

I'LL SWAMP THE CONTEST WITH ENTRIES! THOUSANDS! TENS OF THOUSANDS! LET'S SEE YOU BEAT THOSE ODDS!
SQUIGGS
2nd ANNUAL CONTEST!
WIN A FREE
RULES
YOU FORGET THAT I ONLY NEED ONE ENTRY TO WIN...
...BECAUSE GLADSTONE GANDER ALWAYS BEATS THE ODDS!
I'LL MAKE YOU EAT THOSE WORDS, YOU POMPOUS DANDY!
LOOK! THE ENTRY BLANKS ARE BEING GIVEN AWAY TODAY!
CONTEST
RULES
C'MON, KIDS! I'M GONNA BE THE FIRST IN LINE AT THE SQUIGG CANNERY!
BUT THE CROWD AT THE CANNERY SOON LEARNS THAT ENTRY BLANKS ARE NOT SO EASILY OBTAINED...
MY BROTHER AND I THANK YOU FOR YOUR INTEREST IN OUR SECOND ANNUAL CONTEST!
BROS.
OOLATED© SQU
OOLATED.
SQUIGGS
SQUIGGS
THIS YEAR WE HAVE A NEW METHOD OF DISTRIBUTING THE FREE ENTRY FORMS!
EACH ENTRY WILL BE IN A CAPSULE TIED TO A BALLOON... LIKE THIS! WE'LL RELEASE 10,000 BALLOONS TO SPREAD THE GOOD WORD ABOUT OOLATED SQUIGGS!
SQUIGG OIL
OH, MY SINKING HEART! I'LL BE LUCKY TO CATCH EVEN ONE OF THOSE BALLOONS!
YOU SHOULD KNOW BETTER THAN TO CHAL-LENGE GLADSTONE TO A CONTEST!

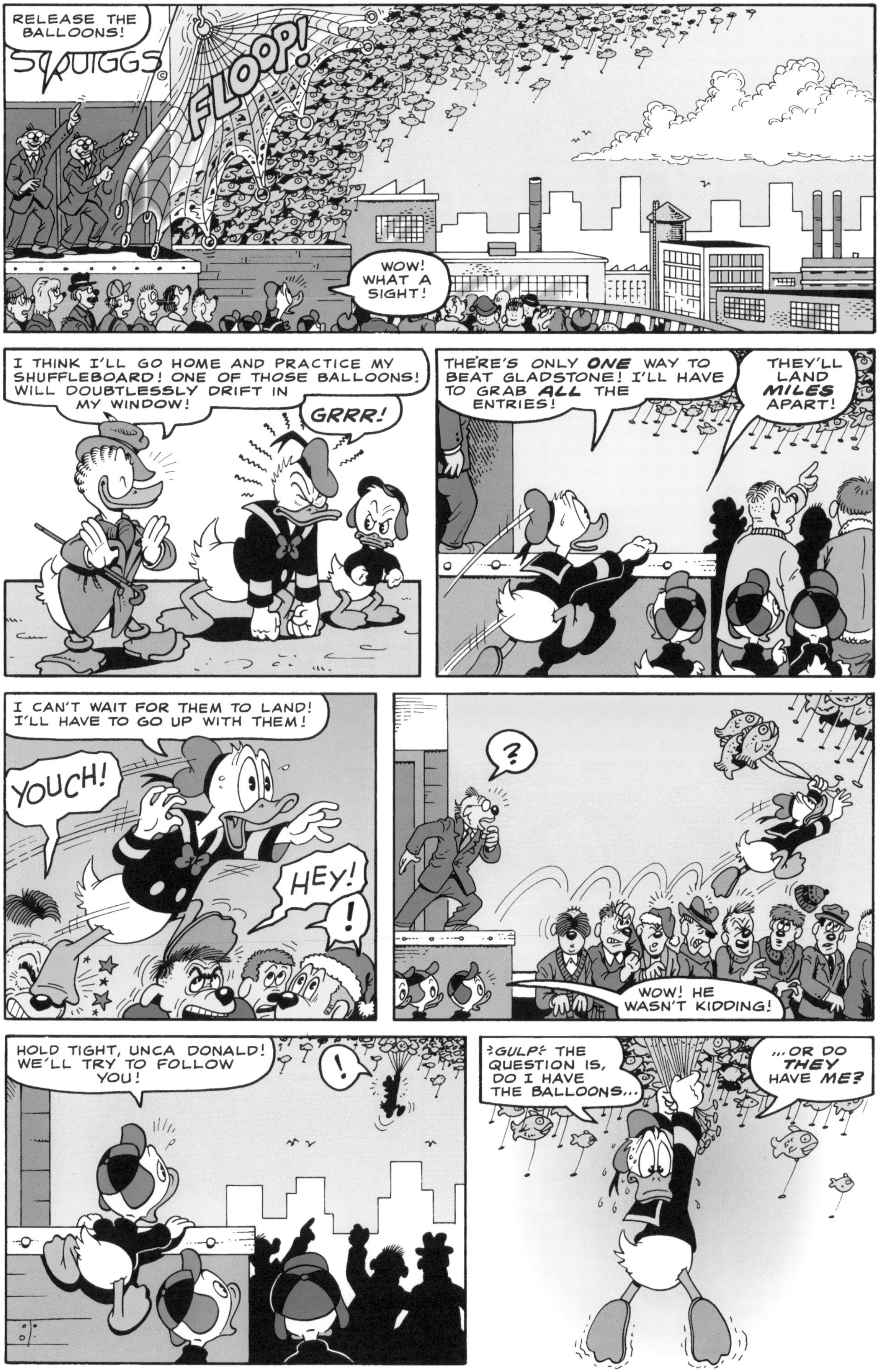
RELEASE THE BALLOONS!
SQUIGGS
FLOOP!
WOW! WHAT A SIGHT!
I THINK I'LL GO HOME AND PRACTICE MY SHUFFLEBOARD! ONE OF THOSE BALLOONS! WILL DOUBTLESSLY DRIFT IN MY WINDOW!
GRRR!
THERE'S ONLY ONE WAY TO BEAT GLADSTONE! I'LL HAVE TO GRAB ALL THE ENTRIES!
THEY'LL LAND MILES APART!
I CAN'T WAIT FOR THEM TO LAND! I'LL HAVE TO GO UP WITH THEM!
YOUCH!
HEY!
!
?
WOW! HE WASN'T KIDDING!
HOLD TIGHT, UNCA DONALD! WE'LL TRY TO FOLLOW YOU!
!
GULP THE QUESTION IS, DO I HAVE THE BALLOONS...
...OR DO THEY HAVE ME?

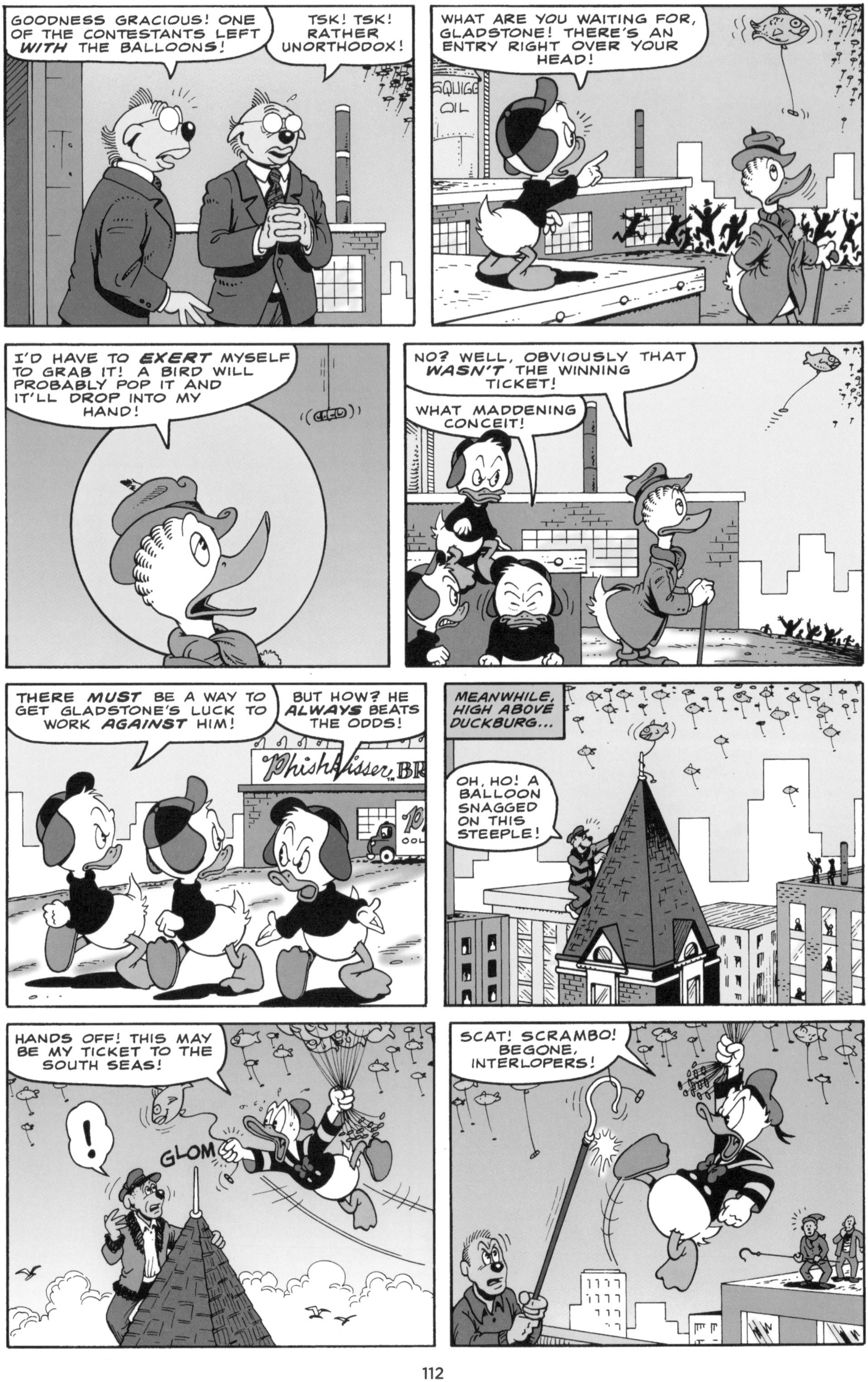

GOODNESS GRACIOUS! ONE OF THE CONTESTANTS LEFT WITH THE BALLOONS!
TSK! TSK! RATHER UNORTHODOX!
WHAT ARE YOU WAITING FOR, GLADSTONE! THERE'S AN ENTRY RIGHT OVER YOUR HEAD!
SQUIGG OIL
I'D HAVE TO EXERT MYSELF TO GRAB IT! A BIRD WILL PROBABLY POP IT AND IT'LL DROP INTO MY HAND!
NO? WELL, OBVIOUSLY THAT WASN'T THE WINNING TICKET!
WHAT MADDENING CONCEIT!
THERE MUST BE A WAY TO GET GLADSTONE'S LUCK TO WORK AGAINST HIM!
BUT HOW? HE ALWAYS BEATS THE ODDS!
MEANWHILE, HIGH ABOVE DUCKBURG...
OH, HO! A BALLOON SNAGGED ON THIS STEEPLE!
HANDS OFF! THIS MAY BE MY TICKET TO THE SOUTH SEAS!
!
GLOM
SCAT! SCRAMBO! BEGONE, INTERLOPERS!

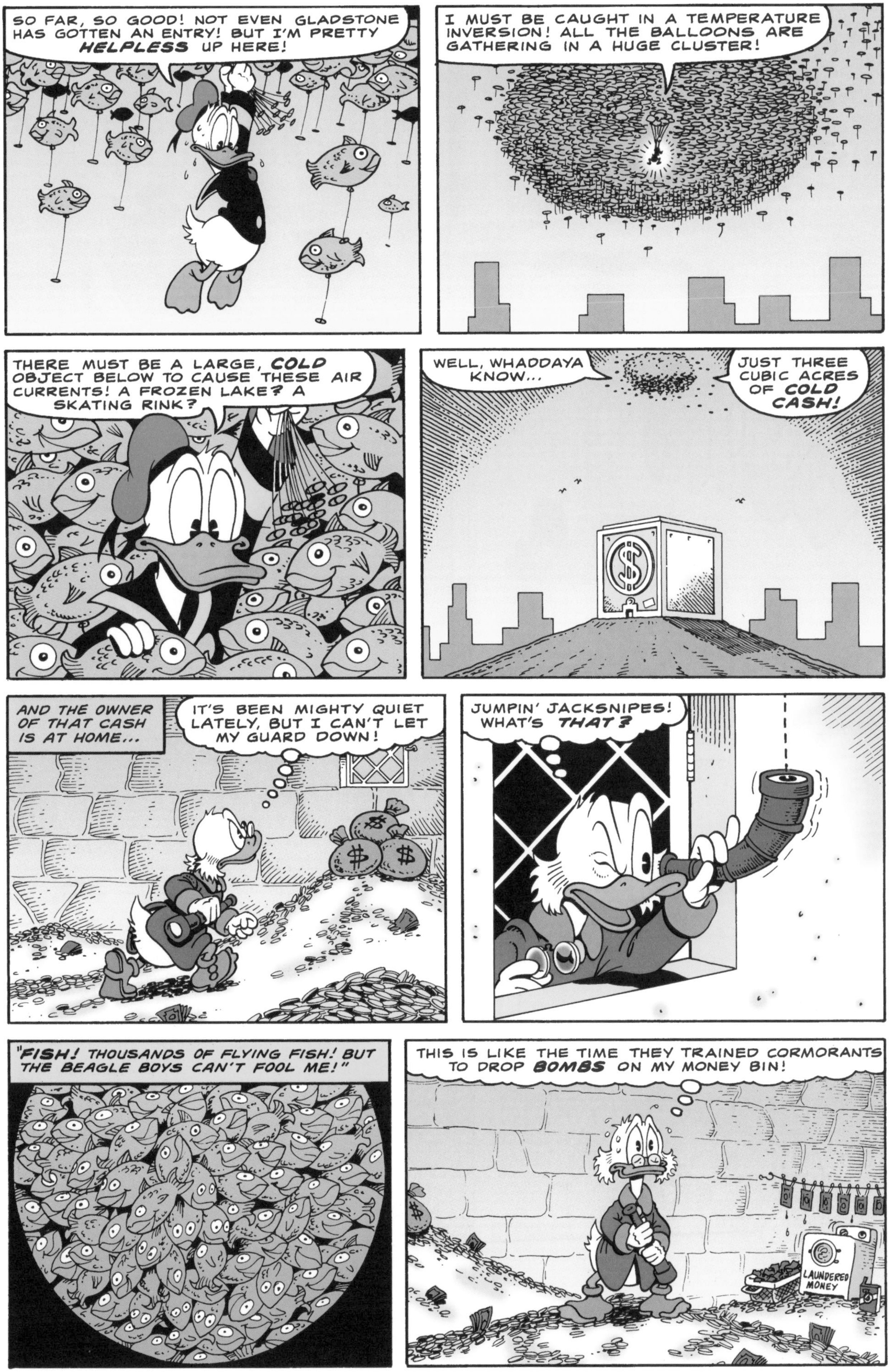
SO FAR, SO GOOD! NOT EVEN GLADSTONE HAS GOTTEN AN ENTRY! BUT I'M PRETTY HELPLESS UP HERE!
I MUST BE CAUGHT IN A TEMPERATURE INVERSION! ALL THE BALLOONS ARE GATHERING IN A HUGE CLUSTER!
THERE MUST BE A LARGE, COLD OBJECT BELOW TO CAUSE THESE AIR CURRENTS! A FROZEN LAKE? A SKATING RINK?
WELL, WHADDAYA KNOW...
JUST THREE CUBIC ACRES OF COLD CASH!
AND THE OWNER OF THAT CASH IS AT HOME...
IT'S BEEN MIGHTY QUIET LATELY, BUT I CAN'T LET MY GUARD DOWN!
JUMPIN' JACKSNIPES! WHAT'S THAT?
"FISH! THOUSANDS OF FLYING FISH! BUT THE BEAGLE BOYS CAN'T FOOL ME!"
THIS IS LIKE THE TIME THEY TRAINED CORMORANTS TO DROP BOMBS ON MY MONEY BIN!
LAUNDERED MONEY

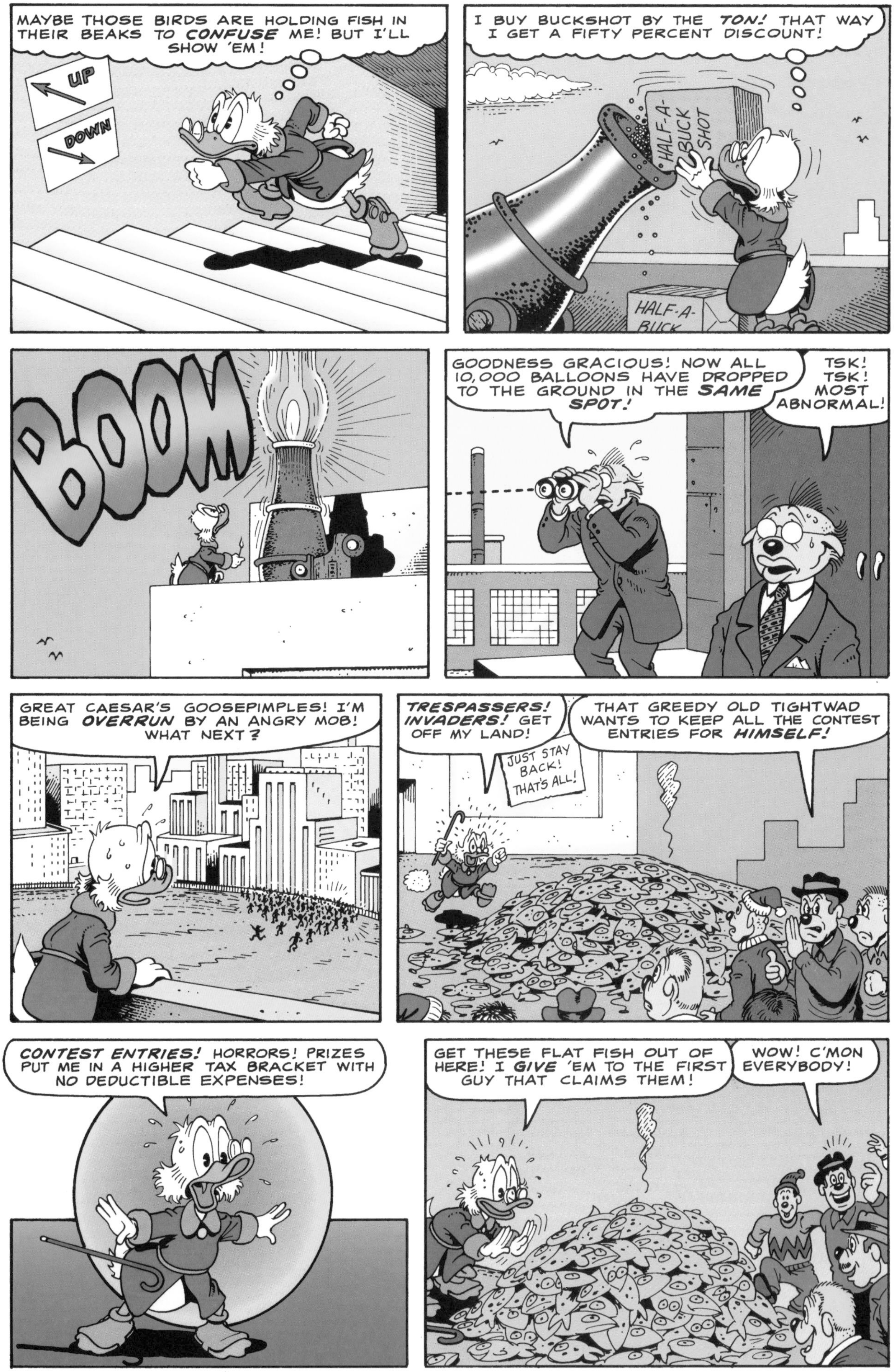
MAYBE THOSE BIRDS ARE HOLDING FISH IN THEIR BEAKS TO CONFUSE ME! BUT I'LL SHOW 'EM!
UP
DOWN
I BUY BUCKSHOT BY THE TON! THAT WAY I GET A FIFTY PERCENT DISCOUNT!
HALF-A-BUCK SHOT
BOOM
GOODNESS GRACIOUS! NOW ALL 10,000 BALLOONS HAVE DROPPED TO THE GROUND IN THE SAME SPOT!
TSK! TSK! MOST ABNORMAL!
GREAT CAESAR'S GOOSEPIMPLES! I'M BEING OVERRUN BY AN ANGRY MOB! WHAT NEXT?
TRESPASSERS! INVADERS! GET OFF MY LAND!
JUST STAY BACK! THAT'S ALL!
THAT GREEDY OLD TIGHTWAD WANTS TO KEEP ALL THE CONTEST ENTRIES FOR HIMSELF!
CONTEST ENTRIES! HORRORS! PRIZES PUT ME IN A HIGHER TAX BRACKET WITH NO DEDUCTIBLE EXPENSES!
GET THESE FLAT FISH OUT OF HERE! I GIVE 'EM TO THE FIRST GUY THAT CLAIMS THEM!
WOW! C'MON EVERYBODY!

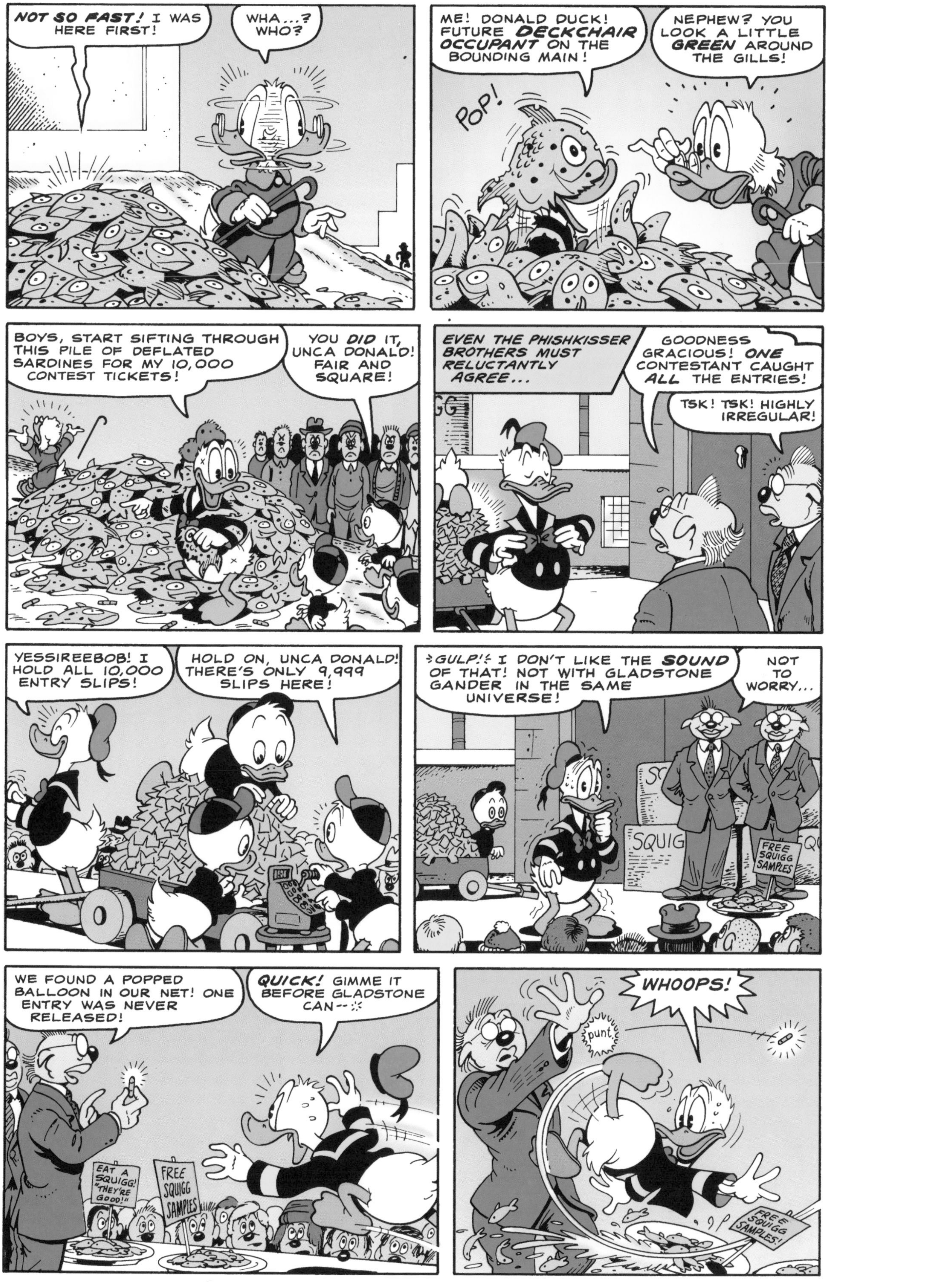

NOT SO FAST! I WAS HERE FIRST!
WHA...? WHO?
ME! DONALD DUCK! FUTURE DECKCHAIR OCCUPANT ON THE BOUNDING MAIN!
NEPHEW? YOU LOOK A LITTLE GREEN AROUND THE GILLS!
POP!
BOYS, START SIFTING THROUGH THIS PILE OF DEFLATED SARDINES FOR MY 10,000 CONTEST TICKETS!
YOU DID IT, UNCA DONALD! FAIR AND SQUARE!
EVEN THE PHISHKISSER BROTHERS MUST RELUCTANTLY AGREE...
GOODNESS GRACIOUS! ONE CONTESTANT CAUGHT ALL THE ENTRIES!
TSK! TSK! HIGHLY IRREGULAR!
YESSIREEBOB! I HOLD ALL 10,000 ENTRY SLIPS!
HOLD ON, UNCA DONALD! THERE'S ONLY 9,999 SLIPS HERE!
GULP! I DON'T LIKE THE SOUND OF THAT! NOT WITH GLADSTONE GANDER IN THE SAME UNIVERSE!
NOT TO WORRY...
SQUIG
FREE SQUIGG SAMPLES
WE FOUND A POPPED BALLOON IN OUR NET! ONE ENTRY WAS NEVER RELEASED!
QUICK! GIMME IT BEFORE GLADSTONE CAN--
EAT A SQUIGG! "THEY'RE GOOD!"
FREE SQUIGG SAMPLES
WHOOPS!
punt
FREE SQUIGG SAMPLES!

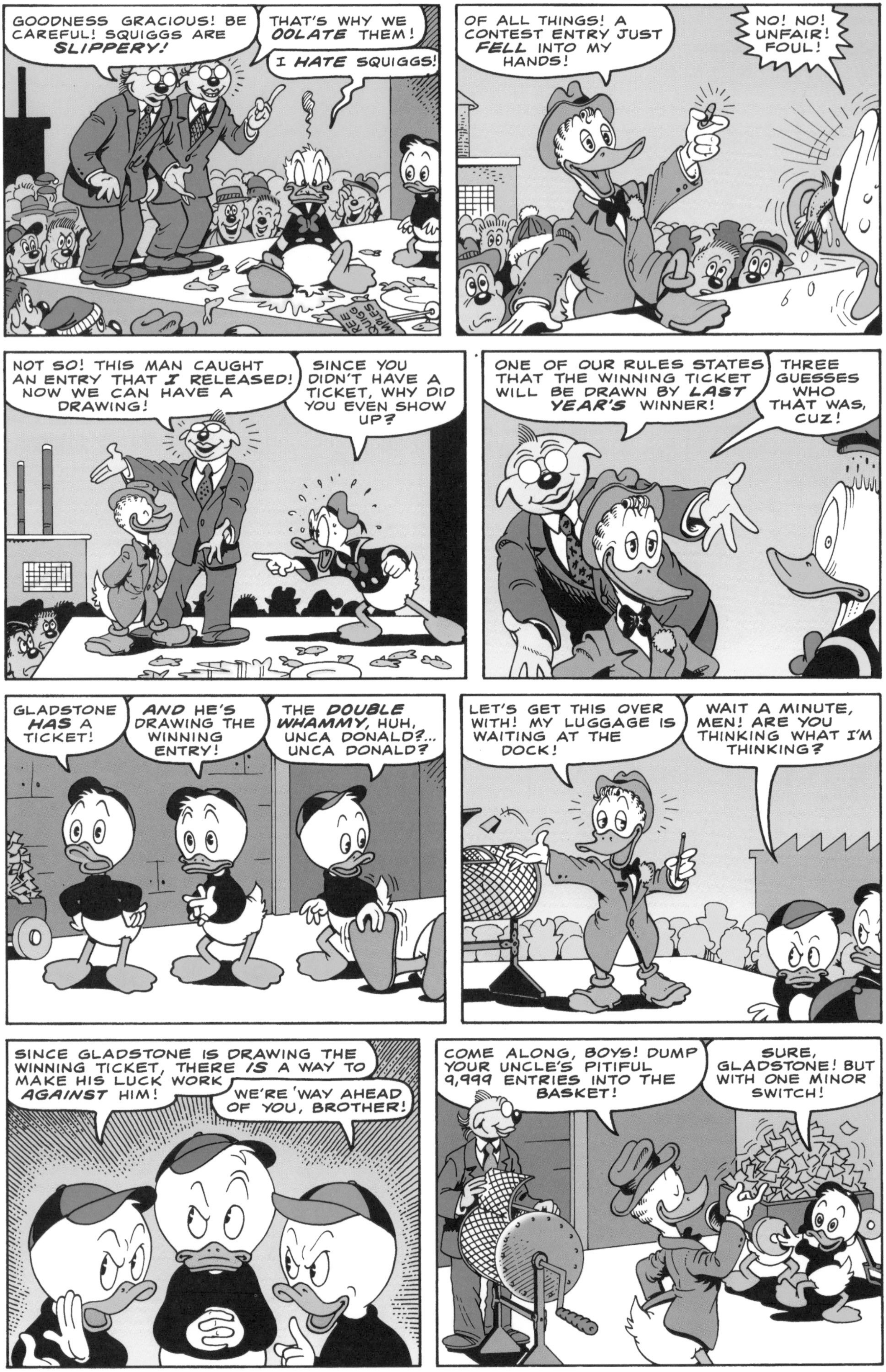
GOODNESS GRACIOUS! BE CAREFUL! SQUIGGS ARE SLIPPERY!
THAT'S WHY WE OOLATE THEM!
I HATE SQUIGGS!
OF ALL THINGS! A CONTEST ENTRY JUST FELL INTO MY HANDS!
NO! NO! UNFAIR! FOUL!
NOT SO! THIS MAN CAUGHT AN ENTRY THAT I RELEASED! NOW WE CAN HAVE A DRAWING!
SINCE YOU DIDN'T HAVE A TICKET, WHY DID YOU EVEN SHOW UP?
ONE OF OUR RULES STATES THAT THE WINNING TICKET WILL BE DRAWN BY LAST YEAR'S WINNER!
THREE GUESSES WHO THAT WAS, CUZ!
GLADSTONE HAS A TICKET!
AND HE'S DRAWING THE WINNING ENTRY!
THE DOUBLE WHAMMY, HUH, UNCA DONALD?... UNCA DONALD?
LET'S GET THIS OVER WITH! MY LUGGAGE IS WAITING AT THE DOCK!
WAIT A MINUTE, MEN! ARE YOU THINKING WHAT I'M THINKING?
SINCE GLADSTONE IS DRAWING THE WINNING TICKET, THERE IS A WAY TO MAKE HIS LUCK WORK AGAINST HIM!
WE'RE 'WAY AHEAD OF YOU, BROTHER!
COME ALONG, BOYS! DUMP YOUR UNCLE'S PITIFUL 9,999 ENTRIES INTO THE BASKET!
SURE, GLADSTONE! BUT WITH ONE MINOR SWITCH!

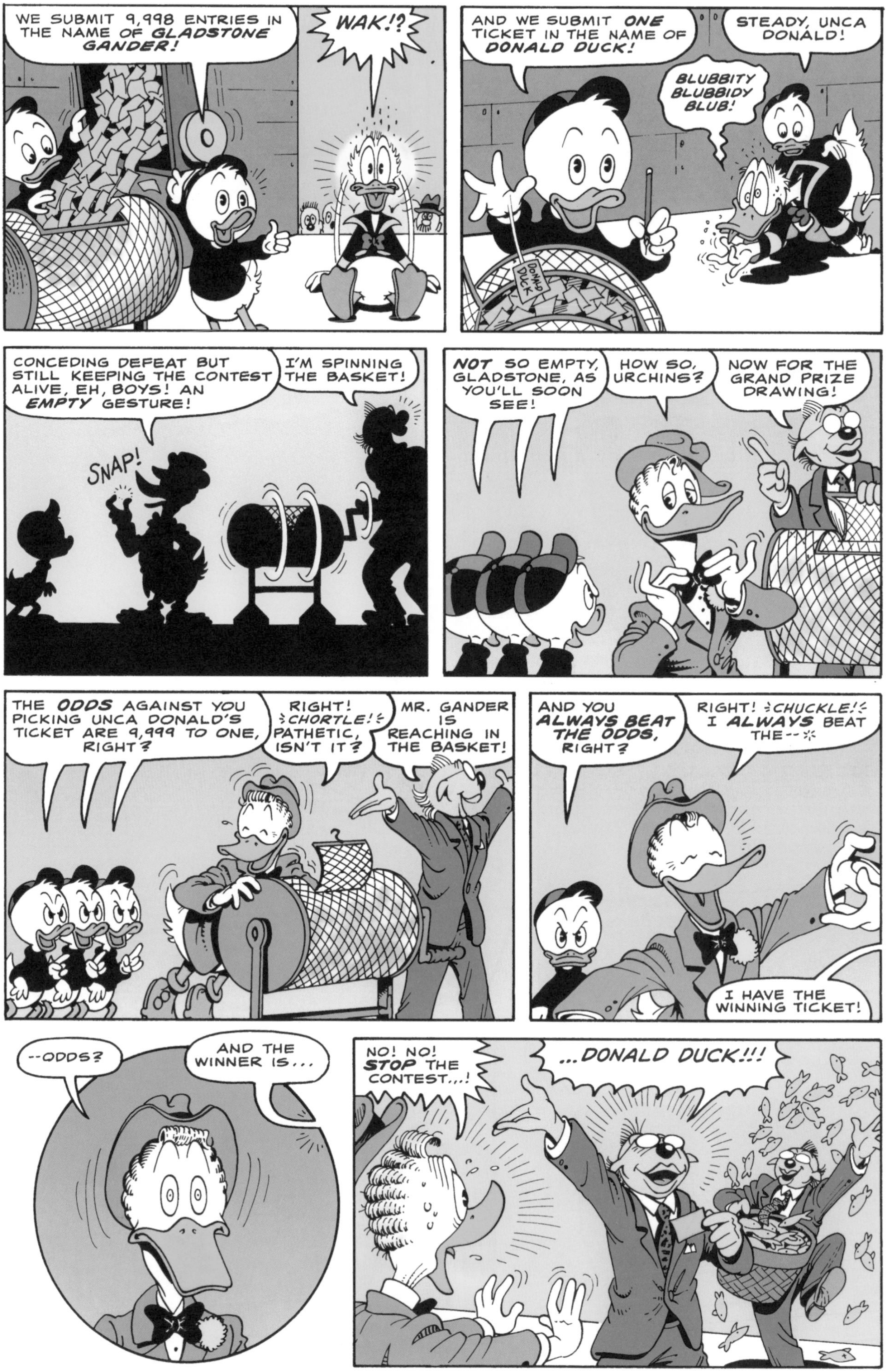
WE SUBMIT 9,998 ENTRIES IN THE NAME OF GLADSTONE GANDER!
WAK!?
AND WE SUBMIT ONE TICKET IN THE NAME OF DONALD DUCK!
STEADY, UNCA DONALD!
BLUBBITY BLUBBIDY BLUB!
DONALD DUCK
CONCEDING DEFEAT BUT STILL KEEPING THE CONTEST ALIVE, EH, BOYS! AN EMPTY GESTURE!
I'M SPINNING THE BASKET!
SNAP!
NOT SO EMPTY, GLADSTONE, AS YOU'LL SOON SEE!
HOW SO, URCHINS?
NOW FOR THE GRAND PRIZE DRAWING!
THE ODDS AGAINST YOU PICKING UNCA DONALD'S TICKET ARE 9,999 TO ONE, RIGHT?
RIGHT! CHORTLE! PATHETIC, ISN'T IT?
MR. GANDER IS REACHING IN THE BASKET!
AND YOU ALWAYS BEAT THE ODDS, RIGHT?
RIGHT! CHUCKLE! I ALWAYS BEAT THE--
I HAVE THE WINNING TICKET!
--ODDS?
AND THE WINNER IS...
NO! NO! STOP THE CONTEST...!
...DONALD DUCK!!!

YOU *WON*, UNCA DONALD!

GLADSTONE *BEAT HIMSELF* WITH HIS OWN LUCK!

OH, THE *SHAME!* THE *DISGRACE!*

DON'T FEEL BAD, MR. GANDER! THE SECOND PRIZE IS A *YEAR'S SUPPLY* OF OOLATED SQUIGGS!

AND SO...

I DON'T GET IT! I *KNOW* THE ODDS WERE 9,999 TO ONE AGAINST ME PICKING DONALD'S TICKET, AND I KNOW I ALWAYS *BEAT* THE ODDS...

BUT STILL ... NO MATTER HOW YOU SLICE IT, IT WAS *BAD LUCK* FOR ME TO LOSE A CONTEST! THERE MUST BE A *REASON*...

OHO! I KNEW IT! THERE *IS!*

OUCH! THIS DARN FISH HAS A *ROCK* IN IT!

Duckburg Times

CRUISE SHIP ICEBOUND

LUXURY LINER GROUNDED ON ICEBERG OFF COAST MUST AWAIT SPRING THAW TO REFLOAT

GRIT!

HMMM! THIS SQUIGG MUST HAVE SWALLOWED SOMEONE'S *DIAMOND RING!* LOOKS TO BE ABOUT TEN CARATS!

HEY, LOOK! I CAUGHT A *SQUIGG!*

THROW THE ROTTEN THING BACK OR I'LL *OOLATE YOU* WHERE YOU STAND!

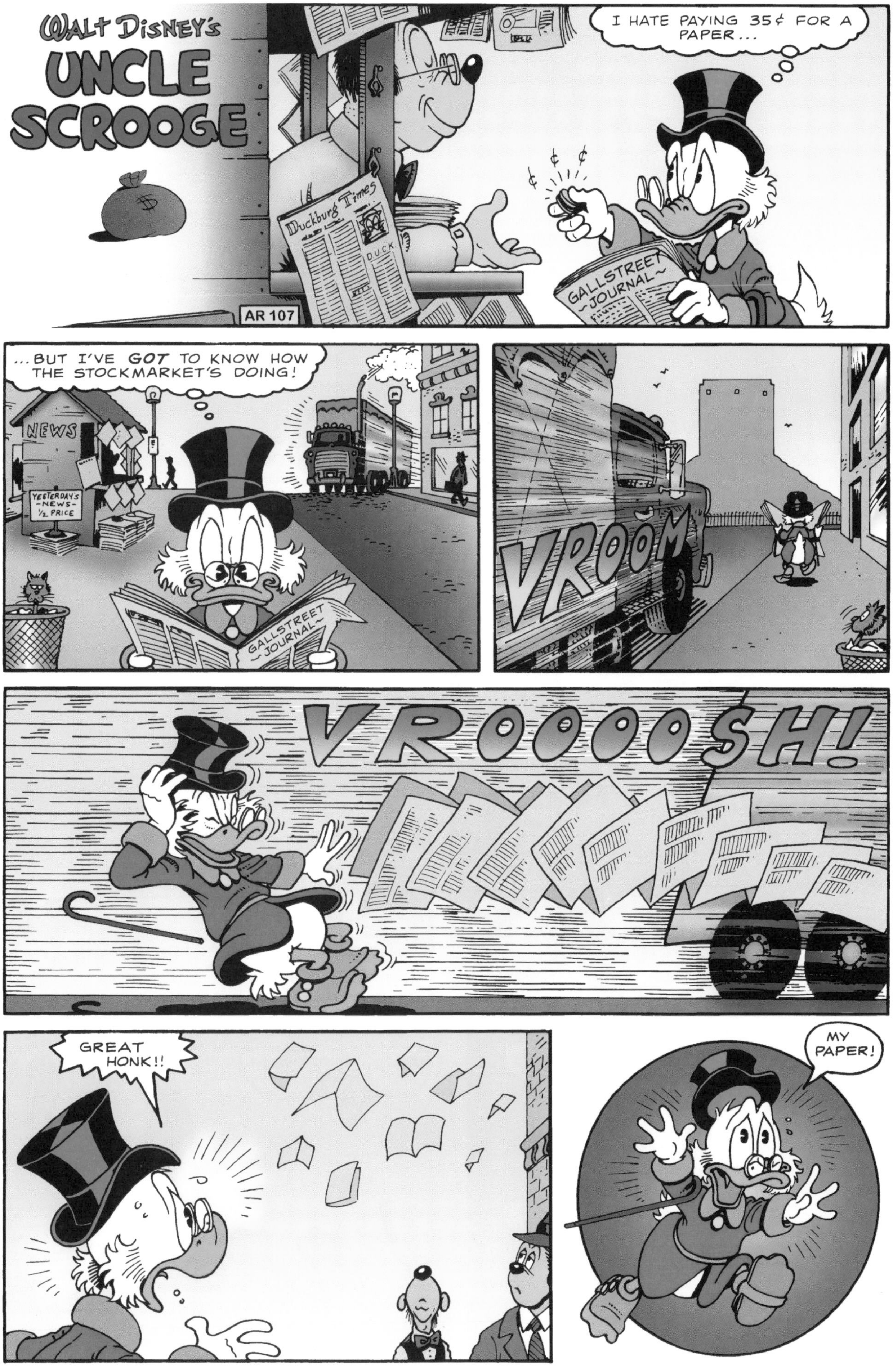
Walt Disney's
UNCLE SCROOGE
AR 107
I HATE PAYING 35¢ FOR A PAPER...
Duckburg Times
GALLSTREET JOURNAL
...BUT I'VE GOT TO KNOW HOW THE STOCKMARKET'S DOING!
NEWS
YESTERDAY'S NEWS 1/2 PRICE
GALLSTREET JOURNAL
VROOM
VROOOOOSH!
GREAT HONK!!
MY PAPER!

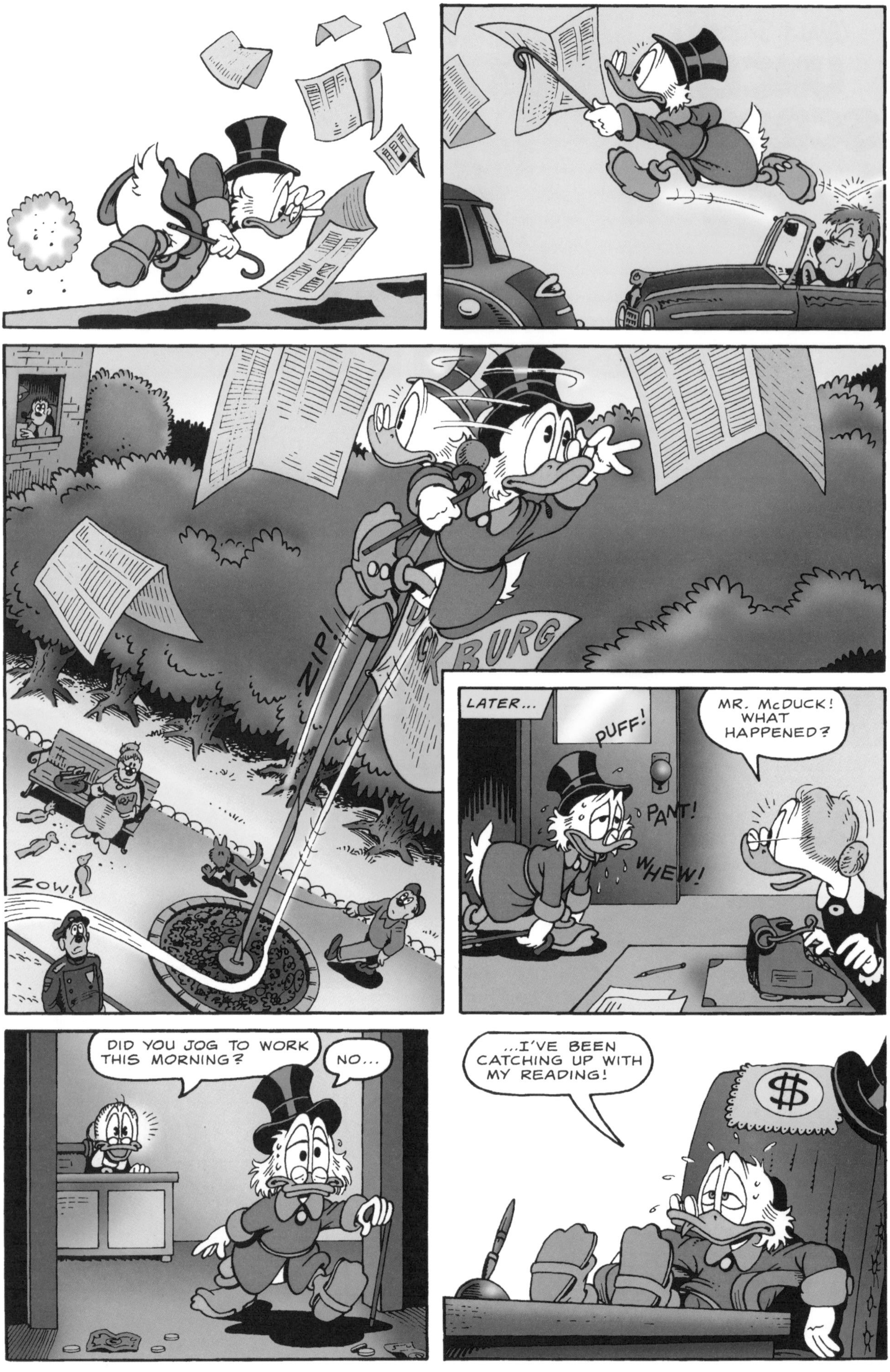
ZIP!
DUCKBURG
ZOW!
LATER...
PUFF!
PANT!
WHEW!
MR. McDUCK! WHAT HAPPENED?
DID YOU JOG TO WORK THIS MORNING?
NO...
...I'VE BEEN CATCHING UP WITH MY READING!
$

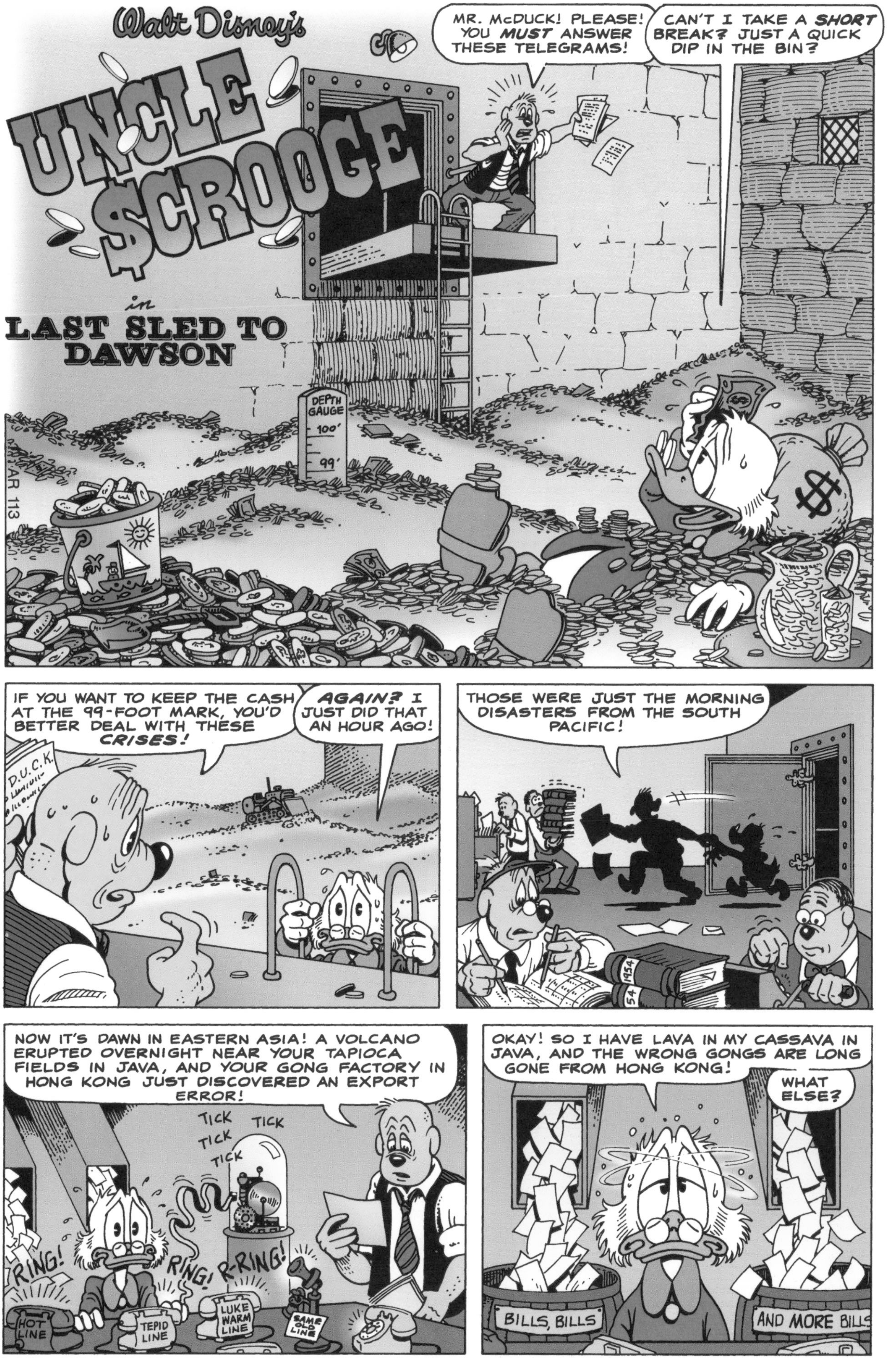
Walt Disney's
UNCLE $CROOGE
in
LAST SLED TO DAWSON
MR. McDUCK! PLEASE! YOU MUST ANSWER THESE TELEGRAMS!
CAN'T I TAKE A SHORT BREAK? JUST A QUICK DIP IN THE BIN?
DEPTH GAUGE
100'
99'
AR 113
IF YOU WANT TO KEEP THE CASH AT THE 99-FOOT MARK, YOU'D BETTER DEAL WITH THESE CRISES!
AGAIN? I JUST DID THAT AN HOUR AGO!
D.U.C.K.
THOSE WERE JUST THE MORNING DISASTERS FROM THE SOUTH PACIFIC!
1954
54
NOW IT'S DAWN IN EASTERN ASIA! A VOLCANO ERUPTED OVERNIGHT NEAR YOUR TAPIOCA FIELDS IN JAVA, AND YOUR GONG FACTORY IN HONG KONG JUST DISCOVERED AN EXPORT ERROR!
TICK TICK TICK TICK
RING! RING! R-RING!
HOT LINE
TEPID LINE
LUKE WARM LINE
SAME OLD LINE
OKAY! SO I HAVE LAVA IN MY CASSAVA IN JAVA, AND THE WRONG GONGS ARE LONG GONE FROM HONG KONG!
WHAT ELSE?
BILLS, BILLS
AND MORE BILLS

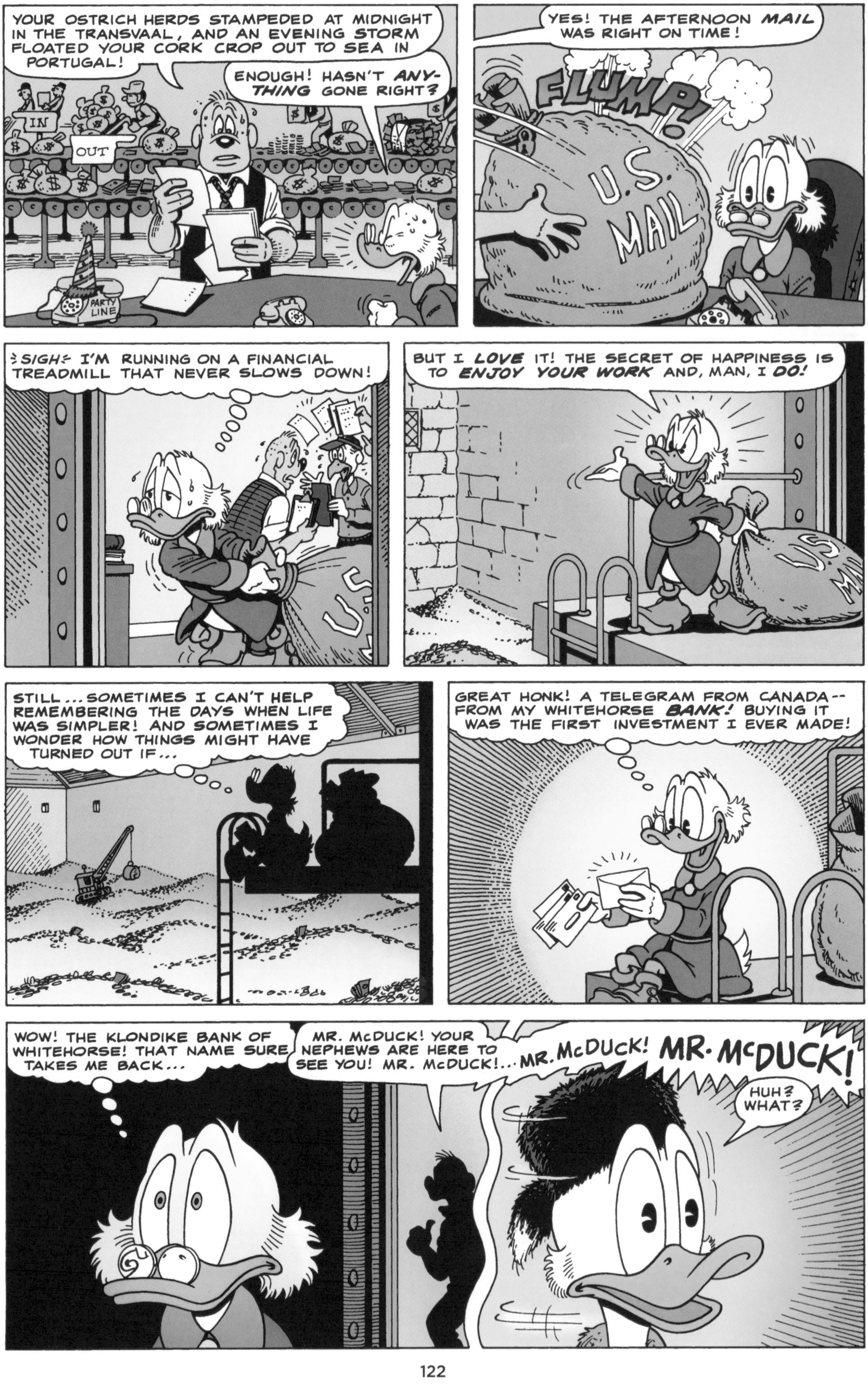
YOUR OSTRICH HERDS STAMPEDED AT MIDNIGHT IN THE TRANSVAAL, AND AN EVENING STORM FLOATED YOUR CORK CROP OUT TO SEA IN PORTUGAL!
ENOUGH! HASN'T ANYTHING GONE RIGHT?
IN
OUT
PARTY LINE
YES! THE AFTERNOON MAIL WAS RIGHT ON TIME!
FLUMP!
U.S. MAIL
SIGH I'M RUNNING ON A FINANCIAL TREADMILL THAT NEVER SLOWS DOWN!
BUT I LOVE IT! THE SECRET OF HAPPINESS IS TO ENJOY YOUR WORK AND, MAN, I DO!
STILL... SOMETIMES I CAN'T HELP REMEMBERING THE DAYS WHEN LIFE WAS SIMPLER! AND SOMETIMES I WONDER HOW THINGS MIGHT HAVE TURNED OUT IF...
GREAT HONK! A TELEGRAM FROM CANADA-- FROM MY WHITEHORSE BANK! BUYING IT WAS THE FIRST INVESTMENT I EVER MADE!
WOW! THE KLONDIKE BANK OF WHITEHORSE! THAT NAME SURE TAKES ME BACK...
MR. McDUCK! YOUR NEPHEWS ARE HERE TO SEE YOU! MR. McDUCK!... MR. McDUCK! MR. McDUCK!
HUH? WHAT?

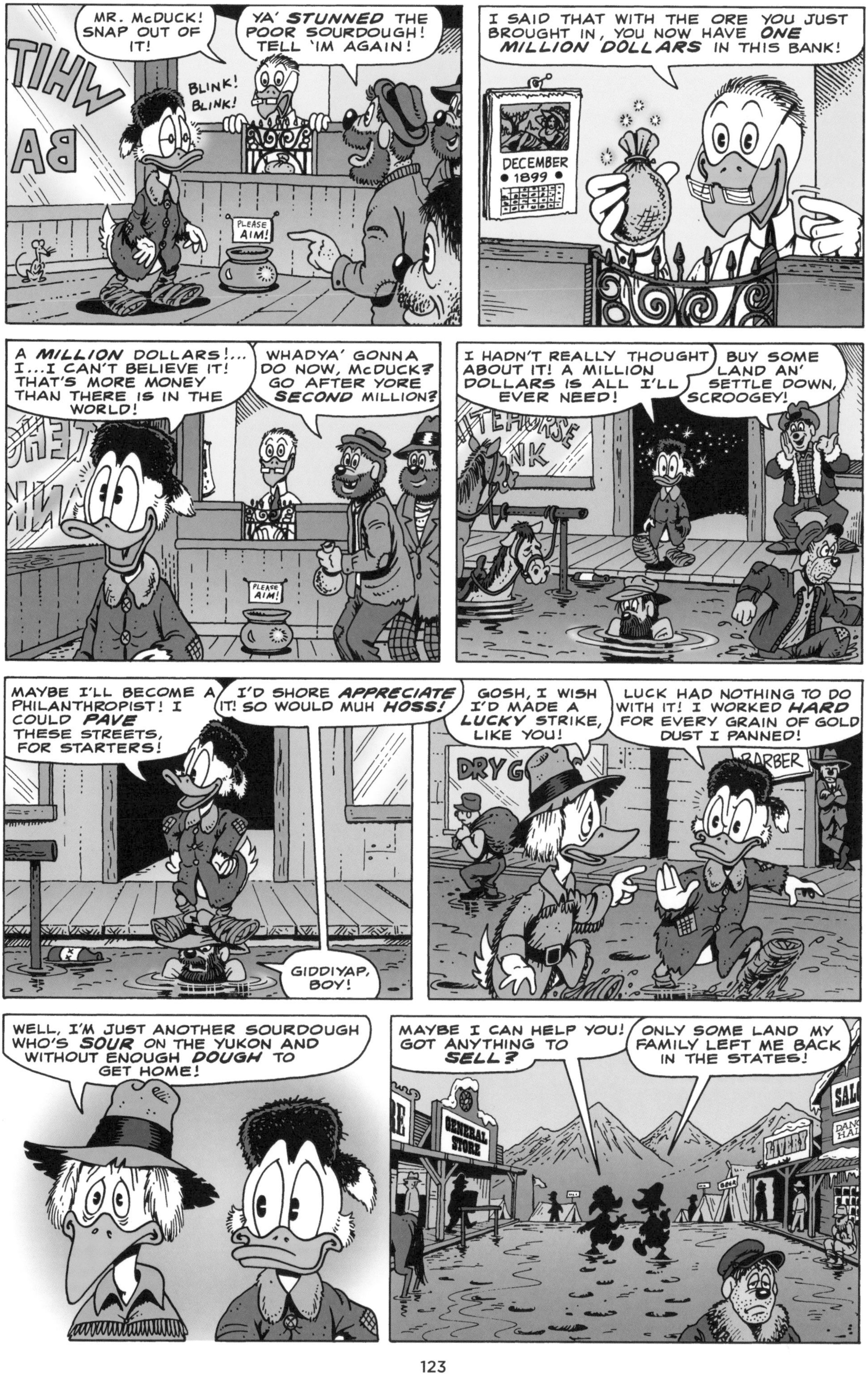
MR. McDUCK! SNAP OUT OF IT!
YA' STUNNED THE POOR SOURDOUGH! TELL 'IM AGAIN!
BLINK! BLINK!
PLEASE AIM!
I SAID THAT WITH THE ORE YOU JUST BROUGHT IN, YOU NOW HAVE ONE MILLION DOLLARS IN THIS BANK!
DECEMBER 1899
A MILLION DOLLARS!... I...I CAN'T BELIEVE IT! THAT'S MORE MONEY THAN THERE IS IN THE WORLD!
WHADYA' GONNA DO NOW, McDUCK? GO AFTER YORE SECOND MILLION?
PLEASE AIM!
I HADN'T REALLY THOUGHT ABOUT IT! A MILLION DOLLARS IS ALL I'LL EVER NEED!
BUY SOME LAND AN' SETTLE DOWN, SCROOGEY!
MAYBE I'LL BECOME A PHILANTHROPIST! I COULD PAVE THESE STREETS, FOR STARTERS!
I'D SHORE APPRECIATE IT! SO WOULD MUH HOSS!
GIDDIYAP, BOY!
GOSH, I WISH I'D MADE A LUCKY STRIKE, LIKE YOU!
LUCK HAD NOTHING TO DO WITH IT! I WORKED HARD FOR EVERY GRAIN OF GOLD DUST I PANNED!
BARBER
WELL, I'M JUST ANOTHER SOURDOUGH WHO'S SOUR ON THE YUKON AND WITHOUT ENOUGH DOUGH TO GET HOME!
MAYBE I CAN HELP YOU! GOT ANYTHING TO SELL?
ONLY SOME LAND MY FAMILY LEFT ME BACK IN THE STATES!
GENERAL STORE
LIVERY

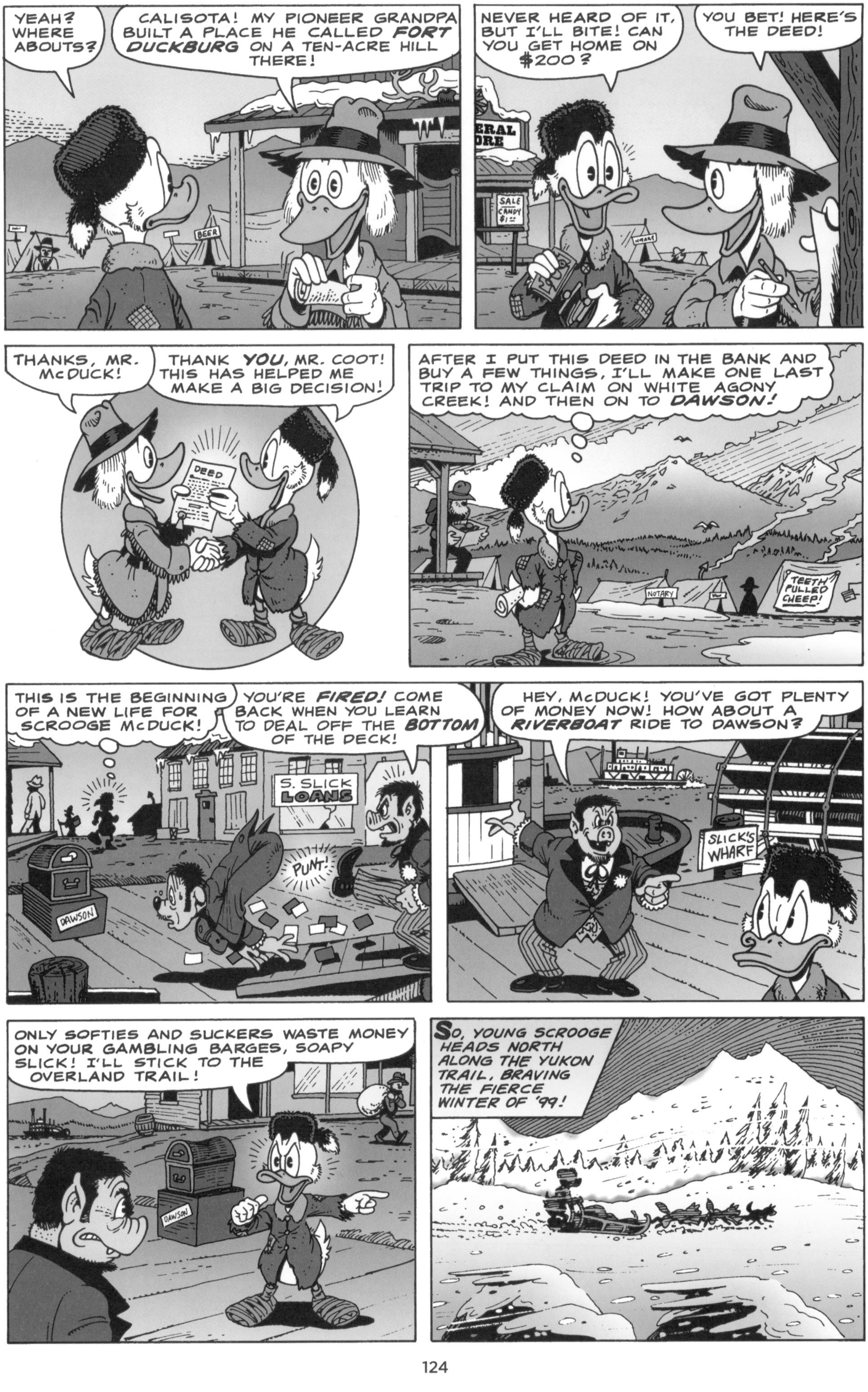
YEAH? WHERE ABOUTS?
CALISOTA! MY PIONEER GRANDPA BUILT A PLACE HE CALLED FORT DUCKBURG ON A TEN-ACRE HILL THERE!
BEER
NEVER HEARD OF IT, BUT I'LL BITE! CAN YOU GET HOME ON $200?
YOU BET! HERE'S THE DEED!
SALE CANDY $1
THANKS, MR. McDUCK!
THANK YOU, MR. COOT! THIS HAS HELPED ME MAKE A BIG DECISION!
DEED
AFTER I PUT THIS DEED IN THE BANK AND BUY A FEW THINGS, I'LL MAKE ONE LAST TRIP TO MY CLAIM ON WHITE AGONY CREEK! AND THEN ON TO DAWSON!
NOTARY
TEETH PULLED CHEEP!
THIS IS THE BEGINNING OF A NEW LIFE FOR SCROOGE McDUCK!
YOU'RE FIRED! COME BACK WHEN YOU LEARN TO DEAL OFF THE BOTTOM OF THE DECK!
S. SLICK LOANS
PUNT!
DAWSON
HEY, McDUCK! YOU'VE GOT PLENTY OF MONEY NOW! HOW ABOUT A RIVERBOAT RIDE TO DAWSON?
SLICK'S WHARF
ONLY SOFTIES AND SUCKERS WASTE MONEY ON YOUR GAMBLING BARGES, SOAPY SLICK! I'LL STICK TO THE OVERLAND TRAIL!
DAWSON
SO, YOUNG SCROOGE HEADS NORTH ALONG THE YUKON TRAIL, BRAVING THE FIERCE WINTER OF '99!

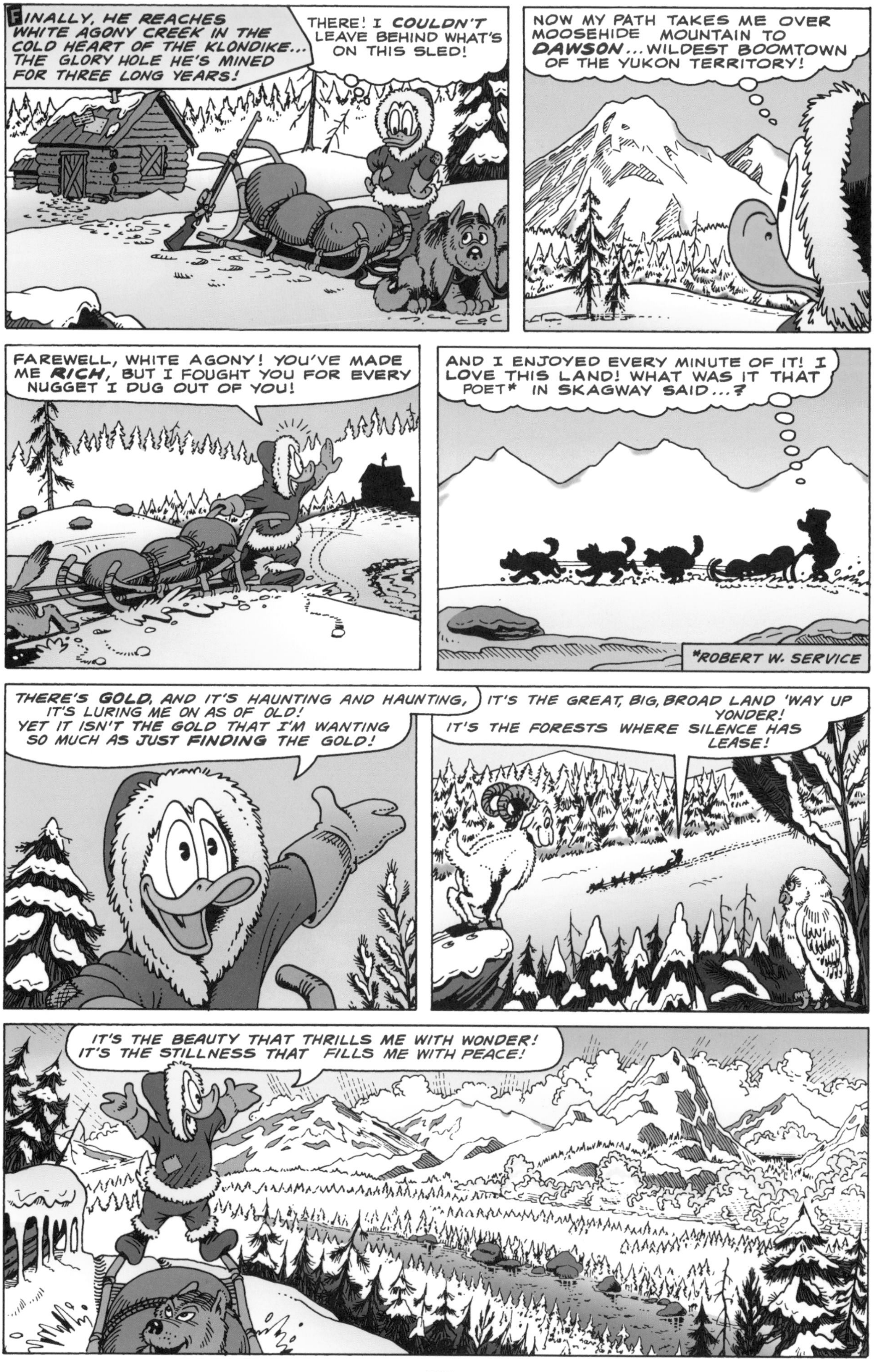
FINALLY, HE REACHES WHITE AGONY CREEK IN THE COLD HEART OF THE KLONDIKE... THE GLORY HOLE HE'S MINED FOR THREE LONG YEARS!
THERE! I COULDN'T LEAVE BEHIND WHAT'S ON THIS SLED!
NOW MY PATH TAKES ME OVER MOOSEHIDE MOUNTAIN TO DAWSON... WILDEST BOOMTOWN OF THE YUKON TERRITORY!
FAREWELL, WHITE AGONY! YOU'VE MADE ME RICH, BUT I FOUGHT YOU FOR EVERY NUGGET I DUG OUT OF YOU!
AND I ENJOYED EVERY MINUTE OF IT! I LOVE THIS LAND! WHAT WAS IT THAT POET* IN SKAGWAY SAID...?
*ROBERT W. SERVICE
THERE'S GOLD, AND IT'S HAUNTING AND HAUNTING, IT'S LURING ME ON AS OF OLD! YET IT ISN'T THE GOLD THAT I'M WANTING SO MUCH AS JUST FINDING THE GOLD!
IT'S THE GREAT, BIG, BROAD LAND 'WAY UP YONDER! IT'S THE FORESTS WHERE SILENCE HAS LEASE!
IT'S THE BEAUTY THAT THRILLS ME WITH WONDER! IT'S THE STILLNESS THAT FILLS ME WITH PEACE!

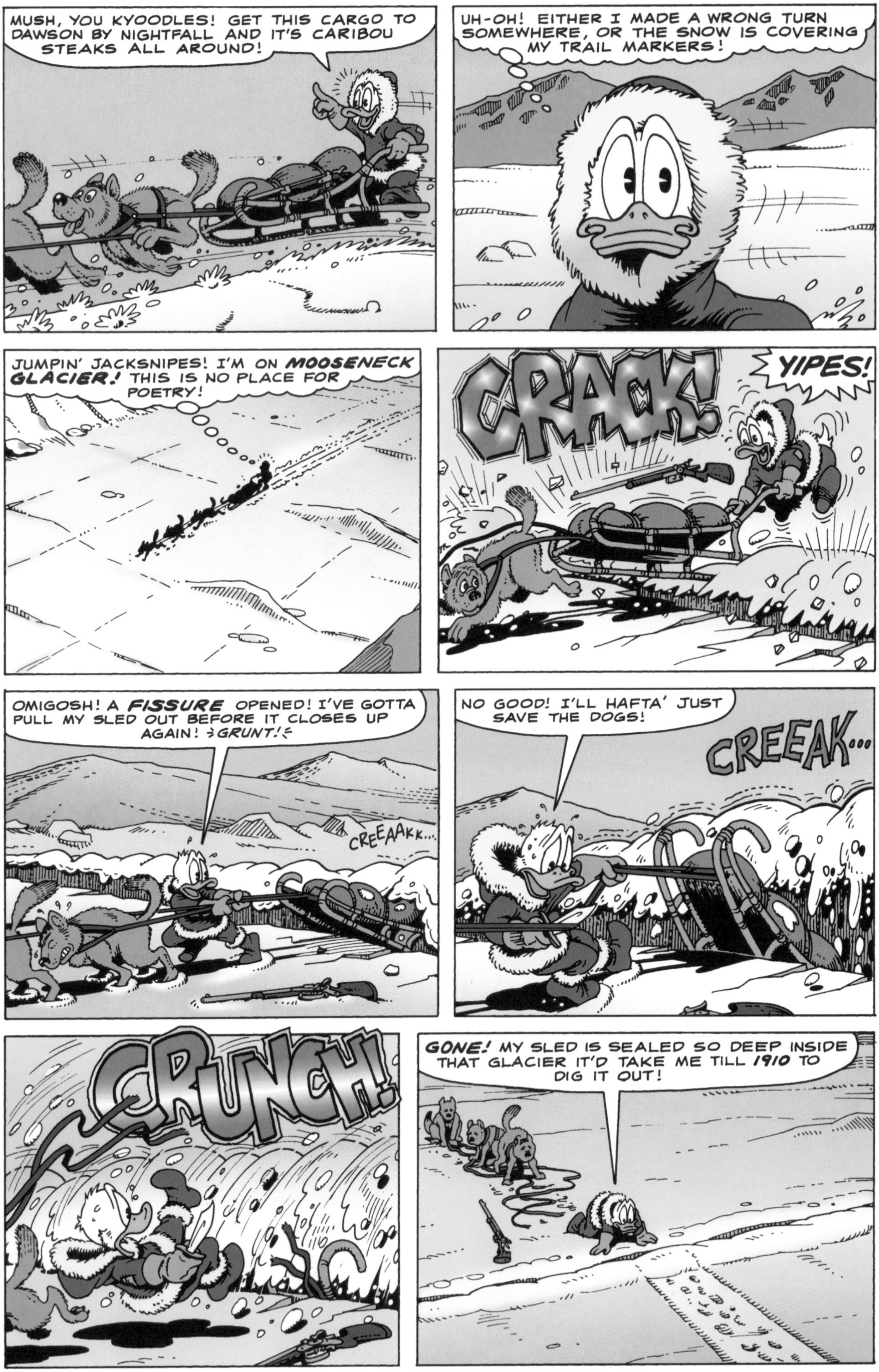
MUSH, YOU KYOODLES! GET THIS CARGO TO DAWSON BY NIGHTFALL AND IT'S CARIBOU STEAKS ALL AROUND!
UH-OH! EITHER I MADE A WRONG TURN SOMEWHERE, OR THE SNOW IS COVERING MY TRAIL MARKERS!
JUMPIN' JACKSNIPES! I'M ON MOOSENECK GLACIER! THIS IS NO PLACE FOR POETRY!
CRACK!
YIPES!
OMIGOSH! A FISSURE OPENED! I'VE GOTTA PULL MY SLED OUT BEFORE IT CLOSES UP AGAIN! GRUNT!
CREEAAKK...
NO GOOD! I'LL HAFTA' JUST SAVE THE DOGS!
CREEAK...
CRUNCH!
GONE! MY SLED IS SEALED SO DEEP INSIDE THAT GLACIER IT'D TAKE ME TILL 1910 TO DIG IT OUT!

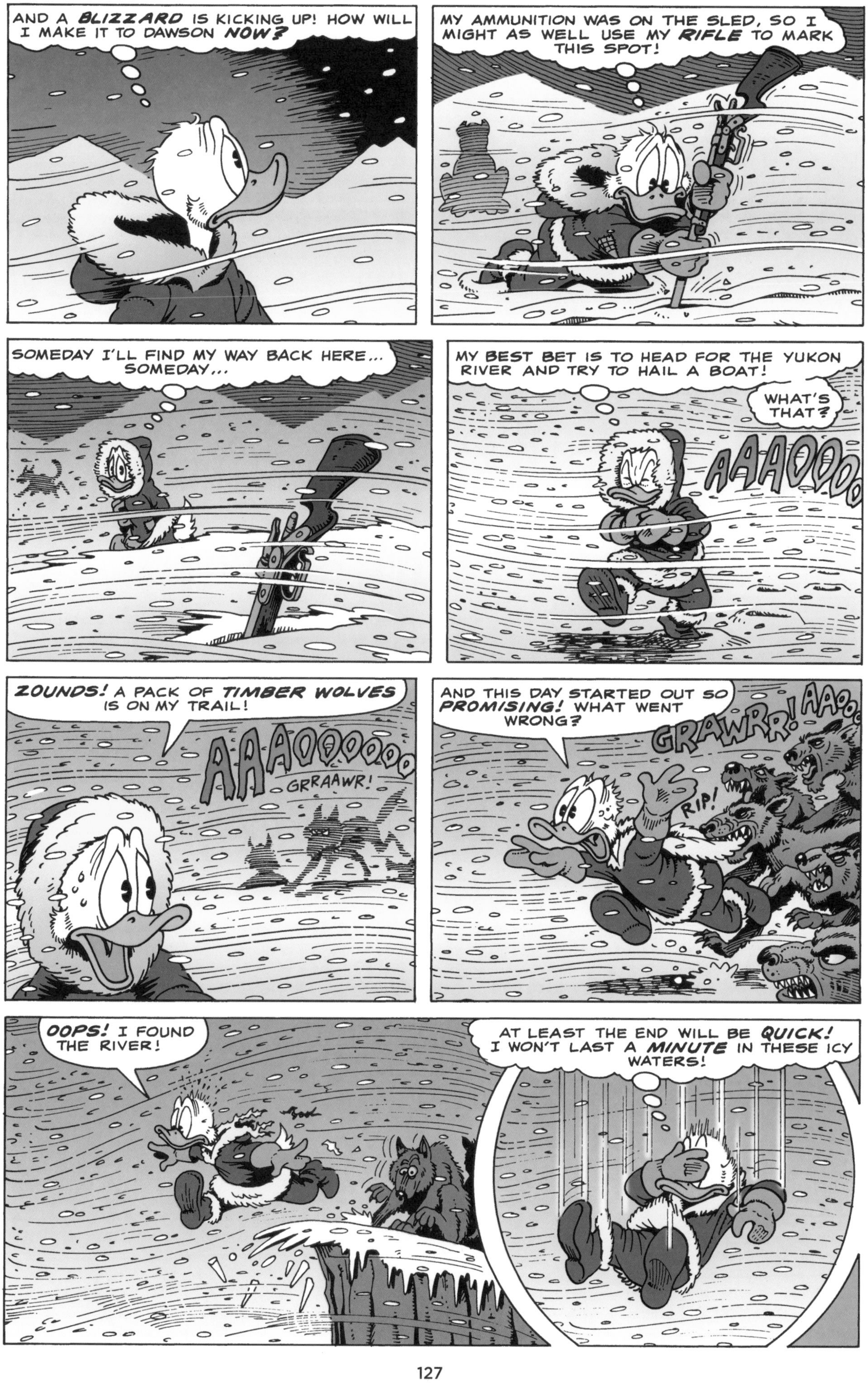
AND A BLIZZARD IS KICKING UP! HOW WILL I MAKE IT TO DAWSON NOW?
MY AMMUNITION WAS ON THE SLED, SO I MIGHT AS WELL USE MY RIFLE TO MARK THIS SPOT!
SOMEDAY I'LL FIND MY WAY BACK HERE... SOMEDAY...
MY BEST BET IS TO HEAD FOR THE YUKON RIVER AND TRY TO HAIL A BOAT!
WHAT'S THAT?
AAAOOOO
ZOUNDS! A PACK OF TIMBER WOLVES IS ON MY TRAIL!
AAAOOOOOOO
GRRAAWR!
AND THIS DAY STARTED OUT SO PROMISING! WHAT WENT WRONG?
GRAWRR! AAOO
RIP!
OOPS! I FOUND THE RIVER!
AT LEAST THE END WILL BE QUICK! I WON'T LAST A MINUTE IN THESE ICY WATERS!

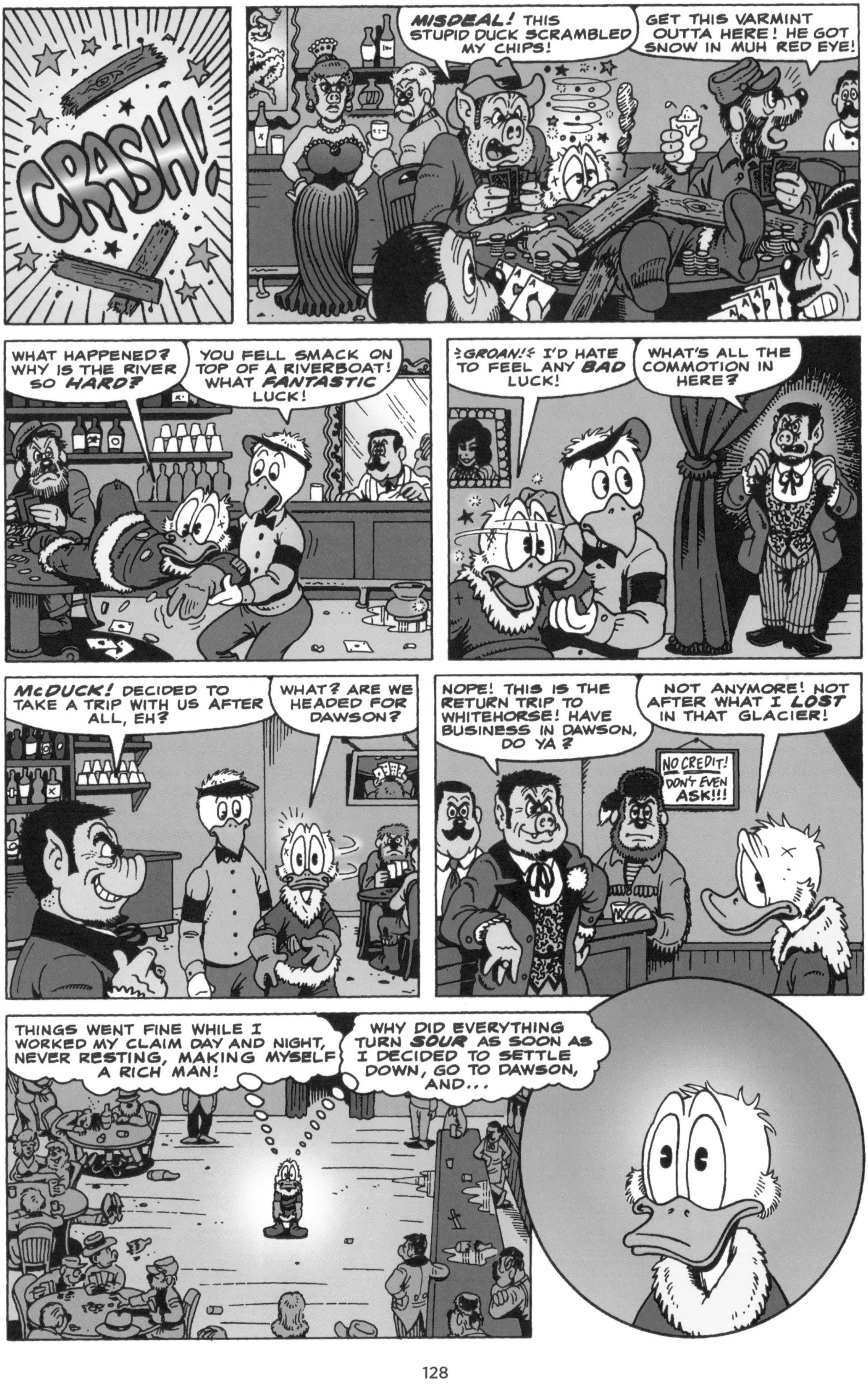
CRASH!
MISDEAL! THIS STUPID DUCK SCRAMBLED MY CHIPS!
GET THIS VARMINT OUTTA HERE! HE GOT SNOW IN MUH RED EYE!
WHAT HAPPENED? WHY IS THE RIVER SO HARD?
YOU FELL SMACK ON TOP OF A RIVERBOAT! WHAT FANTASTIC LUCK!
GROAN! I'D HATE TO FEEL ANY BAD LUCK!
WHAT'S ALL THE COMMOTION IN HERE?
McDUCK! DECIDED TO TAKE A TRIP WITH US AFTER ALL, EH?
WHAT? ARE WE HEADED FOR DAWSON?
NOPE! THIS IS THE RETURN TRIP TO WHITEHORSE! HAVE BUSINESS IN DAWSON, DO YA?
NOT ANYMORE! NOT AFTER WHAT I LOST IN THAT GLACIER!
NO CREDIT! DON'T EVEN ASK!!!
THINGS WENT FINE WHILE I WORKED MY CLAIM DAY AND NIGHT, NEVER RESTING, MAKING MYSELF A RICH MAN!
WHY DID EVERYTHING TURN SOUR AS SOON AS I DECIDED TO SETTLE DOWN, GO TO DAWSON, AND...

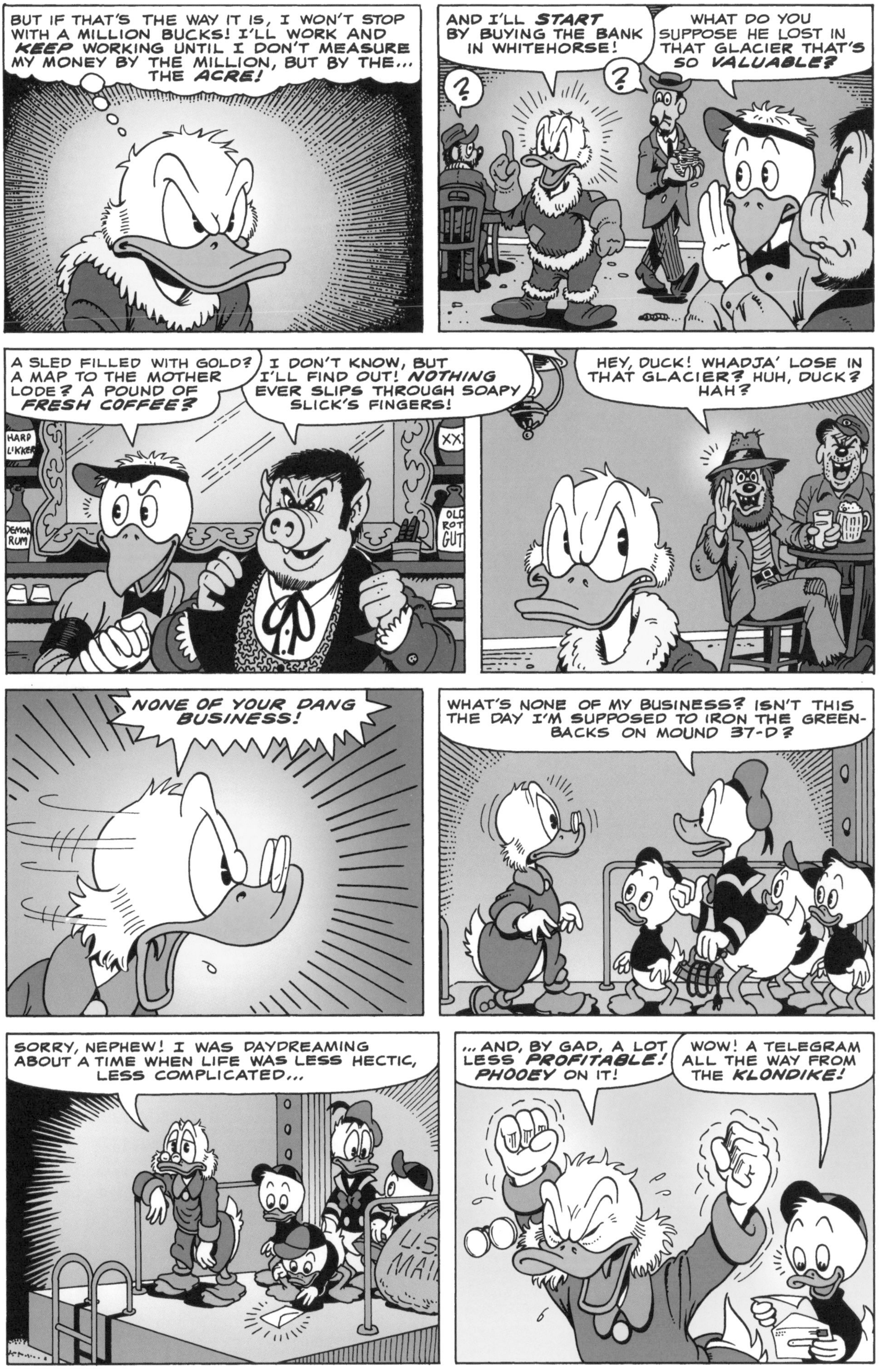
BUT IF THAT'S THE WAY IT IS, I WON'T STOP WITH A MILLION BUCKS! I'LL WORK AND KEEP WORKING UNTIL I DON'T MEASURE MY MONEY BY THE MILLION, BUT BY THE... THE ACRE!
AND I'LL START BY BUYING THE BANK IN WHITEHORSE!
?
?
WHAT DO YOU SUPPOSE HE LOST IN THAT GLACIER THAT'S SO VALUABLE?
A SLED FILLED WITH GOLD? A MAP TO THE MOTHER LODE? A POUND OF FRESH COFFEE?
I DON'T KNOW, BUT I'LL FIND OUT! NOTHING EVER SLIPS THROUGH SOAPY SLICK'S FINGERS!
HARD LIKKER
DEMON RUM
XXX
OLD ROT GUT
HEY, DUCK! WHADJA' LOSE IN THAT GLACIER? HUH, DUCK? HAH?
NONE OF YOUR DANG BUSINESS!
WHAT'S NONE OF MY BUSINESS? ISN'T THIS THE DAY I'M SUPPOSED TO IRON THE GREEN-BACKS ON MOUND 37-D?
SORRY, NEPHEW! I WAS DAYDREAMING ABOUT A TIME WHEN LIFE WAS LESS HECTIC, LESS COMPLICATED...
U.S. MAI
...AND, BY GAD, A LOT LESS PROFITABLE! PHOOEY ON IT!
WOW! A TELEGRAM ALL THE WAY FROM THE KLONDIKE!

IT'S FROM YOUR WHITEHORSE BANK, UNCA SCROOGE!

SO WHAT?! THAT BANK HAS BEEN A WHITE *ELEPHANT* SINCE THE GOLD FIELDS PLAYED OUT!

THEY SAY YOU LEFT STANDING ORDERS TO KEEP TABS ON SOME MARKER IN A GLACIER!

AND THE MARKER AREA IS ABOUT TO FALL INTO THE YUKON RIVER!

MY MARKER? MOOSENECK GLACIER? OH, MY HEAVENLY DAYS! I'VE BEEN WAITING FOR THIS MOMENT FOR *YEARS!*

GLOM!

WHIT!

DIG OUT YOUR OVERCOATS AND PACK YOUR BAGS, BOYS!

WE'RE GOING BACK TO THE KLONDIKE... *AGAIN!!!*

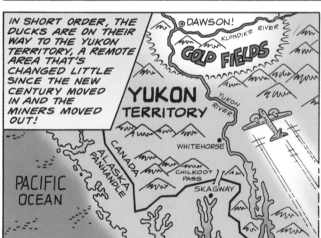

IN SHORT ORDER, THE DUCKS ARE ON THEIR WAY TO THE YUKON TERRITORY, A REMOTE AREA THAT'S CHANGED LITTLE SINCE THE NEW CENTURY MOVED IN AND THE MINERS MOVED OUT!

DAWSON!

KLONDIKE RIVER

GOLD FIELDS

YUKON TERRITORY

YUKON RIVER

WHITEHORSE

CHILKOOT PASS

SKAGWAY

CANADA

ALASKA PANHANDLE

PACIFIC OCEAN

HERE IT IS, UNCA SCROOGE! A GLACIER FORMS WHEN SNOW ON A MOUNTAIN NEVER GETS WARM ENOUGH TO MELT! THE COMPACTED MASS MOVES *SLOWLY*, LIKE A SOLID RIVER, A FEW FEET EACH YEAR!

Z

YES, BOYS...

...THAT'S WHY I HAD THE BANK KEEP AN EYE ON MY MARKER! WHEN MY CHUNK FALLS INTO THE RIVER I'LL *FINALLY* BE ABLE TO RETRIEVE MY DOGSLED!

DAWSON, Y. T.

RAMJET FLYING SER

GOSH, UNCLE SCROOGE! WHAT'S ON THE SLED THAT'S SO IMPORTANT?

NOTHING THAT CONCERNS YOU! YOU GET 30 CENTS AN HOUR TO HELP ME, NOT TO BE SO DANG *NOSEY!*

RAMJET, IN A DIV. OF McDUCK IN

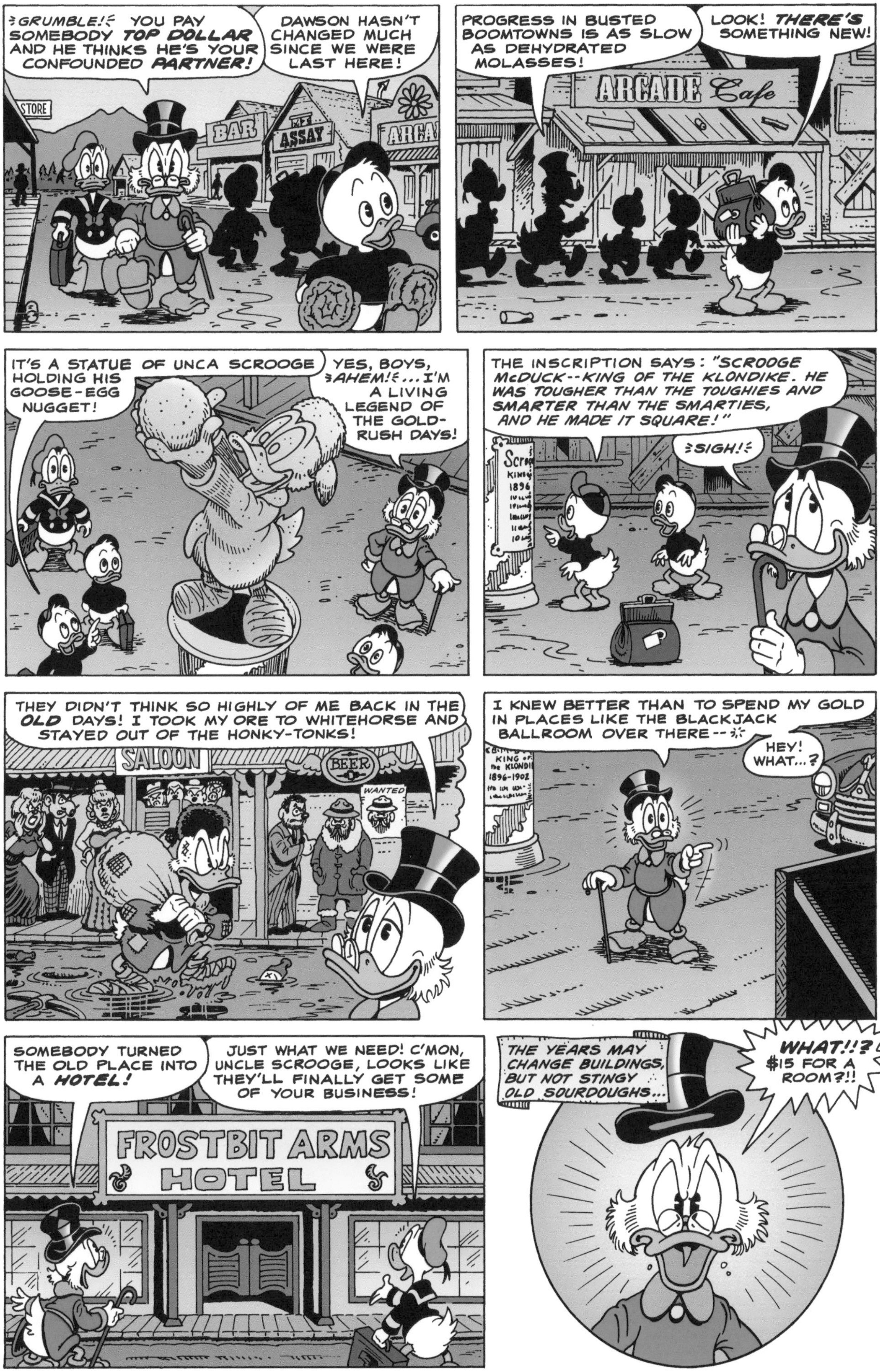
GRUMBLE! YOU PAY SOMEBODY **TOP DOLLAR** AND HE THINKS HE'S YOUR CONFOUNDED **PARTNER!**
DAWSON HASN'T CHANGED MUCH SINCE WE WERE LAST HERE!
STORE
BAR
ASSAY
PROGRESS IN BUSTED BOOMTOWNS IS AS SLOW AS DEHYDRATED MOLASSES!
LOOK! **THERE'S** SOMETHING NEW!
ARCADE Cafe
IT'S A STATUE OF UNCA SCROOGE HOLDING HIS GOOSE-EGG NUGGET!
YES, BOYS, *AHEM!*... I'M A LIVING LEGEND OF THE GOLD-RUSH DAYS!
THE INSCRIPTION SAYS: *"SCROOGE McDUCK--KING OF THE KLONDIKE. HE WAS TOUGHER THAN THE TOUGHIES AND SMARTER THAN THE SMARTIES, AND HE MADE IT SQUARE!"*
SIGH!
THEY DIDN'T THINK SO HIGHLY OF ME BACK IN THE ***OLD*** DAYS! I TOOK MY ORE TO WHITEHORSE AND STAYED OUT OF THE HONKY-TONKS!
SALOON
BEER
WANTED
I KNEW BETTER THAN TO SPEND MY GOLD IN PLACES LIKE THE BLACKJACK BALLROOM OVER THERE--
HEY! WHAT...?
KING OF the KLONDI
1896-1902
SOMEBODY TURNED THE OLD PLACE INTO A ***HOTEL!***
JUST WHAT WE NEED! C'MON, UNCLE SCROOGE, LOOKS LIKE THEY'LL FINALLY GET SOME OF YOUR BUSINESS!
FROSTBIT ARMS HOTEL
THE YEARS MAY CHANGE BUILDINGS, BUT NOT STINGY OLD SOURDOUGHS...
WHAT!!? ***$15 FOR A ROOM?!!***

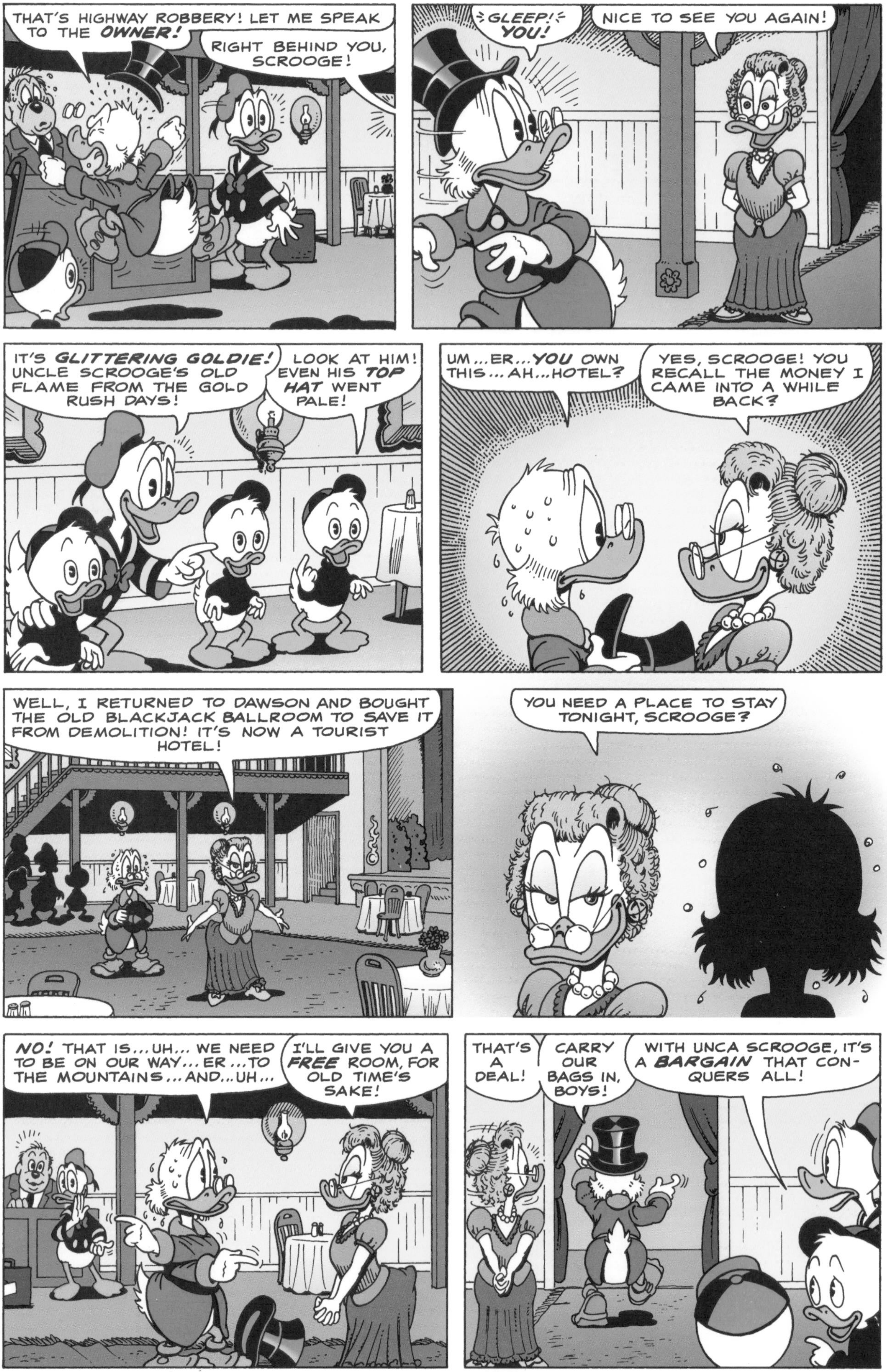
THAT'S HIGHWAY ROBBERY! LET ME SPEAK TO THE OWNER!
RIGHT BEHIND YOU, SCROOGE!
GLEEP! YOU!
NICE TO SEE YOU AGAIN!
IT'S GLITTERING GOLDIE! UNCLE SCROOGE'S OLD FLAME FROM THE GOLD RUSH DAYS!
LOOK AT HIM! EVEN HIS TOP HAT WENT PALE!
UM...ER...YOU OWN THIS...AH...HOTEL?
YES, SCROOGE! YOU RECALL THE MONEY I CAME INTO A WHILE BACK?
WELL, I RETURNED TO DAWSON AND BOUGHT THE OLD BLACKJACK BALLROOM TO SAVE IT FROM DEMOLITION! IT'S NOW A TOURIST HOTEL!
YOU NEED A PLACE TO STAY TONIGHT, SCROOGE?
NO! THAT IS...UH... WE NEED TO BE ON OUR WAY...ER...TO THE MOUNTAINS...AND...UH...
I'LL GIVE YOU A FREE ROOM, FOR OLD TIME'S SAKE!
THAT'S A DEAL!
CARRY OUR BAGS IN, BOYS!
WITH UNCA SCROOGE, IT'S A BARGAIN THAT CONQUERS ALL!

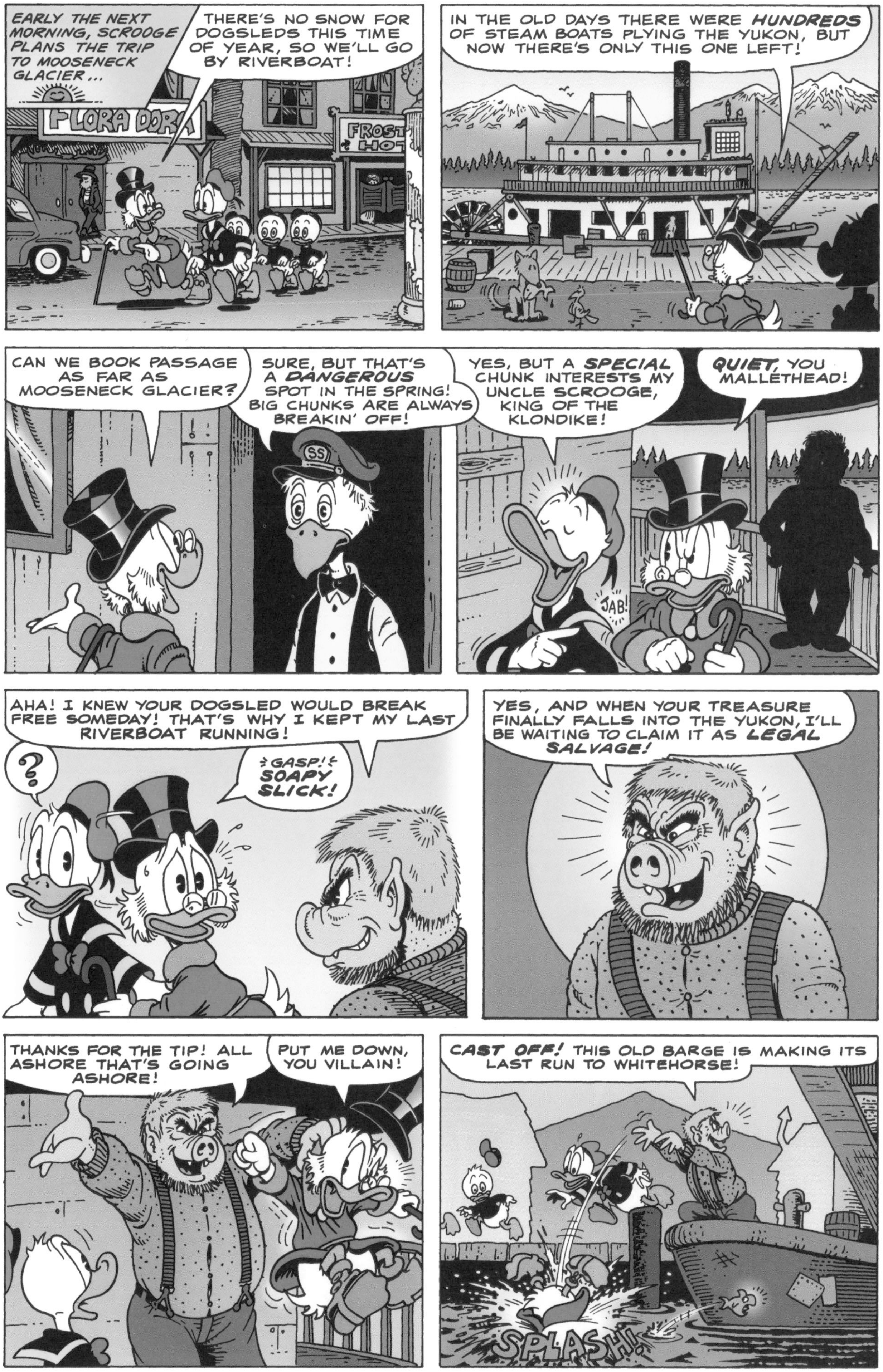
EARLY THE NEXT MORNING, SCROOGE PLANS THE TRIP TO MOOSENECK GLACIER...
THERE'S NO SNOW FOR DOGSLEDS THIS TIME OF YEAR, SO WE'LL GO BY RIVERBOAT!
FLORA DORA
FROST HOT
IN THE OLD DAYS THERE WERE HUNDREDS OF STEAM BOATS PLYING THE YUKON, BUT NOW THERE'S ONLY THIS ONE LEFT!
CAN WE BOOK PASSAGE AS FAR AS MOOSENECK GLACIER?
SURE, BUT THAT'S A DANGEROUS SPOT IN THE SPRING! BIG CHUNKS ARE ALWAYS BREAKIN' OFF!
SS
YES, BUT A SPECIAL CHUNK INTERESTS MY UNCLE SCROOGE, KING OF THE KLONDIKE!
QUIET, YOU MALLETHEAD!
JAB!
AHA! I KNEW YOUR DOGSLED WOULD BREAK FREE SOMEDAY! THAT'S WHY I KEPT MY LAST RIVERBOAT RUNNING!
?
GASP! SOAPY SLICK!
YES, AND WHEN YOUR TREASURE FINALLY FALLS INTO THE YUKON, I'LL BE WAITING TO CLAIM IT AS LEGAL SALVAGE!
THANKS FOR THE TIP! ALL ASHORE THAT'S GOING ASHORE!
PUT ME DOWN, YOU VILLAIN!
CAST OFF! THIS OLD BARGE IS MAKING ITS LAST RUN TO WHITEHORSE!
SPLASH!

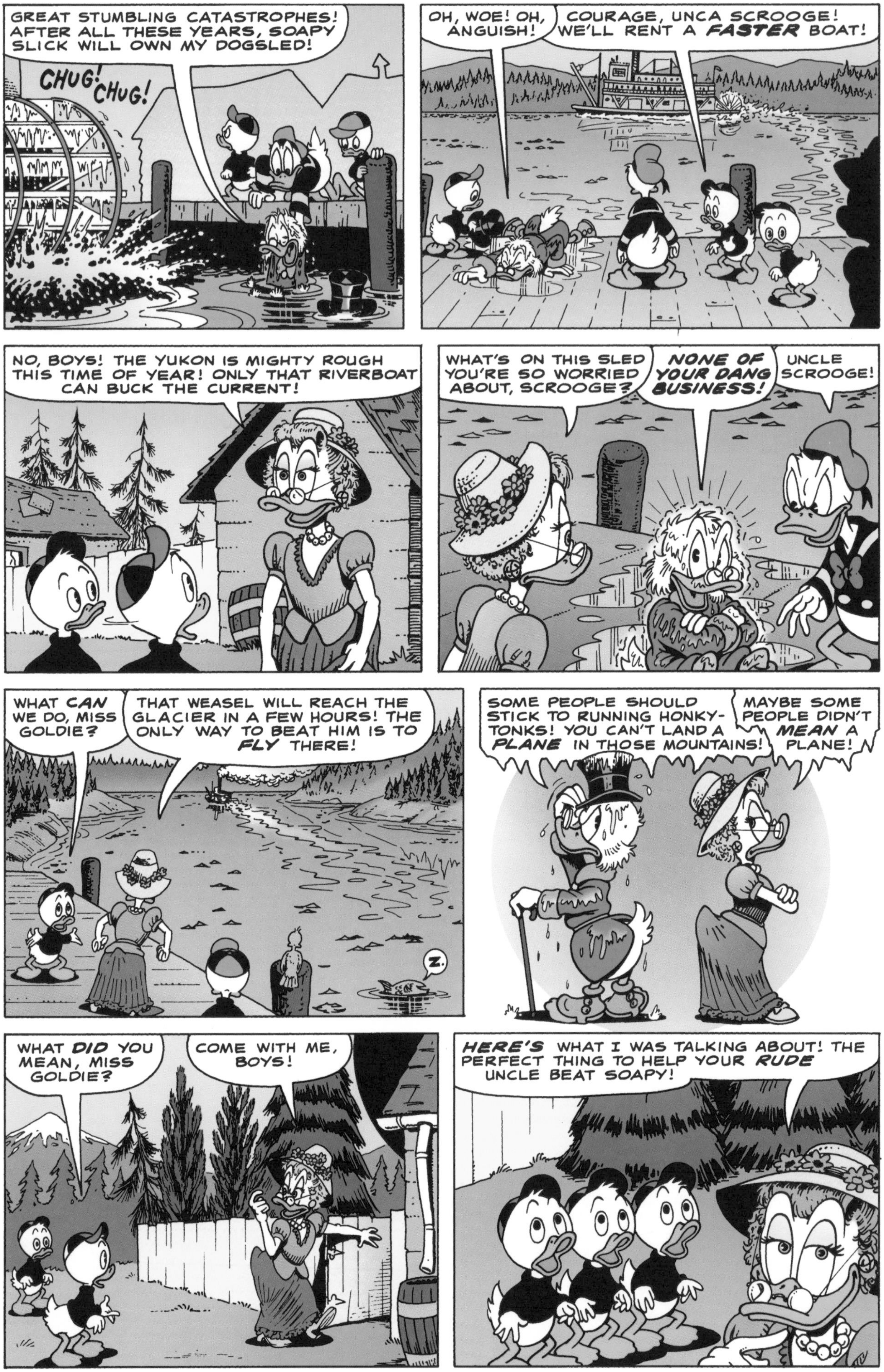
GREAT STUMBLING CATASTROPHES! AFTER ALL THESE YEARS, SOAPY SLICK WILL OWN MY DOGSLED!
CHUG! CHUG!
OH, WOE! OH, ANGUISH!
COURAGE, UNCA SCROOGE! WE'LL RENT A FASTER BOAT!
NO, BOYS! THE YUKON IS MIGHTY ROUGH THIS TIME OF YEAR! ONLY THAT RIVERBOAT CAN BUCK THE CURRENT!
WHAT'S ON THIS SLED YOU'RE SO WORRIED ABOUT, SCROOGE?
NONE OF YOUR DANG BUSINESS!
UNCLE SCROOGE!
WHAT CAN WE DO, MISS GOLDIE?
THAT WEASEL WILL REACH THE GLACIER IN A FEW HOURS! THE ONLY WAY TO BEAT HIM IS TO FLY THERE!
Z.
SOME PEOPLE SHOULD STICK TO RUNNING HONKY-TONKS! YOU CAN'T LAND A PLANE IN THOSE MOUNTAINS!
MAYBE SOME PEOPLE DIDN'T MEAN A PLANE!
WHAT DID YOU MEAN, MISS GOLDIE?
COME WITH ME, BOYS!
HERE'S WHAT I WAS TALKING ABOUT! THE PERFECT THING TO HELP YOUR RUDE UNCLE BEAT SOAPY!

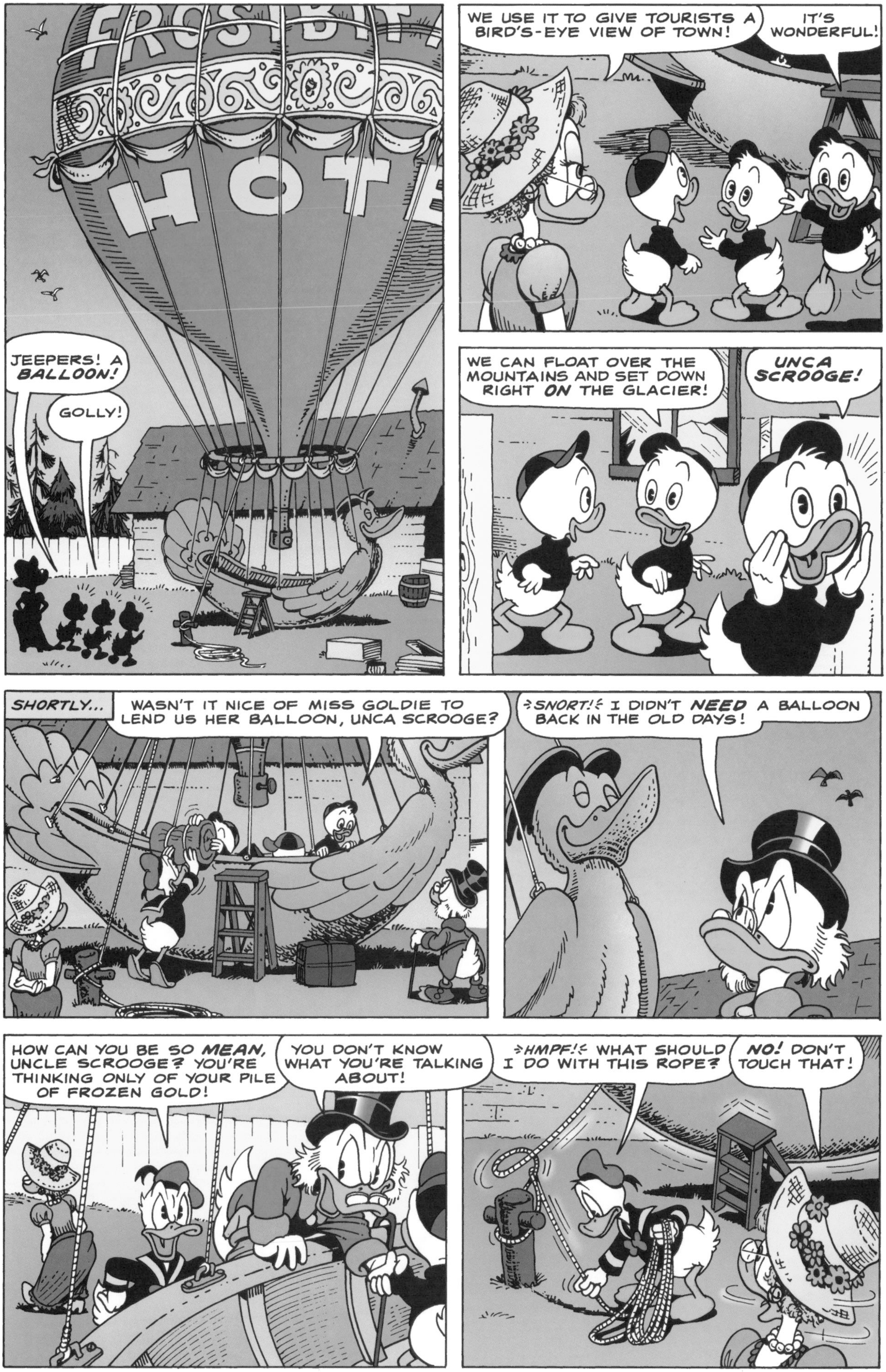

FROSTBITE
HOTE
JEEPERS! A BALLOON!
GOLLY!
WE USE IT TO GIVE TOURISTS A BIRD'S-EYE VIEW OF TOWN!
IT'S WONDERFUL!
WE CAN FLOAT OVER THE MOUNTAINS AND SET DOWN RIGHT ON THE GLACIER!
UNCA SCROOGE!
SHORTLY...
WASN'T IT NICE OF MISS GOLDIE TO LEND US HER BALLOON, UNCA SCROOGE?
SNORT! I DIDN'T NEED A BALLOON BACK IN THE OLD DAYS!
HOW CAN YOU BE SO MEAN, UNCLE SCROOGE? YOU'RE THINKING ONLY OF YOUR PILE OF FROZEN GOLD!
YOU DON'T KNOW WHAT YOU'RE TALKING ABOUT!
HMPF! WHAT SHOULD I DO WITH THIS ROPE?
NO! DON'T TOUCH THAT!

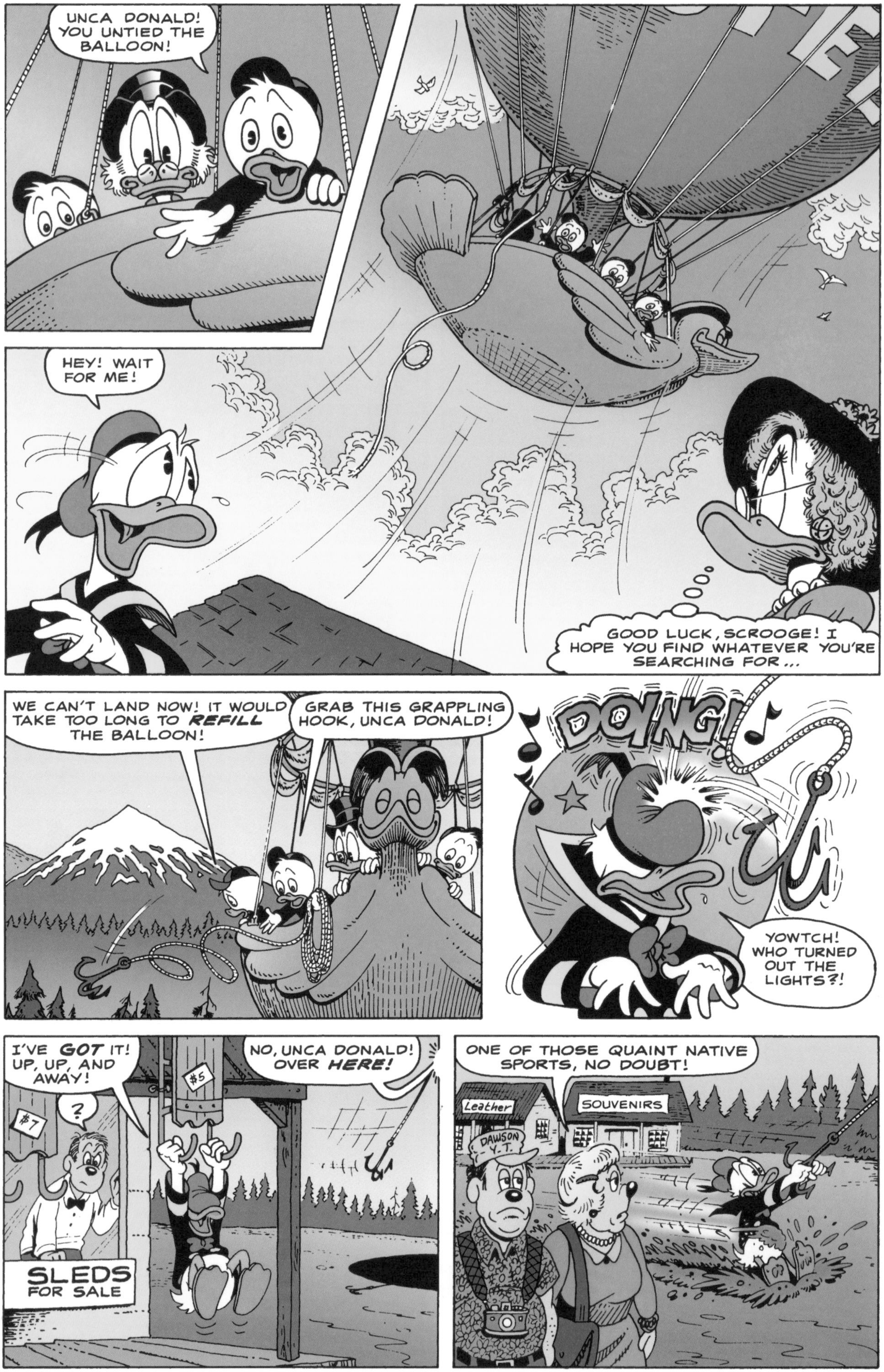
UNCA DONALD! YOU UNTIED THE BALLOON!
HEY! WAIT FOR ME!
GOOD LUCK, SCROOGE! I HOPE YOU FIND WHATEVER YOU'RE SEARCHING FOR...
WE CAN'T LAND NOW! IT WOULD TAKE TOO LONG TO REFILL THE BALLOON!
GRAB THIS GRAPPLING HOOK, UNCA DONALD!
DOING!
YOWTCH! WHO TURNED OUT THE LIGHTS?!
I'VE GOT IT! UP, UP, AND AWAY!
NO, UNCA DONALD! OVER HERE!
?
$7
$5
SLEDS FOR SALE
ONE OF THOSE QUAINT NATIVE SPORTS, NO DOUBT!
Leather
SOUVENIRS
DAWSON Y.T.

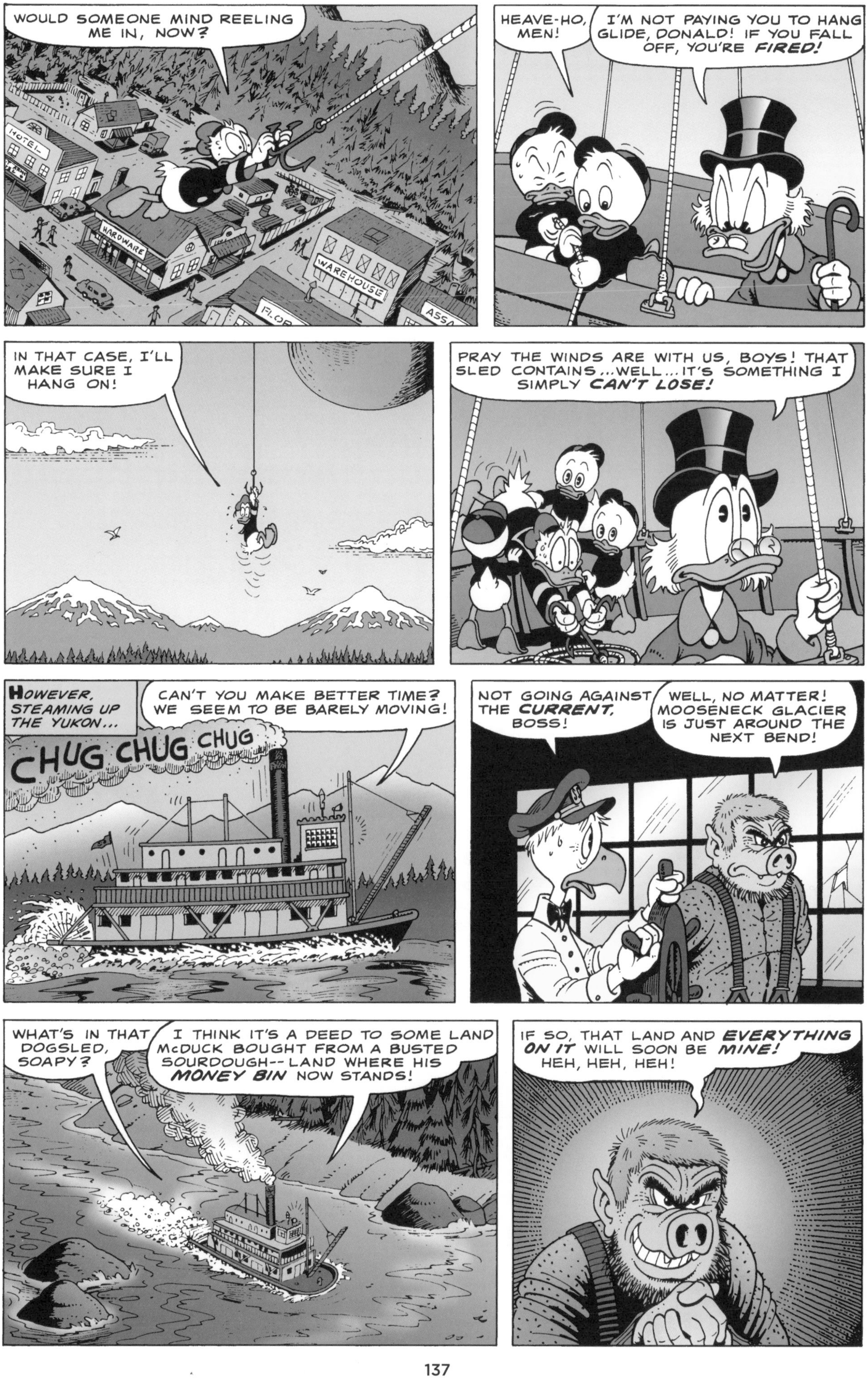
WOULD SOMEONE MIND REELING ME IN, NOW?
HOTEL
WARDWARE
WAREHOUSE
HEAVE-HO, MEN!
I'M NOT PAYING YOU TO HANG GLIDE, DONALD! IF YOU FALL OFF, YOU'RE FIRED!
IN THAT CASE, I'LL MAKE SURE I HANG ON!
PRAY THE WINDS ARE WITH US, BOYS! THAT SLED CONTAINS ...WELL... IT'S SOMETHING I SIMPLY CAN'T LOSE!
HOWEVER, STEAMING UP THE YUKON...
CAN'T YOU MAKE BETTER TIME? WE SEEM TO BE BARELY MOVING!
CHUG CHUG CHUG
NOT GOING AGAINST THE CURRENT, BOSS!
WELL, NO MATTER! MOOSENECK GLACIER IS JUST AROUND THE NEXT BEND!
WHAT'S IN THAT DOGSLED, SOAPY?
I THINK IT'S A DEED TO SOME LAND McDUCK BOUGHT FROM A BUSTED SOURDOUGH-- LAND WHERE HIS MONEY BIN NOW STANDS!
IF SO, THAT LAND AND EVERYTHING ON IT WILL SOON BE MINE! HEH, HEH, HEH!

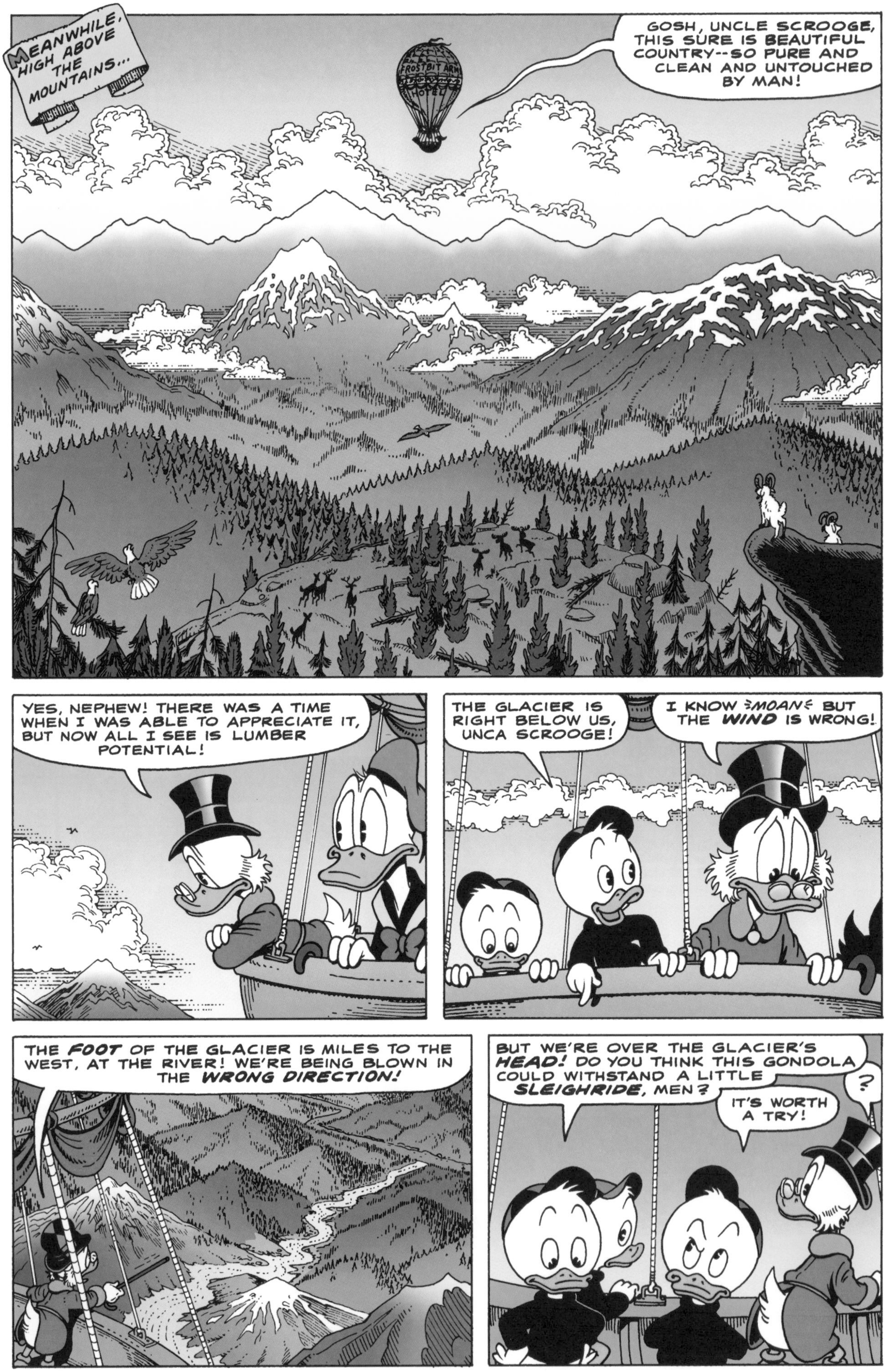
MEANWHILE, HIGH ABOVE THE MOUNTAINS...
GOSH, UNCLE SCROOGE, THIS SURE IS BEAUTIFUL COUNTRY--SO PURE AND CLEAN AND UNTOUCHED BY MAN!
FROSTBIT ARMS HOTEL
YES, NEPHEW! THERE WAS A TIME WHEN I WAS ABLE TO APPRECIATE IT, BUT NOW ALL I SEE IS LUMBER POTENTIAL!
THE GLACIER IS RIGHT BELOW US, UNCA SCROOGE!
I KNOW *MOAN* BUT THE WIND IS WRONG!
THE FOOT OF THE GLACIER IS MILES TO THE WEST, AT THE RIVER! WE'RE BEING BLOWN IN THE WRONG DIRECTION!
BUT WE'RE OVER THE GLACIER'S HEAD! DO YOU THINK THIS GONDOLA COULD WITHSTAND A LITTLE SLEIGHRIDE, MEN?
?
IT'S WORTH A TRY!

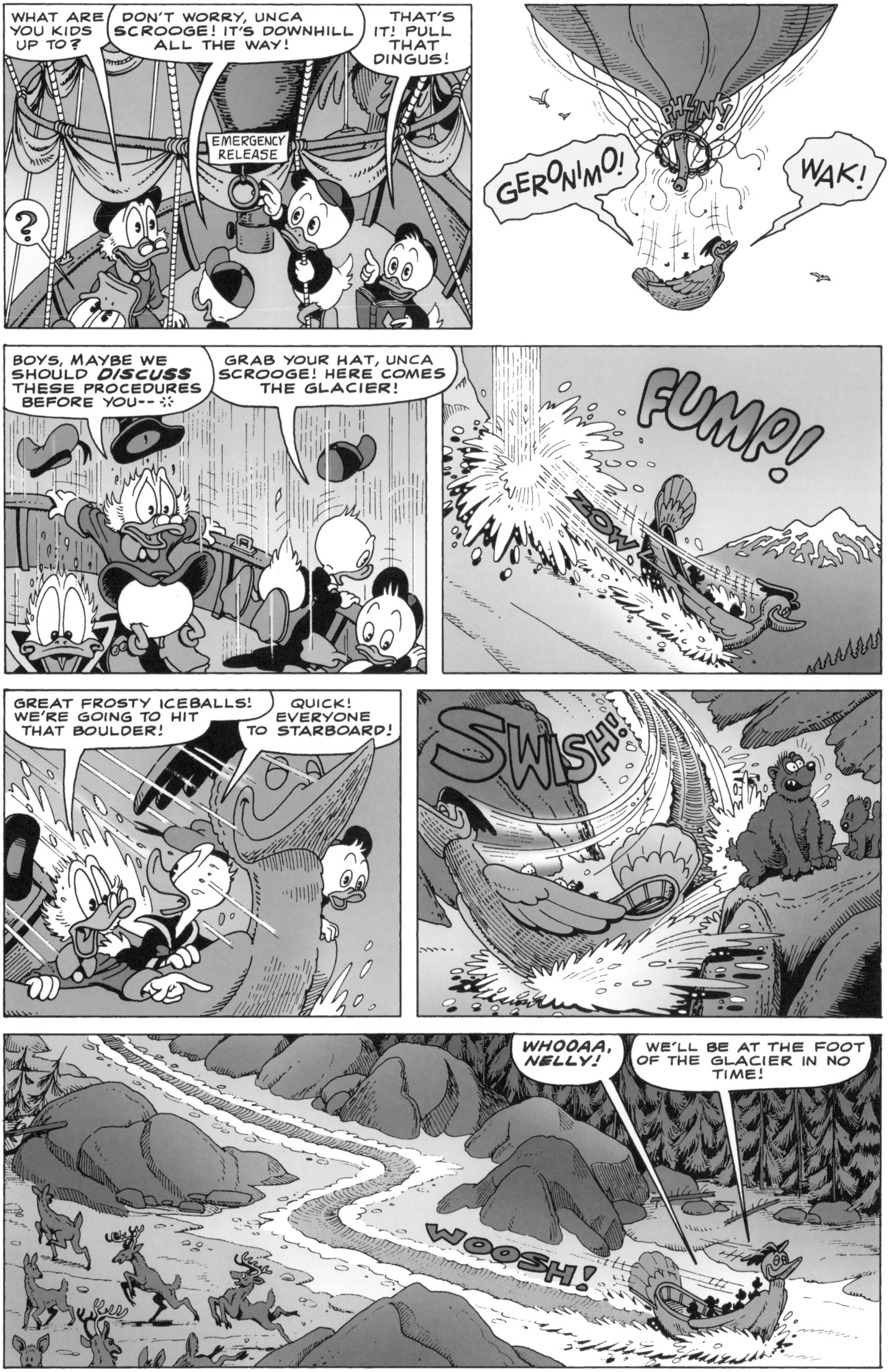
WHAT ARE YOU KIDS UP TO?
DON'T WORRY, UNCA SCROOGE! IT'S DOWNHILL ALL THE WAY!
THAT'S IT! PULL THAT DINGUS!
EMERGENCY RELEASE
?
PHLINK!
GERONIMO!
WAK!
BOYS, MAYBE WE SHOULD DISCUSS THESE PROCEDURES BEFORE YOU--
GRAB YOUR HAT, UNCA SCROOGE! HERE COMES THE GLACIER!
FUMP!
ZOW
GREAT FROSTY ICEBALLS! WE'RE GOING TO HIT THAT BOULDER!
QUICK! EVERYONE TO STARBOARD!
SWISH!
WHOOAA, NELLY!
WE'LL BE AT THE FOOT OF THE GLACIER IN NO TIME!
WOOSH!

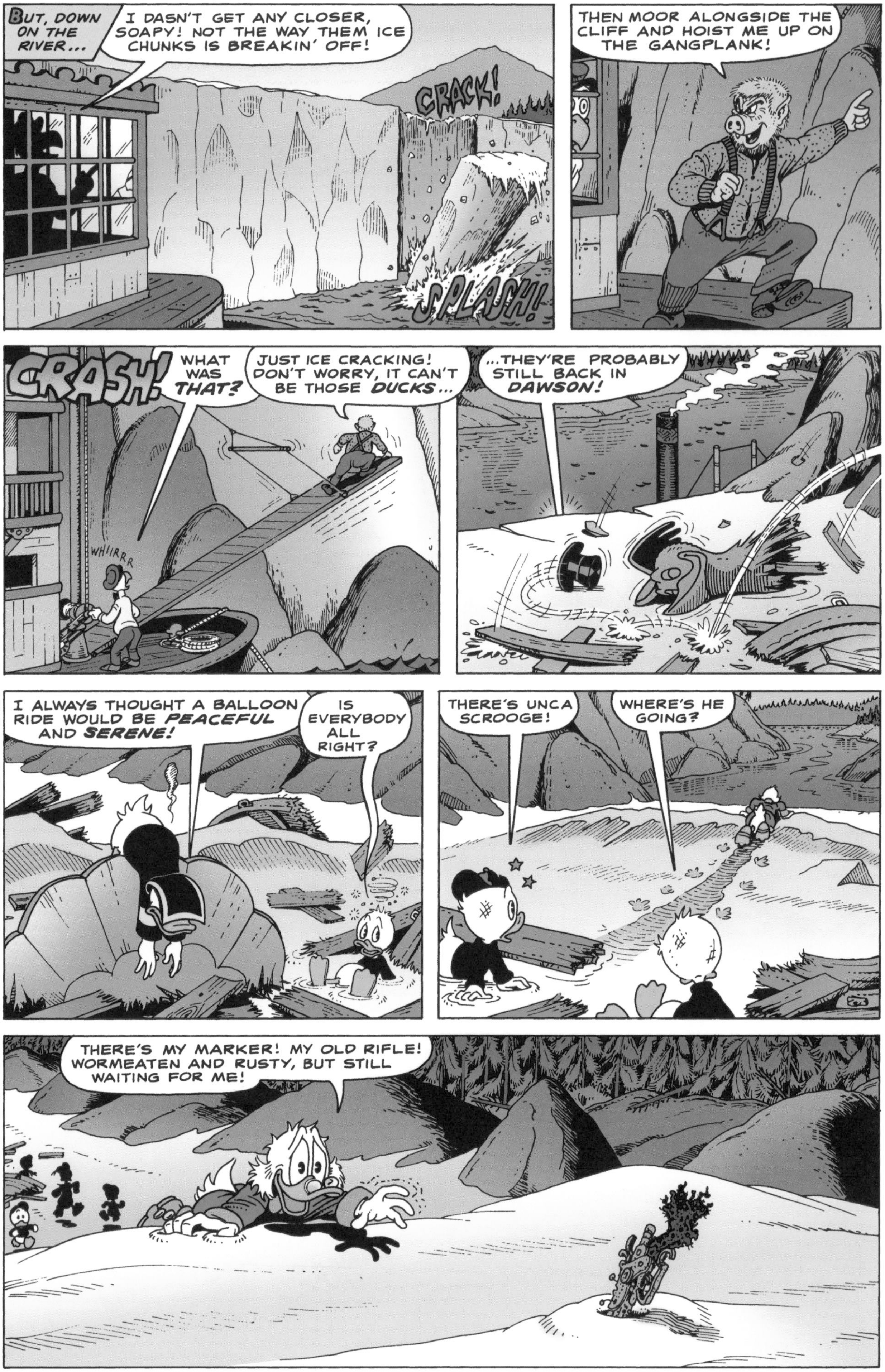

BUT, DOWN ON THE RIVER...
I DASN'T GET ANY CLOSER, SOAPY! NOT THE WAY THEM ICE CHUNKS IS BREAKIN' OFF!
CRACK!
SPLASH!
THEN MOOR ALONGSIDE THE CLIFF AND HOIST ME UP ON THE GANGPLANK!
CRASH!
WHAT WAS THAT?
JUST ICE CRACKING! DON'T WORRY, IT CAN'T BE THOSE DUCKS...
WHIRRR
...THEY'RE PROBABLY STILL BACK IN DAWSON!
I ALWAYS THOUGHT A BALLOON RIDE WOULD BE PEACEFUL AND SERENE!
IS EVERYBODY ALL RIGHT?
THERE'S UNCA SCROOGE!
WHERE'S HE GOING?
THERE'S MY MARKER! MY OLD RIFLE! WORMEATEN AND RUSTY, BUT STILL WAITING FOR ME!

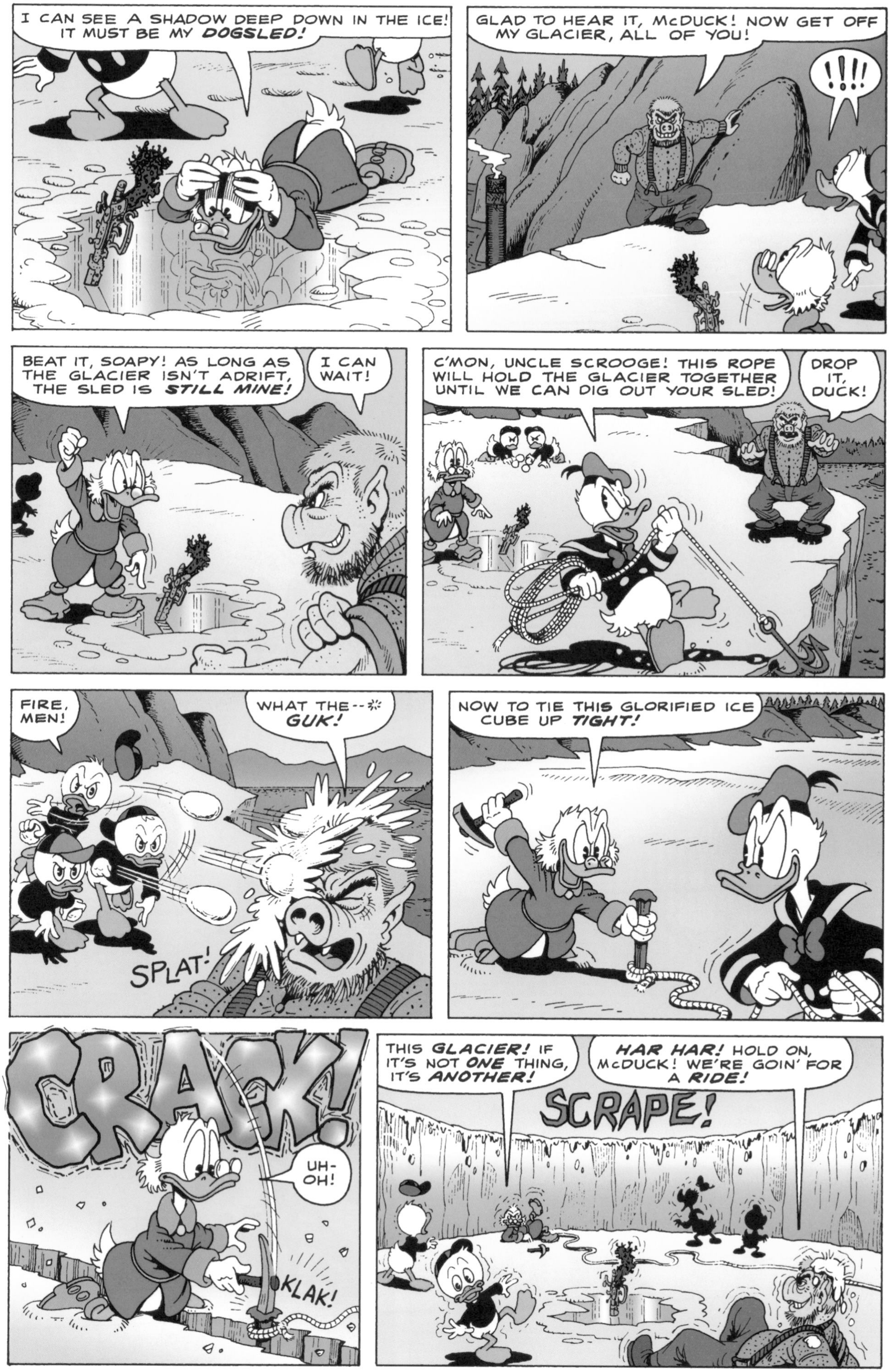
I CAN SEE A SHADOW DEEP DOWN IN THE ICE! IT MUST BE MY DOGSLED!
GLAD TO HEAR IT, McDUCK! NOW GET OFF MY GLACIER, ALL OF YOU!
!!!!
BEAT IT, SOAPY! AS LONG AS THE GLACIER ISN'T ADRIFT, THE SLED IS STILL MINE!
I CAN WAIT!
C'MON, UNCLE SCROOGE! THIS ROPE WILL HOLD THE GLACIER TOGETHER UNTIL WE CAN DIG OUT YOUR SLED!
DROP IT, DUCK!
FIRE, MEN!
WHAT THE-- GUK!
SPLAT!
NOW TO TIE THIS GLORIFIED ICE CUBE UP TIGHT!
CRACK!
UH-OH!
KLAK!
THIS GLACIER! IF IT'S NOT ONE THING, IT'S ANOTHER!
HAR HAR! HOLD ON, McDUCK! WE'RE GOIN' FOR A RIDE!
SCRAPE!

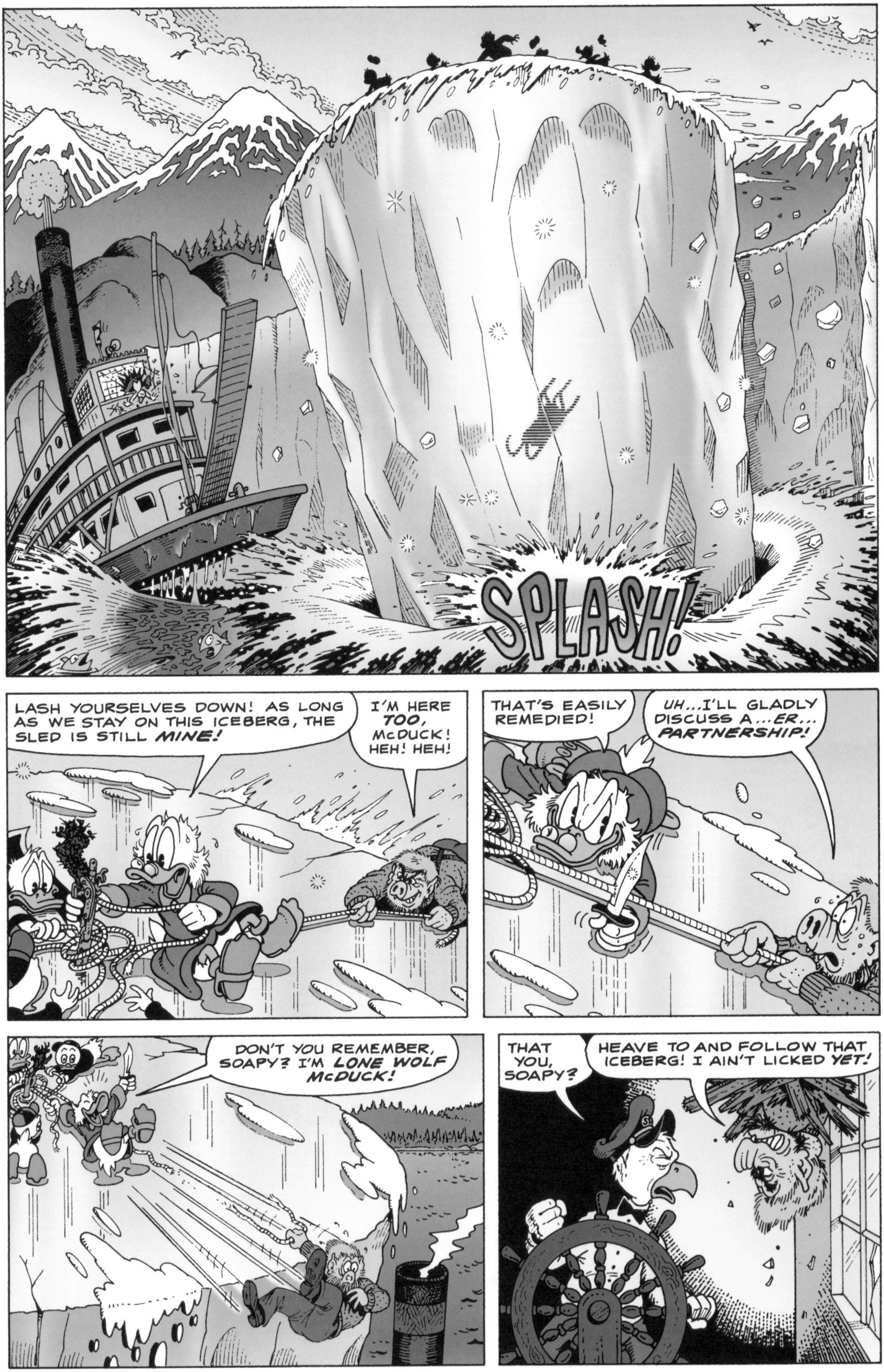
SPLASH!
LASH YOURSELVES DOWN! AS LONG AS WE STAY ON THIS ICEBERG, THE SLED IS STILL MINE!
I'M HERE TOO, McDUCK! HEH! HEH!
THAT'S EASILY REMEDIED!
UH...I'LL GLADLY DISCUSS A...ER... PARTNERSHIP!
DON'T YOU REMEMBER, SOAPY? I'M LONE WOLF McDUCK!
THAT YOU, SOAPY?
HEAVE TO AND FOLLOW THAT ICEBERG! I AIN'T LICKED YET!

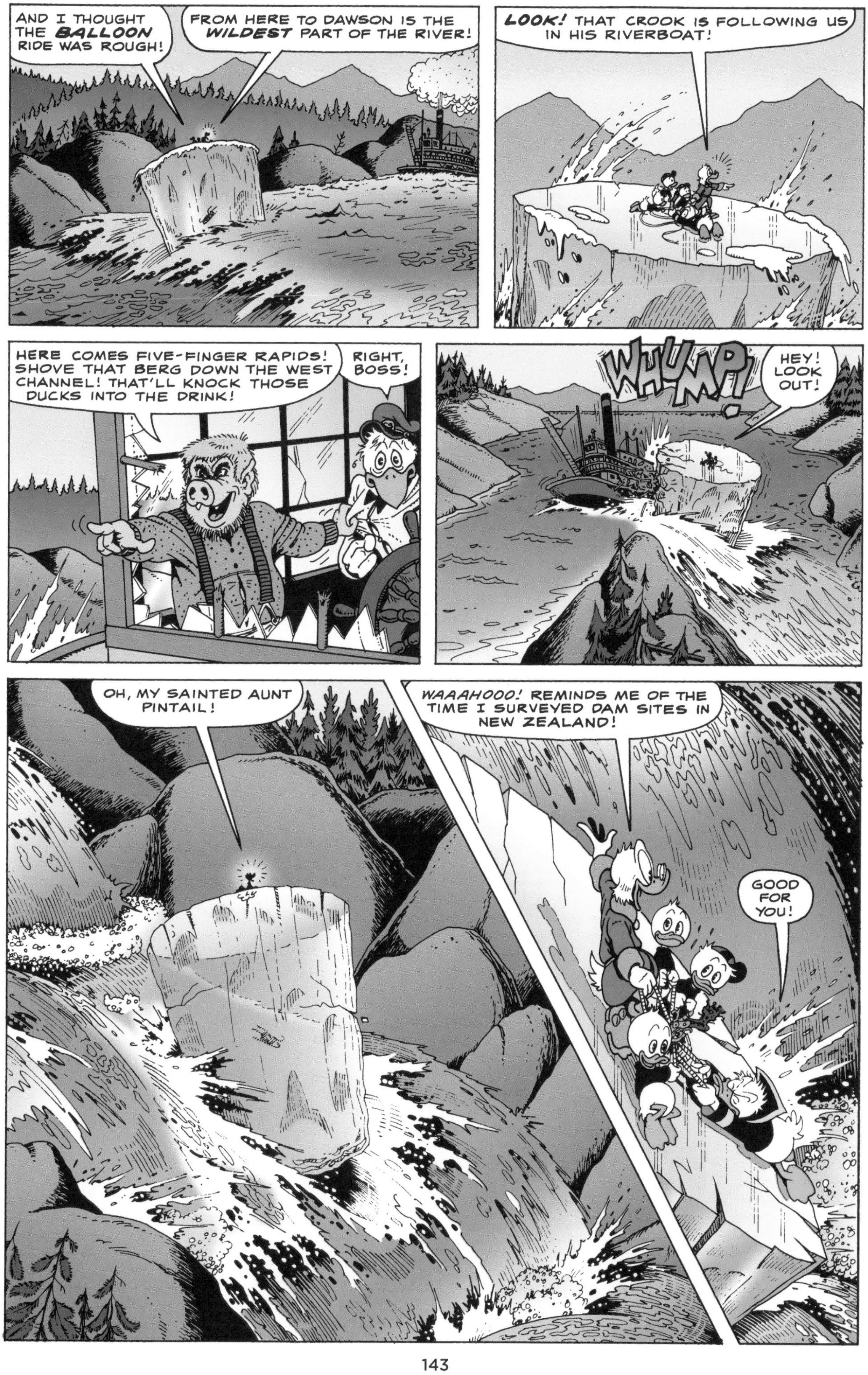
AND I THOUGHT THE BALLOON RIDE WAS ROUGH!
FROM HERE TO DAWSON IS THE WILDEST PART OF THE RIVER!
LOOK! THAT CROOK IS FOLLOWING US IN HIS RIVERBOAT!
HERE COMES FIVE-FINGER RAPIDS! SHOVE THAT BERG DOWN THE WEST CHANNEL! THAT'LL KNOCK THOSE DUCKS INTO THE DRINK!
RIGHT, BOSS!
WHUMP!
HEY! LOOK OUT!
OH, MY SAINTED AUNT PINTAIL!
WAAAHOOO! REMINDS ME OF THE TIME I SURVEYED DAM SITES IN NEW ZEALAND!
GOOD FOR YOU!

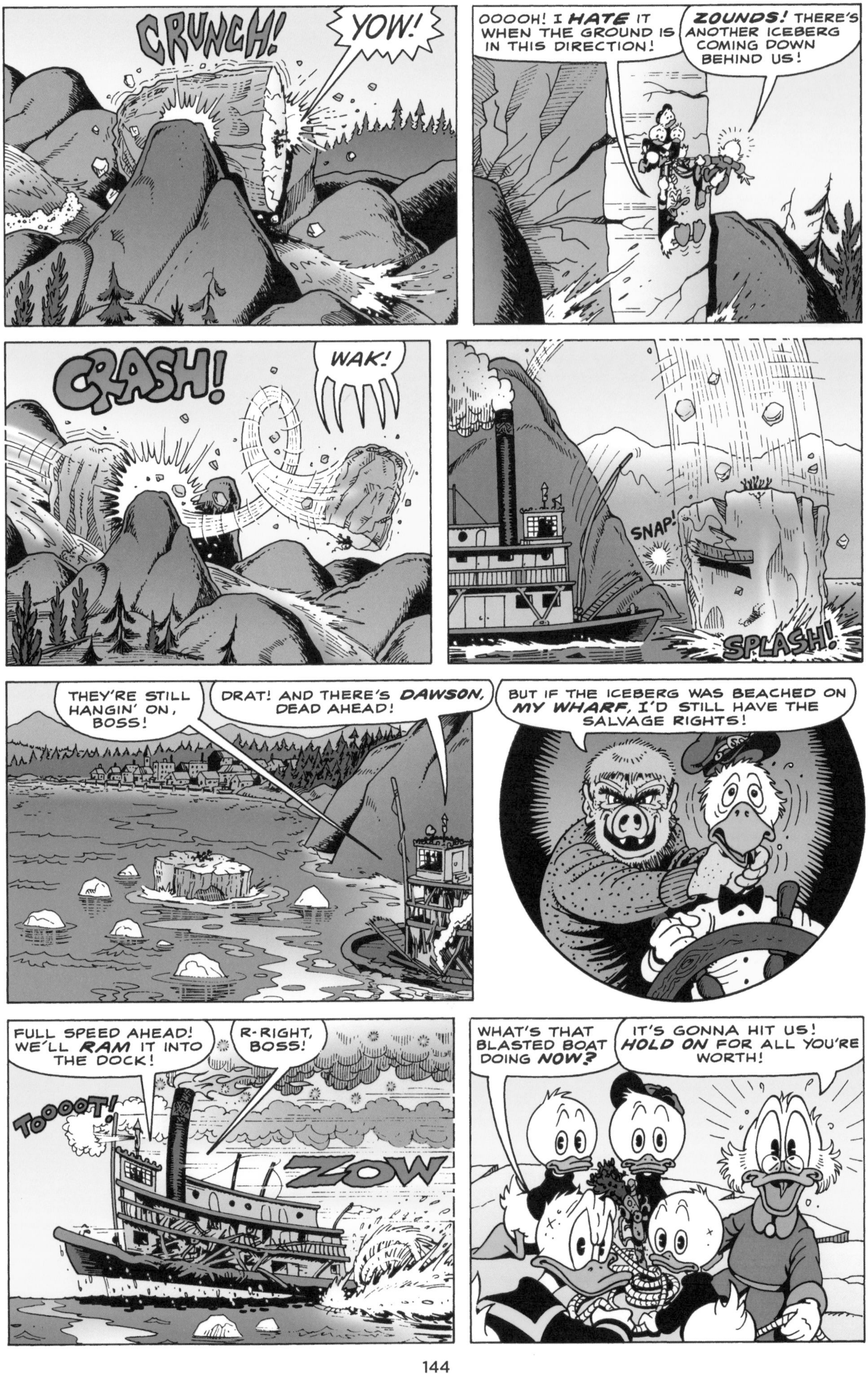
CRUNCH!
YOW!
OOOOH! I HATE IT WHEN THE GROUND IS IN THIS DIRECTION!
ZOUNDS! THERE'S ANOTHER ICEBERG COMING DOWN BEHIND US!
CRASH!
WAK!
SNAP!
SPLASH!
THEY'RE STILL HANGIN' ON, BOSS!
DRAT! AND THERE'S DAWSON, DEAD AHEAD!
BUT IF THE ICEBERG WAS BEACHED ON MY WHARF, I'D STILL HAVE THE SALVAGE RIGHTS!
FULL SPEED AHEAD! WE'LL RAM IT INTO THE DOCK!
R-RIGHT, BOSS!
TOOOOT!
ZOW
WHAT'S THAT BLASTED BOAT DOING NOW?
IT'S GONNA HIT US! HOLD ON FOR ALL YOU'RE WORTH!

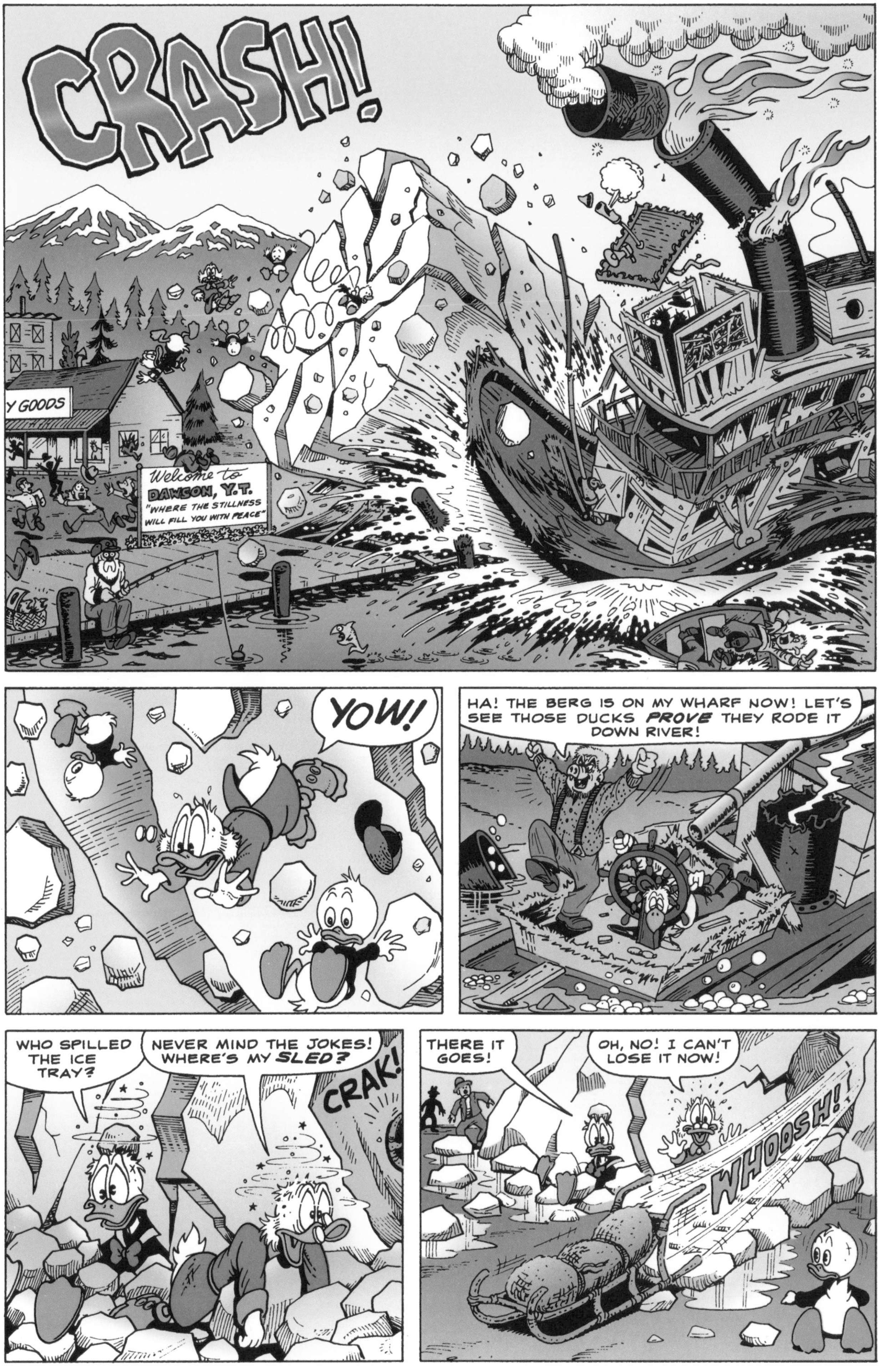
CRASH!
Y GOODS
Welcome to DAWSON, Y.T. "WHERE THE STILLNESS WILL FILL YOU WITH PEACE"
YOW!
HA! THE BERG IS ON MY WHARF NOW! LET'S SEE THOSE DUCKS PROVE THEY RODE IT DOWN RIVER!
WHO SPILLED THE ICE TRAY?
NEVER MIND THE JOKES! WHERE'S MY SLED?
CRAK!
THERE IT GOES!
OH, NO! I CAN'T LOSE IT NOW!
WHOOSH!

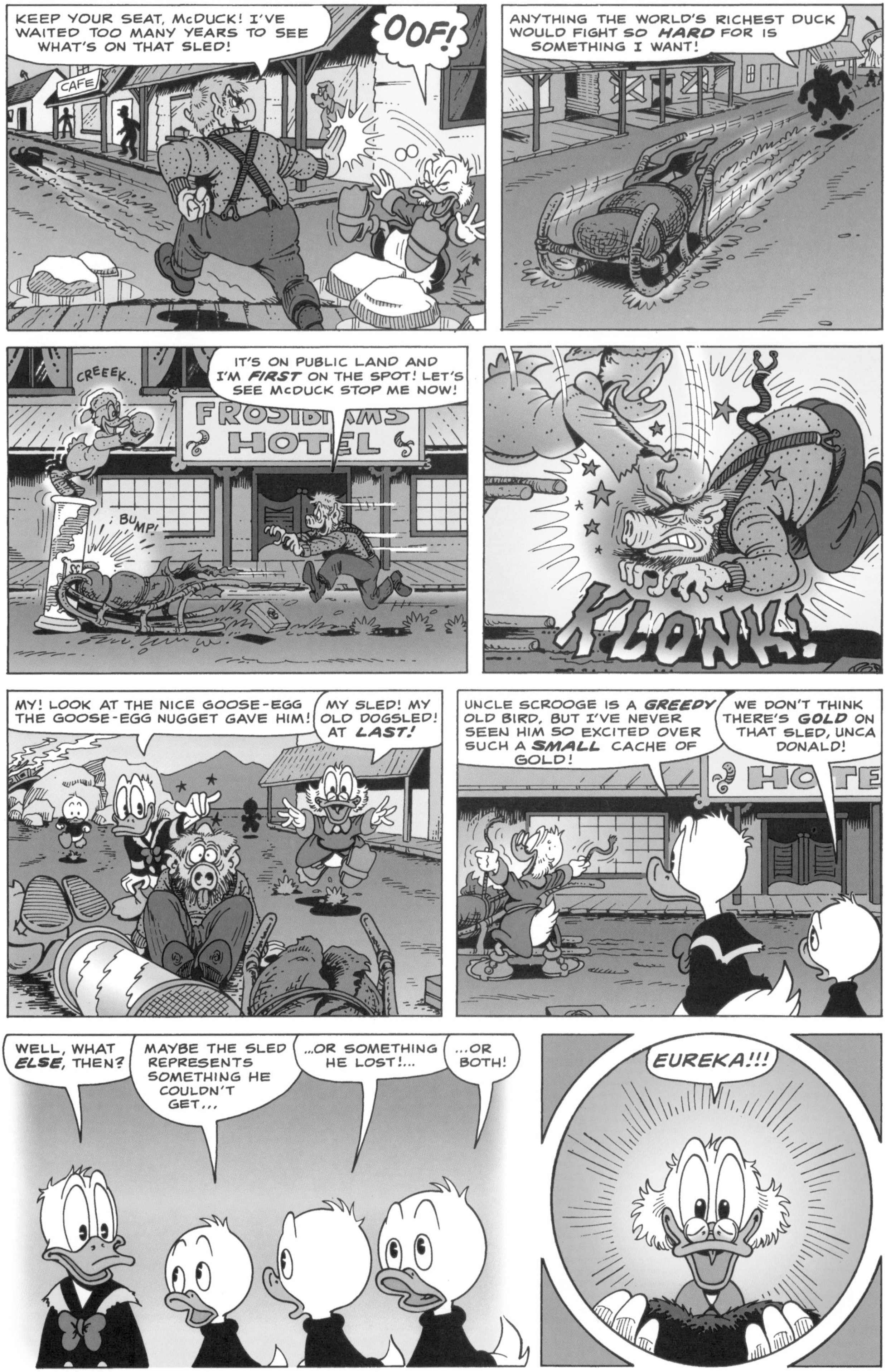
KEEP YOUR SEAT, McDUCK! I'VE WAITED TOO MANY YEARS TO SEE WHAT'S ON THAT SLED!
OOF!
CAFE
ANYTHING THE WORLD'S RICHEST DUCK WOULD FIGHT SO HARD FOR IS SOMETHING I WANT!
CREEEK...
IT'S ON PUBLIC LAND AND I'M FIRST ON THE SPOT! LET'S SEE McDUCK STOP ME NOW!
FROSTBITAMS HOTEL
BUMP!
KLONK!
MY! LOOK AT THE NICE GOOSE-EGG THE GOOSE-EGG NUGGET GAVE HIM!
MY SLED! MY OLD DOGSLED! AT LAST!
UNCLE SCROOGE IS A GREEDY OLD BIRD, BUT I'VE NEVER SEEN HIM SO EXCITED OVER SUCH A SMALL CACHE OF GOLD!
WE DON'T THINK THERE'S GOLD ON THAT SLED, UNCA DONALD!
HOTE
WELL, WHAT ELSE, THEN?
MAYBE THE SLED REPRESENTS SOMETHING HE COULDN'T GET...
...OR SOMETHING HE LOST!...
...OR BOTH!
EUREKA!!!

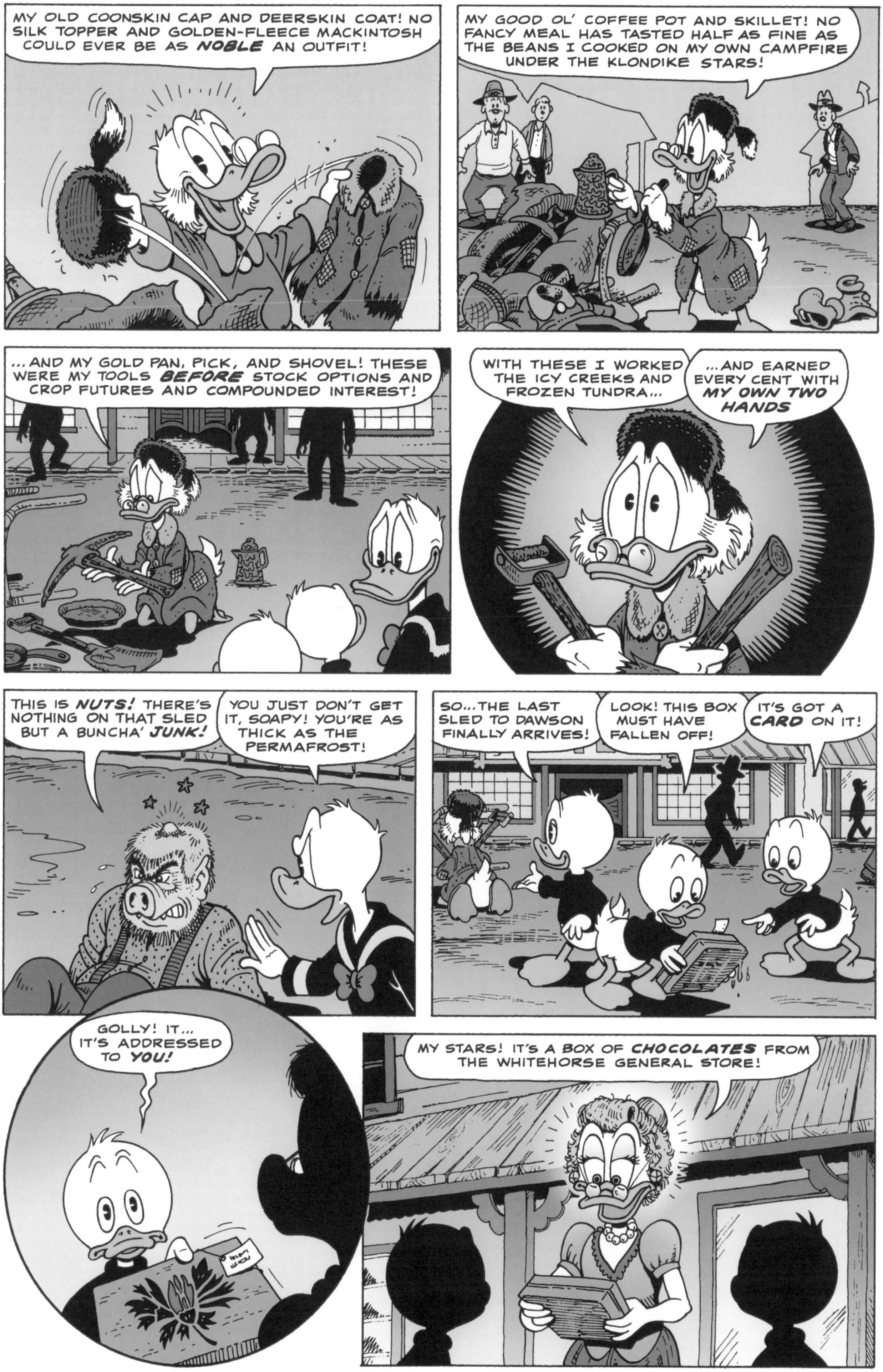
MY OLD COONSKIN CAP AND DEERSKIN COAT! NO SILK TOPPER AND GOLDEN-FLEECE MACKINTOSH COULD EVER BE AS NOBLE AN OUTFIT!
MY GOOD OL' COFFEE POT AND SKILLET! NO FANCY MEAL HAS TASTED HALF AS FINE AS THE BEANS I COOKED ON MY OWN CAMPFIRE UNDER THE KLONDIKE STARS!
...AND MY GOLD PAN, PICK, AND SHOVEL! THESE WERE MY TOOLS BEFORE STOCK OPTIONS AND CROP FUTURES AND COMPOUNDED INTEREST!
WITH THESE I WORKED THE ICY CREEKS AND FROZEN TUNDRA...
...AND EARNED EVERY CENT WITH MY OWN TWO HANDS
THIS IS NUTS! THERE'S NOTHING ON THAT SLED BUT A BUNCHA' JUNK!
YOU JUST DON'T GET IT, SOAPY! YOU'RE AS THICK AS THE PERMAFROST!
SO...THE LAST SLED TO DAWSON FINALLY ARRIVES!
LOOK! THIS BOX MUST HAVE FALLEN OFF!
IT'S GOT A CARD ON IT!
GOLLY! IT... IT'S ADDRESSED TO YOU!
MY STARS! IT'S A BOX OF CHOCOLATES FROM THE WHITEHORSE GENERAL STORE!

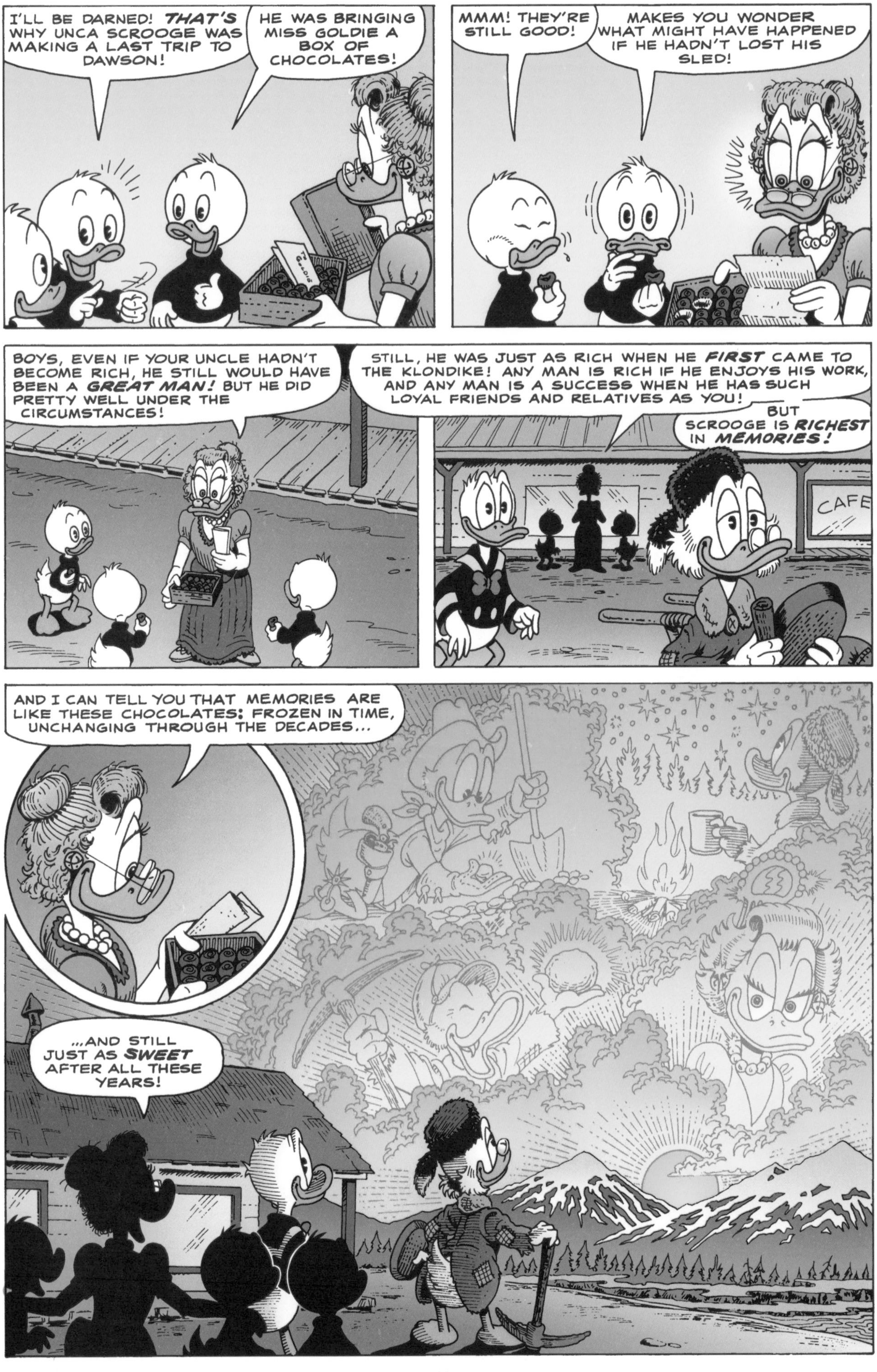
I'LL BE DARNED! THAT'S WHY UNCA SCROOGE WAS MAKING A LAST TRIP TO DAWSON!
HE WAS BRINGING MISS GOLDIE A BOX OF CHOCOLATES!
MMM! THEY'RE STILL GOOD!
MAKES YOU WONDER WHAT MIGHT HAVE HAPPENED IF HE HADN'T LOST HIS SLED!
BOYS, EVEN IF YOUR UNCLE HADN'T BECOME RICH, HE STILL WOULD HAVE BEEN A GREAT MAN! BUT HE DID PRETTY WELL UNDER THE CIRCUMSTANCES!
STILL, HE WAS JUST AS RICH WHEN HE FIRST CAME TO THE KLONDIKE! ANY MAN IS RICH IF HE ENJOYS HIS WORK, AND ANY MAN IS A SUCCESS WHEN HE HAS SUCH LOYAL FRIENDS AND RELATIVES AS YOU!
BUT SCROOGE IS RICHEST IN MEMORIES!
CAFE
AND I CAN TELL YOU THAT MEMORIES ARE LIKE THESE CHOCOLATES: FROZEN IN TIME, UNCHANGING THROUGH THE DECADES...
...AND STILL JUST AS SWEET AFTER ALL THESE YEARS!

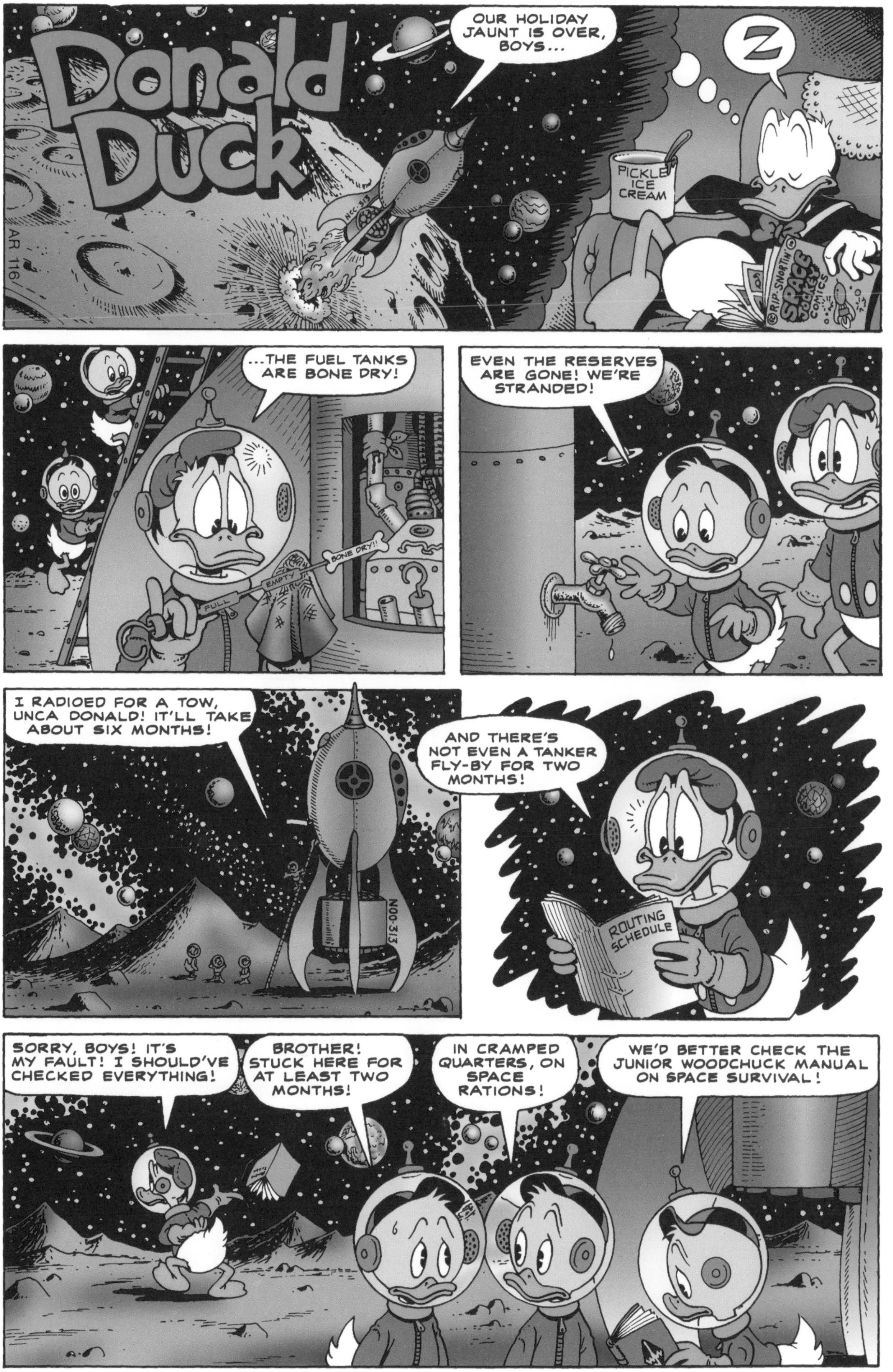
Donald Duck
AR 116
OUR HOLIDAY JAUNT IS OVER, BOYS...
Z
PICKLE ICE CREAM
SPACE COMICS
...THE FUEL TANKS ARE BONE DRY!
FULL
EMPTY
BONE DRY!!
EVEN THE RESERVES ARE GONE! WE'RE STRANDED!
I RADIOED FOR A TOW, UNCA DONALD! IT'LL TAKE ABOUT SIX MONTHS!
AND THERE'S NOT EVEN A TANKER FLY-BY FOR TWO MONTHS!
ROUTING SCHEDULE
SORRY, BOYS! IT'S MY FAULT! I SHOULD'VE CHECKED EVERYTHING!
BROTHER! STUCK HERE FOR AT LEAST TWO MONTHS!
IN CRAMPED QUARTERS, ON SPACE RATIONS!
WE'D BETTER CHECK THE JUNIOR WOODCHUCK MANUAL ON SPACE SURVIVAL!

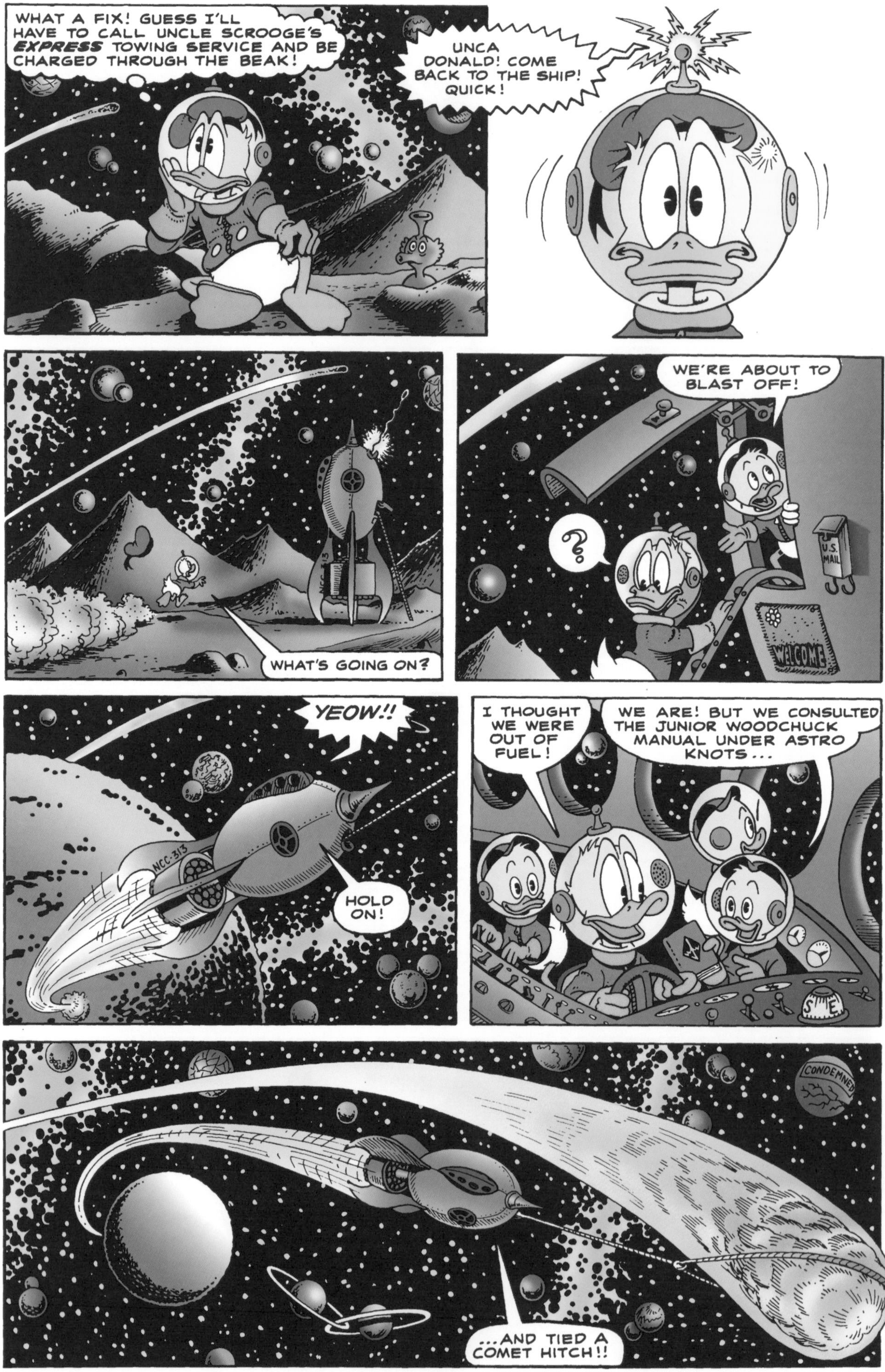
WHAT A FIX! GUESS I'LL HAVE TO CALL UNCLE SCROOGE'S **EXPRESS** TOWING SERVICE AND BE CHARGED THROUGH THE BEAK!
UNCA DONALD! COME BACK TO THE SHIP! QUICK!
WHAT'S GOING ON?
WE'RE ABOUT TO BLAST OFF!
?
U.S. MAIL
WELCOME
YEOW!!
NCC-313
HOLD ON!
I THOUGHT WE WERE OUT OF FUEL!
WE ARE! BUT WE CONSULTED THE JUNIOR WOODCHUCK MANUAL UNDER ASTRO KNOTS...
CONDEMNED
...AND TIED A COMET HITCH!!

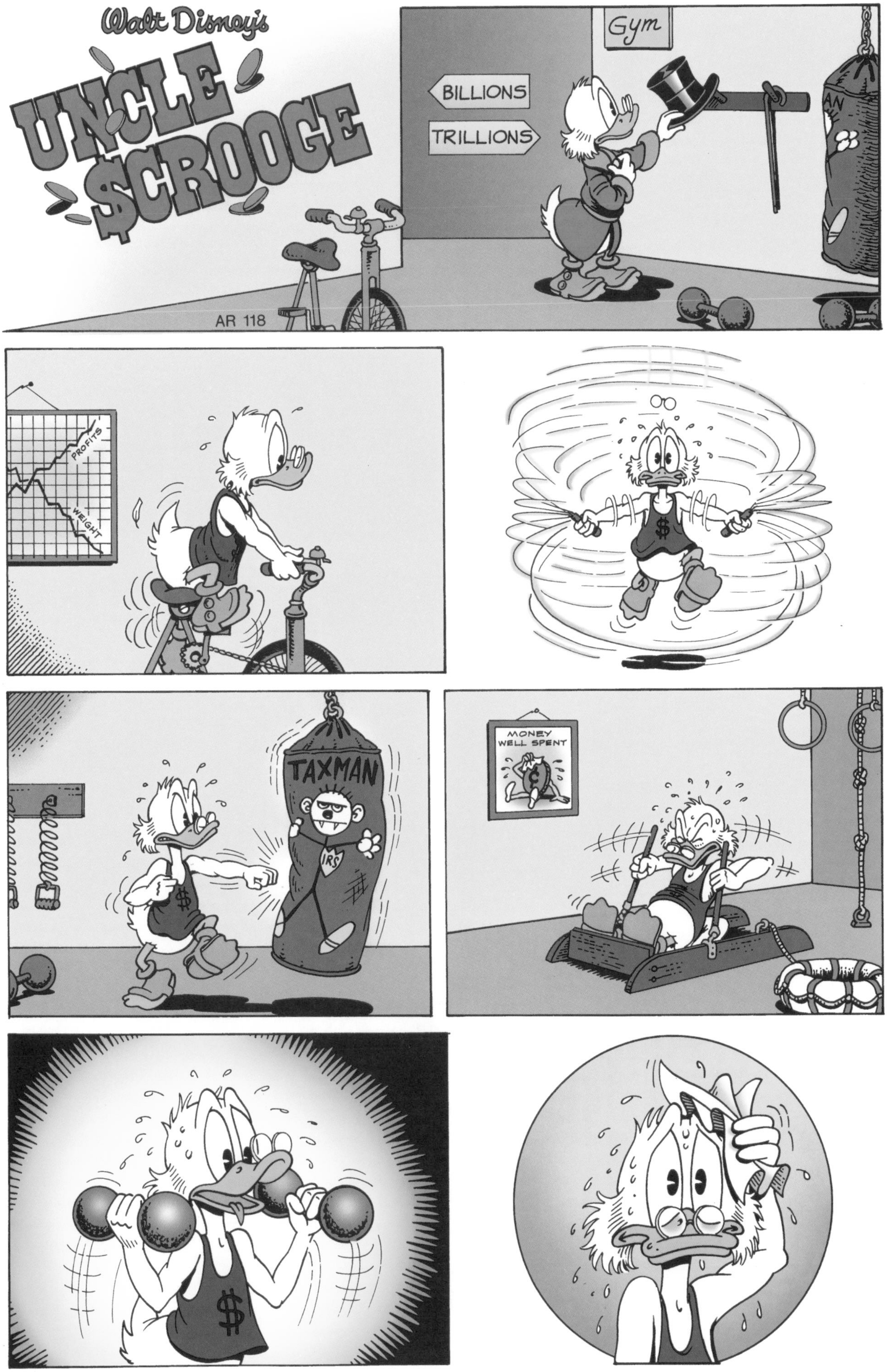
Walt Disney's
UNCLE $CROOGE
Gym
BILLIONS
TRILLIONS
AR 118
PROFITS
WEIGHT
TAXMAN
IRS
MONEY WELL SPENT

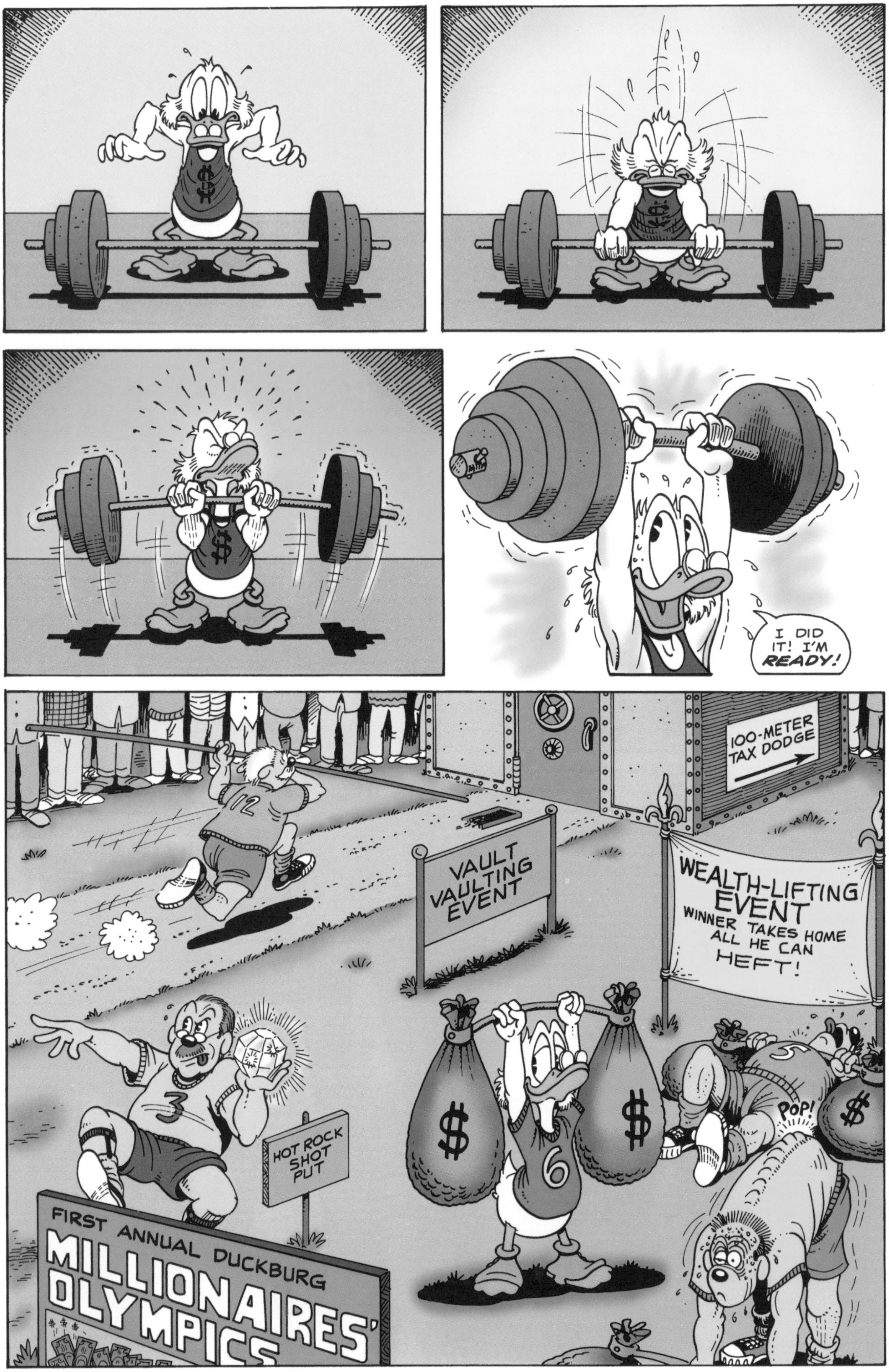
I DID IT! I'M *READY!*
100-METER TAX DODGE
VAULT VAULTING EVENT
WEALTH-LIFTING EVENT
WINNER TAKES HOME ALL HE CAN HEFT!
HOT ROCK SHOT PUT
POP!
FIRST ANNUAL DUCKBURG
MILLIONAIRES' OLYMPICS

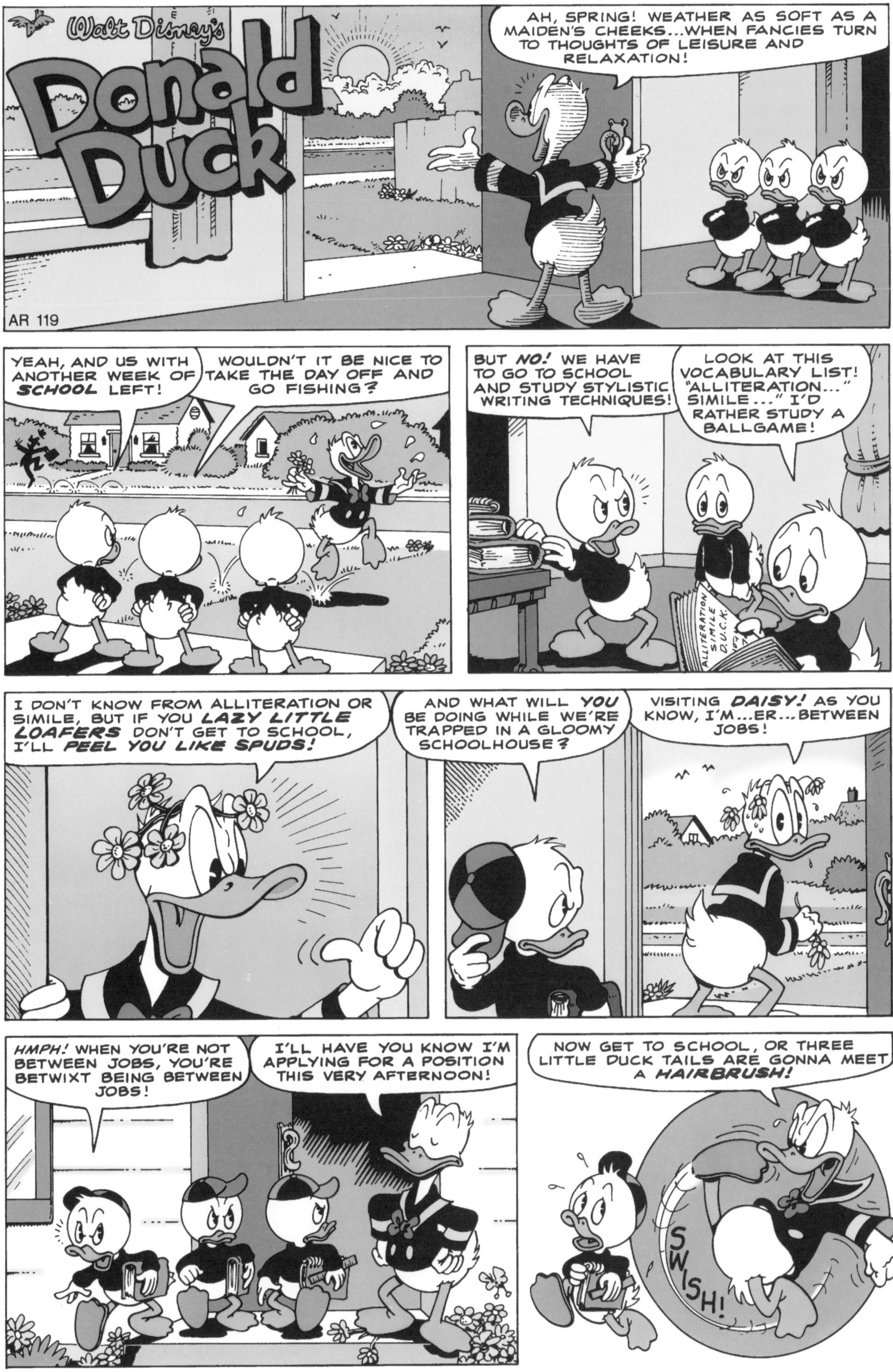
Walt Disney's
Donald Duck
AR 119
AH, SPRING! WEATHER AS SOFT AS A MAIDEN'S CHEEKS...WHEN FANCIES TURN TO THOUGHTS OF LEISURE AND RELAXATION!
YEAH, AND US WITH ANOTHER WEEK OF SCHOOL LEFT!
WOULDN'T IT BE NICE TO TAKE THE DAY OFF AND GO FISHING?
BUT NO! WE HAVE TO GO TO SCHOOL AND STUDY STYLISTIC WRITING TECHNIQUES!
LOOK AT THIS VOCABULARY LIST! "ALLITERATION..." "SIMILE..." I'D RATHER STUDY A BALLGAME!
ALLITERATION SIMILE D.U.C.K.
I DON'T KNOW FROM ALLITERATION OR SIMILE, BUT IF YOU LAZY LITTLE LOAFERS DON'T GET TO SCHOOL, I'LL PEEL YOU LIKE SPUDS!
AND WHAT WILL YOU BE DOING WHILE WE'RE TRAPPED IN A GLOOMY SCHOOLHOUSE?
VISITING DAISY! AS YOU KNOW, I'M...ER...BETWEEN JOBS!
HMPH! WHEN YOU'RE NOT BETWEEN JOBS, YOU'RE BETWIXT BEING BETWEEN JOBS!
I'LL HAVE YOU KNOW I'M APPLYING FOR A POSITION THIS VERY AFTERNOON!
NOW GET TO SCHOOL, OR THREE LITTLE DUCK TAILS ARE GONNA MEET A HAIRBRUSH!
SWISH!

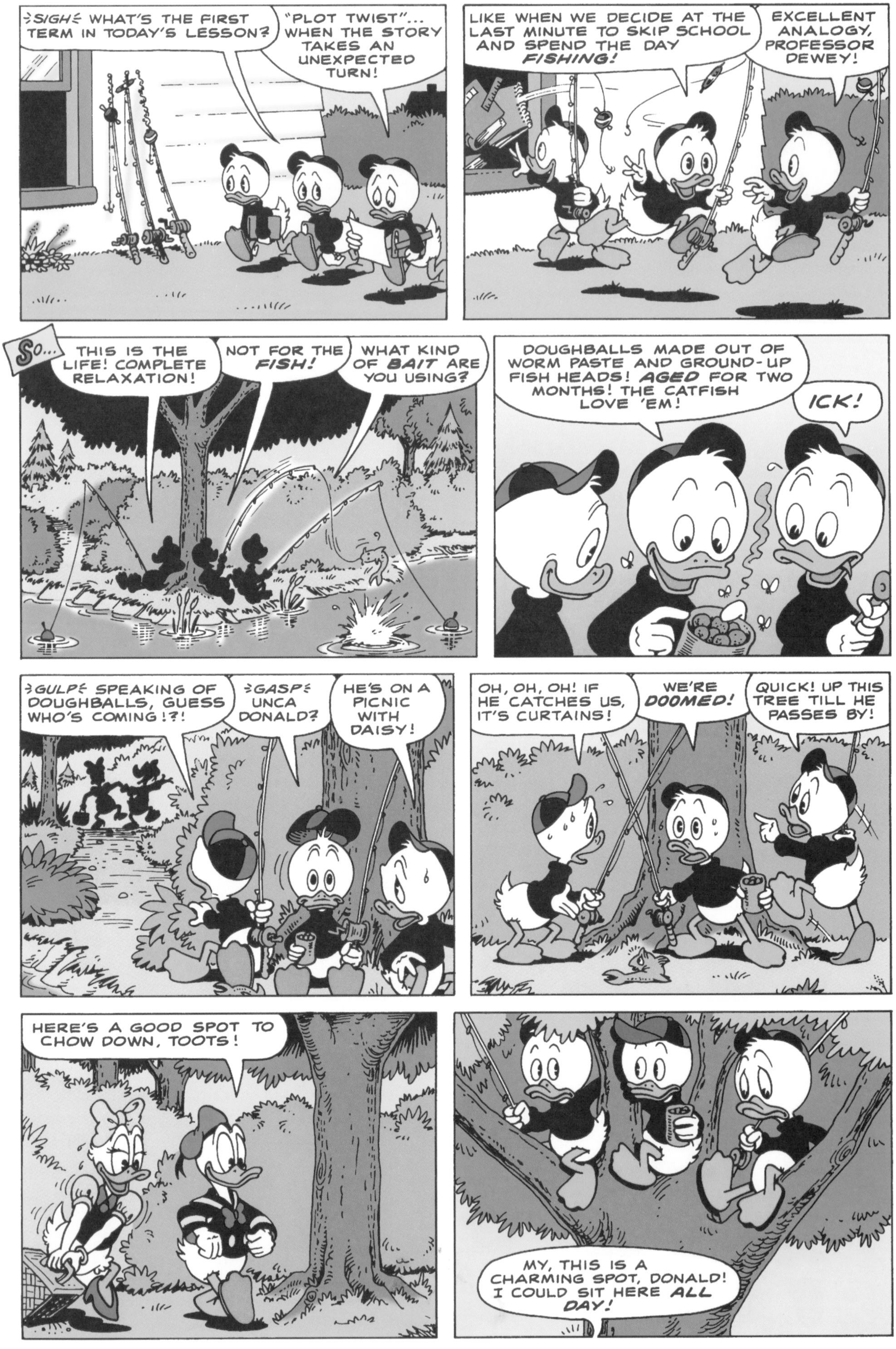

≷SIGH≶ WHAT'S THE FIRST TERM IN TODAY'S LESSON?
"PLOT TWIST"... WHEN THE STORY TAKES AN UNEXPECTED TURN!
LIKE WHEN WE DECIDE AT THE LAST MINUTE TO SKIP SCHOOL AND SPEND THE DAY FISHING!
EXCELLENT ANALOGY, PROFESSOR DEWEY!
SO...
THIS IS THE LIFE! COMPLETE RELAXATION!
NOT FOR THE FISH!
WHAT KIND OF BAIT ARE YOU USING?
DOUGHBALLS MADE OUT OF WORM PASTE AND GROUND-UP FISH HEADS! AGED FOR TWO MONTHS! THE CATFISH LOVE 'EM!
ICK!
≷GULP≶ SPEAKING OF DOUGHBALLS, GUESS WHO'S COMING!?!
≷GASP≶ UNCA DONALD?
HE'S ON A PICNIC WITH DAISY!
OH, OH, OH! IF HE CATCHES US, IT'S CURTAINS!
WE'RE DOOMED!
QUICK! UP THIS TREE TILL HE PASSES BY!
HERE'S A GOOD SPOT TO CHOW DOWN, TOOTS!
MY, THIS IS A CHARMING SPOT, DONALD! I COULD SIT HERE ALL DAY!

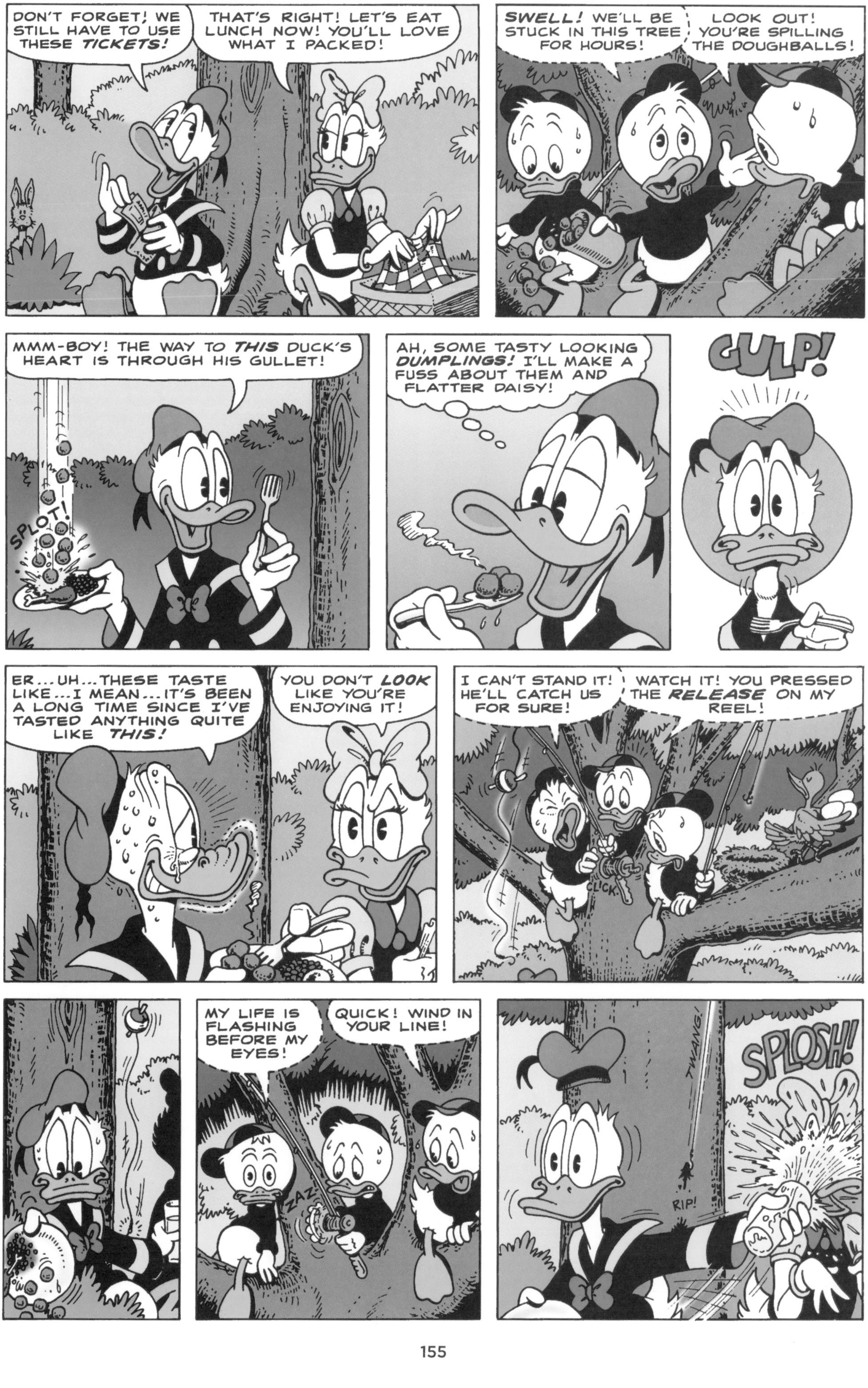
DON'T FORGET! WE STILL HAVE TO USE THESE TICKETS!
THAT'S RIGHT! LET'S EAT LUNCH NOW! YOU'LL LOVE WHAT I PACKED!
SWELL! WE'LL BE STUCK IN THIS TREE FOR HOURS!
LOOK OUT! YOU'RE SPILLING THE DOUGHBALLS!
MMM-BOY! THE WAY TO THIS DUCK'S HEART IS THROUGH HIS GULLET!
SPLOT!
AH, SOME TASTY LOOKING DUMPLINGS! I'LL MAKE A FUSS ABOUT THEM AND FLATTER DAISY!
GULP!
ER... UH... THESE TASTE LIKE... I MEAN... IT'S BEEN A LONG TIME SINCE I'VE TASTED ANYTHING QUITE LIKE THIS!
YOU DON'T LOOK LIKE YOU'RE ENJOYING IT!
I CAN'T STAND IT! HE'LL CATCH US FOR SURE!
WATCH IT! YOU PRESSED THE RELEASE ON MY REEL!
CLICK
MY LIFE IS FLASHING BEFORE MY EYES!
QUICK! WIND IN YOUR LINE!
ZAZ
TWANG!
RIP!
SPLOSH!

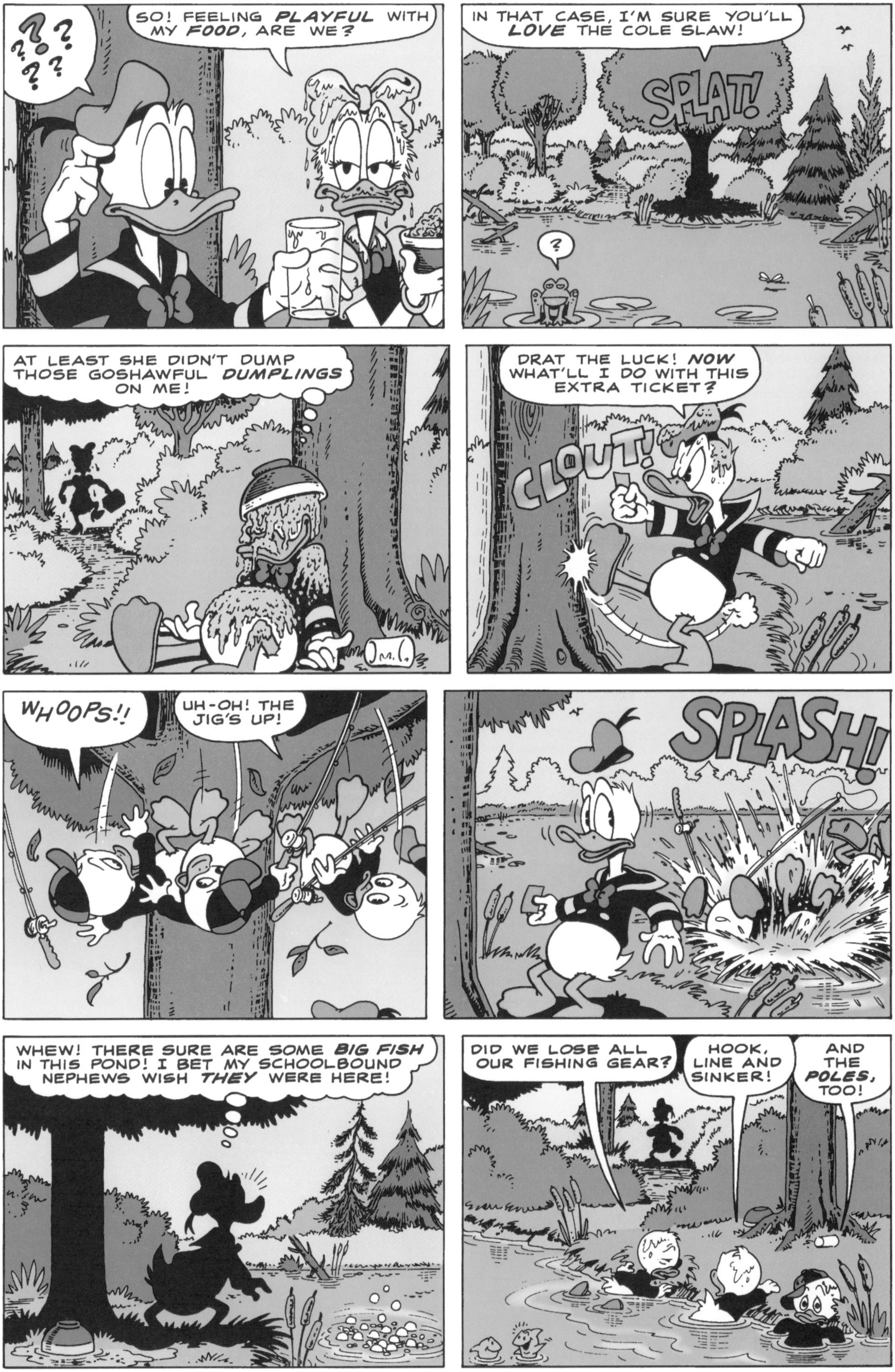
??
SO! FEELING PLAYFUL WITH MY FOOD, ARE WE?
IN THAT CASE, I'M SURE YOU'LL LOVE THE COLE SLAW!
SPLAT!
?
AT LEAST SHE DIDN'T DUMP THOSE GOSHAWFUL DUMPLINGS ON ME!
DRAT THE LUCK! NOW WHAT'LL I DO WITH THIS EXTRA TICKET?
CLOUT!
WHOOPS!!
UH-OH! THE JIG'S UP!
SPLASH!
WHEW! THERE SURE ARE SOME BIG FISH IN THIS POND! I BET MY SCHOOLBOUND NEPHEWS WISH THEY WERE HERE!
DID WE LOSE ALL OUR FISHING GEAR?
HOOK, LINE AND SINKER!
AND THE POLES, TOO!

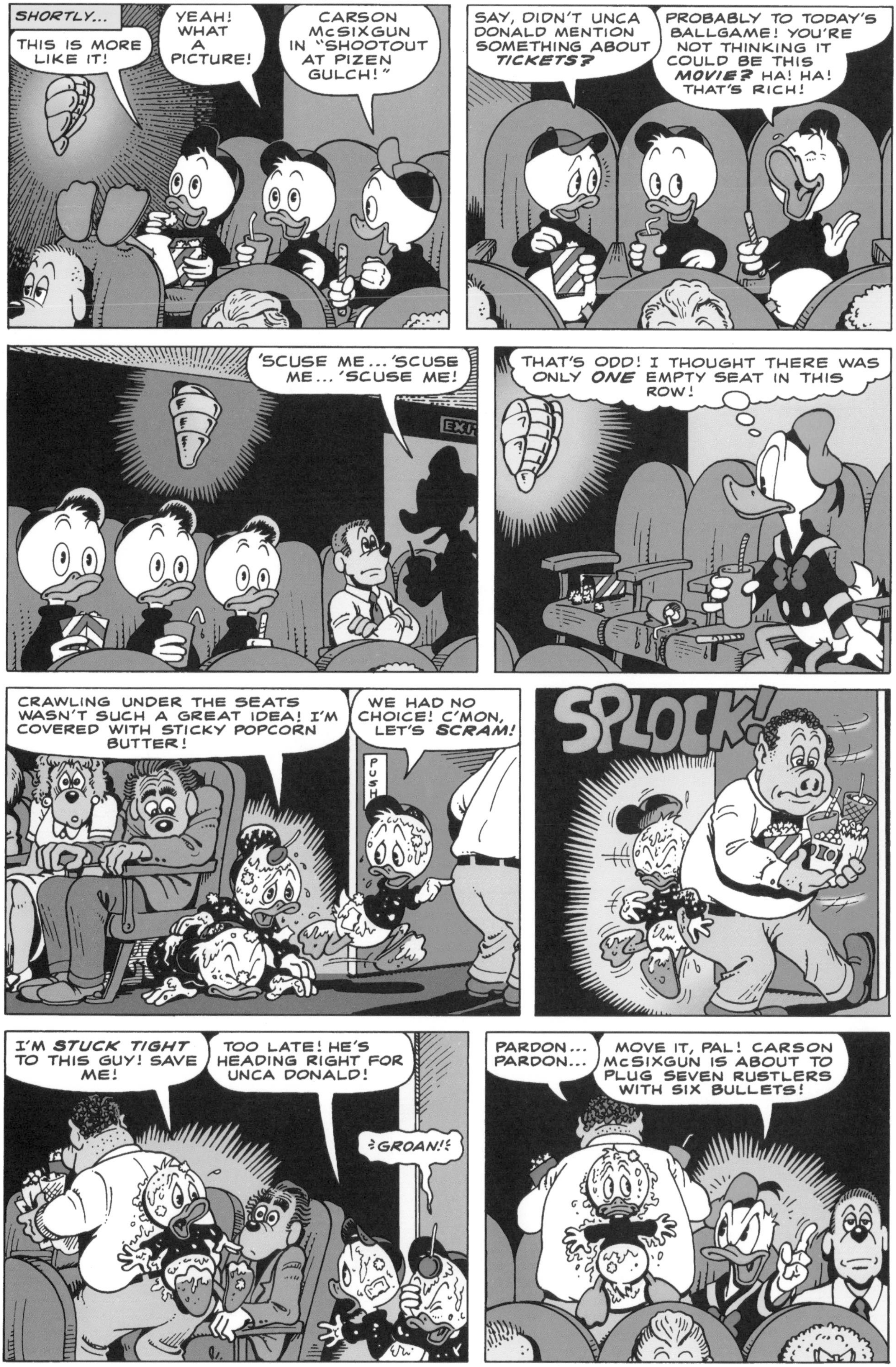
SHORTLY...
THIS IS MORE LIKE IT!
YEAH! WHAT A PICTURE!
CARSON McSIXGUN IN "SHOOTOUT AT PIZEN GULCH!"
SAY, DIDN'T UNCA DONALD MENTION SOMETHING ABOUT TICKETS?
PROBABLY TO TODAY'S BALLGAME! YOU'RE NOT THINKING IT COULD BE THIS MOVIE? HA! HA! THAT'S RICH!
'SCUSE ME... 'SCUSE ME... 'SCUSE ME!
THAT'S ODD! I THOUGHT THERE WAS ONLY ONE EMPTY SEAT IN THIS ROW!
CRAWLING UNDER THE SEATS WASN'T SUCH A GREAT IDEA! I'M COVERED WITH STICKY POPCORN BUTTER!
WE HAD NO CHOICE! C'MON, LET'S SCRAM!
PUSH
SPLOCK!
I'M STUCK TIGHT TO THIS GUY! SAVE ME!
TOO LATE! HE'S HEADING RIGHT FOR UNCA DONALD!
GROAN!
PARDON... PARDON...
MOVE IT, PAL! CARSON McSIXGUN IS ABOUT TO PLUG SEVEN RUSTLERS WITH SIX BULLETS!

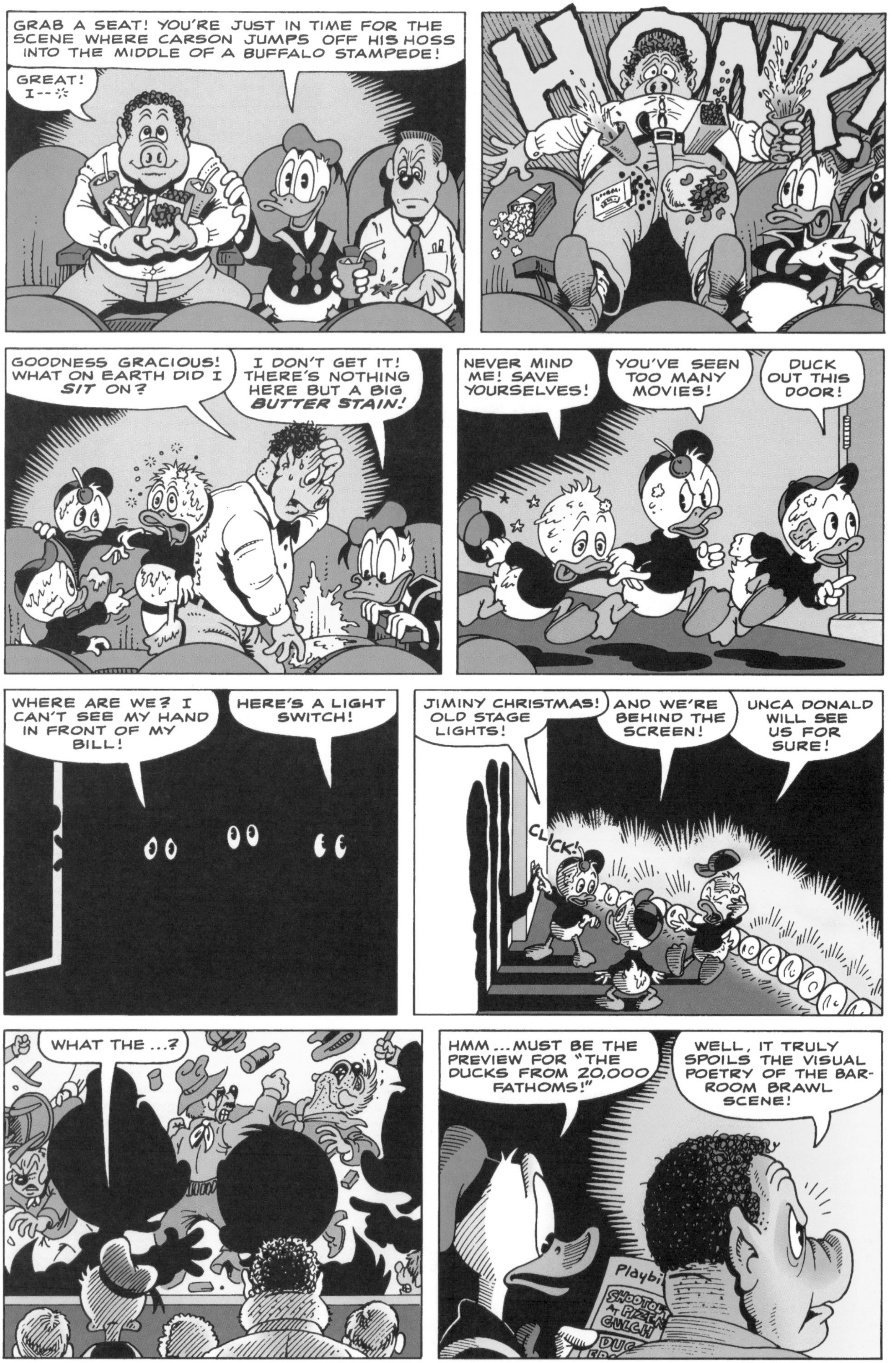

GRAB A SEAT! YOU'RE JUST IN TIME FOR THE SCENE WHERE CARSON JUMPS OFF HIS HOSS INTO THE MIDDLE OF A BUFFALO STAMPEDE!
GREAT! I--
HONK!
GOODNESS GRACIOUS! WHAT ON EARTH DID I SIT ON?
I DON'T GET IT! THERE'S NOTHING HERE BUT A BIG BUTTER STAIN!
NEVER MIND ME! SAVE YOURSELVES!
YOU'VE SEEN TOO MANY MOVIES!
DUCK OUT THIS DOOR!
WHERE ARE WE? I CAN'T SEE MY HAND IN FRONT OF MY BILL!
HERE'S A LIGHT SWITCH!
JIMINY CHRISTMAS! OLD STAGE LIGHTS!
AND WE'RE BEHIND THE SCREEN!
UNCA DONALD WILL SEE US FOR SURE!
CLICK!
WHAT THE ...?
HMM ... MUST BE THE PREVIEW FOR "THE DUCKS FROM 20,000 FATHOMS!"
WELL, IT TRULY SPOILS THE VISUAL POETRY OF THE BAR-ROOM BRAWL SCENE!
Playbi
SHOOTOUT AT PIZEN GULCH

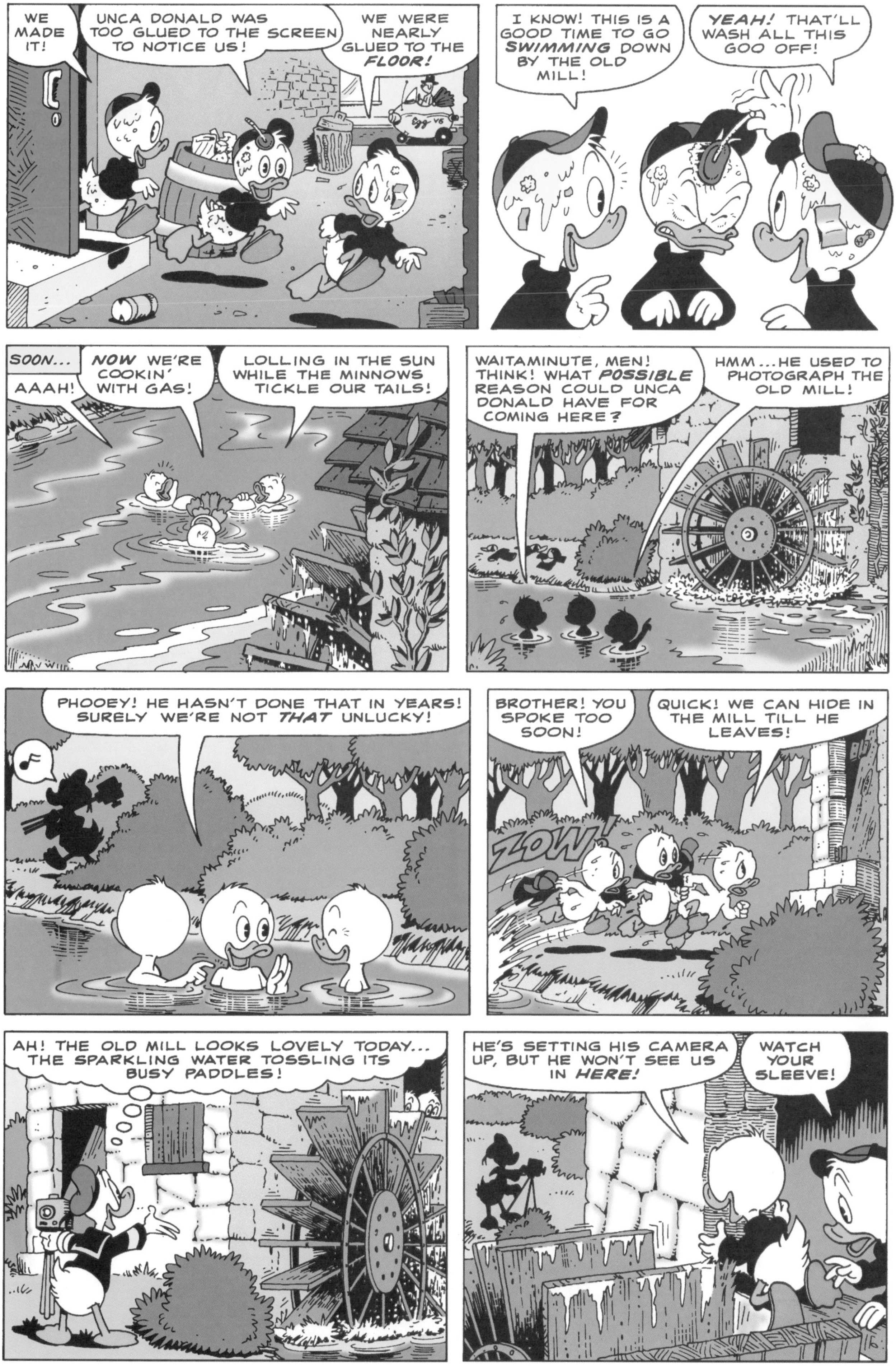
WE MADE IT!
UNCA DONALD WAS TOO GLUED TO THE SCREEN TO NOTICE US!
WE WERE NEARLY GLUED TO THE FLOOR!
I KNOW! THIS IS A GOOD TIME TO GO SWIMMING DOWN BY THE OLD MILL!
YEAH! THAT'LL WASH ALL THIS GOO OFF!
SOON...
AAAH!
NOW WE'RE COOKIN' WITH GAS!
LOLLING IN THE SUN WHILE THE MINNOWS TICKLE OUR TAILS!
WAITAMINUTE, MEN! THINK! WHAT POSSIBLE REASON COULD UNCA DONALD HAVE FOR COMING HERE?
HMM...HE USED TO PHOTOGRAPH THE OLD MILL!
PHOOEY! HE HASN'T DONE THAT IN YEARS! SURELY WE'RE NOT THAT UNLUCKY!
BROTHER! YOU SPOKE TOO SOON!
QUICK! WE CAN HIDE IN THE MILL TILL HE LEAVES!
ZOW!
AH! THE OLD MILL LOOKS LOVELY TODAY... THE SPARKLING WATER TOSSLING ITS BUSY PADDLES!
HE'S SETTING HIS CAMERA UP, BUT HE WON'T SEE US IN HERE!
WATCH YOUR SLEEVE!

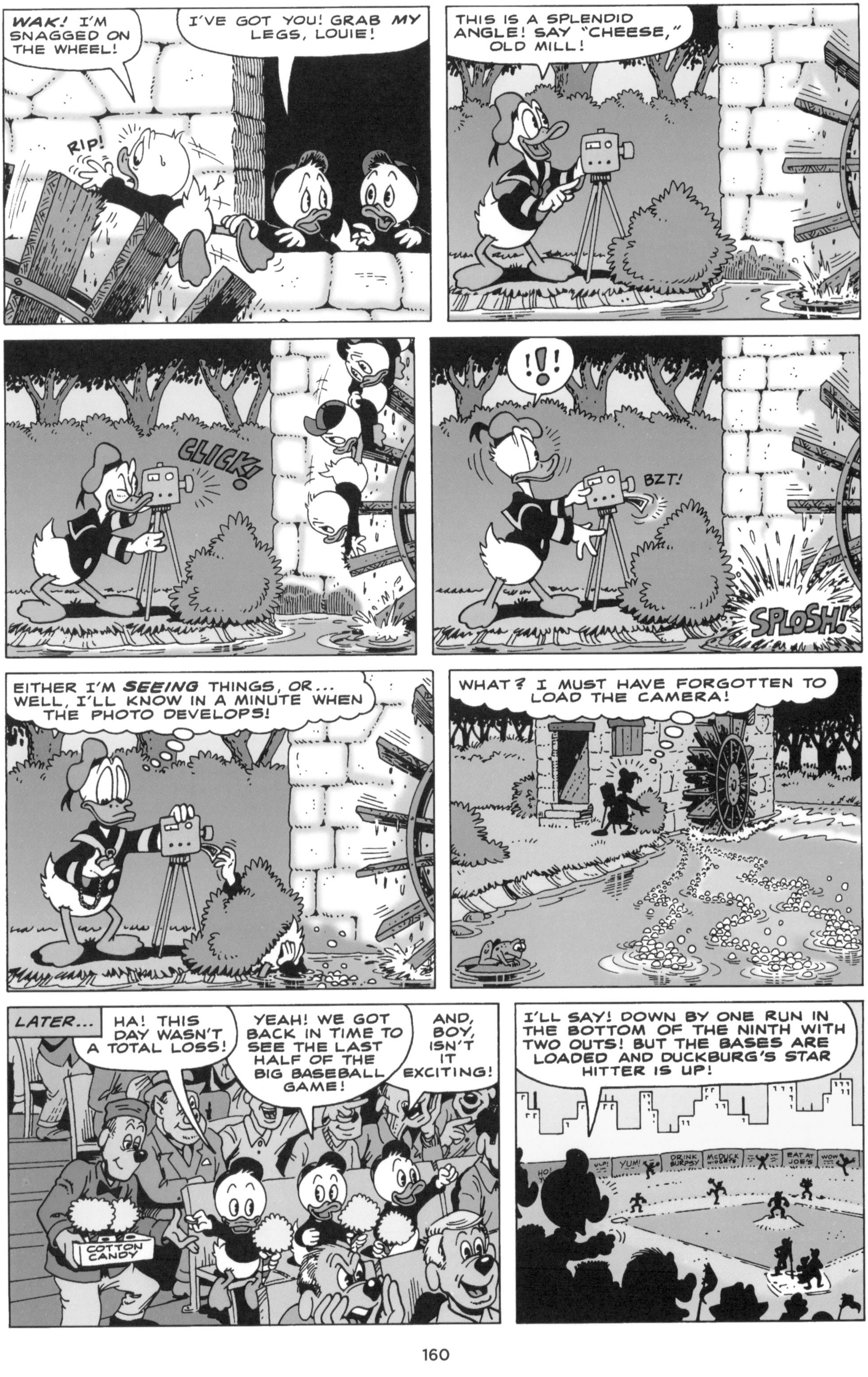
WAK! I'M SNAGGED ON THE WHEEL!
I'VE GOT YOU! GRAB MY LEGS, LOUIE!
RIP!
THIS IS A SPLENDID ANGLE! SAY "CHEESE," OLD MILL!
CLICK!
!?!
BZT!
SPLOSH!
EITHER I'M SEEING THINGS, OR... WELL, I'LL KNOW IN A MINUTE WHEN THE PHOTO DEVELOPS!
WHAT? I MUST HAVE FORGOTTEN TO LOAD THE CAMERA!
LATER...
HA! THIS DAY WASN'T A TOTAL LOSS!
YEAH! WE GOT BACK IN TIME TO SEE THE LAST HALF OF THE BIG BASEBALL GAME!
AND, BOY, ISN'T IT EXCITING!
COTTON CANDY
I'LL SAY! DOWN BY ONE RUN IN THE BOTTOM OF THE NINTH WITH TWO OUTS! BUT THE BASES ARE LOADED AND DUCKBURG'S STAR HITTER IS UP!
YUM!
DRINK BURPSY
McDUCK WIDGETS
EAT AT JOE'S
WOW

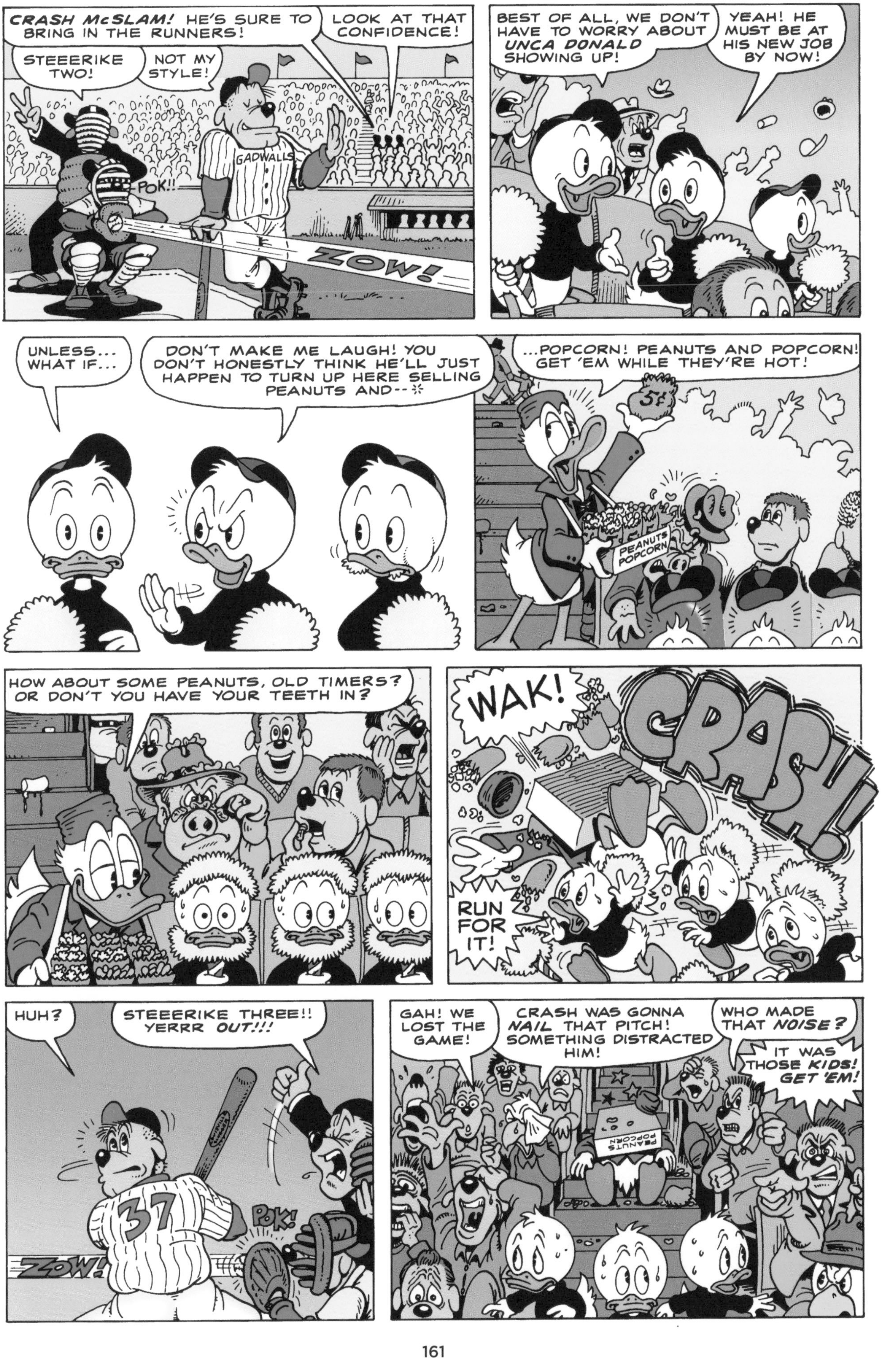

CRASH McSLAM! HE'S SURE TO BRING IN THE RUNNERS!
LOOK AT THAT CONFIDENCE!
STEEERIKE TWO!
NOT MY STYLE!
GADWALLS
POK!!
ZOW!
BEST OF ALL, WE DON'T HAVE TO WORRY ABOUT UNCA DONALD SHOWING UP!
YEAH! HE MUST BE AT HIS NEW JOB BY NOW!
UNLESS... WHAT IF...
DON'T MAKE ME LAUGH! YOU DON'T HONESTLY THINK HE'LL JUST HAPPEN TO TURN UP HERE SELLING PEANUTS AND--
...POPCORN! PEANUTS AND POPCORN! GET 'EM WHILE THEY'RE HOT!
5¢
PEANUTS POPCORN
HOW ABOUT SOME PEANUTS, OLD TIMERS? OR DON'T YOU HAVE YOUR TEETH IN?
WAK!
CRASH!
RUN FOR IT!
HUH?
STEEERIKE THREE!! YERRR OUT!!!
37
POK!
ZOW!
GAH! WE LOST THE GAME!
CRASH WAS GONNA NAIL THAT PITCH! SOMETHING DISTRACTED HIM!
WHO MADE THAT NOISE?
IT WAS THOSE KIDS! GET 'EM!
PEANUTS POPCORN

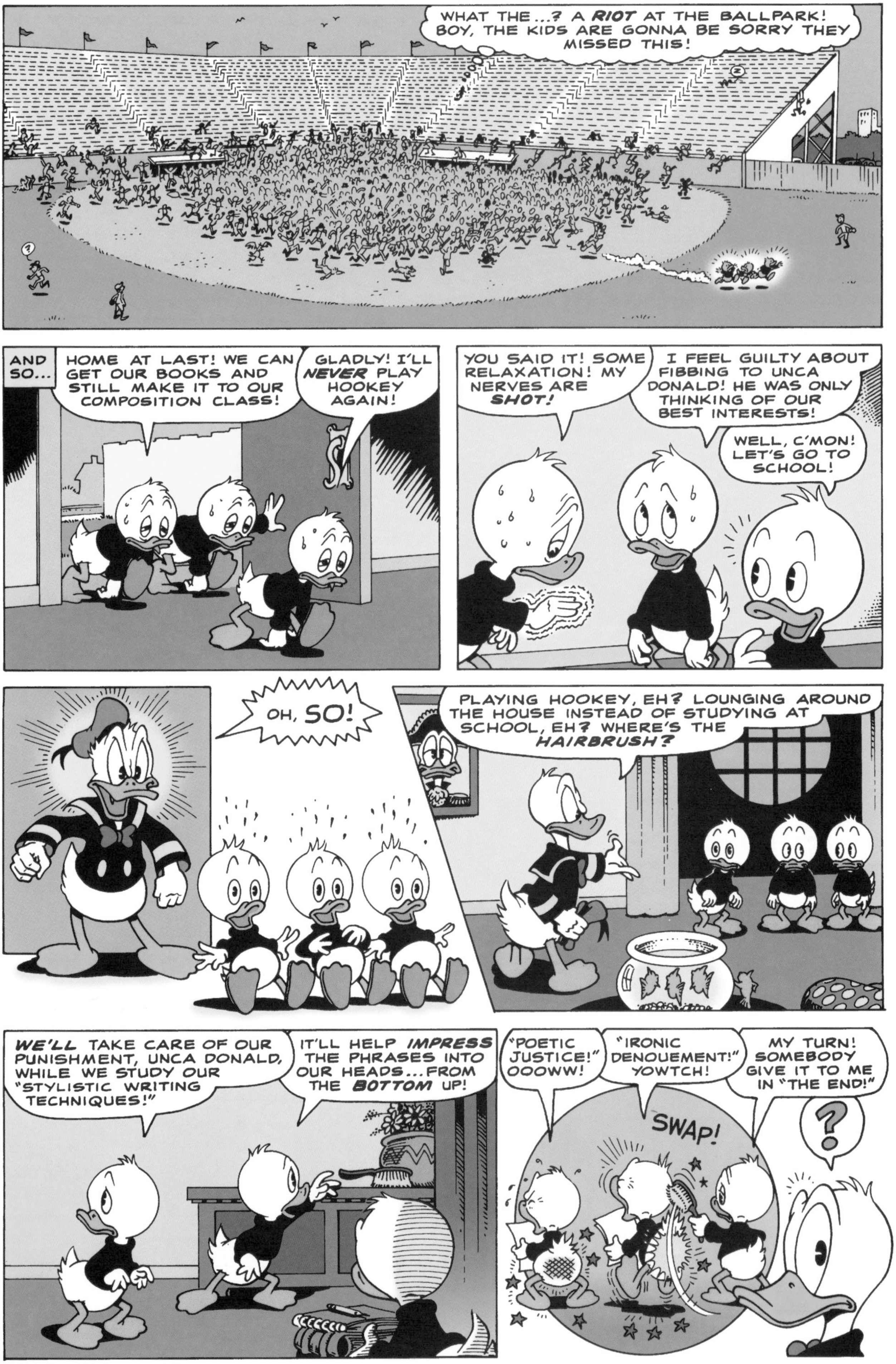

WHAT THE ...? A RIOT AT THE BALLPARK! BOY, THE KIDS ARE GONNA BE SORRY THEY MISSED THIS!
AND SO...
HOME AT LAST! WE CAN GET OUR BOOKS AND STILL MAKE IT TO OUR COMPOSITION CLASS!
GLADLY! I'LL NEVER PLAY HOOKEY AGAIN!
YOU SAID IT! SOME RELAXATION! MY NERVES ARE SHOT!
I FEEL GUILTY ABOUT FIBBING TO UNCA DONALD! HE WAS ONLY THINKING OF OUR BEST INTERESTS!
WELL, C'MON! LET'S GO TO SCHOOL!
OH, SO!
PLAYING HOOKEY, EH? LOUNGING AROUND THE HOUSE INSTEAD OF STUDYING AT SCHOOL, EH? WHERE'S THE HAIRBRUSH?
WE'LL TAKE CARE OF OUR PUNISHMENT, UNCA DONALD, WHILE WE STUDY OUR "STYLISTIC WRITING TECHNIQUES!"
IT'LL HELP IMPRESS THE PHRASES INTO OUR HEADS... FROM THE BOTTOM UP!
"POETIC JUSTICE!" OOOWW!
"IRONIC DENOUEMENT!" YOWTCH!
MY TURN! SOMEBODY GIVE IT TO ME IN "THE END!"
SWAP!
?

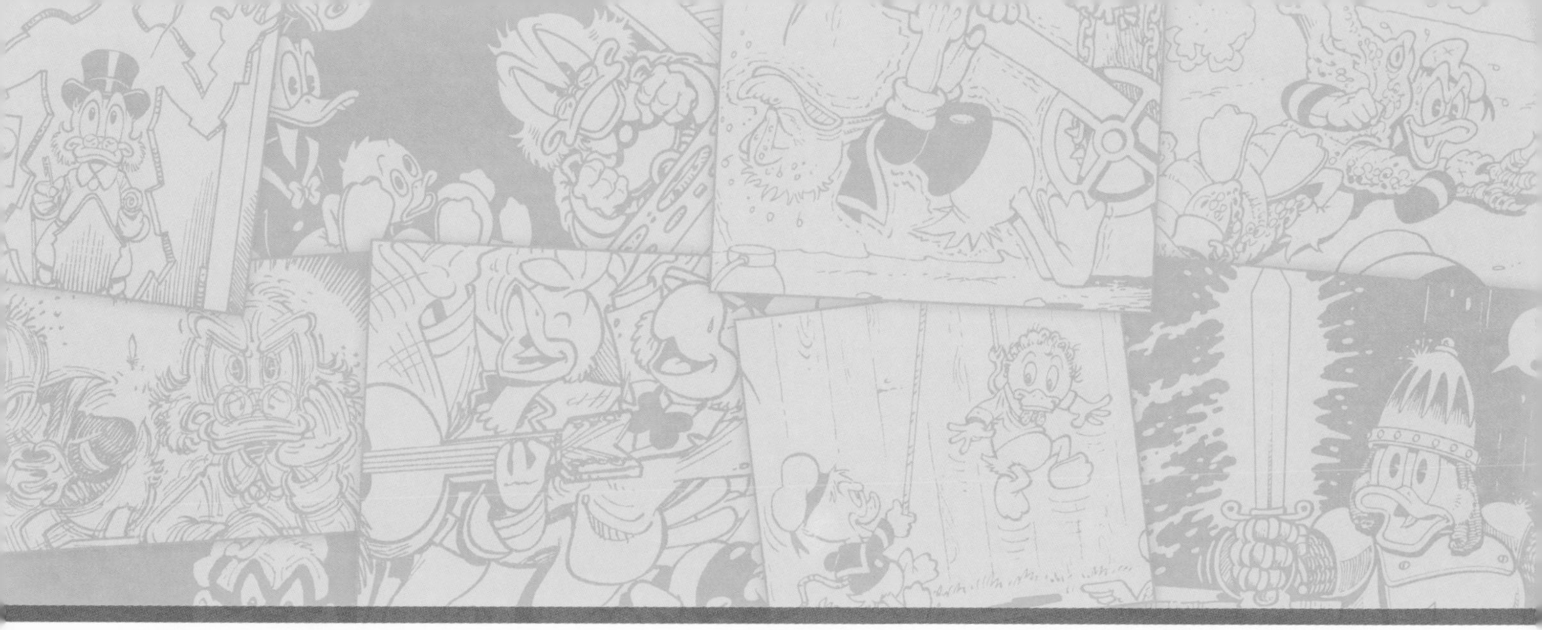

Behind the Scenes

BY

Don Rosa

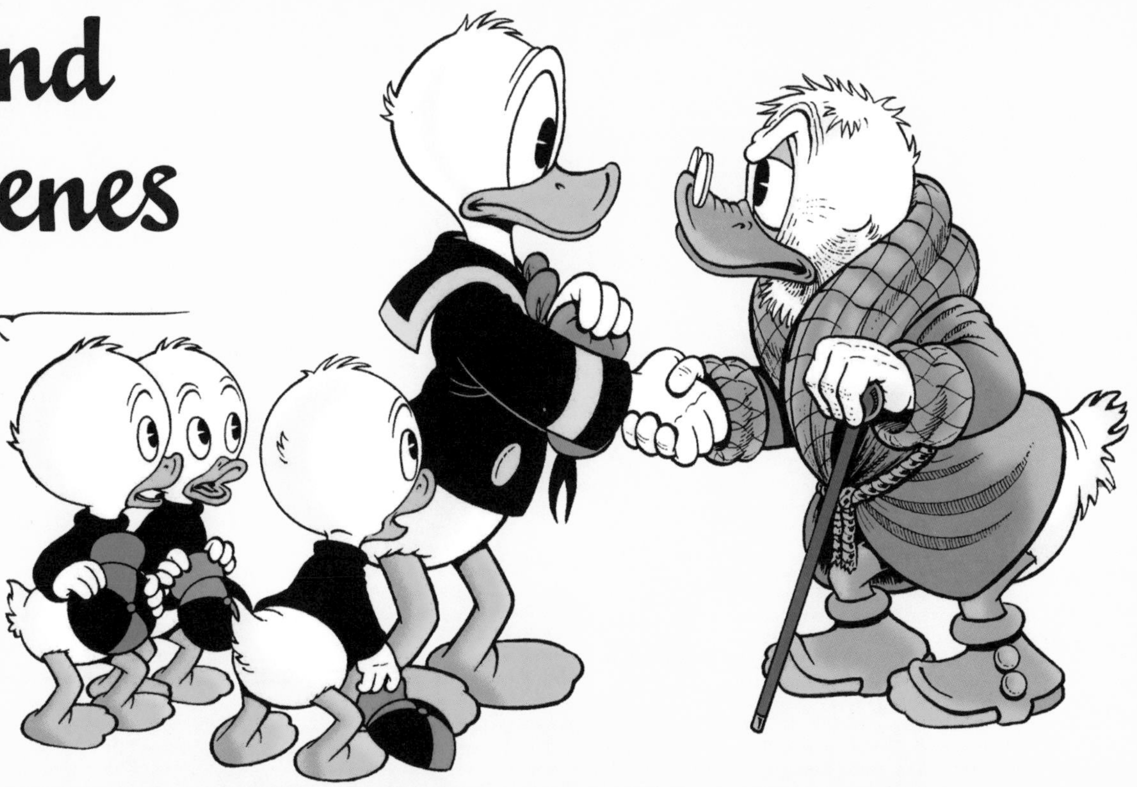

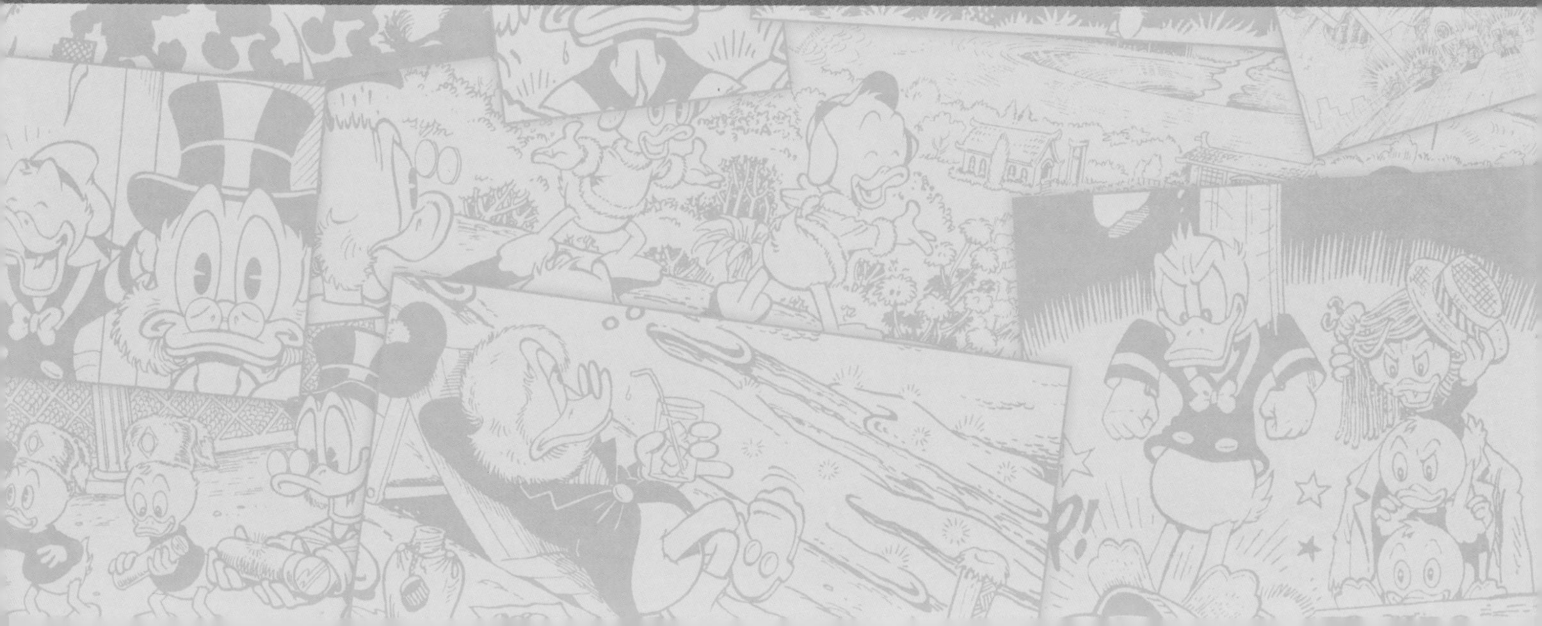

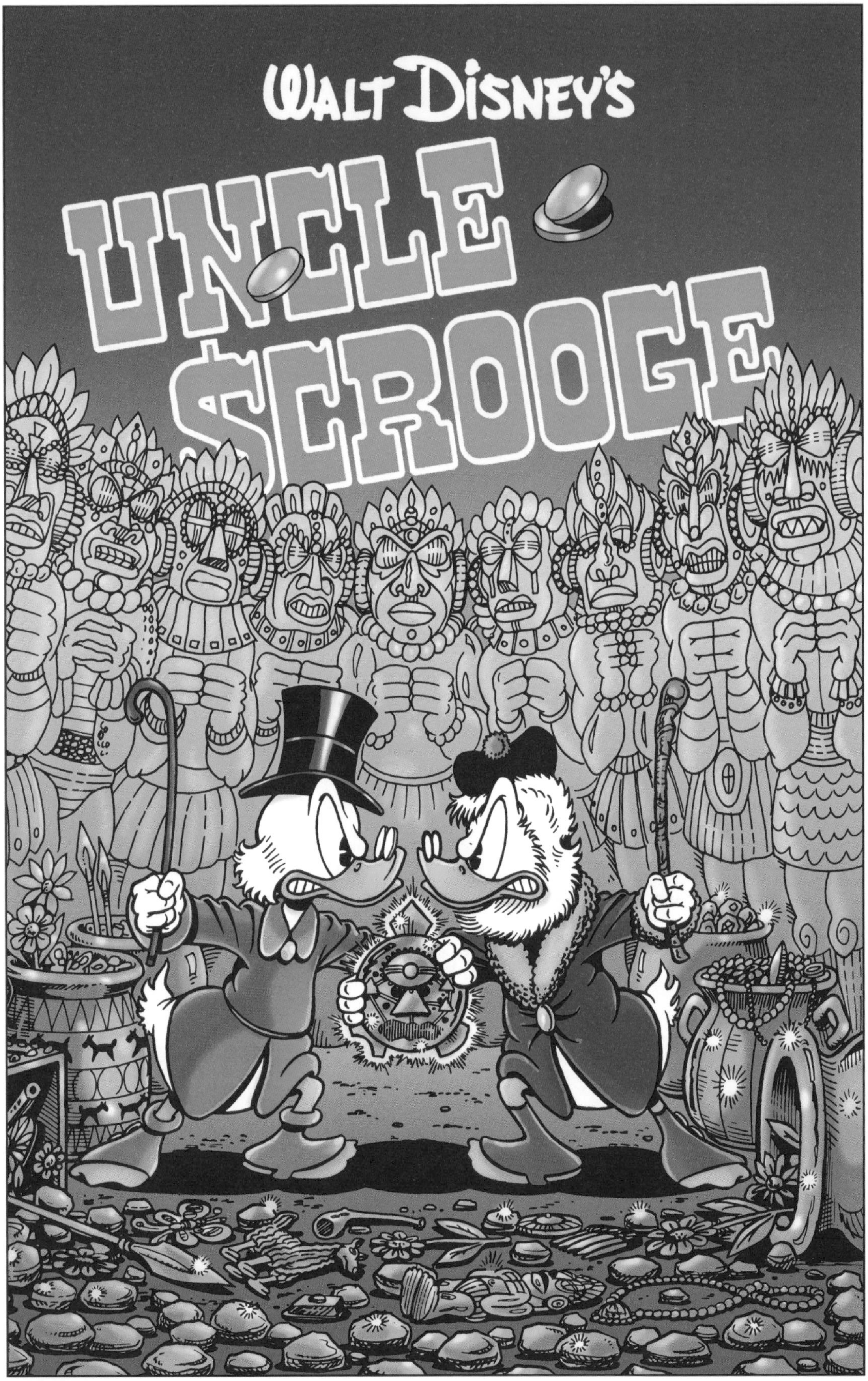
WALT DISNEY'S
UNCLE $CROOGE

THE SON OF THE SUN
Uncle Scrooge 219 (July 1987); new color by Kneon Transitt.
The second Duck comic book cover drawn by Don Rosa. See page 12 for a variant drawn earlier but published later.

A later Rosa-drawn poster illustrating "The Son of the Sun" (French *Picsou Magazine* 315, 1998). New color by Kneon Transitt.

THE SON OF THE SUN *p. 13*

So... there I was in June 1986, with my childhood dream in my hands... I'd been given the go-ahead to write and draw a full-length adventure of Carl Barks' *Uncle Scrooge*, my favorite comics character whose stories were so important to my childhood! But... where was I to begin? Actually, I already knew the whole plot—I'd already written and drawn an Uncle Scrooge adventure back in college as a daily comic strip for the school newspaper. Well, not really... that version had featured my own characters in my *Pertwillaby Papers* strip. But in my *mind* I had written it as an Uncle Scrooge adventure. So it was a foregone conclusion that I would rewrite that story into an actual Scrooge McDuck adventure. An *actual* Scrooge adventure!!! By *me*!

My original version of the story involved my hero, Lancelot Pertwillaby, discovering the golden Incan map disc while dusting some ancient pottery in the history department archives where he was attending college. Naturally, this had to be changed. My first idea was automatically that my story would open and progress exactly like my very favorite Barks adventure, "The Golden Helmet" (*Four Color* 408). Donald would discover the disc while working as a guard in the same museum for the same curator. The first page of my original 1986 script had Scrooge meeting

Huey, Dewey and Louie as they were all on their way to the museum; Scrooge to check on his trophy exhibit, and the nephews taking lunch to Unca Donald. As you saw, I eventually sped up that opening scene—perhaps at editor Byron Erickson's wise direction—so that the story now opened already in the museum. But checking through the remainder of my original script, I see the rest of the story and dialogue is exactly as I first wrote it.

The exhibit wouldn't be of the museum's own artifacts. I made it into a display of Scrooge's trophies from past Barks stories. This was my clue to the readers that this story would be based solidly on Barks' originals, using them as foundation and inspiration; and openly acknowledging my debt to his body of work that so enriched my childhood imagination.

Naturally I also had to change the villain. I'd always gotten a kick out of my Herr Doktor Viktor Dimitrius Smyte character—the Pertwillaby villain—but I was pretty certain that a fugitive Nazi war criminal was not quite right for a *Donald Duck* comic book. But I automatically knew that the villain in my Scrooge story would need to be Flintheart Glomgold! The "evil twin" has always been a staple of pulp fiction—what could possibly be more exciting than stories where a favorite hero matches wits with his misguided equal? Sherlock Holmes had Prof. Moriarity, Nero Wolfe had Arnold Zeck, Doc Savage had John Sunlight, the Shadow had Shiwan Khan, Capt. Marvel had Black Adam. All of these villains had the same powers and abilities as the hero, only they put their abilities to evil purposes. And in Flintheart Glomgold, Barks created a classic "evil counterpart," every bit as ambitious as Scrooge, virtually as wealthy, but with none of Scrooge's redeeming factors, such as his honesty and sense of fair play.

And yet Barks had used Flintheart only three times. I was *so* excited that I would be using Flintheart for the fourth time ever, and the first time in over a quarter-century! (Of course, at that time I had yet to discover that Scrooge comics were still being created in Europe and had been for many years after the American publisher ceased—and that some of these European comics featured Flintheart.)

What of the treasure Uncle Scrooge seeks in "The Son of the Sun"? It remained the same as in the comic strip I'd done nearly fifteen years earlier in college. I had gathered my data on Incan history from a professor of Latin American studies in the university History Department. I had designed my "Eye of Manco Capac" based on gems and precious minerals available to the Incans according to another professor in the Geology Department. Those elements of the story remained the same.

Obviously, I rewrote the details of the old plot to fit the Ducks. And there was one scene that I had originally planned to include, but later deleted for lack of space—it would have taken place when Flintheart is journeying through the Andes with Donald and the nephews. One night around a contemplative campfire, I would have had the Ducks quiz

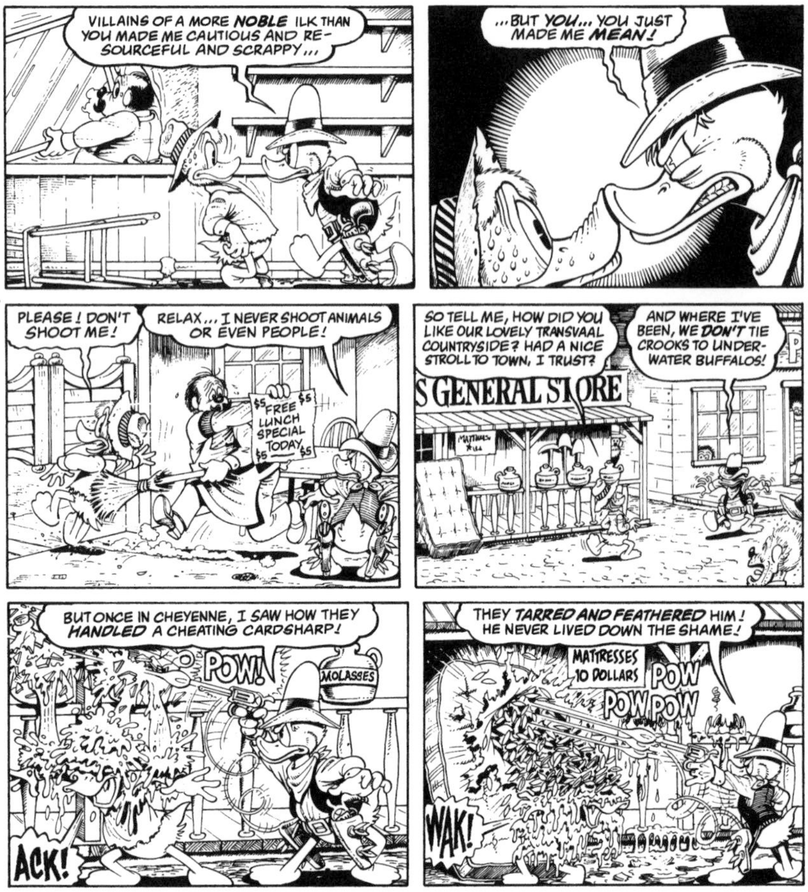
VILLAINS OF A MORE NOBLE ILK THAN YOU MADE ME CAUTIOUS AND RE-SOURCEFUL AND SCRAPPY...
...BUT YOU... YOU JUST MADE ME MEAN!
PLEASE! DON'T SHOOT ME!
RELAX... I NEVER SHOOT ANIMALS OR EVEN PEOPLE!
$5 FREE $5 LUNCH SPECIAL $5 TODAY $5
SO TELL ME, HOW DID YOU LIKE OUR LOVELY TRANSVAAL COUNTRYSIDE? HAD A NICE STROLL TO TOWN, I TRUST?
AND WHERE I'VE BEEN, WE DON'T TIE CROOKS TO UNDER-WATER BUFFALOS!
S GENERAL STORE
BUT ONCE IN CHEYENNE, I SAW HOW THEY HANDLED A CHEATING CARDSHARP!
POW!
MOLASSES
ACK!
THEY TARRED AND FEATHERED HIM! HE NEVER LIVED DOWN THE SHAME!
MATTRESSES 10 DOLLARS
POW
POW POW
WAK!

Rosa's much later "Life of Scrooge" chapter "The Terror of the Transvaal" (*Uncle Scrooge* 290) showed how Scrooge humiliated Glomgold in South Africa long ago.

Glomgold as to why he hated their Uncle Scrooge so much. He would tell the story of how he was badly humiliated by Scrooge in his South African home during the Transvaal Gold Rush of 1887, and how this inspired him to do his best to someday rival this hated enemy. Scrooge would have created his own worst enemy; a well-worn chestnut of plot twists. But I was not able to use this idea until years later when I actually *showed* the story unfolding in Chapter VI of my "Life and Times of Scrooge McDuck."

After rewriting my Pertwillaby story using Barks' characters, it was time to (gulp) *draw* it. Barks fans should easily notice that every Duck pose in this story is familiar to them. The first panel of "The Son of the Sun" was the first time I had ever drawn Scrooge, Donald, Huey, Dewey and/or Louie—except for a few times a year while I was illustrating the fanzine articles I was writing in the mid-1970s; and even *then*, I wasn't trying to draw them too *well*. I am not embarrassed in the least to say that the only way for me to learn immediately—from scratch!—how to draw these Ducks was to copy poses out of old Barks comics. I picked the period when I thought Barks' art was at its apex—1952; hauled stacks of comics to the copy store, copied hundreds of pages, cut out all the individual panels, then sorted them all into piles. The categories were poses and/or expressions such as "happy-standing," "mad-walking," "scared-running," "worried-pointing," and thirty other combinations. I also had about ten other categories for backgrounds such as "Money Bin scenes," "seascapes," "deserts," etc. In order to draw every single individual pose of each individual character in every individual panel I would get a reference pose out of my Barks clip file. Did it take a long time to draw that way? *You bet it did*!

And I was only drawing two days a week, while continuing to work at my construction company the rest of the time. I think it took me something like six months to complete "The Son of the Sun." I can barely stand to look at the art in this story now, but at the time it was the supreme effort I could achieve with my drastically limited experience and total lack of training.

But that didn't matter to me. I was on a mission from God. I was fulfilling my destiny! All my life I'd known that someday I would write and draw *one* Uncle Scrooge story, and this was it! And as yet another tribute to the inspiration to the man who instilled in me that burning passion to tell stories, in the last panel I put that tiny secret acronym. *"D.U.C.K."*... *D*edicated to *U*nca *C*arl from *K*eno. That was to be the epitaph on my one and only Scrooge story.

I won't even try to tell you what a *thrill* it was for me when "The Son of the Sun" first appeared in an actual *Uncle Scrooge* comic... issue 219, July 1987. If you haven't gotten the idea thus far of how I felt when that issue appeared, you haven't been paying attention! (I still feel shivers when I think back about it.) But I was distressed to see that my "D.U.C.K." dedication had been removed from the last panel! As I mentioned earlier in this volume, apparently it looked like an artist's signature; which Disney policy didn't yet allow in those days, so the Gladstone people removed it. But it was supposed to have been the finishing touch on my one-story career as a professional Scrooge cartoonist.

And then another surprise: "The Son of the Sun," my very first story as a professional, was nominated in the very first annual Harvey Awards as the "Best Comic Story of the Year." (In 1987, the Harvey Awards—named for Harvey Kurtzman—were the main equivalent of the Academy Awards for American comic books, though now the Eisner Awards seem to have become more prestigious.)

BUT HOLD! WHAT'S THIS BAKED INTO THE BASE OF THE VESSEL?
DON ROSA
A BEATEN-METAL PLAQUE OF SOME SORT, WITH SOME INSCRIPTIONS ON THE CONVEX SIDE... BUT WAIT–THIS ISN'T JUST ANY METAL... WHY, LANCE OLD BOY, THIS IS...

YOU BLOCKHEAD! YOU'VE BROKEN AN ANCIENT INCAN FUNERARY POT FROM MR. McDUCK'S EXHIBIT!
HERE'S WHY IT SOUNDED SO SOLID! THERE'S A METAL DISK BAKED INTO ITS BASE!
RELICS OF THE INCAN MINES
UK-WHUK!
GREAT SCOTT! LET ME SEE THAT! WHY, IT'S GOLD, AND COVERED WITH HIEROGLYPHS!
HA! MY INSTINCTS TELL ME I'M ALREADY HALF-WAY TO THAT INCAN TREASURE TROVE!
HANDS OFF!
JEWELED CROWN OF THE MAYAS

ONE MORE TURN OF THIS WINDING TRAIL AND WE SHOULD BE THERE!!
DIS ISS IT, MINE KOMRAD!
THERE IT IS! THERE IT IS...
the TEMPLE of MANCO CAPAC the SON of the SUN!!!
DON ROSA
CONTINUED!!!

THE TEMPLE OF MANCO CAPAC!
THE SON OF THE SUN!...
...AND KEEPER OF THE INCA GOLD!

VHAT ISS GOING ON DOWN HERE! VHAT...?
THE SACRED SUNBURST! THE "EYE OF MANCO CAPAC"! THIS IS THE TEMPLE'S ORIGINAL TREASURE!
DON ROSA

JUST AS I THOUGHT! EAT YOUR HEART OUT, SCROOGEY!
BEHOLD! THE ORIGINAL TREASURE OF THE SON OF THE SUN! THE EYE OF MANCO CAPAC!
YE CATS AND LITTLE KITTENS!

BOOM

BLOOEY!

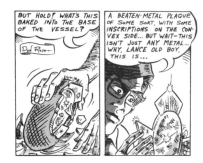

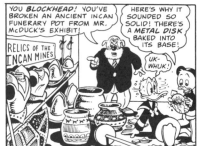

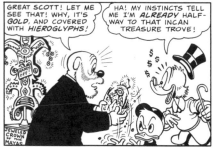

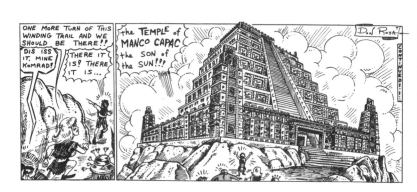

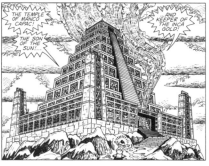

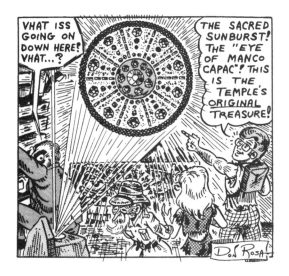

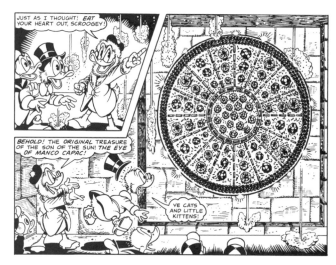

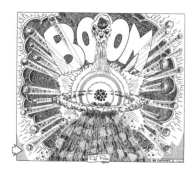

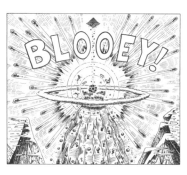

Rosa's *Pertwillaby Papers* story "Lost In (an Alternative Section of) the Andes" sent Lance Pertwillaby in search of Manco Capac's treasure. The story would inspire Rosa's much later Duck adventure "The Son of the Sun." *The Pertwillaby Papers* © and courtesy Don Rosa; *Uncle Scrooge* "The Son of the Sun" © Disney.

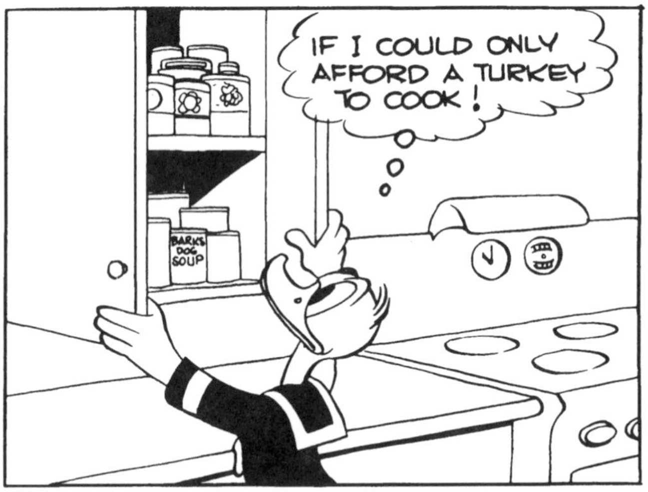
IF I COULD ONLY AFFORD A TURKEY TO COOK!
BARKS DOG SOUP

A can of "Barks Dog Soup" in *Walt Disney's Comics and Stories* 75. Story and art by (who else?) Carl Barks.

My story did not win, but a mere nomination in this superhero-dominated comics culture was absolutely remarkable!

So, I think it was then that I decided, well... people apparently liked that story... maybe I'll do just *one* more Scrooge story, and this time make certain that the "D.U.C.K." dedication remains in my final panel. Just *one* more.

Little did I know what the next twenty years would hold...

INSANE DETAILS TO LOOK FOR: This is the place—in a lot of these story notes—where I'll be describing all the special Barksian items and other references that I include in my Duck work for fans to find. Since "The Son of the Sun" started out as the *only* Scrooge story I thought I'd ever do, I crammed more Barksian details into it than almost any story afterward!!!

At Scrooge's museum display on Page 1, you'll spot some square eggs mixed in with the rock exhibit ("Lost in the Andes," *Four Color* 223). Also sighted are the Candy-Striped Ruby ("The Status Seeker," *Uncle Scrooge* 41); gold bullion from the "Flying Dutchman" ship (*Uncle Scrooge* 25); the Crown of Genghis Khan (*Uncle Scrooge* 14); a rare 1916 quarter (*Uncle Scrooge* 5); and the Golden Fleece ("The Golden Fleecing," *Uncle Scrooge* 12).

Page 2 brings us the treasures of Aladdin ("Rug Riders in the Sky," *Uncle Scrooge* 50), King Minos ("The Fabulous Philosopher's Stone," *Uncle Scrooge* 10), and Sir Quackly McDuck ("The Old Castle's Secret," *Four Color* 189). We see the Philosopher's Stone (*Uncle Scrooge* 10 again); the Goose Egg Nugget ("Back to the Klondike," *Four Color* 456); and pearls from the *Kuku Maru* ship ("Deep Down Doings," *Uncle Scrooge* 37).

Pages 3 and onward feature the Terries' and Fermies' trophy ("Land Beneath the Ground," *Uncle Scrooge* 13); relics of the Incan mines ("The Prize of Pizarro," *Uncle Scrooge* 26); the Crown of the Mayas (*Uncle Scrooge* 44); and sand from the Mines of King Solomon (*Uncle Scrooge* 19).

We also see treasure urns from the palace of King Croesus. I had always thought that the search for the treasury of Croesus was the greatest Uncle Scrooge story never told; Croesus supposedly being the wealthiest figure in history. So I added this exhibit of a treasure that Scrooge had surely sought out, but of which Barks had never told the story. Then, years later—long after I found that I *would* be doing more Scrooge stories than just "The Son of the Sun"—I *did* tell a tale of Scrooge finding that treasure. So the "untold story" in Scrooge's past became one that I revealed myself.

Moving onward in "The Son of the Sun," Barks' "Lost in the Andes" (*Four Color* 223) is referenced again when we get to (of course!) the Andes—and reencounter an elderly vicuna hunter from that story, who still recalls Donald's earlier quest for square eggs. What the old vicuna hunter is *thinking*, each time the Ducks depart from him, is my homage to the similar catchphrase found in all *Asterix* comics, usually in reference to Romans.

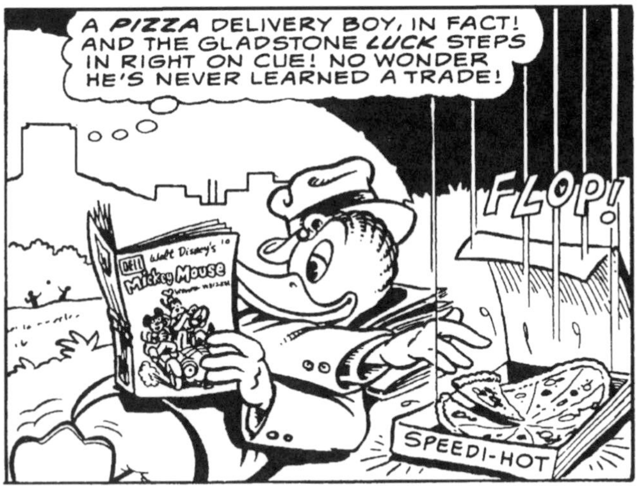
A PIZZA DELIVERY BOY, IN FACT! AND THE GLADSTONE LUCK STEPS IN RIGHT ON CUE! NO WONDER HE'S NEVER LEARNED A TRADE!
FLOP!
Walt Disney's Mickey Mouse
SPEEDI-HOT

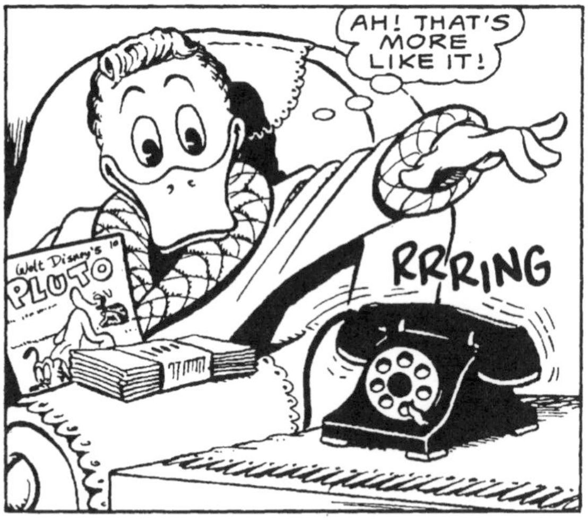
AH! THAT'S MORE LIKE IT!
Walt Disney's PLUTO
RRRING

The first printing of "Nobody's Business" featured Rosa's hand-drawn recreations of vintage Disney comic covers, including *Four Color* 427 (Mickey Mouse in "The Wonderful Whizzix") and 429 (Pluto in "Why Dogs Leave Home"). Rosa's "official" version of the story (>>39) substitutes the comics' actual cover art.

And finally—the matter of Flintheart Glomgold locating an Incan treasure by using a golden disc to reflect sunlight up onto a wall comes from an obscure 1954 Charlton Heston movie titled *Secret of the Incas*. See? I told you these were insane details.

NOBODY'S BUSINESS *p. 39*

"The Son of the Sun" being my first, this was the second Duck story I ever did (1987), and my first short "gag" story. Somehow the art looks like I've actually lost a bit of ground from the already-low ebb I began with in "Son of the Sun," probably because my first love is those long adventure epics! But I was not a professional cartoonist... I had never studied art, and I had only puttered in cartooning as a hobby back in high school and college. In fact, as of about 1982 I had given it up entirely, and when I started doing Duck comics I had not put pencil to paper for five years.

As with anything else, drawing is not a "talent"; it is an ability that you develop through long study and (especially) *practice*. And since I never intended to be a cartoonist for a living, I had never done *any* drawing except for a few hours each week for school newspapers or comic book "fanzines." This is why my art has an "underground" look to it... *not* because I was an R. Crumb imitator who was trying to bring "underground art" into Disney comics (as some critics snidely proclaim)... but simply because that's all the better I knew how to draw! I think R. Crumb and I had a similar style simply because we both grew up making comics for our own amusement as children, never taking cartooning very seriously, and never trying to develop a visual style that would be pleasing to a typical comics editor. We were only drawing for fun. An artist who studies his craft will learn how to draw in the simplest manner possible, with as few ink lines as required to convey an idea, so that he can get as much work done as quickly as possible, and maximize his income. To me, cartooning was simply a way to entertain myself in my spare time... so the *longer* it took, the more spare time it would fill... the more "needless and irritating detail" that I put into my art, the more fun it was. But I could never *un*learn that childhood trait, so I was stuck with an art style that would always be cluttered and always take me extra time to achieve, to the detriment of my paycheck.

I'm just relieved that in the years after I did these early Duck stories, I moved into cartooning full-time; and as a result of that practice, I think (I *pray*) that my art improved *greatly*. As I look back at these early stories, I wonder why Gladstone published them! One thing that Duckfans will be able to easily spot: virtually every Duck pose in this story is copied from an old Barks Duck. I was still giving myself a crash-course in drawing these characters since, though I had loved them all my life, I had never actually *drawn* them until I found myself as a comic book writer and artist so suddenly and unexpectedly.

Anyway, as to the plot of "Nobody's Business," I'm not sure if there's much to say... that's why I laid down that smokescreen above! It's a pretty straightforward little gag story. The punchline was intended strictly for Gladstone Publishing—our Disney comic publisher was named after Gladstone Gander (for luck!), and the end of this tale has Gladstone the Gander taking over Gladstone the comic publisher. I prepare the reader for Gladstone's final business situation by showing him reading comic books all through the story. In fact, all the comics that Gladstone is reading are actual Dell Disney comics of the 1950s (which is when my stories take place).

And even the company that Donald finally ends up with is an in-joke for Duck experts—back in the '40s and '50s there actually *was* a "Donald Duck Soda" brand in America. You can still see Donald Duck soda bottles for sale on eBay every week.

INSANE DETAILS TO LOOK FOR: In panel 6 on page 2, where Scrooge is talking into a can-and-string "telephone," the label on the can is "Barks Dog Soup"—the same as a can that Barks drew into a cupboard in an old Donald story

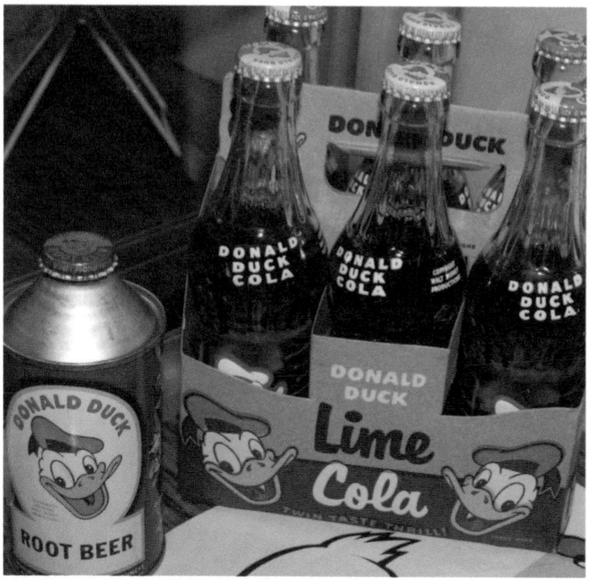
DONALD DUCK COLA
DONALD DUCK
Lime
Cola
ROOT BEER

Donald Duck Cola and other Donald-themed sodas were a popular commodity in the 1940s. Image courtesy Walt Disney Archives.

(*Walt Disney's Comics and Stories* 75). Then on page 7 there are two figures walking past Gladstone's yard who are obviously Azure Blue and Sharky the Lawyer from my favorite "Golden Helmet" adventure (*Four Color* 408). On the last page you see Scrooge's office clerk Clerkly, a character Barks used once or twice—but I rarely ever used him again, since I find that type of character with the bird bill and human ears to look a bit creepy.

I should also mention that this story features my first use of both Gladstone Gander and Gyro Gearloose! And my second use of a certain dedication. Why don't we initiate the...

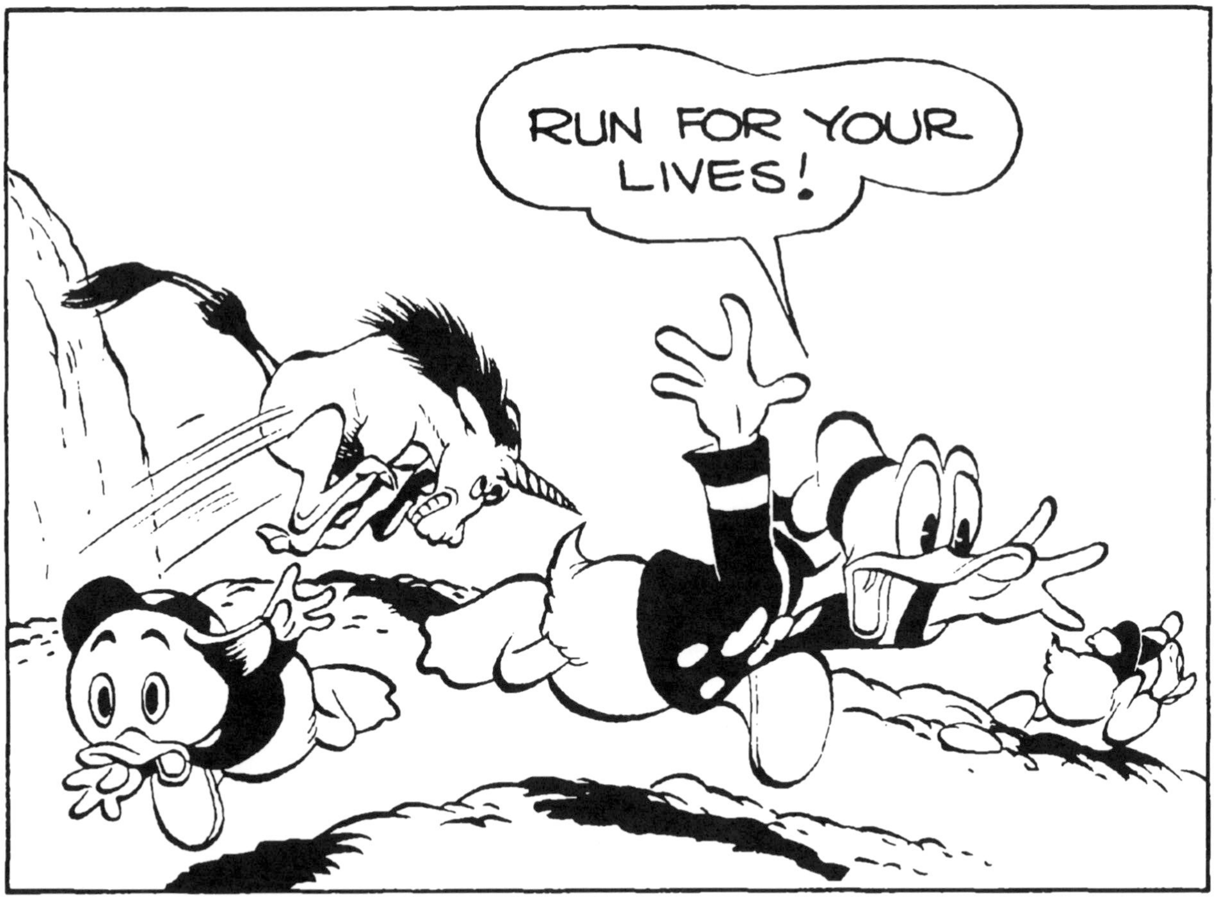
RUN FOR YOUR LIVES!

The Ducks encounter a fearsome figment in Carl Barks' "Trail of the Unicorn" (*Four Color* 263).

D.U.C.K. SPOTTER'S GUIDE: When I did this story, "The Son of the Sun" had not yet been published, so I did not know that my dedication would be removed from it. So I again placed it in the last panel of this story. But this time it slipped into print because it is written to look like the title of a comic book, and does not look like a then-forbidden artist signature.

MYTHOLOGICAL MENAGERIE *p. 49*

This is a special story for a few reasons—it's the third Duck story I created in my career, but it's the *first* "Donald Duck" story; the previous two stories I created for Gladstone Publishing being Uncle Scrooge tales.

I would imagine I chose the plot of Donald trying to show-up his smarty-pants Junior Woodchuck nephews due to how much I loved those stories as a kid. But looking back on the plot, I find it unusual by my current standards that I depict the nephews as being so gullible. Any *real* Woodchuck would know that the animals they are seeing in the Black Forest are quite impossible! But I do have them mention that unicorns are also considered mythological, and yet the Ducks once captured one for their Uncle Scrooge's private zoo—so a precedent had been set (and in an old Barks story!) for them to believe anything they saw. This also might be the first Duck story that I did background research on (since the research for "Son of the Sun" had been done thirteen years earlier). I made sure that all the animals that the kids found in their Guidebook were actual mythological beasts of various ancient cultures.

This is also my first use of the kids as Junior Woodchucks, and of Gus Goose and Grandma Duck... as well as Grandma's old Studebaker Electric car that's such fun to draw (since I love old cars... as you'll see in the next story's introduction).

INSANE DETAILS TO LOOK FOR: As I look back at this old story, I spot something even I've forgotten—in panel 3 of page 6 I can see bundles of old Dell Disney comic books stored in the shack! I can just barely read the titles of *Mickey Mouse* and *Walt Disney's Comics* (and Stories) on the bound bundles of old issues.

D.U.C.K. SPOTTER'S GUIDE: Again, I had not yet learned that any dedication I placed in the story would be removed, so for the third time I simply wrote it in plain sight in the final panel. And *poof*, it disappeared! But as with the last panel of "Son of the Sun," I have sent the editors a scan of that last panel so that you'll see the dedication appearing in this story for the first time.

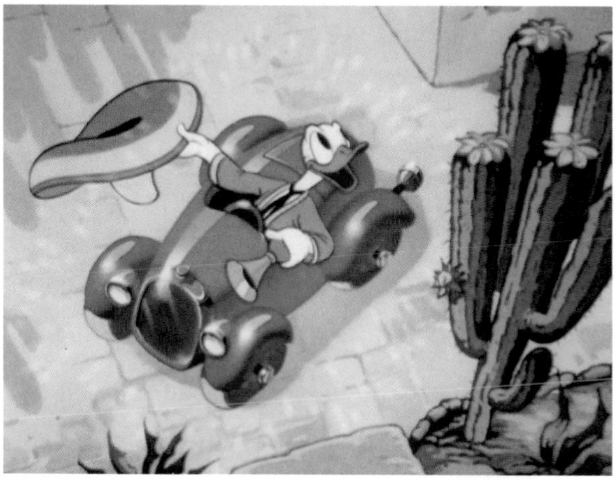

Donald's car in the cartoon *Don Donald* (1937). Its 313 license plate debuted in the Al Taliaferro-drawn newspaper strip for March 22, 1940.

RECALLED WRECK *p. 59*

Yikes... there just really is very little to be said about these short gag stories... they just sorta speak for themselves, y'know? There isn't extensive research for me to brag about, or historical accuracy to boast of, or spectacular volcano explosions or tidal waves to show off. All I recall about this 1987 story is that I decided to do a tale about Donald's famous little car with the "313" license plates.

I hear many Duck fans often try to guess what actual make of car Donald's was fashioned after, as created for the cartoon *Don Donald* and adapted by Al Taliaferro for the *Donald Duck* newspaper strips. There really was never a car that looked much like Donald's (what a strange little car that would have been!). However, in Carl Barks' "Volcano Valley" (*Four Color* 147), he had an incidental character describe Donald's car, and I used that same description in my story: "a 1920 Mixwell engine," a "[19]22 Dudge body," and "[19]23 Paclac axles." These car names are all fictitious, though they are based on actual car makes of that period—"Mixwell" comes from Maxwell (the type of car that the radio comedian Jack Benny always said he drove), "Dudge" obviously comes from Dodge which we still have today, and "Paclac" must be a cross between the two old-time luxury cars, the Packard and the Cadillac.

Anyway, this comment from "Volcano Valley" suggested to me that Donald built the car himself from scrap parts, which might explain why he loves it and never trades it in on a newer or better model. And I also introduce the idea that his license plate number of "313" is one that he pays extra to get each year in one of those "vanity license plate" offers where you can choose your own license plate designation. Otherwise how could he always have the same license plate number?

(On a personal note that has some relation to the above: Since I am as bored by modern car designs as much as I am bored by most modern movies, TV shows and American comics, in 1977 I decided to buy the last car I would ever own. I bought a 1948 Dodge Custom 6 from an old farmer who'd only driven it into town once a week since he bought it new. It was in perfect condition... and still is. It looks a little like a giant version of Donald's "Dudge" car body, except that mine is not a convertible and is midnight blue). And from that time on, each year I've always gotten the same license plate which says "COMICS"! So, if you're ever in Louisville, and see a 1948 Dodge with the license plate COMICS go by, honk at me!)

D.U.C.K. SPOTTER'S GUIDE: Stop looking! By the time *this* story was published, I had been told that I was not allowed to put my "D.U.C.K." dedication into my story. But I had yet to decide: "phooey on 'em! I'll just *hide* the dedication so they won't notice it!" So there is *no* D.U.C.K. in "Recalled Wreck."

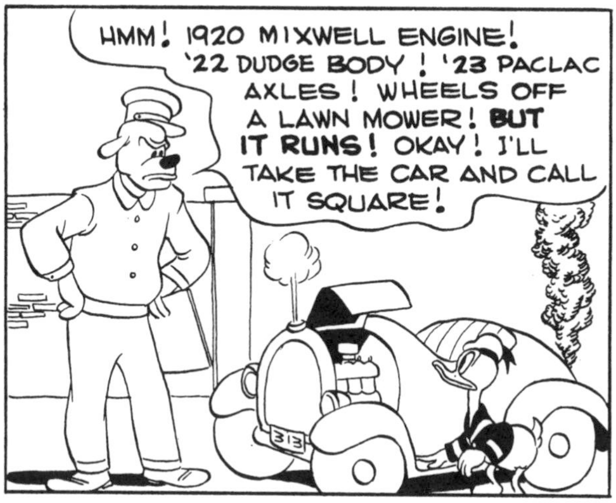
HMM! 1920 MIXWELL ENGINE! '22 DUDGE BODY! '23 PACLAC AXLES! WHEELS OFF A LAWN MOWER! BUT IT RUNS! OKAY! I'LL TAKE THE CAR AND CALL IT SQUARE!
313

Barks' description of Donald's car from "Volcano Valley" (*Four Color* 147).

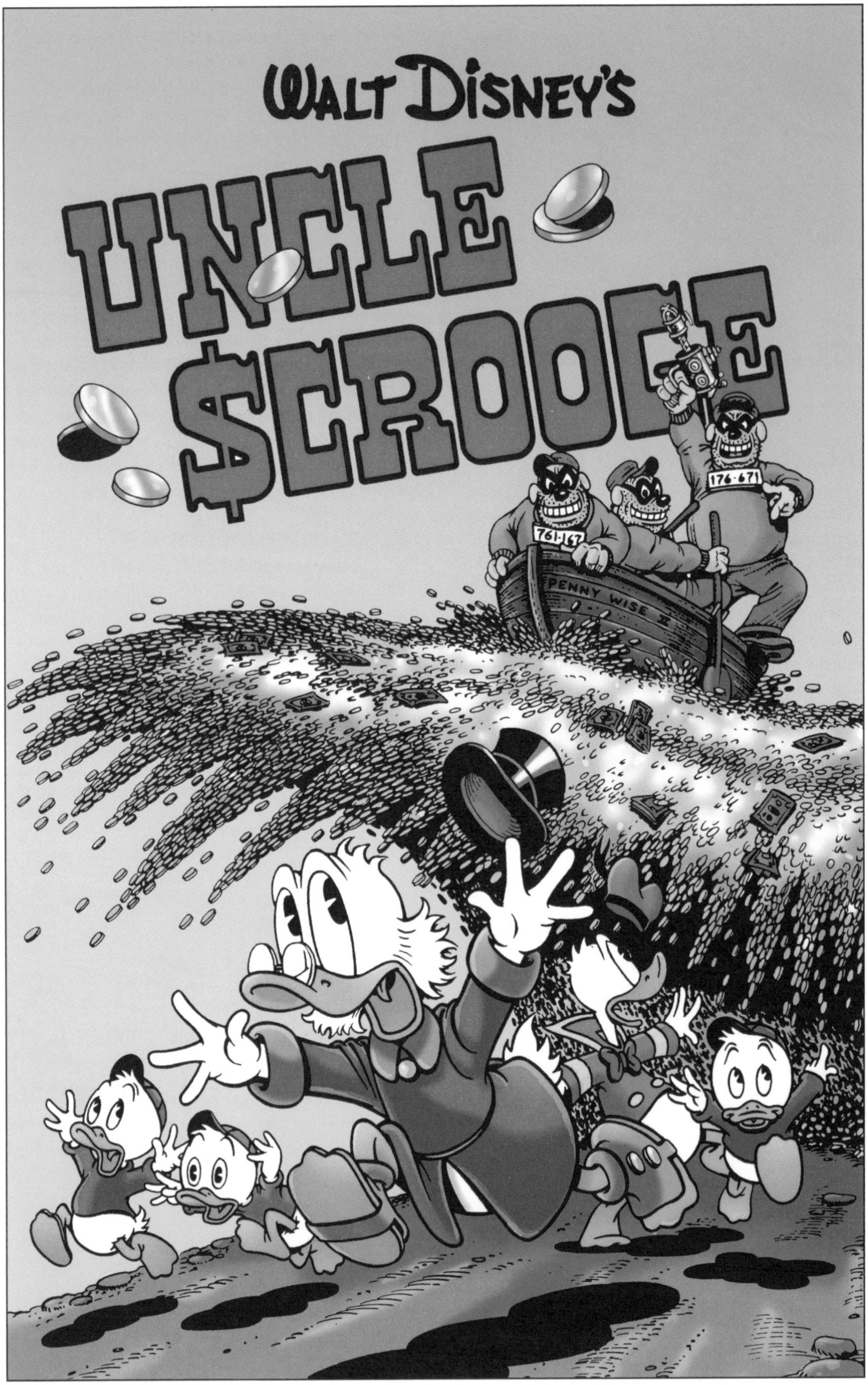
WALT DISNEY'S
UNCLE $CROOGE
761-167
176-671
PENNY WISE II

CASH FLOW
Uncle Scrooge 224, December 1987; new color by Kneon Transitt.
The ray gun held by 176-671, seen here approximately as originally drawn,
was omitted in all previous American printings. Restoration by Jesper Sichlau.

AND WHEN WE WANT TURKEY FOR BREAKFAST, WE'LL HAVE TURKEY!
AND WHEN WE WANT PRUNES FOR BREAK-FAST —
176-1
BEAGL BOYS INC
176-167
BEAGLE BOYS INC.
SHUT UP! WE HAD PRUNES FOR BREAKFAST EVERY MORNING IN PRISON! ARE YOU GETTING HOMESICK?
BUT I LIKE PRUNES!
BEAGL BOYS INC

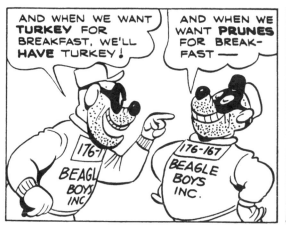

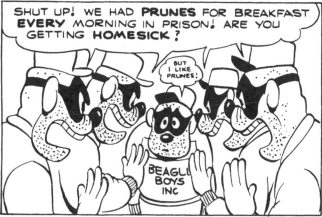

176-167's prune fetish is born in *Uncle Scrooge* 8. Both Barks and Rosa would make several uses of this endearing cliché.

CASH FLOW *p. 69*

As we all know, inertia is the tendency of a body's resistance to changes in momentum or, simply put, a body's inertial mass. The mass of a body determines the momentum P at given velocity v; it is a proportionality factor in the formula:

$$P = mv$$

The factor m is referred to as 'inertial mass'. But obviously mass as related to 'inertia' of a body can be defined also by the formula:

$$F = ma$$

Here, F is force, m is mass, and a is acceleration.

By these formulas, we can easily see that the greater a body's mass and velocity, the greater the force that body will exert on a resistance to its movement. Thus, mass is the quantitative measure of a body's inertia; that is to say, of its resistance to its force being resisted. Therefore, a body's *inertia* is its tendency to maintain momentum; or, the measure of how difficult it is to cease the momentum of the body which—

Excuse me... do you understand any of that baloney? Me neither! Not after 40 years since I graduated from engineering college! I still recall how, while taking notes in my Thermodynamics class or my Mechanics of Deformable Solids class, I would not ponder how physics would solve the mysteries of the universe—I would sit and daydream about what would happen if there was no inertia?! What a laugh riot! Or, what if the coefficient of friction were suddenly zero?! Haha—everybody would fall on their butts!

Meanwhile, to keep myself from going crazy during those four years, I drew editorial cartoons for the college newspaper, and even a comedy-adventure comic strip (discussed in other sections of this volume). But I couldn't resist trying to make physics have more *meaning* for my life by using some of the concepts I was studying in my comic story... and negate them. In one storyline, my college-student hero Lancelot Pertwillaby created a new substance during a lab accident which neutralized the coefficient of friction. He named it "anti-abrasium." Ergo, proceeding, I next used the formula:

$$(wi) + (dh) = CH$$

...where ***(wi)*** stands for "wacky invention," ***(dh)*** represents "desperate hero," and ***CH*** denotes "cartoon hijinks." This is a very useful scientific equation in comic strip theory.

My "anti-abrasium" was too funny a plot gimmick not to introduce to a bigger audience, just as I'd done with my old "Incan Treasure" plot, so for my second overblown

Uncle Scrooge 8 also introduced this unnamed Professor—and his quixotic quest to create stink-free cabbage.

AND HERE I ALMOST PERFECTED MY FUMELESS CABBAGE, BUT EVERY TIME I TOOK OUT THE FUMES, I ALSO TOOK OUT THE TASTE!
TSK! TSK!

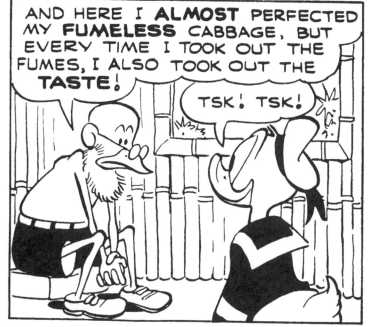

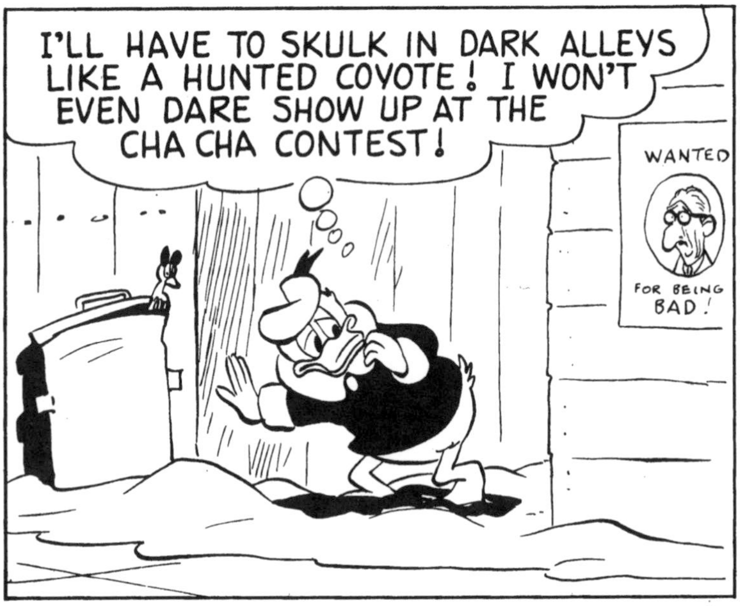
I'LL HAVE TO SKULK IN DARK ALLEYS LIKE A HUNTED COYOTE! I WON'T EVEN DARE SHOW UP AT THE CHA CHA CONTEST!
WANTED
FOR BEING BAD!

Barks' original version of himself on a wanted poster. From "The Christmas Cha Cha" (*Dell Giant* 26).

Scrooge adventure I brought it back as a new ray beam invented by Barks' wacky "Cabbage Scientist." But to make the story even more interesting, I also came up with another engineering-class-daydream, the "anti-inertia" ray gun to further enhance the above formula for even more potent ***CH***.

But I wasn't writing for a college audience now. Would some younger readers not understand these principles? I didn't worry about that—I knew, since I had been a young comics fan myself, kids do not like being talked down to. They enjoy and appreciate some concepts that challenge them and make them think a little harder. That's one of many reasons that Barks' stories are so popular—he, too, showed respect for the intelligence of his young readers. And, as it turned out, I never saw any evidence of readers having trouble understanding my "anti-inertia" or "anti-friction" ray guns. And it made a fun story! I just wish my drawing ability was improving quicker! Today, this story looks even more crudely drawn to me than "The Son of the Sun."

Actually, there was *one* moment in "Cash Flow" that confused some readers: if a flying cannonball would not

Rosa, like Barks, featured giant statues of Cornelius Coot. Scrooge and Blackheart Beagle even battle on top of one in Rosa's later "A Little Something Special" (*The Adventurous Scrooge McDuck* 2).

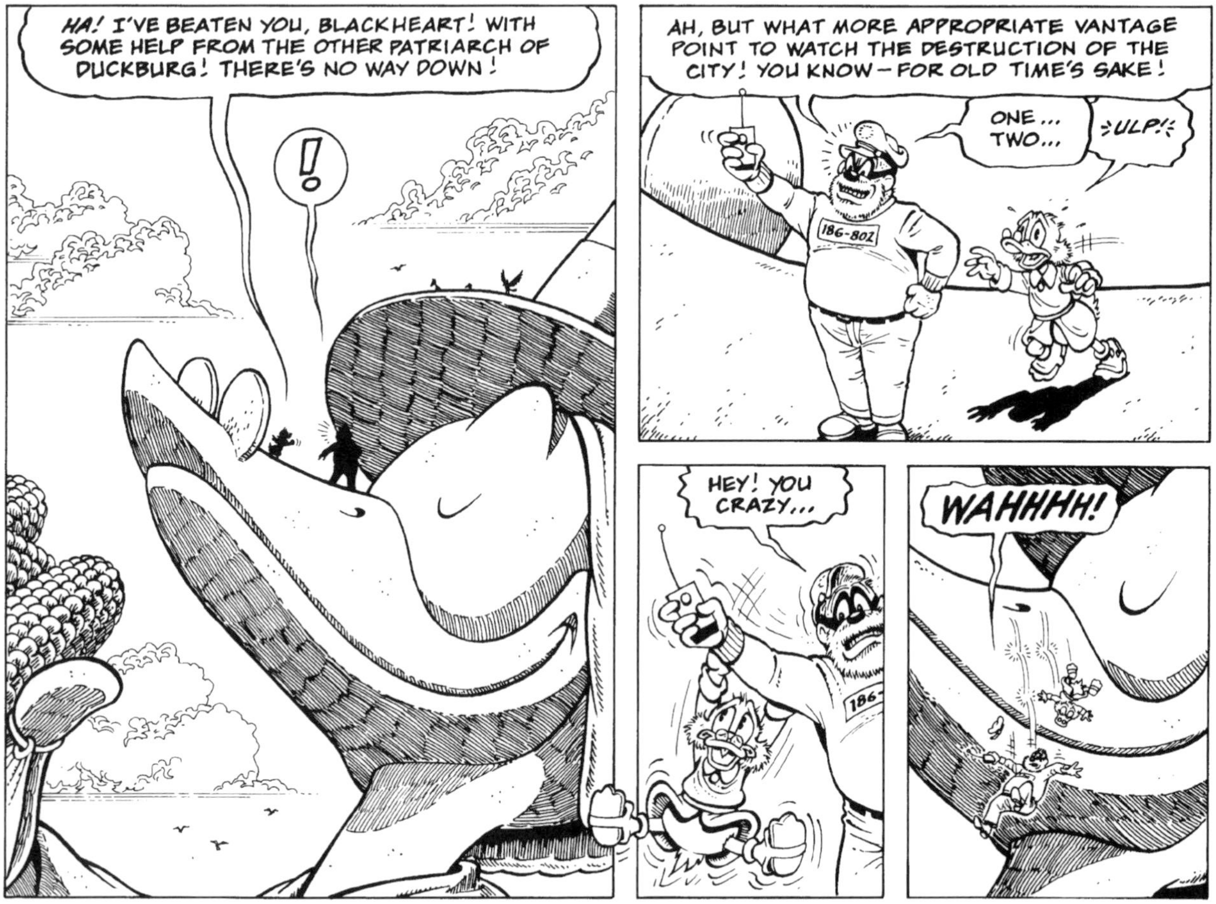
HA! I'VE BEATEN YOU, BLACKHEART! WITH SOME HELP FROM THE OTHER PATRIARCH OF DUCKBURG! THERE'S NO WAY DOWN!
!
AH, BUT WHAT MORE APPROPRIATE VANTAGE POINT TO WATCH THE DESTRUCTION OF THE CITY! YOU KNOW—FOR OLD TIME'S SAKE!
ONE... TWO...
ULP!
186-802
HEY! YOU CRAZY...
WAHHHH!

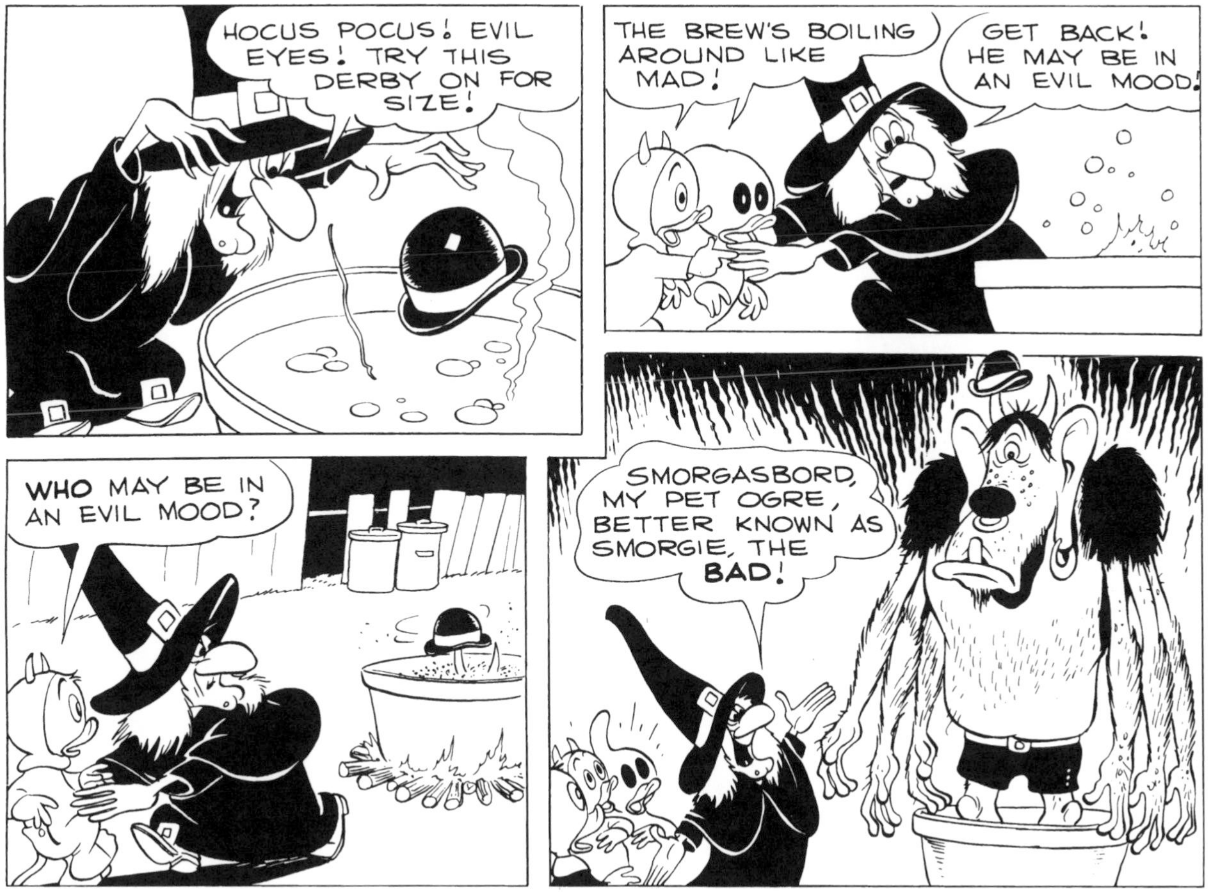
HOCUS POCUS! EVIL EYES! TRY THIS DERBY ON FOR SIZE!
THE BREW'S BOILING AROUND LIKE MAD!
GET BACK! HE MAY BE IN AN EVIL MOOD!
WHO MAY BE IN AN EVIL MOOD?
SMORGASBORD, MY PET OGRE, BETTER KNOWN AS SMORGIE, THE BAD!

Witch Hazel's ogre Smorgasbord, as created for Barks' "Trick or Treat" (*Donald Duck* 26).

hurt a Beagle Boy's nose, and a car falling off a cliff hit the ground without crushing force due to its mass and velocity, then *why* did those lobbed cannonballs hurt the Beagles' heads and toes? Well, even though there was no force exerted on the Beagles by the gravitational velocity of those cannonballs, the cannonballs *still* had their full 150-pound weight after coming gently to rest on a noggin or tootsie.

But I beg your pardon! In my opening remarks I failed to mention the 'coefficient of friction.' This value, symbolized by the Greek letter ***μ***, describes the ratio of the force of friction between two bodies and the force pressing them together. For surfaces at rest relative to each other, blah blah yakkety yakkety... *zzzzzzzzzzzzzzzzzzzz!*

Oops, there I go again. Not very interesting.

The aspects of this tale that I find *more* interesting, as I look back at it, are all of my references to the Barks stories that I grew up on! This being my very second Scrooge adventure (and my first use of the Beagle Boys), I can see I was really enjoying the idea that I, me, Don Rosa, myself, was writing and drawing stories based on the Barks adventures that I had loved so much as a kid!!! I seem to be piling the Barks references on thick and fast here. In fact, the first page reads like an outline for the "Life and Times of Scrooge McDuck" series I would do about four years later.

One aspect about this story that I well recall: As always, I wanted to show readers that I was not taking a single shortcut in my writing or drawing, so I was determined to use *lots* of Beagle Boys. I had already penciled about five pages of the story in which I used up to *ten* Beagle Boys in every panel where they appear as a group. Then I recall that I needed to double check a Barksian fact such as, perhaps, what numbers might have been used on the mug shot prison-number plates they are wearing (as they did in their earliest Barks appearances).

Looking through my old issues, I suddenly realized that even though Barks implied that there were sometimes a dozen Beagle Boys involved in a caper, he never showed more than *seven* in any single panel (except in about three instances in his career). But I had been using an even *ten*! It was important to me that fans know that I was only trying to do honor to Unca Carl's work, and *not* trying to *top* him in any way! So I went back through all the panels I'd already penciled and *erased* three of my ten Beagle Boys!

INSANE DETAILS TO LOOK FOR: The Beagle Boy 176-167 who loves prunes (*Uncle Scrooge* 8 and 58). The wacky cabbage-loving professor who invented the stone ray (*Uncle Scrooge* 8), and the Beagle Boys remembering that escapade. A mention of Scrooge's old flame Glittering Goldie ("Back to the Klondike," *Four Color* 456). A mention of Super Snooper (*Walt Disney's Comics and Stories* 107). The Oso Safe vault door (various stories) with the seven combination dials. A mention of "Impervium", a substance that Scrooge had his safes made of (various stories). The fact that Scrooge built the Duckburg storm drain system ("Clothes Make the Duck," *Uncle* Scrooge 32). The Tulebug River ("Only a Poor Old Man," *Four Color* 386). A Cornelius Coot statue in the park (*Walt Disney's Comics* 138). A cityscape view which shows Mount Demontooth (*Walt Disney's Comics* 157) and two rocky pinnacles that Barks showed in a story about Donald selling feather mattresses (*Walt Disney's Comics* 187). A wanted poster with my first-ever drawing of Magica De Spell. And even *Carl Barks* appearing on a wanted poster, being a duplicate of one that he, himself, once drew into the background ("The Christmas Cha Cha," *Dell Giant* 26).

D.U.C.K. SPOTTER'S GUIDE: By this point, I had begun to realize that I might still include my dedication if I made it harder to spot, so you'll see it written on an obscure dollar bill in the first panel. Not especially clever, eh? If I didn't improve on that idea, my dedications would still often be spotted and deleted.

FIT TO BE PIED *p. 95*

I must try hard to say anything interesting about this tale. It's not bad, but it's another very straightforward short gag-story. I wrote/drew this ten-pager in 1987, the same year as my first Uncle Scrooge story appeared!

This is the last time I ever used Barks' great Neighbor Jones character. In fact, I think that—to this day—"Fit to Be Pied" and "Recalled Wreck" are the *only* times I used the character, since he is mostly a face from the cast of Barks' ten-page gag stories, and I specialize in the long adventure sagas.

It's been years since I glanced through this story myself. One thing I notice is the Halloween costume that Donald considers wearing—it's Smorgie the Bad, the ogre character featured in the pages of Barks' "Trick or Treat" story which were cut from the original 1952 publication (*Donald Duck* 26), and have only more recently been restored to the reprints. At the time I drew this story, no readers except Barks scholars of the first order would even know who Smorgie *was*, since those pages had never been printed anywhere except in clusters of photocopies circulated among us collectors. But gad... at this point I could sure draw a better ogre than I could a Duck! Even my Ducks look a bit ogre-ish! I wish I could reach in and redraw all of those Ducks. Some of them are just painful to look at!

I'll say something about the story titles of the ten-page "gag" stories like this one. While we're now referring to these stories as "Fit to Be Pied," "Recalled Wreck," and so on, I personally *never* gave them any titles. I always gave titles to my early adventure tales, but since the Barks ten-pagers I grew up on never had titles, I saw no reason to give my short stories any titles. The titles that have been used on these tales since their first appearances in 1987-88 were created by the editor at Gladstone Publishing. And they are good titles, but they are not my own invention (this is the sort of fact that comic scholars want to know).

D.U.C.K. SPOTTER'S GUIDE: Look in the branches of the bush in the foreground of the first panel.

FIR-TREE FRACAS *p. 105*
THE PAPER CHASE *p.119*

I specialize in the long adventure stories, and like to do an occasional short "gag" story just to add variety to the mix. But I have never been interested in doing the ultra-short

The Barks tale that gave us "Barks Dog Soup" (*Walt Disney's Comics and Stories* 75) was also the birthplace of oolated squiggs.

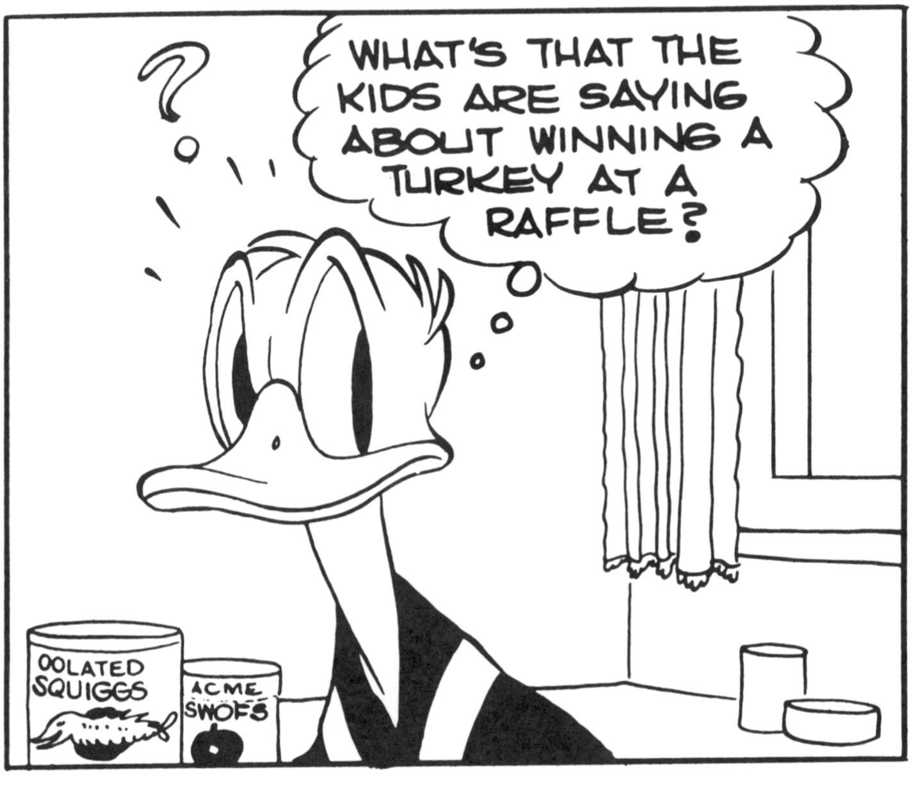
WHAT'S THAT THE KIDS ARE SAYING ABOUT WINNING A TURKEY AT A RAFFLE?
OOLATED SQUIGGS
ACME SWOFS

> I AM *NOT* LUCKY ALL THE TIME! ON MY BIRTHDAY I'M THE *UNLUCKIEST* GUY IN DUCKBURG!

> YOU *ARE?* HOO HOO! TELL US MORE!

Gladstone suffers a daylong jinx in Rosa's later "Sign of the Triple Distelfink" (*Uncle Scrooge* 310). That's Donald covered in cake frosting at right.

one- or two-page "jokes"... I just need more than that to sink my teeth into; complexity fascinates me. That's probably why I collect so many different things and have so many interests and hobbies... it's probably some of that engineer that rubbed off on me in college (though I tried to avoid it).

However, when I was working for Gladstone Publishing they told me they needed some two-page gags to fill certain holes in certain issues. I declined to do any, but they said that they had some jokes already supplied by staffer Gary Leach, and would I please just do the drawing? Well, okay, if they really needed the work done... after all, I was the only artist they had at the time.

They also needed one four-pager to fill a hole they had in a Christmas issue, and that one got printed first. Four pages was just long enough that I could get interested in the job, and I wrote a quick story about Donald and a Christmas tree that the editors titled "Fir-Tree Fracas." Anyway, for only being four pages, it's not half bad.

Published a few months after that yuletide quickie was "The Paper Chase," the first two-pager written by Gary Leach. It might be most notable for its punchline... which might be an untranslatable gag. When it appeared in other countries, what was the joke?

D.U.C.K. SPOTTER'S GUIDE: In "The Paper Chase," the "D.U.C.K" is acting as a headline on the newspaper in panel 1, page 1. But that seems to be the only time I put the dedication into Gary's short gags. Perhaps I was thinking that since I was only doing half the work, I had no right to speak for the writer in dedicating the entire job to someone.

"Fir-Tree Fracas," meanwhile, is one of the first stories

where I realized that I could play a game with the fans if I *hid* the dedication in the art! That seemed like a great idea (even though it feels like a dedication is a bit pointless if I'm forced to *hide* it). Nonetheless, fans seem to enjoy this bit of extra sport in reading a Rosa story, so it's now a tradition. So, here is the first real "spoiler" if you've given up looking for the "D.U.C.K." on your own: look in the Christmas tree in panel 2 of page 1.

OOLATED LUCK
p. 109

This story concerns a promotional contest held by the makers of some sort of canned fish called "oolated squiggs." Now, wait! Don't run for your dictionaries! There are no such words as "oolate" or "squigg." As with the "Barks Dog Soup" can that I showed in "Nobody's Business," "oolated squiggs" was a label on another can in a cabinet in Donald Duck's kitchen in that same old Carl Barks story (*Walt Disney's Comics* 75), and it is a famous "nonsense word" to Barks scholars. There was a picture of a fish shape on the can, so I've always assumed that an "oolated squigg" was something like a pickled herring.

This story was one of very few times that I did a story centered on Gladstone Gander's incredible good luck. It seemed to me that just about every possible idea dealing with Donald trying to beat Gladstone's super-luck had been done by then... but I wanted to figure the only possible way that Gladstone's good luck could logically work *against* him. And I think this story might have found that way! Yet... having done that, I spent years unable to think of *another* plot for a short Gladstone Gander gag story, until finally doing "From Duckburg to Lillehammer" in 1992. I also did a special Gladstone Gander 50th anniversary story in 1998 at the publisher's request, but that had Gladstone being incredibly *un*lucky for one day, which is a whole different idea... a whole different can of squiggs!

Uh... and that's all there is to say about this story... so I'll get right to the

D.U.C.K. SPOTTER'S GUIDE: the dedication is hidden in the footprints in the snow below Gladstone in the fifth panel of the first page. This was done back when I had not yet decided to always hide the thing in the *first* panel of all my stories, so that I would not drive the readers *too* totally crazy looking for it.

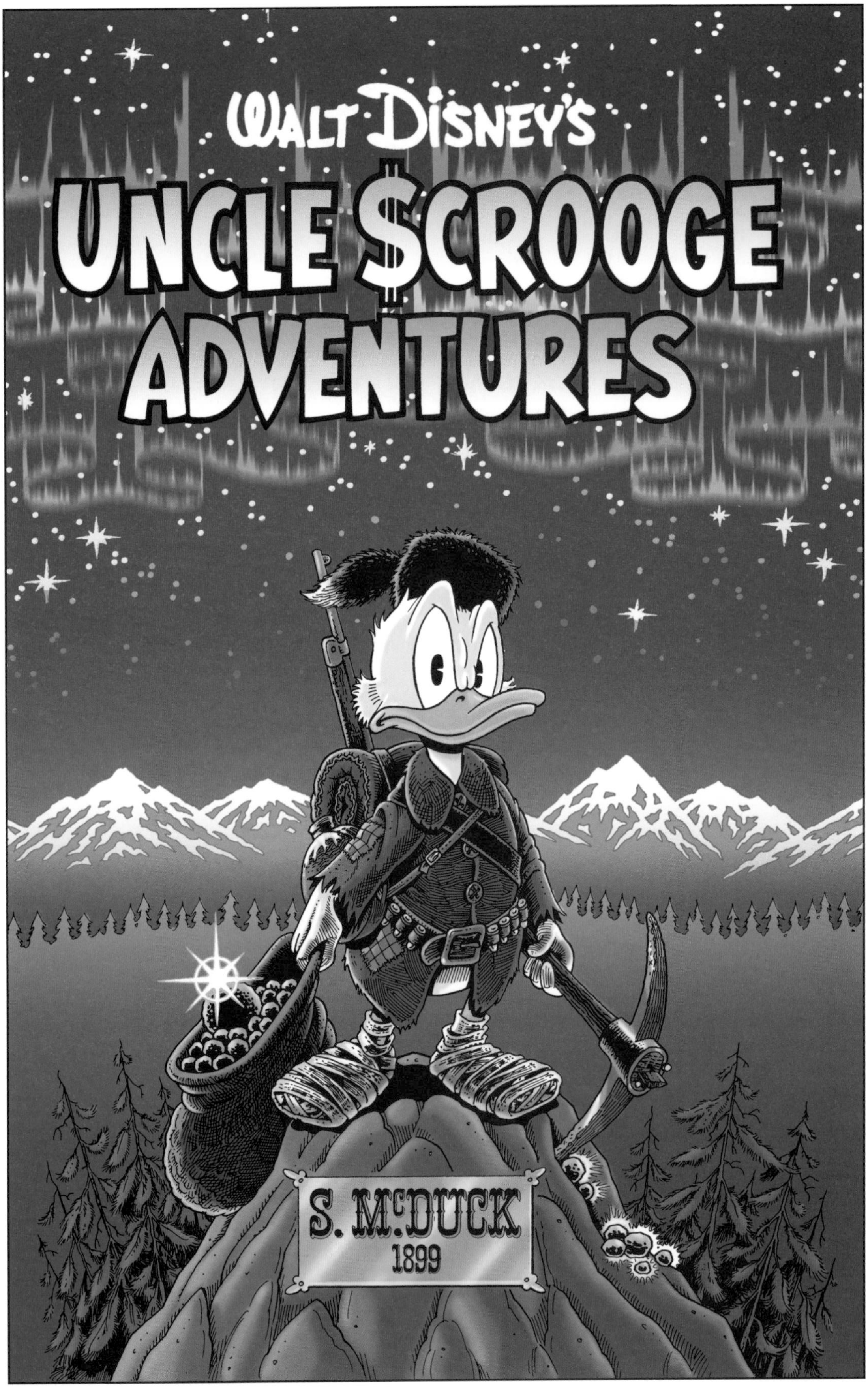
WALT DISNEY'S
UNCLE $CROOGE ADVENTURES
S. McDUCK
1899

LAST SLED TO DAWSON
Uncle Scrooge Adventures 5, June 1988; new color by Kneon Transitt

"SUDDENLY GLITTERING GOLDIE WAS THERE — IN A LONG DIVE FOR THE NUGGET!"
WHAT A JEWEL!
DON'T BE SO DOGGONED GRABBY!
BARTENDER! I'M HAVING COFFEE WITH THIS FABULOUS MINER!

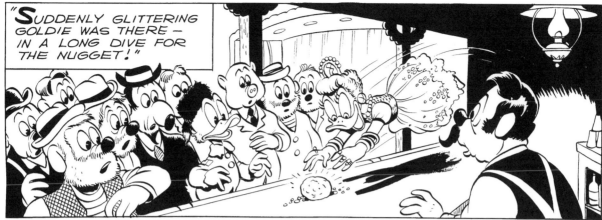

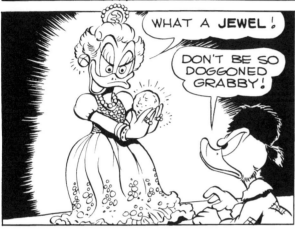

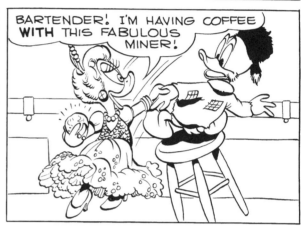

Above and overleaf: Excerpts from the flashback in "Back to the Klondike" (intended for *Four Color* 456). Goldie swindles Scrooge out of his Goose Egg Nugget—and Scrooge gets even with the entire Blackjack Ballroom. This long-lost sequence was first restored to Barks' story in 1978.

LAST SLED TO DAWSON *p. 121*

My first long adventure story ("The Son of the Sun") had been my favorite type of Barks plot: a quest for a historic treasure of antiquity. My second Scrooge adventure ("Cash Flow") had to involve the other type of Barks Scrooge plot, saving his Money Bin from a Beagle Boy attack. And when Gladstone said they were ready for my *third* big Scrooge adventure, I knew what it would be...

Of all the Barks Scrooge stories I grew up with, there was one that had the deepest effect on me of all... but not until nearly 25 years after it was first published. Barks' 1953 "Back to the Klondike" (*Four Color* 456) was a great story in itself, and it also gave us some clues to Scrooge's early life and *how* he became so wealthy. There was a reference to a long-ago dance hall girl, about whom Scrooge seemed to become mysteriously introspective for one mere panel—but nothing more was explained about that. We eventually meet an aged and haggard woman who is living destitute on Scrooge's old gold claim, and whom we discover was the dance hall girl he had known during the Gold Rush days. He finally allows her to find a gold cache he had left on his property; and in the story as I first read it, we assume he's doing this out of simple charity to the poor old woman.

Then in the early 1970s I got into contact with fellow comic book collectors and Barks fans. One thing the fans shared with each other were copies of a four-page Scrooge flashback sequence that had been cut—actually censored—out of "Back to the Klondike" in 1953. Discovering these four pages was a life-changing experience for me! For the first time I saw my favorite character in his youth, a truly bigger-than-life hero right out of American folklore; and I saw the young and beautiful version of his lost love, Glittering Goldie. Finding those pages was like discovering the lost original versions of Frank Capra's *Lost Horizon* or Orson Welles' *The Magnificent Ambersons*, or finding the "Spider Pit" sequence from *King Kong*... but *better*! As much as I already loved Barks' Scrooge, this short sequence gave me an entirely new insight into him. This young Scrooge was a much richer character than I had dreamed, with a fiery lust for life right out of a Jack London novel or a John Ford western film. And *that* is what I wanted my next Scrooge adventure to explore. I also wanted to show my ideas of how different a personality a young and innocent Scrooge McDuck may have had, and how random events can change the course of a life (as had been proven to *me* by the wonderful serendipity of my own recent life!).

And I knew what my plot would involve—as I was basing my story on the events of those four long-lost pages, I would also borrow an incident from the favorite *non*-Barks Duck story of my youth: one called "The Secret of the Glacier." It appeared in 1957 in *Donald Duck* 51, and (as I would later learn as a collector) was written by Carl Fallberg and drawn by Tony Strobl and Steve Steere. That tale had a brief flashback to Scrooge losing a sled into a glacier crevasse during the Gold Rush, and retrieving it decades later when the section of the glacier moves far enough to finally "calve" into the ocean. Here was a flashback to Scrooge's Gold Rush days that I read fifteen years before I knew of Barks' previous censored flashback! I ignored the rest of the old Fallberg/Strobl story, but I never hid the fact that I "borrowed" a bit of the plot from it, no more than I would ever deny all the Barks bits I make use of—I'm proud to bring attention to the old masters' works!

"Dawson" was perhaps the first story where I gave readers a clue that my Duck adventures were happening not in the present, but in the mid-1950s; how else could Scrooge still be alive if he was a sourdough in 1898 or a cowboy in 1882, as Barks' stories stated? It's a better solution than something silly such as saying these are "immortal characters living in a fairy tale universe." That robs Barks' characters and plots of their dramatic and realistic qualities. If you look at the business ledgers in panel 3 of page 1, you'll see the year 1954, showing that this tale takes place one year after Barks' "Back to the Klondike." In fact, my original title for the story was "Back to the Klondike *Again*," to pay even more direct homage to Barks' original.

The final fact to tell you about this story is a dandy: I knew that this would be a story very close to my heart, and to my love of Barks' classics. So I contacted my friend Prof. Don Ault, who was one of the very first fans to discover that Carl Barks was the hitherto unidentified "good artist" of Donald Duck. Prof. Ault was a longtime friend of Carl's and had been given many wonderful bits of memorabilia by the Old Master, one of which was the drawing board that Barks would lay on top of his worktable to act as a movable work-surface. Most of Barks greatest stories were drawn on that one surface! I borrowed that very drawing board from Prof. Ault, laid it atop my own drawing table, and drew all of "Last Sled to Dawson" on top of this magic surface!!! What a thrill!!! Charles Foster Kane never felt so rich!!!

And a final question for the reader: what is written in that note in Goldie's box of chocolates?

INSANE DETAILS TO LOOK FOR: Scrooge mentions his Klondike Bank in Whitehorse, this fact gleaned from an old Barks story. He meets the grandson of Cornelius Coot—whom we all know that Barks says founded Duckburg—and buys the land there that he will later make his home base. (This is one scene I did not repeat in my later "Life and Times of Scrooge McDuck" series.) I use Barks' Soapy

"I DON'T KNOW WHAT GOLDIE PUT IN MY COFFEE!"
MORE COFFEE?
"BUT I AWOKE HOURS LATER IN A SNOWDRIFT SIX MILES FROM TOWN!"
MY POKE!... THE GOOSE EGG NUGGET — GONE! I'VE BEEN DRUGGED AND ROLLED!
NOBODY CAN TAKE GOLD FROM SCROOGE McDUCK! THERE'LL BE A HOT TIME IN THE OLD TOWN TONIGHT!

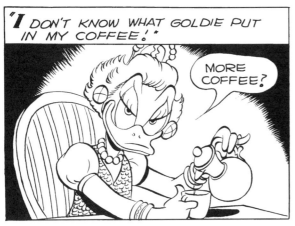

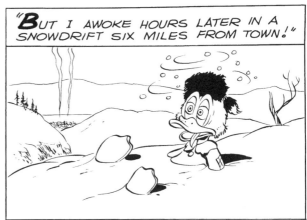

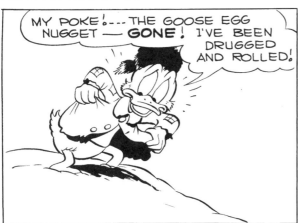

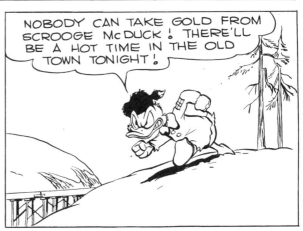

Slick (from "North of the Yukon," *Uncle Scrooge* 59) as the villain. Not only do I recreate Barks' version of Scrooge's cabin on White Agony Creek—but if you look in the panel where Scrooge is leaving his claim, you'll see the four rocks in a square on a hill, which is where Barks said that young Scrooge hid a fortune in gold in "Back to the Klondike."

In case a reader makes a closer comparison between "Last Sled to Dawson" and the later "Life of Scrooge" series, I should not try to hide the fact that when I wrote the Yukon chapter of that series, I apparently decided to change one geographical fact. In "Last Sled to Dawson," White Agony Creek and Scrooge's claim are apparently east of the Yukon River, in the normal goldfields of the 1898 Gold Rush. But in the eighth chapter of my "Life of Scrooge," I decided to place Scrooge's claim in a special place that only *he* was brave and smart enough to venture: *north* of the actual goldfields and on the *opposite* side of the Klondike River (see the maps in both stories). Everything would still work out okay if we say that in "Dawson," Soapy's riverboat is in the Klondike River rather than the Yukon River—but I'll bet the Klondike is not a large enough waterway for such a large craft!

"Last Sled to Dawson" contains other esoteric references done for movie fans like me. At the end of the story, when the characters are all offering opinions as to what Scrooge's sled means to him, movie buffs will notice a number of thematic similarities to *Citizen Kane*. Also, you'll note that there is a box of chocolates which are meant to represent the most important thing that Scrooge lost from his pre-tycoon days; that box, too, bears certain Kane-like significance. (If you are not a movie buff, you won't understand any of this. Too bad!)

D.U.C.K. SPOTTER'S GUIDE: This story was originally published out of production order—which means that unlike the few that preceded it in this book, it was done when I had not started hiding the dedication yet. You'll see it simply written on the paper held by the clerk in panel 2 of page 1.

COVERING IT: I based the general spirit of my first cover for "Dawson" (page 178) on a Barks oil painting titled "Always Another Rainbow," from which Gladstone's parent company, Another Rainbow, derived their name. But while Barks' prospector Scrooge looked as if he was wistfully considering the next rainbow's end, my Scrooge shows the toughness and determination that I loved in Barks' "Back to the Klondike."

ROCKET REVERIE *p. 149*
FISCAL FITNESS *p. 151*

Time for the last of the group of shorties that I did for Gladstone based on Gary Leach scripts. His "Rocket

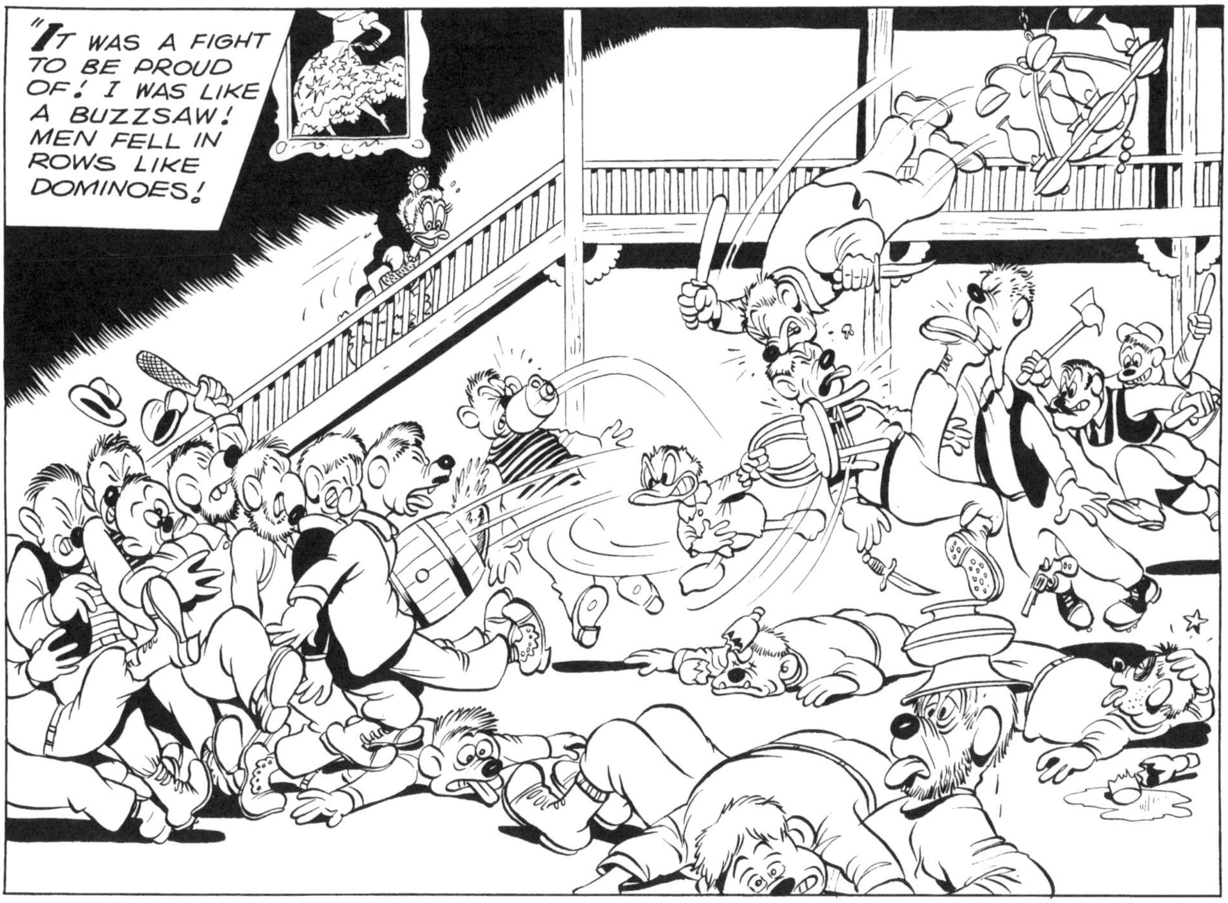
"IT WAS A FIGHT TO BE PROUD OF! I WAS LIKE A BUZZSAW! MEN FELL IN ROWS LIKE DOMINOES!

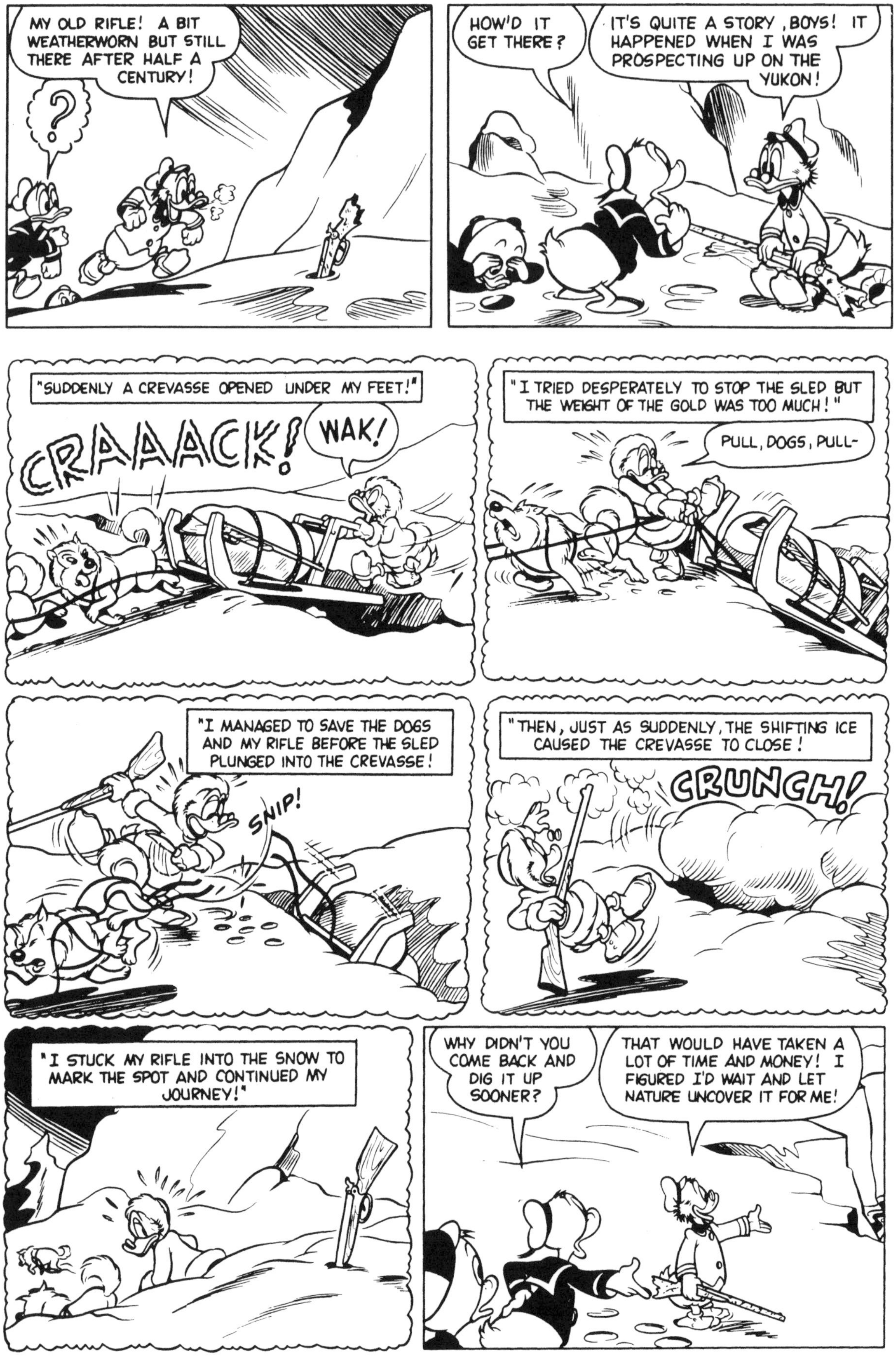
MY OLD RIFLE! A BIT WEATHERWORN BUT STILL THERE AFTER HALF A CENTURY!
?
HOW'D IT GET THERE?
IT'S QUITE A STORY, BOYS! IT HAPPENED WHEN I WAS PROSPECTING UP ON THE YUKON!
"SUDDENLY A CREVASSE OPENED UNDER MY FEET!"
CRAAACK!
WAK!
"I TRIED DESPERATELY TO STOP THE SLED BUT THE WEIGHT OF THE GOLD WAS TOO MUCH!"
PULL, DOGS, PULL-
"I MANAGED TO SAVE THE DOGS AND MY RIFLE BEFORE THE SLED PLUNGED INTO THE CREVASSE!
SNIP!
"THEN, JUST AS SUDDENLY, THE SHIFTING ICE CAUSED THE CREVASSE TO CLOSE!
CRUNCH!
"I STUCK MY RIFLE INTO THE SNOW TO MARK THE SPOT AND CONTINUED MY JOURNEY!"
WHY DIDN'T YOU COME BACK AND DIG IT UP SOONER?
THAT WOULD HAVE TAKEN A LOT OF TIME AND MONEY! I FIGURED I'D WAIT AND LET NATURE UNCOVER IT FOR ME!

Excerpts from the flashback in "The Secret of the Glacier" (*Donald Duck* 51), drawn by Tony Strobl.

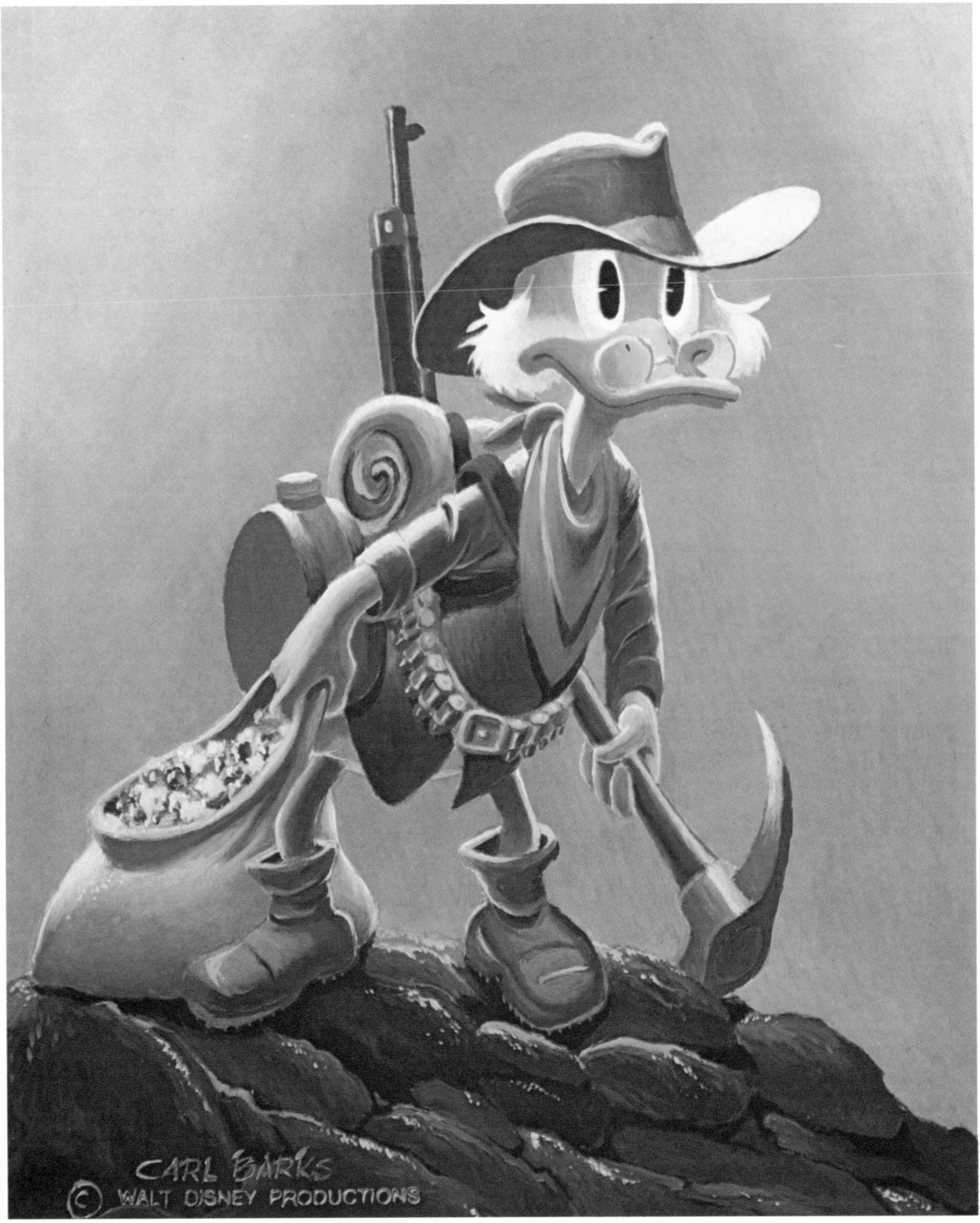
CARL BARKS
© WALT DISNEY PRODUCTIONS

"Always Another Ranbow" (1974), a Carl Barks painting that inspired Don Rosa's first comic book cover for "Last Sled to Dawson."

Reverie" posed a problem for me. It had Donald and the nephews apparently making a casual flight in a rocket ship. What? Characters in Duckburg don't hop in their rocket ships and go jetting off to Mars for the afternoon! And even though it's funny, what the Ducks do to a comet is too absurd to consider. I didn't know what I could do with this script—until I realized I could add one panel of my own showing that the entire bit is only a nutty dream that Donald is having when he falls asleep reading an E.C.-style science fiction comic after eating pickle-flavor ice cream.

And after deciding the whole thing was a dream, I went on to add all sorts of zany details in the background;

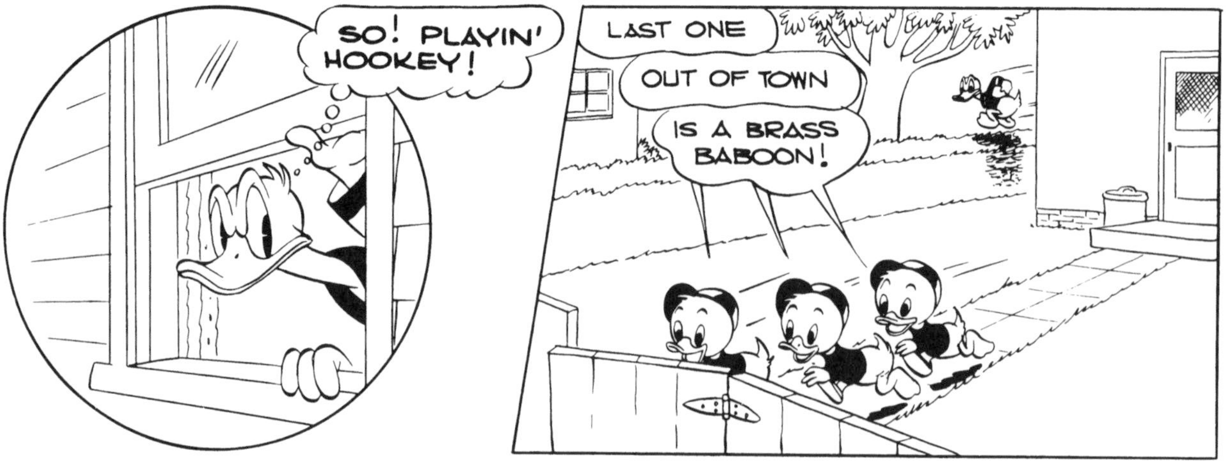
SO! PLAYIN' HOOKEY!
LAST ONE
OUT OF TOWN
IS A BRASS BABOON!

Before Rosa was reading: earlier, brattier versions of Huey, Dewey and Louie skip school in a vintage Barks ten-pager (*Walt Disney's Comics and Stories* 72).

like signs on condemned planets, a compass on a spaceship dashboard, a doorknob on the rocket hatchway, Donald losing his hat *through* his helmet... lotsa other silly stuff, even a group of planets that seem to resemble a certain Mouse.

"Fiscal Fitness": wow, what a difference in art detail between these sparse panels and those in "Rocket Reverie"! Maybe I was pooped after all that outer space zaniness? This might have been a one-page joke that they needed me to expand to two pages to fill out some space—notice how little is happening on the second page and how it's padded with a half-page panel (a half-page panel in a two-page gag?). I recall adding some extra visual jokes to this one to fill the space, such as the millionaires replacing a "pole vault" with a "vault vault."

D.U.C.K. SPOTTER'S GUIDE: None here (see my explanation at "The Paper Chase" for why).

METAPHORICALLY SPANKING *p. 153*

There's not a great deal of background to discuss regarding this story. It was simply intended to be a standard ten-page gag strip. I am most often unsatisfied with my own work, but I actually thought this short story had a few pretty good laughs. It's also the only Duck story I ever wrote where Huey, Dewey and Louie are somewhat less than perfect examples of kidhood. The stories I grew up with were from the mid-years of Barks' work; where Donald's nephews were depicted as Junior Woodchucks of the noblest ilk, and where they usually acted more adult and more responsible than either Donald or Scrooge. So I don't see them as the mischievous rascals of Barks' earlier stories. But, at least for this one tale, I thought I had a pretty good plot that could have the nephews taking a rare endeavor into the realm of hooky-playing.

Um... about the only additional thing I can think of to say about this tale is that you should take a look at the riot scene in the top panel of the last page. If you look closely, you'll see a certain Mouse in the running crowd.

INSANE DETAILS TO LOOK FOR: Donald calls the weather "soft as a maiden's cheek," which is also what he called it in a 1947 story with the nephews as truants (*Walt Disney's Comics and Stories* 79).

D.U.C.K. SPOTTER'S GUIDE: The dedication is written in a list of English words in a nephew's textbook in the third panel of page one.

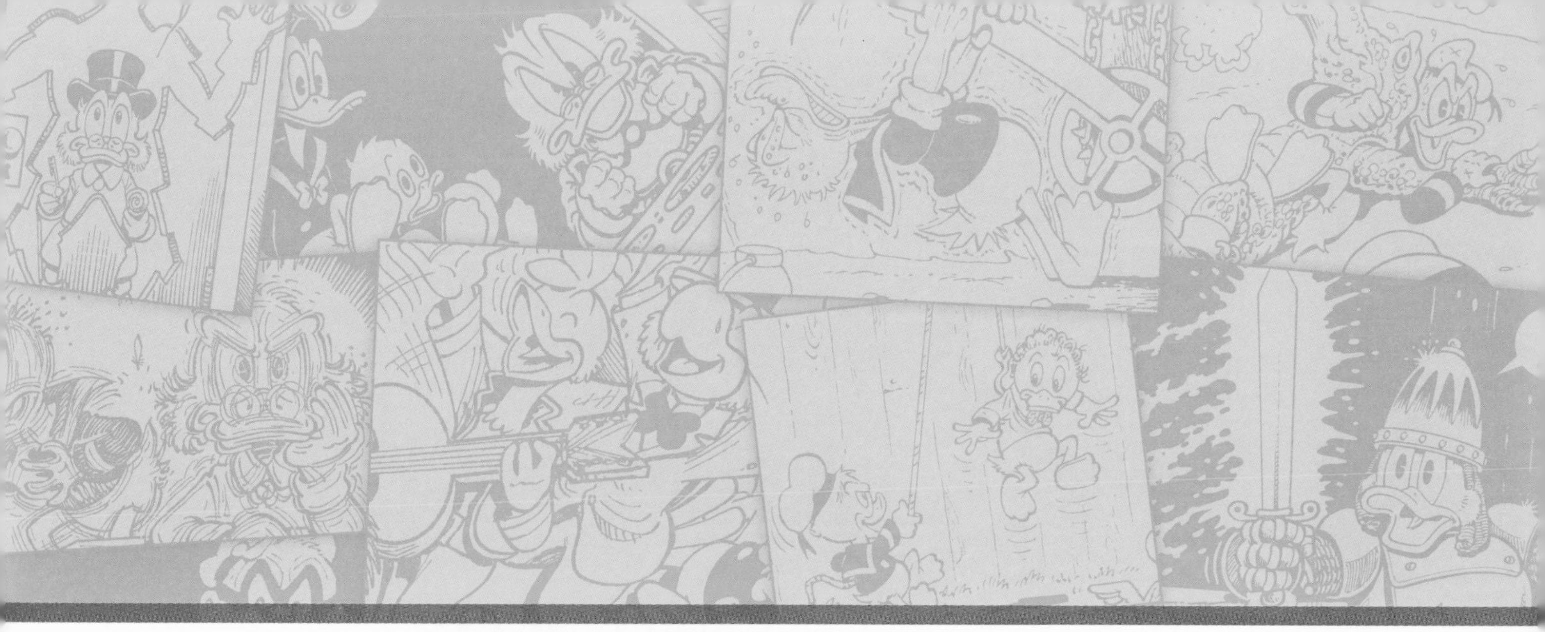

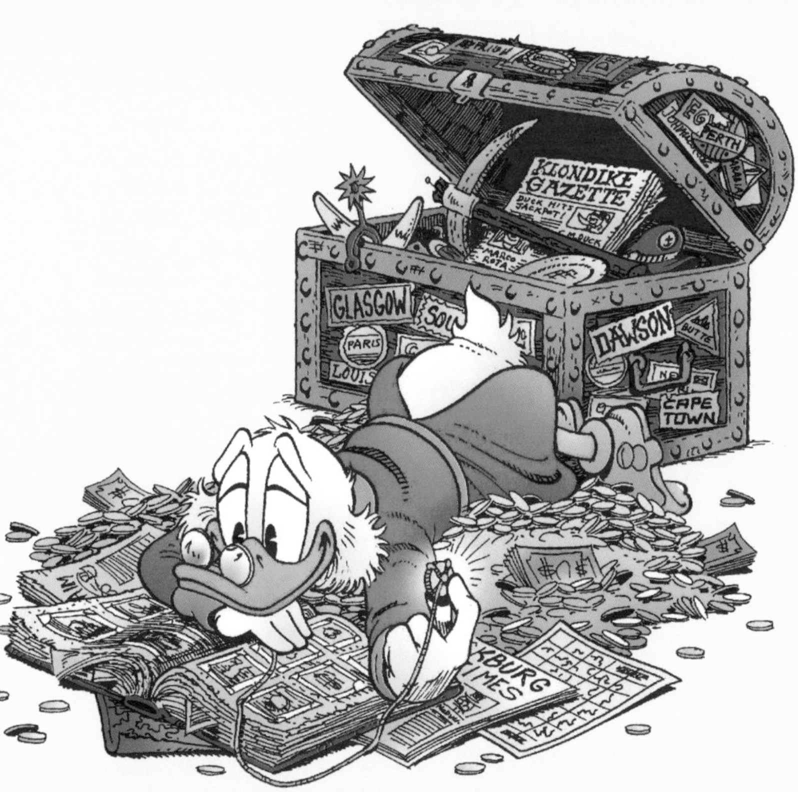
KLONDIKE GAZETTE
GLASGOW
PARIS
DAWSON
CAPE TOWN

The Rosa Archives

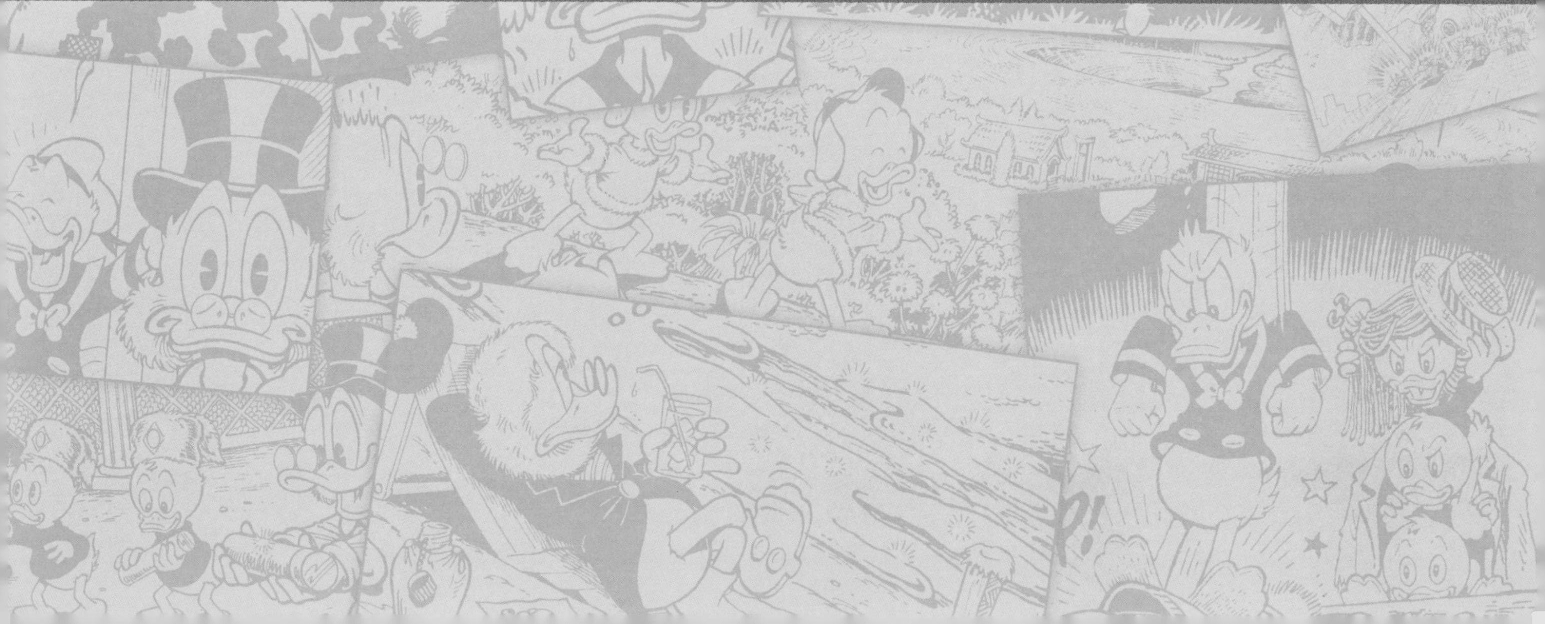

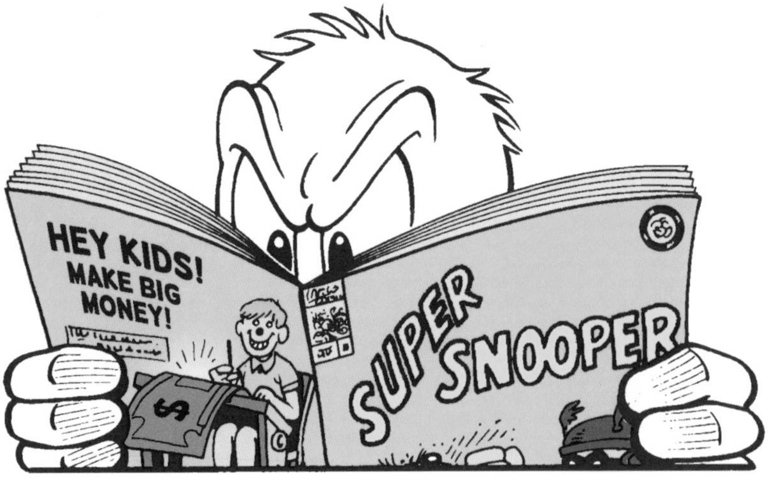
HEY KIDS!
MAKE BIG
MONEY!
SUPER
SNOOPER

This Should Cover It All!

(Additional Covers, 1987-1989)

By Don Rosa

Earlier on in this volume you've seen the "Don-Rosa-story-specific" covers that I did in my first years of doing comics. To be precise: if I did a cover for one of my Duck stories near the time of its first printing, then Fantagraphics has run that cover either alongside the story itself, or alongside my "Behind the Scenes" annotative text.

But what about all the covers done not for my *own* stories, but for Barks classics and other projects? That's what *this* gallery is for. And just so our Fantagraphics books balance out neatly, the covers in this volume will extend a bit further than the stories, giving us a preview of 1989.

Turn the next few pages for a spin through these "non-Don-Rosa-story-specific" covers. Or look below for my comments on many of them:

LAND BENEATH THE GROUND *p. 187* • This was the *first* time I did a cover based on an old Barks story that I grew up with. Barks seldom did covers illustrating his stories in the '50s. Such a coverless story was his 1956 classic "Land Beneath the Ground"... so Gladstone called on me to supply a cover for their reprint. I can imagine what a thrill drawing this scene might have been for me in 1988!

MOLTEN/SOFT/COLD GOLD *p. 188* • This was the *only* cover I ever did for a comic book that did not depict a scene from a specific story in the issue. This is just a *gag* cover. I didn't like doing these, since my overly-complex art is far better suited to scenes of full-speed action and adventure.

HAWAIIAN HIDEAWAY *p. 189* • Even after 26 years this is still one of my favorites of my own covers. I like the animated depiction of Scrooge dangling from the Beagle Boy's grasp, the erupting volcano, the worried Ducks, and the other gloating Beagle Boys. And tropical scenes are always my favorites. The only bad spot in this job is Donald's lower jaw, which looks too small.

THE MOUNTLESS MOUNTIE *p. 191* • This is one of very few covers I ever did for a story by someone other than Barks or myself. I wanted to do a pose of Donald having *just* changed into his Mountie uniform so that I could show his usual clothes hanging on a nearby coatrack.

THE MAGIC HOURGLASS *p. 192* • This Barks story was later problematic to me since it contains a fact about Scrooge that I had to *ignore* in my "Life and Times of Scrooge McDuck" series. In this early story about Scrooge (before Barks had finalized his new character) we are told that Scrooge's entire fortune is due to a *magic hourglass* bought in Morocco when he was a cabin boy on a cattle boat. I could *never* attribute Scrooge's fortune to magic, so I had to ignore Barks' magic hourglass. (But I still had Scrooge sail to America as cabin boy on a cattle boat.)

THE GOLDEN FLEECING *p. 193* • Years after creating this cover I was asked to do a sequel to this Barks story, but I couldn't get into the proper spirit. I love Barks' stories with critters like these "Larkies" (Harpies) or his Terries and Fermies... but I couldn't bring myself to tell stories with such absurd beings. On the other hand, I *did* do stories involving ghosts or the supernatural, which Barks never would do. Every storyteller is different, I guess.

LOST BENEATH THE SEA *pp. 194-195* • Dell and Gold Key didn't always have Barks draw the cover ideas he suggested to them. One unused sketch was for a cover to this 1963 story. The Gladstone editors obtained the sketch from Barks' personal files, and sent me a copy that I traced and inked for the reprint issue.

THAT'S NO FABLE *p. 196* • This cover illustrates the fact that it's very difficult to draw a cover *or* comic story panel with both Ducks *and* a normal sized *human* character. If I draw the entire human figure, the Ducks would be too small in the scene. So even though I tried to have this armored man rising from behind the mound, his legs are still too stubby!

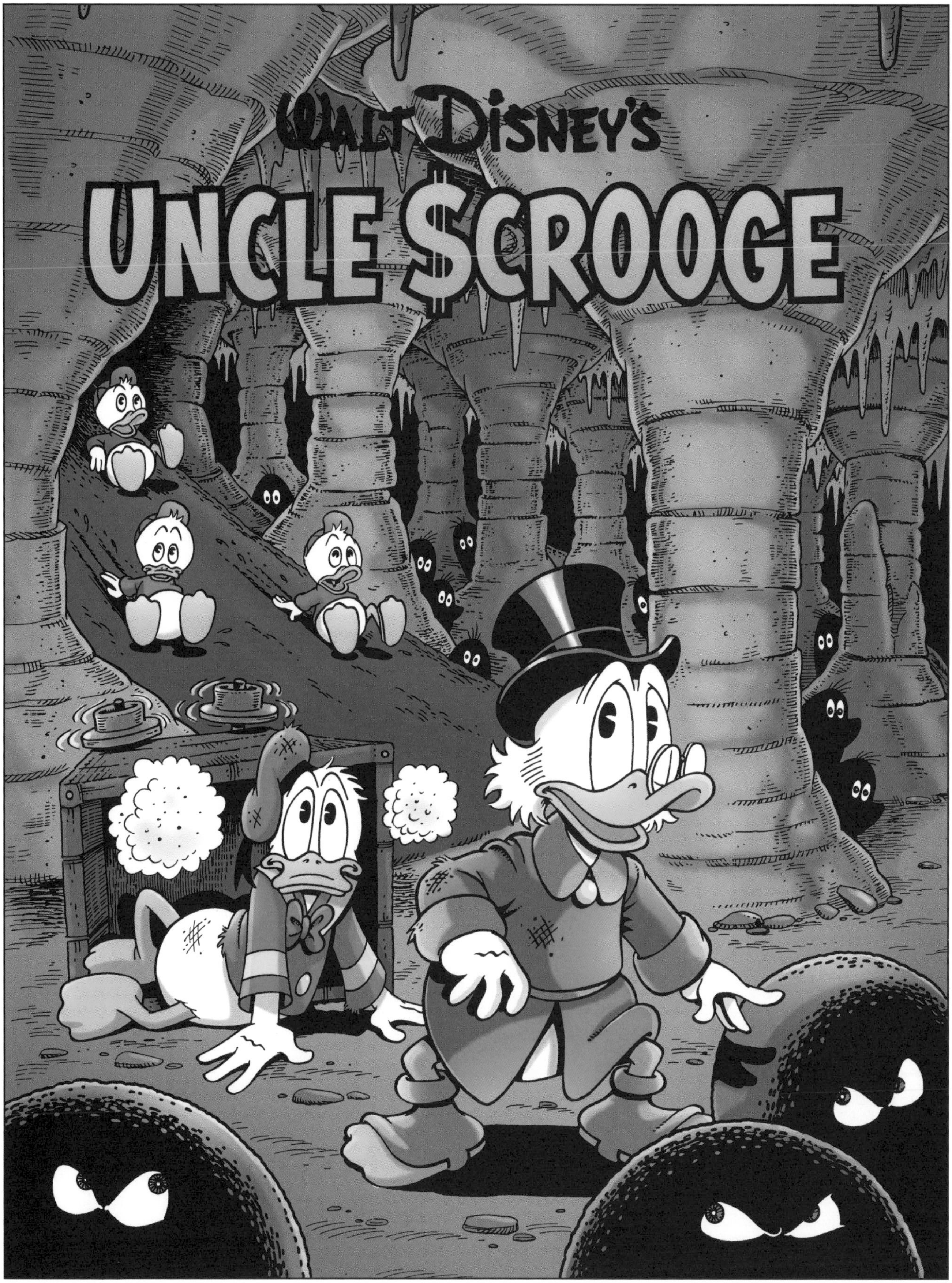
WALT DISNEY'S
UNCLE $CROOGE

LAND BENEATH THE GROUND • *Gladstone Comic Album* 6, June 1988; new color by Kneon Transitt. Illustrating a story written and drawn by Carl Barks (*Uncle Scrooge* 13, March 1956)

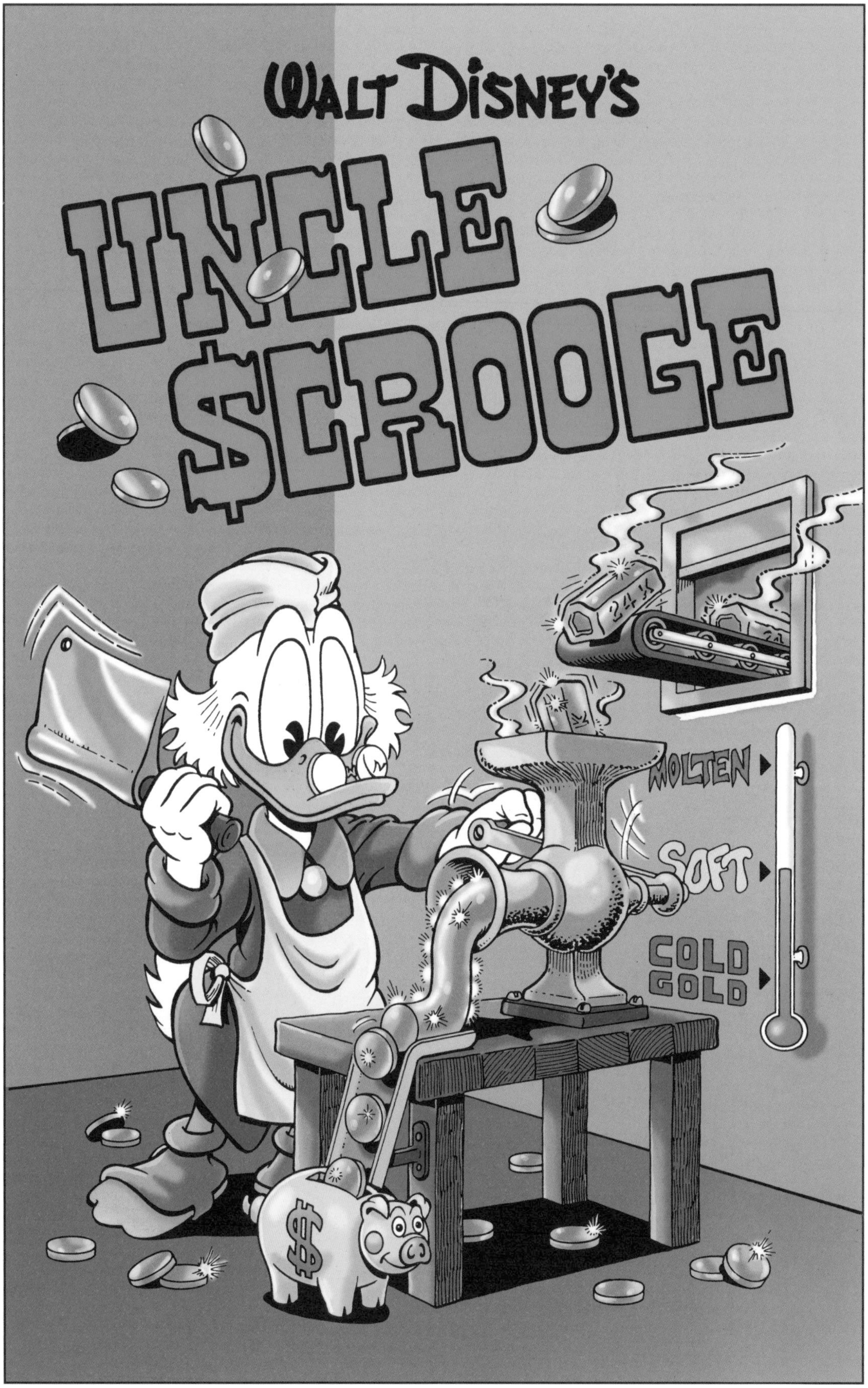
WALT DISNEY'S
UNCLE $CROOGE
24 K
MOLTEN
SOFT
COLD GOLD

MOLTEN/SOFT/COLD GOLD • *Uncle Scrooge* 231, November 1988; new color by Kneon Transitt

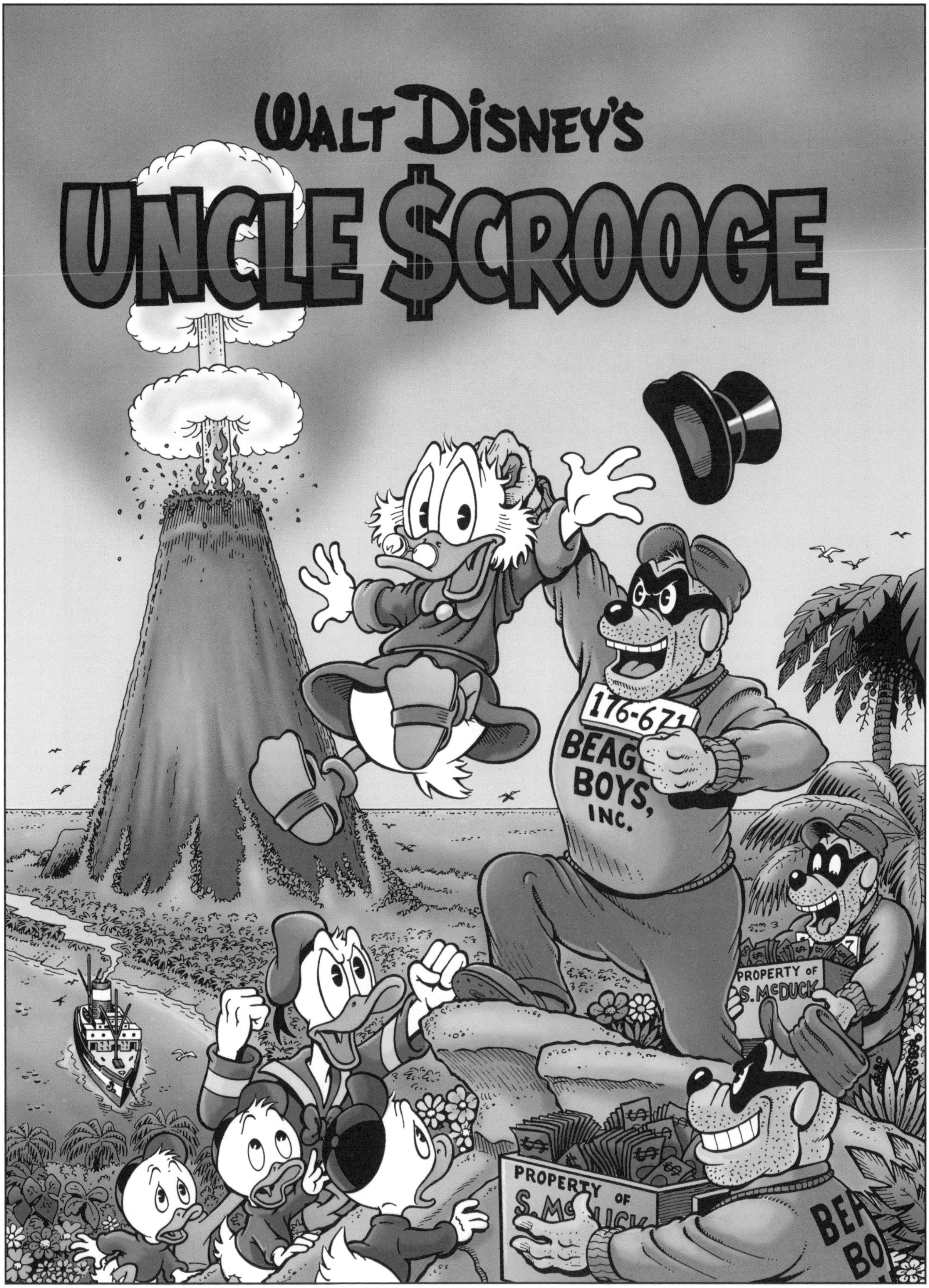
WALT DISNEY'S
UNCLE $CROOGE
176-671
BEAGLE BOYS, INC.
PROPERTY OF S. McDUCK
PROPERTY OF S. McDUCK

HAWAIIAN HIDEAWAY • *Gladstone Comic Album* 11, December 1988; new color by Kneon Transitt. Illustrating a story written and drawn by Carl Barks (*Uncle Scrooge* 4, December 1953)

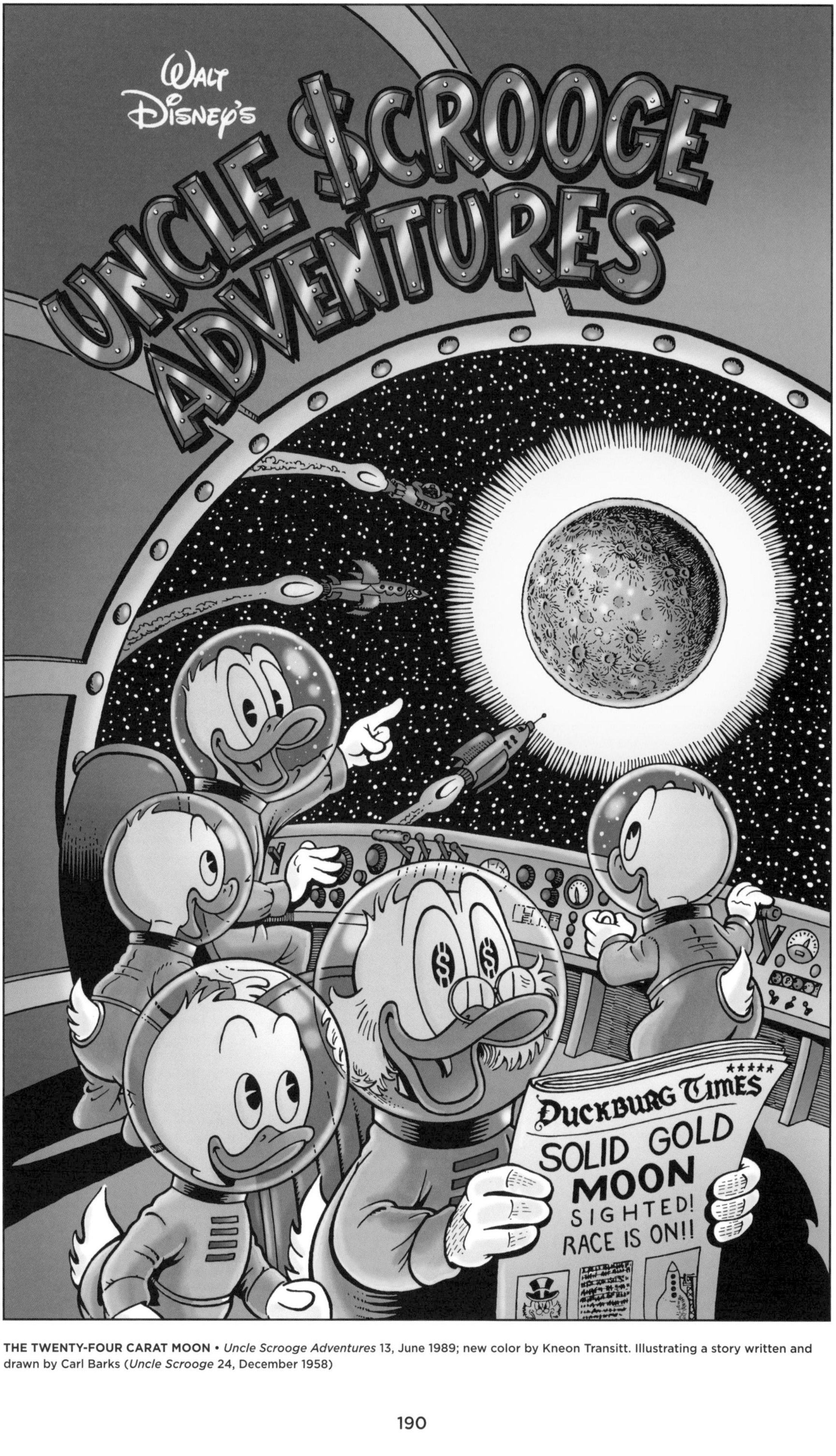
Walt Disney's
Uncle $crooge Adventures
Duckburg Times
SOLID GOLD
MOON
SIGHTED!
RACE IS ON!!

THE TWENTY-FOUR CARAT MOON • *Uncle Scrooge Adventures* 13, June 1989; new color by Kneon Transitt. Illustrating a story written and drawn by Carl Barks (*Uncle Scrooge* 24, December 1958)

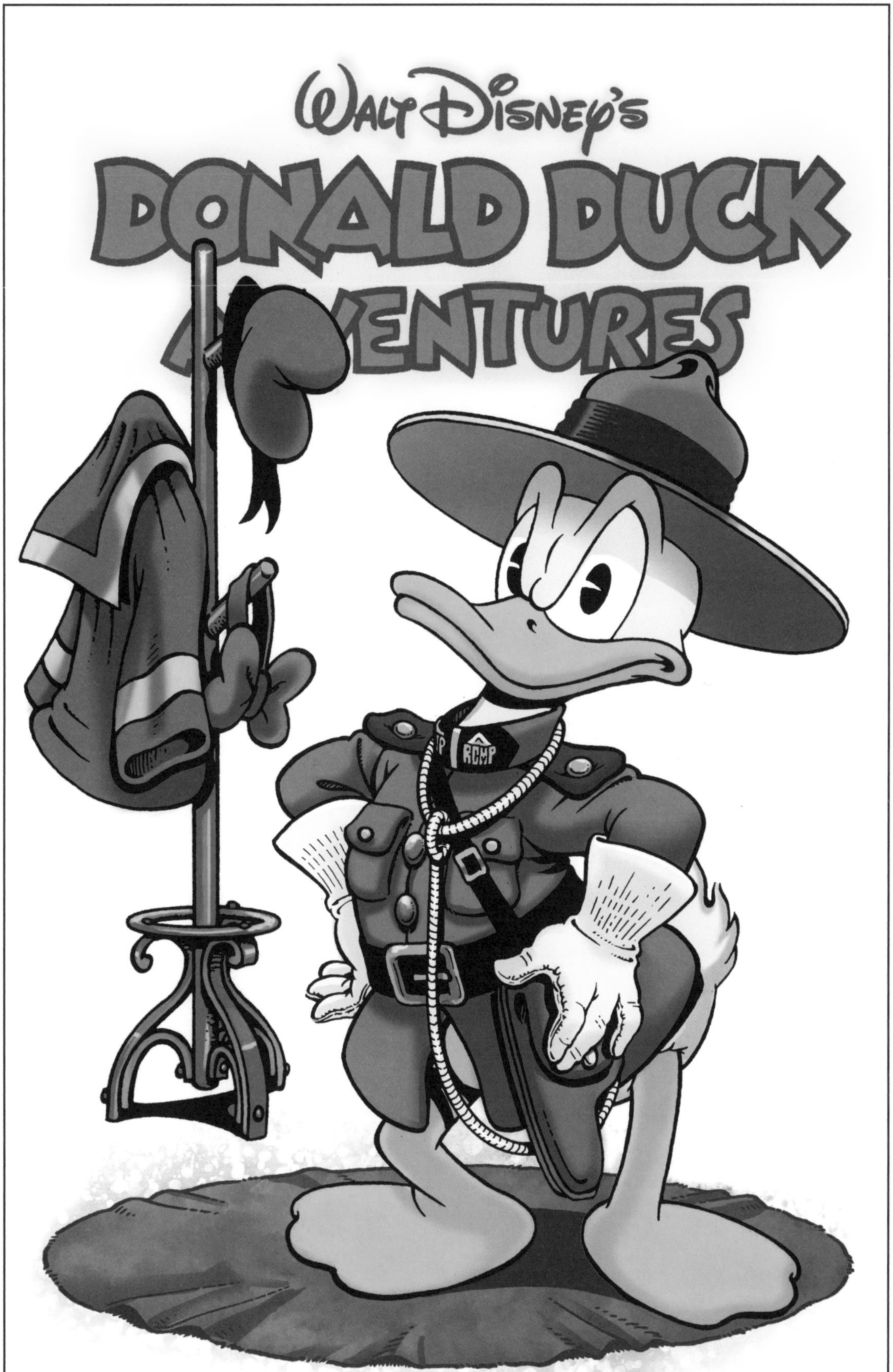
WALT DISNEY'S
DONALD DUCK
ADVENTURES
RCMP

THE MOUNTLESS MOUNTIE • *Donald Duck Adventures* [series I] 13, July 1989; new color by Jake Myler. Illustrating a new story drawn by Daniel Branca. Donald's coatrack, seen here as Rosa first drew it, was reduced in size in all previous printings to make way for cover text.

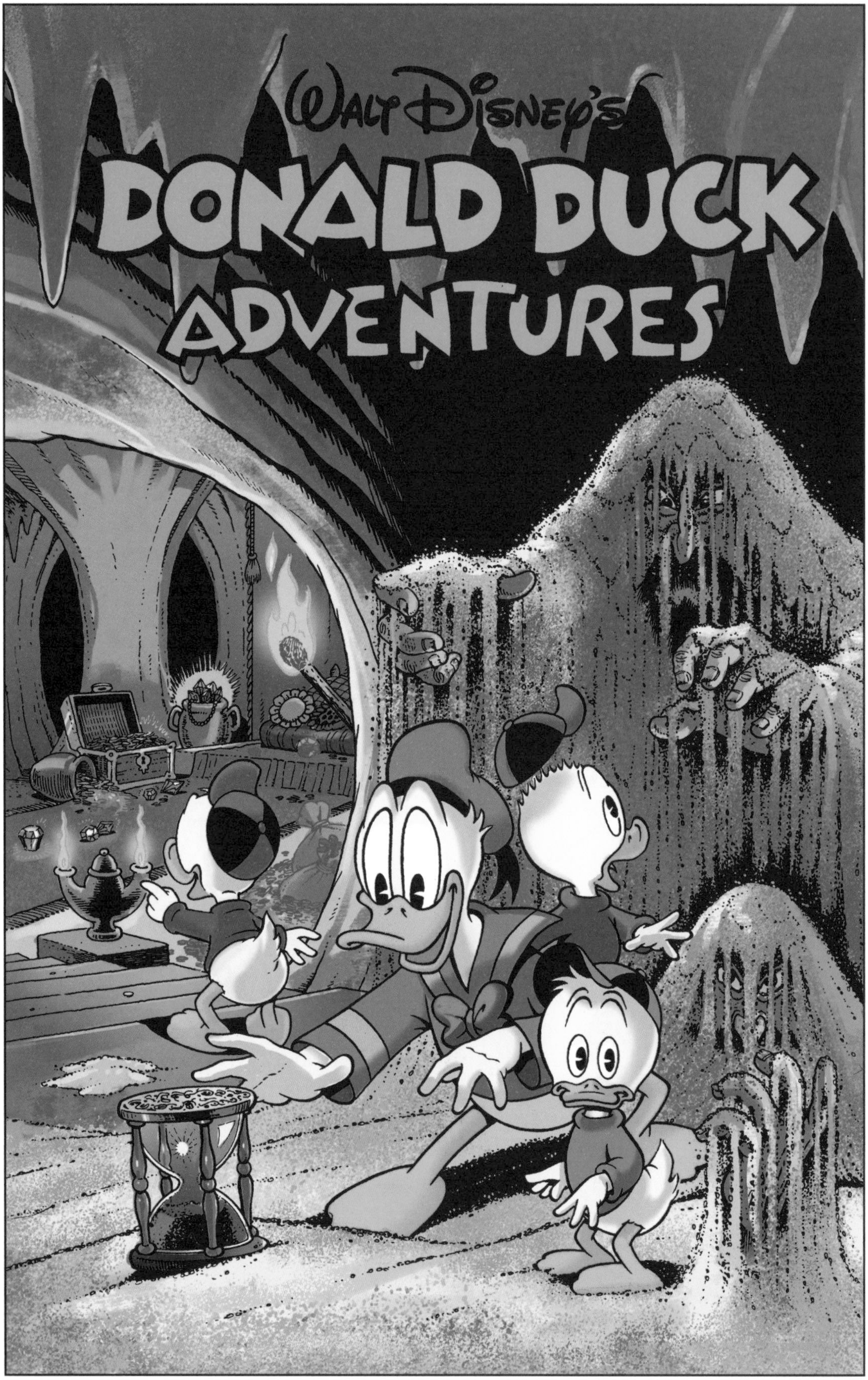
WALT DISNEY'S
DONALD DUCK
ADVENTURES

THE MAGIC HOURGLASS • *Donald Duck Adventures* [series I] 16, October 1989; new color by Jake Myler. Illustrating a story written and drawn by Carl Barks (*Four Color* 291, September 1950)

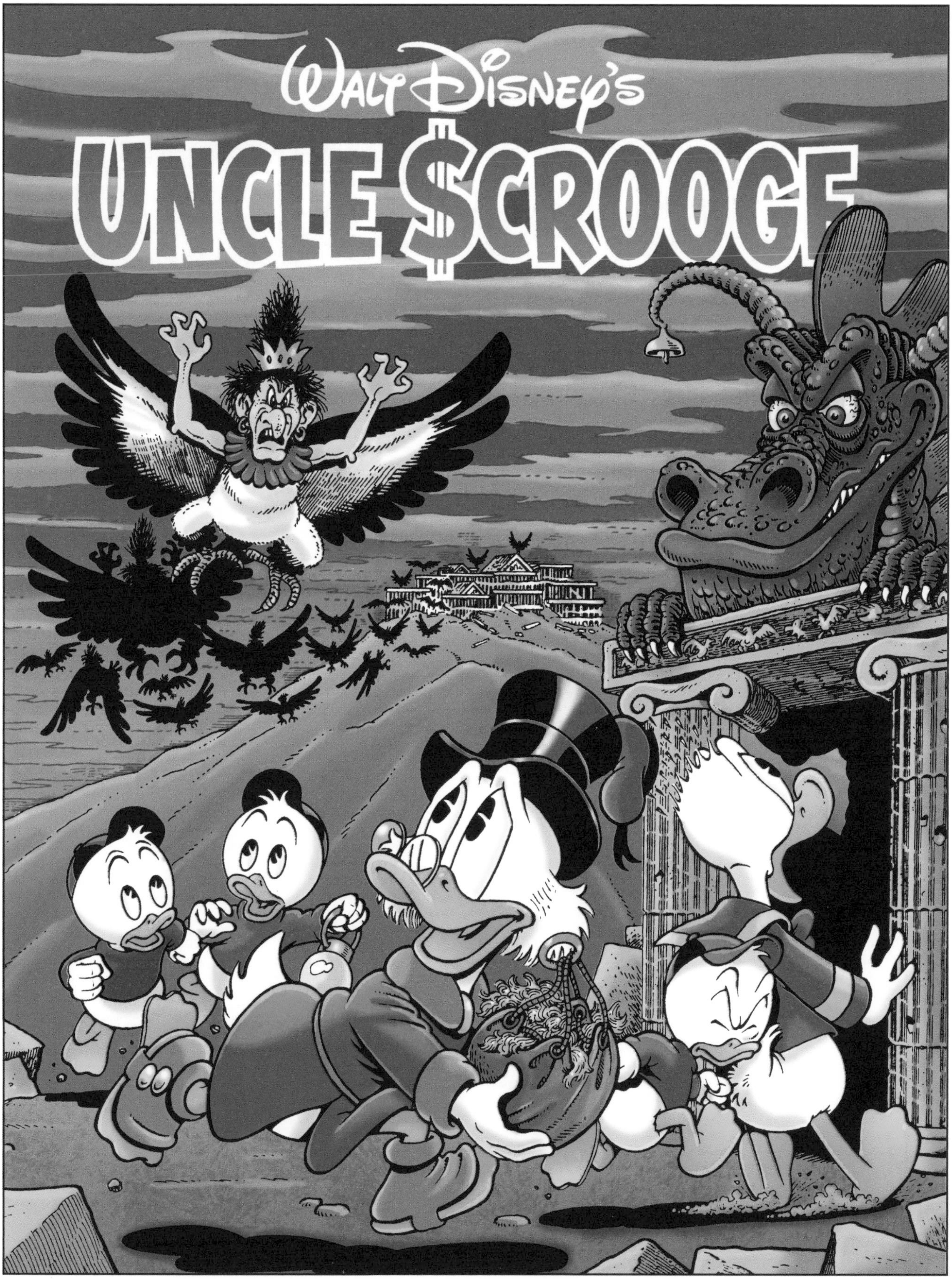
WALT DISNEY'S
UNCLE $CROOGE

THE GOLDEN FLEECING • *Gladstone Comic Album* 19, October 1989; new color by Kneon Transitt. Illustrating a story written and drawn by Carl Barks (*Uncle Scrooge* 12, December 1955). The dragon's silhouetted body, seen here as Rosa first drew it, was replaced in all previous printings with an expanse of solid black.

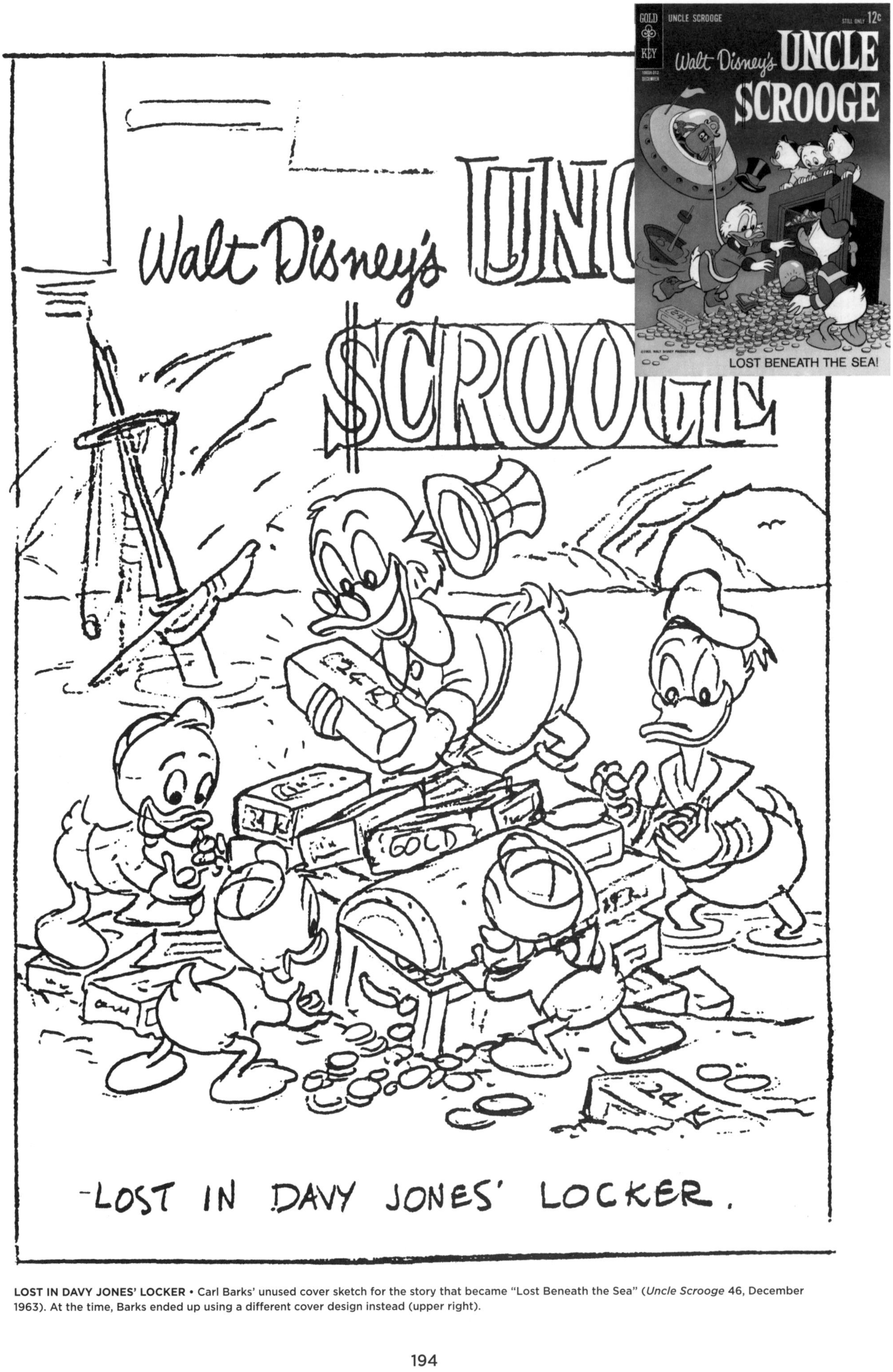
Walt Disney's
24 K
GOLD
-LOST IN DAVY JONES' LOCKER.
GOLD KEY
UNCLE SCROOGE
STILL ONLY 12¢
Walt Disney's UNCLE SCROOGE
LOST BENEATH THE SEA!

LOST IN DAVY JONES' LOCKER • Carl Barks' unused cover sketch for the story that became "Lost Beneath the Sea" (*Uncle Scrooge* 46, December 1963). At the time, Barks ended up using a different cover design instead (upper right).

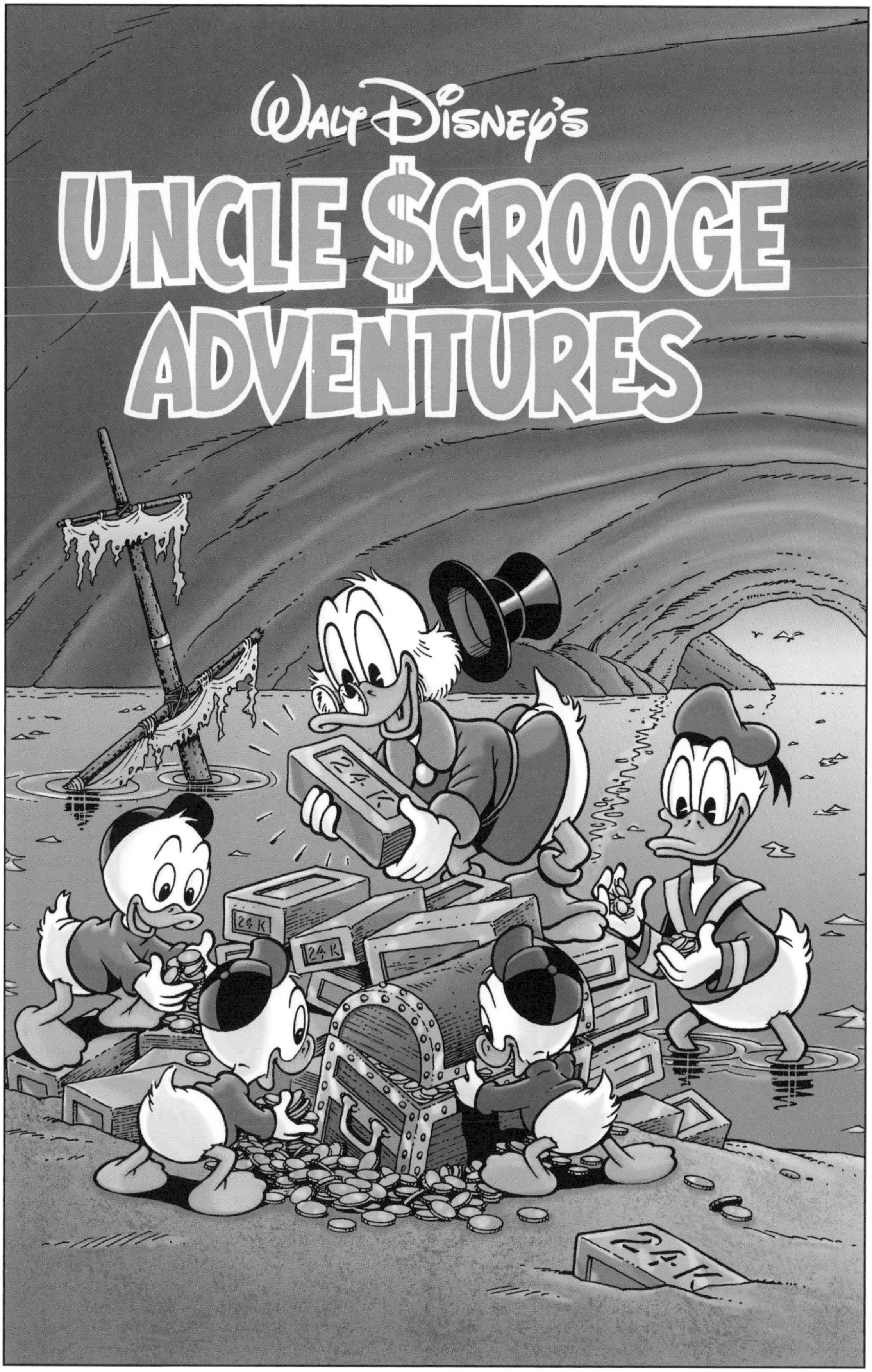
WALT DISNEY'S
UNCLE $CROOGE
ADVENTURES
24 K
24 K
24 K
24 K

LOST BENEATH THE SEA • *Uncle Scrooge Adventures* 17, November 1989; color by Kneon Transitt. Barks supplied his unused sketch so that Rosa could complete it; one of the only Barks/Rosa art collaborations ever done.

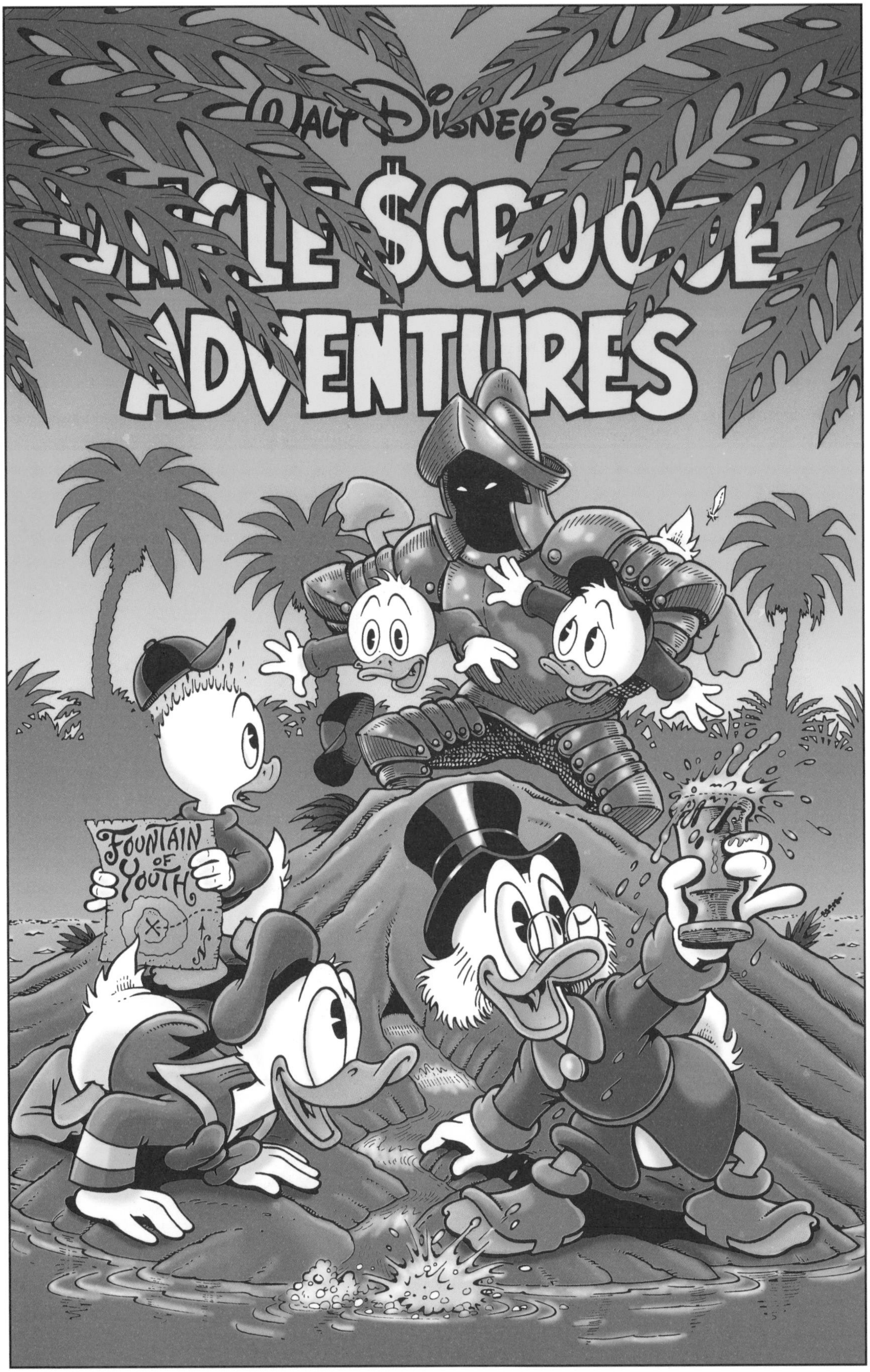
WALT DISNEY'S
UNCLE $CROOGE
ADVENTURES
FOUNTAIN OF YOUTH

THAT'S NO FABLE! • *Uncle Scrooge Adventures* 18, December 1989; color by Kneon Transitt. Illustrating a story written and drawn by Carl Barks (*Uncle Scrooge* 32, December 1960). The palm fronds at the top of the image, seen here as Rosa first drew them, were omitted from all previous printings.

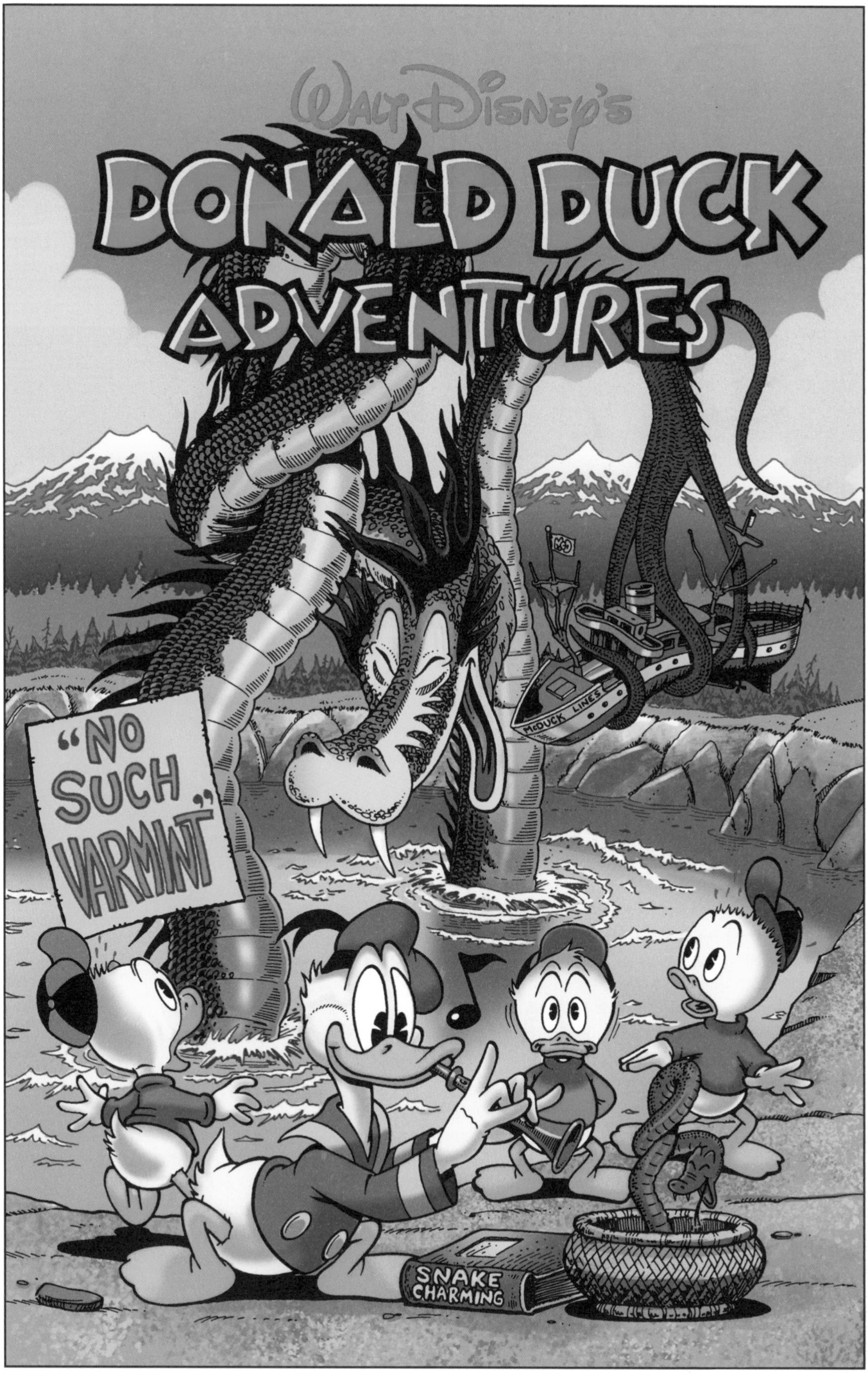
WALT DISNEY'S
DONALD DUCK
ADVENTURES
"NO SUCH VARMINT"
McDUCK LINES
SNAKE CHARMING

THE MAGIC HOURGLASS • *Donald Duck Adventures* [series I] 18, December 1989; new color by Jake Myler. Illustrating a story written and drawn by Carl Barks (*Four Color* 318, March 1951)

The Life and Times of DON ROSA

PART 1: "The Last of the Clan Rosa"

Everything seemed to be going along just fine, when suddenly, without any sort of polite warning, I was born. June 29, 1951. St. Joseph's Infirmary Hospital in Louisville, Kentucky.

Undoubtedly, as I lay in my bassinet, I heard the vocal displays of another fellow—a future TV announcer—who was born in the same maternity ward on the same day. Had he known how to speak, he would have told me his name was Ray Foushee. Speak yet or not, I couldn't tell him *my* new name, because that was still the subject of a family controversy.

The problem was that I was the first male Rosa born in America. My grandfather, Gioachino Gostaldo Rosa, had left his home in Maniago, Italy, as a teenager in 1896 to seek his fortune. Although poor and uneducated, he somehow managed to reach America early in the year 1900, when he was only twenty-two years old. The only thing I know for certain is that he arrived with all his worldly possessions in a large trunk, which I still have on display in my home. From Ellis Island he then travelled here to Louisville, Kentucky, for unknown reasons—it was said that he saw a pretty girl at the Louisville station and got off the train without his ticket. But Louisville seemed to be good to him—he worked hard and in 1905 established the Keno Rosa Tile & Terrazzo Co., using his new nickname "Keno," which he'd decided was easier for Americans to pronounce than was Gioachino. Then, in 1908, leaving his company in the care of his brother who had also moved to America, Keno returned to Italy to find a proper Italian bride. The illiterate country boy had made it big in the Land of Opportunity, and he could have any girl he chose as his wife! In Venice (near to his hometown of Maniago) he chose beauty, brains, talent and prestige by marrying the daughter of a school principal who could trace direct lineage back to Venice's most famous son, Titian! They soon had four children (including my father Ugo) and moved back to America in 1914 to escape World War I.

Anyway, as I was the first American-born Rosa boy, the patriarch of the Rosa family fully expected me to be named Keno, after him. But my father named me after himself, Dante Ugo (which he thankfully Americanized to Don Hugo). This so outraged my grandfather that he disowned

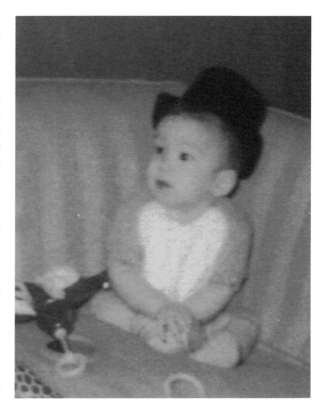

Don Rosa as photographed by his father at less than one year of age—already wearing a top hat in the style of his future hero. All photos with this article © and courtesy Don Rosa.

my father and would not allow him into the family construction company. This may have been the beginning of my dysfunctional family life. And it was all my fault!

There was one other American Rosa when I was born, my sister Deanna. She outranked me by a full 11 years, and what little money there was to be spent on us two kids, it seemed to all go to buy her comic books. She loved comic books! She hoarded comic books! She'd saved every comic she ever had—they filled a closet! The house was already filled with my sister's old comics when they brought me home from St. Joseph's Infirmary, so those were what I was allowed to use for toys. I was looking at comic books long before I could read. Like every other American kid (and still most kids around the world), my very favorites were

The family of Gioachino Rosa (Americanized name "Keno" Rosa, Don's grandfather) ca. 1925. From left to right: Lena, Leonardo, Keno's wife Celestine Tizian, America, Keno, and Ugo (Don Rosa's father).

the Duck stories by that one "good artist", whoever he was. Oh... and another favorite were the *Mad* comics and magazines she bought later as a teenager.

If I wasn't reading comic books, I was watching TV. In the mid-1950s there weren't many animated cartoon shows on TV, but there were lots of old movies. So, ever since my very earliest memories, I loved comics and old movies. But if there wasn't a movie on either of the two (two!) TV stations, and if my sister had not let me get a fresh stack of her comic books, the only other way I had to entertain myself was to create my own comic stories.

I would make comic books on loose sheets of paper. Or out of folded sheets of paper sewn together with yarn. But mainly in blank business ledgers that my father would bring me home from the Keno Rosa Co.

Hm? Oh, yes... by the late 1950s, my father had been *un*-disowned and was now my uncle's partner in the family company. One year before he died, my grandfather had paid my father one thousand dollars to change my name to Keno Don Hugo Rosa. I never saw a share of that money made off my name, but thank gosh my first name was changed to Keno and later made my famous "D.U.C.K." dedication possible (explained earlier in this volume on page 10).

Well, life had changed for the Rosa family after that! I was enrolled in a small private school, the St. Thomas Aquinas Preparatory Academy, where it was intended I would hobnob with the sons of the local construction company executives, car dealership owners and bankers. And my father bought some land in the woodland hills outside of town and built a huge home

which was a showplace for the work of the Keno Rosa Co. artisans. From the age of eight I grew up in this magnificent home that was featured in newspapers' Sunday magazine sections—all the floors were of solid terrazzo or ceramic tile, with a three-story ceramic mosaic of a Chinese Ming tree on the wall of the main staircase. I had my own private bathroom with mosaic designs around the sunken tub, two sinks in a vanity of Italian marble, and a separate room for the commode. I also had a five-acre back yard to play in and a twelve-acre private woodland beyond that to explore. If the folks back in Maniago could see the Rosas now!

However, this new home was another key ingredient in shaping my personality. I was more isolated than before from having any playmates or nearby sources of entertainment. From that point on, I spent even more of my time reading comics, watching TV and creating my own comic stories. And, to give a complete idea of my environment, it must also be mentioned that my family life was never very happy. My parents did not get along with each other, and partly due to their somewhat advanced age and partly due to that dysfunctional family life, they generally ignored me, leaving me more or less to grow up on my own. My older sister had married as soon as she could in order to move away from home, but I was stuck there. My comics and my TV were my whole life. But I can't say that I felt miserable—thankfully, I didn't know what a "happy childhood" was like, so I didn't miss it. I was comfortable in that big house out in the

The Keno Rosa Co.: office of the family construction company, ca. 1927. Keno Rosa (Don Rosa's grandfather) is seated at left.

Portraits of the artist as a young man. From left to right: ca. 1955; ca. 1957; ca. 1969; and 1970, moments after buying five thousand old comics for two cents apiece!

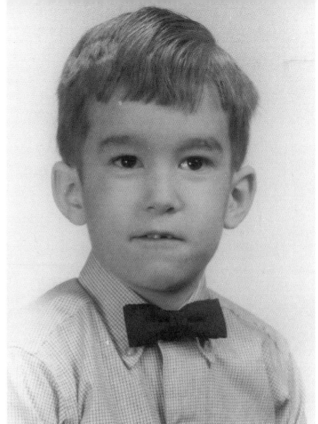

country, and I knew my future as the owner of the highly successful Keno Rosa Co. was in the bag; I was the last of the clan Rosa.

As I grew up in this lonely solitude, my interests expanded (as they still do to this day). In 1962 I began collecting magazines about monster, science-fiction and adventure movies. I also became an inveterate builder of plastic model kits that pertained to movies or TV or comic book heroes—I guess those were the forerunners of the much smaller modern "action figures." But kids in my day liked to build and paint stuff ourselves. And, if you know my drawing style, you can imagine how detailed my models were!

But I also continued to write and draw my own comics. My stories were always comedy-adventures; as were my favorite comics by that "good artist," and as were my favorite movies. But as I got older and my drawing abilities improved, my characters still all remained stick figures. To me, it was only the story that was important, not the drawings. Besides, I never tried to show my comics to anyone—I just enjoyed telling stories to myself.

Living out in the country, far from any stores, I was reduced to endlessly rereading my sister's old comics (which I had inherited when she bailed out). But those dated back to before I was born, and I was starting to get tired of them. Sometimes if I rode with my mother into town on an errand, I could find a magazine stand, and was able to select some comics for myself for the first time. Naturally I tried some *Donald Duck* comics. But... they weren't much good. I figured that "good artist" must have stopped doing them, so I lost interest in those. The whole problem had been that the "good artist" did not have work in the *Donald Duck* title any longer, as in my sister's ancient issues... his stories were now in the *Uncle Scrooge* title, which was only published quarterly. But I was too young to analyze the situation, so I decided I'd try something new—some comics my sister didn't have—and I became enthralled with the large *Superman* family of comics. Furthermore, I started to actually "collect" these comics; in the sense that, rather than just piling them randomly in a closet, I paid attention to the issue numbers and kept them in numerical order, making lists of the back issues I needed.

Just to get away from home, my father would spend even his Saturdays in the empty offices of the Keno Rosa Co., and I would ride into town with him and visit used magazine shops looking for old issues to fill in gaps in my collections. I gradually traded off all of my sister's thousands of old comics for old *Superman* comics or bits of cash with which to buy new issues.

Away went all the Disney comics by that "good artist," which I figured it was time for me to outgrow. And yet, there were two of his stories that I could not bear to part with! One was a *Donald Duck* issue with a story titled "The Golden Helmet," which had always been my favorite—I loved how it created such an exciting plot, involving historical intrigue in the search for a fabulous treasure. The other was an *Uncle Scrooge* issue with a story titled "Only a Poor Old Man," which I absolutely loved since it revealed

bits and pieces of the early life of my favorite character Scrooge—and since it had an ending that so brilliantly summed up all that I loved about the personalities of both Scrooge and Donald. That issue, a Dell *Four Color* one-shot, had the number 386 on the cover, so I had no idea that it was the very *first* story starring Uncle Scrooge in his own title! I tucked those two wonderful comics into a drawer and busied myself collecting only *Superman* comics.

I still vividly recall how, a few years later, one of the most important moments in my life occurred. In 1964, on a visit to one of the dusty little used comic shops, I spotted a recently published large-size comic titled *The Best of Donald Duck and Uncle Scrooge*, with a cover blurb that said "reprinted by popular demand." The two stories in the comic were both by that "good artist" (though the stupid comic still didn't reveal his name), and one story was my own top favorite, "The Golden Helmet!"

This was a classic moment of epiphany! I realized that I had loved these Duck stories not simply because I was a dumb li'l kid—these were apparently regarded by many *others* as great stories, too!!! I didn't need a reprint of "Golden Helmet," but the other reprint story was from a comic predating those my sister had, titled "The Old Castle's Secret" (*Four Color* 189). I bought that comic instantly (half price, too!). Reading the "Castle" story brought another shock—it was still the "good artist," but he was drawing with a much more realistic and atmospheric art style! It was like an old movie! With a really scary-looking ghost! *Wow*! It had been a few years since I'd drawn any of my own comics, but I was now super-charged with inspiration!!!

I immediately started copying these two stories into the blank business ledgers that I still had. No, I wasn't going to pass the stories off as my own work—as I said, no one ever saw any of the hundreds of comics I'd spent my childhood making. They were only for my own private amusement.

One of four-year-old Rosa's first attempts at an action scene was this storm-at-sea drawing; replete with foundering ocean liner, treasure ship, octopus, swordfish, and deep underwater grotto. All non-Disney Rosa artwork with this article © and courtesy Don Rosa.

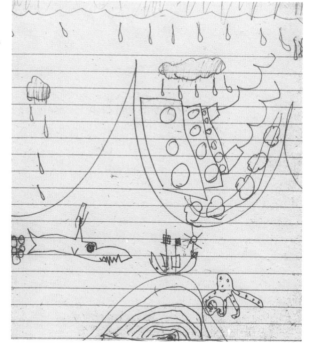

Pluto At the Store:
STORE
One Day. pluto. went to The SToRe. He said I will Buy some-THing.
So He went in and Bought what He wanted. He Bought a hat. He liked it. He said oh Boy!! He liked it so much
So Then Pluto went home. to try on the Hat.
But when He Tried it on. it was too little.
CLOSED
But when He looked at the sign CLOSED!!! He said oh.! no.! my Hat, He said.

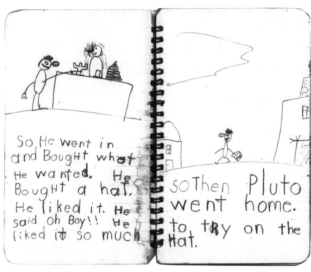

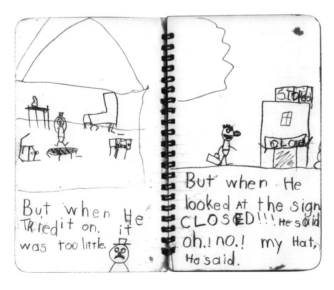

Don Rosa's first-ever comic story (ca. 1958), drawn in a blank business ledger. While "Pluto" is not the Disney character, we can't help but note his round, black Carl Barks-style nose.

But... the thrill of telling such wonderful stories with my own hand... I could not resist it! I created my own characters and then copied the two stories, panel by panel, into the ledgers.

In 1965 my father decided that small private school was too exclusive and didn't offer me enough opportunities for the future, so I was switched to a much larger private all-boys' high school, St. Xavier. School was no longer as easy as it had been back with those stupid rich kids, where I was always the smartest kid in the class. At St. X I realized I was not the academic achiever I thought I was. But as in grade school, I was still the only cartoonist! I was immediately working on the school newspaper and being asked by the teachers to draw covers for band concert programs, school magazines and even yearbooks. And then, in my sophomore year, came another turning point in my life.

I'd missed meeting him during my previous year in that big school, but in 1966 I again ran into Ray Foushee, whom I noticed had grown since I last saw him at St. Joseph's Infirmary in 1951. If being born on the same day in the same hospital, then ending up in the same high school fifteen years later wasn't enough of a coincidence, consider this: we were both lifelong comic book collectors and fans... and we were the *only two* such fans either of us had ever encountered. The only difference is that I was a cartoonist, maybe only because Ray did not grow up in the isolation and solitude that had compelled me to tell myself funny stories. But Ray was smarter and sharper than I was, and could write! So we became a team!

Of equal importance was that, unlike myself, Ray had found contact with the national network of other comic book collectors, which in those early days numbered no more than a few thousand. But they existed! I wasn't the only one! We weren't the only two! Another epiphany!!! Ray introduced me to "fanzines," the amateur magazines published by our fellow hobbyists, that featured articles about the history of comics as well as (yow!) people selling the old comic book issues that I needed for my *Superman* collection!

Sure, these didn't cost half-cover price like I was accustomed to paying—these old comics from the 1940s or '50s might cost fifty cents or even up to a whole dollar apiece! There were people selling a 1938 *Action Comics* 1 (first appearance of Superman) for (gasp) $100!!! That's more money than I'd ever dreamed of having! Luckily, I was more interested in recent issues—I wasn't going to waste $100 on an *Action* 1! (Note: an *Action* 1 sold in 2011 for $2 *million*.)

And now I learned of the universe of comic books my sister did not have! Unlike the miserable American comic industry of today, in the 1940s and '50s American comics covered every possible type of character or story or art style or... my head was gonna explode!!! And I could also complete my collection of *Uncle Scrooge* and *Donald Duck* comics! Look, I said to myself—here's an ad for the original 1948

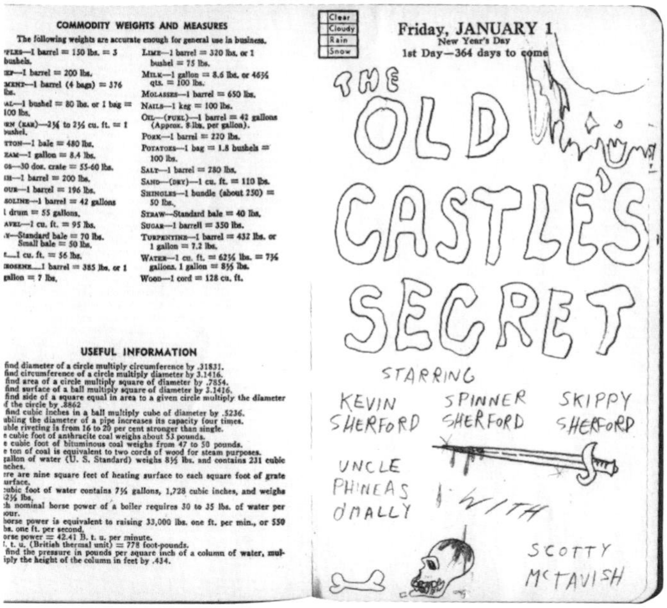
COMMODITY WEIGHTS AND MEASURES
USEFUL INFORMATION
Clear
Cloudy
Rain
Snow
Friday, JANUARY 1
New Year's Day
1st Day—364 days to come
THE OLD CASTLE'S SECRET
STARRING
KEVIN SHERFORD
SPINNER SHERFORD
SKIPPY SHERFORD
UNCLE PHINEAS O'MALLY
WITH
SCOTTY McTAVISH

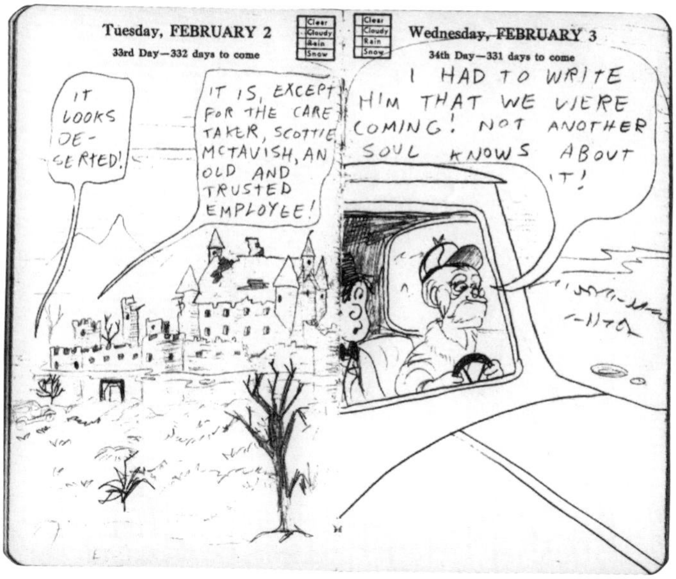
Tuesday, FEBRUARY 2
33rd Day—332 days to come
Wednesday, FEBRUARY 3
34th Day—331 days to come
IT LOOKS DE-SERTED!
IT IS, EXCEPT FOR THE CARE TAKER, SCOTTIE McTAVISH, AN OLD AND TRUSTED EMPLOYEE!
I HAD TO WRITE HIM THAT WE WERE COMING! NOT ANOTHER SOUL KNOWS ABOUT IT!

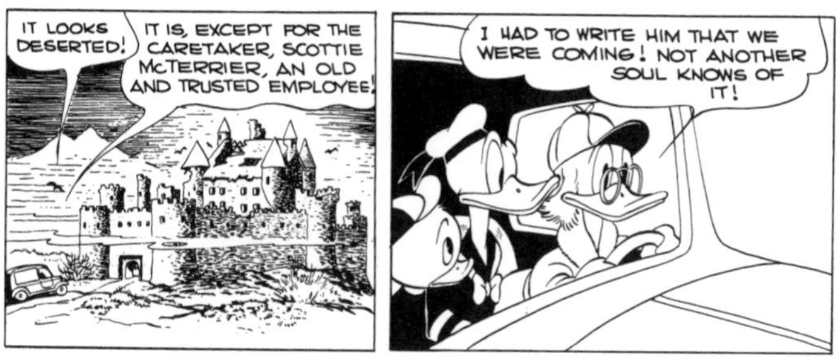
IT LOOKS DESERTED!
IT IS, EXCEPT FOR THE CARETAKER, SCOTTIE McTERRIER, AN OLD AND TRUSTED EMPLOYEE!
I HAD TO WRITE HIM THAT WE WERE COMING! NOT ANOTHER SOUL KNOWS OF IT!

Carl Barks' work (*Four Color* 189, 1948) inspired the teenage Rosa's self-created human characters. Carl Barks art © Disney.

Donald Duck comic with "The Old Castle's Secret" that costs only $1 and... what's this? "Story and art by *Carl Barks*."

Carl Barks.

The "good artist." His name was Carl Barks.

But also... I discovered *The Spirit* by Will Eisner. *Pogo* and others by Walt Kelly. *Prince Valiant* by Hal Foster. *Flash Gordon* by Alex Raymond. So many more! And the best comic books ever published, the EC comics of the early 1950s! Epiphanies were coming too fast! Stop! Stop!

I still never found another type that I loved as much as the Uncle Scrooge stories by the "good arti—" I mean, by Carl Barks. But there was still so much else! I went crazy! Within a year I'd started collecting virtually every comic book published, eventually channeling all the money I made working summers at the family business into it. And to this day I still am collecting old comics, forever filling holes in my vast collection, one of the largest comic book collections in the USA.

And Ray Foushee also gave me an audience for my comics besides only myself. With Ray scripting, we created parodies of school events and current movies or TV shows like *2001* and *Lost in Space* starring ourselves and our friends, some in full color. On my own, I wrote and drew comic strips also starring Ray and other school pals as themselves or as funny super-heroes—one of my continuing comedy-adventure stories ran over 500 pages! Also there were the "mini-comics" I would draw in class or study hall about the day's events. And yet my entire audience had increased from only one (myself) to still no more than a half-dozen pals.

Ray and I graduated high school in 1969 and we attended different colleges. I went to the University of Kentucky to study civil engineering. Why? I really don't know. As the proverbial "boss' son" in a construction company, there was no sort of formal education that would do me any good. But I knew that wasn't the point—I figured that the important thing about attending an institution of higher learning was not simply to learn a trade, but to learn of the universe of things there are to learn about! I still recall how glorious it felt to be living in an "intellectual community," not to mention how nice it was to get away from my unhappy home for most of the year.

But still, why civil engineering? That's probably the most difficult four-year college course there is! I suppose my father thought I would meet future building contractors, the people for whom we would work as "finish" contractors (tile, marble, etc.). I would have preferred studying art or cinema, the things in which I was interested, but which my father thought were idiotic. My future was to be owner of the family company, and my father was not going to let me waste his tuition payments on my silly hobbies!

But there was no reason I couldn't still *participate* in my hobbies. The first day on campus I went to the Journalism Building to see if the school newspaper needed a cartoonist. As always, the reception was startlingly positive!

CREW
CAPT. DON KENO
LEADER OF THE MISSION
LT.
RAIMUND
FOOSHAI
SECOND OFFICER
PASSENGER
DR.
CLARENCE
JOSEPHS
CRACK BIOLOGIST
POST
NO
SWISH!
FINANCIAL WORLD
FINANCIAL WORLD
COCK

The opening of Rosa's and Ray Foushee's high school sci-fi parody (ca. 1968).

I became the first freshman to ever earn a spot on the core newspaper staff. Yes, it was as a political cartoonist, and I was not particularly interested in politics due to my too intense (modern parlance would describe it as nerdy) interest in my hobbies. Even though the years I was in college would be the most politically active years in college history, I would not become very politically minded until sometime after college. Nonetheless, for the next four-and-a-half years I kept quite busy providing editorial cartoons, illustrations and even ads for the college newspaper.

Also I became increasingly active doing art for the comic collector fanzines, drawing covers and illustrations of favorite comic characters. With a friend I did a comic called *Khulan*, a story of sword and sorcery (which was a very popular new genre at the time). I still stayed in constant mail contact with Ray Foushee, and together we tried an EC-style science fiction story titled "Off Limits." But in our college environments we had both discovered the new art form of "underground comix" by greats like Robert Crumb and Gilbert Shelton—people like us who created comics just for the love of the medium. Ray and I decided we'd try something like that...

We'd do an "underground"-style parody—but not really as vulgar as the typical underground comics, since we wanted to submit it to a comics fanzine. By 1970 Carl Barks had retired; American Disney comics had dropped from being the best comics on the market to what I considered pathetic hackwork. They were on the verge of disappearing altogether as the American comic-buying market continued to collapse. I suggested we do a story that revisited the entire Duckburg crowd and see what had happened to them in the years since their days of glory in the 1950s. Thus was born "Return to Duckburg Place" (the title being a reference to the movie *Return to Peyton Place*, which also involved a revisit to the sordid lives of residents of a small town). When the nine-page story was complete, we took it with us to a New York City comic convention and showed it to some fanzine publishers. But they were very not interested—we had naively not anticipated that nobody was insane enough to print an "underground" story of revolution and mayhem using Disney characters, even if it *was* obviously a one-time parody.

But also at the convention was a young guy who had friends in the "underground" comix movement, and said he would try to get a publisher interested in our comic. So, unable to make copies (copy machines were not very common in 1970), I gave him the original art to see what he could do.

Later I was horrified to realize that, while I knew his name, I had no idea where he lived. Of all the comics I had ever done—all the way back to drawings when I was five years old!—"Return to Duckburg Place" became the only story for of which I did not have the original art.

Meanwhile, civil engineering classes continued. But I could take some elective courses now and then; and one was ancient history, which was a subject I liked due to my love of Barks stories like "The Golden Helmet." The lecturer for that course was one Prof. John Scarborough, and during one class he made a reference to *Asterix*. Now, *Asterix*—the comic adventures of a Gaulish warrior battling the ancient Roman empire—has never been too well-known in America; but in the late 1960s, attempts began to publish *Asterix* books in the USA. At the time, they went unnoticed—except by a comic fan like me, or a professor of ancient history like Prof. Scarborough. I struck up a conversation with him after class and found that, while not a collector on my intense level, he had a deep respect for the comics of his youth. As with everyone, his favorites had been those by Barks, from which he'd gotten his interest in history that resulted in his career as a history scholar. In 1972 we decided that together we would create a comedy-adventure comic strip like *Asterix*, except ours would be set in ancient Greece (the Professor's specialty), and would be done in a daily newspaper strip style. Thus was born *Phalanx*. We submitted about two weeks worth of *Phalanx* to the local city newspaper editor, who naturally rejected it. But if that life as the owner of a construction company hadn't already been waiting for me, I think I could have enjoyed a career of doing *Phalanx* with the Professor, and I would have continued to submit the strip to actual comic strip syndicates.

But a daily comic strip was still in my future. *Doonesbury* had recently debuted and was an instant sensation, so—also in 1972—the college newspaper editor asked me if I'd create a similar daily comic strip set on a college campus with a cast of wacky characters. I was glad to oblige, but, rather than creating a *Doonesbury* clone, I secretly had plans of my own.

This time as my co-writer I chose someone I had met who had the same dry sense of humor as I did, even though he was not a comics fan. Ron Weinberg was a graduate student in radiation-biology. (I liked to work with people who were lots smarter than I was!) Together we created *The Pertwillaby Papers*, which ran two semesters in the school paper. During the first semester, we introduced a cast of characters and involved them in a college-based adventure involving an anti-friction chemical. But then, between semesters, Ron left the university to take a job at the nuclear research labs in Oak Ridge (and later Diablo Canyon), so I had to carry on alone. As I'd intended, my second *Pertwillaby* story was a Barksian comedy-adventure involving a search for the lost treasure of the Incas. In my mind I saw it as a Scrooge McDuck adventure (with my own characters), and even titled it "Lost in (an Alternate Section of) the Andes," a Barks reference that I knew no one else would understand besides me (as if that mattered)!

Then in 1974 I graduated college. A bachelor-of-arts degree in civil engineering. Far out. What now?

I went to work at the Keno Rosa Co. But somewhere along the line, I'd been double-crossed! My uncle, who had been a confirmed bachelor until his fifties, had married a widow who had a son older than me. While I was in college, this stepson had already taken the spot I would have occupied in the office force. So, with an engineering degree I became a manual laborer for my own company, doing

Rosa as photographed by his wife, Joyce Ann Rosa. From left to right: with pencil in hand, 1980; with his statue collection, 1980; promotional shots, 1979; and posing as Captain Kentucky, ca. 1980.

"grunt" work with grade-school dropouts. Mixing mortar, pushing wheelbarrows, carrying hundred pound bags of marble chips. I missed college! But at least now there were no thermodynamics exams.

To stay sane I intensified my comics fanzine activities. I was a main contributor of data to the first *Price Guide*, a book that revolutionized comic book collecting. And I took over the writing of a well-known column that had been in fanzines since 1961: "The Information Center," which answered readers' questions about comics. I had previously helped the retiring author with information; such as indexes to Barks' Duck comic stories, illustrated with my own drawings of Scrooge and Donald. But I expanded the column to also include readers' questions concerning my other fields of knowledge, movies and TV. And as with everything I'd ever done, I poured every ounce of my enthusiasm and spare

time into this project, even though work done for fanzines is all done for free. It's a hobby. For fun.

I was still living in that large and unhappy home, but now kept entirely to three rooms like a boarder—my bedroom, my office/library and that large bathroom. I bought and prepared all my own meals. My "Information Center" became the new center of my life. I researched the questions using my vast collections of materials concerning visual entertainment, and included numerous illustrations with my answers (very often of Barks' Ducks, since they were still my favorite comics). To my knowledge, in those days if anyone wanted to know who played a bit part in some 1936 movie, or how many episodes of a TV series had been shown in 1958, I was the only public source in the world for such answers. Nowadays we have at our fingertips the answer to those and every other question in the universe on the Internet. And how wonderful that is!

After several years of that, I realized I enjoyed writing that Q&A column, but that my thirst to tell stories was not

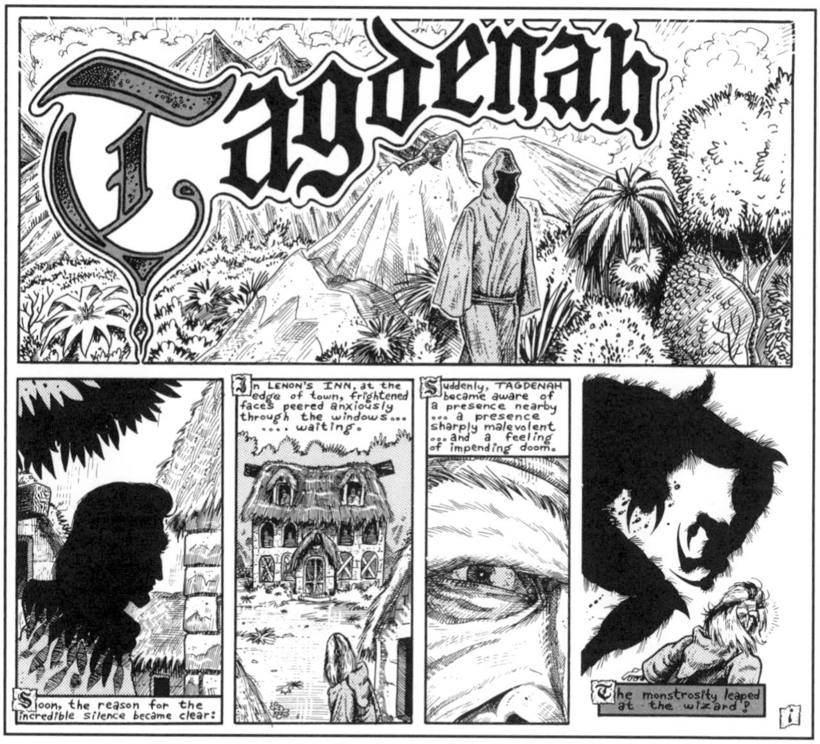
Tagdenah
Soon, the reason for the incredible silence became clear:
In LENON'S INN, at the edge of town, frightened faces peered anxiously through the windows... ...waiting.
Suddenly, TAGDENAH became aware of a presence nearby ... a presence sharply malevolent ... and a feeling of impending doom.
The monstrosity leaped at the wizard!

Excerpts from *Tagdenah* (1977). Two four-page installments of this sword and sorcery series were drawn by Rosa.

being satisfied. So the fanzine editor had other cartoonists illustrate my columns while I brought back my *Pertwillaby Papers* in comic-book-style stories rather than as a daily newspaper strip. In the next few years I had my cast of characters search for looted Nazi art treasures, rescue the earth from a "universal solvent" which had bored a hole directly to the earth's core, and meet King Arthur.

In-between *Pertwillaby Papers* adventures, with another friend as my writer, I drew two more "sword and sorcery" comics for fanzines about a wizard named "Tagdenah."

Due to various newspaper articles and TV interviews about my activities, over the years I had become a minor celebrity in Louisville. So in 1979, the features editor of the major Louisville newspaper asked me to create a weekly comic strip for their Saturday entertainment magazine. I decided this was a fabulous opportunity to do something I didn't think had ever been done anywhere else—I would create some sort of hero who would have adventures with actual local personalities in actual Louisville locales! Thus was born *Captain Kentucky*, a superheroic version of Lance Pertwillaby. The salary was $25 a week for the Sunday-size comic strip, though it would take me about 12-15 hours of my spare time to do it.

The editor didn't tell me to create something with such complex art and plot, but you know me! Now I poured every ounce of my enthusiasm into this new project while still working full-time at the family business and writing fanzine columns, so that I needed to stay up at least one whole night a week to get the work done in time for each Saturday's magazine. But... within a few months I could tell something was wrong. I could never tell anyone was even reading the strip. I would never get any reactions from readers—not even complaints! But just like when I was a kiddy, I enjoyed telling stories even if nobody was reading them. So I wrote and drew *Captain Kentucky* for three years—150 big episodes.

1982. My uncle had died, so I was now working in the office at Keno Rosa. I also had met a young lady who could tolerate my intense interest in my hobbies, as well as my "hermit"-like life, and I'd gotten married. And bought a home. And had dogs, and... life was getting complicated! *Captain Kentucky* would no longer fit in, so I gave it up with no reluctance. I no longer had the luxury of boundless time to indulge my hobby of drawing comics. And why bother? Though I enjoyed writing and drawing comedy-adventures, there was no interest in that genre in America. Why have a hobby that's frustrating and too time-consuming? So I threw away what few artist supplies I had, and carried my beat-up little drawing table down into the cellar. I would never draw again. That part of my life was over and done with. Now I would go ahead and accept my life of running my grandfather's construction company, just as I'd been brought up to do. I bid on contracts, managed the workers, then spent most days reading a book. It was easy... but so boring. And uncreative.

I recall that one night in 1985 I noticed that a popular local radio call-in show had the topic of "what do you regret most in life?" The host was a friend of mine—I'd even used him in a "Captain Kentucky" adventure, and I appeared regularly on his show with my ol' pal Ray Foushee to answer callers' questions about comics, movies and TV. I found myself dialing the number and telling him that what I deeply regretted was that I had always blindly followed what my family had planned for my life without ever trying to pursue my own dreams, and now I could see that those childhood dreams would never be realized.

For better or worse, that was about to change—and *that* brings us back to the Foreword of this very book. If you'd like, you can turn back there now and re-read what came next: 1986, and the start of my experiences writing and drawing real Uncle Scrooge and Donald Duck adventures!!!

As for what came next after *that*... well, I'll pick that up in the next volume of Fantagraphics' *Don Rosa Library*. •

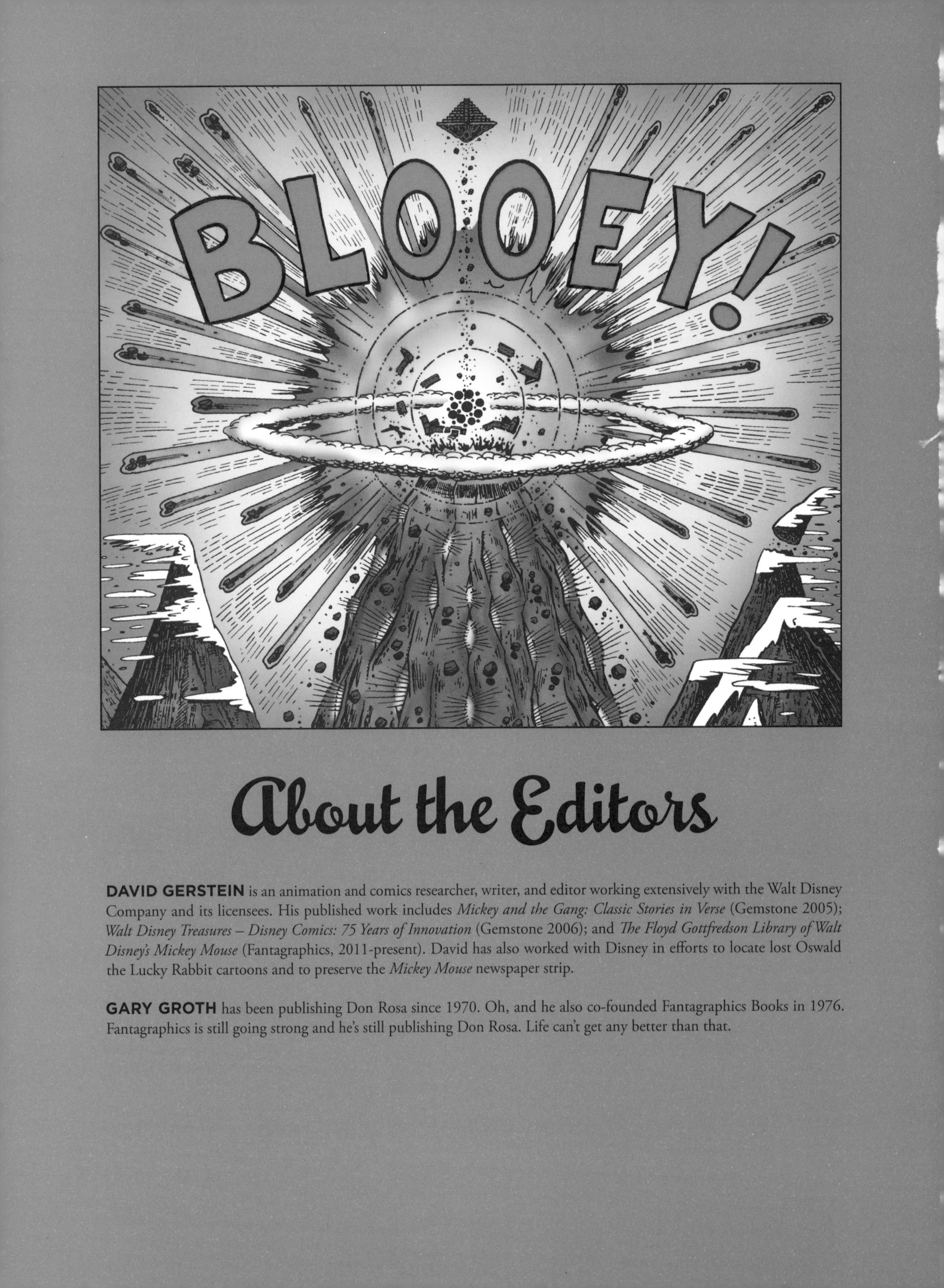
BLOOEY!

About the Editors

DAVID GERSTEIN is an animation and comics researcher, writer, and editor working extensively with the Walt Disney Company and its licensees. His published work includes *Mickey and the Gang: Classic Stories in Verse* (Gemstone 2005); *Walt Disney Treasures – Disney Comics: 75 Years of Innovation* (Gemstone 2006); and *The Floyd Gottfredson Library of Walt Disney's Mickey Mouse* (Fantagraphics, 2011-present). David has also worked with Disney in efforts to locate lost Oswald the Lucky Rabbit cartoons and to preserve the *Mickey Mouse* newspaper strip.

GARY GROTH has been publishing Don Rosa since 1970. Oh, and he also co-founded Fantagraphics Books in 1976. Fantagraphics is still going strong and he's still publishing Don Rosa. Life can't get any better than that.